W9-AFB-212

ISAAC M. WISE

ISAAC M. WISE

His Life, Work and Thought

by JAMES G. HELLER

THE UNION OF AMERICAN
HEBREW CONGREGATIONS

Library of Congress Catalogue Card 64-24340

Produced in the U.S. of America

To My Father
His Disciple
Max Heller

Foreword

ISAAC MAYER WISE'S PHILOSOPHY OF JUDAISM AND HIS PENETRATING insights into its essential truths have withstood the grueling test of time and the searing examination imposed by its adherents who have suffered humiliation, torture and death for its sake. No other religion in the world has invited such venomous and vicious attacks upon it, and upon its protagonists, by pagans and Christians, by virtually every nation in history, and sometimes by those within the family of Judaism itself. No other religion in the world has been compelled to struggle so tragically and majestically to be allowed to live at peace with the religions it spawned, nor has any other had a more profound influence upon the ethics of men. Underlying much of modern-day psychiatry, woven into the fabric of our Western law, undergirding the Constitution of the United States are the fundamental insights and prophetic comprehensions of those ancient sages who first divined the oneness of God, nature, and man and who first perceived that a corollary to natural law is moral law.

This definitive study of Isaac Mayer Wise, who brought with him from Bavaria a deep commitment to Judaism and the gleaming vision of its potential in the fertile soil of a free land, could hardly have been written by a more scholarly and devoted disciple than

James G. Heller. Himself one of the giants of Judaism in our time, James Heller is a man of many parts: a rabbi of illustrious stature, his resonant voice has ever been heard in behalf of justice and liberty; staunch champion of his people and of the restoration of the land of Zion; profound interpreter of his faith, a musician of quality and sensitivity; a naturalist of near professional proportions; a singularly brilliant intellect informed by a compassionate heart.

It is often said that "great times beget great men." It is surely true that great men beget great biographers: Johnson had his Boswell, Lincoln his Sandburg and now—happily for our own and countless generations of students of all persuasions in the future—Wise has his Heller.

In tracing the motivations and objectives of Rabbi Wise, his successes and failures, Rabbi Heller has here given us more than a portrait in depth of one individual, albeit a gigantic one. He has given us the sweep of a movement, the Reform Jewish Movement in the United States during the past revolutionary decades. The forces and counterforces which have shaped, and are shaping, the destiny of mankind are clearly discerned through this encompassing chronicle of one personality, one burgeoning religious group. To read this book is to enlarge one's perspective of the century past and thus to reach a greater understanding of the impact of religion on society and of society on religion. For Wise, like Judaism itself, was ahead of his time and time is now catching up to his ideas as it is coming abreast of Judaism's age-old insistence that God is the Father of all men and thus all men are brothers.

MAURICE N. EISENDRATH

Preface

I KNEW ISAAC M. WISE, AS IT WERE, AT SECOND HAND IN MY FATHER'S oft-told memories of him. When I came to Cincinnati as one of his successors in the pulpit of K.K. B'nai Yeshurun, I acquired an acquaintance with him more vividly through the recollections of some of those who had labored at his side and loved him. I knew him in his own lengthened shadow in the organizations and institutions he had brought into being. And later I came to know him in his own writings, in the recorded evidence of his labors and of his thought.

With the years I felt a steadily increasing admiration of him as a man, and developed a steadily rising estimate of his importance, not only for Reform Judaism in America, but for the burgeoning of the whole Jewish community in the United States. Clear traces of his influence I discovered in many places, often among those who little suspected to whom and to whose work they owed much.

But, above and beyond the evidence of his influence, he himself interested me. As I read more and more of the record of his life and work, I found myself wondering about his personality, constantly caught up in amazement at his quality of indomitableness, of indefatigability. The bare tale of his days, his speaking, his writing, his organizing, his travels, remains almost incredible. And yet, as in the case of many men —not with all, for with some the external seems to outweigh the inward—all this that he pursued and achieved seemed shadowy compared with his own robust personality, with what his own living presence must have been.

As the years passed, too, I observed that there were many who spoke in his name, who appealed to his views as precedent for their own, as a kind of "classical" point of view, a "norm" from which Reform Judaism ought not to have strayed. And in many such instances I was certain—to judge from his own recorded opinions—that Isaac M. Wise would have been volubly indignant at this distortion, this misrepresentation of his ideas: concerning Hebrew customs and ceremonies, the theology of Reform and of Judaism in general, etc. Perhaps, to single out a matter of more than passing import, he would have thundered most vigorously against the notion that any period or any person should be regarded as a "norm," that Reform should thus repudiate its essential principle of freedom, of the possibility—no, the duty—of review and change. This is not intended to throw out of court the obvious fact that in some of his attitudes and opinions he was very close to some of those who now hark back to him. . . . But all this will appear in the record, which is far more complex and absorbing than any schematic, tendentious account of it.

The material about Isaac M. Wise has been increasing steadily in volume. I have drawn upon all that I could find. In regard to his life my main sources have been: the volume devoted by the Alumni of the Hebrew Union College to his selected writings and to a brief biographical sketch by David Philipson and Louis Grossmann (this was intended to be no more than a preliminary study, in 1900, the year of Wise's death); his own *Reminiscences* (translated from the German and published in 1901); a full-length biography by his grandson, Max B. May, published in 1916; but especially Isaac M. Wise's own published works—his innumerable lectures, editorials, editorial paragraphs, articles—published chiefly in *The American Israelite* from the time he founded it in 1854 until his passing in 1900, also in *The Asmonean*, *The Occident*, *Sinai*, and various other American Jewish periodicals.

All these I found interesting and useful, and I have drawn freely upon the information they furnished, both about his life and about his system of ideas. Wherever possible, I have acknowledged the source. Where I have used books about him, I have attempted to check back from their references to the original. Nonetheless I became convinced that another and more comprehensive work on

Isaac M. Wise needed to be written. Those that existed seemed to me partly too hasty and partly too pedestrian. They seemed to me to fail in several essential respects—some in their externality, their neglect of the historic setting in which he was born and lived; others in their self-declared inability to deal with his opinions on Jewish theology, on revelation, on the "Law," on the Talmud, and on various problems of Judaism and Jewish history, in which Isaac M. Wise maintained a lifelong, absorbing interest. On the other hand, there was one book, Dena Wilansky's *Sinai to Cincinnati*, which was in substance a long-drawn and discursive plea against his views on Zionism, a thesis to the effect that these views had been of a piece with his universalistic concept of Judaism and of the messianic and millennial probabilities of the future of mankind. I became convinced that a new work was imperative, one to interpret his life genetically, to relate him to his eventful and moving time, to devote itself equally to a systematic exposition of his views as a whole and in the light of their development and modification during his lifetime.

This is the reason for this book. Its plan is to consider Isaac M. Wise under two chief headings. The first part will be dedicated to a straightforward narration of his life and his achievements. Wherever possible here and in the latter half, we shall permit him to speak in his own words, though not so frequently or at such length as to interrupt the continuity of the story. He wrote vividly and well, with a highly individual style, which always bore the imprint of his education in the German language, but which matured steadily from his first awkward wrestlings with English to a considerable degree of facility and rhetorical strength. Quite naturally (and to discern this most clearly his style should be compared with that of many of his public and religious contemporaries) he exhibited the somewhat stilted, flowery and often grandiloquent flair of the day. But, if one strips away the temporal garb, one finds at once beneath it his own warmth, his quick enthusiasm, his deep Jewishness, his cleaving to life rather than to impersonal ideas. Some of this should filter through to the reader from all that I have inserted straight from his own pen.

I do not intend this work to be one of propaganda. In fact, I shall do my utmost to avoid this. In every case, especially those in which the matters under discussion are still controversial, the attentive or skeptical reader may substantiate every statement made in my text from the notes which will be appended. These notes will invariably indicate the source which justifies the assertion. In most cases it will be found that a large number of instances, of statements by Isaac M. Wise, back up the apparent *obiter dicta*.

At the outset I debated with myself whether to follow Judge May in singling out for continuous and separate treatment Wise's long and difficult road on the way to the creation of the Union of American Hebrew Congregations, the Hebrew Union College, etc. I decided against this. It seemed better to me to lay the emphasis upon Wise as a man and only in the second place upon the history of his plans, struggles, defeats, and creations. Anyone who may wish to follow all the phases of his propaganda for a Union and a College may do so by diligent use of the Index, which will furnish all the references to these in chronological order.

It is my earnest hope that from this study several important things will become apparent:

I. That, like most other men, Isaac M. Wise changed his mind from time to time; that consistency was no bugbear to him. Not only is consistency the fetish of small minds, but it is not infrequently evidence of a failure to grow. When men hold a great objective constantly before them, they are likely to bend on lesser matters, to modify as they proceed. It seems obvious to me that this is precisely what Wise did as his life progressed. And this the record will display clearly.

II. That the bitter charge made then and still made against Reform Judaism that it was intended as a "way out of Judaism" never had conceivable validity in reference to him, to his concept of Judaism, or to his life and work. On the contrary, everything he did and said gave evidence of his deep Jewish loyalty, his passion to prevent the dissolution or enfeeblement of the Jewish tradition, his ecstatic appreciation of the faith of his fathers, his unvarying emphasis upon Jewish unity, his angry disavowal of any intention of founding a Jewish "sect." It cannot be within the purview of this book to go on from this point, to consider what has happened to Reform Judaism in the American and in the world Jewish scene since his death. This will have to be left to the reader to follow for himself, and perhaps to other studies to be made later on.

III. That in spite of many statements to the contrary—usually by men who have not taken the trouble to read him—Isaac M. Wise was far from being a man ignorant of the Jewish sources. True, he was not a great creative scholar. This he would have been the first to concede was not his *métier*. But he had a good Jewish grounding, especially in rabbinics and he did not neglect this in his studies during his very busy career. Some of the pioneering work he did remains intensely interesting, not only in his constant and violent reaction to biblical criticism, the controversy about which raged in his day, but especially in the field to which he gave himself angrily and steadily for many years: the origins of Christianity, the veracity of the gospel accounts, and the relation of early Christianity to its Jewish sources and its Jewish contemporaries. In the opinion of the writer, some of his published work in these fields remains remarkably interesting. In general, Isaac M. Wise was a better scholar than he has been given credit for being, and he took the trouble later in his life, at great cost to himself, to become grounded in the humanistic classics, in philosophy, and even in the contemporary great sources of scientific development and theory.

IV. That he had a pervasive and consecrated sense of Jewish unity, an unvarying consciousness of the meaning and direction of Jewish history, an impassioned longing to bring back the wanderers among his people to awareness of their noble heritage and of what he regarded as their millennial opportunity for service in that time.

V. That he was patently and deeply a product of what many times he was wont to call "the spirit of the age." This sprang especially from the experiences of his childhood in Bohemia and of his rabbinical career as a young man. It was responsible for his decision to pluck up himself and his family by the roots and to migrate to America. But it had its origin equally in prophetic conviction, in the belief that the world was moving perceptibly and rapidly toward brotherhood, toward universal democracy, toward the general acceptance of rational goals, the simple truth of Judaism, as he conceived it. This is so central in its relation to his own genesis and development that I have begun with three chapters, one on Europe—and America—at the end of the eighteenth and the beginning of the nineteenth centuries, and two others on the conditions that obtained then among European Jews, with especial reference to his own community in the Austro-Hungarian Empire and in Bohemia.

VI. That his concept of America, of the principles that animated its founding fathers, of those spiritual bases of its democracy which he equated often with the Mosaic tradition—that these played a major role in his thought and in his life. This will be shown in many of the incidents of that life, and in many of the words he spoke and wrote.

VII. That, over and above all else, he was a most remarkable and interesting human being—vivid, lovable, sometimes mercurial, not always as pacific as he claimed to be; with a capacity to make friends even of many of his enemies; and all his life filled with a burning purpose that, like the thorn-bush at Horeb, never consumed him. It is my hope that he himself will appear out of the chapters on his career and out of the multiplicity of his writings and opinions.

Within the limit of my capacity and understanding, I shall present Isaac M. Wise and his ideas just as they were, without distortion, without reference to my own point of view. I shall not argue with him. I shall not attempt as others have done to contend that, had he lived a decade or more longer, he would have changed his mind about this or that. It will, however, be necessary to elucidate, especially for the lay reader, the intellectual, historic, and Jewish sources of many of his attitudes and concepts. This, too, I shall try to do as impersonally and as fairly as I can. If—perhaps inevitably, as in all human undertakings like this—some of my own differences with him, some of my own experiences of two generations later, should creep in, I beg the reader's indulgence. I can assure him that they will have crept in inadvertently. Many years ago we had as our teacher in history at the Hebrew Union College a fascinating and lovable man, Gotthard Deutsch. Dr. Deutsch used to launch into his courses with a lecture on the writing of history. According to him it was simply the reverent and scrupulous assembling and recording of *fact*. Since his day this point of view has become outmoded. History is now seen to be a creative task, deriving always from the principle of selection and interpretation. It may be too much to hope, therefore, that I shall be able entirely to avoid the interposition of my own opinions. But it will not be for lack of trying!

I am very grateful for the help I have received from many in the making of this work: to Dr. Jacob R. Marcus and Mr. Maxwell Whiteman of the American Jewish Archives of Cincinnati; to the Union of American Hebrew Congregations, which made available to me photostatic copies of the complete files of *The American Israelite*; to the lamented Dr. Jonah B. Wise and his twin-sister, Jean W. May, for permission to use excerpts from private letters of their father; to the New York Public Library for access to the files of *The Asmonean*, *The Occident*, etc.

I am also very grateful to Rabbi Chaim I. Essrog for his tedious editorial work, to Mr. Ralph Davis for his fine technical knowledge and aid and to Dr. J. H. Kanner for preparing the index.

It is my ardent hope that this book will contribute to an understanding and appreciation of the life and work of a pivotal figure in American Jewish history; and beyond this—quite simply—that the book will be found interesting and enjoyable.

JAMES G. HELLER

Contents

Part Three
Isaac M. Wise, His Thought

Appendices

Part I
The Setting

1

"The Spirit of the Age"

No words were oftener on the lips or at the tip of the pen of Isaac M. Wise than these that are the title-head of this chapter. They were not exclusively or especially his. At this period of human history one comes upon them almost everywhere, as a basic postulate. But, if we are to try to understand Isaac M. Wise; if we are to hope to comprehend his characteristic ideas concerning history; if we are to describe and judge correctly what he thought and wrote of Judaism as a religion and of Israel as a people; if we are to assess with some degree of discernment his concept of Reform Judaism, of Jewish theology and Jewish practice: then it must be in the light of his time, in terms of the unique period after which and into which he was born. He entered the world four years after the battle of Waterloo. At the Congress of Vienna a reaction had set in against the ideas and the political devices of the French Revolution in the governments of Western Europe, and perhaps even more strongly in his native Bohemia, under the Austro-Hungarian Empire. But the magic of the Revolution had not been banished. Europe and the whole Western world were still smoldering with that ardent vision. Military defeat, the triumph of the Holy Alliance, were not to prove enough to drive that magic, that glowing hope, forever underground. The new force in men's minds burst into the light again and again, culminating—after Wise's own flight to America—in the European Revolution of 1848.

The antecedents of the Revolution were to be found in the evolution of ethics and of political theory, in profound changes that were germinating within the body and spirit of Western Europe. Its more remote causes must be sought in the Renaissance; in the birth and growth of commercialism and of the middle class; in the emergence of the vernaculars; in the rise and prevalence of monarchy; in a whole new panoply of science and of philosophy; in the invention of gunpowder and of printing; in the transmission of biblical ideas about the dignity of man and the equality of souls before God; in the broadening which the Crusades—certainly without their having willed it so—had brought to circumscribed lands and peoples; in the concept and elaboration of the Common Law—especially in the Norse lands and in Britain; and in many other causes and in many other directions that might be enumerated. For all this the reader must be referred to any good modern history of Europe, especially to a history devoted to the understanding of intellectual and emotional processes. Our own purpose in these introductory chapters is simple: firstly, to present succinctly the background of European history and of the spirit of the time; secondly, to parallel this with a rapid description of the condition and fluctuating lot of the Jews of Europe during the same period; and, thirdly, to turn to the milieu of the Austrian and Bohemian Jews, among whom Isaac M. Wise was born.

The central descriptive word of the eighteenth century was "Enlightenment" (*Aufklaerung*), a "self-conditioned revolt of the trained human intellect against tradition for tradition's sake, and against whatever the intellect holds to be superstition or prejudice."[1] To this we shall append a résumé of an address Isaac M. Wise gave under the title, "A Comparison of the 18th and 19th Centuries."

He began with a plea against the pessimistic interpretation of history, and with a strong argument in favor of the concept of progress. Up to this time wars had been waged, not to advance the interests of man, but for purely dynastic and selfish reasons. Nor had the Napoleonic Wars been better. But utterly different from these was the informing spirit of that time, which drew its inspiration from the contagion of the American and French Revolutions. Napoleon—Wise claimed—was victorious only as long as he held aloft the banner of progress. Only in the United States (this was written in 1884) "does there now exist a government with the consent of the governed." Wise then went at some length into a comparison of governments in the eighteenth and in the nineteenth centuries:

> Despotism pure and simple is gone in Church and State, except perhaps in Russia. . . .

Tyranny had dug its own grave:

> The Academy of Science, established in 1666, was one starting point. In England John Locke and Peter Bayle revolutionized the conceptions. . . . But all these geniuses did not reach the masses as did the French literature of the 18th century, as did Montesquieu, Voltaire, Rousseau, Diderot, d'Alembert, and a host of minor spirits. Great as was Isaac Newton, and Buffon, and other scientists, they did not reach the people as did David Hume, or Gibbon, or Bolingbroke of England, as did the Deists in England, and the Encyclopedians [sic!] in France. . . .

Wise continued with an account of the fathers of the American Revolution, who learned—he wrote—from the common law in England, and from the French literature of the eighteenth century. French ideas climaxed in American patriots. Parallel to the burgeoning of ideas was a growth of commerce and industry. Some have said that the eighteenth century was idealistic and humanitarian, and that the nineteenth was proving to be realistic and selfish; but this is not true. This century (the nineteenth) is realizing the ideas of its predecessor in institutions and in private charity:

> We are children of the nineteenth century, proud of our mother, and her motto shall be our watchword: emancipation of the mind, mental culture, redeems the human family from the misery of existence in all its forms.[2]

Few epochs in human history have been as decisive, as deep and comprehensive in purport as the latter half of the eighteenth century. Surely this was among the few great turning points in the history of the human race: like the birth of critical thought among the Greeks, the coming of the Renaissance, the death-blow to ancient cosmology dealt by Copernican astronomy and Newtonian physics. Since primitive times man had been dominated by a parochial attitude toward his life. Little by little, during these eventful years, world-perspective was born. The natural and the social sciences challenged the logic and the theology that until then had been sovereign guides to knowledge, complementary approaches to truth in a system such as that of Thomas Aquinas. Eventually the inner spirit of the Renaissance affected philosophy, which turned from heaven to earth, which began to busy itself with the observable facts of experience, in an effort to deduce truth from what man saw, what man was and did, and to perfect a method of finding truth inductively. Ethics was progressively divorced from the supernatural, and much thought was devoted to ways of attaining freedom, where freedom was conceived as freedom from restraint. More and more man was depicted, not as the creature of divine grace or of predestination, but as one who could—if he would—control his own destiny, transform his environment, and pave the way for uninterrupted progress. Not for all this period, but certainly and centrally in most of it, the chief emphasis was upon Reason, a word to conjure with.[3] Utopian visions, first spun by Sir Thomas More a century before, were multiplied and elaborated.

It would, however, be erroneous to believe that most, or all, of the changes of this time were in the realm of the mind, of man's concept of himself. In the late eighteenth and early nineteenth centuries, scientific principles—which for the most part had been discovered in the previous century—were applied to industrial purposes. Steam was used in the mines. Power was introduced into factories. Steel took the place of iron. Railways were built. The nature of electricity was discovered and the force itself harnessed. Oil was found and employed in the internal combustion engine. Printing was made much more efficient by the invention of power presses. Scientific thought was widely disseminated in a large number of popular works.[4] From Newton to Laplace, the victories of science grew in momentum and number.

Parallel to these developments—as we shall learn in more detail a little later—there was a drive against dogmas, especially against those considered inconsistent with reason. A group called the Rational Supernaturalists, their tenets set forth by John Locke, asserted that, underlying all religious beliefs and practices, there were three central principles: One God; the obligation to live a virtuous life; and a future life with reward and punishment. Even miracles must be capable of rational elucidation.[5]

Such were the chief content and direction of this remarkable time. Of its historical background we shall give only the barest essentials, for it cannot be the purpose of this work to sketch in the men and events that led up to the Revolution. The era begins, perhaps, with the Peace of Utrecht, in the second decade of the eighteenth century. The inheritance of the Spanish Empire was parceled out, and a balance of power created between Hapsburgs and Bourbons. There were three partitions of Poland, which fell prey to Prussia, Austria, and Russia. England was engaged in a rapid expansion of her colonial possessions. The maritime and colonial sway of France entered upon a decline. Parliamentary institutions in Britain were developing rapidly and fascinatingly.[6] Interested men and women on the continent followed all of this eagerly. John

Locke formulated his celebrated "Principles of 1688," which (according to Sir Leslie Stephen) became the "political Bible of the eighteenth century." In fact, Locke was progenitor to most of the fathers of the American Revolution.[7]

Frederick the Great made of Prussia a European power, invading Silesia, thwarting the ambitions of Joseph II of Austria. Under Maria Theresa, Austria was growing weaker. Russia, under Catherine the Great, was entering into the politics of Western Europe. Yet, outside of dynastic wars, of the upward or downward movement of ancient regimes, of the ambitions of individual rulers, nothing essential appeared to have changed in Europe as compared with the seventeenth century.[8] Yet it was not so! Benevolent—or malevolent—despotisms were a thin veneer over seething unrest. Goethe contended that a characteristic fault of the century was its impatience with "the inevitably slow processes of historic growth.[9]

Later we shall dwell at greater length upon the plans and acts of Joseph II of Austria (at first co-regent with his mother, Maria Theresa, and then for too brief a time Emperor); his attempted reforms, his clash with the Catholic Church, his "Patent of Tolerance," and his death on February 10, 1790.[10]

Beyond all else, these were the years in which the French Revolution was in gestation. Here too we can give no more than the barest outline. For detailed treatment of fact and interpretation, the reader must be referred to any one of the many excellent books on the French Revolution. But we must pause to observe that this was what a recent writer called "The Age of the Democratic Revolution":

> In one way, it [the Revolution] signified a new feeling for a kind of equality, or at least a discomfort with older forms of social stratification and formal rank. . . . Politically, the eighteenth century movement was against the possession of government, or any public power, by any established, privileged, closed, or self-recruiting groups of men. It denied that any person could exercise coercive authority simply by his own right, or by right of "history," either in the old-fashioned sense of custom and inheritance, or in any newer dialectical sense, unknown to the eighteenth century, in which "history" might be supposed to give some special elite or revolutionary vanguard a right to rule. . . .[11]

Perhaps the *locus classicus* for the time may be found in a speech by Robespierre in the Convention of February 5, 1794:

> Democracy is a state in which the people, as sovereign, guided

> by laws of its own making, does for itself all that it can do well, and by its delegates what it cannot. . . . Democracy is the only form of state which all the individuals composing it can truly call their country. . . .[12]

Or, as it was put by the General Court of Massachusetts in 1776:

> It is a general maxim in every government, there must exist, somewhere, a supreme, sovereign, absolute and uncontrollable power; but this power resides always in the body of the people; and it never was, or can be, delegated to one man, or a few.[13]

The growth of revolutionary sentiment in Europe, and especially in France, is readily explained from within the continent, in its political and intellectual history. Yet there can be little doubt that the preceding revolution in America had greatly influenced many, in theory, and in the example of the establishment of representative institutions. A contemporary writer speaks of this influence in these words:

> The effects of the American Revolution, as a revolution, were imponderable but very great. It inspired the sense of a new era. It added a new content to the conception of progress. It gave a whole new dimension to ideas of liberty and equality made familiar by the Enlightenment. It got people into the habit of thinking more concretely about political questions, and made them more readily critical of their own government and society. It dethroned England, and set up America, as a model for those seeking a better world. It brought written constitutions, declarations of rights, and constituent conventions into the realm of the possible. The apparition on the other side of the Atlantic of certain ideas already familiar in Europe made such ideas seem more truly universal, and confirmed the habit of thinking in terms of humanity at large. . . .[14]

The French Revolution emerged from attempts at moderate reform—the "Declaration of the Rights of Man," the creation of a single legislative chamber, the seizure of church lands. But the flood could not be dammed.[15] The Bastille was stormed in July, 1789, the Tuileries Palace taken, and the monarchy came to an end. Noblemen fled when they could, and begged for armies to bring them back. The Revolution began by defending itself, but soon, after incredible victories, carried the gospel of revolution into neighboring lands.[16] In France itself, one leader after another fell to the guillotine. The Assembly witnessed an internecine struggle for power. At last not one leader was left, and France could be heard to breathe a great sigh of relief. The government was turned over to a Directory, and the way was open for a young Corsican, Napoleon Bonaparte.[17] From general, to consul, to emperor, he moved his triumphant and bloody way. He initiated some remarkable reforms: a Code of Laws, a thorough-going financial reform, the establishment of the Bank of France, a system of public education, and a Concordat with the Vatican. He could give France everything but peace! Again and again he crushed his—and their—foes, but he bled France white in the process and impoverished it. His first defeat was at Leipzig in October, 1814. The Congress of Vienna was convened. Napoleon returned from Elba, and, after the Hundred Days, was finally beaten at Waterloo by Wellington and Bluecher, and confined to St. Helena.[18]

We shall not follow Europe through the period of reaction that followed the defeat of Napoleon: the acts of the Congress of Vienna; the restoration of the German states; the various outbreaks of revolutionary ardor, until the coming of the time, in 1848, when victories for the human spirit were won—and lost! It was into this very post-revolutionary period that Isaac M. Wise was born, and under its lowering air that he spent his youth and young manhood. As we shall describe it in some detail in the third chapter of this Part, he lived under a curious and confused amalgam of reactionary reality and revolutionary hope; under an oppressive regime but with a sense of the presence and unweakened validity of the ideals of 1789. Most of his ideas—as was true of most of the visionaries and idealists of the time—stemmed from a long antecedent line of thinkers, especially in England and in France. To understand Wise, it is imperative to add to the moving pageant of the history of the time something of the currents of the mind that converged upon it in conviction and in hope.

First, briefly, as to the beginnings of liberal thought in England:

Though a mechanist and materialist, Thomas Hobbes was a pioneer in the field of political philosophy, and prepared the way for John Locke. Hobbes struggled for the separation of Church and State, and for a concept of the veritable basis of sovereignty. The king is only a symbol; it is the people who rule. All this in his *magnum opus*, the *Leviathan*. Authority, for Hobbes, came not from "the divine right of kings," but solely "from the principles of reason." He was the founder of the English school of Deists. He pursued a strict analytic method, or what he regarded as that; he took men as he found them, and wished to build upon reality.[19]

For John Milton, too, it was the people alone that chooses kings, and that may put them to death. His constant note is liberty: no muzzling of the press, no state-initiated or state-fed Church, no bondage to ceremonies. In full-throated magnificent prose he expounded his concept of a genuine democracy and of civic duty as a religious obligation.[20]

Most outstanding of all, for America and for the progenitors of French revolutionary thought, was John Locke (1632-1704). Few more seminal thinkers have lived in the modern world. We may begin with one of his axioms:

> All the compact that is or needs to be, between the individuals that enter into or make up a Commonwealth, is barely agreeing to unite into one political society.

Implicit in this is the idea of the Social Contract, which we shall find in the writings of Rousseau. Locke broke with Roman law and taught that government is only a trustee for the ends for which society exists. His trust was in the people, the "irrevocable depository of all powers." From this came the American Declaration of Independence and its implicit point of view: the right and duty to resist tyranny; that the people cannot create government and then retire forever into limbo. All along its course, the people are in the government, inalienably possessing the right to resist and to change it. Subjection without consent is unthinkable. Locke's treatises on government, written in 1689, became the central texts of the revolution. He insisted upon toleration, upon the concept of utility. His heritage is best summed up in these four words: Reason, Utility, Toleration, and Property. For him all were in reality subsumed under the first.[21]

After Locke, and varying viewpoints that followed in the writings of Hume, Bolingbroke, and others, the line continued in France. During his sojourn in England, Voltaire had read and learned a great deal.[22] The epoch found one of its points of crystallization for the first time in the eighteenth century that writers began to create the *Encyclopedia*, which was published in France from 1751 to 1771, a work that insisted again and again upon the doctrine of popular sovereignty. The principles central to the thought of the period were: that all men are equal; that they possess a natural right to happiness and self-preservation, to freedom from control of their persons and property, to resist oppression, by force if necessary, and to entertain and give expression to their opinions. Reason was regarded as omnipotent and infallible.[23] No law enacted against nature could be valid. Related to this, logically and humanly, was the concept of Progress. This, too, was deeply imbedded in the "spirit of the age." The term was perhaps first used in an essay by Turgot (1727-1781), though its ultimate source is in Cicero and the Stoics in general.[24]

Germany was not unaffected by these currents. The *Aufklaerung* under Wolff and Lessing was weakening the belief in old institutions and religions. The *Sturm und Drang* period in literature was largely one of revolt. The French Revolution was welcomed by Wieland, Schubart, and even by Wilhelm von Humboldt. Klopstock regretted that he had not a hundred voices with which to celebrate the birth of liberty, and he was joined by Hoelderlin, Herder, and others. The salons of Henrietta Herz and Rahel Levin spoke of naught else.[25]

We must come now, in greater detail, to the line of men who were the chief proponents of the new ideas prevalent in France. Obviously the sequence of events in France cannot be ascribed solely, or perhaps even chiefly, to the ideas that began to be disseminated. There were deep-seated social and political ills prevailing in the country for generations, which had become more and more acute. It was probably because large numbers were seeking an intellectual basis to justify their own sense of unrest, their own passion for change, that France began to produce a series of remarkable men, who created a new philosophy of government. They owed much, it is true, to the English philosophers, but they also struck out new paths of their own—Montesquieu in his *Lettres Persanes* (1720) and *Esprit des Lois* (1748)[26]; the Physiocrats under Turgot; followed by Voltaire (François Marie Arouet—1694-1778). Beginning with a passionate campaign against torture (*Ecrasez l'Infâme*), Voltaire continued in his *Letters on the English People* to wage an intensive campaign against the existing order of government, church, and society. This polemical activity continued for half a century. A large part of his great popularity may be explicable by the fact that he was usually proclaiming loudly the very opinions held by the man in the street. It was he who shouted from the housetops that the king was naked. He startled men out of their complacency, shook the monarchy, though perhaps neither was in the clear line of his purpose. He did not idealize the lower classes; to him they were barbarians, incapable of true culture or the use of reason. He predicted the crumbling of the Church, and its supersession by "natural religion." He advocated the reform of the criminal law, appealed constantly to common sense, and had a rooted distaste for what he called "ideologues." Like most others of his age, he had boundless confidence in reason. In most ways his labors were negative, serving to clear away obstructions, holding the flood back for a little space.[27]

Vauban (1633-1707) wrote of the misery of the French people; Saint-Pierre, of the perfectibility of mankind. Much was said of the dignity of man. Sieyès (1748-1836) asserted that the application of reason to politics would enable man to alter the entire course of his own political development. Condorcet (1743-1794) and Saint-Simon (1760-1825) denounced Christianity and advocated compulsory education. The *Encyclopédie* was edited chiefly by Diderot, d'Alembert, and Grimm. This, as we have noted, became the great repository of rationalism. It represented a concerted and capable effort to rouse the people.[28]

For the last, we have kept the name and work of a man, the most interesting and influential of them all, Jean Jacques Rousseau, who became the polestar of the actual leaders of the Revolution. A man of the people, of humble origin, all his life he was motivated by a deep sympathy for the depressed classes. He was not as rationalistic as his predecessors, but believed rather in the validity of simple human feeling. Two *Discours* (1750 and 1755) and *Émile* (1762) pleaded for a simpler life and for the reform of education. The publication of these works was followed by an electric shock-wave throughout Europe. They were a cry against the artificialities of an outworn civilization, a revolt against convention. This mood lasted for three generations. Rousseau was responsible primarily for one of the most tenaciously held, seminal ideas of the time: that man is free by nature; that left to his own devices he would found and perpetuate a free society, from which happiness would flow simply and directly. This cult of the natural had a thousand results in literature and in politics. In *Le Contrat Social*, Rousseau wrote what was intended to be an explanation of the legal origins of human societies. But it had more than a didactic purpose; he intended it to lead to the removal of artificial constraints upon human action.[29]

It is difficult to overestimate Rousseau's influence upon his time, and upon the amazing period that followed him. Beyond all others, it was he who gave concrete and complete expression to what hosts were feeling. Voltaire was the guest of princes; Rousseau was unalterably of the people. It was he—not alone, but perhaps primarily—who proclaimed that the rule of the popular majority was the will of God; that only natural rights exist among men. Robespierre and the men of "The Mountain" were surely children of Rousseau. He was the rallying point for the inchoate longings of men, for their half-formulated will toward liberation and reformation.[30]

These are but a few of the lineaments of a strange and remarkable time. With the gradual transition from mediaevalism to modernism, civilization groped for a new pattern of life, intellectual and social. It evolved from the feudal to the sovereign national state, an institution that crystallized most recognizably during the Napoleonic era in Western Europe; from the universal Catholic Church to numerous differentiated Christian sects; from the *lingua franca* of Latin to the vernaculars; from a purely agricultural economy toward commercial capitalism and at length to the genesis and rapid development of industrialism; from the period of liege-lord and varlet to the emergence and power of the middle class.

On the cultural side changes were equally clear and equally new. Supernaturalism began to yield to naturalism—though both these terms need to be understood in the way they were used during this period. Triumphs in the field of physics and astronomy convinced many that the universe is regulated by fixed and immutable laws. Instinct and revelation were relegated to a subordinate status, and reason came to be regarded as supreme and as the single avenue to knowledge. It was in the seventeenth century that the popularization of the concept of Reason took place (we have followed only some of the main persons and steps). But by the eighteenth, this opinion was held to be so sure as to require no further demonstration. Upon almost every field of human thought—science, philosophy, religion, and especially social and political theory—this conviction of the supremacy of reason exerted an incalculable influence.

But, over and above directions of thought, this was an era of awakening and prevailing optimism, of boundless confidence in man, in his capacity to lift himself by the process of thought, in making "progress" a universal dogma, and in the widening espousal of purely secular values. It was the age of two great revolutions—in America and in France. The waters of humanity were churned up. The masses were in motion. Millions were led to believe that, though reverses—occasional reverses—might be inevitable, a millennium of freedom, of brotherhood, of peace, and of perpetual progress, was attainable. Besides the major upheavals, there were countless skirmishes on the front of popular liberty, against entrenched privilege, against age-old barricades. Wherever a man might be, at the heart of events or far away in some backward land, if he were alert, if he read what was being written, if his ear was attuned to the prophetic voices declaiming from many forums, he would be swept along in the conviction that great things were in the making, that the concepts of freedom and progress were only beginning to be adopted and pursued. Against stubborn opposition, it was true, they were on the march, and to certain victory![31]

It was into this revolutionary and exciting age that Isaac M. Wise was born. That there had been a temporary setback, not long before his birth, at the Congress of Vienna, mattered little. From the students who were his companions, from the very air, from the books and periodicals he read, these ideas, these events, this vigorous, invigorating spirit, became his own. It is not difficult to discern that all of this was the unvarying substratum of his thinking and feeling. As we have seen in a passage cited at the outset of this chapter, he quoted often the words of Rousseau, of d'Alembert, and of others. Not only the heritage of the French Revolution, but the report and the inspiration of the American Revolution (which eventually drew him across the seas) were his own. From them he derived his own conviction of the meaning of freedom, of the impending doom of all tyranny, of the approaching brotherhood of man, of a certain universality of faith, of the probable nearness of the millennium. The manner in which he phrased all this, and the forms which pursuit of these ideas and ideals took in his own career, in the goals he strove to attain and the ends he proposed for himself, were equally his own. Yet they were also deeply of his generation. It is, therefore, imperative to bear this "setting" in mind, as one reads the tale of his life, and as one peruses his own writings. It is imperative to retain it as a constant background. It was this complex of events and this hope that Isaac M. Wise meant, when again and again he employed the words we have set at the head of this chapter: "The Spirit of the Age."

2

The Jews of Europe

ISAAC M. WISE WAS A MEMBER OF A MINORITY GROUP WHICH HAD suffered more than others from the vestiges of mediaeval oppression, from being hemmed into ghettos, from being forbidden to own or till land, from being excluded from many trades and guilds, from being forced to wear distinctive garments or badges of shame, from living in incessant terror of exile or of deadly slander. Jews had always believed in the coming of a time of peace, justice and brotherhood among men. Even during the darkest days they had not faltered in this faith, hard as it was to cling to when persecution, death, or exile confronted them. That any hopes for an amelioration of their existence, a relaxation of the myriad repressive laws that limited life, business, even worship for them, that any rumor of an utter change of political, cultural, even religious climate, should stir them, arouse in them new strivings and new and often pathetic reachings-out, is not difficult to credit. Who could be more aware than the Jews of Europe of the impending revolution? Who would follow the various preludes to it with such alternations of vaulting hope and obsessive fear? And when at last full political equality was granted them in France in 1791, who would greet it with more frenetic joy, and with more touching gratitude, than they?

Isaac M. Wise was reared in the recollection of these things. His views concerning the position of the Jews, civically and religiously, were shaped by the recollection of these hopes, which had by no means been abandoned, by his own recollection of the response of the European Jewish community during his younger years, as well as later on by his experiences in America, after he and his family had migrated hither in 1846. Together with the movement of ideas and ideals in Europe as a whole, which we have attempted to outline in the preceding chapter, it is also, therefore, essential, that we should begin with some understanding of the conditions and events of the European Jewish community from the middle of the eighteenth century to the middle of the nineteenth.

In the various lands of Europe, Jews were in a position not markedly different from that in which they had been since the end of the Middle Ages. Disabilities hedged them about. In not one European state had they yet been granted even a modicum of civic equality. Special taxes and special legal limitations and discriminations were chronically and continuously saddled upon them. In most lands and in many cities their continuance of residence was precarious. At a moment's notice, at the whim of some tyrant, or because of hate-surcharged suspicions hurled by milling mobs, they could be forcibly ejected. Down through the ages had descended thronging myths concerning them, myths that had become an integral part of the folk beliefs of the ordinary Christian. These myths conditioned the status of Jews, their security of life and property.

The Jewish population of Western Europe at this time (the 18th and 19th centuries) was not numerous. Later on we shall give a few typical figures for some lands. The masses of Jews lived in Poland, before its three partitions. And after these they became citizens,—or rather subjects, of Russia, Prussia, and Austria. In most places Jews were striving to live their own lives, even under the untoward conditions that surrounded them, faithful to a traditional Judaism which had changed not too greatly over the course of centuries, speaking their own version of the vernacular in some lands—like Germany and Austria, and in many places dwelling in their own special quarter of the city (in which they were usually confined), often under the jurisdiction of courts and codes of laws of their own making.

But even before the French Revolution a spirit was beginning to stir in the diverse Jewish communities of Western Europe. In some lands sovereigns indulged in experiments concerning their status, prompted not by any alteration of sentiment, but with the hope of making their bitter lot a bit more bearable, perhaps even—in some cases—to compensate for ancient historic injustice. As a comprehensive rule, it might be laid down that almost always the purpose of these proposals and these measures was to make Jews less conspicuous. The thought entered many minds that the "Jewish problem" might be solved by persuading the Jews to disappear. Few themes are more hypnotically constant—even in the debates and proposals of the French Revolution, and clearly in Napoleon's dealings with Jews—than that the antecedent condition by which Jews might acquire new rights was that they should eliminate, or at least diminish, the differences between themselves and their neighbors.

Nor was this policy lacking in proponents within the Jewish community. Many Jews had felt strongly the magnetic attraction of German culture. In Bohemia Jews had long preferred the German tongue to the Czech. Their children were taught the German language and German literature. This was far different from Eastern Europe, where, for a Jew to devote himself to non-Jewish culture, to draw away from recognized educational and communal agencies, was to be denominated a heretic, an apostate. In the west, however, it became more and more possible for a young Jew to follow this new pathway without suffering any serious consequences in his relation to the community, though there were not wanting occasions and places when and where bitter charges and counter-charges went along with the phenomena of "assimilation."

Up to this general period Jews had more or less taken themselves for granted, had been animated by pride concerning what they regarded as their intellectual and moral superiority over the masses of men about them. They had usually been aware of no compulsion to defend themselves before the world, or to elaborate excuses for their existence. About them might be reiterated charges that they, the Jews, were a pestilence or a tragedy. Their long and not uneventful history might be described as a result of divine anathema. This had never caused them to deviate seriously from the belief that they were "a kingdom of priests and a holy nation."

With the exception of the "Golden" period in Moslem Spain, and in some of the enforced disputations of the Middle Ages, it was for the first time in the eighteenth century that Jews began to create an apologetic literature and to scrutinize their own heritage critically. This was an integral part of their hope to gain essential human rights. That Christians had contended consistently that State and Church were aspects of one indivisible corporate body, Jews were only too well aware. To have the temerity to differ—essentially—in religion, was, to this way of thinking, to make equality of civil position, rights and responsibilities difficult or even impossible. The authorities of some states thought that Jews might be tolerated. But this did not lead them to believe that Jews could be incorporated organically into the state. Again and again Jews heard the contention that the central creative role in western civilization had been and was that of Christianity, invariably without more than a mean-spirited acknowledgment of the debt Christianity owed to Judaism. Our contemporary term, "the Judaeo-Christian tradition" would have aroused the voluble scorn of religious—and many secular—theorists. It was against this immemorial background that the great —though tragically temporary—improvement in the Jewish situation in Europe took place, beginning with the latter years of the eighteenth century.[1]

It is tempting to review the specific conditions under which, at the beginning of this era, Jews lived in various European lands. In Spain there were only crypto-Jews, and *autos-da-fe* were still taking place early in the eighteenth century. Though Jews were not yet full citizens in Holland, they enjoyed freedom of worship and an autonomous communal administration. In the Papal States of Italy, Jews were still in ghettos and subject to incredible special taxes. The partition of Poland severed the members of its community, and threw millions into the feudal arms of Russia. In England, after a century, Jews were permitted to be naturalized, and were certain that full civil rights would soon be theirs. Prussia set the pattern for the German states. The number of Jews was strictly limited by absurd laws about marriage. There was much governmental interference, even with the choice of rabbis, etc. Some of the rulers of Prussia had a mercenary interest in Jews. But the latter were hedged about with petty annoyances and with the status of an inferior group.[2]

Two events occurred which began to bring the problem of the place and position of Jews before the European public: the naturalization of Jews in England and Voltaire's insensate attacks upon them.[3]

We shall next place before the reader, again much too superficially, one of the pivotal figures of the era.[4] A great literature exists about him. Opinions concerning him are widely diverse, and we shall refer in passing to these differences.

Moses Mendelssohn himself summed up the position of the Jews of Europe as it was during his own lifetime in these words:

> It is wonderful to note how prejudice assumes the forms of every country in order to act despotically towards us and place difficulties in the way of our obtaining civil rights. In superstitious ages we were said to insult sacred objects out of mere wantonness, to pierce crucifixes and cause them to bleed; secretly

> to circumcise children and to stab them in order to feast our eyes upon the sight; to draw Christian blood for our Passover; to poison the wells. . . .
>
> Now times have changed, calumny no longer makes the desired impression. Now we in turn are upbraided with superstition and ignorance, lack of moral sentiment, taste and refined manners, incapacity for the arts, sciences and useful pursuits, especially for the service of war and the state, invincible inclination to cheating, usury, and lawlessness, all these have taken the place of coarse indictments against us to exclude us from the number of useful citizens and reject us from the motherly bosom of the state. They tie our hands and reproach us that we do not use them. . . . Reason and the spirit of research of our century have not yet wiped away all traces of barbarism in history. Many a legend of the past has obtained credit because it has not occurred to any one to cast doubt upon it. Some are supported by such important authorities that few have the boldness to look upon them as mere legends and libels. Even at the present moment there is many a city of Germany where no circumcised person, even though he pays duty for his creed, is allowed to issue forth in open daylight unwatched, lest he kidnap a Christian child or poison the wells; while during the night he is not trusted under the strictest surveillance owing to his well-known intercourse with evil spirits.[5]

Some, like the historian Graetz, held the highest opinion of Mendelssohn, and asserted that he had initiated a period of Jewish "rebirth." Others contended that Mendelssohn helped destroy Judaism, not of course wilfully, but that he was the "prototype" of the time when Jews began to chafe at ancient restrictions and set forth to acquire secular culture, to loose the bands of Judaism.[6]

Mendelssohn, born in Dessau, September 6, 1727, was the pupil of a fine scholar, David Frankel. He followed the latter to Berlin, and earned a livelihood by copying.[7] Little by little he learned—Maimonides, mathematics and logic, and also the field of general German literature.[8] Perhaps the most important incident of his early life was his friendship with Gotthold Ephraim Lessing (1729-1781), the first modern German free-thinker. Lessing admired Mendelssohn for his nobility of character, cogency of thought, and devotion to ethical and spiritual verities. Through him Mendelssohn met many leaders of thought, and eventually wrote for them some remarkable essays in philosophy. He won a prize in 1763 in which even Immanuel Kant received only honorable mention. Mendelssohn's major philosophic work was "Phaedon, or the Immortality of the Soul," in Platonic form, a work which won immediate and great popularity, and which captured the assent of many minds. Later Lessing plunged into controversy, and then wrote "Nathan the Wise," a glorification in dramatic form of the virtues of his friend.[9]

Mendelssohn translated the Pentateuch into German (in Hebrew characters) to wean Jews from the use of Judaeo-German to classical, pure German. In spite of orthodox fulminations the translation exercised a widespread influence. It was read even by the Wilna Gaon. In 1783 Mendelssohn published a large work, "Jerusalem, Upon Ecclesiastical Power and Judaism." This work was replete with warm Jewish conviction. In it he argued that Judaism had never possessed a creed, that it was not a revealed religion but "revealed legislation." Mendelssohn died January 4, 1876, before the historical consequences of his life could become clear. He was a great and dedicated Jew, who believed implicitly in the religion into which he had been born. In two ways he cleared the path for much that followed: in his own acquisition of secular culture; and in paving the way for a critical study of Judaism.[10]

We shall now devote ourselves to the consequences of Mendelssohn's life and work, and to the years that immediately preceded the French Revolution.

Many liberals, even before the Revolution increasing in number and influence, discerned that the problem of Jewish rights was an integral part of the whole context of repression. Together with this latter it had to be attacked and solved. They understood that the ghetto was the very sign and symbol of the Middle Ages. But the majority of the people, even of the intellectuals, continued to think of Jews as they had thought of them for centuries.[11]

Those who followed Mendelssohn gave themselves to a rationalist program, to educate Jews, to eliminate all characteristic differences save in the field of religion. A "Jewish Free School" was organized in 1778 with a whole new approach to Jewish education. A habit of mind became prevalent among many Jews, and non-Jews, distinguishing between the national consciousness of Jews and their religious distinctiveness. To what extent this opened the portal for assimilation—that is, assimilation in the negative, or passive, sense—it is not easy to determine.[12]

Christian Wilhelm von Dohm, in 1781, published a book, "Concerning the Improvement of the Condition of the Jews."[13] Dohm did not go to the length of advocating that Jews be permitted to occupy public office. But he wanted to withhold nothing else. This was in the later years of Mendelssohn's life, and the latter hailed it with these words:

> Blessed be Almighty Providence, that has allowed me, at the end of my days, to see the happy time when the rights of humanity begin to be realized in their true extent.[14]

Under the successors of Frederick the Great some of the archaic laws that applied to Jews were repealed.[15] Some Jews went too far and too fast, notably Karl Ludwig Boerne, journalist and essayist (1786-1837), and Heinrich Heine (1797-1856), one of the truly great poets of modern Europe. This was also true of Lassalle and of Karl Marx.[16] There was no little evidence of indecent haste and eagerness in grasping at even the weak beginnings of emancipation. This was especially true in two remarkable *salons,* those of Henrietta Herz and Rahel Levin. To one of these Mendelssohn's daughter, Dorothea, was wont to go.[17] The magazine, to which Mendelssohn had contributed, *Ha-Meassef,* advocated the commingling of old and new, and led to the formation of nuclei of the "enlightened" in various communities. There were some remarkable Jews in diverse creative fields: Marcus Herz, a disciple of Kant, a physician and noted personality; Solomon Maimon, the author of a bitter and very modern autobiography; and Lazarus Ben-David, a mathematician and lecturer on Kant, in Vienna and Berlin.[18] Against such men and their program some of the orthodox leaders thundered, notably an eminent scholar, Ezekiel Landau of Prague. The "enlightened" formed a "Society of Friends," which placed at its masthead a motto from Mendelssohn:

> To seek for truth, to love the beautiful, to desire the good, to do the best.

More than a few of these went over to Christianity.[19] One of the most extreme instances was a letter of David Friedlander to Pastor Teller, expressing his—and others'—willingness to be received into Christianity, providing they would not be required to believe in Jesus, or to follow some of the rites of the church. Perhaps the nadir of the absurdity of assimilationism![20]

Now we come to the sequence of events in France, which influenced vitally the position of Jews, in France most, but to some extent in all European countries. In France itself lived between forty and fifty thousand Jews: Sephardic Jews in Bordeaux and Avignon, about five hundred in Paris, and all others, of German derivation, in Alsace and Lorraine.[21] There had been no material improvement of Jewish status under the Bourbons. In the National Assembly, after the fall of the Bastille, one of the problems often discussed as part of the thesis that all men, regardless of religion or previous condition, should be accorded equal rights, was that of the civil equality of Jews. The Assembly wavered. It temporized. Deplorably, the Portuguese Jews dissociated themselves from those of Alsace and Lorraine. The Constituent Assembly had, on November 3, 1778, adopted a noble historic document (based, as we have noted, on the American Declaration of Independence) known as the "Declaration of the Rights of Man." In this the principle of religious liberty was proclaimed. Some, like Mirabeau and Abbé Gregoire, advocated the immediate application of this declaration to Jews.[22] Three years of delay ensued. But on September 28, 1791, a decree was promulgated, bestowing upon the Jews of France full civic equality.

News of this decree spread like wildfire among Jews, and was received with the most exuberant manifestations of gratitude and joy. Men everywhere were listening to news of the Revolution, and the Jews were no exception. Jews threw themselves into the service of the Revolution, especially during its most precarious years. Some Jews, in spite of their loyalty, died under the blade of the guillotine in the Reign of Terror. But the strong injunction of the new law stood unshaken:

> No one shall be molested on account of his religious opinions, in so far as their outward expression does not disturb public order as established by law.[23]

There were, however, some ominous undertones. At the time of the emancipation one statement was made that needs to be examined closely in all its implications:

> The Jews, conscious of the error of their ways, have felt the need for a fatherland; we have offered them ours.[24]

In general, the experience of Jews during these turbulent years was that they were able to win new rights, rights welcomed with inexpressible joy, only to discover, after the storm had passed, that all that they possessed had been conceded under duress, and that little permanent or genuine improvement in their position had been attained.[25] This was especially true in most lands adjacent or near to France.

The Jews of Holland (about 50,000 of them) had labored under some disabilities. They were given complete emancipation, and this was never taken away from them.[26] In Italy the Revolutionary armies had destroyed the ghettos and torn off the Yellow Badge. But, in 1814, with the loss by France of the Papal States, all Jewish rights disappeared once again.[27] Some German principalities granted Jews freedom: Baden, Westphalia, the cities of Cologne, Lübeck, and

Bremen. Three German princes stood stubbornly unmoved by the stirring of the age: those of Bavaria, Austria, and Saxony. Grudging progress was made in Prussia. For a short time Jews were recognized as citizens, and enlisted under Stein and Hardenberg. But, when the war was over, all this was canceled.[28] In Switzerland (concerning which we shall come to a very interesting chapter in Isaac M. Wise's life), where there were only about two hundred Jewish families, Jews did not enjoy equal rights.[29] The Czar appointed a commission to find a "solution" for the Jewish problem, to civilize Jews by force, and compel them to recognize the superiority of the Russian variety of Christianity. Whatever promises had been made to and concerning Jews at the time of the "Napoleonic menace" were promptly withdrawn after Waterloo.[30]

In time the Revolution spent itself. Perhaps by historic logic it led through the Commune, to the Directory, and to Napoleon as Emperor. Napoleon himself knew very little of Jews. All the evidence appears to indicate that he entertained fantastic and wildly warped ideas concerning them. At the time of his conquest of Egypt, and his invasion of Palestine, he had issued a grandiloquent pronunciamento, urging Jews to accept him as defender, and to come and march under his banners. In return he promised them the Holy Land and the Holy City. Jews paid no attention to this and helped the Turks defend Jerusalem. And like a meteor, Napoleon had come and gone, leaving his army behind him.[31]

A complaint against Jews in Alsace and Lorraine convinced Napoleon later that Jews had to be treated in a way utterly different from the remainder of the nation. He decided to try part persuasion and part compulsion.[32] For a time he considered putting in force again all the discriminatory legislation of the Bourbons against Jews. But he was afraid of appearing to coddle the reactionaries. At long last, and in his own characteristic way, he proceeded to action. He was reported to have said before the *Conseil d'État:*

> The Jews are to be regarded as a nation and not as a sect. They are a nation within the nation. The proper law to apply to them is not the civil but the political law, for they are not French citizens.[33]

This point of view, however, was hard to reconcile with the French constitution, still technically in force. Sometimes Napoleon considered expelling Jews from France, but this might have been interpreted as weakness. Perhaps—who knew?—Jews might be metamorphosed into Frenchmen? But, in exchange, they, the Jews, must cease being a nation and become no more than a religious sect. A way to do this might be by compelling every third Jew to marry a Frenchwoman, and every third Jewess a French husband.[34]

A discussion before the Council led to the appointment of a committee, headed by Count Molé, a very ambiguous individual. After some time he brought in a report retailing all the old slanders. The older members derided this.[35] At a second meeting Napoleon spoke in milder terms. He was not overfond of Jews, but he would not tolerate persecution. Then he had what seemed to him a brilliant inspiration: to summon a formal meeting of Jews, to ask them point-blank whether Judaism required of its adherents hatred and oppression of Christians. Thus Jews would decide their own fate. Other ends were to be: to do away with usury, and to revive among Jews that "civic morality" lost "during the long centuries of a degrading existence."[36]

A decree was drawn up (May 30, 1806), summoning representatives of the French Jewish community.[37] This assembly came to be known as "the Assembly of Jewish Notables." It held sessions from July, 1806, to February, 1807.[38] It began with a communication from the Emperor, concerning Jewish history, the religious and moral separateness of the Jews, and the necessity of withdrawing the sanction of usury. Twelve questions were laid before the Assembly: whether Jews regarded France as their country and Frenchmen as their brothers; did they look upon the laws of the land as binding upon them; can Jews legally intermarry with Christians; is usury from non-Jews forbidden or permitted by Jewish law? There were other questions about the influence of rabbis, polygamy, and divorce.[39]

Most of the questions were easy to answer. The Notables were eager to proclaim their loyalty and that of Jews. They replied with a resounding affirmative about their patriotism and their relation to their fellow-citizens. They were glad to serve France, "Aye, unto death!" They claimed that the Jewish nation as such had ceased to be:

> At the present day the Jews no longer constitute a nation, since they have had the privilege of being incorporated into the great nation in which they expect to find their political salvation.[40]

Nor did they encounter any difficulty on the topics of polygamy or the validity of civil divorce. But concerning intermarriage there were extended and heated debates. Finally they hit upon a "clever" answer.

The Bible had forbidden marriage with "idolaters." Even in the Talmud, however, intermarriage was not prohibited. Nonetheless, the rabbis were opposed to such unions. This had nothing to do with civil marriage, and had to do only with the religious character of the union. But thereafter the community would regard as a Jew or Jewess one who had contracted an intermarriage.[41] The latter part of the Notables' statement was a fairly servile word of gratitude to the Church for protection and benevolence.[42]

This reply was submitted to the commissioners and then to the Emperor, who expressed his gratification. He received the Notables, and found them not cringing, as he had supposed, but including many men of fine character and intelligence.[43] He issued a public statement on September 18, that he had been satisfied, but wanted a guarantee. For this he had another dramatic plan: to summon "the great Synhedrion," to make known to all synagogues that these decisions were henceforth to be "the Law."[44]

The pattern of the ancient Sanhedrin was restored. In the main, nevertheless, all that that body actually did was to put its imprimatur upon the decisions of the Notables. A proclamation was drawn up in February, 1807. This asserted that only religious laws were immutable, and that the political regulations of Judaism had remained inoperative since the fall of Jerusalem. They desired to surrender jurisdiction in civil matters.[45]

The Napoleonic Council issued two decrees: one creating the Consistorial system, still prevailing in France, by which in effect the rabbis became officers of the state; the remainder regulating the civil position of Jews. Jews had to get permits to engage in trade; they were not, like other Frenchmen, allowed to employ substitutes for military service. No more Jews were to be permitted to live in Alsace-Lorraine.[46]

To this day Napoleon is customarily depicted as a friend of the Jewish people. He was nothing of the kind. True, he was not among those who persecuted them. But he was filled with impatience with them for having the temerity to survive. For anything genuine in the way of knowledge about Jews and Judaism he had neither time nor patience. By compulsion, if necessary, he was going to cure them of their obstinacy.[47]

All of this, in spite of some of its coloration, aroused great hopes among Jews all over Europe. Perhaps not all that had been gained in the Revolution would be lost; Jews might be permitted to retain some rights and some opportunities. It was not to be so! The *ancien régime* came in after Waterloo. Hatred of Jews came to new life. One of the wiliest of statesmen, Metternich, turned freedom into a by-word. Rights, painfully gained, were swiftly lost. This was the more distressing to Jews, for they had responded with wild eagerness—often with excessive gratitude and haste—to the opportunities for European culture and political life. In June, 1815, a resolution was proposed to the Vienna Congress, which read as follows:

> The Congress of the allies will consider how the civil improvement of those professing the Jewish faith in Germany is to be effected in the most harmonious manner, and how in particular the enjoyment of civil rights, and participation in civil duties, may be secured to them. The rights already conceded them in the several federated states will be continued.[48]

This sounded more than innocuous, even promising. A deputy from Bremen proposed the alteration of the tiny word "in" to "by," in the last sentence. The simple and drastic effect of this was to render at a single stroke all ameliorations, introduced after the Revolution, null and void.[49] The Holy Alliance united to keep its populations in subjection. In cold fact, Jews had no shred of genuine rights left in the German states.[50] Perhaps the only hopeful connotation of the Congress of Vienna could be taken to be that this was the first time the Jewish question had been regarded as of sufficient importance to be considered as part of the problem of general European political life.[51]

But old conditions could not be restored in their entirety. Jews in France did not lose all their rights. Many improvements in the position of English Jews continued. In Germany, anti-Semitic libels were revived. Pope Pius VIII reintroduced the Inquisition. There were brutal outbreaks. In Russia a storm of reactionary fanaticism was released, and the Czars let it break unhindered over their Jews. Everywhere there was heightened nationalism, intense and exclusive.[52]

But beneath the surface, the forces that led to the Revolution, and the forces unleashed by the Revolution, were still seething. Secret societies and capable journalists fostered the spirit. The days of the privileged nobility and the landed aristocracy were numbered in many lands, and no reactionary forces were to suffice to keep them in power. Sometimes underground, but often in overt tentatives at revolution, the struggle for democracy was going on.[53]

Adolphe Crémieux, in France, was the leading battler against the reactionary policies of Louis Philippe. Nor did he ever fail to spring to the defense of his fellow-Jews.[54] In Germany, Gabriel Riesser (whom we shall encounter in Wise's reading and in his experiences) was the leading proponent of Jewish rights. Riesser had refused to accept baptism to become a professor of law. At a meeting of all German states in Frankfurt in 1848, Riesser served as a vice-president. But the revolution of '48 failed, and many liberals fled, especially to the United States.[55]

One final section must be added to this chapter, concerning the internal movements that were agitating the Jewish community during this momentous period. Unfortunately we have not the space to enter into this more than superficially and briefly. Many aspects will be found in the second part of this book, in Wise's experiences as a young man, in his attendance at the rabbinical conference at Frankfurt in 1845, in his experiences in relation to Reform Judaism in the United States. For a full treatment of the programs and philosophies of Reform, Conservatism, and Orthodoxy in Central Europe, the reader must be referred to any of the standard works which are listed in our bibliography.

Again and again we have emphasized the fact that the stirring events in the life and mind of Europe—beginning with the middle of the eighteenth century—had affected Jews not only in regard to their civil status, but also in their concept of themselves, in the manner in which they lived, in the language they spoke, the books they read, in their general cultural orientation. Jews were led to believe that they might begin to enter into full participation in the life about them. All of this was intensified by the rapid development of commercialism and industrialism. Very germane to this was the historic experience of Jews with the character and use of capital. In many cases, cultural assimilation led insensibly into national assimilation. Jews had a deep and natural interest in the metaphysical, in the burgeoning art of music, in the German language, and in the breadth, depth, and richness of German *Kultur*.[56] Time again forbids our entering into a discussion of the pathos of some of these responses, the sharp contrast between the eager assimilation of many Jews, and the grudging—often vicious—reception accorded them, individually and nationally. Schleiermacher, for example, criticized acidulously those Jews who got civic advantages by the road of conversion.[57] Even Riesser, in a work entitled "Concerning Those Who Profess the Mosaic Faith in Germany" (1830), defended Jews against the charge that they constitute a nation. Communal autonomy, he asserted, had nothing to do with patriotism. Riesser went so far as to write: "We are either Germans, or we are homeless." From the vantage-point of our time, almost two centuries later, we can see to what tragic consequences this struggle for citizenship and participation in German culture led.[58]

In this time and atmosphere Reform Judaism came into existence. Certainly its purpose was not, as its detractors claimed and still claim, to open an easy way out of Judaism. Nor did it propose to liquidate anything it regarded as fundamental to Judaism. Little by little, by way of changes in ceremonies, ritual, the use of Hebrew, it came to an evolutionary concept of Judaism, an adaptation in form and idea to the shifting needs of its age. Its first stage was devoted largely to the synagogue, to the institution of choral music and the organ, the use of the vernacular, emphasis on the sermon, the family pew, a change in the status of woman, etc. Intense struggles followed with the orthodox in various communities, and often appeals were made to the state by one side or another. The *Piutim* (largely mediaeval liturgical poems) were taken out of the liturgy (we shall come across this issue a number of times in Wise's own career in America). Those sections in the prayer book that had to do with a personal Messiah, and with a return to Palestine, were excised. In some strange way, the use of the pipe-organ at services became the chief *casus belli.* In the course of the prolonged and bitter debates, engendered by all this, a third party began to make its appearance, a party which propounded a more moderate approach to the problems of authority and revelation, which contended that "historical Judaism," the continuity of tradition and practice, must be the primary desideratum.

Farthest apart were such men as Samuel Holdheim for the Reform group, and Samson Raphael Hirsch for the Orthodox. Holdheim believed in extreme changes in practice and belief, the discarding of all that he regarded as outworn and outmoded. Hirsch spoke and wrote eloquently of the literal truth of the revelation on Sinai. Without Torah—in the traditional sense—Hirsch contended there would be no Israel. Against the divine, reason could be accorded no validity.[59] There were also moderates, like Abraham Geiger and Zechariah Frankel. It was Geiger who labored diligently upon the theoretical foundations of Reform, by tracing the actual record of Judaism as a living movement, not a fossil, not a changeless reality, but a growing entity, of which the forms—and even sometimes the ideas—had altered and would continue to alter. For him this did not connote that the core and heart of the message of Judaism was to be tampered with. With most of this, Frankel went along. His main difference concerned the manner in which changes were to be regarded as permissible. These, he argued, must come into being by themselves, without conscious deliberation, and always in complete accord with the consistent direction of the Jewish tradition.[60] Certainly it must be conceded that in almost all its earliest manifestations Reform declared Jews to be a "religion only." It renounced entirely, not merely the national concept of Jewish life, but often even that of the distinctiveness of the Jewish people.

A most important and seminal movement, in 1819, was the "Society for the Culture and Scientific Knowledge of Judaism" in Berlin. A magazine was launched to display Judaism as a faith possessing a rich culture and a continuous and creative meaning of its own. The greatest giant on its roster was Leopold Zunz (1794-1886), and through it he elaborated a towering structure of scholarship. By 1840, when he became a member of the faculty of a teachers' seminary in Berlin, he had produced most of his remarkable works: "The Religious Discourses of the Jews"; "The Names of the Jews," etc.[61] It was in fact Zunz who had suggested the name of the society.[62] He favored some innovations—like choral singing—and some revision of the content of belief. But he was consistently opposed to the calumniation of the Talmud, in which only too often and unjustly some men were indulging. This he regarded as no less than suicidal. Nor did he favor discarding fundamental Jewish observances like *Milah* (circumcision), or the seventh-day Sabbath.[63]

The general character of the time, for the Jews of Europe, should now be apparent: a time of glowing new hopes, of the lifting of the pall of many centuries! A time of wavering advance and retreat! A time in which—behind the sequence of events—lay in the minds of many a bold optimism, the conviction that nothing could stay the forward march of freedom, of brotherhood, of democracy! A time that seemed to many Jews to fit snugly into the context of Hebrew prophecy! A time that led some—perhaps too swiftly and too trustingly—to believe that a Messianic age was at hand, and—like the old parable of the man concerning whom the sun and the wind made a wager—to strip off the old protective cloak of Judaism!

Again, without the picture we have drawn of the causes, the character, and the progress of liberalism in Europe, especially in England, France, and America, and of the effect all this had upon the status, the hopes, and the self-concept of Jews, Isaac M. Wise himself, his career, his essential opinions and ideas, even his plans, would be utterly unintelligible. It is far from easy today for men, who are heirs of a very different time, to move backward in thought to this unique period, from the middle of the eighteenth to the middle of the nineteenth century. Too much has intervened between us and it. But without this understanding, nothing else in the life and work of the man of whom we shall write can be comprehended. In every sense he was a child of his time, both non-Jewish and Jewish. Its hidden or overt hopes were his own. He dreamed its dreams, and clasped to his heart its revolutionary fervor. As we shall see, his own Jewish background moved out of the parochial into the broadly human. His reading shifted more and more into the field of liberty, of universality, of the need of adjusting to a new day. He was a European Jew. Despite his childhood in Bohemia, he shared the aspirations and often the disappointments of the European community as a whole. This does not mean to say that he was completely explained by external factors. Far from it! But without the setting of this time, his life and his dearest ideals would remain obscure and sometimes fantastic!

3

The Jews of Austria and Bohemia

LET US DEVOTE SOME PAGES TO A CLOSER LOOK AT ISAAC M. WISE'S native land, to Bohemia, and to Austria of which it was then a part. Inevitably both these lands were affected by the general course of European history, between 1750 and 1848, which we have described. Despite its autocratic character and its age-old devotion to Catholicism, the Hapsburg Empire was unable to prevent the infiltration of ideas, the contagion of the excitement that throbbed through the very air of Europe. It was, moreover, occupied several times by French troops under Napoleon, saw the tricolor waving from its flag-staffs, and must have had to listen—however unwillingly—to the bombast of French officers and soldiers. As a government, however, and in relation to its Jewish inhabitants, Austria and Bohemia were less altered by the Revolution than almost any other country except Czarist Russia. They succeeded in resisting the blandishments of freedom and the insistency of change.

From of old, Austria had set an example in the maltreatment of and discrimination against its Jews. Its statute-books contained a multiplicity of laws that regulated what Jews might do and what Jews might not do. All of this was part of the general context of extreme paternalism in the Austro-Hungarian monarchy, by which the life and even the beliefs of its subjects were kept under incessant surveillance. In the eyes of the Emperors the existence of Jews appeared to impair the homogeneity of their Empire, although how anyone could regard as homogeneous a state which comprised Germans, Magyars, Slovaks, Slovenes, and Czechs, not to omit Serbs, Croats and others, it is difficult to imagine. Through the centuries Jews had been regarded as utterly different, not only by religion, but by race and nationality, by laws, customs and costumes, and even by places of residence. The new fashion was to hold them at arm's length, rather than to torture and slay them, as had been the historic wont; to strive to make them objects of derision, to represent them as backward and barbarous.[1]

Jews had been expelled from Vienna in 1670. But this edict was from the beginning a dead letter; for some Jews continued to do business in the capital city, even though they were not permitted to reside there officially. Jews helped furnish the sinews of war with which to repel the Turks in the crucial war of 1683. In 1722, as a result of the malignant fanaticism of the clergy, the mob destroyed the synagogue and drove out the congregation in the city of Aussee,—all following upon trumped-up charges by a lying priest.[2] In modern times in Europe, and up to the partition of Poland, Austria had the largest Jewish population, not for any lack of effort on its part to reduce that population drastically. Sometimes Jews were tolerated, and sometimes they were expelled. An ardent disciple of the Jesuits, Leopold I (1675-1705) was wed to a Spanish Infanta, and later appointed a group of experts to make a study of the "Jewish problem." As might have been anticipated from the personnel of this commission, the gist of its report was that by their very existence Jews constituted an anti-Christian conspiracy. Followed new measures expelling Jews from Vienna and Lower Austria. The *Judenstadt* in Vienna was rechristened the *Leopoldstadt.* But the only immediate and concrete result was a rapid decline in trade, a rise in prices, and a dearth of funds in the imperial treasury. Perhaps, it was whispered, Jews were—at least economically—more useful than had been thought. Thus a new Jewish community was suffered to begin, though it was as usual surrounded with crushing rules and discriminatory regulations.[3]

Heavy taxes, especially devised for them, were often levied upon Jews. Charles VI taxed them to defray the expenses of his coronation in 1711. In 1717, a large loan was extorted from the Austrian Jews. Underlying all the vagaries of this record, upon which we have only touched, was the principle that at best, Jews were a nuisance, that they required constant surveillance, and that without the exercise of unremitting caution they could and would become vicious. It was the same Charles VI, who first issued the decree—upon which we shall come again and again—that no more than one member of a Jewish family might marry. This iniquitous law was enacted on September 23, 1726.[4]

Maria-Theresa—a remarkable woman in many ways, but also a thorough-going bigot—reigned in Austria from 1740 to 1780. In most of her acts she exhibited consistent hostility toward Jews. One of her less successful wars was against Frederick the Great. Some of her adjutants, probably for want of a more plausible reason, spread the word that her defeat had been due to the treason of Jews—a recurrent practice in European history. Upon these selfsame Jews, therefore, she levied a huge fine, and in 1744 expelled all those who dwelt in Bohemia, including Moravia and Silesia. There were 20,630 of them, and it was in the depths of winter.[5] Actually the edict was held in abeyance, but for this imperial clemency Jews had to pay a tremendous annual sum.[6]

Strangely enough Maria-Theresa sometimes evinced a deep interest in matters pertaining to the synagogue. A statute of 1754, concerning the Jews of Moravia, is a classic in the field of paternalistic (or, in this case, shall we say "maternalistic"?) legislation. In it the duties of the district-rabbi are set forth in great detail, the mode of his election, and even a curriculum for the Talmudic seminary. All Jewish books were to undergo examination by a Jesuit member of the commission. In 1760 all Jews were ordered to don a yellow badge, if they did not already wear beards.[7] Only upon one occasion, apparently, did Maria-Theresa display any mitigating signs of humanity; this was on February 15, 1769, when she decreed that no Jewish child was to be baptized against the will of its parents. On occasion, also, she tried to improve somewhat the material conditions under which Jews lived. It was enacted (April 10, 1772) that Jews might sell new garments, made by themselves, and engage in the craft of jewelry. But they were forbidden to employ apprentices. Jewish learning was restricted to rabbinical disciplines.[8]

In her later years Maria-Theresa ruled jointly with her son, Joseph II. Between the two was a wide gulf as to the desirable directions of royal policy. Perhaps by disposition, and certainly as a result of his rearing and experience as a young man, Joseph was a sincere devotee of liberalism. Although we are not fortunate enough to have any concrete evidence, his reading must have included the books referred to in Chapter One, the intellectual and moral pabulum of the Revolution. After his mother's death in 1780, he became sole monarch of Austria and Hungary. His reign lasted only ten years.

One of the duties Joseph set himself was to alleviate the condition of the Jews. On October 21, 1781, he had all laws abrogated requiring Jews to wear a distinctive garb or sign. He urged Jews to become assimilated into their environment, to use the language of the land, and to establish new schools in which a modern education might be sought (*Normalschulen*). Jews were also accorded permission to enroll in public high-schools and universities, to lease land for agricultural purposes (though they might still not employ Gentile labor), and to engage in the mechanical trades, arts, and in commerce. All of these provisions were in the legislation of October 21, 1781. On December 10, he abolished the iniquitous poll-tax, and informed the citizens of Austria that henceforth Jews were to be treated as fellowmen (*Nebenmenschen*).[9]

One can imagine the deep sense of gratitude, even of adulation, all of this aroused in the Jews of Austria, especially in the light of the many centuries of their suffering in these lands. By all odds the most important document of Joseph's decade of sovereignty, so far as Jews were concerned, was the *Toleranz-Patent* of January 2, 1782, which was preluded by the statement that the Emperor's purpose was to enable all his subjects—without distinction as to creed or nationality—to share in the welfare and the freedom of the country. Some few restrictions as to residence for Jews remained in force. But as a whole, the document breathed in every line the spirit of a new era.[10] All economic restrictions inhibiting Jews were abolished. Jews might appear abroad before noon on Sunday. Jews were enjoined to adopt family names and to serve in the army. These measures were the very first of their kind in modern Europe.[11] It should not be difficult to imagine how all this raised the hopes of the Jews in Joseph's domain, and even among the Galician Jews, 100,000 of them, who had been taken into Austria after the third partition of Poland.[12]

It is sad to have to record that this harbinger of a new day of freedom proved very brief. Unfortunately, Joseph was not robust. He fell ill and died at the age of forty-nine. The succession fell to his brother, Leopold II (1780-1792). But his reign too was not long, —and it was almost entirely uneventful. With the passing of Joseph, the Catholic bishops of Austria were sure that the country would revert to the good old days of oppression and repression. They petitioned Leopold to abrogate all the new laws Joseph had had passed, and to return the Jews to the status of crown-vassals (*Kammerknechte*), dependent for all their so-called rights upon the whim of the ruler. But Leopold proved unwilling to take so drastic an action, and replied evasively.[13]

Meanwhile, Jews had responded promptly to the liberalism of Joseph. New schools had been established in Prague and in Trieste. Other cities soon followed this example, though Galicia continued on its wonted way. A number of Jews adopted the suggestion that they should enter mechanical and agricultural pursuits. Later a "Society for the Promotion of Mechanical Occupations" was founded in Vienna (1840), and still another in Prague (1846). For the first time, a Jewish kindergarten was opened, and a school for the blind.[4]

Leopold II was succeeded by his son, Francis I (later Francis II, after he became Holy Roman Emperor), in 1792. It must not be forgotten that his accession to the throne was in the most tumultuous years of the French Revolution, when Austria was again and again occupied by French troops. Under his rule all the purposes and acts of Joseph II were canceled, and new humiliations were saddled upon the Jews of Austria. On many new classes of objects burdensome taxes were levied. Many were intended merely to constitute petty annoyances, as those upon candles, wine, and meat. Every Jew who entered Vienna had to pay a special toll. As though they were spies or criminals, Jews were kept under constant surveillance. Under the old, inhumane regulation of the *Familienrecht*, marriages were restricted. Under Francis and his chief minister, Metternich, Jews were herded back into ghettos.[15] Some sections of the country—the Tyrol, for example, and the mountain cities of Bohemia—were closed to Jewish residence. Everywhere there were especial Jew-streets. In Galicia the oppression became worse than in the Middle Ages. Under Francis, a few Jews were given patents of nobility. While military service was required of Jews, they were not permitted to become officers.[16] Jewish books were subjected to strict censorship. By exacerbation and petty annoyance everything seemed intended to drive Jews toward baptism.[17] No Jew in Vienna could own his own home in his own name. A special permissive act of grace was required for the building of a synagogue.[18] To evade the restriction concerning homes, some Jews bought houses under the names of Christians. This attempt to circumvent the "law" aroused the intense indignation of the Emperor.[19] Added to all these there were many galling interferences in the internal affairs of the Jewish community. Jews might not have music on Chanuccah, or dance on Purim (1802 and 1824).[20] Jews were forced to take an examination on religion, the examination based on Herz Homberg's *Bene Zion* (1810).[21]

Some other legislation was perhaps intended in a kindlier spirit, though it played havoc with the ancient government of Jewish communities. There was a *Patenz* for Bohemia, August 3, 1797, which held forth the hope that eventually all Jewish disabilities would be removed. The only new law actually put on the books was one requiring all candidates for the rabbinate to take a course in philosophical studies. This law—originally for Bohemia alone—was later applied to all other parts of the Empire (1810 and 1826). But it remained a dead letter until the days of Isaac M. Wise's youth, in the 1830s and '40s.[22]

While the Assembly of Jewish Notables was meeting in Paris in 1806, and during the time of the Great Sanhedrin in 1807, Francis and some of his sage advisers thought that Austrian Jews might become unduly excited by these world-shaking events and seek to serve Napoleon's cause in Austria. Repeated protestations from Jews themselves as to their unswerving loyality fell on deaf ears. Jewish letters were seized and read. One Jew—Bernhard Eskeles—had actually been invited to come to Paris, but had publicly refused, and had turned the invitation over to the police. For the Jews of Austria it was a time of suspicion, of dark whispering, and of fear.[23]

On November 10, 1829, the Emperor established a "scientific" institution for the education of rabbis at Padua, which—it must be remembered—was under Austrian rule. In 1817, Francis issued a permit to the Jews of Vienna to build a "Temple" on the model of that in Hamburg. But a foolish clause was appended, that they might not style themselves a "congregation," but only "The Jews of Vienna."

The reign of Francis was followed by that of Ferdinand I (1835-1848). No scintillating intellectual, Ferdinand was a ruler who exerted little influence upon the actual course of affairs. His ministers were bent upon maintaining a patriarchal state in the traditional pattern, the policy which Metternich had regarded as the surest guarantee of public order. Nonetheless, the tacit progress of the age, the continued stirring of revolutionary ardor, the whole heritage of the eighteenth century were perceptible in Austria too. The status of the Jews of Vienna was changed mildly for the better. They were allowed to transfer to their children the right of residence in the capital. Many of the old repressive laws fell into desuetude, simply because the police did not bother to enforce them. On June 14, 1841, Jews were again granted the right to own farms, provided they worked the land themselves. The ancient and galling restrictions upon marriage—in force since the beginning of the eighteenth century—were interpreted more liberally. Of this particular problem we shall hear in detail, when we come to the time of Wise's ministry in Radnitz. Teachers and rabbis were permitted to marry without restriction. On August 18, 1846, the oath *more Judaico* (a particular insult to Jews, which had come down from very ancient European practice) was abolished. Jews were urged once again to acquire German, and the Emperor declared himself interested in the reform of public worship.

Almost without exception the Jews of Austria were completely traditional in their religious practices and beliefs. In Vienna there was a single attempt to introduce the "Hamburg" reforms—under one M. L. Biedermann—but this was limited to the omission of some of the *Piutim*, the use of a trained choir, a greater degree of decorum at services, and a German sermon. All this in 1826. Two other places tried these things, Tarnopol and Brody.

And thus we come to the conclusion of this depressing chapter in Jewish history. When the Revolution of 1848 came (after Wise had left Bohemia), it turned at once into a struggle between the Hapsburg dynasty and the people. A young Jewish medical student in Vienna, Adolf Fischhof by name, was one of those who came to power under the revolution. Other Jews took part in Austria, in Bohemia, and in Hungary. The first martyrs of the Revolution, Gentiles and Jews, were buried in a common grave. At the funeral, Rabbi Isaac Noah Mannheimer was one of those who officiated. It was true that the Revolution, in Austria as in Germany, was defeated, and the old regime returned to its former power. But not a little had been gained. In the next twenty years, emancipation for Jews and the extension of democracy in a number of directions was to come. Jews became citizens of Austria on March 4, 1849. Most of the mediaeval restrictions in respect to trades and professions were rescinded, and Jews were given the right to own land. Finally, in 1867, the Constitution bestowed upon Jews full citizenship.[24]

The latter part of this chapter we shall devote to the Jews of Bohemia. Here, certainly since the tenth century, and perhaps even earlier than that, they had lived. The repressive legislation of Austria, which we have reviewed, hemmed them in. They could not buy land or pursue agriculture. The institution of the *Familienrecht* applied to them too, beginning with 1744, and remained in force until 1848. Bohemia was permitted to have no more than 10,000 Jews, and not more than 5100 families.[25] Only the eldest son might marry. When such a marriage was without issue, the *Familienrecht* could be acquired by someone else.[26] Periodically Jews were exiled. Usually they were then permitted to return (to Prague, for example, June

30, 1745) because "their departure would entail a loss of many millions," but always under degrading conditions. They were forced to pay into the imperial treasury an annual sum of 200,000 Gulden, and this hard requirement remained in force until the Revolution of 1848.[27]

In 1757, after her war with Frederick the Great, Maria-Theresa praised some of the Jews of Bohemia for the help they had given, and said some words concerning their patriotism.[28] But this was the sole sign of alleviation in a reign—as far as the Jews of Bohemia were concerned—characterized by unremitting prejudice. Jewish trade was hedged about with limitations. Jews had to wear a Yellow Badge, which was abolished only in 1781, under Joseph II.[29] On one occasion the Jews of Prague presented a petition to Maria-Theresa. They brought respectfully to her attention that they were not permitted to buy victuals before a certain hour; that Jewish druggists found it almost impossible to do business; and that the general and special taxation upon them was intolerable. They filed a special objection to a specific tax on the *Esrogim* they used for *Sukkoth* (1747).[30]

On July 1, 1789, a provision—similar to that in force in Galicia—was drawn up to be applied to the Jews of Bohemia. This was promulgated on February 15, 1790, only a few days before the death of Joseph II. The number of synagogues that might exist in Galicia had been fixed at 141. But only one was authorized in Bohemia, that in Prague.[31] Like other Jews in the Empire, those of Bohemia had been greatly heartened and their condition greatly ameliorated by the "Patent of Toleration" of Joseph in 1782. The ghetto was abolished. Jewish physicians were permitted to treat Christian patients. Jews could serve in the army.[32] An essential feature of Joseph's intent was to induce more Jews to take up agriculture.[33]

A strange man, by name Anton von Riegger, was entrusted with the duty of dealing with the "Jewish problem." His publicly avowed purpose was to metamorphose Jews into full citizens. Riegger was called to the University of Prague in 1778, and was also given a government office. He left Prague, but returned to it in 1785 from Vienna. He claimed to be a man of the Emancipation, and a Free Mason. While he asserted that his purpose was to improve the conditions of Jewish life, he was opposed to any increase in the number of Jews, asserting that such an increase would create problems both for the State and for themselves. Through all his words and deeds one could discern the conviction that Jews belong to a different nation, in speech, customs, and character; that Jews had contributed much to "immorality" in many lands. In this he was referring to what he regarded as chronically unethical Jewish business practices. And, to complete the bewildering picture, he claimed to have a strong dislike of religious prejudice in general.[34]

In April, 1786, Riegger issued a *Gutachten.* How was the "morality" of Jews to be improved? Primarily through education! With this thesis Riegger coupled an extensive criticism of traditional Jewish education: no real grammar; only the text of the *Siddur* (the prayer book), the Bible, and the Talmud; their only speech a corrupt "*misch-masch*"; a regard for the Talmud greater than that which Jews entertained for the "Old Testament" (so Riegger said!). Schools for Jews under State guidance and control were the prerequisite, but this alone would not suffice. Riegger continued with an ancient and characteristic Gentile slander: that Jews loved their "neighbor" only when that neighbor was of the same religion. He cited the much misused passage in Deuteronomy (Chapter 23, verses 20-21), which he contended meant that Jews were permitted to take usury from non-Jews. Among the Jews, he said, one might come occasionally upon enlightened men, but in most cases these were no longer Jews. Centuries had made it too difficult for Jews to be like other men. A long and arduous course of training would be required before Jews would be ready for emancipation. . . . And this was a man who claimed to be of the "Enlightenment"! His specific proposals were: to attempt to transform the Israelitish nation into a religious community; private instruction to be replaced by public; the abandonment of *Juedisch-Deutsch*; the prohibition of printing books in this "Jargon"; the new schools to have Christian principals; schools for women; and all religious instruction in German.[35]

During the reign of Leopold II there were two parties among Bohemian Jews: one conservative, bent on retaining the rights gained under Joseph; and a more aggressive group, who wished to go beyond these. The latter sought assurances from the Emperor.[36] At the outset there was some small improvement. Taxes were lightened. Some congregational unions were to be permitted. The *Familienrecht* system was to be made more endurable. A petition was sent to Leopold from Prague on May 6, 1790, asking for the protection of the Jewish faith, and the undisturbed application of Jewish laws and customs. A second petition followed on May 12, asking for the free right to marry. The Emperor was informed that marriage was a religious commandment, a *Mitzvah,* among Jews; and they petitioned not to be compelled to work on the Sabbath. Leopold asked for comments upon these petitions from his Chancellery. The Jews of Bohemia were permitted to hope for some amelioration, especially in regard to the marriage regulations. A few minor concessions were put into effect: some marriages with relatives were permitted, where these accorded with Jewish law.[37] A marriage with the sister of a deceased wife was forbidden. Divorce was to be legal only in cases of proved adultery. Jews were still to be compelled to furnish recruits for the army.[38]

As in general in Austria, suspicion at the time of the Assembly of Notables and the Sanhedrin in Paris, in 1806 and 1807, settled upon the Jews of Bohemia. The letters of Jewish leaders were opened and read. The Orthodox Jews of Prague issued a public declaration, dissociating themselves from the Sanhedrin, which they feared might recommend dogmatic innovations. Nonetheless, they were following the Assembly and the Sanhedrin closely in the press. A few Jewish leaders were inclined to agree that certain reforms might be necessary.[39] The young Jewish *intelligentsia* were enthused about Napoleon and his creations. Many letters were actually exchanged with French and Dutch Jews.[40]

At the Congress of Vienna, representatives of the Jews of Bohemia and Moravia approached the Emperor and Metternich, and presented a petition asking for equality of inheritance, and in trade and ownership rights. The men who composed this delegation were called the "head of those for Jewish emancipation."[41]

Subsequent to the Congress the position of the Jews of Bohemia—as of Jews almost all over Europe—deteriorated. Various decrees, enacted in 1827 and in 1828, introduced new varieties of discrimination. In Prague and elsewhere Jews were forced back into a ghetto. Emigration was made very difficult. A special and onerous system of taxes was levied upon them.[42] The provisions of the *Familienrecht* were reinstituted. Coming as all this did after the high hopes aroused by the French Revolution, it was doubly bitter. In 1834, some representatives of Bohemian Jews—headed by Juda Porges, Samuel Lippmann, and Nathan Dormitzer—presented a petition to the Emperor, Francis, asking that full rights of citizenship be accorded the "Israelites" of Bohemia.[43]

At the beginning of the nineteenth century, the time of the birth, childhood, and youth of Isaac M. Wise, Jewish children were instructed chiefly by tutors in their own homes, in the Hebrew of the Torah and of the Mishna. There were some excellent Yeshivas, in which students were instructed in the Talmud. In 1797, it was proposed to found a Jewish university. And such an institution actually enjoyed a brief existence until 1806. To it came also some foreign students, about whom the government made constant trouble.[44]

The revolution of 1830 had little effect in Austria in general, and the general status of Jews in Bohemia did not improve materially until after the revolution of 1848.[45]

From this somewhat hasty sketch it should be clear that the position of Jews in Bohemia was not radically different from that of their coreligionists in the remainder of Austria. In their own history there were some special incidents of expulsion and of oppression. They were swayed by the same visions of deliverance, and plunged into the same depression when the old order returned. Rich as it was in Jewish learning and in Jewish loyalty, their life was lived under the darkness of fanaticism, of inherited repression, of the absence of any veritable humanity.

For the end of this preliminary section, concerning the time and place into which Isaac M. Wise was born, we have kept a résumé of some articles he himself wrote for the *Asmonean* in 1854, at the very end of his tenure as a rabbi in the city of Albany.[46] Unfortunately these articles were never finished. This was an eventful time in his life, just at the time of his election to the pulpit in Cincinnati, and the removal of himself and his family thither—a major undertaking. He did not find time, then or later, to complete the series, as probably he had planned it. But what we have is picturesque, furnishing us with some scattered sketches of the life Jews lived in Bohemia during his young manhood.

> It is admitted by all travelers who bestow sufficient attention on Jews, that those of Bohemia are as a class the best educated, and the wealthiest in the Austrian empire.

In the United States—at the time Wise was writing this—there were four rabbis, and no less than ten physicians, who had come from Bohemia. . . . The commercial interests of Bohemia, he wrote, were largely in the hands of Jews, and the country was the seat of many ancient Yeshivas.

> In the center of the village, where Jews live, usually stands the Synagogue, often a beautiful stone building, with a brick roof, and a *Mogen David* on top. Most of the synagogues inside are plain, arched, and have high bow-windows. Next to the synagogue is the dwelling of the minister and the school-rooms. Around the synagogue are usually the best houses of the Jewish families.

Services were well attended. *Minyanim* were always present. In general liturgical use was the *Minhag Polen* except in a few places where the *Minhag Ashkenaz* was employed. In many cases the minister was also the *Hazan*, and often also the *Shochet*, the teacher, and even the *Shamash*. Even in places where there were no more than two Jewish families—Wise claimed—there was a good synagogue; and, where there were thirty Jewish families, they were wont to have an organ, a choir, and both a rabbi and a *Hazan*.

The children attended both public and Hebrew schools, and were instructed in three different languages: Slavonic (Czech), German, and Hebrew. Rich families employed private teachers, and for this purpose expended large sums of money. During the time of which he was writing, the great subject of study was the Talmud. Exceptionally bright boys were sent away from home to study, and were supported—in conformity with a time-honored Jewish custom—at the tables of the wealthy. Even poor boys were thus enabled to attend the higher institutions of learning. At a Yeshiva, life was strange. Sixty or a hundred lads—ranging in age from fourteen to twenty—came into a single room twice a day to be instructed by a venerated master. The boys had previously studied a passage from the Talmud, upon which the master was to comment. The teacher's purpose was to correct their own reading and interpretation, and to indicate to them the methods of Jewish disputation:

> Outside the schoolroom there was perfect liberty. There was not in a Bohemian Yeshiva that bigotry as in Hungary and elsewhere, that the students were prohibited from reading belletristical works, or that it was considered a crime to know Ibn Ezra's commentary on the Bible, or Maimonides' *Moreh Nevuchim*. On the contrary it was considered an accomplishment to have read Schiller's, Goethe's, Lessing's, or Wieland's works; and the young man spent a considerable time in philosophical-theological books, such as the *Kuzari*, the *Moreh*, *Chovoth* ("Duties of the Heart," by Bachya ibn Pakuda). We remember distinctly that we had formed a secret Club for the study of *Cabalah*, and we met for this purpose three times a week from nine to twelve P.M., but, when our old master found out the secret of our Club, he earnestly exhorted us not to spend our time with such an impractical study, calculated to make young men bigots and phantasts; he said it would be better for us to read Moses Mendelssohn's, Abarbanel's, or de Rossi's works.

Gradually the system in Bohemia was making way for modern

education. When Wise left Bohemia, there were hardly any traces of Talmudic instruction left in the villages and small towns. Most places were demanding rabbis who had gone to a university. Bright boys were studying Latin, geography, history, etc., instead of Talmud. They would go to an Academy, to a Gymnasium, or to a University. Only those intending to become "rabbins" studied Talmud, "and they must do so in private schools, and after the college hours." An attempt to establish a rabbinical college had failed.

In Bohemia there was no good education at all for girls:

> But this is a common fault in Europe, and it is not quite rectified in this country.
>
> The country Jews in Bohemia are very religious, sometimes superstitious, have good morals, are industrious and enterprising.

In the second place, Wise turned to the nature of family life, as it was in Bohemia. This—he wrote—was still entirely patriarchal in character. The father was the "independent sheik of the house." There were old laws and rules of love and reverence, "but sometimes this degenerates into a kind of petty tyranny." Children were required to be unconditionally obedient. They were not accorded the right of selecting their own vocation, or their partner in marriage. Only married children were regarded as independent. But they too were expected to pay due respect to their parents. Domestic quarrels were very rare, "and almost never grew up to violent differences."

No one was idle. All the men were in business. They worked hard, as did the women in the home. Upon sabbaths and holidays they placed a very high value. For them the house was thoroughly cleaned and the clothing changed. The man went to the synagogue. At home the lamps were lit and a white cloth spread upon the table. The mother read the ancient prayer. All was festive and clean. The father returned from prayers, blessed the children, and all washed their hands, sat at the table and sang *Sholom Aleichem.* The special sabbath-bread was broken. There was no meat, which was however not missed, and "fish must grace the table." After the meal the family sang *Zemiroth*, and the blessing over the meal was recited.

> The poor are sent flour, oil, money, and meat on Thursday, to have them for the Sabbath.

In general the same procedure was followed on the eve of holidays.

But much more ado was made about the *Seder* in the month that preceded and that which followed it. In the home there were many additional festivities; for example, betrothals, which were always held at night and in the house of the bride. A porcelain cup was broken in the presence of a number of friends, and those nearest the couple got each a piece of the cup. Customarily, about a year intervened between the betrothal and the wedding. In the olden days, a wedding-feast was given for the entire community; a band played before the house of the bride, and afterward there was a dinner and a breakfast. Formerly, weddings were held in an open place, but later in the synagogue. It had been the custom for the bridegroom to give a public Talmudic discourse. Every guest came with a present for the young couple. Often professional comedians were employed. Before 1848, there was a law that no Bohemian Jew could marry without a license. And such a license was granted only to the first-born son. Many were thus excluded from their natural right of legal marriage. Jews went to much trouble and expense to get a license:

> But the Jews were by no means deterred by those inhuman measures of the government; they married by thousands without legal permission. In such cases the ceremonies were performed by some private person and in a secret place, because the laws set a heavy penalty upon the act; the wives were considered by the government as mistresses, and the children who received the family name of the mother were considered bastards. The subordinate officers of the State saw the impossibility of enforcing the law, and so thousands of families lived in this manner.
>
> It is really a matter of surprise that, notwithstanding that inhuman law, a high state of morality and regard for female innocence was maintained among the Jews of Bohemia, merely by the religious sentiment of the people and the unlimited authority of the parents.

In Wise's days, most of the Jews of Bohemia lived in cities. Formerly they dwelt chiefly or only in villages. This had caused many changes among them. Few traces were left of old Bohemian ways, "everyone is modernized, or at least assumes the appearance of being so." There were synagogues with choirs, organs, and good preachers. It was rare to discover a real Talmudic celebrity. The sacredness of ceremonial was almost lost; and "many a merchant violated the Sabbath."

Younger rabbis were wont to regard the Talmud as a secondary affair:

> It is remarkable that the renowned Rabbi Rappaport [to whom we shall come in detail later] is considered more as a philologist, antiquarian, and historian than a learned Talmudist. When he first came to Prague (he is a Polander) his reputation was very low in this respect, and we remember distinctly that he was looked upon as a third-rate man in this respect.

Rappaport was Chief Rabbi of Prague, but not of all Bohemia. The latter had twelve district rabbis, who did not however enjoy too much authority outside their own congregations. There was no real hierarchy among Bohemian Jews, "and there never was one," though men of great learning had always enjoyed especial respect. Congregations were not as large as in Germany. . . . Here, in mid-air, the article ends.

This was the country, and these were the conditions, into which Isaac M. Wise was born in 1819. Two things should have become clear: neither Austria nor Bohemia was entirely unaffected by the revolutionary spirit of the time, especially during the hopeful years under Joseph II; but—compared with France, or with the German lands contiguous to it—Austria and its provinces responded weakly, during short periods, to the tide of liberalism, and then swiftly returned to the even tenor of its reactionary history. Eager young men must have felt the infinite attraction of the new spirit and been embittered by the galling repudiation of it in theory and practice. For them—perhaps even more than for the East-European Jews behind the Czarist curtain—there was a smarting sense of defeat, of hope deferred, of the stark contrast between the new freedom and their immemorial lot. All of these elements, as the tale will reveal, were commingled in Isaac M. Wise!

> In [illegible] the first [illegible] called Rapoport, for which he [illegible] is considered [illegible] and Rapoport, what a learned [illegible]. When [illegible] came to Prague (he was [illegible]) the [illegible] was very low [illegible]

Rapoport was Chief Rabbi of Prague, [illegible]. The latter [illegible] much authority [illegible] their own congregations. There was no real [illegible], and there never was one, though [illegible] always [illegible] special respect. Congregations [illegible] the [illegible].

This was the [illegible], and these were the conditions into which Isaac M. Wise was born in 1819. Two things should have become clear [illegible]. Bohemia [illegible] was entirely unaffected by the revolutionary [illegible] of the time, especially during the Napoleonic [illegible] under French [illegible] with France, or with the German lands contiguous to it. Austria and its provinces responded weakly, during short periods, to the ideals of liberalism, and then swiftly returned to the [illegible] of its reactionary masters. Eager young men must have felt the whole attraction of the new [illegible] and been embittered by the [illegible] and practice. For them—perhaps even more than for the [illegible] European [illegible] the [illegible] century—there was a smarting sense of defeat, of hope deferred, of the stark contrast between the new [illegible] and their [illegible] lot. All of these elements, as the tale will reveal, were commingled in Isaac M. Wise.

Part II

Isaac M. Wise
His Life and Work

1

Family, Childhood, and Early Education

NOT NEARLY AS MUCH IS KNOWN ABOUT THE ANCESTRY, CHILDHOOD, and training of Isaac M. Wise as we would like to know. Throughout his life he exhibited a certain reticence about this period. For what particular reason, it is not apparent.[1] As will be seen, what exists about these early years comes from his own *Reminiscences,* and from a few other sources. But our material seems to lack warmth, vividness, detail. A person who grew into so versatile and colorful an adult must have had a childhood filled with incidents, replete with tales that might have been told. From the description he himself penned at one time of what Jewish life in Bohemia was like, which in outline we have reproduced in the third chapter of the foregoing section,[2] it is easy to surmise that his own home life must have been rich and vital. Yet we can find no more than accounts of scattered episodes, which serve only to whet our appetite for more. And especially later on, during his student years, when he studied at various schools in various communities, when he began to attend a Gymnasium and universities, and when, as he confessed, his own thinking underwent a "sea-change" decisive for his whole life, when he began to gain an acquaintance with the great European classics, when with the utmost zest and sympathetic enthusiasm he felt the wind of freedom, brotherhood, and hope that was sweeping Europe and the world: we want more, more of what he was reading, more of the impressions it was making upon him, more of the way in which it was beginning to transform his concepts of life, of man, and more especially of Judaism and its destiny. Some of all this we can infer for ourselves. And this we shall attempt to do. But, as will become apparent, all lies far too often in the realm of conjecture and of inference.

All this by way of initial complaint! We must not, however, delay too long in launching into the actualities of his parentage, of his life as a child and as a boy.

What we possess about his family has to do almost exclusively with his father's side of it.[3] Isaac M. Wise himself was a child of the Central European Jewish community in every sense. Just how far back the residence of his family in Bohemia, or in the neighborhood, went, it is impossible even to guess. The earliest record extant has to do with his paternal great-grandfather. Several things conduce to indicate that the family had a tradition related to medicine. Two of his immediate forebears were physicians; and there is some evidence that for a time, shortly after he had come to America, Isaac M. Wise himself wavered between medicine and the law instead of the rabbinate, which at the moment seemed to offer him no future.[4]

For centuries there had been famous physicians among the Jewish people.[5] Because medicine was part of the Jewish heritage as bearers of culture between East and West, part of their long and fruitful contact with the great Arabic civilizations of the Middle Ages, and surely because medicine was a calling that opened doors into the larger world, a port of entry to courts and princes and positions of power and influence, many of the ablest Jews went into the profession. The ancient line goes back to the rabbis of the Talmud, to some of the Gaonim, and to so massive a figure as Moses Maimonides, who, by the side of his great treatises on the Law and on Aristotelian and Jewish philosophy, left a number of monographs on the medical art.[6] These, too, testify eloquently to his learning, his originality, and his theoretical and practical wisdom. For centuries this was the single calling open to gifted Jews outside the confines of their own people.

Once Isaac M. Wise wrote rather wryly of this and of related matters:

> My grandfather was a district physician, and I knew next to nothing about medicine. My maternal grandfather was a prosperous broker, and I was never out of debt. How is that? The point is that a man should be proud of his own accomplishments.[7]

Certainly all the evidence goes to show that for some generations and on both sides the family included men of learning, of professional calibre, and that Isaac M. Wise's own qualities did not come out of thin air.

His paternal great-grandfather left Bohemia to study medicine. The sources differ as to precisely where he went to seek his professional training. One asserts that he studied in Padua, a very ancient and famous Italian university; another, that he repaired to Salerno, which is not far from Naples.[8] The name should be well-known to Americans, located as it is only a little to the south of the Amalfi Drive, and poignant in its recent memories of a great landing of American boys there during World War II. It had been a noted school for centuries and many physicians had gone forth from it to all parts of Europe.

Leo, Isaac M. Wise's great-grandfather, completed his studies, either at Padua or Salerno, and returned to his native land. At this point it would be well to make note of the fact that the name Leo recurred in the family. Isaac M. Wise's own father bore it, and his own eldest son. The first Leo determined to practice medicine in Marienbad, a popular resort, a "watering place,"—that is a town having baths of some real or supposed medicinal quality. But he discovered that by old laws Jews were not permitted to reside there.[9] So he made his residence in a village within calling distance, by the name of Durmaul. Here he lived, but through all his career his practice was largely in the resort itself.

To the family, their paternal great-grandfather was always known as "Dr. Leo," but to his coreligionists, according to Isaac M. Wise, —for reasons that do not appear in the record—he was the *Chacham.* Perhaps this title was derived from his position in the little synagogue in Durmaul. Perhaps it was conferred upon him because in addition to his medical knowledge he was learned in the Law. The word simply means "wise," a "wise and learned man." Without doubt it was from this nickname that the family acquired their last name of "Wise."[10] Many years later, when Isaac M. Wise had leveled one of his many attacks against Robert Ingersoll, the voluble and flowery atheist, Ingersoll was reported to have heard of it and commented: "I knew a man once whose name was 'Gross' and he was four feet tall; I knew another man whose name was 'Kraft' and he couldn't lift any real weight. This man's name is 'Wise'! . . ."

This was the period in which Jewish families in Central Europe were compelled to take last names, when they were haled into court and forced, *faute de mieux*, to adopt some nominal appendage, often a ridiculous one, which a judge bestowed upon them.[11] The likelihood, however, is that the Wise family did not get their last name in this fashion, but that it was simply a continuation of the honorific title conferred upon Dr. Leo.

We do not know how long Dr. Leo carried on the career of medicine, nor whether he achieved anything in the realm of medical theory besides his regular care of his patients. We do not know what manner of man he was, nor whether anything in his life foreshadowed the bents and talents that were to be so marked in his great-grandson.

His son, or one of his sons, was named Isaiah. He studied medicine at Padua and also settled in Durmaul to practice in Marienbad.[12] The probability is that he took over his father's practice. Isaiah lived a long and useful life, surviving until his ninetieth year. One of our references informs us clearly that Isaiah practiced medicine by day but devoted his evenings to assiduous study of the great volumes of Hebrew lore, that he was well and deeply versed in the Talmud, the great compilation of rabbinic decisions and discussions upon the text of the Mishna, and in rabbinic literature in general. About the Talmud—contemporary to it and subsequent to its completion in Babylon (there was also a Jerusalem Talmud, which did not become the central authority in rabbinic Judaism)—sprang up a great mass of commentaries, additions, other compilations, codifications and selections, etc. It was in all this that Isaiah busied himself by night.

Precisely how many children he had, how many sons and how many daughters, we are not told. One of his sons, perhaps the eldest in accordance with Jewish custom, was named after his own father, Leo. And to the education of this son Isaiah devoted himself.[13]

Not long after he had completed his training under his father, Leo the second decided to leave Durmaul.[14] He had never intended to be a physician, had not gone to a university to study medicine, and had no reason to remain in the vicinity of Marienbad. What the reasons were that prompted his choice of a home we have no means of telling. Especially in the light of the fact that the place where he settled was a tiny village, it seems likely that he must have had some good and sufficient reason for selecting it. Its name was Steingrub; it had about one hundred inhabitants and was quite close to the borders of both Saxony and Bavaria. My own father, writing in 1899 on "Dr. Wise as a German," declared that he could not find Steingrub on any large map of Bohemia:[15]

> Whether it is or is not in the Boehmerwald, near the Bavarian frontier, as some vague recollection urges it is, the name is

> sufficient indication of the fact that the locality must belong, or at least has belonged, to the German portions of Bohemia.

Most of the population of the little town were Catholic.[16] We have no means of knowing just how many Jews lived there. But let us hazard a guess that there could not have been more than thirty or forty in all. All the recollections of Isaac M. Wise about his early life show that he had little or nothing to do with the Czech language. It must be borne in mind that there were large sections of Bohemia even in those days, and increasingly toward the period of World War I, which were ardently and often belligerently nationalistic in speech and in political tendency, that they hated German, and cultivated Czech language, music, folk-lore, art, etc. This was never true of the majority of Jews in the land, for they were closely related by familial and cultural ties to Germany and Austria. Almost always, they sent their children to "German" schools, and were proud of the books they read and the tongue they spoke. This must not be taken to imply, however, that at this period the Bohemian Jews had the habit of speaking pure German. They had their own dialect, *Juedisch-Deutsch*, not as far from modern German as Yiddish had come to be in Poland, but still not identical with it, and printed and written in Hebrew characters. In my father's library was a considerable number of prayer books and other volumes which Jews in Germany and Austria used during this very period, all of them *Juedisch-Deutsch* in Hebrew letters. If it had been true for a long time that the Jews of Bohemia were really Germans in sympathy, as my father puts it "heartily and without exception" (he should certainly have known, for he himself was born in Prague in 1860, educated there, and graduated from the Gymnasium in 1879, when he migrated to America); then this fact was even more intensely true at this time, for Germany was then regarded as "the country of enlightenment and progress, the fatherland of Lessing and Schiller." While Austria itself, of whose empire Bohemia was an unwilling part, labored still under reactionary domination, immersed in "mediaeval slumber," Germany was seething with the fever of liberty.[17]

But we have gone fairly far afield in an effort to evoke some faint idea of the air of Steingrub and of the little Jewish community that lived in it. We must return to Leo the second, the grandson of our first Leo. The record indicates somewhat more precisely that Steingrub was one mile from Saxony and three from the Bavarian frontier, that despite its tiny size, its location at a kind of cross-roads lent it somewhat of a cosmopolitan atmosphere. There, German and Bohemian, Catholic and Jew, mixed on amicable terms.[18]

Leo conducted the village Jewish school in his own home. Exactly what he was paid it is impossible to tell. But surely, according to the custom of the time, it must have been pitifully little, since we are informed that he was able to provide no more than the barest of necessities for his family. We learn also that he was married twice. Of his first wife we can ascertain nothing, not even her name. His second wife was Regina, a name that recurs in the Wise family in later generations. According to the family tradition she was a handsome woman, in character bright and cheerful, deeply devoted to husband, children, and later to grandchildren. More than twenty years after Isaac M. Wise she made the journey to America, in 1867, in the company of another son, Samuel. They lived in various American cities. At length Regina settled in Peoria, Illinois, in the home of her daughter, Caroline Korsosky. She died in 1880 at a ripe old age.[19] In *The American Israelite* Isaac M. Wise wrote that he paid her a visit in Peoria in 1877, three years before her death, on his way to the Pacific Coast. He wrote delightfully of her, and we quote some sentences:

> You need not laugh, we must stop to see the ladies. Here is one of them, a wonderful woman. She is eighty-six years old, speaks, hears, and sees like a young woman, and goes every Sabbath to the temple even if it rains or is right hot. She tells beautiful stories of sixty to seventy-five years ago, and laughs over a good joke of today. She is never cross, never displeased, and has a kind word for everyone. She speaks, thinks, and feels as I do, and like me she laughs over the world's numerous follies. She looks like me, and is as incurable an optimist as I am. She is my mother. God bless her. I stopped over to see her and my baby sister.[20]

By both his wives Leo had thirteen children, seven of whom died in infancy. The oldest surviving child was Isaac Mayer. Now at long last we come to the day on which the subject of this book was born into the world, the day on which he began the career that was to go so far in space and in achievement. It was on March 29th, 1819. Later he himself liked to observe the Hebrew date which was the third of Nissan in the traditional year after the creation of the world, 5579.[21]

Certainly Isaac M. Wise did not find himself in a wealthy home. His father was a typical teacher, living from hand to mouth, trying desperately to keep the wolf from the door, to provide food and clothing for his wife and himself and their six living children. The fact that his school met in the house doubtless compelled his wife

Regina to resort to many expedients to keep her own brood quiet. The school cannot have been very large. How many children of school age could there have been among the Jews of Steingrub? To earn his pittance Leo was a general factotum for his fellow-Jews. He read the prayers at *Minyanim* (the daily services in the synagogue), served as ritual butcher, *Shochet*, and sometimes officiated at weddings and funerals. Whether he was also the village *Mohel*, the specialist in the rite of circumcision, we cannot ascertain, but the probability is that he did this too, although there may have been a district *Mohel*, as there often was.[22]

To be more accurate, as Isaac M. Wise himself wrote, he was the first son but the second child. The first died in infancy. Concerning Isaac we know nothing whatsoever, from birth until his fourth year. Then, like every Jewish child, he began to study. And it is fitting that our first knowledge of him should be of this. We may like to picture him in the very first of all his contacts with Hebrew learning. Like the father, vividly described by Shmarya Levin in "Childhood in Exile," the first volume of his remarkable autobiography, Isaac's own father may have taken him into the school-room, where honey had been placed on the first letter of the Hebrew Alphabet, put the child's finger on it and have had him lick it off, thus fulfilling the biblical word:

> More to be desired are they than gold, yea, than much fine gold; sweeter also than honey and the honeycomb. (Psalm 19:11)

Isaac attended his father's school, since there was no other. Beyond this he received private instruction from his father. Though he himself did not say so, either in his *Reminiscences* or elsewhere, it is not difficult to conjecture that from the beginning he must have been a child of quite exceptional brightness. It is fair to assume that his father must have discerned that in his oldest living son he was dealing with one of those upon whom God had conferred a quick, inquiring, and retentive mind, a voracious eagerness for learning, a willingness to spend long hours perched above a great tome, foregoing often the distractions of childhood, the boys clamoring for him outside window or doorway. The boy himself, Isaac, wrote later that he began the study of the Talmud at the age of six.[23]

One cannot help pausing here in wonder. Not that Isaac M. Wise was unique in this. The record of Jewish life teems with tales of such boys, boys who dashed through *Chumash* (the Five Books of Moses), and *Mishnah* (the Code of the Law, cir. 200 C.E.) like racehorses. And yet, for most of us of this later day and of this other world, it is not easy to picture this child, taking his first avid taste of the *Gemara* (the Talmud), sitting there before a huge folio of one of the Tractates open before him like the portals of a great gate upon an entire world.

He was always short of stature. In later years he was occasionally called "the little giant." And certainly, upon the fare his father was able to furnish, he cannot have been too robust, too ruddy. There he was at the outset of his career in far-off Steingrub with the Talmud open before him. It is hard not to dwell on this picture. Later on he would be accused of not possessing a mastery of the rabbinic sources or of cherishing them too lightly. We shall look into this charge much more than superficially when, in the third part of this book, we come to his mature attitude toward the Talmud and toward rabbinic authority in general. But beginning at this very point it is clear that now and in the years that follow he had a good training in "The Law," that he mastered and remembered it well, and that all his life he could and did make use of that mastery.

Three more years passed. Isaac had reached the age of nine. His father could teach him no more. That small chalice was filled to its brim with a devouring thirst for knowledge. Isaac wanted more—more to read, more to learn. Since his first lesson he had given evidence of precocious mental ability. His father had tried to keep pace with him. He had singled him out for individual instruction. But this was not enough. It was far from satisfying the child's hunger. Therefore, doubtless after long discussion between Leo and Regina, it was decided to send him to his paternal grandfather, to Isaiah, the second in the line of doctors, at Durmaul, near Marienbad.[24]

But before we leave Steingrub, forever be it said, it is necessary to add one subsidiary episode not without interest and humor. In an essay written many years later in *Die Deborah* as part of a serial, Isaac M. Wise recounted this tale from his own childhood. It is worth reproducing for itself and for the light it casts on the qualities that developed in him as a man.

He was, he wrote, always defying the world. Once when he was a schoolchild his father was forced to scold him gruffly. Obviously this was not in the tenor of his father's habitual treatment of him. In his account, Isaac M. Wise does not inform us at what precise period of his childhood the following episode took place. But it must have been before he left Steingrub and therefore before his ninth year.

In their neighborhood of the village lived a rich butcher. Leo, as we know, was among other things the *Shochet* for the Jewish community. This must, therefore, have been a Gentile butcher. This the facts themselves imply, but we like to think also that the temperament of the rich butcher's son must have been derived from this and not from a Jewish source. The son was Peter, a few years older, and perhaps a bit taller and stouter than Isaac. And Peter had the disgusting habit of beating up Jewish children. Nor was Peter alone in these forays and attacks. Other boys allied themselves with him. Once, wrote Isaac M. Wise, he was walking alone, when he was suddenly ambushed by Peter, and set upon by Peter's more adult fists abetted by a stick he had in his hand. Isaac looked about him. He could discover neither friend nor ally. He could see nothing for it but to take his own part as valiantly as he could. And this he did. He rushed upon Peter in his turn, grasped the stick and wrested it from the bully's hand. Thus the anticipated roles were reversed, and Isaac thrashed Peter roundly and soundly. Bullies make execrable losers. Peter turned and ran home bawling at the top of his capable lungs. His mother, who received him into her arms, was horrified. Who is a mother to look deliberately into the origin or the justice of a cause? Especially when her son and heir rushes into the house with the red welts of a stick upon his tender skin and the wild sounds of fear and pain in the welkin? In her turn she ran to Peter's father's butcher-shop, where doubtless he was serving customers and chatting with them, as is the custom in butcher-shops all over the world. Peter's father too was greatly angered. He was not used to having Peter thrashed by others, though possibly he had not excited himself unduly when others had rushed to him complaining about their sons' injuries. The butcher ran to the home of the *Melamed* and in a spate of words told of Isaac's misdeeds. He demanded that Isaac be punished forthwith and roundly. . . . What was Leo to do? Here was a dilemma! Almost surely he knew a bit about Peter. Possibly he was even a little proud of his son's courage. But a Jew—at least a Jew in those days, as he tended to think of himself—could not afford such displays of Maccabean intrepidity. When Isaac came home, his father reproached him with what sternness he could muster. He said to his son: "We mustn't create any *Rishus* ("prejudice"); we are in *Golus* (the traditional Jewish term for 'exile,' for homelessness, for being defrauded of human rights, for the destruction of the national home and the Temple, in general for helplessness!)." To this the boy replied (as he himself wrote): "I've been in *Golus* long enough. Let Peter be in *Golus* from now on. If I catch him again, he'll be beaten again."

The matter did not quite stop here. By this time Isaac was a student of the Talmud. And a good Jewish discussion between father and son must not spend itself merely with warning and rejoinder. So (says Isaac) his father set himself to quoting passages from the Talmud, to prove that "our teachers, blessed be their memorial" said plainly that those who do not fight back are God's favorites. Isaac was not impressed or convinced. Perhaps even at this age he was able to quote other verses in rebuttal. He may even have appended a little Jewish history for good measure. And he ends the tale, much, much later on, by adding (this was written in *Die Deborah* in 1896-97, when Isaac M. Wise was about seventy-eight years old) that all his life he had never been able to resist fighting back.[25]

2

The Later Years of His Education

IN OUR FIRST CHAPTER WE TOOK ISAAC M. WISE THROUGH THE RECORD of his ancestry, his infancy and early childhood in Steingrub, and up to the day when his father Leo decided that there was little or nothing more he could teach the boy. It had been decided therefore to ship him to his grandfather Isaiah, the second in the line of physicians living at Durmaul but practicing in Marienbad.

Thither at the age of nine Isaac Mayer went. There was a *Cheder* (a Hebrew day-school for elementary instruction) in Durmaul. His study of the Talmud went on, except on Friday when the class studied *Chumash* (the Pentateuch in Hebrew), together with the first Aramaic translation, the *Targum,* and the wonderful and beloved commentary upon the text, *Rashi.* But this was not all. In his turn the grandfather discerned how gifted the boy was, how great his capacity, and how boundless his hunger for learning. Therefore, after his busy days of visiting patients, diagnosing their ailments, prescribing cures, his grandfather gave him close personal attention in the evenings, entering more sharply into the concise and closely reasoned debates and discussions of the *Amoraim* (the Talmudic generations of rabbis), teaching him the principles of Talmudic logic, the shorthand of its system of reasoning, and the great religious and ethical principles that undergirded the Law.

Isaiah also taught him "allied subjects" (he tells us). Concerning what these were, we can only hazard a guess: perhaps *Midrash* (various compilations of homiletical material on the biblical text, chiefly on the Torah), something of mediaeval and modern Hebrew, perhaps a glimpse into Jewish poetry and philosophy. Isaac M. Wise's occasional comments and his later interests seem to indicate that all this was so.[1]

The boy was sent to bed at ten o'clock, late enough for nine years of age. He was, however, aware of the fact that his grandfather sat up in the same room under the same lamp, poring over other books after he had been bidden to his slumbers. Isaac was keenly curious about these vigils of his beloved grandfather. What did he read? Why did he wait until Isaac was safely in bed? The boy had noticed a large wooden box from which Isaiah would occasionally extract a book. One day, when no one was near, Isaac tried the lid of the box, discovered that it was not locked, that in fact it opened readily. In it he found a hidden treasure, a number of Cabalistic books (perhaps the *Zohar*, and various others: mystical books, full of hidden symbolic lore, regarded as forbidden to those who were supposed to busy themselves only with the clarity and the authority of the Law). It was with these Isaiah was busying himself in secret. All this we find in Isaac M. Wise's *Reminiscences*. It is likely that he did not rest content with having discovered what was there. It is likely that he read them himself, sneaked them up to his own room and hid them under the pillow to be conned over in the light of early morning, or perhaps, like Johann Sebastian Bach, by the flickering flame of a candle.[2]

This period lasted again for three years. From the age of nine until that of twelve he lived in Durmaul, studied at the *Cheder* and under the personal guidance of his grandfather. How much learning he gathered in during this time we cannot ascertain. But it must have been a considerable amount. He had already demonstrated his own eagerness and his ability to learn. Boys in those days went farther and faster, and they developed memories that had not become weak by leaning upon crutches. Unfortunately for him, when he reached the age of twelve, his grandfather died.[3]

It is a pity that we cannot find some picture of Isaiah, some ancient Daguerreotype, or, lacking that, some pen-picture by his grandson, Isaac. It would be very good to be able to see him, to summon him out of that remote time more than a century ago. All one can do is to try to imagine them together: the venerable old man and the quick, avid boy. I see them sitting at a table under a lamp with its wick in sperm oil. I see the rest of the room immersed in deep shadow and only about the table and upon the spread book a cone of yellow light. I see the doctor with a long white beard, a silk skull cap upon silvery hair, bent head, kindly old eyes and lips well used to encouraging patients and moving with the accents of Bible, Midrash, and Talmud. I see his look bent upon his grandson, filled with hope and pride, full too of tender concern that the budding mind should unfold upon the immemorial lore of faith and people. And I see the boy, long brown hair, bulging brow even then, his lips moving as he reads the complex text, his eyes lighting as its involute sense reaches him. And behind the eyes and lips of the boy I feel all the years that are to come, all the corridors of the new world he is to traverse, the seas he is to cross, the dreams he is to dream, the valiant battle he is to fight. All of this seems implicit to me in that little room in Durmaul and in that vision of a grandfather and his grandson studying together.

Even as early as this, Isaac had decided to become a rabbi.[4] As far as we know, unless one goes back quite a distance or to collateral branches of the family, his forebears had not been rabbis. But they had been lovers of the Law, "pupils of the wise," as the old Jewish phrase had it. Nor was it exceptional for a boy to make up his mind thus early. Entry into life, decision as to a career, was made much sooner in those days of more than a century ago. Isaac knew he could not depend upon his parents. He knew clearly that they were in no position to care for him. His father was heavily burdened. As we have noted, his pay had always been pitifully inadequate. And with the coming of more children it had had to stretch farther and farther. At this tender age Isaac felt thrown upon his own resources. It was necessary for him to decide and to find ways and means of beginning to move toward the goal of his profession. A professional career was by all odds the best choice. Europe was full of young men who had to employ various devices by which to get an education: to find a generous patron; to learn while they earned. My own father did this in the selfsame city of Prague, after his family had left for America in 1877. He supported himself by tutorial work while he completed the last two years at Gymnasium.

This then was Isaac's decision after his grandfather had died, after he realized that he could no longer live in that hospitable home in Durmaul. He chose Prague, the capital city of Bohemia, one of the oldest and best seats of Jewish communal life and learning in Europe. This it had been for many generations and this it still was in the third decade of the nineteenth century. The manner of his getting there too was time-honored, not by stagecoach, for this he could not afford, but on foot, his small possessions—chiefly clothes—tied in a bundle and slung over his shoulder. As he walked, doubtless he was imagining Prague and what he would find there. For years he had heard of it as of a metropolis, a great center of schools and noted rabbis. Like a magnet the city drew him from afar.[5]

In his pocket was the magnificent sum of twenty-seven kreutzer (a kreutzer in 1831 was worth about half a cent). But does that trouble a boy of twelve? He lives on air and on hope. He eats where he can and when he can. Thank God the world is not without kindly men and kindlier women who will give you a piece of bread, a slice of *wurst*. Alone though he was, with nothing before him but the unknown, he did not walk the roads of Bohemia in dejection, but looking keenly about him, with quick and intense interest, singing as he walked. On the way he stopped in the little city of Mies. Here he knew that he had cousins, but whether on his father's or on his mother's side we do not know. To his wealth they added five florins (a florin in 1831 was worth about 48 cents). Apparently he was not poor in relatives. For next he paused in Pilsen, famous for its golden beer. In that city lived an uncle, serving in the Austrian artillery corps, an occupation rather unusual for a Jew. Generous as had been the others, his uncle gave him ten florins more. Surely, Isaac must have said to himself, he had little to worry about. As he went, he was becoming not poorer but richer. He had enough in his pocket to begin with in Prague, enough perhaps to find quarters and to buy enough to eat for several weeks.[6]

How long it took him to walk to Prague from Durmaul again we do not know. The distance is not great and young legs make nothing of it. On some day in 1831 he arrived at the capital city. As he approached it, from a distance he could see the mountain rising in the midst of it, crowned with its cathedral in which, encased in silver and glass, lie the mortal remains of the city's patron saint, John of Nepomuk. He could see the red roofs of the castle of Wallenstein, the *Pulverturm* (powder, or rather shot, tower) by the Moldau, and all the spires of the old churches, especially those about the square where John Huss had roused the people before he went to the stake at Constance. Isaac wasted little time in round-eyed staring. He went straight to the *Beth Hamidrash* (Hebrew school). This was to be found immediately next door to one of the most venerable religious edifices in Europe, the *Alt-Neu Schul* ("old-new synagogue"): a small building with a gabled roof, several feet below the level of the city about it, dark within, a great faded banner over the rafters, a banner given the Jews of Prague by one of the rulers of Bohemia; closely wrought grill-work behind which the women sat; and up a narrow stairs in the attic the *Golem* of the *hohe Reb Loew* (Judah Loew ben Bezalel, end of the sixteenth century), the automaton with the tetragrammaton upon it, the automaton about which so many tales had been and were yet to be written. What a venerable and fascinating place! And how many great rabbis had spoken in that golden old pulpit and taken the *Sifre Torah* (scrolls of the Law) from behind the curtains of the Ark![7]

Well! At least he was there! Where he expected to study and to become a rabbi!

But how was he to live and where? Happily he was not entirely friendless. He had relatives of a kind. One had been Rabbi Bezalel Ronsperg, an uncle of his mother. The Rabbi had been *Dayyan* (Judge) in the Jewish community. He had died, but his widow was still living and might lend the boy a helping hand. He called on her and found her as kind as all the rest of the family. She welcomed him to her house and often had him there for meals during the various periods of his dwelling in Prague.[8]

It was, however, not enough. For his daily bread and for his regular lodging he could not depend upon Frau Ronsperg. A fortunate chance, the exact nature of which we do not know, brought to young Wise the patronage of a rich and liberal Jew, by name Moses Fischel. Fischel cherished an ambition that was far from exceptional among wealthy Jews of this era, that was one of the greatest traditional devices for the promotion of scholarship. Doubtless Fischel's life in the world of commerce had been too busy to permit him to amass learning. But he knew, as did almost all Jews then, that it was learning alone that counted, that learning had kept Israel alive. And Fischel had a daughter or daughters. He wanted a learned son-in-law. In Central Europe, and much longer in Eastern Europe, there was an understanding that a son-in-law who was a scholar did not sully his hands with earning a livelihood. It was the duty and the privilege of the bride's father, a duty usually stipulated in the marriage contract, to have the young couple live in his home, to support them generously, and to bask in the light of his son-in-law's glory. When such a *Shidduch* (match) had been arranged, everything went according to precedent. After the betrothal, not wishing to take everything on trust, the father would have the prospective groom appear at an assembly in the synagogue and in public give a sample of his Talmudic learning, his powers of casuistry, his command of the voluminous sources of knowledge and wisdom. Once, walking past a synagogue on a Sabbath afternoon together with a number of his companions, Isaac M. Wise heard through the doorway such a prospective groom holding forth. They entered and sat down to listen. Full as he was then and most of his life of a youthful and exuberant spirit, and probably by this time having laid up a good arsenal of Talmudic methods and problems, Isaac and some of his friends tried to confuse the groom, firing involved and difficult *sh'eloth* (questions) at him. In this case the occupation proved to be not so innocent and not so without effect. The groom was actually an *Am Ha'aretz* (an ignoramus), and became swiftly and completely embarrassed and confused. The questions soon reduced him to stammering incoherence. At last, after several futile attempts to pull himself together, he made public confession of his inability to answer. Unhappily for Isaac, his patron Moses Fischel was in the congregation. Fischel rose from his seat, turned angrily upon Isaac and his comrades, boxed Isaac's ears soundly—for the latter appeared to have been the chief organizer of the fun and the chief offender in the malicious questioning. The matter might have ended very unfortunately for young Wise. Certainly he was genuinely beholden to Fischel. The end, however, was far from tragic. The very next morning something thoroughly astonishing occurred. To Wise's great amazement—he was only thirteen years old at the time—Fischel called upon him and humbly begged his pardon. The action is not easy to explain from a much older man to someone not yet a man. Its real reason is not far to seek. Isaac M. Wise himself thought that it resulted from the boundless respect Jews of that day and that place had for learning. When his anger had subsided, Fischel reminded himself that the youths who had come into the synagogue, Wise among them, were the keenest and most talented students of the *Beth Hamidrash*. Said Isaac M. Wise, Fischel's action speaks for itself.[9]

This same man, Moses Fischel, now insisted that the boy become a frequent guest in his home, chiefly at mealtime. This too was the custom in those days, for understanding Jews let their houses be open to "the wise." Often, when Isaac was there, he lifted his plate to find generous sums beneath it; and these gifts went far toward enabling him to continue his studies in Prague.[10]

Thus Isaac remained at the *Beth Hamidrash* preparing for the rabbinate for between two and three years. One experience came to him which was probably among those that accumulated toward the shaping of his viewpoint and his character, that culminated later on in his attitude toward Orthodoxy and toward modern Western culture. In what precise way it happened his own recollections do not inform us, but we are told that he became acquainted with Prof. Moses Koref, who taught mathematics at the Normal School. Koref took an immediate fancy to the quick-witted lad and after some chats with him asked Wise whether he would not like to add to his rabbinical studies some hours in the disciplines that were totally outside the intent and the purview of a Hebrew institution, notably arithmetic, algebra, and geometry. Isaac leaped at the chance. He devoured the new knowledge. And although he does not go further in speaking of it, it is fair to assume that this was the initial step in his penetration into the undiscovered continent of the humanities.[11]

Now begin some of his *Wanderjahren.* The narrative of these next few years of fairly rapid removal from institution of learning to institution, of his trying now this, now that, may read quite strangely to an American reader or an American student. But so it was done then and there. The very German word we have used at the beginning of this paragraph was one often on the lips of German students, and Austrian too. It was part of the title of the first novel in German, Goethe's long and rambling tale of Wilhelm Meister and of his *Lehrjahren* and his *Wanderjahren,* his years of study and his years of wandering. One recalls also the "Grand Tour" which the scions of the aristocracy in Britain used to make. German and Austrian students did not feel it necessary to take their entire professional training in one university, but might study at two, three, or four. And there was close enough coordination of method and of subject-matter among them so that this was not too difficult. The custom must also have communicated itself at least somewhat to Jewish schools.

Isaac left Prague when he was about fifteen or sixteen years of age (that is in 1834 or 1835) and repaired to the *Yeshiva* (an institution of higher Jewish learning) of Rabbi Loeb Schlesinger, who had for some time been serving as *Kreisrabbiner* (district-rabbi) for that section of Bohemia known as the Braun area. Here Wise remained a year.[12] At the end of twelve months he returned to Prague. We must infer that before he departed for Braun he had learned all that was taught at the *Beth Hamidrash* and was ready for the next step. This second time in Prague he attended the chief rabbinical school of the city, the famous Yeshiva of Rabbi Samuel Freund, who was serving as spiritual head of the so-called *Zigeuner Schul* (the "Gypsy" Synagogue) and was accounted by many the greatest Talmudical scholar of the age. How long Isaac stayed there and what he learned we are unable to ascertain.[13]

The likelihood is that it was not for very long. He himself later wrote that the greatest Yeshiva of the time in Bohemia was at the town of Jenikau, and its head was Rabbi Aaron Kornfeld, a man of both wealth and deep, broad scholarship. To Jenikau he went, probably in the fall of 1835, and remained at the seminary for two years. The institution was a fairly large one, for Wise informs us that it had one hundred and fifty students.[14]

3

His Education *(Continued)*

WE HAVE SELECTED THIS POINT AT WHICH TO BEGIN A NEW chapter, not because it marked an epoch in Isaac M. Wise's life, that is, of the outward circumstances of his life, but because in Austria and Bohemia themselves, and in the processes of his own intellectual and spiritual development, began a change which was decisive, which proved to be one of the central factors guiding his future course. This does not mean that it was only at Jenikau, and during the years from 1835 to 1837, that he began his long career of delving into general knowledge. He had already had a taste of it in mathematics under Koref. And with his quick intelligence, his capacity to employ even a little knowledge as a starting-point from which to launch into far-reaching speculation, to draw all the obvious and all the more recondite inferences, Isaac had doubtless before this more than an inkling of the cultural world outside.

In 1837, the Imperial government at Vienna promulgated an edict. That government was forever intervening in the communal and individual life of its Jews, sometimes in petty and sometimes in tragic ways, as later we shall be forced to recount. The edict in question provided that thereafter no candidate might enter the rabbinical profession in all of Austria unless he had taken courses at Gymnasium and University.[1] There and in Germany the rabbinical office was one that in part derived its authority and sometimes its compensation not only from the Jewish community but also from public taxation. Until this time to become a rabbi had meant to study at some recognized Jewish school under recognized masters, and to have one's qualifications passed upon by a rabbinical *Beth Din* (court). Thereafter *Semicha* (literally the "laying on of hands"; actually ordination) was bestowed in regular order.

This edict was a body-blow. Far more than authority was involved in it, far more than interference with the ancient regimen of a Yeshiva. All over Europe at this time, varying in degree and in kind in Western and in Eastern Europe, a conflict was in progress. Judaism had preserved itself for centuries, ever since the destruction of the Temple at Jerusalem by Titus and his legions, ever since the establishment at Yavne of the school of Rabbi Jochanan ben Zacchai, by its system of education, by its primary schools for younger children, and by its institutions of higher learning which trained scholars and rabbis and served as repositories of its own rich, deep, comprehensive heritage. These schools had survived century after century in the midst of encompassing violence and of almost universal illiteracy among the Gentiles. They had continued to teach the principles of the good life, of righteousness, charity, and peace. They were islands surrounded by a sea of anarchy, feudalism, the glorification of force, and often the minutiae and unreality of scholastic learning. With the exception of isolated periods and places—Alexandria where Jews strove to bring into accord Hellenistic and Hebrew culture; Spain under the Moslems, where the Aristotelian treatises and the vestiges of Greek and Indian science created a kind of Golden Age—the Jewish school had nothing to learn from its hostile neighbors. More and more as the ages circled, it had cut itself off. At this very time many of its leaders, in Poland, in Russia, and certainly in Germany and Austria, were fighting with might and main to prevent the contamination of the minds of their students. Some students in Eastern Europe escaped into what they called the *Haskalah* (the "enlightenment"). The masters did not wish their students seduced by what they called *Chochmath Yavan* (the wisdom of Greece). They feared its siren voice, its power to entice minds from traditional disciplines and from traditional problems. A most amusing instance of this is to be found in a novel by Sammy Gronemann, published some forty or fifty years ago, entitled *Tohu vaBohu* ("waste and emptiness," the term in Genesis, Chapter I, for Chaos). Here we discover a Talmudical student with one of the great folios open before him. He is sitting on a park bench. But within the great pages is a copy of Goethe's *Faust*, which he is reading so assiduously that he does not hear his teacher and rabbi coming up behind him and taking in the whole revealing and damning spectacle.

Moses Mendelssohn himself had been an example of a *Bochur* (a young man, a student) who had studied in a Yeshiva, had migrated to Germany and there become a great master of Western learning, especially in the field of philosophy. There was by this time a host of others. And to the list of famous men might doubtless be added that of countless unknown students who had yielded to the temptation of adding to their Talmudic learning something of the West, in letters, science, philosophy, etc. One must be on guard against the conclusion that *all* Jewish scholars, or all schools, had set themselves unanimously and unalterably against the commingling of secular and sacred studies. At this very time there were great scholars who commanded both, and seminaries already established or in the process of founding which required university degrees of their rabbinical students.

In Jenikau, however, the news of this edict precipitated a very real crisis. Rabbi Kornfeld came to his Yeshiva. He said not a word, but sat on the ground, like the prophets of old, as a visible sign of his deep mourning. Had he had sackcloth and ashes he would have garbed himself in the one and cast the other upon his head. The students had until this not been apprised of the decree. They asked one another what was wrong, what had caused the Rabbi's symbolic gesture. After a time the venerable rabbi rose. In measured and solemn words he told them of the new law and declared that it constituted a death-blow to his Yeshiva. Nor was he mistaken. Perhaps this institution and its Rabbi were too firmly fixed in their immemorial way, too adamant to bend, to adapt, to re-form. Isaac M. Wise himself informs us that this day proved to be the beginning of a steady and fatal decline which ended in the disappearance of the seminary.[2]

While he was living and studying in Jenikau, the process that had been initiated by Koref in Prague continued for Wise. Not, as the edict required, in the local Gymnasium! That was to come later. But from an unexpected source. There was in Jenikau another rabbi, by name Jonathan Altar. Altar had been, according to the sources, a bitter opponent of Rabbi Aaron Chorin of Arad. Altar appears to have been one of the first rabbis in Bohemia to seek secular culture. At this very time he had two sons studying at the University, which—in the light of what we have written above—could not be regarded except as an unforgivable crime. That any Jew should do this would have been shocking enough. But that two sons of a rabbi, and with their father's consent and blessing, should attend the University, become infected with this alien learning, was utterly incredible, more than enough to create a whole library of pamphlets and a whole barrage of eloquent sermons. They and he, sons and father, were filled with enthusiasm for *belles lettres.* They adored Schiller, Goethe, Herder. Although these are the only authors Wise mentioned in his *Reminiscences,* there must have been many more, of a literature rich in its past and richly creative in that day, whom they read and in whom they took joy. Isaac joined their company. By them he was introduced to the German masters. The significance of this was not only that a new world began to unfold for him, but also that he was learning to read—and speak—in pure German, instead of in the *Juedisch-Deutsch* that had been his vehicle of expression until then. Nor did Altar and his sons remain content with drinking all this in. They were fired with the ambition to do something themselves, to contribute their mite toward the winning of their fellow-Jews for German and for a wider culture. They undertook the translation of the *Machzor* (part of the traditional prayer book used on holidays) into classical German. Although Wise does not say so, there can be little doubt that the concept of this undertaking was in the pattern of the translation of the Pentateuch into German by Moses Mendelssohn. This translation had become the center of bitter controversy. Mendelssohn had intended it as a device for Germanizing and modernizing his fellow-Jews. In this task of translation Isaac aided his three friends.[3]

At this point it is necssary to insert a paragraph which Isaac M. Wise wrote much, much later in *The American Israelite;* in 1889 in fact.[4] Its context seems to show that it had to do with this very period in his life and with the spiritual changes that were evolving within him. It should be borne in mind that this was written from the vantage-point of more than fifty years later. But Isaac M. Wise had a vivid and for the most part an accurate memory, as we shall discover many times. It is good to have his own words:

> . . . The late Gabriel Riesser, whose literary works, indeed, influenced us largely in our boyhood years, leading us into a new sphere of right and freedom then unknown to the masses of our coreligionists, and especially to the students of the Talmud. We only wish to add that another book, which appeared when we had entered upon the twenty-second year of our age, exercised a similar influence upon the formation of our character, and that was Dr. Samuel Hirsch's great work on Jewish philosophy. This book impressed us among the then small band of disciples of Saadia, Maimonides, Albo, and their compatriots at a time when, wavering between two standpoints of the crystallized

> *Halacha* (the Talmudic law) and the progressive theology of the Moorish-Spanish savants, Rappaport taught us the method of research, Sachs gave us the rules of pulpit oratory, Riesser made us feel free, and Hirsch led us to think free. . . .

This paragraph would be almost meaningless alone. Let us, therefore, pause before going on, for a brief sketch of the lives and books to which Isaac M. Wise refers.

Gabriel Riesser was one of the earliest and boldest advocates of Jewish emancipation. His life extended from 1806 to 1863. He found himself excluded from teaching in a university, and admittance to the bar, both because he was a Jew. He began to write, to strive to induce men of light and leading to rectify this great and ancient wrong. Isaac M. Wise probably read his "*Ueber die Stellung der Bekenner des Mosaischen Glaubens in Deutschland*" (second edition, 1831) "*On the Status of the Adherents of Mosaic Faith in Germany*," and several later works. Riesser drafted a petition to the Senate of Hamburg in 1834, asking for the Jews of that city the rights of citizenship. Later he played an active role in the "revolution" of 1848, and traveled in the United States.

Samuel Hirsch was an American rabbi, born in Prussia, living from 1815 to 1889. While he was rabbi in Dessau he published several works, by all odds the most important and interesting of which was "*Religions Philosophie der Juden*" (*The Religious Philosophy of the Jews*). He was an active participant in the three conferences (at Brunswick, Frankfort, and Breslau), and became a vigorous exponent of Reform Judaism. The rest of his life was spent as rabbi of Keneseth Israel Congregation in Philadelphia. His major work is a defense of Judaism and its central principles from a Hegelian point of view. It is also a defense of Judaism against Hegel's assertion that it could not be ranked as an "absolute religion." It is a powerful and original book, deeply thoughtful, systematic in character. Later Hirsch became a contributor to Wise's German paper, *Die Deborah*.

Michael Sachs we shall refer to later, at the time Wise left Bohemia and prepared to set forth for America (p. 97).[5] We have interrupted the narrative so that the implications of the edict of the Austrian government might be made clear to the reader and so that he might form some idea of its effect upon Wise himself. Thirty students of the Yeshiva out of one hundred and fifty decided to attend University, to go in fact to the old and famous one at Prague. Isaac M. Wise was among these thirty. But this transfer was more easily planned than carried out. Probably few if any of these students had ever attended a secular school at all. Whatever they had learned outside their Jewish knowledge had been self-acquired, and in all likelihood it was sporadic, ill-organized, and inexact. How were they to pass the entrance examinations to the University? Their average age was nineteen. They were too old to enter a Gymnasium, which is a six-year course beginning for most boys at about the age of fourteen. The Austrian government proved fair enough to recognize that it had created special problems for young men like these, and that it must not show itself too unbending in helping them to find a solution. They applied for and were granted a special dispensation, permitting them to take examinations for University without having to attend a preparatory school. All of them proceeded at once to buckle down to the most intensive study in German, Latin, and Greek. They studied night and day. They aided one another and they examined one another.[6]

Upon his return to Prague for this purpose Isaac M. Wise was lucky enough to find the means of supporting himself. He became tutor in the home of a wealthy Jew, by name Leopold Jerusalem. And not long after he had come to live in Jerusalem's home and with his fellows, he had crammed for some weeks, he took and successfully passed an examination which covered the work of the first half of the Gymnasium course, three years.[7]

It would have been fortunate for him if this could have lasted, if he could have gone on tutoring the children, studying and taking examinations until he was ready to enter the University. But the course of his life was never to be smooth. His plans were rudely interrupted by the death of his patron and friend. The future of the whole household was in jeopardy. It became evident at once that they could no longer afford to permit him to live there and to teach. Unexpectedly, and while he was still grieving for Jerusalem, he found himself compelled to seek *Parnosoh* (support) elsewhere. Days of search in Prague proved fruitless. He began to scour the countryside round about. Day after day went by without success and in the evening he would return to the Jerusalem home, where he still lived, downcast and discouraged. Suddenly the clouds were dispelled and he found work, again as a house-tutor, in a village not far from Prague, the village of Grafenried, and in the family of Hermann Bloch, a merchant. Here he came upon another stroke of luck, a curious one. Through what accident or incident we do not know, but he records that he formed the acquaintance of the assistant to the Catholic priest in a near-by town called Wassersuppen. Every evening the two met. The candidate for the priesthood taught the prospective rabbi Greek. And in return Isaac taught him Hebrew. Both profited greatly by this barter of learning.[8]

For a year and a half Isaac lived in Grafenried. In addition to his work with the family he must have been busying himself with his own studies to complete the last three years at the Gymnasium. At the behest of the father he took the two sons of the house, Joseph and Edward Bloch, and with them returned to Prague. The boys went to school and he himself entered the Gymnasium as a regular student. The information we have at this point is a bit confusing. It appears to imply that somewhere in between Isaac had passed the fourth year of Gymnasium. Whatever the case, he remained at the Gymnasium as a regular student for only six months. Young men of his day, young men like Isaac M. Wise, did not have time to lose. They could not content themselves with the pedestrian pace of their fellow-students. Their minds, moreover, had been sharpened and their powers of acquiring and retaining knowledge enhanced by the discipline of the Talmud. After this half-year he took examinations covering the whole fifth and sixth years. He had been laboring with great diligence, attending classes, but racing ahead on his own time outside them. The examination was successfully passed and he was at long last ready to enter a University.[9]

But in the meantime and once again he had to find a way to support himself. His life had brought him into contact with Solomon Judah Rappaport, the great scholar and rabbi in Prague.

Rappaport, an Austrian rabbi and scholar, was born at Lemberg in 1790 and died in Prague in 1867. Despite the fact that he began in business, his great talent for learning and his critical Jewish intelligence soon displayed itself. A series by him on mediaeval Jewish sages, beginning with Saadya HaGaon, sent his name far and wide. He left his occupation and after some intervening years, became rabbi of Tarnopol in 1837, and of Prague in 1840. In his religious views he was conservative, not far in position from that taken later by Zechariah Frankel. He took issue in writing with Geiger, Jost, and others. Primarily, Rappaport was a man who took a critical, "scientific" attitude toward Jewish studies. His most important works are: *The Travels of Benjamin of Tudela;* an encyclopedic dictionary of Judaism called *Erek Millin;* and numerous polemical works.[10]

By law no one could become a teacher unless he had behind him his *Abiturienten-Pruefung* (entrance-examination) for University. But the distinction between this requirement and Wise's own position at that time was slight. After all he had passed all the classes of the Gymnasium and was only waiting to enter a University. Whether this explains the situation or not, he was successful in securing a commission from the government and with Rappaport's help went to the Jewish community of Ronsperg as a teacher. Here he remained for a single year, doing his tasks, and most likely saving the money that would enable him to forge ahead.[11]

At the end of that year he left Bohemia and journeyed to Pressburg in Hungary for the purpose of taking his examination for entrance into a university. He himself does not state why he had to go so far. But the reason lay in the legal state of things. In Austria no one was permitted to graduate from Gymnasium and to matriculate at the University unless he had spent at least one year in actual attendance upon classes in the upper half of the Gymnasium.[12] This must have resembled the rule in American universities by which no one can obtain a graduate degree without spending a certain proportion of his time "in residence." Apparently Hungarian law was not so strict. In Pressburg he remained for six months, studying hard, took his examination and went forth jubilant in the possession of his papers of matriculation. Not all his time in Pressburg was spent in this preparatory study. He attended classes at the Yeshiva, one of the most famous in Europe, of the celebrated Rabbi Moses Sopher[13] (*Chasam Sopher*).

Moses ben Samuel Schreiber (Moses Sopher was actually a kind of pen-name) was a German rabbi, who lived from 1763 to 1839. He was a child-prodigy in Jewish learning and as such won great fame. He studied chiefly in Frankfort and Mainz, devoting himself more and more to the Talmud. But he did not scorn secular knowledge, and learned much of astronomy, mathematics, and history. He held various teaching and rabbinical posts, being the head of Yeshivas in Pressburg and Mattersdorf, in Hungary. He was an open and belligerent opponent of Reform. Sopher was noted for his great learning, his preaching, and his unfailing modesty. His most famous work is the *Chasam Sopher* (published in Pressburg from 1855 to 1864), a collection of deep comments on the Talmud. He wrote Cabalistic poetry, a commentary on the Pentateuch, and some autobiographical works in Hebrew.[14]

Isaac M. Wise was now twenty-one years of age. In some places the chronology of his own account is a little difficult to follow and to piece together. But we must take his word for it, for he sets down the fact that a crucial event found him at this age. Once again he returned to Prague and with his matriculation-papers from Pressburg in his hand registered at the old University. For two years he remained there, living in the home of Rappaport. This time he supported himself by giving instruction, not in a home but going from one home to another, probably in the evenings.[15] He earned additional money by copying music.[16] Later we shall find that he had learned to play the violin, that he had acquired a deep and lifelong love for music and knew not a little about it. All of this was germinating during these years and was sharpened and trained by his work upon musical texts.

Once again he decided to pursue his education in more than one place. He wanted a more varied experience, to sit, too, at the feet of other teachers of whom he had heard. Perhaps, too, he thought that it would add prestige to his degree, if part of it had been earned in a greater city and at a larger college. He left Prague and traveled to Vienna. With him he took warm letters of personal recommendation from Rappaport, Samuel Freund, and M. L. Landau, the editor of the *Aruch* of Nathan of Rome (a Talmudical Dictionary written in 1100). Besides he had with him several letters from professors at the University of Prague.[17] During these years in Prague and in Vienna, and without question from the whole undocumented direction and detail of his life and work from his fifteenth to his twenty-fifth year, Wise began to move toward liberal ideals. He became attached to German as his "mother-tongue," and formed a deep and enduring admiration for "the best of the German spirit." He bore with him a lifelong impression of the *Schwarz-Roth-Gold* (black, red, gold) colors under which German youth then marched.[18]

On arriving in Vienna, Wise went first to the home of Isaac Noah Mannheimer, a celebrated preacher, to whom some of his letters of introduction were directed. Here he was accorded the kindest of receptions. Mannheimer insisted upon his remaining in his home until he could find permanent quarters.[19] This was in 1842, when Wise was twenty-three years old. He remained in Vienna for two years, the last two years of his studies. Every *Shabbos* he took dinner at Mannheimer's house, and spent every Sunday with Salomon Sulzer, the famous cantor, the composer and compiler of the *Shir Zion* (Born March 30, 1804; died in Vienna, January 17, 1890), the friend of Beethoven and Schubert and one of the great formative influences in the music of the modern synagogue. Is it too much to assume that Isaac M. Wise's consistent and deep interest in synagogal music, his constant effort to improve it, to employ it as a force making for worship, stemmed in part from the years of his friendship with Sulzer?[20]

He was quickly registered at the University and found employment as a teacher in the family of a wealthy Jew, Herr von Wertheimstein. With this family he lived and here he tutored some of the children. For some time Isaac had been nursing the notion that he might possess some literary talent. It is not unthinkable that he cherished a hidden ambition to become a great writer of fiction. Later in his career, he was to toss off some secular, light-hearted German plays in a style then quite conventional, not unlike those Theodor Herzl wrote for the Viennese stage. He was also to spin out, installment by installment, novels for the *Israelite*, some on themes from Jewish history or Jewish life, others not Jewish at all. He himself recorded that during this Viennese period he wrote several novels of which only one title is extant. This was entitled *Die Belagerung von Mailand* ("The Siege of Milan"), and it found a publisher in Prague. No copy of it, as far as we know, still exists.[21]

Here ends the account of Isaac M. Wise's childhood, his youth, and the years of his training. Before we go on to the next chapter, to the years of his actual pursuit of the rabbinical profession, it may be wise to pause for a moment and to recapitulate.

Wise came from a good Jewish family which had probably lived in Bohemia for centuries. In the family was a tradition of the professions and of Jewish learning. A few of them were merchants, but for the most part they were doctors and teachers. His own way was not easy. It was full of wandering from place to place, of an education acquired piecemeal and together with the invariable need of earning his own way while he was still of tender age. The good days when he was with his grandfather, attending school in the town and sitting at his grandfather's feet in the evenings, lasted far too brief a time. But he was filled with energy, with physical and intellectual zest and strength. By one expedient or another he forged ahead, acquiring a complete rabbinical education, and then, as the law of Austria and his own widening horizons demanded, coupling it with a good grounding in the classics and in some of the wider reaches of secular education: in German literature, in mathematics, in philosophy, in the beginnings of Liberal Jewish learning and thinking, in the great field of political and spiritual freedom. It must be clearly understood that all this was the merest beginning. Isaac M. Wise was far from regarding the years of his wandering and learning as having completed or concluded his education. The exigencies of his own career, his contacts with other men, the inherent fascination books exerted upon him, the quality of that optimistic and burgeoning time in the early decades of the nineteenth century, all these worked upon him year after year and forced him to go into other fields of knowledge, to learn more and more.

Probably many if not most of the essential directions of his personality and of his characteristic modes of thought and feeling were formed by this early period of his life; his feeling for the inestimable value of Judaism, his habit of relating it to the spiritual and ethical tendencies of the age, his conviction that this was a millennial time of progress, liberty, and brotherhood. He had acquired a solid grounding in the Hebrew Bible, in Talmudic literature, and in at least some of the aspects of culture in the West. Many of the traits of his character had rounded into their permanent quality: his immense self-reliance, his tenacity of purpose especially in regard to spiritual fundamentals, his warmth toward and his knowledge of men.

A young man like Isaac M. Wise is a ship about to set forth from the home port. The wide seas lie before him. He has not been idle, he has learned how to trim his sails to the weather, how to judge the currents of the great ocean, how to navigate by sun and stars, and how best of all to set his course toward a chosen port. Thus we come to his first posts and his crucial experiences as a young rabbi in some of the towns of Bohemia.

4

Rabbi of Radnitz

ISAAC M. WISE HAD SECURED HIS SECULAR DEGREE.[1] HE HAD complied with all the conditions laid down by the Imperial government. After so much hardship and so much struggle he was ready at last for the profession toward which he had directed his steps ever since the days when he had studied with his grandfather at Durmaul. The period that follows covers less than three years. Yet it would not be extravagant to contend that these years proved to be the turning-point in his life. These were the years in which he discarded the main principles of Jewish Orthodoxy, in which he came to the momentous decision to leave his native land forever and migrate to America. Can there be any question that he arrived at all this because the ideas that had been germinating within him came to full and sturdy growth? Yet, to anyone who has followed closely the account of his education in the preceding three chapters, the motives that entered into this revolutionary change and into this decision, apparently so precipitate, are not far to seek. As he went and as he learned, he had been discovering them and becoming very sure of them. As a matter of fact, the key to most of his life, to most of his ways of thought, especially concerning Judaism, is to be found here in this very period: his acquaintance with and his admiration for Western culture, especially in its wider and deeper aspects; his profound commitment to liberal ideals in religion, in politics, and in regard to the destiny of man; his essential informing beliefs concerning the meaning of revelation, the authority of Scriptures and of the Talmud (to an exposition of all of which we shall come in detail in Part Three of this volume); even his feeling for America, while he was still in Bohemia.

It is to be deplored sincerely that all the information we possess about his ministry in Radnitz, all that he wrote later concerning his first pulpit and the incidents of his life from the autumn of 1843 until his emigration to America in the summer of 1846, all that we can piece together of the swiftly mounting sum of his discontent, is so meager in amount and so vague in detail. Yet it is enough to enable us to feel our way through to the truth, as that truth is also revealed in the years that followed, in the gradual unfolding of plans and ideas that must have been incipient then. When he left Radnitz he was a man of twenty-seven years of age, well-matured in self-reliance and in thought. By every indication he had already by then been wrestling with the central problems of his life and of his time. No perilous assumptions need then be made to conclude that these three years were the crucial period in which much in him converged, in which his career and his purpose adopted the direction from which they would not greatly depart.

When precisely he was ordained none of our sources tells us. He himself wrote that he had received his *Hatarat Hora'ah* (ordination) from his teachers, Rappaport and Samuel Freund, and, as the third member of the *Beth Din*, Ephraim Loeb Teweles. At their hands he became *Morenu* (our teacher), and was given full license to practice the rabbinical profession.[2] An early biography of Wise —written by two of his disciples and depending doubtless upon information derived directly from himself—asserts that his examination in the essentials of Judaism before the three rabbis gave evidence of full competence in Hebrew knowledge and exhibited his brilliance as a student and scholar.[3] He was by this time equipped also in ways quite other than those of the majority of rabbis in Bohemia and in Austria, by reason of the excellent secular education he had had in Prague, Pressburg, and Vienna and his voracious reading in various fields of European literature. Also by this time and as a result originally of his work with Altar and his sons, by his own dogged continuance in this direction, he had acquired a good mastery of pure German in writing and in speaking.

A congregation in the city of Radnitz, not far from Pilsen, wrote to Rappaport, asking him to recommend a competent man to serve as their rabbi. Rappaport, as we have seen, had already befriended Isaac M. Wise in many ways. He had also become convinced of the fine mind and dedicated spirit of his pupil. He wrote therefore to the officers of the Radnitz congregation, telling them that he had just the man for them, that in fact he would send them an *Or Chodosh* ("a new light"—from the prayer-book). Isaac M. Wise went to Radnitz, delivered a sermon, and was immediately elected by the congregation.[4] This was to prove the usual sequence in his life. When he was young and in the later years of his life, his effect upon congregations was decisive, and he never experienced any difficulty in getting pulpits. He was inducted as rabbi on October 26, 1843. The text of his inaugural sermon was Isaiah, Chapter 51, verses one to three:

> Hearken to me, ye that follow after righteousness, ye that seek the Lord; look unto the Rock whence ye were hewn and the hole of the pit whence ye were digged. Look unto Abraham, your father, and unto Sarah that bare you, for I called him alone and blessed him and increased him. For the Lord shall comfort Zion and He will comfort all the waste places, and He will make her wilderness like Eden and her desert like a garden of the Lord; joy and gladness shall be found therein, thanksgiving, and the voice of melody.[5]

In October, 1893, fifty years later, Isaac M. Wise wrote of this induction into the first and only rabbinical office he occupied in Europe, in these words:

> Fifty years ago this day the oldest son of a Bohemian village schoolmaster and a minister of a small congregation, preached his inaugural sermon before the large and highly respectable congregation of Radnitz, Bohemia. I was humbly aware of my imperfections and with little confidence in my ability to do justice to the sacred office.[6]

Radnitz, as we have noted, was a city not far from Pilsen. The size of its Jewish community, or the number of members affiliated with this congregation, we cannot ascertain. But to judge from Wise's own words, just cited, it cannot have been too small. Certainly it impressed him as offering an excellent opportunity and a serious responsibility. He launched into his task at once, in the fall of 1843. His sermons were usually not in *Juedisch-Deutsch*, but in German. There was at that time but one other rabbi in all Bohemia, outside the capital city of Prague, who spoke German or preached in it.[7] Before long, with the consent and aid of most of his people, he opened a day-school, but not without some opposition. Until then only the Catholics of Radnitz had had such a school. They were strongly opposed to permitting the Jews to open their own. Neither Wise nor any of his biographers give us the reason. Perhaps the Catholics wished to use this pressure to urge Jews toward conversion, and with this purpose to keep Jewish education personal and irregular. Wise got around this opposition by going to see the minister of education in Prague and securing from him a specific permit to launch the institution. With this permit went also the right to use the title of "Professor."[8]

Another event of primary importance in his life took place a few months later. The careful reader will recall that he had lived and worked as tutor in the home of Hermann Bloch, a merchant in the town of Grafenried, not far from Prague. He had taken two of Bloch's sons, Edward and Joseph, to Prague with him and had taught them there. While he was in Grafenried he had fallen in love with Theresa Bloch, who was two years younger than he.[9] At this time she was, therefore, twenty-three years of age, beautiful, small of stature and of a most lovable and tender character. Her grandson wrote of her that she possessed a great fund of common sense and a lifelong and abiding faith in her remarkable husband. Isaac and Theresa were married in Grafenried on May 26, 1844. Their married life proved to be one of great happiness for thirty years. But one child was born to them during Wise's Radnitz days, Emily, on February 22, 1846.[10]

While he was in Radnitz, Isaac M. Wise did not neglect his Jewish studies. Many years later he wrote that at this time a friend, whose name he does not give, required aid to prepare himself for his rabbinical examination. By an ancient praiseworthy custom, rabbis were accustomed to help such young men. He himself had had assistance like this a number of times from older men. Some of his time he devoted to studying with this young man, reading with him parts of the *Shulchan Aruch*, the Code of the Law, especially the two books known as *Orach Chayim* ("the way of life"), on ceremonial law, and *Yoreh Deah* ("who giveth knowledge") on religious law. The study served Wise as well as his pupil, for it stimulated in the former a quickened curiosity concerning the origin of each of the laws Caro cited. Thus he was led back again to the Babylonian Talmud, to substantiate the references, and also to make note of the divergent opinions that had been discarded by Caro. Nor was this all. There were other codes besides the *Shulchan Aruch*, especially the *Mishne Torah* of Maimonides, and the *Tur*. Wise compared these with the *Shulchan Aruch*, and noted their —often different—judgment as to what was the authoritative and authentic tradition. He acquired the habit of entertaining every traveling Talmudic scholar, taking him to his home, and engaging him in endless casuistical argument. All of this served the purpose of renewing and refreshing his Talmudic knowledge and the breadth of his approach to the problems of rabbinical legalism. The friend, whom he had been tutoring, came up before the District Rabbi (whose name was given earlier as Kafka, though in this passage Wise refers to him as Kufka—which may be a misprint!), and he in his turn was made *Morenu.*[11]

The picture, however, would be quite incomplete, were we to infer that during the Radnitz period Wise was devoting himself exclusively to rabbinic studies in the narrow sense. Just the contrary was the case! The most intensive field of study for him, and equally the most decisive in its influence upon his own ideas and projects, was in two other directions. The one was in the field of what had come to be known as *Die Wissenschaft des Judenthums* ("The Science of Judaism"), a rational, "scientific" approach to Jewish learning and Jewish history, leaning heavily upon an evolutionary interpretation. This had been creating a whole new spirit in Jewish scholarship, closely associated intellectually and historically with the origin and character of Reform Judaism.[12]

Isaac M. Wise was beginning to be conscious of his own one-sidedness. Many things contributed to this: his growing knowledge of German literature, his readings in science and philosophy, the whole spirit of liberalism of which Riesser had for him been the primary symbol. Many years later he wrote that he had, as it were, changed his library, had thrown himself "in the arms" of Samuel Hirsch, Formstecher, Reggio, Krochmal, Moses Mendelssohn, and Baruch Spinoza . . . "until he was convinced that he had mastered Spinoza and survived Mendelssohn." It was thus through his reading and as a result of the processes of thought it initiated in him that he began to move toward Reform. It was thus also—he writes—that he was led to busy himself with the Jewish thinkers and poets of the Middle Ages, especially of the Golden Age in Spain.[13]

Some of his time, too (it is always a mystery with him, now and throughout his life, where he found time!), was given to attempts to write poetry in German and in Hebrew. A physician, Dr. Starkenstein, who was married to an older sister of the director of the seminary in Budapest, claimed to have discovered a not inconsiderable poetic gift in Wise, flattered him, and kept urging him to write poetry. Most of his early efforts, Wise tells us, he condemned to the flames. Nor did he ever give evidence of any genuine poetic flair. Later in his life, under the constant pressure to fill space in the *Israelite*, and because of the dearth of hymnal poetry, he did write not a little verse, in most cases printed anonymously, often set to music, and some still sung in the synagogue.[14]

It was during these years that he began to think of America. What first led him toward this we have no way of knowing. In the following chapter we shall find that by some premonitory sense, or perhaps as a result of some half-formed plan, he had begun to study and to read English. But at the beginning it was chiefly through some of his reading that his boundless admiration for the United States began to crystallize. One must bear constantly in mind that the two great formative influences in the minds of liberals of this era were the American and French Revolutions and the ferment of ideas that preceded and succeeded both. In the third chapter of his *Reminiscences* Isaac M. Wise wrote:

> I was an enthusiast on the subjects of America and freedom, and was convinced that everyone thought and felt just as I did. Consequently I could begin at once to reform and improve the world.[15]

In July of 1845, Wise left Radnitz for the purpose of attending the second meeting of the "Conference of the Rabbis of Germany," held at Frankfort-on-the-Main. Many of the leaders of liberal Judaism were there, among them Samuel Adler, David Einhorn, Z. Frankel, Abraham Geiger, Samuel Holdheim, Samuel Hirsch, and I. M. Jost.[16] The presiding officer of the Conference was Leopold Stein, who had recently become rabbi of the Frankfort congregation. Geiger acted as vice-president, and Jost and Hirsch as secretaries. These conferences, of which the first had been held at Brunswick in the summer of 1844, were decisive meetings by which the history of Judaism in Germany, its whole direction and character, were deeply affected. Nor did they exist in a vacuum. All of them, but especially this conference, its character, its utterances, its whole point of view, were bitterly attacked and as valiantly defended. Primarily these comings-together of rabbis were intended to grapple with the theological and practical problems of Reform. In Germany the first stage of Reform had consisted of minor changes having to do with music, decorum, the status of woman, the liturgy, the vernacular. But it had become obvious in the course of time that the problems of Reform went much deeper than all this. Certain of the ideas embodied in the text of the liturgy, some of the tenets which had been held central to Judaism, seemed incompatible with the liberal spirit, with the whole concept of Judaism that had been maturing among some of the best minds and loftiest spirits in Germany and Austria.

The Frankfort Conference used most of its time for a report submitted by the Commission on Liturgy. Not all those in attendance were forthright, or even mild, "reformers." One in fact, Zechariah Frankel, became the chief founder of what came later to be called Conservative Judaism. It was at this Conference that he first employed the phrase, indicative of his own interpretation, "positive historical Judaism." As the result will show, it was obvious, however, that the majority of those present wished change.[17]

The chief questions reported and taken up for discussion were: the retention of Hebrew as the language of the liturgy; what was to be done with those sections—very many of them—which prayed for a return of all Jews to the Holy Land; prayers for the restoration of the sacrificial cult; the custom in the Orthodox synagogue of calling men up to the reading of the Law; and the use of a pipe-organ for services.

We shall review briefly the decisions of this Conference, though it would be unwise to enter at length into the interesting discussions that took place. The recommendation of the Commission in regard to Hebrew was adopted, though not by a large majority. In substance this advocated the retention of Hebrew in the most traditional and representative parts of the liturgy, but that the remainder of the service be in German.

The Commission recommended the adoption of a "universalistic" rather than a "particularistic" interpretation of Judaism, and as a consequence of this theoretical stand an abandonment of the belief in a personal Messiah and in the restoration of a Jewish State. This was not to be taken to imply the abandonment of the Messianic idea, "but all politico-national elements are to be eliminated." The Conference adopted this resolution:

> The Messianic idea should receive prominent mention in the prayers, but all petitions for our return to the land of our fathers and for the restoration of a Jewish State should be eliminated from the prayers.

This too was adopted, with the addition of another resolution striking out all references to the sacrificial cult. The "triennial" cycle of readings from the Torah was adopted. The majority favored retention of the custom of calling up to the reading of the Law. A unanimous vote approved the use of the organ. Other matters also came up for consideration: circumcision, the status of woman, the

Sabbath, revision of marriage laws, and so forth. No record exists of Wise's participation in the debates on these topics. But he was there, listened attentively, and without question was deeply and permanently influenced. The very fact that he, rabbi of an Orthodox congregation at Radnitz, under the suzerainty of the constituted rabbinical authorities of Austria, found the courage to go to this Conference, and in the general atmosphere of bitter controversy that surrounded the meeting, its predecessor, and its single successor, is intensely significant. Certainly Wise had come or was coming to a basic decision, that he would align himself with those who favored a free change in thinking and in acting. Whether this was the end of a process, or the beginning or middle, we cannot know. But that it was part of it every fact corroborates. At the Conference too he met a number of those with whom he was to have far-reaching and long-lasting relations in the remainder of his life, men like Hirsch whose book had already taught him so much and changed him so deeply, men like Einhorn who was to be his bitter and constant opponent later in America. With some of those at the Frankfort Conference he corresponded for many years, on points concerning which he himself was embroiled. From them he received counsel and aid.

Another point that must be noted before we pass on is that this same Conference, at the suggestion of Ludwig Philippson, editor of the *Allgemeine Zeitung des Judenthums*, and one of the most influential and far-seeing of the "reformers," adopted a resolution which called for the founding of one or more rabbinical seminaries in Germany, intended to train men for the rabbinate in the spirit of liberal Judaism, for service in German-speaking lands. A committee, consisting of Geiger, Philippson, Stein, Holdheim, and Solomon, was appointed to further this project. This too, and the discussion which preceded it, must have exerted an abiding influence upon Wise. We shall soon see that among his earliest plans for uniting and serving American Jews, among the plans for which he fought hardest and longest, was the establishment of a "university," a "college," a "seminary." Some of his convictions upon this must have received their original impetus at this meeting in Frankfort.[18]

It is, again, to be deplored that we possess nothing from him concerning his own reactions to the Frankfort Conference, or about the part it played in his own spiritual and intellectual life. But it does not require much in the way of imagination to believe that it was a decisive factor, added to the diverse currents already urging him along.

He returned to his post in Radnitz (this was a little more than a year and a half after he had become rabbi there) deeply dissatisfied with his own position, with the city in which he was living, with the narrow discipline under which he was compelled to labor and to think. How could he help comparing his own environment, his own people, with the freedom and the depth of what he had heard at Frankfort? The restrictions of many kinds that hemmed him in were becoming more and more painful.[19]

What were these restrictions?

They were in reality of three kinds. He came into conflict with the representatives of the Austrian government on two counts: his own relation to the government, and the cruel and oppressive laws that still in that period of "enlightenment" restricted the freedom of Jews. He had trouble, in the third place, with his own rabbinical overlords, to whom in many ways he was accountable. His independence of judgment and action soon precipitated this.

At this point, before detailing specific cases and episodes, it might be wise to pause briefly and to inquire: why did he do these things? Why was Isaac M. Wise filled increasingly with impatience? Even as so young a man! Three things were probably the causes of his own attitude and his line of conduct: his inherent character, one of sturdy independence, his refusal thus early to accept as immutable the iniquities he had to encounter; secondly, the contact he had begun to seek and to find among Jewish liberals, from the days of his first acquaintance with the writings of Gabriel Riesser to his attendance at the Frankfort Conference; thirdly, the "spirit of the age," as he and many others loved to term it, the whole air of unrest under inherited and legitimatized wrong that was stirring over Western Europe. All this we shall have occasion to examine much more closely later on, as we have already sketched the general outlines of the background in Chapter One of Part One. Not superficially, but carefully and closely, we shall examine Isaac M. Wise's own concept of the time in which he lived, its principles and its probable implications for mankind's future. We shall also later attempt to define what he came to regard as "Reform," certainly—as we shall discover—neither very far to the right nor to the left of Jewish center. It is sufficient to discern for the present that he had abundant reason, native and acquired, for chafing at the bonds he felt about his young limbs.

Quite early in his occupancy of the post at Radnitz he had trouble with the representatives of the Austrian government.[20] Beneath the apparent triviality of the episode must be descried his scorn of such constituted authorities. Later, after he had settled in the

United States, he was to deliver a lengthy fulmination entitled "The End of Popes, Nobles, and Kings" (N.Y., J. Muhlhaeuser, 1852), in which he consigned them all to a receding past. One of the reasons too for this chapter in his early career was that he had been known to give expression, perhaps in personal conversations, perhaps from his pulpit, to democratic and "radical" opinions. Whatever the precise setting, this is what occurred:

An order had been issued that all houses of worship of all faiths and denominations were to conduct a special service in honor of the birthday of the Emperor Ferdinand. Had it been Joseph II, son of Maria Theresa, Isaac M. Wise might not have been as uncompromising. But Ferdinand was a ruler of the good old type, autocratic and repressive. One of the reports avers that police spies had been placed in the synagogue at Radnitz to see what the young rabbi would do. Instead of a special service and a fulsome sermon Wise contented himself with informing the congregation somewhat curtly that it was the Emperor's birthday, and appended to the announcement some characteristic utterances of a "radical" nature. What these were, or even what was meant by "radical" at that time and place, we can only conjecture. Rabbi Wise was at once summoned to appear before the *Kreishauptmann* (Governor of the District) in Pilsen, the nearest center of office. He was interrogated thus: "Is *er* (he) a local citizen?" He vouchsafed no answer, and stood there stiffly silent. After the third repetition of the question in this form, Isaac M. Wise said—or so we are told—"Whom are you addressing? I am not an *er!*" The Austrian official had spoken to him not as *Sie*, a term of address reserved for superiors, etc., not even as *du*, a term either of familiarity or of endearment; but in the third person, as though he were not there. This was one of the many signs of the disdain in which the *Schutzjuden* were held in Austria. And doubtless its employment was habitual with such petty officials.

The account states that Wise's boldness was not punished. Perhaps impressed by his republican firmness, the officer condescended to question him in the second person; and thereupon Isaac M. Wise, though not apologizing for his conduct in regard to the Emperor's birthday, gave "satisfactory proofs" of his loyalty.[21]

The second incident was much more serious and had to do with one of the most poignant injustices against the Jews of Austria. Under the law only a certain number of Jewish families were permitted to live in a given town or village. These Jewish families thereby enjoyed a right that had come to be known as *Familienrecht*, that is, an authorization to found a household and to have children. The very statement of this ought to suffice to make the blood boil. In the course of their wanderings and their residence in a diversity of backward lands, Jews had had to endure many varieties of restrictive and discriminatory measures; but to be told who might and who might not marry, might or might not have children? To what could this be compared except to the first of all anti-Semites, the unnamed Pharaoh of Moses's time, "And the king of Egypt spoke to the Hebrew midwives . . . and he said: 'When ye do the office of midwife to the Hebrew women, ye shall look upon the birthstool: if it be a son, then ye shall kill him; but if it be a daughter, then she shall live' " (Exodus 1:16). This is the Malthusianism of hatred.

If a young man did not belong to a family that possessed *Familienrecht* and wished to marry, he had under the law to wait until a vacancy in the list was caused by the death of a holder. Imagine a youth, deeply in love with a maiden, perhaps grown up side by side with her in some town of Bohemia, their love deep and sure, and utterly unable to be married to one another! The authorities had before them constantly a long waiting-list of young men who wished to acquire *Familienrecht*, and some of whom must have died wifeless and childless. Up to that time all this had not moved the rulers of Austria to moderate, much less to abrogate, the law.

The result might have been foreseen. A large number of couples would not wait. Nor for the most part did the rabbis insist that they should. The "law of the land was the law," according to time-honored Jewish polity, but not when it violated simple and fundamental human or religious rights. A touching tale by Kompert exists of this time and of this cruel practice, called "*Ohne Bewilligung*," which draws a deeply affecting picture of all that this situation involved. Rabbis or laymen married couples who did not have *Familienrecht*, but they were unable to register the marriage with the state authorities. The wives were recorded in the necessary documents as cooks, housekeepers, etc. to their husbands, and by Austrian law their children were illegitimate.

Believing the law profoundly iniquitous—as indeed it was—Isaac M. Wise officiated at a number of such marriages in Radnitz. It must be recalled in this connection that a rabbi was in many senses a public functionary, exercising some of his prerogatives by virtue of legal authorization. He was therefore guilty of a misdemeanor. Moreover, Wise had asserted openly that he would disobey the law and that Jews in general had every moral right to evade it. Once again he received a summons to the office in Pilsen. Face to face with the officials he delivered himself of a statement, carefully considered in advance, denouncing the law and the entire practice, announcing frankly that he would continue to marry Jewish couples without *Familienrecht*, and telling his inquisitors that he would go to prison rather than refuse marriage to a single such couple.

As far as we can learn, he suffered no legal consequences, and the matter remained for a short time *in status quo*. But there must have been repercussions, for not long thereafter he was summoned to Prague. A member of the Imperial Council which governed Bohemia, that member in fact who was in charge of "Jewish affairs," a certain Count Fuerstenberg, had had a question directed to him: why were there so many illegitimate births among the Jews of Bohemia? Fuerstenberg invited Isaac M. Wise to come to Prague and to confer with him upon this matter. Wise went and explained everything in history and in present experience having to do with this law. The Count understood and promised to make a serious attempt to have the law repealed. The attempt was successful, and after a short space this barbarous law disappeared forever from the statute-books of the Empire. To what extent this consummation resulted from Wise's courage and his explanation to the Count, or how much it was to be ascribed to the long mounting weight of many instances, many iniquities, many infringements, cannot now be determined. Without question, however, the whole sequence of these circumstances tended to deepen Isaac M. Wise's own feeling that he was living in a mediaeval land, which the whole new climate of freedom had failed to affect.[22]

The third experience which added to his dissatisfaction had to do with the rabbinical authorities. The district rabbi, whom we have already mentioned more than once, was by name Abraham Kafka. Bohemia was then divided into twelve districts, over each one of which a rabbi was made the head; and from such a "district rabbi" local rabbis had to obtain permission to perform most of the essential local functions: marriages, funerals, etc. This was a preposterous arrangement, without reason and without purpose, except to annoy, to complicate, and to keep subservient. Isaac M. Wise paid no attention to it. He performed all the functions appertaining to his post in Radnitz without consultation with Kafka and without even informing him. Thus for some months things went. The probability is that Kafka was well aware of this and was biding his time to call his inferior to account. The chance was not long delayed. Wise listened to a case and granted a divorce to a woman who was a relative of Kafka, who had himself refused to grant the divorce. If the earliest biography of Wise is to be believed —and doubtless it depended more or less upon his own personal statements—Kafka had refused the divorce for purely personal reasons, and without valid cause in Jewish law. At any rate and quite understandably Kafka was furious, summoned Wise to Pilsen, had him charged before a *Beth Din*, a district Jewish court. But to Kafka's amazement and chagrin Wise was acquitted. This action would appear to bear out the interpretation of the facts given above. Naturally after this Kafka bore a deep grudge against him and tried to make things as unpleasant and difficult as possible. Another incident soon turned up. Soon after coming to Radnitz Isaac M. Wise had become sure that there was need for an improvement of the liturgical material then in use in the synagogue. This proved to be a lifetime interest on his part. This time he had compiled and published a collection of hymns and prayers intended to be used as a supplement to the *Siddur*. Not by an inadvertence, but most likely with full intent, it had omitted the customary prayer for the life and health of the Emperor. And again he received a summons from Kafka, and again was haled before a *Beth Din*, with what result our sources do not state.[23]

Thus in reality ended the Radnitz period. His cup was full. He had had more than he could endure: an oppressive government; Jews hemmed in by restrictions and apparently not brave enough to defy them or to strike out for liberty; even a modest effort at reform checkmated at the outset; rabbinical authorities who were jealous and reactionary. After not more than a year or a year and a half in Radnitz he had begun to perceive that he must depart. In the next chapter we shall recount first the evidences for this decision, for his attraction to America, his efforts to acquire English, and his sudden resolve to leave the land in which he had been born and in which his family had lived for many generations.

5

Departure and Arrival

ISAAC M. WISE HAD NOW COME TO THE PARTING OF THE WAYS. AS we shall read soon in his own words, he decided that his position in Radnitz had become intolerable and that therefore he would leave it. The idea of emigration was no unique or rare one in those days. Some of his friends and connections had already plucked up their roots out of the ancestral stepfatherland and settled in America. The dream of America was in the air. European literature of the time was full of roseate reports about America, the glory of its new freedom, its limitless opportunities, its thrusting aside of the ancient roadblocks of Europe.

Nor was the decision to depart a sudden one for Isaac M. Wise. All the available evidence indicates that he had been mulling it over at least from the first days of his rabbinate in Radnitz. Why is it that one man goes and another stays? That the same intellectual and spiritual conditions will gall one unbearably and not unduly disturb another? Why does one mind turn toward greater independence and another rest relatively content under the yoke of authority? Men will give diverse answers depending upon their predilection for doctrines of necessity or of the freedom of the will. A more circumspect explanation would be that it is both, the man and the time, his own character and the things that happen to him, meshing and intermeshing, the thrust now from one factor, now from the other. Many incidents and many choices in his youth, his education, his affinity for certain friends, his own growing response to Jewish tradition and Jewish authority, his hunger for general culture, added to his own traits of character—his sturdy independence, his eagerness to strike out along his own pathway without let or hindrance: all these conduce toward the impression that he was bound to get to the point where he could endure no more, where even with a wife and a very young child he would resolve to cut the Gordian knot, to take his leap into the relatively unknown. There are times and there are men who cannot and will not "rather bear those ills we have than fly to others that we know not of. . . ."

Later on, glancing back over his shoulder at this period and at himself in it, Isaac M. Wise was sure that he had decided quite early to become an American, that he had already—as it were—enfranchised himself in the spirit of America while still in Bohemia. To what extent this is to be ascribed to the distortion of memory it is not easy to determine. Great lover of the United States that he was and became still more, it was natural for him to think so. Later too he was of the opinion that he set forth for America with comprehensive and precise plans in regard to the American Jewish community as it then was.[1] In the light of the evidence this is doubtful. That is not to say that Isaac M. Wise was unaware of the disunity, the ignorance and the general ineffectiveness of American Jewry in the fifth decade of the nineteenth century, nor perhaps of some of the concepts and plans that needed prompt and vigorous initiation on its behalf. But what he did after he arrived, his first months of doubt and vacillation, make highly improbable the thesis of preliminary, inclusive, sharp vision. That he was a deeply passionate Jew, that like Joseph he was constantly seeking his brethren, that by this time he must have arrived at a fairly complete notion of what he wanted for himself and for Jews religiously and in the field of civil rights, there can be little doubt. But one cannot believe that it went much farther than that.

We must, however, resist the temptation to conjecture further concerning the roots of his state of mind, of his decision to migrate, to indulge ourselves in futile attempts to see him as he was in the spring and summer of 1846. It will be wiser to adduce the evidence and permit the thoughtful reader to judge for himself.

One of the chief evidences in support of his assertion that he had long been nurturing an interest in and an impulse toward America is to be found in the unquestionable fact that he had begun to busy himself with the English language some time before he left Bohemia. He himself wrote:

> In an antiquarian bookstore in the city of Prague I found a collection of American-English prints, and in it a set of

> journals from the years 1770-1790. I purchased the whole and read with the heart perhaps more than with the reason. That literature made of me a naturalized American in the interior of Bohemia [an oft-quoted statement of his]. It inspired in me the resolution to go to America, and against the will of my friends I did go and my family with me.[2]

Among other things he read the letters of Richard Henry Lee, who had written under the *nom de plume* of "Federal Farmer," on the adoption of the proposals for a new Constitution in 1787.[3] He immersed himself also in the novels of James Fenimore Cooper which were widely read and greatly admired in Europe in the middle of the nineteenth century, the *Leather-stocking Tales* with their romantic treatment of the frontiersman and the Indian.[4]

Where he got practice in speaking English he does not say. But this he must have had, for upon his arrival in New York he was not tongue-tied like most "greenhorns." All that he read contributed to his conviction of a natural and profound affinity between the ideals of America and his own, and, judging by many things he said and wrote in later years, that in fact there was a profound and natural nexus between the ideals of America and the ancient teachings and visions of Judaism.

Some time, perhaps late in 1845 or early in 1846, his mind was made up. He would give up his post in Radnitz and leave the country. It was certain that he could not teach or preach Judaism as he conceived it. The Frankfort Conference of 1845 had served to bring his dissatisfaction to a head. He became sure that all his own leanings were toward Reform Judaism, and that his political convictions and inclinations were strongly democratic.[5] He must escape from the excesses of public and ecclesiastical authoritarianism. Like many others he believed that his primary loyalty was not to one nation but to humanity, not to his birthplace but to the appropriate home of his spirit. Why should he remain in Austria which denied him and millions of others the "rights of man," which was saddled with a state church "that treated its serfs worse than the slaves in the South?" With all his valiant heart he chafed at remaining "an imperial-royal-Bohemian Tolerated Jew." His own words ring strongly and significantly: "Therefore I never had a fatherland!" It was senseless to wait for the coming revolution in Austria. It might never come. In its first faint and timid beginnings it had been defeated in the time of Joseph II. What hope was discernible on the horizon now?[6]

Most vividly and characteristically, in a sermon Isaac M. Wise delivered in Cincinnati on the celebration in 1894 of the fortieth anniversary of his occupancy of the pulpit of the Plum St. Temple (as it was then called), he described what had been his state of mind in 1846:

> I was well satisfied with my condition materially and yet I was morbidly dissatisfied with everything: the country, the city, Judaism and Christianity, everything in any State appeared to me a disappointment; my ideals were far above the realities, and I could see no prospect of improvement. I felt sick of home. The irresistible longing for other conditions, another state of things generally, became to me finally the message of Abraham—"Get thee out of thy country, and far from thy kindred, and far from thy father's house, unto the land which I shall show thee" (Genesis, chapter 12, verse 1). All my considerations as to such a venturous step were silenced by the charge to Eliezer—"He will send His angels before thee" (Genesis, chapter 24, verse 7). "You must emigrate" became to me a divine commandment which I could not overcome in spite of myself.[7]

He began preparations to leave Radnitz. A friend (who it was, we do not know!) tried to persuade him to go to France and live there.[8] Isaac M. Wise declared that France, even France, was not far enough ahead in political and spiritual independence (this, one must recall, was thirty-one years after Waterloo and after the restoration of the Bourbons). He said once, speaking of himself at this period: "I had the American fever!"

He applied to a man he regarded as his friend, Count Fuerstenberg, for a passport. Fuerstenberg answered him haughtily and summarily: "Do you think we opened schools for you to take your learning to America?"[9] That is to say: you got your education here; you owe this country a debt; stay here and pay it!

By this time Wise's resolve was much too sure and his eagerness to depart much too intense to be deterred by so peremptory a reply. He must have turned away from Fuerstenberg with impatience, determined to leave with or without the Count's blessing. The obstacles did not daunt him. Nothing is clearer in his personality and in his career than the fact that obstacles, even seemingly insurmountable obstacles encountered again and again, did not deter him.

Without having secured a passport he resigned his post in Radnitz.[10] He gathered together his little family, his few belongings, and proceeded to the border. Together, his wife, his little girl and he crossed the line into Saxony. One imagines them doing this at night, possibly with the aid of some fellow-Jews who would have been only too familiar with exigencies like this. Germany was not then free, but it was freer than Austria, especially in some of the Catholic states not yet under the domination of Prussia, states like Bavaria and Saxony. Isaac M. Wise crossed the border and went on to Leipzig. There he was fortunate enough to come across a friendly and understanding official who welcomed him as a political pilgrim and furnished him and his family with the necessary papers.[11] Now he was no longer a man utterly without a country, entirely without status, as later after both World Wars were millions of Jews, thrown into statelessness!

In one of his later writings reviewing this time Isaac M. Wise asserted that, on his way from the Bohemian border to the port of embarkation, he made "mighty plans for the future." But he does not pause to tell us what those plans were, nor how they were related to his future in America.

Now there was nothing to prevent his proceeding to the sea and taking ship for the United States of America. But, for good and sufficient reasons, he did not go at once nor directly. In Leipzig itself he spent some time with three eminent men. The best known of them was the German-Jewish novelist, Berthold Auerbach, born in the Black Forest in 1812, trained to be a rabbi, a defender of Jews and Judaism, the composer of artless but deep tales. Auerbach was an ardent and brave Jew, as well as a warm-hearted artist. The two deepest and most consistent strands of his character were his love for the country in which he was born—the Black Forest—and his enthusiasm for the spirit and the cause of Israel.[12] The second was Franz Delitsch, a Christian Hebraist, a contemporary of Auerbach, one of that small group of Christians who have devoted their lives to rabbinical learning and to sympathy for the Jewish people. At this time Delitsch was professor of Semitics at the University of Leipzig. In his writing Delitsch was a progressive student of the Bible and of post-Biblical literature, a vigorous defender of Jews and Judaism against anti-Semites (notably in regard to the "blood-accusation"). He was just then in a public controversy with Rohling, an anti-Semite raving and ravening in the German press.[13] The third was Julius Fuerst, an older man, born in 1805, a German Hebraist and Orientalist, then at the University teaching Chaldaic, Syriac, Hebrew grammar and literature, Biblical exegesis, etc. Only two of his works have survived as useful: one on the Karaites, and a Hebrew bibliography.[14]

With these men Isaac M. Wise sat and discussed many things. First they spoke of Austrian affairs. A movement was on foot to erect a statue to the memory of Joseph II, of whom we have written many times in the preceding pages. He was the first ruler in Europe to initiate steps looking toward the complete emancipation of Jews. An amusing incident in connection with these conversations of Wise with Auerbach, Delitsch and Fuerst is to be found in the first biographical sketch of Wise by Philippson and Grossmann. While they were speaking of this proposed monument, Fuerst turned to Auerbach: "What Biblical verse would you suggest for this statue?" Quick as a flash Auerbach replied: " 'Joseph recognized his brethren, but they did not know him' " (Genesis, chapter 42, verse 8).[15]

From Leipzig Wise traveled to Breslau, where he spent some time with the great scholar and thinker of liberal Judaism, Abraham Geiger.[16] Geiger was nine years older than Wise and had already had an embattled career as rabbi and as author, historian and critic. Beginning as a child-prodigy he had given evidence of an analytic and encyclopedic mind. His chief interest was in the very *Wissenschaft des Judenthums*, the "scientific" approach to Jewish history and Jewish studies, of which we have written earlier. Wise had met and heard him in Frankfort and wished to go more deeply into some of the controversial topics discussed there. Geiger had been rabbi in Breslau since early in 1840. He did not go along with the middle-of-the-road position of Zechariah Frankel, nor was he content with a compromise when it came to what he regarded as the truth. His greatest single work was on the text and the translations of the Bible.[17] From him Wise could have learned and doubtless did learn much, did find a sharpening and clarification of his own ideas and a strengthening of his resolve. He must have canvassed with Geiger not only the problems of Reform in Judaism, but probably also the status and future of Jews in the United States.

Wise's next stop was in Magdeburg, where he spent some time with Ludwig Philippson, the widely known editor of the *Allgemeine Zeitung des Judenthums*, and translator of some of the Hebrew prophets.[18] Philippson had been called to Magdeburg as rabbi when he was but twenty-two years old and had been there for fourteen years when Wise visited him. Later Philippson took an active part in the abortive liberal revolution of 1848. He too was a learned and vigorous proponent of Reform.[19]

Now back to Frankfort where Wise wished to spend more time

with Leopold Stein, another of the men he had met and heard in Frankfort the previous year.[20] There appears to have been a special feeling of warmth and mutual understanding between Stein and Wise, for they corresponded with one another frequently over the course of many years, and Stein was invariably cordial and helpful. Stein had come to Frankfort as rabbi in 1833, and although he had retired as rabbi twenty years earlier, remained there until his death in 1882. He was also one of the great leaders of Reform in Germany, a prolific writer of poetry, of works chiefly on the liturgy, and of some dramas.[21]

Last of all Isaac M. Wise traveled to Berlin and spent some days with Michael Jehiel Sachs, who had been rabbi in Prague until 1844.[22] There Wise had come to know him. Sachs then went to Berlin and lived there until his death in 1864. At this very time, in 1846, Sachs was having a long and bitter controversy with his own congregation in Berlin on the subject of his adherence to Reform. In the end he withdrew into private life and devoted himself exclusively to study. He was himself a poet, and indited some excellent works on Hebrew poetry, notably of the Middle Ages. Some of his researches on the relation of the Talmud to the Greek and Roman world were pioneering studies of great fertility and originality. He was regarded by many as the foremost Jewish preacher of his time.[23] It was, as we have said, in the midst of these controversies that Wise came to Berlin. In the following year there was a secession and the establishment of the *Juedische Reformgemeinde* (Jewish Reform Congregation).[24]

What was the probable reason for these peregrinations? Without question it was to crystallize and clarify his own feelings about Reform in Judaism. Thirty-six years later (December 15, 1882), on receiving news of the death of Leopold Stein, Wise wrote:

> It may be put down as a fact that reform among American Jews was accelerated by Leopold Stein, because many of our leading men and women in this country were educated under his influence and felt a rare attachment to him and his teachings.[25]

The entire trip took no more than several weeks and was thoroughly successful in its purpose, to judge by Wise's own comments upon it and the course he pursued when he came to America.

Several days before *Shabuoth* (The Feast of Weeks) Wise arrived in Bremerhaven with his family. For the holiday he was invited to preach in the neighboring town of Bremerle. In his *Reminiscences* Wise writes that he had "gone with wife and child to Bremen without a passport." This is hard to understand. It may mean that the papers he had secured from the friendly official in Leipzig were of another kind, but this conjecture too leaves the entire matter somewhat up in the air.[26]

The day after *Shabuoth* he and his little family set forth from Bremen on the S.S. Marie, a sailing vessel. In those days a voyage was no swift transition between continents. Long and often arduous the journey assuredly was. This one took sixty-three days, lengthened by storms encountered on the way. It was May 20, 1846 when they left the land and started out through the North Sea and the English Channel into the wide Atlantic.

Isaac M. Wise was but one of many. These were the years, before and after the crisis of liberalism in Europe, when many forsook the Old World to try their chances in the New. They came for a variety of reasons: to throw themselves into the arms of liberty; to test their fortunes in a land where horizons were still open and society in the early stages of formation; because of extravagant reports of easy wealth; or because their dear ones had already settled here. Few of them, very few, were there whose coming meant as much as did that of Isaac M. Wise, few who were temperamentally and in vision as fitted for America, few who were to respond as immediately, as vigorously and ardently—and as creatively—to the hope and promise of America.

In his *Reminiscences* Isaac M. Wise wrote[27] of but one time during the sixty-three days of rolling and tossing upon a small sailing ship. It was two months after they had set sail, precisely on July 20. The captain told them that they were but fifty miles out of Boston. It was late at night. Most likely Isaac M. Wise had put his wife and child into the cabin and was alone on the deck. He thought how foolish and daring he was, how much he had—perhaps heedlessly—placed in jeopardy. Everything was behind him and he did not know what lay ahead. Usually so buoyant and resilient, his spirits sank within him. He grew despondent, he wrote, and at last he went to sleep. The rest it would be best to let him tell in his own words:

> Finally I dropped off to sleep, and dreamed the following unforgettable dream:
>
> I dreamed that a great storm which drove the ship toward the land had arisen. Every one swayed, trembled, feared, prayed; the inky waves rose mountain-high, and broke into seething masses, only to give way to other watery heights. Convulsively I embraced wife and child, and spoke words of calm and

> comfort. It then appeared to me as though a high, steep, rocky mountain was hurrying toward us and threatened to crush us. "Here we must land, or we sink," cried the captain, with quaking voice. Scarcely had these words been uttered ere the ribs of the ship, which had been hurled on the rock, cracked. I took a daring leap, and stood on the rock with wife and child. The ocean still roared; a wave seized the ship, and cast it far out into the seething waters; in a few moments it was swallowed up in the night, and disappeared from my gaze. So, then, here we were on the rugged rock; at our feet the waters, agitated by the wild storm, raged; above us, and about us, were forbidding rocks, while the darkness added its terrors. Finally, after a long interval, morning dawned, and revealed a dangerous situation. "However steep the mountain appears, we must ascend it," said I to my wife. I took the child on one arm; tremblingly my wife clung to the other, and then forward, in God's name! It seemed to me as though an inner voice called, "Up above there is help." With difficulty we clambered from rock to rock, higher and higher, constantly, untiringly. Then, as though the measure of woes was not yet full, hollow-eyed, ghostly, grinning dwarfs, lascivious, ragged goblins, and tiny poodles, with large, hollow, puffed-out heads, came towards us on the narrow path, opposed our further progress, and mocked me mercilessly. I brushed them aside; but for every ten that I pushed away a hundred arose from out the bare rock. They came in the shape of night-owls, and deafened me with their cries; they sizzed about me like angry wasps, and stung me; they placed themselves, like stupid blocks, in my path; in short, they did everything to harass me and prevent my further progress. My wife at my side wept bitterly, the child in my arms cried for fright, but my courage, strength, and confidence grew. I begged, implored, avoided, circumvented them, all to no avail. Then I marched straight through the crowd of dwarfs, paid no attention to their ravings, dashed them aside to the right and to the left, until finally, weary and perspiring, we reached the summit of the mountain. Arriving there, I saw the most beautiful and glorious landscape, the richest, most fertile meadows, but I sank fainting; thereupon I awoke, and found it was all a dream; but I have often thought of that dream.[28]

The dream is so patently symbolical in character and so perfectly fits the coming tenor of his life, his climbing a spiritual mountain, the petty people who were forever opposing and vilifying him, his victory and the pleasant fertile land that he was to find beyond, that it is hard to refrain from thinking that some of it must have been written retrospectively from the vantage-point of later years. After all, these *Reminiscences* were written almost thirty years later. And yet men do have dreams like this, premonitory in character, compounded of trepidation and hope, of past and future. Certain it is that Wise was poised between two worlds, the world he had incontinently left and the world he was about to explore. Certain it is that he had abundant reason for foreboding. This mood might have pursued him from his waking into his sleeping hours.

The long voyage was almost over. Three days later the Marie had sailed from near Boston to New York and was made fast to the land. This was on July 23, 1846.[29] In his *Reminiscences*—regrettably—he passes over what he must have felt when first he looked upon, when first he set foot upon, the soil of America. In a man so deeply sensitive, so given over to inner musings, to translating every moment into its relation to himself and his "mission," there must have been a crowding multitude of thoughts and emotions, racing through mind and heart. In his biography his grandson (Max B. May) declared that Isaac M. Wise came to America with very definite plans and purposes, most of which derived from his determination to liberate Judaism and American Jews from the condition of their bigotry and their disunity, to secure for them complete equality in political and religious rights in the new land, to raise the whole level of Jewish life, Jewish dignity and self-respect, so that the Jew would be and would feel himself to be a respected citizen of the community.[30] Much of this may have been inchoately within him. But it is not likely that it was so clear-cut, that it rested then upon a sharp and comprehensive analysis of the situation and the needs of Jews in America. That he came to all this very quickly the record establishes. Within an amazingly brief time after his arrival he had learned the essentials, had discerned the direction in which improvement must lie and had begun to speak, to propose, to act.

But on July 23 of 1846 he was taken up with the necessities of getting his wife and child off the sailing-ship. In his *Reminiscences* he informs us that he had come with much luggage and little money, as a matter of fact, with only two dollars in his pocket. A burly German, doubtless among the many shouting at the dock, offered to take his luggage to Essex Street for the sum of six dollars. It was too high and he did not have it to pay. An Irishman cut the price and offered to do the job for two dollars. As all such price wars are wont to, this infuriated the German driver, who heaped objurgations, not upon the Irishman, but upon the "greener." This in turn roused Isaac M. Wise's wrath. So here it was again! The old Jew-hatred, which he had just left home to escape! But what good would it do to bandy words with a hack driver? He turned his back on the scene and on the shouting. Deep down, he tells us, it did not trouble him, for he realized to the depth of his soul that he was no longer a *Schutzjude*, but had come to free air, to equality, to right and opportunity.[31]

His wife and child did not go with him and the luggage, but were taken to the home on Staten Island of a certain John Lindheim, who "had a clothing-store on the Bowery." Wise's brother-in-law, Edward Bloch, then sixteen years of age, clerked for Lindheim. This was the first chapter in a long record of friendship between the Wise and the Lindheim families. But Isaac M. Wise could not let his little family remain there, for he had promised to be the guest of a certain Joseph Cohn, whom he had married half a year before in Radnitz. When Wise had officiated at the marriage, Cohn had confided to him that he was about to emigrate to America, and, instead of paying Wise a fee, invited him and his family to stay with him, Cohn, in New York. There too the three Wises did not remain long, but moved into a house on Broome Street, a house belonging to a Mr. Friedmann. There they set up housekeeping.[32]

Let us leave Isaac M. Wise for the moment, safely arrived and ensconced in New York and conclude this chapter with two addenda: New York and American Jewry in 1846.

His first glimpse of New York was not prepossessing. It seemed to him no more than a large and noisy hamlet. The faint, embryonic beginnings of a "metropolis" were to be found in lower Broadway, but "elsewhere it was like a village." It was "like a large shop where every one buys or sells, cheats or is cheated." There was no art, execrable architecture, no good taste, and an incredible amount of "rushing, hurrying, chasing, running." Noise, too, everywhere and all over! Wagons, street-gamins, newsboys, "dealers in popcorn!" "All this shocked my aesthetic sense beyond expression." He liked some negro dance-music he heard a fiddler playing. But in general, humanly and aesthetically, it all seemed on a small scale and paltry.[33]

And what was the condition of American Jewry at this time? Many times in later years Isaac M. Wise was to advert to what it was then, to its appalling state of ignorance, disaffection and disunity. It is not a little astonishing, in the first place, to know that the Jewish population of the United States was estimated to be, in 1848, two years later, about 50,000.[34] Jews were settled for the most part in the larger cities of the Eastern seaboard. Some—but not a large proportion—had been drifting westward even in the early years. Between 1840 and 1850 there were recognizable Jewish communities in Albany, Syracuse, New York, Buffalo, Rochester, Pittsburgh, Cleveland, Cincinnati, Louisville, Chicago, St. Louis, New Orleans, and a few other places in the South.[35]

The first Jews in America had been of Portuguese origin, via Brazil, Holland, the West Indies. They had founded congregations and some Jewish institutions in a few cities. They had their own characteristic ritual, their own religious customs. They brought with them—and further deepened here—a sense of aristocratic distinction real or fancied, as compared with other Jews. They had been here almost two hundred years when German-Jewish migration to America began. A deep cleavage naturally followed. Social and religious crossing of the lines was minimal. Many Portuguese Jews had already intermarried, and there had been a large degree of assimilation—in speech, in garb, in culture, in habit—into the ways of the land. They looked down upon the newcomers, in many cases unmercifully, and had little commerce with them.[36]

Immigration from Poland and Germany (the former often by way of England) had begun lightly about 1830. It was recruited chiefly from among Jews who had lived in small towns and villages. Cincinnati, for example, had most of its German Jews from Bavaria, from towns in back areas and with strange names. These Jews had lived cramped and oppressed lives. They had come, lured across the Atlantic by rumors of immediate economic opportunity in the New World. This was a society not yet congealed into classes, and a land whose resources had only begun to be discovered and exploited.[37]

At the time the German and Polish Jews began to come, there were Portuguese synagogues in Newport, R.I., New York, Philadelphia, Richmond, Charleston, S.C., Savannah, and New Orleans.[38] These the newcomers did not think of joining. As institutions they were too remote from the newcomers' habits, and the people much too frigid in their bearing. Instead the German Jews simply organized their own congregations, transplanting their own immemorial customs and beliefs, using local German and Polish forms and pronunciations of the liturgy. Even here there were difficulties. In Cincinnati, the German Jews did not feel at home in K.K.B'nai Israel, which used the *Minhag Polen.* They soon seceded and established K.K.B'nai Yeshurun, which used the *Minhag Ashkenaz.* As soon as a *Minyan* (the "ten" sufficient for most worship) had come to a community, they united to form a congregation, in these early years always along strictly traditional lines.[39] The same abuses, the same intractabilities, the same eclipse of the spirit in the letter, that had been plaguing German and Austrian Judaism, were simply grafted upon America with a few trivial variations of time and place.

But the beginnings of Reform Judaism were already to be found. Charleston, South Carolina, was first, on November 21, 1824; Har Sinai in Baltimore next on April 19, 1842; then Emanu-El of New York in 1845, and Wise's future congregation in Albany was fourth in line.[40] But these were only a handful, and all the remainder were strictly orthodox when Wise landed in New York. There were in all about forty organized congregations in the country: nine in New York, three in Philadelphia, three in Baltimore, and about twenty-five more from Boston to Cleveland to New Orleans.[41] The religious life that prevailed in almost all of them was not calculated to arouse much in the way of enthusiasm or of hope. The habitual indecorum of the synagogue was usually in evidence. There were deplorably few men who had a modicum of Jewish education. Later we shall give somewhat more detailed comments by Isaac M. Wise on the status of religious leadership at the time, how few rabbis of any kind there were, and what were the qualities—or the lack of qualities—of the *Hazanim* ("cantors"), *Shochetim* ("ritual butchers"), and *Mohelim* (specialists in circumcision), who were serving as spiritual guides.

By the side of the synagogue at that time there were tragically few public Jewish institutions. Genuine religious instruction of any but the most sporadic and rudimentary variety did not exist. In 1838 Rebecca Gratz had founded the first genuine religious school in Philadelphia. She called it a "Sunday School," the characteristic name by which it was and still is known. Only a few cities (New York, Albany, Philadelphia, Richmond, Charleston and Cincinnati) boasted the possession of any school at all. The American Jewish community possessed but one "organ," *The Occident*, under the editorial leadership of Isaac Leeser of Philadelphia.[42] Ere long we shall come upon Wise's caustic comments upon Leeser's lack of courage and of even the most elementary Hebrew and Jewish scholarship (though, as we shall see, Wise wrote for the *Occident* for some years and had a sneaking affection for Leeser). An American Jewish Publication Society was born in Philadelphia in 1845, but lasted only a few years and did not achieve much. With the single exception of Max Lilienthal, then the spiritual head of three congregations in New York, there was not in the whole land a single rabbi officiating in an orthodox pulpit.[43] The *locum tenens* was either a cantor, a ritual butcher, or some other minor servitor, quite without learning, leadership or vision. Most of the so-called German congregations then used the *Siddur* (prayer-book) according to *Minhag Polen*, others the *Minhag Ashkenaz*. They retained the custom of calling men up to the reading of the *Torah* and of selling *Mitzvoth* (privileges of participation) to the highest bidder. Many old customs—for the most part without deep religious significance—were still observed.

Perhaps we have been drawing the picture too much in dark colors. There were some remarkable men then among the German Jews, remarkable in their sturdy independence, in their refusal to make compromises with intolerance in Central Europe, remarkable certainly in their capacity to adjust to the new land and to make their way in it. Among them, even thus early, there must have been many of liberal views. In no other way can one explain reasonably the rapid transition of some of the congregations from orthodoxy to reform. The congregation to which Isaac M. Wise came eight years later, K.K.B'nai Yeshurun of Cincinnati, where he remained until the end of his life, began technically as orthodox, had some ridiculous quarrels in its early years on specific points of orthodoxy, was unable to keep James K. Gutheim as its rabbi, yet in 1854 called Wise, and had quite surely made up its mind to become Reform. And it followed Wise unswervingly, loyally and almost unanimously from that day forward.[44]

For the sake of completeness and fairness it must be added that already in 1846 there were two other rabbis besides Lilienthal on the American scene, both in Reform pulpits: Leo Merzbacher at Emanu-El in New York, and Gustav Poznanski in Charleston: both German rabbis, and both to become fast friends and constant co-workers of Isaac M. Wise.[45]

But, taken all in all, it would have been hard to imagine a community for which the diagnosis would have been more discouraging than that for American Jews as they were more than a century ago. Wise's swift perception of all that was ailing Jews in America did not extend in the least to the country, its political institutions and its public leaders. He was not blind to American faults or shortcomings, but almost from the outset he fell in love with America, felt himself at home in it, glowed when he thought of its contrast with the land whence he had come, believed in it, predicted for it a glorious and speedy millennial future and a boundless influence upon the cause of justice, equality, freedom, brotherhood and peace among all men. His affinities were all with Jeffersonian democracy, its ways of thinking, and its assertive individualism, in the beginning and throughout his life. His heroes, whom he chose as he began to know them and their place in the American drama, were men whose lives and ideas were close to his own: men like Seward of Civil War and Alaska fame; Stephen Douglas, Lincoln's great opponent in the debates in Illinois; Daniel Webster, Henry Clay and Horace Greeley.[46] Nor did he admire them from afar. Almost all of them he came to know and to converse with, and his feeling for America gained in clarity and in strength almost from day to day.

Such was the man, such was the city, such was the Jewish community, and such the country, to which Isaac M. Wise came on that July day in 1846. It was from here that his life began to move in expanding circles of vision and leadership. Let us follow him!

6

First Weeks in America

ISAAC M. WISE AND HIS WIFE AND CHILD, AS WE HAVE SEEN, WERE established in a house on Broome Street, belonging to a Mr. Friedmann. From his own account in the *Reminiscences* it is clear that his first days in this country were confused, that he was by no means certain of the way he would go, even of the profession or occupation he would follow. This we shall describe in detail in a moment. But first it would be wise to attempt to estimate his position, his situation, as it was for a short time, and as it seemed to him.

He himself was convinced that he had gone through a very difficult time and that it was not of short duration. One of the amusing evidences of this is the perhaps unconscious and symbolical shift of dates in the *Reminiscences*. We have noted that he arrived in New York on the S.S. Marie on July 23, 1846. He was elected to his first pulpit in Albany just after Rosh Ha-shono, which cannot have been much later than the latter part of September. Thus it follows that between his landing and his finding himself launched upon his rabbinical career in America not much more than two months can have elapsed. Yet several times in the *Reminiscences* he refers to his first meetings and tentatives at work in New York as happening on or about July 1st.[1] This was a manifest error, for he was then upon the high seas. Doubtless he meant August 1st, after he had been in New York about a week getting settled.

But there can be no question that it was a time of very real and acute worry, of shifting and perhaps desperate plans, of seeking friends and at last finding them, of wondering whether he would be able to follow the profession for which he had so long been trained and for which he was so eminently fitted, of rapid adaptation to his own situation in America. Indeed, considering the condition of American Jewish life as we have rather superficially described it, the number of Jews then in America, the remarkable fact is not his preliminary period of searching, but its brevity, the promptness with which he found a post and embarked upon the career he was to follow from then onward, his rapid and eagle-clear discernment of what was needed and of how best he could serve.

In an essay in the *Deborah* many years later he wrote that he had "decided to conquer America," but that he had no weapon save the "living word."[2] While on shipboard he had been told by a Boston teacher of some works in English that would help him, notably the eight volumes of Addison's *Spectator* and Blair's Lectures on *Rhetoric*. To the reading and study of these, during his early unoccupied days, he devoted himself assiduously.

Meanwhile the insistent question was: what should he do? He had no money, and, though living in New York in 1846 was cheap as to rent and food, he had nothing at all. His brother-in-law, Joseph Bloch, was living in San Francisco earning a livelihood, as were many, many Jews then, as a peddler, not having too easy a time of it and burdened by many debts. Nonetheless he made the long journey to New York and offered Isaac M. Wise some money. Whether Wise accepted this offer he does not say in his *Reminiscences*.[3] But he does inform us that he managed to get along in these early days, that his landlord at Broome Street did not press him, but was even kind enough to lend him money to buy food for his wife and child.[4] Others whom he met offered to lend him money. But all this could not continue. As quickly as he could he had to begin to earn a living.

His coming to America did not pass completely unnoticed. We have remarked that at that time there were only three ordained, well-educated rabbis in the whole country. The arrival of another, even though he was at that time but twenty-seven years of age, was news. The *Occident*, Leeser's paper, carried a paragraph informing the Jews of the land that Isaac M. Wise had arrived in New York. It referred to him in tentative and inaccurate terms as "a young schoolmaster who also preaches, and is said to possess some Hebrew learning."[5] In the light of Wise's opinion, often reiterated later, that Leeser lacked practically all Jewish or Hebrew "learning," this rings somewhat sardonically. On August 3 (in the *Reminiscences* he writes "July 3rd") Wise was introduced to a man named Von Eichtal, the editor of the *Daily and Weekly Express*, and through him met some leaders of the Whig Party. From the latter he received the gratuitous advice not to follow the rabbinical profession but to pursue a literary career.[6] This kind of counsel he was to get quite frequently and from various sources during these earliest days. He records also that he met a certain "Mr. Robinson." Under what circumstances, we are not told. Robinson must have been much taken with the young man, for he offered to take the whole Wise family into his home and to care for them until they could make a start. But this, with his customary sturdy independence, Isaac M. Wise refused.[7]

Wise had come to America with a number of letters of introduction. These he now decided to use. Two of them were directed to Jewish physicians in New York, both practicing chiefly among Jews. He visited them, shook their hands and received their counsel. Both depicted the American synagogue to him in raven color, and American Jews in the most unflattering terms. They advised him strongly to abandon his profession, to follow the precedent set by the majority of German-Jewish immigrants and to take up peddling or some trade. Wise listened, refrained from arguing, but turned away in disgust from this kind of short-sighted, faint-hearted advice.[8]

Later he had a number of talks with a certain Mr. Joachimson whom he met at Lilienthal's house. Joachimson he found to be an intelligent Jew of genuine loyalty and good will. With him he discussed his own future. Wise believed then that he might be able to find work as a "professor" in some school or college. This would appear to indicate that he was himself wavering as to his future. Joachimson begged him not to abandon Judaism, not to forsake the convictions and the hopes he had acquired in Frankfort, in Radnitz and in his meetings with Geiger, Sachs, Philippson, and Stein. Joachimson told him that the Jews of the United States needed him desperately, whether they realized it or not. The earnestness and the wide vision of this man moved and convinced Wise and did much to keep his feet upon the pathway upon which they had been set so long. Also—he writes—he had not forgotten his dream on shipboard.[9]

During these first weeks he opened a night-school in the basement of Cohn's house. Here he gave instruction in English to earlier immigrants, most of them factory-workers. Under his tutelage were sixteen students, and in a few days his name was known all over the German quarter of New York, from Houston Street to Grand. But his pupils were poor men, able to pay little or nothing for lessons, and he himself—he said—was a very "poor teacher," in both senses of the word. This experiment lasted only one or two weeks and was completely abortive, financially and educationally. In a much later work Wise asserted that this school lasted for four weeks, that he was followed—as teacher—by a tailor's apprentice from Posen (across whom he came years later in the role of an itinerant salesman of such objects as *Tefillin* (philacteries), *Mezuzzoth* (scrolls for the doorpost of a Jewish home), and so forth.[10]

In the meantime he was acquiring an acquaintance with Jewish life in New York. In the foregoing chapter we have already enumerated some facts about it. There were then seven congregations in the city, two community schools and some early charitable organizations, German and English. Wise began a round of visits to synagogues. He went first to the oldest in New York, the Portuguese synagogue, *Sherith Israel* (The Remnant of Israel). Here he was on *Shabbos Nachamu* (the Sabbath after *Tisha b'Ab*, the Ninth of Ab, the day on which the Temple on Zion was twice destroyed, and on which the wonderful passage at the beginning of Chapter 40 of the prophet Isaiah, beginning "Comfort ye, comfort ye My people," was read). He found—he writes—that the ritual was tedious.

Later he attended services at the "English-Polish" synagogue on Elm Street. This followed the Polish *Minhag*, which had probably been acquired on the way from Poland in London. In this synagogue occurred an absurd but interesting incident. Wise recounts that he was hungry "for the sight of a Hebrew book." He asked for a volume of the *Mishna* (the first codification of the Law by Judah HaNasi about the first half of the third century C.E.): "that individual laughed so mockingly, that I readily perceived what a sign of 'greenness' it was on my part to ask for an ancient Hebrew book in the New World, and that too in an orthodox synagogue. . . ."

Another synagogue was the "Polish Synagogue" on Center Street, at that time on the second story of the building. Here Wise listened to a very ignorant reading of the commentary of Rashi on the Torah. There were then in New York three "ultra-orthodox" congregations, one on Henry Street, the two others on Attorney

Street. At this time Max Lilienthal (of whom some personal details, shortly) had been rabbi of all three for about six months. Every Saturday Lilienthal preached in a different pulpit of the three.

Wise also visited the Henry Street Synagogue on *Shabbos Hazon* (the Sabbath before *Tisha b'Ab*, on which the denunciatory first chapter of the prophet Isaiah is read). Here the old German *Minhag* was used. There was—he reports—a large attendance, but with a deplorable lack of decorum. The services were conducted by a cantor who sold *Mitzvoth* in the old and—to him—disreputable way.

Wise listened to Lilienthal preach and found him to be a splendid speaker with a glowing diction and a most dignified carriage. He did not, however, care for what Lilienthal had to say about *Tisha b'Ab*. By this time Wise had come to the point of view, which was that of Reform Judaism, that there was no longer occasion to mourn the loss of the Temple and the sacrificial cult. He wrote: "what he said about the season of mourning had long since lost all significance for me, and I was really and truly moved to mournful feelings, not for the destruction of Jerusalem, but for the disappearance of Judaism in the Polish-cabalistical rabbinism and supernaturalism." Wise indites also an extravagant but amusing description of the *Hazan*, who "had on a Christian gown, trilled like a mock nightingale, and leaped about like a hooked fish."

The youngest congregation was Emanu-El, which had just undertaken to build a synagogue. Wise visited the place where the building had been begun, found there about fifty men and thirty women, "the latter in a section partitioned off," which opened some doubts in his mind as to the genuineness of the congregation's "reform." There was a boys' choir reinforced by a few male adult voices, and they sang Sulzer—very poorly, he says. But the service was at least conducted with some degree of dignity and decorum. The rabbi was Merzbacher who soon became his very good friend. Merzbacher spoke concerning the end of the *Galuth* (exile), "of the morning that was dawning also for the house of Israel." "His words made me feel at home, although he did not treat the *Tisha b'Ab* as drastically as I could have wished."[11]

Outside of Lilienthal and Merzbacher, Wise writes, there was not one leader of a congregation who could read unpunctuated (unvocalized) Hebrew, or who possessed any genuine knowledge of Jewish history, or of Jewish literature. There were here and there a few individuals, not rabbis, who had a smattering of knowledge, but no more! In his *Reminiscences* Wise adds here the description of a number of instances of *Am Ha'aratzuth* (Jewish ignorance). A prominent Jew "denied emphatically" that *Rashi* had written a commentary to the Book of Samuel. And another ". . . imparted to him, as though it were a secret and wonderful piece of knowledge, that Maimonides had written a Code," and asked Wise whether he had ever seen "a copy of this valuable work."[12]

Things were in not much better state in regard to secular culture. "No Jew who had recently immigrated was fitted to occupy a public position creditably." Among the Portuguese Jews, Mordecai Noah had achieved some prominence through "literary and political activity." In the world of business some Jews had already registered considerable successes, and some even as long ago as this were striving assiduously to conceal their Jewish origin.[13]

It was somewhere about August 1st (Wise writes "July 1st" in his *Reminiscences*) that, as we have written, he met Merzbacher, a learned and sincere man, the then rabbi of Temple Emanu-El. There was an immediate and hearty liking on both sides. Merzbacher had already had to endure a number of disheartening experiences before Wise met him. He had been rabbi of the orthodox "German" congregations, where Lilienthal was at the moment. They had discharged Merzbacher incontinently. In their first conversation Merzbacher asked Wise whether he intended to be a rabbi or to follow an academic career. Wise replied: "I can sacrifice everything except principle." Merzbacher wished him luck, but was doubtful of the possibility of "preaching Reform" at that time. Merzbacher, Wise informs us, was receiving the munificent salary of two-hundred-and-fifty dollars a year.[14]

By all odds the most interesting and the most fertile of Wise's contacts in these early days was with Max Lilienthal. The latter, as we have already noted several times, was then serving as a rabbi of three orthodox congregations in New York. He was a German Jew, born in Munich, November 6, 1815, educated in the same city and graduated from its University in 1837. He then took the position of preacher and teacher in Riga on the Baltic. In 1841 he was sent on an official mission about Russia by Uvarov, the minister of public instruction. It was the proclaimed purpose of the Czarist government to establish Jewish schools for secular and religious instruction. The Jews of Russia regarded this plan with the utmost suspicion and probably had good reason for so regarding it. They believed that the real purpose of these schools was to be conversionist. Lilienthal's task was to investigate the reasons for this attitude, and to attempt to allay fear and suspicion. Before long he became convinced that his task was utterly impossible. The result, it was evident, was very far from being what the government had said it hoped. He himself was looked upon as a foreigner, perhaps a traitor. Between him and the Russian Jews a deep gulf opened. Suddenly in 1844 he left Russia and made the voyage to the United States. During the time of his occupancy of the three orthodox pulpits in New York his advanced liberal views led to constant friction with leaders and members. In 1850 he resigned all three pulpits and established an institute for Jewish education which was not unsuccessful. Wise was hardly installed in Cincinnati as the rabbi of K.K.B'nai Yeshurun in 1854, when he established the *Israelite*, made Lilienthal its correspondent, and then soon thereafter was instrumental in persuading K.K.B'nai Israel of Cincinnati (later the "Rockdale Avenue Temple") to elect Lilienthal as their rabbi. Here Lilienthal officiated for twenty-seven years, aiding in the labors of the *Israelite*, teaching later on at the Hebrew Union College, and contributing frequently and productively to the *Israelite*, the *Occident*, *Die Deborah* and other Jewish journals. He found time to write poems, dramas and several volumes of sermons and addresses. He played a prominent role in civic affairs in the city of Cincinnati, serving as a member of the Board of Education and of the board of the University of Cincinnati. He had become and remained a whole-hearted and consistent advocate and leader of Reform Judaism. Between him and Wise from the beginning to the end was the warmest of fraternal relations, full of affection and admiration on both sides. On all the causes which led to the laying of the cornerstones of Reform Judaism in America they labored together.[15]

Their first meeting is therefore of quite exceptional interest. It proved to begin, quite soon, the launching of Isaac M. Wise upon his American career. It is good to note that, just as Lilienthal was the primary instrument in aiding Wise to find a hearing and a pulpit, so after the passage of not many years it was Wise who brought Lilienthal to Cincinnati and helped him to the post where he was happy in the free exercise of his religious liberalism, in civic helpfulness, and in his noble participation in that era of great trials, great plans, and—ultimately—of great achievements.

Our records do not reveal to us exactly when Isaac M. Wise went to see Max Lilienthal in New York, presenting to him a letter of introduction which Wise had brought with him from the old country. Based on what happened thereafter the probabilities would place their first meeting at some time in August, 1846. Wise had the most cordial, friendly, even brotherly reception from Lilienthal and from his wife. Wise's own description in his *Reminiscences* is worth quoting, for it gives us a vivid picture of that first meeting:

> A man in a dressing-gown, with a black velvet cap on his head, opened the door.
>
> "I would like to speak to Dr. Lilienthal."
>
> "I am he; step in."
>
> We stepped into the rear room, which was his library.
>
> "I come from Bohemia. Here is a letter from Dr. W., your school friend, and here are some of my papers."
>
> Dr. Lilienthal read the letter and the first of the twelve documents I had given him, when he went to the door and called: "Wife, bring coffee and cigars. I have received a guest." Turning to me, he gave me a friendly and hearty *Shalom aleichem* ("peace be with you"). "Hold up your head! Courage!" cried he. "You are the man. We need you." In short, Dr. Lilienthal was the first man to encourage me and inspire me with hope, and at that time this was of prime importance and significance to me. After a few minutes *she* [italics his] came into the room; *she* whom later I had the frequent opportunity of admiring as the most lovable and amiable of wives and mothers; she who surpassed even Munich's daughters in charm; who with clear insight penetrated into the very heart of conditions and persons, and cast a glamour of love on all about her. I mean the sainted Peppie Lilienthal. Within ten minutes I felt at home, and the impression which I received in the Lilienthal home, perhaps decided my career in America. . . .[16]

So auspiciously begun, this friendship was to last until Lilienthal's death in 1882. Officiating at his funeral obsequies Wise could hardly speak, by reason of the sobs stifling his voice and the tears streaming from his eyes. It became a friendship without blemish or interruption, founded on mutuality of tastes and principles, and upon truly fraternal cooperation.[17]

Wise goes on to say that he might have continued indefinitely in the hack-work he had been doing, living from hand to mouth, had it not been for Lilienthal's active interest, his seeking out ways by which Wise could make a beginning. Once again we prefer to tell it in Wise's own words in his *Reminiscences:*

> I would have continued thus for some time longer, had not the following occurrence taken place:

> "Are you a good preacher?" Dr. Lilienthal asked me one day.
>
> "At home they considered me a passable pulpit orator," I answered, not without hesitancy, for I did not want to preach in New York for various reasons, and had already refused several invitations.
>
> "Well, then, go on Thursday to New Haven, in the State of Connecticut," said Dr. Lilienthal. "They invited me to dedicate a synagogue there. I cannot leave New York. Go and do your best."[18]

This was in the last week of August, 1846. For the occasion for which he was to go Isaac M. Wise wrote two sermons in German. It is hard to picture to ourselves that he went to New Haven not by road and not by rail but by steamer from New York. He was cordially received by the members of the Jewish community.

The situation among the Jews of New Haven is briefly described in the *Reminiscences.* There had been a congregation for some time, but a group under the leadership of one Leopold Wasserman had seceded from it. The reasons that underlay this split are not given. According to Wise, Wasserman was a fine man, a poet, many of whose compositions appeared later in the *Deborah.* He was also a genuine idealist, with whom Wise formed a life-long friendship. The place of worship was only a room in the upper story of a building. Wise was conscious of some trepidation on his own part. The place was small; the number of worshippers present cannot have been large. But he writes:

> I seemed to myself very small and childish. . . . I had never preached in so small a place.

He delivered sermons Friday night and Saturday morning, and on Sabbath afternoon was asked also to speak in the older congregation. A peddler from Albany who was present at the earlier services assured Dr. Wise that "he had heard no better German preacher in Poland—and that, if I would come to Albany, my fortune would be made."[19] But the praise of the president, Mr. Wasserman, pleased him much more. The New Haven *Palladium* of August 29, 1846 contained the following account:

> The hall in the fourth story of Brewster's building was consecrated as a Jewish synagogue. A lecture was delivered in German by Dr. Wais [sic!], a rabbi who has but recently arrived in this country. This is spoken of by those who understood the language as a most excellent discourse, and the speaker certainly in his manner gave evidence of a most perfect style of oratory.[20]

It is appropriate to note here that it was this mis-spelling of his name that prompted Isaac M. Wise to adopt the spelling of his name which became permanent. In Bohemia it had been "Weis." He discerned that this was too difficult for Americans, and that the native spelling for the same meaning would be easier and better in every way. Thus it became and remained "Wise."[21]

For the two addresses he had delivered for the dedication of the synagogue in New Haven he received what seemed to him the munificent sum of sixty dollars. This would have been three hundred gulden in Bohemia, and, compared with what he had had until then, and what he had brought to the United States, it was wealth.[22]

On the steamer returning to New York he chatted with a certain Mr. Isaacs, who was a preacher in New York, in what congregation Wise does not inform us. From the height of his superior knowledge and his longer residence Isaacs delivered to Wise a sententious lecture, because Wise had been reported to have said a few things in New Haven about reform and progress. Wise writes that he did not understand most of this harangue and paid little attention to it anyhow.[23]

Returning home he regaled his devoted wife with an account of his experiences in New Haven. After all, this was the first time. It was a beginning, though doubtless even he did not realize how swiftly it would lead to other things. Like most rabbis, even young ones, he had had many laudatory things said to him, and these—as is the case with rabbis—had warmed his heart. All this he told Theresa and boasted of his wonderful success. She laughed at him fondly, for she knew perhaps better than he how paltry all this was for her wonderful husband and how many wider prospects really lay before him.[24]

Lilienthal too had heard from New Haven regarding his substitute, and the reports indicated that he could have confidence in Wise and go on giving him assignments with the certainty that they would be filled not only with competence but with distinction.

In passing, it is worth recording that Isaac M. Wise wrote that until this time it had been his custom, especially while he was in Radnitz, to write out all his sermons. This was a habit he shared with most of the rabbis of the time. When he had come to America, he had left behind more than a hundred sermons, and he had to begin again. Upon mature consideration he resolved that he would no longer speak in this way, no longer interpose a manuscript between himself and his audiences. To this resolve he adhered consistently. His notes he kept in his head. Since, later on, he published many of his sermons and addresses in the *Israelite*, often serially, it was necessary to get them down on paper. This he was accustomed to do after their delivery. When one reads many of them, as they lie within the pages of the *Israelite*, usually at considerable length and often on recondite and complex subjects, this procedure becomes the more amazing. His memory both before and after delivery must have been astonishing. At any rate, we insert this for the edification and instruction of those who preach, and perhaps as a "word to the wise" as to how to speak to congregants and auditors.[25]

The following week, early in September 1846, Lilienthal had another assignment for him, this time in Syracuse, and again for the dedication of a synagogue. A "rich man," J. D. Walter, president of a congregation in New York, was present when Lilienthal said jokingly that he had appointed Wise "assistant bishop" and had decided to send him to Syracuse. Walter advised Wise to go via Albany. The former's brother-in-law, Moses Schloss, was serving as president of the congregation in Albany. Walter declared that they had never listened to a good preacher in Albany and that it would do them and him good. He was kind enough to despatch a letter to Schloss at once. The results were prompt. Wise received an invitation to come to Albany for the next following Sabbath, three weeks before *Rosh Ha-shono*.[26]

Wise began at once to prepare for both Albany and Syracuse. He sat down and wrote three sermons, two for Syracuse and one for Albany. The next Thursday he took a steamer up the Hudson. He left his wife and child with sadness. In his *Reminiscences* he writes of this moment touchingly:

> I parted very reluctantly from my wife, for she, who fulfilled the wifely ideal of my youthful imagination so completely, and to whom I clung with my whole heart, had become still dearer to me, now that she had followed me so trustingly and without a word of objection to an utterly strange land, and that, too, though she was the only daughter of well-to-do parents, and was well justified in indulging better prospects. . . .[27]

He writes also of the deep impression the Hudson made upon him, especially the Palisades which seemed to him to have been set up by God especially to shut off the Old World:

> And the steep heights in the vicinity of West Point were for me the mighty door, the giant gate, opening into the New

> World. Overcome with awe and devotion, I could have embraced every mountain, every rock.[28]

On the boat he helped a peddler, who bewailed the fact that he had "lost the English language," that is, a piece of paper on which some friends had written down the English terms he would need in his trade. Wise took a pencil and "gave him back" the "English language."[29]

Having arrived in Albany probably toward evening, he repaired to Stern's Hotel. He went to visit those to whom he had letters of introduction. From one of them, Moses Schloss, he had a most cordial reception. But from then until the Sabbath he was left to his own devices. No one worried about him. None of the members called upon him, or invited him to their homes. He felt himself very much alone, walked the streets of the city, observed what it had to offer, and in the evening sat in his room and read by the light of a lamp.[30]

The text for his sermon on the Sabbath was taken from *Ki Setze* (Deuteronomy, chapter 21, verse 10), which is the opening sentence of the *Sedre*:

> When thou goest forth to battle against thine enemies, and the Lord thy God delivereth them into thy hands, and thou carriest them away captive. . . .

What use he made of this text, or to what he applied it, we have no idea. It is interesting to speculate upon this, for its immediate homiletical aptness is not apparent. One imagines that he used it to speak concerning the status of Judaism in America at that time and what had to be done to defend it against its enemies without and within, against misrepresentation and calumny, against sloth and ignorance.[31]

The services had been held in the old synagogue on Herkimer Street. This was an ancient wooden building, the interior in a traditional arrangement with the benches in four squares on two sides. There was a *Hazan;* they were still indulging in the old practice of selling *Mitzvoth.* But the decorum was not bad. Wise himself thought that his sermon had not been too well received. This was quickly borne out when after the services he dined with the president who told him in a kindly way that his sermon "was greatly liked," but that very few could understand it. "Your language is too lofty and your thoughts too deep for these people." Despite the gentleness of the reproof Wise thought he had failed utterly and was greatly aggravated with himself. He felt humbled, for he was keenly conscious of his own powers and of his ability to instruct and to stir.[32]

It cannot, however, have been quite as bad as Wise was told, for he was invited at once to return to Albany and to officiate for *Rosh Ha-shono* for an honorarium of one hundred dollars. He promised that he would think it over and write to Schloss from Syracuse. When he left Albany, he was far from sure that he would come back.[33] He did not relish the criticism and was besides contemplating going on from Syracuse to Cincinnati. This latter fact is interesting. Precisely what it was that attracted him to Cincinnati, that caused him to feel thus early that he wanted to go there, is not easy to determine. In New York he had met a number of people from the Queen City of the Middle West. Unquestionably these had described Cincinnati to him in glowing terms: its burgeoning future, its fine Jewish community, its pressing need for Jewish leadership. All of this stirred his imagination and tempted him to go and see for himself.[34]

He left Albany on Monday morning, not caring to linger in the city. Much later on, in writing of this time, Isaac M. Wise asserted that the criticisms leveled against him in Albany, chiefly by Moses Schloss, had aroused more than resentment in him. Perhaps on Sunday and on the way to Syracuse on Monday he mulled things over. He was not the man to adhere stubbornly to his own opinion and his own practice in matters like these. Perhaps they were right! Perhaps he had assumed too much about the learning and the intelligence of his auditors. Perhaps he had been following too blindly what he had been used to in Bohemia. Of what use were sermons and addresses, if those who listened to them could not understand? How would his words be able to reach the mark, achieve their purpose, if they were not comprehended with the heart as well as the intellect? If he was to move toward the purposes he was beginning to envisage, if he was to become a force in the American Jewish community and help it realize itself, a prerequisite would be that he be clearly and readily understood.[35]

He tells us that he took the lesson to heart and that he reworked the sermons he was about to give in Syracuse into more popular form. No doubt all this is true, as the record displays. And yet! When one peruses some of his published addresses with the great demands they made for an understanding of scholarly arguments and often of involved metaphysical reasoning one can only come to the conclusion that Jewish audiences, not merely in Cincinnati but in many other places, must have been far different from those encountered today. Yet his sermons *were* understood and appreciated, for they exercised a profound influence upon an entire generation, laid the basis for a broad approach to Judaism and to American life, were greeted—as he recorded later in the *Israelite*—with wide acclaim and often published and bought in book-form.

From Albany he could not take a boat to Syracuse. So he rode upon the train for the first time since his coming to America. He read the *Torah*, together with the *Targumim* (Aramic translations) and *Rashi* (perhaps the best commentary). On the seat next to him sat a Yankee. One must picture the latter glancing sideways at the sturdy, short-statured foreigner, wondering what he was reading, what were the strange books with the outlandish characters he was holding and perusing so assiduously. The Yankee did not stop with wonder; he spoke to Isaac M. Wise, asked him what the books and what the language were. When he was told, it seemed to take his breath away. That a man could be so learned! Wise, he said, must be at least "a Jewish bishop." Nor, for all his amused attempts, could Isaac M. Wise disabuse him of this conviction.[36]

Arriving in Syracuse, Wise discovered that he had come too early. Not through any misunderstanding on his part! He should have been notified, but communication was not so simple in those days, even by post. The synagogue, it turned out, had not been finished on time. There had been various delays. Two weeks had to elapse. Wise hated wasting those two weeks. He had the feeling that his life was beginning to move out of the time of doubt and of idleness that had followed his arrival in America, and that he ought to be at work. But there was nothing for it. He had to wait. Aided by a Mr. Stein, he devoted himself to some books on ethnology, the science of human races.[37]

He had been met at the train by a reception committee and accompanied to his hotel. There they left him. The local paper carried a few words apprising the general community of his coming, to the effect that "Bishop Wess (or Wiss) of Jerusalem" was in town; also that he spoke no less than half a dozen languages. Wise writes that like Byron he woke one morning to find himself famous.[38]

While in Syracuse he learned much; especially in conversation with Stein. Through him he met some people and had the opportunity to orient himself much more thoroughly in regard to American Jewish conditions. He began to believe that the German Jewish immigrants had not lost their love for their ancient faith.

To this their promptness in founding synagogues attested. But they lacked culture and they seemed as yet incapable of organizing themselves, of meeting some of the deep and urgent needs of themselves and their children. All this stimulated his eagerness to serve, and his dawning conviction that he would find a way. Little by little, even in these first difficult months of transition and exploration, he was becoming aware of his vocation and his mission.[39]

He received a visit from a committee of the congregation who took him almost certainly to a private home for a Kosher meal. He found time to pay a visit to Niagara and, like millions of others before and after him, to stand in open-mouthed amazement, certainly to utter a silent prayer of praise and thanksgiving to the God who had created such wonders. In Syracuse during these weeks he made many friends, not only among the members of the new synagogue, but also among others from nearby towns who came for the dedication.[40]

At last this event took place on the Friday and Saturday preceding the New Year. Everything went well. The services were most impressive, and what Wise said found immediate lodgment in many hearts. The accounts in the newspapers of Syracuse "teemed with praise." Certainly this must have done much to take out of his mouth the faintly bitter taste of his first experience in Albany. He felt reassured. Perhaps he had already learned "to temper the wind to the shorn lamb" and to speak directly and intelligibly to his people![41]

In the meantime he had notified Schloss in Albany that he had decided to come back to officiate for *Rosh Ha-shono*. There was little time left. The night before the New Year he took a train back to Albany. In the midst of the excitement there was a corner of his consciousness in which he felt regret that he had been unable to carry into effect his plan of going to Cincinnati. Probably a number of considerations prompted him to return to Albany: their insistence, and his own hope of canceling the first impression he had made. This time he would elicit from them the same enthusiasm he had been able to call forth in Syracuse.[42]

> I came to the conclusion that logical and rhetorical addresses were beyond the people and a special pulpit diction incomprehensible to it.[43]

According to his own words he had no idea that he was going to become rabbi of Albany. He had about made up his mind that he would have to return to New York and follow the profession of teaching. Nevertheless he sketched his sermons for *Rosh Ha-shono* with the utmost care. If only he could hew to the line he had decided upon, he must succeed.[44]

He reached Albany on the morning of *Erev Rosh Ha-shono* (the morning of the day on which *Rosh Ha-shono* begins). No one paid overmuch attention to him, except the officers and a few who had come to feel friendly toward him on the occasion of his first visit about three and a half weeks before. His landlady, Mrs. Stern, regaled him with much chatter, especially of concern about his health, for he looked "pale and sickly."[45] He was thinking of other things, deeply and with intense concentration upon the coming services. At last the time had arrived. A large congregation was assembled. The old melodies were sung and the old prayers intoned. The *Hazan*—writes Wise—could not read Hebrew decently, but in this respect he differed little from most of his ilk. Finally the service wound around to the place for the sermon.[46]

This time Isaac M. Wise had chosen his text and his whole approach with great care. He began with the story of Hagar and Ishmael (Genesis, chapter 21), using them as symbols of body and soul. He expounded the story in the sense that, when these two had been sent away by Abraham at the behest of Sarah his wife, the wilderness in which they wandered was like human life itself. All this he did not permit to remain in the realm of the abstract, the allegorical. He came to the verse (verse 14) that says: "And she departed and strayed in the wilderness of Beer-sheba." "Here," he writes, "I was able to bring all my weapons into play." This going astray he likened to the "faults and mistakes" of centuries, and the angel who appears to open the spring of water at which they assuaged their thirst he likened "to the voice of conscience and the perennial fount of religion." He concluded with a peroration about "the hoped-for reconciliation and brotherhood of mankind." He was sure that it was a good sermon. It had come straight out of the well-spring of his own heart. And instinctively and immediately he was aware of the fact that it had found its way into the hearts of his hearers.[47]

The people had listened avidly. At the conclusion of the service they crowded about him. They deluged him with flattering, gratulatory, fervid sentences. A procession accompanied him to his hotel. The presiding officers of another congregation came to see him and invited him to preach the next day at their synagogue. He accepted. Policemen had to be placed at the doors of this house of worship on the second day of *Rosh Ha-shono* "for fear lest the great mass of people should break down the old house. . . ."[48]

He writes that "his fortune was made" in so far as Albany was concerned. Even before the Holy Days were over a committee visited him to begin negotiations to induce him to remain in Albany. He received a visit from a certain Mr. Goldman, a Freemason, later a resident of New Orleans. Goldman had the reputation of being a learned man and he had espoused Wise's cause warmly. All this did not immediately imply, as one would be tempted to assume, that Wise was offered the pulpit as rabbi. Among most American congregations at this time, he himself tells us, there was a grotesque prejudice against rabbis. Jews were earning their living the hardest way, by peddling, and culture and rabbis seemed senseless impedimenta to them. If they wanted anything, it was a *Hazan*, who would be a "Reverend," and who would suffice for their simple needs. He would serve as reader and cantor, "teacher, butcher, circumcisor, Shofar blower, gravedigger, secretary. . . . He was *sui generis*, half priest, half beggar, half oracle, half fool, as the occasion demanded." True! not one of them had even a "common-school education," or possessed the merest smattering of Hebrew learning.[49]

Albany wanted Wise to preach and teach, but not to be rabbi. They asked him to submit an application toward this end. Thereupon Wise laid down the rule he followed all the rest of his life. He declared that he "did not apply" for pulpits. But he intimated that, if he were to be elected not "preacher and teacher," but rabbi, he was likely to accept.[50] They had informed him also that he would be expected to open a school, to teach in it and to superintend it. This, as the record shows here and in Cincinnati, he was more than willing to do, for he knew that a good school was one of the most imperative needs of Jewish children in America at that time. But only as a rabbi would he come, for that is what he was, that is what he had been trained to be, that is what he had been at Radnitz, and that was what American Jews needed: more direly than they knew!

By all accounts the excitement at Albany had been very great. This had been something entirely new to the Jewish community: a man of learning; a man of burning eloquence; a man of dignified bearing; a man who could speak to minds and hearts; a man who had a clear and penetrating vision of what he wanted and what American Jews needed; and, above all this, a man who knew his own mind!

He told them besides that he would not argue about salary, that they could fix that for themselves. And that very evening, after the conclusion of the second day of *Rosh Ha-shono* 1846, he left for New York. He had been away for almost a month. This had been far from easy for him, to be separated from wife and child in a strange land, to leave them in a city where they and he until that time had few friends and no relatives. But the congregation in Albany lost no time. When he got back to New York, got off the boat the next morning, and arrived at his home, he was greeted by his landlord, Friedman, with a broad smile upon his face. He congratulated Wise and told him that his wife, that is, Wise's wife, had already received a telegram informing them that Wise had been unanimously elected rabbi of Congregation Beth El in Albany, at a salary of two hundred and fifty dollars a year. The sum sounds absurd. But it was not in those days, as we have already remarked in the case of Merzbacher.[51]

Only one week was needed by the Wise family to make ready. They packed their little store of possessions. Wise took a ship and got to Albany shortly before Yom Kippur. His wife and child arrived a week later. They moved into a house at Number 77, Ferry Street. And Wise went to work.[52]

7

Initiation at Albany, First Period

UPON HIS ARRIVAL IN ALBANY ISAAC M. WISE WAS LAUNCHED UPON the real beginning of his career. All that had gone before was preface: his childhood in Steingrub, his studies with his grandfather, his acquisition of a secular and religious education, and finally the convictions in regard to Judaism in the modern world to which he had come slowly and painfully. All these were now to be put to the test of American actuality. It is no hyperbole to assert that these eight years in Albany, from 1846 until 1854, were the crucial formative period of his entire later life, that in them were conceived and formulated most of the central convictions which he carried through his career, and that most of the projects —which it was to take him years to translate from the realm of the possible to that of the actual—were then born in his mind.

Albany was for Isaac M. Wise also a time of testing. The "storm and stress" which had played so large a role in the psychology and in the literature of a revolutionary generation in Europe came to him in abundant measure during these years. Certainly the ideas about America which he had brought with him from Bohemia were corrected, elucidated, or intensified. His characteristic concept of Judaism, of a system of ideas and beliefs poised between past and future—which we shall see to have been his particular system of tenets—was born here and later years served only to sharpen and deepen it. In its essentials he adhered to it all his life.

Here he began and completed the first volume of his "History of the Israelitish Nation," made his first sketches and plans for a *Minhag America,* sent forth his first proclamation calling for a Union of all American Israelites, and formulated under this general program various subsidiary projects of equal importance. Here he came into violent conflict with the forces that were opposed even to his mild variety of Reform, and—it is clear—learned to handle himself with more wisdom, with more comprehension of the difficulties to be overcome.

The Albany period is most simply divided into two parts: that from his arrival in the city in the fall of 1846 until his forcible ejection from Beth El in 1850; and that from the creation of the new congregation, Anshe Emeth, in 1850, until his decision to accept a call to Cincinnati in 1854—two periods of approximately four years each. So that this may be a little more clearly envisaged, let us recall that the beginning of most of his literary and historical work was in the second four years, and that it ended in April 1854 when he left Albany for the Middle West.

The first period of four years was for him a time of both bitter strife and besetting doubt: whether he should continue in his chosen work of the rabbinate; whether it would not be the part of wisdom to leave it and enter some one of the other fields of which good friends had spoken to him, and in which ready and easy opportunities appeared open to him. We shall later come upon precisely what these were and who the people were who spoke to him of them. At the outset it is only necessary to note—as a characteristic of the first four years—that his own personal troubles, the inertia of indifference, ignorance and obtuseness he was forever encountering, affected his health and brought him to hours of melancholy and doubt. But with his quality of indomitable conviction and hope he swung back from these promptly enough and returned to the belief that in spite of everything he would find a way to do what he wished to do and what he discerned to be imperative for the American Jewish community. This became increasingly true after the first four years, in the latter half of his service in Albany.

There is a letter in the *Occident*—under the date of February 1, 1847—from Albany and signed "Leopold," which gives some of the facts about the congregation to which Isaac M. Wise had come.[1] It had been organized, says the writer, nine years earlier —that is, in 1837—by German Jews. Its membership had been very small in the beginning, but in 1847 had increased to a roster of 130 contributing members. It was already ensconced in a "fine synagogue," which had been built in 1841. In the city—and closely associated with the synagogue—were also a benevolent society and a ladies' benevolent association. Before Wise's advent—writes Leopold—nothing had been done for the improvement of the ritual, except in 1842 when a Rev. Mr. Traup had devoted himself to improved methods of singing and to better education for the children.

It must also be borne in mind—as we have already described somewhat superficially in Chapter Five—that in 1846 the great majority of German Jews in America were unable to read English, that most of them were adhering closely to the customs and observances which they had brought with them. This seems to have been the case, but important reservations of fact need to be made, reservations upon which Isaac M. Wise harped many times. The piety of many—he and others claimed—lay more in protestation than in actual fealty. The Sabbath was habitually desecrated. Many of them were peddlers or traveling salesmen. When they were away from home, they forgot about *Kashruth* (the dietary laws), or to lay *T'fillin* (the phylacteries with the morning service). It was only when they returned home that these men insisted stubbornly and inconsistently upon their orthodoxy. There was also a veritable Babel of customs and ceremonies, usually associated with diverse *Landsmannschaften* (Jewish groups from the same land): Portuguese, German, and Polish. All this Isaac M. Wise himself described in some detail in his *Reminiscences*. Let us give a single example, which has to do with the congregation that played the largest part in his life, K.K.B'nai Yeshurun of Cincinnati. A group of energetic and gifted German Jews began to come to the Queen City in the late thirties and early forties of the last century. At first they joined K.K.B'nai Israel, sometimes known as the "English Congregation." Disagreements, clashes of personality and *Minhagim* soon made their appearance. The groups spoke different languages and had strongly contrasted ways of worship, or so it seemed to them. This is obvious from some of the words of the first Constitution of K.K. B'Nai Yeshurun:

> . . . And whereas, also, the mode of worship in the established synagogue of our beloved brethren, K.K.B'nai Israel, in this city, is not in accordance with the rites and customs of the said German Jews.

Both congregations were orthodox in the beginning, but B'nai Israel used the Polish *Minhag*, and the forebears of K.K.B'nai Yeshurun wished to use the *Minhag Ashkenaz*. This was quite typical of similar situations in many communities.[2]

Before proceeding to the narration of the actual course of Wise's life, beginning in the fall of 1846, it might be well to pause yet a while. In the *American Israelite* of 1895 Wise published a series of articles, chiefly memoirs, under the rather curious title, "The Difficulty in Defining Judaism." In one of these he entered into some detail about himself in these earliest years in America. What follows should probably be read with some caution. It was written almost forty years after the time which it described. Almost certainly memory had distorted and perhaps colored with rose some of the events of that distant time of his life. It must be remembered also that by 1895 Wise was the head of a large and powerful movement, under the Union of American Hebrew Congregations (organized in 1873), the Hebrew Union College (founded in 1875), and the Central Conference of American Rabbis (begun in 1889). To some extent he must have seen himself—retrospectively—as the one man to whom American Jewry owed its essential forms and its place in the cultural and spiritual economy of America. He wrote of his own spirit in these early years:

> It may be unknown to many that Isaac M. Wise was the first man coming to this country who had lived contemporary with all those distinguished literati of Judaism [he refers here to the founders of *Die Wissenschaft des Judenthums*]. In Germany and Austria from 1830 to 1845, he had not merely read and studied the productions of the century, but had lived himself deeply into that spirit and a profound sympathy with the reform movements of that age, up to the second, nearly to the third, *Rabbinerversammlung* (conference of rabbis) in Germany in 1846. This was with him the very period of a man's life when he forms his convictions and his character. All he learned in the schools was outbalanced by that literature and the problems under discussion in that age. He was a disciple of that memorable period, not of any school or system, hence a novelty, a *unicum* (unique phenomenon!) in America. He had lived, learned and preached long enough in Bohemia to arrive at a conviction that those problems, as far as Judaism is concerned, could not be solved in any monarchical country with its inherited prejudices and stereotyped habits; and he went to America, a free country, and a young people.[3]

It was his opinion that Judaism, as he found it in the United States of 1846, would not have been strong enough to outlive the end of the nineteenth century. "He could see but one way out of this labyrinth of confusion." That was to be discovered in a new formulation, one purified of the dross of legalism. Later on, in the second half of this book, we shall examine in some detail Wise's concept of the Talmud, of rabbinic legalism. But for the present we must simply take his word for the broad outlines of his attitude, which was quite common at that time among men like himself:

> And so he arrived in New York with a finished plan of action ready for immediate execution. It was mapped out on paper ready to be submitted to the masters in Israel.[4]

All the evidence appears to indicate that this is an exaggeration, that though he may have had general ideas as to what was needed and what he hoped to do, it was far from being "on paper," or in so precise and clear a form even in his own mind.

But he found himself to be a stranger in a strange land. He had to calm himself and learn to wait. " 'With this program,' said one of his friends, 'you will stand alone in this country, none will aid, none will assist you. This is a land of practical men,' said he, 'your program is utopian.' " In the beginning—as a result of advice like this—he felt crushed. He says he preferred not to speak; "he would not appear in the sanctuary with a false face." Nonetheless, as we have seen, he overcame this initial revulsion and spoke in New Haven, Syracuse, and Albany.

All this may be taken largely as retrospective wisdom, for the record to which we come now indicates unmistakably that he was groping, that his mind had not yet been made up either as to the ritual or dogmatic outline of Reform Judaism for America, nor as to the exact ways in which it would be possible to work toward the unification of the American Jewish community. It is not unlikely that he saw very quickly and very clearly that something must be done, that he hoped that it would be given to him to be the instrument in uniting American Jews, in making their worship and their belief appropriate to the American scene, and in bringing Judaism into a position of respect and understanding.

Upon receipt of the news that he had been elected rabbi of Congregation Beth El in Albany, Isaac M. Wise boarded a steamer and arrived in the capital of the State on the eve of *Yom Kippur.*

Within a week by the same route he was followed by his wife and child. They took up residence in a home at Number 77, Ferry Street.[5] In the early days he was quite satisfied with his new post. True! he did not have enough money, but soon he found ways of supplementing his small income. His yearly salary at the outset was two hundred and fifty dollars.[6] He was expected also to open a school and to collect from each child a tuition-fee of six dollars *per annum*, out of which all the expenses of the school had to be met. This latter task he liked. He found little difficulty in establishing a school, as it were "out of nothing," to set its curriculum, and to make sure of affectionate relations with the children. He had had a school in Radnitz. But there he had been diverted constantly by the necessity of giving separate instruction to students in the Talmud, students preparing for a higher Jewish education. In the Albany school the language of instruction was English, and Hebrew and German were taught as well as the elements of a general primary education.[7]

Wise waited until after *Yom Kippur* for his inaugural address, which was delivered to the congregation on the first day of *Sukkoth*. In this he devoted himself to the task of defining Judaism and laying down plans for his own work as he was beginning to envisage it.[8] Unfortunately we do not possess the text, or any excerpts, of this sermon, which might give us some insight into what kind of definition and what plans he described. After this address his friend Moses Schloss said to him somewhat wryly:

> Our people like and admire you so well because, perhaps, they do not understand you.

As the sequel exhibits, this may well have been a very perceptive comment.

Much later in the *Deborah* Wise wrote a series of articles entitled "The World of My Books." This was reissued in pamphlet form by the American Jewish Archives in June, 1954. The original articles appeared in 1896 and are—like those we cited from the *American Israelite* of 1895—open to the same questions about accuracy of memory. But they deserve review for the general light they cast at least upon his recollection of his interests at the time, and of some of the opportunities of which he availed himself.

Albany, Wise writes, had two very good libraries: the New York State Library in the Capitol itself, and that of the Young Men's Association. The latter he joined in order to be able to take advantage of its facilities, and the former he was invited to use. Before long he came to know the staff at both places and many of those who came to them regularly to read. In his first months these two places were his primary contact with what he calls "the educated world." "These well-meaning people made a great man out of me, long before I had the faintest idea of my 'greatness,' " This was, of course, written tongue-in-cheek.[9]

His time was largely taken up with preaching and teaching. A little later we shall give some idea of his schedule for a typical week. Despite the large amount of labor he was devoting to the congregation and to the children, this did not suffice to fill his mind. He yearned for a nameless something. Earlier in his life, before his coming to America, he had found solace and inspiration in reading the Jewish philosophers of the Middle Ages. But in these libraries there were no Jewish books whatsoever. Even the *Occident*, the only Jewish periodical in America at that time, was not read in Albany. He asked his friend Lilienthal to send him some books, and soon received a copy of one of the sections of the *Shulchan Aruch*, that known as *Eben Hoezer*, to which we have referred above. He had from him also a compilation of Jewish laws and *responsa* on marriage and divorce. From Joachimson on Houston Street, New York, he received a copy of the Cabbalistic work, *Reshith Chochmah*.[10]

In one of the libraries he found copies of the works of Josephus and of Josippon. So much reading awoke in him in turn the impulse to write. He was in touch with Leeser—as we shall see—and began to write for him with a fair degree of regularity. A paper in Albany, called *The Young Presbyterian*, published a series of articles, which were later reproduced in the *Occident*. These propounded the thesis that most of the Christian dogmas were in reality secret doctrines of Judaism. This is interesting in the light of the recent discoveries of the Dead Sea Scrolls. Wise entered the lists on this and on other subjects. But he says that he was at a grave disadvantage, for his only sources were from various Roman Catholic books that were to be found in Albany. When at last some of his own books, that had been following him from Bohemia, caught up with him, and when he had begun once again to acquire Jewish books, he soon had his adversary—whose name was M. R. Miller—utterly at his mercy.[11]

In another one of the articles in the *American Israelite*—under the general heading of "The Difficulty of Defining Judaism"—he wrote of himself as rabbi in Albany in these earliest years:

Eighteen hours out of every twenty-four, five days of the week,

> he was steadily at work, six hours daily in his school, and twelve hours at his desk. All the reading was done between Friday evening and Sunday evening, excepting three hours in Temple. He had become a writing apparatus, and remained in this anomalous state. . . . Outside of his school he was dead to practical life, dead to society. He could not write a sermon, and preached all that time *ex tempore* without any preparation. . . .[12]

It was probably against his will that he was drawn slowly but surely into polemics. His real wish was to continue the work of the great German-Jewish scholars, on *Juedische Wissenschaft* ("Science of Judaism"), to transplant many things from the original German.[13] This at least he tells us. At first he thought he would translate Josephus's *History of the Jews* ("Jewish Antiquities"), the last volume of which had just appeared in German. But he thought that probably this work would prove too difficult for the public. He considered the project of a general history of the Middle Ages, one of the chief purposes of which would be to display the influence upon that era of Arabs and Jews. He soon realized, however, that this would involve an entire decade of preparatory labor. Finally he determined to write a history of Jewish literature from the tenth to the fifteenth centuries. Upon this he concentrated for some time, giving out in lectures from the pulpit the material he had assimilated —a habit he was to continue throughout his life. His favorite reading was in the fields of history and of philosophy. In fact, he wrote, he lost all other interests. For a long time he wandered in the realms of mythology, of Asiatic religions, especially those of India, China and Persia. For years, as he puts it, he lived "behind a Chinese wall."

A friend, Dr. Joseph Lewi, forced him out of this intellectual isolation. Lewi had just returned from abroad. He took Isaac M. Wise in hand, forced him to eat and drink, for he found him greatly run down physically.

An association of scholars, to which bishops and statesmen belonged, was founded in Albany. Its primary, declared purpose was to found a "University of the United States." Nothing concrete ever materialized from this grandiose plan. But the group did establish a teachers' college, in which also medicine and law were taught. And it did found a geological museum. Wise was part of this group, acted for a time as its recording secretary, and participated in its discussions and debates. Its entire accent was on the natural sciences. This, he writes, was very good for him, for he was forced "to look squarely into nature's face."[14]

Meanwhile his school was flourishing. The necessity for such a school, as in Cincinnati—where the Talmud Yelodim Institute was established in September, 1849—was due to the weakness of the public-school system of that time and place. The enrollment of children increased from seventy-six in the fall of 1846 to one hundred and twenty by the spring of 1847.[15] His salary was raised by the congregation to an annual stipend of $400. But it was the school that was his and his family's main support in all the four years of his ministry at Beth El. In it he found congenial work and also peace. Some of the teachers, whom he used in the early years, had fine careers later and in other places. Not all of them were Jews, for he mentions a Kennedy who later became a Bishop, of what church we cannot ascertain.[16]

The sessions of the school would begin just after *Simchath Torah*. It was housed in two rooms on the ground floor of his home. In the beginning it employed two teachers, one who taught English, and Wise himself. Later in the same year, with the enlargement of its enrollment, he employed two assistants. Once, according to his *Reminiscences*, a pupil rushed home saying: "The Dutchman (Wise) is a fine teacher, but he does not even believe in Jesus Christ." Wise loved the school and loved the boys and girls who came to it.[17]

The congregation itself paid so meager a salary—as did almost all in America at that time—because its own status, or that of its members, was modest in the extreme. The yearly dues of a member were six dollars. Additional money came in from *schnodering* (offerings at the reading of The Torah). The Jews of Albany lived modestly. Few of them had parlors with carpets. Most of them lived in two or three rooms. Silk dresses were rarely to be seen on wives or daughters.[18]

It is important to emphasize the fact that his school was for both boys and girls. Of this he writes: "This was reform enough for the start to show what the synagogue would look like in after times. It was the first school of its kind in America; none protested against it."[19]

His general position in Albany at that time is hard to imagine more than a century later. A rabbi was an unknown quantity in almost all American communities. To Bible-loving Americans he was of intense interest. They assumed that *ipso facto* he must be a great scholar. And when, in spite of his being a "greenhorn," a rabbi could speak passable English, the matter ascended into the realm of the miraculous.[20] He was recognized universally by the "aristocracy" of Albany, became a close friend of many whose names and careers we shall come to more specifically later. Some of them employed him as a teacher in their own homes and for their own progeny, and for this he was well paid.

The synagogue itself he found in chaotic condition. Or that at least was his judgment. It was not long before he came to the conclusion that he must make a bold stand for certain changes. Of his basic objectives he writes at length in his *Reminiscences*: to introduce order and decorum, to improve the aesthetic and rational appeal of the services, to make the synagogue respected by the churches.[21]

It was the custom at the time of the reading from the *Torah* to apportion the sections to the highest bidders. This Wise altered at the very outset. Cards were passed around, and the number of special blessings was limited to two per person.[22] Also from the beginning he discovered that one of his main problems would be that of his relation with the president, or *Parnass*, of the congregation. This was a general pathological condition in American Jewish congregations. The *Occident*, and later the *Asmonean*, abound with references to it and discussions of it. The *Parnass* dominated the congregation. He was not so much *primus inter pares* (the first among equals) as an overlord, a dictator. No debatable sermon could be delivered without his consent, and he had no hesitancy in reproving or in enjoining the rabbi.[23] Wise informs us that Leeser, of whom we shall write later, had not been permitted to preach in his own pulpit in Philadelphia without the permission of the *Parnass*. Wise's words in his *Reminiscences* are worth quoting at this point:

> At that time the *parnass* was an autocrat in the congregation. He was president, *shamash* (sexton), *chazan* (cantor), rabbi. He ruled the quick and the dead. He was the law and the revelation, the lord and the glory, the majesty and the spiritual guardian of the congregation. He suffered no rival; all were subject to him. This was an inheritance from olden times, brought to these shores from the small European congregations.[24]

Doubtless some of this forensic bitterness is due to Wise's own experiences—soon to follow—with his own *Parnass* in Albany. But it does not seem to go too far beyond the truth.

Added to all this tyranny, the *Parnass* was usually an ignorant and narrow-minded man. In general, when he came to Albany, Wise found the trustees of the congregation well-disposed toward him, and of many of them he made warm friends and adherents. One of his best friends was Moses Schloss, with whom he felt a close intellectual companionship, but Schloss was too young to be of much help to him when crucial issues arose.[25]

One of his first proposals was for the formation of a choir. He undertook to train it himself. Throughout his life Isaac M. Wise had a keen sense of the central importance of music in worship. He wished to modernize the musical tradition of the synagogue, to teach its members to sing, and to give them hymns to sing, to make available for the synagogue music and musical forces of an amplitude commensurate with its spiritual needs and its spiritual message. He himself played at the violin, and—though he was no expert—loved and understood music.

There were but two copies of Sulzer's *Shiray Zion* then in America. The congregation voted him fifty dollars to employ a teacher of music. Wise had great dreams. He engaged a violinist, Topp, to help, at fifty cents an hour. He was able to discover only two singers, both bassos. The only solution upon which he could hit was to have the children of his school take the upper voices of the four-part harmonies. Even with all these obstacles to be overcome the choir was trained and within a few months was ready to take part in the services.[26]

One of his next steps was to take the prayer book in hand and to free it of some of the liturgical poetry—chiefly of the Middle Ages—which seemed to him turgid and spiritless. From the services for the High Holy Days he excised many of the *Piutim*, *Kinnoth*, and *Selichoth*.[27] The order attendant upon the *Mitzvoth*, at the reading from the Torah, he had already seen to. That he did not encounter a very strong reaction against these steps in the very first months is remarkable. The opposition to him and to his "reforms" took time to gather itself, to descry the danger, to become clear, and to mobilize for attack.[28]

In addition to these alterations he proceeded to eliminate all prayers for the "restoration of the throne of David, the coming of a personal Messiah, the returning of Israel to Palestine, and the restoration of the sacrificial polity." And again, he writes, "nobody protested against this radical change of basis." Most of these excisions were in the direct spirit and action of the rabbinical conferences in Germany, especially that at Frankfort in 1845, which Wise had attended, and which—as we have seen—devoted itself primarily to problems of liturgy. But they were also deep in the spirit of the beginnings of Reform in America, and in Wise's underlying concept of Judaism and of its place in the modern world and in America. With this entire aspect of his views we shall come to grips thoroughly only in the third part of this work.[29]

He followed the same general line in his sermons, and some of the key phrases which became characteristic of Reform were already then in his mind and upon his tongue: "This is our holy land, the land of promise."[30] He preached also and strongly against the desecration of the Sabbath, the iniquity of habitual card-playing, the frequenting of saloons, and the bearing of false testimony.[31]

One of the most important incidents of this first year of his Albany ministry took place in October, 1846. This was only two and a half months after his arrival in America. Lilienthal suggested the convoking of an authoritative synagogal body to be called a *Beth Din* (a court of law), which was to consist of learned men deciding upon ritual and religious questions. He invited Wise, Felsenheld (apparently a teacher), and Kohlmayer (then a student, later rabbi in New Orleans). Wise writes that he did not relish the proposed name of the organization, because it smacked too much of legal formality. But he wrote to Lilienthal that he would cooperate gladly. A meeting was to be held in New York. It was clearly understood that the *Beth Din* would be vested with no hierarchical powers. Lilienthal himself was to be the head of it. At this first session it was decided that its first task would be to undertake some specific assignments. Lilienthal was to get to work at once to prepare a Jewish history for Jewish schools; Felsenheld, a catechism; and Kohlmayer, a Hebrew grammar. Wise's task—significantly—was to get up a *Minhag America*, a modification of the liturgy appropriate for America. They resolved to meet again in the spring of 1847 just after the Passover. Each was to devote the next six months to hard work upon his task and to bring the finished product with him in the spring.[32]

This proposal of Lilienthal was centrally important. It was the very first actual attempt at finding some effective form of national Jewish cooperation in America. As its chief problem it conceived the beginnings of ritual authority, the creation of texts and instruments for instruction and worship, and the improvement of Jewish knowledge in general. Unfortunately it died aborning. It proved to be little more than a pious hope. Without question, however, it helped define Wise's own ideas and ambitions, and to unite him with Lilienthal in lifelong friendship and cooperation toward the attainment of these very ends.

For his part Isaac M. Wise went to work with a will upon a *Minhag America*, a project that was not to be realized then, but to which he returned until it was accomplished.

8

Initiation at Albany, First Period *(Continued)*

IN ADDITION TO ALL THE ACTIVITIES IN WHICH ISAAC M. WISE WAS engaged at this time, his own description of which we reproduced in the main in the preceding chapter, he was also laboring hard at improving his command of the English language, and at learning more about good style in public speaking. On Sundays it was his habit to go to two churches in Albany and to listen to two sermons. Every day for some two hours he read classical works in English.[1] Simultaneously he was using every spare moment to complete the task which he had accepted from Lilienthal's *Beth Din*, the preparation of a *Minhag America*, which had to be ready for the spring of 1847. An outline of this latter he succeeded in completing at the end of April of that year.[2] Some of his English lessons, he himself tells us, were with Chief Justice Wood of New York, and with Professor Amos Dean, the latter a pupil of Daniel Webster. These two he had met at the public library. Dean was a lawyer and a scholar, and later became Professor of Criminal Law.[3] In his *Reminiscences* Wise gives a vivid sketch of the friends he had made, chiefly in the library.

After the *Pesach* week had passed, Isaac M. Wise again made the journey to New York, carrying with him a manuscript for an outline of *Minhag America*. To his intense disappointment he found that the others had done nothing. Kohlmayer had left the East and gone to a pulpit in New Orleans. Neither Lilienthal nor Felsenheld had apparently found either time or will to finish their assignments. A writer in the *Occident* gives a report of his submission of the *Minhag* to this last actual meeting of the *Beth Din*:

> Rabbi Wise then proposed a Minhag America for Divine Service. He had been charged with such a work, because experience teaches that in most places different congregations are set up and the strength of the Israelites is divided, because the emigrant brings his own Minhag from his home, and the German will not give way to the Polish, nor he to the English, nor the latter to the Portuguese. Such a cause for dissension would be obviated by a Minhag America, which would promote the harmonious development of the young congregations. The project of the Minhag as introduced by Dr. Wise treats of the Tephillah (prayer-book) according to the *Din* (the law), that is, religious authority, upon scientific principles and the demand of the times, and shows plainly that the new Minhag must be based on these three pillars to be entirely satisfactory. The plan was read to the meeting and a resolution was passed to lay the whole question over until the next meeting in order to give the members time for deliberation and they were not to give their opinions until then, the question being one of paramount importance.[4]

The impression one derives from this contemporaneous report is: first, that—if it is correct—Wise did not actually have with him a complete text, but a plan for such a text; and secondly, that the others (here Lilienthal and Felsenheld) were not ready even for this and found a method of postponing action.

There is more in the *Occident* having to do with the whole meeting. We are told that it was held on the second of *Iyar*, 5607 (April 18, 1847), and that there were present: Lilienthal, Wise, and "*Morenu*" H. Felsenheld (in various places this name is spelled Felsenfeld, and in others Felsenheld. Since Wise himself gives it as "held" in his *Reminiscences*, we assume that this is correct). The meeting began with an address by Lilienthal on the purposes with which these three had come together. The *Beth Din* was to rest upon no "hierarchical assumptions," "and will act only as an advisory council. It must be of great beneficial service to the young and rising congregations of North America." Lilienthal asked that they concentrate upon an English reader for Hebrew Schools. Letters were received from various rabbis in Europe concerning the ceremony of *Halitzah*[5] and the problems of *Agunoth*.[6] There were at hand as well queries (*Sh'eloth*) from some American congregations. Each of those present was asked "how the organization of the young congregations in America could best be promoted." All agreed that the education of children must come first. It was decided that the next meeting be held in Albany. All the minutes were to be sent to Kohlmayer in New Orleans.

Wise left New York filled with certainty that the *Beth Din* was dead, that it would never meet again. And in this he was entirely right, for it never did. This was one of the first abortive attempts at some kind of cooperative effort on behalf of and by the Jews of America. Later we shall come to the claims of Leeser and of Wise as to priority in this whole field.[7]

To all this should be added that Leeser, the editor of the *Occident*, had certainly seen the plan or the text of Wise's *Minhag America*, for in that publication soon thereafter appeared a strongly worded note against some of Wise's ideas for a reform of the liturgy. As he claims he had already done in Albany, Wise had proposed the elision of all prayers for the restoration of the sacrificial system. On this Leeser wrote:

> We most emphatically object to any such form of prayer, which, as proposed by Dr. Wise, should exclude the petitions for the rebuilding of the temple, and the re-establishment of the sacrifices. We believe, in common with all orthodox Jews, in the literal fulfillment of Scriptures.[8]

And Leeser asked that his readers remain under no misapprehension as to his own stand. He claimed also that later on he received numerous communications from readers who agreed with him heartily.

In presenting his version of the liturgy Wise had insisted upon the priority of Hebrew as the language of prayer.

> If the effect of prayer is to be objective, our service ought to be conducted in the Hebrew language; for it is that which our prophets spoke. . . . There exists no [other] language that possesses a character for such sublimity.[9]

Wise proposed also the omission of those prayers which asked for vengeance upon former persecutors of Israel. He thought that the morning service for the Sabbath should be not more than two and a half to three hours long.

Isaac M. Wise went back to Albany heavy of heart. He spoke to many of his friends of what he regarded as a fiasco. They did not understand why he felt so acutely about this. But he could not let the matter rest here. It is plain that already by this time he was consumed by the deep feeling that nothing could be done with or for the Jews of America until laymen and rabbis would learn to come together. For many years—certainly until the birth of the Union of American Hebrew Congregations in 1873—this need obsessed Wise, gave him no rest, drove him past defeat after defeat, obloquy piled on obloquy. It was the central theme in his thinking and in his striving.

In order to put into words what he felt, to begin the task of making it plain in thought and in proposals for action, he embodied his ideas in two lectures in English, which he delivered before a circle of his friends in Albany. One of these friends—a certain Mr. Koschland—deeply impressed, asked him for the manuscript, which in this case Wise had prepared with some care. Without asking Wise's consent Koschland sent it on to Isaac Leeser. To his astonishment, Wise came across the lectures in the *Occident*, with notes appended at the bottom of the pages by Leeser, who was in fact thoroughly aroused and incensed by the document. This was the first real encounter between the two men who were to be the real protagonists of two contrasted schools of thought in regard to the present and future of American Judaism, Leeser for an orthodox interpretation, and Wise for what he called "progress." This difference persisted through a number of decades of occasional clashes, but, fully as often, of friendship and cooperation. As it unrolls in the following pages, the record will—we believe—show that at least some of this latter was due to Leeser's forbearance and kindliness, and his considerable degree of modesty.[10]

Again in this case Wise called for changes in regard to temple, Palestine, and sacrifices, and Leeser added a note: "We must emphatically object. . . ."

Much personal correspondence ensued between the two men. It is to be deplored that we do not possess it, not a single letter of it. But one of the biographies, one certainly tendentious and prejudiced in Wise's favor, contends that in this correspondence Leeser maintained that progress in Judaism was "unnecessary" and the proposals of Reform "destructive." Leeser wrote: "But we say in all candour that any synagogue reformation except such a one as looks to raising the standard of decorum and propriety cannot be supported by us in our journal."[11]

Wise rejoined in a later issue of the *Occident*. He was perhaps beginning to sense the violence of the storm that was gathering. His letter to Leeser—he says in his *Reminiscences*—was "drastic." It began as usual with an appeal to the "spirit of the age," a habit with him as with many others then. He cited nine rabbinical authorities. He inquired why, if there was no real need for change in Judaism, so many were leaving the fold in America. He contended that between the years 1620[12] and 1829 hardly two hundred of the families that had come to America had remained Jews.[13] Leeser answered coldly, decidedly, and frankly. He would have nothing of Reform. Here Wise added a note—again as he writes in the *Reminiscences*—upon a theme and in a manner that was chronic with him and that was probably correct. Leeser—he said—could not read unpunctuated Hebrew. He knew nothing whatsoever of rabbinics. His Judaism was entirely that of the Bible, the prayer-book, and *Minhagim* (customs and ceremonies).[14]

About this time a young Presbyterian minister had sent Leeser some papers on the "dogma of trinitarianism." Leeser did not see clearly or quickly—Wise contends—through the content or purport of these fulminations and the inappropriateness of printing them. As a result, some cogent criticism was flung at Leeser. To get Leeser out of this dilemma Lilienthal advised him to go to Albany and talk to Wise. This he did, and Wise agreed to write a series for the *Occident*, expounding Deuteronomy, chapter 10, verse 12:

> And now, Israel, what doth the Lord thy God require of thee, but to fear the Lord thy God, to walk in all His ways, and to love Him, and to serve the Lord thy God with all thy heart and with all thy soul. . . .

Leeser signed the articles "Rev. Dr. Wise," though Wise—as he himself says—"never claimed title or handle to this name." It was, Wise contended later, in his writing for the *Occident*, beginning at just this time, that he learned to wield a pen.[15]

At any rate, it was thus in the autumn of 1847 that Leeser came to Albany and that the two men met for the first time face to face. Wise writes that he found Leeser honest and well-meaning, thoroughly sincere in his orthodoxy, a man who was not having too easy a time—a friendly and kindly man. He was glad to comply with Leeser's request and to write articles for him, answering the Christian missionary point by point. The articles were characteristically entitled: "Reason and Faith," and in them—he tells us—he quoted Maimonides' rationalism *in extenso*, and also some relevant material from the *Zohar*. The articles attracted much attention for their bold polemical forthrightness and for their scholarliness. He himself—he asserts—thought them poor when he read them later in cold type. They did not seem logical enough, in fact in some places quite obscure. From another source we learn that the name of the young Presbyterian clergyman was M. R. Miller, who wrote under the pseudonym of *Talmid* (Hebrew for "pupil"). Wise's articles bore the sub-title: "Rejoinders to Talmid's Thoughts on Deuteronomy, Chapter 30, Verse 6—Based on Maimonides' rationalism, etc." The verse referred to from Deuteronomy is:

> And the Lord thy God will circumcise thy heart, and the heart of thy seed, to love the Lord thy God with all thy heart, and with all thy soul, that thou mayest live.

It may be well to pause here briefly, to insert a sketch of the life of Leeser, since we shall come across him not infrequently in the pages that follow.[16]

Isaac Leeser was born in the province of Westphalia in Prussia on December 12, 1806. He was thus Wise's senior by a little more than twelve years. In spite of Wise's strictures upon it, his education was not actually meager. He went to the Gymnasium at Muenster, and studied some of the tractates of the Talmud under Hebrew masters. He migrated to America at the age of seventeen, arriving in Richmond, Va. in May, 1823. His uncle was a merchant of that city and sent Isaac to a private school. This lasted but a short time, and Isaac worked for the next five years in his uncle's employ. During this time, however, he aided in teaching at the Jewish school on Saturdays and Sundays, and sent various articles to papers in defense of Jews and Judaism. In 1828—probably as a result of some of his articles—Leeser was chosen *Hazan* of Congregation Mikveh Israel (the Portuguese Congregation of Philadelphia). Thither he went in the summer of 1829, in his pocket the manuscript of his first book: "The Jews and the Mosaic Law." Leeser's hope was to move promptly from the cantor's desk to the pulpit, and this he achieved. His first discourse in English was delivered in the early summer of 1830, and thereafter he preached regularly though always "on sufferance," until some thirteen years later when the congregation made the sermon regular. Leeser continued to write and to publish books: a Hebrew spelling-book, a catechism, books on the civil rights of Jews, historical works, prayers, until 1867. He founded the *Occident* in 1843 and edited it until his death in 1868. He retired from his post at Mikveh Israel in 1850, but returned to the pulpit in 1857 in a new congregation, called Beth-El-Emeth. Here he remained until his death. When Leeser came to the United States there were only between twelve and fifteen thousand Jews in the country. He participated in a host of Jewish movements. Later he became President of Maimonides College, one of the early, abortive attempts at a theological seminary. His translation of the Bible into English was for many years the only one that American Jews could use, until the Jewish Publication Society issued its authoritative translation in 1917. Leeser was a consistent conservative and never faltered in the belief that in the end all opposition to this interpretation of Judaism would die away.[17]

Let us return for a moment to Wise's certain plan and possible text for a *Minhag America*. In an article much later he contended that this was the first draft of the book which he brought out somewhat later in Cincinnati, and which was more widely used by liberal congregations than any other until the appearance of the Union Prayerbook in 1894. He contended also that it was the precursor of "all the synagogue reforms which followed." The suggestion for this form of liturgy was revived nine years later at the "Cleveland Conference" in the fall of 1855.[18]

It was also during this year in Albany that Isaac M. Wise first joined battle with Christian missionaries and conversionists. Two things need to be noted at the outset in relation to this: this was a lifelong interest and concern with him in speaking and in writing. We shall have many occasions to observe that his primary purposes were: to defend Jews and Judaism; to attempt to clarify and remove Christian prejudices and misconceptions; to raise Judaism to its rightful place in the esteem of good men everywhere; and to try to put a stop to what he rightly regarded as the scandal and the insult of most conversionism. It should be remarked in the second place that every source indicates that there was a veritable fever of such conversionism at this particular period. Wise found this "pursuit of souls" deeply distasteful. This had been one of his deeply imbedded dissatisfactions with his and his people's lot in Europe. There it had not been possible for Jews to oppose the conversionists with their own weapons. As his father had reminded him while he was yet a child, Jews were forced to display humility and often hypocrisy. It is true that in some ages Jews took part in public disputations with Christians, often at the command of some absolute ruler or overlord. But even then they were not granted genuine freedom to speak their minds, to rebut the slanders and the unctuous claims of superiority of their Christian opponents.[19]

In Albany—Wise says—the missionaries were for the most part pious but excessively ignorant men, in the tradition of revivalist Christianity of the period, so well described by Mrs. Trollope in some of her strictures upon religion in America around 1828.[20] Usually the missionaries let Jews alone and devoted themselves to revivalist shouting at their fellow-Christians. A German Methodist came to Albany and established a "place of business," but enjoyed no success.[21] Little by little, one case at a time, some one or the other of them hit upon the dramatic device of trying to convert Jews. Wise soon got into public controversy with them. This was helpful to him in a number of ways. It forced him to acquire command of a simple, clear, virile English. The aid of his prominent Gentile friends proved invaluable: the Hon. Bradford W. Wood, a member of Congress from 1845 to 1846 and later American Minister to Denmark; Chief Justice Wood, whom we have mentioned before, and also Amos Dean, later Chancellor of the University of Iowa. Isaac M. Wise was especially much in the company of Wood and Dean.[22]

He decided to give three lectures in English in answer to the weekly attacks leveled against Jews and Judaism by a Baptist clergyman. His subject was "The Messiah." It was in this, clearly and unmistakably, that he first repudiated the concept of a personal Messiah, a point of view that resulted in violent troubles within two and a half years in Albany.[23]

In the Albany *Argus* appeared a notice to the following effect: "Rev. Rabbi Cohn from Jerusalem, a missionary of the London Society for the Improvement of the Condition of the Jews, will speak this evening in Dr. Wykoff's church, with the purpose of forming a branch organization for this holy and humane work. The lower floor will be reserved exclusively for the clergy, the church officers, and their ladies. The general public will be accommodated with seats in the gallery."[24]

Wise determined to go there and speak. In the *Reminiscences* there is a long and vivid account of what followed. We shall reproduce it in somewhat abbreviated form.

Wise went home, donned his frock-coat, presented himself at the door of the church, and said that he was a "clergyman," in fact a "protestant clergyman," if that meant one "who protests against you all." Two ministers, Unitarian and Universalist, sat near him and had agreed to second him. The church was filled and the three men were generally eyed askance. First prayer and song, then Wykoff explained the purpose of the meeting with some display of embarrassment. He inquired from the platform whether anyone wished to speak on the subject. This was planned as a gambit to introduce ex-Rabbi Cohn, the missionary. But Wise anticipated him. He jumped to his feet and asked for the floor. He did not wait for recognition by the chairman but began to speak at once. He writes: "It was the first time that the voice of a Jew had been heard on this question, and I could count with assurance on the undivided attention of the public." He analyzed the situation and the subject, the hypocritical sympathy that underlay it. He defended Jews as a pious and charitable people, who did not need "conversion." He was about to go on to theological problems, but the rousing applause convinced him he had said enough. He then moved that the meeting adjourn *sine die*. The Unitarian minister rose and seconded the motion "with solemn mien." There was a rousing thunder of "ayes." No one had the temerity to say "no." "The play was over, the audience went home, their faces a yard long. No similar meeting ever took place in Albany. . . ."[25]

His own enemies in the Jewish community attempted to make capital of this incident, claiming that Wise was engendering *Rishus*, and had even had the effrontery to invade the sacred precincts of the *Goy* (Gentile). This was not said to him directly in person, but came to him at second or third hand.

Certainly this had been a dramatic act exhibiting a quite extraordinary degree of courage. It is to be doubted that many rabbis would be capable of this in our own day. Much of it stemmed from Wise's own character, but also doubtless from his boundless confidence in America and Americans. The conversionists were routed in his community. The task had been begun. Upon it he labored—through one channel or method or another—for many years.

Another episode of the same variety came to pass when a young Christian preacher on Pearl Street delivered himself of a fanatic attack on Jews and Judaism, both of which he knew only by name. Isaac M. Wise treated him more gently, wrote him a letter asking him to refrain. But to no effect! The young zealot waxed in extremism. Wise wrote a second letter which served only to add fuel to the flames. Then, perceiving that so considerate an approach was futile, he published the letters in an evening paper with a demand that the denunciations cease. Wise spoke also from his own pulpit, and the synagogue was crowded with both Jews and non-Jews. Ten days later the preacher had to leave the city. The Christian clergy—says Wise—had succeeded in outraging the convictions of the intelligent people in Albany, and as though in poetic justice the church where the clergyman had spoken became his synagogue three years later.[26]

Constantly and consistently, too, Wise was taking a bold stand on the matter of Sabbath-observance. This he conceived to be an inescapable part of his duty as a rabbi. Again and again throughout his career he returned to this matter. His forthrightness, however, his lack of regard for individual offenders, began to make enemies for him even in his own congregation. All this came to a head in 1850 in a crisis that can be traced to several causes. But at the time of which we write, in 1847, Wise paid little or no attention to the grumblers and calmly pursued his way. Later he was to learn that he had greatly underestimated the hatred of a number of those whom he had offended. His articles appearing in the *Occident* were being carefully read and noted by a small group of his own members. A storm was brewing, of which he himself appears to have had little inkling. In his *Reminiscences* he defends himself on this score by claiming that he could not believe that all this was serious. He was not trying to alienate people. He was not motivated by hatred, by ambition, or by "greed." Only two years later did he come to comprehend the intensity of the emotions he had aroused. About him were warm, close friends, who loved him, who believed in him, who knew that he had at heart nothing but the weal of Judaism in America. These served as a buffer between him and the others, and his fearlessness and his progressivism went on without apparent let or hindrance.[27]

9

Initiation at Albany, First Period *(Concluded)*

THE YEAR 1848 WAS FILLED WITH POLITICAL FERMENT, PRIMARILY IN Western Europe. The news of its events traveled swiftly throughout the world and aroused great interest and much hope. If this was true of men in general, if it connoted a stirring up of the whole human brew, how much more must this have been so for one like Isaac M. Wise, who had left Europe because he had been forced to the regretful conclusion that liberty could win no swift or decisive victories there, that the ancient tyrannies were too securely entrenched. Suddenly there were revolutions, or incipient revolutions, in France, in Germany, Austria, and in Italy. He devoured every word in the newspapers and from whatever other source he could lay his hands on. The streets of Paris were ablaze. The barricades were up again! Louis Phillippe had been deposed, had abdicated. At any moment a Republic of Europe was expected to be born. Wise delivered an address at a meeting called on the spur of the moment in Albany, entitled "Universal Republic and the Brotherhood of Man." For him this was the long-awaited eruption of the repressed masses, of the long and sorely tried. He waited fourteen more days while the news poured in. He made up his mind to leave the United States and return to Europe. After all, it had been for the lack of this hope that he had severed his connection with his homeland. Now it seemed to be here; now the "new age" was dawning. He must go back and play his part in it. He informed the *Parnass* of his congregation of his intention of resigning. He had long discussions with his beloved wife, who protested energetically, strove to calm his excitement, and told him that, if he went, he would have to go alone, without her and their two young children. This deterred Wise and he wavered. But he handed in his resignation anyhow. The city of Albany was full of bonfires and torch-light processions, as though at an election. There was constant speech-making in many languages. Most of this was at the end of March, 1848.[1] Wise had the good fortune to meet William H. Seward, a native of New York State. Practicing law at Utica and later at Auburn which was his home for the remainder of his life, Seward had drifted into politics. He was in succession a National Republican, an Anti-Mason, and a Whig against Jackson. He was elected Governor of New York for two terms, and had to his credit some splendid liberal laws. Before long he had become one of the leaders of the anti-slavery wing of his Party. At the time of which we write Seward had completed his second term as Governor and had returned to the practice of law. A year later he went to the Senate, where he was courageously and unmistakably anti-slavery. As the Whig Party became moribund, he helped lead its remnants into the Republican fold. He was passed over in nominations for the presidency, for Fremont in 1856 and for Lincoln in 1860. But Lincoln chose him as Secretary of State, and a wise choice it proved to be. Seward believed then that the Union could be saved without recourse to war, but he soon perceived that neither facts nor the President would long countenance this possibility. In the end, after distinguished service in the Cabinet, he was attacked by a fellow-conspirator of Booth, was wounded but survived, served in Johnson's Cabinet, purchased Alaska in 1867 from Russia, and died at Auburn on October 10, 1872.[2]

It was this distinguished American, distinguished in record and in his splendid spirit, whom Wise had come to know. The subject of their conversation could have been nothing else but the world-shaking events in Europe. Seward saw what was to come with sad but prophetic vision. He was much clearer-sighted than Wise and perhaps more deeply versed in historic probabilities in Europe. Europe—he told Wise—was not yet ready for freedom. The revolution would prove abortive and would end in the supremacy of the army. Nor was this only in personal conversation. Seward repeated the substance of this prediction on the floor of the Senate.

Seward's realism troubled and vexed Wise. But the course events in Europe were taking appeared to bear Seward out. As ardors have a habit of doing, Wise's first excitement was cooling. At a great celebration held in Albany he listened to a Hungarian heap abuse on Germans, and the Germans heap abuse upon the Jews. As a final step in this episode he left Albany for New York to consult another friend of his, Horace Greeley.[3]

Here we shall pause for a brief paragraph about Greeley's life, for he too played a considerable role in the Americanization of Isaac M. Wise, in personal contacts with him in later years, and in his influence upon Wise's opinions and courses of action.

Greeley was also somewhat older than Wise, having been born at Amherst, N. H., on February 3, 1811. As a lad Greeley lived on a farm, physically feeble, but intellectually precocious. There was a tale that he learned to read before he had uttered his first word. Reverses forced his family to move off the land. His earliest ambition was to become a printer, but it took him some time to find a way to make a beginning. Very early in life he became interested in politics. He made his way to New York in the summer of 1831, all his earthly possessions slung over his shoulder. He found work putting the New Testament into type. Two years later he formed a partnership with a fellow-workman. They founded the *Morning Post* which soon failed. Other ventures were more successful. Their greatest success was with a paper called *The New Yorker* which was published for seven years.

Greeley's reputation was growing in the Whig Party and he helped edit various campaign papers. This led to the publication of a weekly campaign paper, called *The Log Cabin*, which soon leaped into what was a large circulation for those days. In 1841 he launched a daily newspaper, *The Tribune*, which soon had a circulation of 11,000. Much of the profit he made from this Greeley dissipated in wild speculations. Later he merged his various papers, which attained a circulation of 150,000, for that day tremendous. He was read all over the land. For many years Greeley was the most widely quoted editor in America, and he succeeded in establishing a warm personal relation with many of his readers. The columns of his paper were open to all sides of public questions, but his own opinions gradually became apparent. For a time he was a Fourierist, a believer in a high protective tariff, opposed to woman-suffrage, had rigid views on the sanctity of marriage and against easy divorce, favored total abstinence, and was zealous for Irish "repeal."

But first and foremost it was his record as an advocate against the institution of slavery that causes him to be remembered. He was one of the great forces leading to the nomination and election of Abraham Lincoln. At one time he printed an article, called "The Prayer of Twenty Millions," which contended that there was no recourse save unremitting and unyielding endeavor to put slavery down. The Emancipation Proclamation, during the Civil War, followed close upon the heels of some of his correspondence with Lincoln. He was one of the fathers of the Republican Party, but held very few offices. He was opposed to Seward as a candidate, and therefore went to the convention in 1860, not as a delegate from New York, but from Oregon. Seward's failure to get the nomination was in part owing to Greeley's opposition. Greeley ran for the Senate of the United States in 1861 but was defeated. In his earlier years he favored allowing the Southern States to secede, but later urged the most vigorous possible prosecution of the War. Day after day he printed a masthead: "On to Richmond!"

At the conclusion of the War with fine magnanimity he urged general amnesty and impartial suffrage on the basis of "Reconstruction." In that time of revenge and hatred this put an effective stop to his political career. He went so far as to sign a bail bond for Jefferson Davis. He was a sharp critic of the administration of General Ulysses S. Grant. This led to the creation of a new Party, the Liberal Republican, which met at Cincinnati in 1872 and nominated Greeley. The Democrats also nominated him, but this hurt rather than helped him.

All this had put too great a strain upon his health, and in November 1872 he passed away. Despite his personal foibles, which were generally ridiculed, and his many eccentricities, he was held in very high public regard. His death brought this home to many. Whittier once called him "Our later Franklin." He had been in great demand as a lecturer, drew large audiences, was a voluminous writer, a Universalist by religion, and unquestionably a great formative influence in the stormiest and most momentous of American historic experiences.[4]

When Wise went to visit him, having become a friend of his in Albany on the occasion of several of Greeley's visits there, he found to his chagrin that Greeley shared Seward's opinion at least in regard to the Europe of 1848 and advised Wise to remain quietly in the United States. Wise sat down to think it over. The memories of his childhood and his youth streamed over him. He had realized what it meant to be a *Schutzjude* in Bohemia. He recalled his experiences in Radnitz with the authorities, lay and rabbinic. He reviewed what he had heard about the "struggle of humanity against the stupid and stupefying elements," which had come to him in reports of the revolution of 1848, but also the many accounts of defeat and disillusion. He decided to take the advice of his many friends—and especially of his beloved wife—and not to go.[5]

One of the immediate results of the frustration of the "spirit of '48" was the streaming of a new immigration to the shores of the United States, an immigration headed by Carl Schurz and many other fine spirits. This was a new and intelligent German group, freedom-loving, unable any longer to brook the cribbed, cabined and confined air of Europe. Among them were many titled men and women and many with the highest education. The Jews who came were for the most part young people, ready to enter vigorously into a new life. Here is the instance of a single young man—of whom Wise wrote—who began as a canal-boat driver and was then, in rapid succession, schoolmaster, itinerant musician, and actor. Thereafter he underwent baptism and was preacher, soldier, etc.[6]

Probably it was this new immigration, the "spirit of the times," and the general impetus of 1848 that prompted the formation of a German Literary Society in Albany in that year. Wise informs us that German life and thought had been "in a sorry plight" until then in the United States. Germans spoke a wretched jargon. The French and the Poles were respected because of their deep dedication to liberty. The Germans had hitherto been looked upon as stupid tradesmen. But the events of this year tended to raise the Germans in the general estimation. And this Society accelerated the process in Albany. There was speaking and debating, public reading of fine literature, plays produced, and much warm social intercourse. The Society began humbly but it grew. A singing society was organized, at first without good female voices. But even then they ventured to give concerts. A German school came into being, and served to protect and to aid later immigrants. Wise recounts other interesting and sometimes amusing incidents about this Literary Society, into which we need not go. What does need to be remarked, however, is that he took a very active part in it. All his life he regarded as a central interest his own early acquaintanceship with great German literature. He had many contacts with Germans in Albany and later in Cincinnati, and he found many warm, true friends among those he met.[7]

At this time there was another most important incident in Wise's life, obviously connected with the failure of the *Beth Din*, but also derived from his perennial concentration upon "Union."

He began a fairly extended correspondence with Leeser, most of it having to do with a plan for the unification and "elevation" of American Israel. He himself comments in the *Reminiscences* at this point, that this constant fixation of his upon this subject, and for many years later, was a "sickness"; that he had the usual passion of one striving to "reform the world," and that it brought in its train the usual results.[8]

Again at this point Wise turns aside to comment upon the utterly incredible and intolerable conditions that prevailed in the American Jewish community. There were then—he writes—only six Jewish schools in the United States: in New York, Baltimore, Cincinnati and Albany. The instruction in them was tragically inadequate in quantity and quality. Most of the teachers were "ladies." There were few text-books and these unmitigatedly poor. Few communities maintained any real charitable organizations and those that did exist were mostly on the decline. There was no provision for widows and orphans, and no hospitals. The only real institution that was to be found was the synagogue, and it was surrounded with a cloud of missionaries. Without many and speedy changes there was no apparent future for Judaism in America. Aggressive, constructive action was imperative. Obviously this could not even be begun without some agency, some instrumentality, and the only pragmatic chance seemed to be through representatives of congregations. This Leeser agreed to advocate in Philadelphia and on journeys to the West and South. Wise was to concentrate his attention upon New York and the East.[9]

One of the immediate results of this tentative alliance with Leeser was a visit by Wise to New York to consult with Lilienthal and Merzbacher. Lilienthal—who should certainly have known—was of the opinion that the orthodox congregations were far from ready for such an undertaking. At Lilienthal's home Wise met some Cincinnatians who displayed a considerable degree of enthusiasm for his ideas and predicted that the congregations in Cincinnati would embrace the plan and help forward it. This proved to be true, at least in the case of one, and it was sharply prophetic of Wise's future. Lilienthal himself was cordial as always and agreed to help to the extent of his ability. He asked Wise to preach in one of his pulpits on this very topic. Wise accepted and the place was crowded. He was moved by the attendance and the response. He used a text from the *Sedrah* (the portion of the Torah for the Sabbath of that week), from *Tetzaveh* (Exodus, chapter 27, verse 20 to chapter 30, verse 10). This sermon Leeser published and called a "veritable thunderstorm of a sermon." Wise had chosen for his text, Exodus chapter 27, verses 20 to 21:

> And thou shalt command the children of Israel that they bring unto thee pure olive oil beaten for the light, to cause a lamp to burn continually. In the tent of meeting, without the veil, which is before the testimony, Aaron and his sons shall set it in order, to burn from evening to morning before the Lord; it shall be a statute for ever throughout their generations on the behalf of the children of Israel.

The sermon went far and wide and found readers and commentators as far West as Cincinnati and Louisville, then the farthest outposts of Jews in the United States. It reached South as far as Richmond and Charleston. The *Occident* recorded also that it roused those who were there when it was delivered. The officials of the three German congregations in New York promised to lay the plan before their officers and members.[10]

All of this reached its climax in a "Call," which Wise wrote and which was published in the *Occident.* It was headed: "To the Ministers and Other Israelites." We quote from it somewhat at length. It is a historic document, one of the first and certainly the clearest of calls for American Jewish union:

> The Reverend Editor of this periodical has granted me the favour to give publicity to my views about the association of Israelitish congregations in North America, to produce one grand and sublime end—to defend and maintain our sacred faith, to the glory of God, and for the benefit of Israel and all mankind.
>
> Brethren! though I am a stranger among you, unknown and unimportant—though I am aware that there are men among you much better than myself . . . though my years are but few in number . . . yet God's choice of Israel prompts me to speak. Our cause is that of all mankind, and our fall theirs. . . . But now in order to fulfill our sacred mission, to send our important message to mankind, it behooves us to be united as one man; to be linked together by the ties of equal views concerning religious questions—by uniformity in our sacred customs, in our form of worship, and religious education.

Most of the congregations in the United States had been in existence only a few years. Their government was in the hands of men with no real knowledge of religion. Therefore the synagogues were built on sand. There was no inspiration for youth "and no nourishment for the spiritual Israelite."

> This naturally produces an enormous amount of indifference; and each congregation pursues its own way, has its own customs and mode of worship, its own way of thinking about religious questions, from which cause it then results that one Jew is a stranger in the synagogue to the other Jew. It is a pity to observe that any man who is so happy as to have a license (*Kabalah*) to kill, from an unknown person, can become the minister of a congregation, and the teacher of the youth, without any proof of his knowledge of religion, and in the absence of any evidence of his conduct as a Jew.

What will become of the synagogues under such conditions? It is a manifest duty to strive to improve them, "and to institute a reform in their synagogues on modern Jewish principles"; if we do not do this quickly, "the house of the Lord will be desolate, or nearly so, in less than ten years." Many conversions will follow. He went on to protest solemnly:

> Nor is it too late; everything can be done, if we are all united before God. . . . But who are the men who shall lay the cornerstone to this reunion? Are not the ministers of Israel those who must take the first step? . . . Are not included in this class (those who must and will help) the pious laymen who sigh now over the downfall of the ancient customs and forms, without the establishment of the modern ones?

It was the patent duty of all to unite and to labor for the "reunion" of all congregations:

> Arise, ye men of piety and wisdom, ye shepherds, ye fathers of Israel, let us all meet *Ish lo ne'edar* (Isaiah, chapter 40, verse 26: "Not one faileth!"); let us first take counsel what should be done, and how it must be done; let us amicably consider what we ought to do as men and Israelites for the spiritual welfare of the present and coming generations; let us earnestly deliberate on a plan to unite all Jews to defend and maintain their sacred religion for the promotion of the glory of God and the bliss of Israel. I call upon all my honoured friends, both ministers and laymen, and all who have an interest in the promulgation of God's law—come, let us be assembled in order to become united! Exercise all your influence on your friends and acquaintances, to bring together all men of zeal and piety, of wisdom and knowledge, to consider what should be done for the union, welfare, and progress of Israel. Let the place of assembly be Philadelphia, it being nearly the centre for the Jews living in North America; let the time of the meeting be the second day of the *Rosh Hodesh* Iyar, 5609. I trust in God to meet in the

> next number of the *Occident* many honourable names who will join this meeting, and also their divers view about it; but I particularly call on the Reverend Doctors Lilienthal, Kohlmayer, Merzbacher, the Reverend Messrs. Isaacs and Felsenheld, not to be the last ones in offering their view. O pray them to assist my weak voice, and call on all Israel, *Chazak venischazek b'ad amaynu* (II Samuel, chapter 10, verse 12: "Be of good courage, and let us prove strong for our people"). And may God, the great Father of all, unite and bless the house of Israel! May He enlighten all men with the shining light of truth, be gracious to all that seek Him, and merciful to all that have forsaken Him. Amen!
>
> Signed, Isaac M. Wise, D.D.
> Rabbi of Albany.

This was marked as having been issued in Albany the ninth day of Marcheshvan, 5609 A.M. It was followed in the *Occident* by a note by Leeser to the effect that Wise had written this call at his suggestion, that he does not endorse beforehand all that "this gifted son of Israel" has said in the document, but that he seconds earnestly Wise's emphasis upon the necessity for a meeting. He himself had favored New York as the locus for it. He asked also that letters be written to the *Occident* commenting upon this Call.[11]

What were the implications of this Call? It was obviously Wise's hope then, as indeed for many years later, to create a union of all American "Israelites," regardless of their attitude toward Reform, regardless of their adherence to a Conservative or an Orthodox interpretation of Judaism. He believed that this was a possible consummation, and—as he contended many times—that the reforms he proposed were moderate, that they could be justified on the score of traditional Judaism, and that they represented neither theologically nor practically any fundamental departure from historic Judaism. Whether it was he or Leeser who was first responsible for the plan of such a Call, or for the first concept of a Union, is debatable. Neither achieved it in the sense of an all-encompassing Jewish body, though for a time Wise was not far from it.

Responses began to come in to the *Occident*. One commented that in Europe the government stands behind the congregations and helps them with funds and organization. In the United States the minister is a "dead letter." All matters are decided not by authority but by a majority of the members. And the writer asks for a meeting principally of members of congregations, so that the decisions of the rabbis may prove effective.[12]

Leeser had entered the field even earlier, writing strong articles favoring a Union. As early as October 1848 he had published an editorial on "Association," which asked New York to take the lead:

> Could not a meeting of elected members of various congregations be held as a friendly reunion? This idea was first broached to us by the learned rabbi of Albany, Dr. Isaac M. Wise; he wishes to see ministers West and East meet and exchange ideas.

Leeser called upon rabbis to heed this appeal and to send in their names and their comments to Wise.[13]

Delegates were chosen by some. Three German congregations in New York (Lilienthal's) formed committees to start the convention. Lilienthal issued a public statement in favor of this move toward Union. Wise himself commented upon the general condition many years later:

> Leeser and Wise understood well to advocate and agitate, but not to organize and execute. The matter was left to the New York Boards and let go by default.

The entire call and the entire venture proved a failure. But the seeds had been planted and later they were to germinate.

Wise himself felt that nothing further could be done for the moment and retreated into his library. Twenty-seven years were to intervene before he achieved his aim—and even then only partially.[14]

Some details in regard to this call and its consequences should be noted for the sake of completeness. Congregation B'nai Yeshurun of Cincinnati responded, endorsed the project, and elected delegates to go to Philadelphia.[15] In addition to Cincinnati the list of those that responded favorably was: Mikveh Israel of Philadelphia; Beth El of Albany; Shaarai Chesed and Nefutzoth Yehudah of New Orleans; Shaaray Shomayim of Mobile, Ala.; Shaaray Tefillah of New York; and Beth Shalom of Richmond, Va.[16]

One of the causes responsible for the abortive conclusion of this attempt was the difference of objectives among various people. Certainly Wise and perhaps some others hoped that a "Union" would foster moderate Reform. One person suggested it should be used specifically for the establishment in the United States of the institution of the Chief Rabbinate, as in other lands, the office to be supported out of the profits of *Shechitah* (ritual slaughtering) and *Kashruth* (the sale of dietary foods). Lilienthal feared that the conservatives would outvote the reformers and might go so far as to outlaw "modernism." One reader of the *Occident* referred to the "terrible" rabbinical conferences in Germany. But the inescapable fact is that the end came as a result of apathy rather than of vocal or conscious opposition. Another generation had to pass, as in the Wilderness, and during the years that followed, Wise had to learn much as to objectives and methods.[17]

Meanwhile, Wise was not idle in Albany. He tells us that he bore patiently the lack of restraint and the viciousness of some of his opponents. His home was a deeply happy one. He was idolized by his pupils. He possessed many brilliant and warm friends, Jewish and non-Jewish. As indeed all through his life, he devoted himself to the poor who came his way. His wife often railed at him for his incorrigible optimism and his daemonic energy.[18]

In his recollections of the time he himself declares that he was perhaps extravagantly independent, that he differed strongly from many members of his congregation on religion, politics, and social conditions, and that publicly and privately he did not hesitate to give expression to his views rather recklessly. It must be borne in mind that he was still quite young, but twenty-nine years of age in this very year, and that—with its intense convictions and abounding energy—young manhood is often intolerant and assertive. Perhaps, as he understood later, his hearers were not ready for all that he was forever dinning into their ears, were not ready for his much too frequent and unmodulated references to their vices and defects. Often after personal conversations and after some of his addresses in the pulpit, individuals felt that he had been indulging in a direct, personal attack upon them and their manner of life.[19]

One of his "campaigns" in 1848 was again for the strict observance of the Sabbath. Wise is rarely given credit for this. Yet it was one of his habitual and perennial interests. In the third part of this book we shall take note of his many utterances as to the character and obligation of Sabbath-observance, his unvarying opposition to a "Sunday-Sabbath," the trouble in which he found himself as a result of his getting down to individual cases. The very heart and core of his Judaism—as again we shall describe in the third part of this book—was his belief in the divine inspiration of the Ten Commandments. And was not the Fourth Commandment an explicit, detailed, and majestic injunction as to the Sabbath day?

To a large extent—he writes—he met with success in his efforts to secure Sabbath-observance in Albany. He was aided in this endeavor by a number of friends. But curiously enough he was denounced by the orthodox—so he says—as a zealot and a hypocrite. He claims in his *Reminiscences* that in Albany the anomalous situation prevailed, that Reform Jews observed the Sabbath, and the orthodox did not. The orthodox, again he says, did nothing but mock at him.[20]

There were acute social problems in Albany, not uncharacteristic of this time in America. Women complained that their husbands spent too much time in saloons, drinking and playing cards. Wise remonstrated with the men but to no avail. He was told—sometimes sharply—to mind his own business. But this did not deter him. This *was* his business. He went into his pulpit and thundered forth scathing denunciations of drink, cards, and idleness.[21] Precisely in what connection we do not know, but he referred also to the taking of false oaths. He had had a report that a judge in Albany had demanded in his court that Jews take an oath *more Judaico* (a mediaeval reference, to the time when it was thought Jews had no regard for the Christian Bible and had to have their own form of oath in court to make them feel bound). Upon investigation this report proved false, and Wise asked the forgiveness of the judge in question. He tried to ferret out the lie. The next Sabbath he took the Torah out of the Ark, held it up solemnly before the eyes of the congregation, and said: "I swear by this Torah that the perjurers, who disgrace the name of Israel, will not live their full quota of years." This was going rather far and risking the disproof of his prophecy and the disdain of his warning. But it did succeed in making a deep impression upon the congregation, and faces were "deathly pale." It was too much for him too, and he claims that he fell back in his chair on the pulpit fainting and was led home from the synagogue. A tempest followed. There was even a lampoon printed against him, exactly where and what we cannot ascertain. But all this did not diminish the number of enemies he was accumulating.[22]

He writes too that occasionally he was greatly depressed by doubts that crept in upon him. He thought that it was not difficult to "disturb people in their religious convictions," but that this did not appear to lead toward any of the great goals he had envisaged for himself and for the Jews of the country.[23] His health was none too good. His friends were constantly remonstrating with him, not to read so much and for such interminable hours. Perhaps sarcastically one recommended that he turn to mythology. Wise took this friend at his word. This had been as a matter of fact Chief Justice Theophilus Wood. Wise waded through many tomes of Asiatic and "African" mythology, and informs us that he learned much from them, so that later on, when he came to the works of Ernest Renan and Max Mueller, these contained few surprises for him.[24]

In the *Occident* a controversy was going on between two *Hazanim* concerning the new ceremony of Confirmation, its Jewish permissibility, and so forth. Wise had introduced Confirmation in

Albany the previous *Shabuoth*. Portions of these articles from the *Occident* were copied in the Albany press and stirred up what he calls a "wasp's nest." Most of his people in Albany liked the innovation and found nothing disturbing in it. But this was one additional element of combustion added to the already glowing mass.[25]

In the summer of 1848 he felt constant premonitions of physical disaster. He was certain that he would die young. Probably at one time or another most young men have this presentiment. He thought his lungs were affected, that his vitality was depleted. The doctors warned him to take better care of himself. But he paid little heed, would take none of the medicines prescribed, and went his way with "rings under his eyes, and listless gait." At the same time a friend advised him to leave the pulpit and to live among people who would not tend to make his life so contentious and miserable. One thought he ought to let himself be baptized and become either a clergyman or a professor. "But," said Wise, "I could have done all this in Austria, had I wanted to shuffle off the coil of Judaism." In America, to which he had come "to be able to live as a free man in accordance with his convictions, this was unthinkable." Another friend, who had often heard him speak and who knew the quality of his mind, told him that he would make a fine lawyer. This advice Wise did not thrust from him, for he began to read Blackstone, Kent and others for a time. Probably one of the causes of his sickness and unrest lay in the hardships his family was enduring. He had little money, hardly enough to provide the merest necessities. Not that he had to listen to complaints on this score by his wife! She was a rock of trust and strength, and her love and confidence buoyed him up, so that in the end he escaped from all these doubts and temptations and knew as clearly as ever that there was but one road for him, the broad highway of his own convictions and his own visions. He consulted an old friend, Dr. Joseph Lewi, fellow-Bohemian, who had come to Albany as his guest. Lewi prescribed for him more nourishing food, beer, cold plunges, and especially more outdoor exercise. To this regimen Wise submitted. He began to take long walks together with a chosen companion, and in a few months this did serve to strengthen him somewhat. In the same year there was a great conflagration in Albany, and his second child fell very ill. His worry over the latter brought on a return of his earlier condition, so that his doctor absolutely forbade him to go on with his incessant and endless reading. For a time he was not permitted even to go to his favorite haunt in the State Library.[26]

Meanwhile the choir he had instituted in his synagogue was improving. It was directed by a Mr. Brand, who worked without compensation. Wise himself studied Sulzer and learned a great deal about "modern" Jewish music. He attended all the rehearsals. But the choir was a thorn in the sides of some of the obscurantists and reactionaries, for there were women in it. They hated it and wanted nothing but a *Hazan.* This led to further bickering. In addition, Wise had begun to write hymns, at least their words, and to try to introduce them into the services and to have the congregation join in singing them. This was a lifelong enterprise of his, and later on he published a collection of his own in Cincinnati. This again was—or seemed to be—an innovation and aroused further opposition. He was asked by some of the officers to recite the *Y'kum Purkan* (a prayer usually antipathetic to reformers). This he refused to do. Further discord!

A congregational meeting was held and a resolution was passed by a majority of those present enjoining him to eliminate the hymns from the service. Wise was of the opinion that this did not represent the opinion of the congregation and that those who had voted this had actually been a minority of his flock. He got around this injunction—he tells us—by transferring the hymns to Sabbath afternoons, and limited them to the times just before and after the sermon in the morning. But even this moderate use of hymns infuriated the "conservatives," who felt—perhaps justly—that he was defying the edict of the congregation.[27]

Another element in his dissatisfaction was what he regarded as the shameful neglect of youth in the community and in the country in general. No education worthy of the name was given to girls. Boys concluded their pedagogic training at the age of thirteen, when they were sent out to earn a living. All this Wise was striving hard to improve. Two "academies" existed in Albany. With the heads of both Wise enjoyed cordial relations. The graduates of his own school he sent to one or the other of these, to help his pupils educationally and socially. His intention was misinterpreted by some, as was almost always the case. These detractors claimed that Wise's real purpose was to make Christians of these children by daring to send them to a Christian institution.[28]

Another element of misunderstanding and controversy, which proved to be more serious, had to do with the status of women in the synagogue. This was one of the chief items in the program of Reform both in Germany and in America, and it was a lifelong concern of Wise himself. We shall later turn in detail to the problem of the place of woman in Jewish life and Wise's views and actions in relation to it, in the third part of this book. When he came to Albany, women had been seated in the balcony of the synagogue, as was then the custom almost everywhere. The hall itself was very small. This meant that there was no place for the new choir. Wise wished to solve the difficulty by setting aside half of the ground floor for women. Today this procedure—even in some orthodox synagogues—would not cause much excitement. But another terrific wave of excitement followed in Albany. Strong opposition crystallized against Wise's proposal. The Board went along with the Rabbi and then tried to compromise by putting the choir in the balcony along with the women. This the women regarded as an affront. They liked Wise's solution far better. The women "rose in their wrath" and began a campaign against the choir. This was a rather complete and sad misdirection of anger and energy, but it did not serve to make Wise's task easier. Bitter feelings were growing day by day. At last the Board had to yield, and to take the choir out of the "new portion of the gallery" in which it was to be placed. The next chapter in this war of nerves, in this somewhat tragi-comic embroilment, was that the choir refused to go on singing. Wise writes that the final arrangement, which is not entirely intelligible in his description, was that the choir was placed in a new section of the balcony, built next to the women's part. This established a *modus vivendi.* He himself, he writes, was blamed for everything. And on top of all this his wife chose this moment to deliver herself of a "curtain-lecture." What was going to happen to his wife and children, if he continued to raise whirlwinds everywhere? He must learn to be more cautious and to handle human beings better than recent events had seemed to indicate he was in the habit of doing![29]

During this same year of his life he discovered the psychology of Herbart and was so taken with it that he wrote a series of articles upon it. These he gave to his friend, Amos Dean, to read. Dean thought they might make more trouble for him and advised him to let them lie.[30]

The summer was over. The fall began. He prepared for the Holy Days, and was so weary that he decided to refrain from introducing into his sermons any polemical topics. People came and filled the sanctuary. They were somewhat astonished when the preacher said not a word about "reform," or "progress." There was much talk, but no one understood his true state of mind, that mere fatigue and discouragement were the sufficient cause.[31] That summer he made a trip to New York at the invitation of Merzbacher at Temple Emanuel, which was then on Christy Street. Wise does not tell us what he said there, but it must have been somewhat of an incendiary character, for afterward the Board of Emanu-El adopted a resolution that no one was to be permitted to occupy the pulpit without their express consent. A visitor to Albany explained to Wise: "You . . . give expression to ideas of reform and progress, and for that reason they are prejudiced against you." He was also called an "agitator and disturber," and a "radical."

Just about the same time, in the early fall, Wise had a visit from the *Parnass* of the Louisville, Ky. congregation. A new synagogue had been founded there, which Wise was asked to dedicate in the spring of 1849 before *Pesach.* He was asked also whether he would consider leaving Albany and coming to Louisville as rabbi, with the assurance that his salary would be considerably larger. This offer attracted him somewhat, but he made no commitment to consider it favorably. In the spring he discovered that the journey to Louisville would be much too difficult. He would have to go to Buffalo, then by wagon to Sandusky, Ohio, and then down the rivers through Ohio and Kentucky to Louisville. The rivers would be full of ice. He abandoned the idea and remained at home.[32]

In Albany itself the gossip about these last two events began to spread broadcast: that is, about his speech at Emanu-El in New York, and the offer of a pulpit in Louisville. In spite of all the difficulty in Albany, the incessantly quarrelsome attitude of some of his members, the constant harassment, Albany did not want him to resign. A congregational meeting was convoked. He was elected unanimously as rabbi for a period of three years. His annual salary was raised from $600 to $800. The news was communicated to him by a committee composed of his best friends, who told him also that the action had been "unanimous." He found that his wife wished to remain in Albany. There she had friends and felt at home. He informed the committee that all this was acceptable to him and that he would remain. The decision was greeted—not only by the committee, but by the entire community—with great enthusiasm. Even his bitterest and most irreconcilable opponents were silent. Perhaps they had repented them of their ways and had become friends. Wise himself was overcome by the apparent unanimity of feeling and thought that this might herald the advent of peace. The following evening a banquet was held, a custom invariably followed in those times when banquets and innumerable and interminable toasts were the order of the day. There was an especially fine toast by his friend, Moses Schloss. Good will and harmony seemed unshakable and eternal.[33]

Several things are clear from the record of this year in Wise's life. His last backward look toward Europe was in this year and thereafter he was unswervingly certain that his own happiness and his own duty lay in America. Even the minor reforms he had instituted in Albany: Confirmation, hymns, Sulzer's music, seating of women, elimination of the *Piutim*, etc., change of the prayers about a return to Palestine, Messiah and sacrifices, were raising in the congregation—and probably in other communities in the East who knew of all this—a strong and determined opposition, which was sure that Wise had as his intention to destroy traditional Judaism. Though apparently this opposition was waxing and waning in numbers and in hatred, the sequence of events and the culmination followed the inevitability of Greek tragedy, moving through 1849 to the crisis in 1850.

It had also been the year of Wise's first strong, clear call for Union, his first description of the reasons that ought to convince American Jews that, if they were to save their faith, keep their children loyal and aware, they must come together. The call is interesting, for negative as for positive reasons. For, like many others that will follow, it implied in every word and line that Wise wanted a union of *all* Jews, of *all* congregations, and that he had not then the slightest conception of the fact that his own program of Reform, or the steps he and others were adopting would militate against an all-inclusive union. His own mind, at least, was fixed upon essentials, upon Judaism as a great world-faith, upon worship, education and learning in general. He had no apparent comprehension of those who, he felt, concentrated upon *minutiae*, would let small differences of opinion impede the great work of cooperation, or divide Israel into warring factions.

10

Initiation at Albany, First Period *(Concluded)*

THE MATTER OF THE PROPOSED UNION RESOUNDED IN VARIOUS quarters for some months. Early in 1849 the *Occident*[1] published a large number of communications bearing upon it. The March issue contained a circular sent to congregations, setting forth the evils it was hoped to correct: the want of "prayer concert," teachers in Jewish schools who lacked proper qualifications; the dearth of good schools; no knowledge among Jews of their own history or of the essentials of their religion; no authority in Jewish life to which to refer questions; no institutions or means to instruct poor children; the absence of proper devotion in homes and in synagogues. As a remedy the circular suggested: a union of congregations to be represented by chosen delegates; the establishment of schools; the discussion at national meetings of subjects introduced by congregations; a plan to have delegates meet in New York, each congregation sending one representative. If a congregation should be represented by more than one, the unit rule should prevail. When twenty congregations would have declared their readiness to come together for this plan, action was to begin.

Wise himself began a vigorous campaign on behalf of the idea, in lectures which he delivered in a number of cities, and in articles from his pen. The same issue of the *Occident*—doubtless spurred to it by many rumors and direct charges—replied to the accusation that

Wise was an agitator, a reformer, an office-seeker. Wise himself wrote:

> I will never accept a salaried office from this convention; I will not give up the plan. You aver that I am a reformer to prejudice people against a sound plan. To be sure I am a reformer as much as our age requires, because I am convinced that none can stop the stream of time; none can check the swift wheel of the age, but I always have the *Halacha* (authoritative legal decisions in rabbinic literature) for my basis; I never sanction a reform against the *Din* (the decision).[2]

To show his earnestness and his desire that whatever plan should in the end be adopted, whatever should be the attitude on controversial points of those who would come together, it should truly represent the judgment and the need of American Israel, he urged his opponents—as many as there might be—to send delegates also:

> We will go on and erect a memorable monument in the history of Israel and bring it about that our children and grandchildren may still look upon it with confidence; that the house of Israel may have a solid center to maintain its sacred faith, to justify and develop our principles before the eyes of the world.[3]

In the same issue, which is fairly full of this one subject, Leeser had an editorial on "The Union of Israelites." He wrote that the specific occasion that had evoked Wise's "Call" had been a meeting which Wise and Lilienthal had had with some gentlemen from Cincinnati. He himself had written of the need for a Union in the *Occident* in the numbers for *Tammuz* and *Av* of 5605 (1845). This was his claim to priority. The article had been entitled "Union for the Sake of Judaism." He had received promises of support from one Lindo of Cincinnati, from the German congregations of New York, and from others in Cincinnati. It was his notion that the Union should not be "self-constituted," that each congregation should have one vote. Leeser expressed the hope that the assemblies would be held annually, and he asked for a first meeting not later than the third Monday of *Sivan* (late May or June) in New York. The circular, which was sent to congregations, the contents of which we outlined in the previous paragraph, was signed by Wise and Lilienthal.[4]

Resolutions were adopted by Lilienthal's congregations favoring the project. Wise himself records the meeting he had with three gentlemen from Cincinnati. It was to this occasion that Leeser referred. Their names, apparently, were: Lewis Abraham, Elias Myers, and Frederick Lindo.[5]

The *Occident* also recorded that on March 3, 1849 Wise had delivered a lengthy sermon in Albany on "The Light," a plea for the vital necessity of a Union, if Judaism in America was to be saved. Wise foresaw the failure of the current proposal, and spoke of it thus:

> But, brethren, I have been terribly undeceived; I have discovered that our priests are but shadows; the great majority are men without knowledge, without importance, without influence; and, what is still more destructive, without love or regard for Judaism; the great majority of our priests, including the Mishna heroes [by this unquestionably he meant the conservative or orthodox rabbis, who hung upon a literal interpretation of rabbinic sources], have forgotten their duty; they love their place, their bread, their salary more than their duty; they are become but the instruments, the echo of their congregations, and repeat composedly what the bestowers of their bread con [sic!] over to them, or what they wish them to hear.[6]

This was much too strong for Leeser—as might have been expected —and he appended a note by way of demurrer, asserting that the ministers could not, even if they would, act without the consent of their congregations. Nor for the present was it within the power of individuals to alter this condition. In the past he himself had not spared words about the supineness of many, but they are not without excuses. The change would have to be in the whole relation between congregation and rabbi, so that the profession of the Jewish ministry might become more useful to itself and to the cause of Judaism. This, he believed, would come about gradually. But Wise was neither impressed nor convinced by this—to him—tepid attitude. He abandoned hope in the rabbis and called upon the laymen.

Wise did not stop with generalizations. He asked the congregations to act, to adopt decisive measures. Once again he went, one by one, over the pressing needs that ought to have induced them to set to work: the education of youth, the need for text-books, books to "promulgate Judaism," material with which to resist missionaries, ministers who would have the capacity to instruct, a theological seminary, hospitals and orphan-asylums. He feared that he would not be able to persuade all congregations:

> . . . to accept at once the plan of union, and to act right away in this spirit; if but twenty congregations were to send their delegates, could not such a convention form a nucleus, and be thus a good commencement for an entire union of all the congregations, which would fall in by degrees?

Such a preliminary meeting could adopt a constitution and devise a plan of action. Nothing could be more short-sighted than to let petty fears prevent this. He called once again upon all native and "foreign" Jews, orthodox and reform, to respond, and to pay no attention to differences in *Minhagim.* And he ended by beseeching his friends everywhere not to remain silent, but to send in their views and their proposals.[7]

The question as to who was the first mover for union among American Jews is a vexed one, and does not perhaps deserve to be dwelt upon at length here. A pamphlet by Joseph Buchler, entitled "The Struggle for Unity, Attempts at Union in American Jewish Life: 1654—1868," in the publication of the Hebrew Union College Archives,[8] asserts that Leeser was the first, in 1841, together with a Philadelphia colleague, but that the attempt enjoyed a singular lack of success. In the *American Israelite* Wise wrote forthrightly that Leeser was not responsible for the original idea of a Union:

> The facts in the case, however, are that we moved Leeser to this enterprise, and we called the meeting in New York in 1849; it took a large amount of persuasion to assuage Leeser's fears and apprehensions about the then rising reform movements. All these things, however, are on record in the *Occident* of 1849, and it is useless now to discuss the subject.[9]

In the *Occident*, for *Kislev*, 5610, Leeser printed an interminable editorial on "The Union." Its gist was as follows:[10]

No one should harbor the impression that the Union was Wise's idea only. Wise had decided that it was a total failure. Should you call it that when eight congregations (New Orleans, Mobile, Albany, New York, Richmond, and Philadelphia) had responded and had appointed delegates? What right had Isaac M. Wise to expect more success than Leeser and his associates had met with in many years preceding? Wise could not now incontinently withdraw into his study. Leeser then noted that Wise had written as follows:

> I am candid enough, sir, to know and sufficiently meek to confess publicly, that I *myself* [italics his] am the real cause of the disappointment. A stranger, unknown and unnamed as I am, scarcely able to read and write the language of the country, having no popularity, no especial renown either for piety or learning, could not possess the confidence of the people; the most energetic words and efforts rather tended to arouse the suspicion of the true-hearted; it was feared that I probably had a design of my own to be effected by such a convention, or that

> I, probably a heretic, or at least a wild reformer, intended to overthrow the rock of venerated Judaism; and, making machines of my own of the majority of the delegates, I might accomplish what I liked and orthodoxy disliked. But I was innocent of any such chimerical motives, and so I retired disappointed, yet with a pure self-satisfaction of having done what I could; I am to blame for not having studied circumstances enough.

Leeser could not be blamed for being irritated by this document. Its self-accusation seemed excessive and did not ring with entire sincerity. Nor could it fairly be said that the failure of the enterprise could be ascribed exclusively to Dr. Wise's personality or to his point of view. As Wise knew well, the *vera causa* inhered in the chaotic condition of American Jewish life, which, unlike the dry bones of Ezekiel's valley, could not be made into a sound and living whole by the mere breathing over them of his spirit. Leeser's reaction was quite valid: he asserted that Wise was assuming far too much blame, that the Union was not Wise's idea or his responsibility alone. He admitted that Wise had been a powerful advocate, but contended also that Wise did not stand like a solitary apostle of the concept. For his part Wise then asked the *Occident* to take up the cause, or—to put it in the bombastic manner of the day—to accept the banner from his hand! Wise would not return from his closet, unless he was needed. If that proved to be so, he would await a call. To all this Leeser appended some reasonable remarks to the effect that the charges against Wise were trivial, and not deeply related to the problem of a Union. A good end to the project might even yet not be beyond the reach of possibility. And with his customary modesty Leeser added that it was not impossible that neither Wise nor he might be the best man to unite the Jews of this country.

Wise claimed in his *Reminiscences* that he had come to understand that the plan would probably divide Judaism into two warring camps, that this was only a temporary defeat, that in the end he would overcome all this thick indifference, and find his way through the combat and struggle that would lead to union and strength. Some of this—which came from many years later—was doubtless the clarity and the dauntlessness of retrospect. All the available evidence of the period indicates that Wise was deeply, tragically discouraged. He was in New York where he preached a powerful sermon on the necessity of union. But the Society, "The Friends of Light," would not cooperate, and without New York the whole enterprise seemed doomed. Wise was gloomy, indignant, and profoundly dejected.[11]

While Wise was in New York, Lilienthal asked him what he intended to do. Wise replied—he says—that he would go on with the fight:

> as truly as I am a son of a Jewish mother. I shall divide this American Judaism into two inimical camps, and they shall overcome the abominable indifference, repair the damages, and achieve the triumph of a new life by fight and struggle.[12]

This too comes from the *Reminiscences* and reads more like the dramatization of memory than fact. In the same passage Wise asserts that he was like all incorrigible idealists, that he could not believe that this great idea could die. He thought he had planted seeds which the future would cause to sprout. But at the time this was "cold comfort." Not everything was to be written down as loss, it was true! Some strong adherents had been won. He himself—he acknowledged—was not yet a "hardened fighter." He was still much too sensitive, much too ready to smart under a rain of blows, and to accept defeat. He could not find the courage to tell his wife of all this. He did not wish to poison her joy, nor disturb the happy tenor of his home life.

He returned to Albany. At the time of the Passover there had been a congregational meeting, at which some members had lodged violent objection against the previous action electing Wise for three years. Some came to blows. Wise had rushed to the meeting. He had listened, taken the contract out of his pocket, and torn it up. Telegrams followed him to New York, asking him not to do anything hasty and asserting that the contract was still valid. In April, 1849, a new contract was drawn up.[13]

At this time Wise thought that the congregation needed a newer and larger building for worship and instruction and he broached the proposal to a number of his friends. Some of these must have had an inkling of what was coming, for they tried instead to persuade Wise to leave Beth El and to form a new congregation with them. But Wise did not wish to disrupt the congregation with which he had been identified. In the main he was weary. His essential depression was evidenced by the circumstance that on his own time he was studying law, often until two in the morning. Occasionally he wrote for the newspapers in Albany, and was still giving private lessons to scions of the wealthy.[14]

Upon his return from New York, moreover, he had been expected to review all that had happened in the pulpit, and, as we have noted, to thunder against his opponents. The synagogue was crowded and all awaited the fulmination. They were doomed to disappointment. Wise spoke on the last two days of the Passover, but passed over the entire subject of Union. His description of the congregation is not without humor:

> Cohn and Moses whispered as usual; Bernhard Smith slept softly as always; Rosenbaum was enchanted; Mayer Isaac and Wolf Simon cracked their jokes after the service; Tschasky had never heard such a sermon in Poland; Kastanienbaum had experienced the like at the time he was living in service; the women were moved to tears, a fact that Marianne Smith imparted to me dutifully after dinner; the choir sang beautiful selections; everything proceeded as usual; everything was as it had been.[15]

When the matter of his contract had been finally adjusted, his salary was set at $800 *per annum* and he was asked to go to the meeting. All begged his forgiveness and promised him peace and friendship. He was touched and spoke to them of complete reconciliation. There was much joy, feasting and—as usual—speechmaking. The next morning he went to his school. The children had heard rumors in their homes that Wise might leave them. They crowded about him—he says—kissing his hands and his coat. It was half an hour before he could persuade them to be quiet. Even the teachers grasped him by the hand and expressed their happiness.[16]

In spite of these occasional spasms of peace and good will, all was far from well. A petition had been circulated among the members demanding that the principal reforms Wise had instituted should be abolished, that all traditional prayers should be restored, especially the references to a personal Messiah and a return to Palestine. Fortunately, Wise wrote, the petition did not have enough signatures and was forgotten.[17]

His own personal life was not uneventful during this same year. In the summer of 1849 there was an epidemic of cholera, a dread disease in that era. Among those who fell victim to it were very few Jews. But his own home was to suffer one of the casualties. His little daughter Laura, but two years old, contracted the dread disease, and died of it within a single day. Theresa and he were grieved to the heart, to the very center of their lives. They had loved Laura greatly. They were both ill and exhausted after the swift, incredible tragedy. Wise himself contracted a persistent and distressing cough.[18]

The funeral for Laura was held and at it Wise followed the course of his own convictions. There was an old Jewish custom (*Keriah*) a *Minhag*, which still obtains, of the cutting of one's garments as a sign of mourning. This stems from the biblical tales about "sackcloth and ashes," and especially the custom which goes back to many biblical instances of "rending the garments." Injunctions in orthodoxy as to this are quite specific. Of this Wise disapproved, and on this occasion he refused to follow it. Nor did he sit on the floor after the funeral and he kept his shoes on his feet. This served to inflame yet further some of those who were constantly offended by what they regarded as his heterodoxy, his disregard of immemorial Jewish laws and customs. Violent dissension ensued all over the little community. Wise's own health appeared to be deteriorating steadily, with results to which we shall soon come.[19]

Only a few other matters need to be described, matters that came within this year. In the *Occident* appeared the first of a series of articles on "The Messiah." This was in reality the text of a sermon which Wise had delivered in Albany on January 30 of that year. In this he had reviewed the history of the idea of the mission of Israel, which, as he conceived it, was to publish a great truth among the nations. The second installment was more than equivocal about the concept of a "personal Messiah." Wise seemed to be implying that the Messiah was to be a man of any nation who would bring into the world an era of perfect peace and justice. This he may have intended to serve as a compromise, but it could not be acceptable to any traditional Jew for whom the Messiah was to be of the house of David.[20]

Once again the missionaries were very active in the eastern part of the United States. The country—Wise wrote—swarmed with them. Most Jewish leaders were afraid to say or do anything. From Albany at least the missionaries stayed away, as a result of the incidents related above. Wise had a visit from Leeser, who told him that he, Leeser, had been greatly worried by the prevalence and virulence of the conversionist frenzy, that he had tried to secure contributions to combat it, but without success. Wise inquired why he, Wise, had not been asked to help. Leeser replied frankly: "My readers are much displeased at me for accepting contributions from your pen. They cannot stand your rationalistic views." "Rationalism" was with him—and with some others—a synonym for Reform. But Leeser then went on to say that he had decided to take the risk and asked Wise to help him. They talked over the strategy for an offensive. They would try to tell Christians why some essential Christian dogmas were dangerously wrong. This led to one of Wise's first attempts at polemics against Christianity, the forerunner of many extended works. The articles appeared in the *Occident*. Their gist consisted of a critical examination of the New Testament, with especial reference to the Westminster Confession. These were striking articles, courageous, and for the first time constituted a counteroffensive by a Jewish leader. They attracted considerable attention. Wise received congratulations from Theodore Parker, a Unitarian leader. Some of his friends in Albany told him warmly of their enthusiasm. But he had again made many enemies, not only among orthodox Christians, but also among orthodox Jews, for he spared neither in these articles. The preachers of Albany were greatly incensed and tried to prevail upon the governor to strike Wise's name from the list of members of the Library Committee. But the governor stalwartly refused to be intimidated and Wise's name continued to appear. Within his own congregation his opponents attempted to make capital of all this, asserting that he was causing *Rishus* ("prejudice"). Wise claimed that no "cowardly or malicious" action or slander was too low for them.[21]

It was in this year that Lilienthal became utterly discouraged with his own task with his three congregations in New York, presented his resignation, and began to teach. The quarrel, however, had nothing to do with orthodoxy or reform.[22]

That trained rabbis were deplorably few in number in America was also evidenced this very year by the extravagant acclaim that greeted the coming to New York of a rabbi, Morris J. Raphall, who arrived late in October of 1849.[23] Since we shall meet Raphall again at one of the most crucial occasions of Wise's life, it would be well to give a sketch of his origins and life. Raphall was born in Stockholm, Sweden, in 1798. He died in New York in 1868. He was educated at a Hebrew grammar-school in Copenhagen. Later he went to England and traveled extensively on the continent. One of his especial fields was Hebrew poetry and he published much on it in the *Hebrew Review.* He wrote also on Maimonides and Albo, made a translation of most of the *Mishna* and began one of the Pentateuch. At the time of the blood accusation in Damascus in 1840 he wrote a striking refutation of this slander, published in four languages. The following year he was appointed rabbi of the Birmingham synagogue in central England and the head of a school there. There he served for eight years. He arrived in New York, as we have noted, and served as rabbi of B'nai Yeshurun until 1866, when ill health compelled his relinquishment of his duties. He had to his credit also a post-Biblical Jewish history, and had received a Ph.D. degree from Erlangen in Germany. He was one of the staunchest and ablest defenders of orthodoxy and was reputed to have been a very eloquent speaker.[24]

At the time of Raphall's arrival in America the *Occident* carried somewhat hysterically ecstatic notices of his coming and of his first sermon at B'nai Yeshurun. The journal reported that Raphall was paid a very exceptional salary for those days, a salary of $2000. Next to this was Mikveh Israel of Philadelphia, which paid $1700 to married and $1300 to single ministers. The average was between these figures, and the low was $500 a year. Raphall not only served his congregation, but was greatly in demand for lectures in various parts of the eastern seaboard.[25]

It was also in the latter part of this year, to be exact in October 1849, that the first issue of a new Jewish periodical appeared. Its editor was Robert Lyon, an English Jew, and its masthead was significant for the time and also of Wise's intense interest in it: "The *Asmonean* is a journal devoted to the advocacy of a congregational union of Israelites of the United States." This frankness and courage would have been enough. But before long Wise had many kinds of relationship with Lyon and the *Asmonean*, which in the years that followed were of much more than passing importance.[26]

11

Crisis at Albany, First Period

THE YEAR 1850 WAS ONE OF THE MOST CRITICAL IN ISAAC M. WISE'S life. In it he learned much that for all the remainder of his life shaped his convictions about and his loyalty for America. In it he discovered to his astonishment that his health was good and that most of his apparent physical troubles had been of psychic origin. For the remainder of his life—with occasional intervals of relatively mild sickness—he enjoyed magnificent health and abounding—almost incredible—energy for work. But, much more important than these, in this year the troubles that had been muttering in his congregation in Albany came suddenly to the surface, and erupted in hatred and violence. No longer in this period do we depend upon his own words alone, or upon his own interpretation of the events of his life. There is abundant correlative material: in the records of the Albany congregation, in the pages of the *Occident* and the *Asmonean*, in court records, and in the daily press of Albany. The picture which we shall draw will rest upon all of these, and will weigh the evidence of them all.

Perhaps Wise should have foreseen what was to come. Perhaps he should not have been so taken by surprise. From the vantage-point of our own time more than a century later the accounts of growing dissatisfaction, the obvious development of an opposition-party within the congregation, the records of congregational meetings, seem to point unmistakably toward the approach of a tragic climax. Such climaxes always seem to come suddenly. Vague feelings and groping wishes converge and interlock toward violence. That all this came as a rude awakening to him and to his friends is more than a little astonishing. As the record will show, it is equally clear that this crisis had a deep and enduring influence upon his feeling about himself, his future, and his plans for American Jewish life. A careful reading of this and of the following chapter will reveal all this.

Early in 1850 Wise's health seemed on the road to serious deterioration. He himself wrote later that he had been ill all winter:

> partly as a result of the cholera in the summer of 1849 (which had carried off his little daughter Laura), and partly because he was overworked and prostrated. He suffered disturbing spells of melancholia, ate little, and looked wretchedly. Some thought him consumptive. He was advised to go South. This he did in February, 1850.[1]

He had a constant and annoying cough. It was his friend, Dr. Joseph Lewi, who advised him to take a trip and to seek some warmer climate. All this was communicated to the officers of the congregation and he was granted a leave of absence. The trip that followed—he himself wrote—proved a turning-point in his life and career.[2]

He left Albany for New York City. Travel in those days was not easy. In his *Reminiscences* he describes the trip down the state. Here are some sentences from this section:

> There was at that time no direct railroad connection between Albany and New York. The traveler had to go eastward first *via* the Boston Road, then southward to Bridgeport *via* the Housatonic Road and from there to New York by steamer. It took generally from sixteen to eighteen hours to make the trip in case the Hudson was frozen over. This was the case during four or five months of every year.[3]

During the long hours of this journey Wise looked deeply into himself. With a certain degree of self-dramatization he saw himself at the age of thirty-one as a "broken man" with little hope for the future. He said to himself that he was enduring the lot of all "dreamers." But even melancholy reflections like these induced a reaction and he could not help growing more cheerful.

Arrived in New York, he called on his friend Lilienthal, who complained to him bitterly of his dealings with M. J. Raphall, then rabbi of B'nai Yeshurun. Lilienthal and Wise sat and exchanged their sad experiences and their fears as to the future. Lilienthal informed him of his decision to leave the rabbinate and to devote himself to education. This action he took shortly thereafter and did not return to the rabbinate for five years, that is in 1855, when Wise induced his sister-congregation in Cincinnati, B'nai Israel, to call Lilienthal to its pulpit. Wise in his turn recounted all that had been happening to him in Albany, and—at some length—the failure of his first efforts toward a union of American Jews. Two of our sources quote Lilienthal as having said to Wise—not too cogently or elegantly—that, if he—Wise—insisted on acting like Christ, he would have to expect to be crucified.[4]

From New York Wise went on to Philadelphia chiefly for the purpose of visiting Leeser. In his *Reminiscences* he informs us that he found Leeser living in a "Christian house," which did not appear to Wise conduct entirely consistent for an orthodox leader. Leeser got around the difficulty by eating no meat. Leeser too was in trouble and told Wise that he expected to lose his position in Philadelphia. He discussed with Wise his proposed translation of the Bible into English. Somewhere Wise wrote the rather captious remark that Leeser had really translated from the German and not directly from the Hebrew. As he listened to Leeser, especially anent Leeser's fears as to his own future in his pulpit, Wise mused to himself that everybody seemed to be in the same boat. Leeser—he said—admitted that the Reform congregations in New York, Baltimore and Charleston were making some progress, but that this did not alter the general picture of retrogression and feebleness. From Leeser also he heard much of Raphall, his lectures in New York on Hebrew poetry, the invitation that had come to Raphall to deliver the same addresses in Charleston, and there also to champion the cause of orthodoxy.[5]

From Philadelphia Wise proceeded to Washington. This was a grave time in the capital. Polk had finished his term as President in 1849, and the Congress had come to its end, leaving the status of California and New Mexico undetermined. Zachary Taylor, a general and hero of the Mexican War, had taken office as president. Taylor was himself a Southern slaveholder. The South hugged to itself the belief that its rights were secure. But California soon adopted a Constitution—without waiting for Congressional authority—prohibiting slavery within its borders. Thereafter it applied for admission into the Union. The slavery issue was paramount. Even now, with the perspective of more than a hundred years, it is not easy to picture to oneself the immense pressures, the continuous political maneuvering, and the towering figures that made up the total scene in Washington a little more than a decade before the Civil War. The South was certain that, to maintain slavery as the country grew, it must extend the institution to new states, or very soon it would be outvoted. The North understood equally well that, unless slavery was to become a permanent and ruinous feature of the American system, the territories then applying for statehood must not be permitted to give sanction to the iniquitous institution. Behind all this were also the writing and speaking of the Abolitionists, who combined humanitarian with religious zeal. More of them later![6]

A crisis was at hand at this very time when Wise came to Washington. Henry Clay, old and sick, proposed a typical panacea, one of the compromises for which he had become famous: to admit California as a "free state"; to admit New Mexico also without slavery; but, to assuage the feelings of the South by tightening the provisions of the law concerning fugitive slaves; also that Congress was to agree not to interfere with slavery in the District of Columbia. Texas was to be indemnified for that part of the territory it claimed that would become part of New Mexico. A bill to this effect was introduced in both houses in January, 1850, and an epochal debate on the so-called "Missouri Compromise" was in progress when Wise came to the Capital. Hour after hour and day after day Wise sat in the gallery of the Senate. He was utterly and completely absorbed by what he heard. He felt himself a witness at the making of American history. The level of the speaking by such giants as Clay, Calhoun, Webster, Seward and others, was a revelation to him in dignity, cogency and power. He listened to a speech by Calhoun on the right of slave-owners to transport slaves into California. The speech seemed to him unanswerable. Then Seward took the floor in opposition and spoke of the right of all men to be born free in the spirit of the Declaration of Independence. Between the extremes were the measured utterances and proposals of Clay and Webster. Wise could not tear himself away from the sessions. He sat there, chin in hand, listening with complete absorption. He was finding his way into the heart of America at this most perilous and bitterly controversial of times. From Washington he carried away a faith that he had always had, but that was then infinitely strengthened and clarified. That he did not form stronger or clearer convictions on the subject of slavery as a result of these experiences is no less than remarkable. The extensive record of his speaking, writing, and acting, after he had removed to Cincinnati, will furnish irrefutable evidence that he had not. To this we shall come in detail in the years between 1854 and 1861. In this connection it is sufficient to call attention to the fact that this was the case.[7]

There were others in the Senate, too, either beginning or ending glorious careers: Benton of Missouri, Seward, Chase, and Hale, and, from the South, Douglas and Jefferson Davis. Wise met Seward several times. They were already good friends from Albany and New York. From him Wise had a most cordial reception. Seward took Wise to the White House to meet President Taylor. The Washington papers came out with an article under the headline: "The First Rabbi to Visit a President."[8]

Wise was struck—he wrote—by the fine faces and figures of the senators, and he was listening morning, noon and night. Calhoun was in his last days and could but rarely be on the floor of the Senate. Wise was taken to visit him and recounted that, as he was there by Calhoun's bedside, he felt strongly the truth of the doctrine of immortality, for this giant with "one foot in the grave" still had a mind cogent and clear. In the midst of all this excitement and in his intense concentration upon all he was seeing and hearing in the Senate of the United States, Wise forgot all about his own supposed ill health.[9]

On the same visit he was introduced to Daniel Webster. He asserted that Webster had heard of him through his friend, Amos Dean, of Albany. Dean had lent Webster Wise's copy of Herbart's psychology. Webster invited Wise to dine with him that evening at eight o'clock. Wise must have made a favorable impression upon the great man, for Webster offered to obtain Wise a position at Boston University. Seward had made him a similar offer. In his *Reminiscences* Wise put down these sentences of his impression of Webster:

> Webster is a grand man. His voice is powerful and well modulated; His face is good, kindly, and handsome. There is fire in his glance. Sublimity sits on his brow. He is well balanced throughout.

With Webster he chatted about Herbartian psychology and the tenets of Unitarianism.[10]

The next evening he was received by the Ambassador of Austria and to his astonishment given a cordial reception. To himself he thought what news this would have made in Austria.[11]

What total impression did this remarkable visit to Washington make upon Wise? It was thus he wrote of it:

> If anyone desires to know how it happens that I have always moved on the lofty platform of humanity, and have always set in motion broad and inclusive projects, even though they have not been great—and God knows I have never concerned myself with trivialities—I could answer him that I learned this from our national politicians and statesmen. . . .

He asserted also that he had gained new confidence and experience as a speaker and a renewed and deepened faith in America, that he had made many new friends and was filled with hope instead of the despondency he had taken with him from Albany. In an interesting essay on Dr. Wise, Jacob R. Marcus writes that after this visit America had truly become his country, the source—for him—of all genuine political liberalism.[12]

After these stirring experiences Wise left Washington and proceeded to Charleston, S.C. He had had an invitation from the Reform congregation there to come and speak. They wrote to him of Raphall's visits and of his attacks upon the "liberals." Wise now knew that his illness had been imaginary and he undertook the trip to Charleston with alacrity.

The congregation in Charleston was called *Beth Elohim* and was still composed chiefly of the Portuguese Jews who had founded it. Its preacher was Gustave Poznanski, who despite his Polish-sounding name was German. Reform in Charleston was not of yesterday, for it had begun as early as 1824, when the congregation had had forty-seven members. Poznanski had taken over in 1836 and more "radical" reforms followed. There had been a fire and the synagogue had been rebuilt in 1838. In 1843 the second days of the holidays had been abolished. The congregation worshiped without hats. It was the most "advanced" congregation in the United States at that time.[13]

Wise went by train to Wilmington, N.C. and then by boat to Charleston. He had thirty hours to himself and decided to take as the subject-matter of his address "Will Ruled by Reason." This was to be a sermon on Biblical theology. The belief of heathens, he thought, makes history rest on chance alone, but in Judaism its essential cause is Providence. This and his experiences in Charleston were to prove critical in his life, within himself, and in precipitating the crisis in Albany.[14]

At the steamer he was met by leaders of the Jewish community. The reception was "stiffly formal." The *Hazan*, a member of the delegation, appeared to be assuming that Wise was unfamiliar with the liberal principles of the congregation, and gently Wise made his mistake clear to him. Wise's sermon, delivered the following Sabbath at *Beth Elohim,* was in fact entitled "The Effect of Biblical Theology," and was later published in the *Occident.* Before long, too, he met Raphall who was still in Charleston. Both of them spoke to various audiences practically every day, and each was soon defending his own position.[15]

For his visit to Charleston Wise was given a spacious room in the main hotel with a Negro slave at his disposal. He was treated like the guest of aristocrats. There was—he wrote—but one German Jew then a member of the congregation. The members enjoyed excellent standing in the city and were very proud of their lineage. Nor was this without justification, for they possessed a high degree of culture and refinement. Many of the leading Jewish citizens paid him visits, among them Poznanski, who in the first days seemed patronizing and had even tried to instruct Wise in German and in English.[16]

Wise recorded that, when he spoke, the temple was crowded to capacity. Here was he, a newcomer, but four years in the land, speaking in this important place and to these impressive people. He was filled with trepidation. If he could have beat a retreat with honor, he would have done so. But all he needed was to begin, and a consciousness of his own powers, a deep immersion in what he proposed to say, came over him. His sermon was cordially received and he was flattered on every hand. The *Parnass* gave a dinner for him. Several visitors came to see him from the other local congregation. One of them gave him a detailed description of what Raphall had been saying and of some of the strictures he had been making against Reform, which—the visitor said—Raphall had "demolished." As a matter of fact, Wise had had all this in mind in his initial sermon, of which he wrote: "This was the time and place, the Albany rabbi thought, to define Judaism as the Universal Religion of Mankind." Leeser liked the sermon and did not until later perceive how destructive it was of his own point of view. But—Wise wrote—it was always his own chief concern to emphasize the positive aspects of Judaism and to let others judge the negative implications of what he had said.[17]

At one of his personal meetings with Raphall—they had got to like one another and Raphall had predicted a great future for him—Raphall informed Wise that Wise was cogent but on the wrong side, and that there was no future for Reform Judaism in America. Wise replied that he stood upon his own convictions and there would be little left of orthodoxy in America within twenty years.

With this exchange of courtesies they girded themselves for battle. The general feeling in the community, Wise claimed, was that Raphall expressed himself beautifully, but that Wise carried more power and conviction.[18]

The end of the *contretemps* came when a public debate was arranged between Raphall and Poznanski. With his usual scorn for most other rabbis in America, Wise remarked that neither of these men had any first-hand knowledge of rabbinical literature. But the debate was to be a high occasion and the house was filled with adherents of both sides. Wise went as an auditor. Whether he was sitting in the audience or on the platform it is hard to tell, for the records are contradictory on this point. Obviously the debate did not absorb him much, for he commented that he had indited a German poem while it was going on. There was no agreed procedure and there were no judges. As things progressed, it seemed to Wise that Raphall was being worsted. The debate was on Sunday, and both men had come armed with large folio volumes which they placed each on a table in front of himself.[19]

Poznanski was a dialectician. He entangled Raphall in contradictions and in fine, logical points. Of course, it is fair to recall that all of this comes from Wise's account of the debate, and no one could claim that he was a disinterested auditor. Much later on in the *Israelite* Wise wrote that everyone listened attentively (except himself possibly!) and that the first hour had to do with subjects that did not interest him greatly:

> It became annoying to him [Wise]. He had forgotten these things years ago; how to pray and chant, to dress for prayer, etc. There was much reference to the Talmud and no mention of the Bible. It was all *Pilpul* (casuistry), at which Poznanski was much better than Raphall.

Finally, wrote Wise, Raphall "turned up two burning questions of that day, viz. the belief in the coming of a personal Messiah, a son of David, and the resurrection of the body from the grave." Raphall maintained that these were dogmas of Judaism and Poznanski rejected both. The temper of Raphall and of some men in the audience was rising rapidly. Poznanski remained "restrained and cool." It is probable that this very restraint tended to make Raphall more excited. The rejection and denial of these "essential principles" touched him in some deep spot of his orthodoxy. His convictions were outraged. He could not credit the fact that a rabbi could be so heterodox, that he could deny publicly what had been fundamental dogmas of Judaism through so many ages. In desperation Raphall then turned toward Wise, whom he knew was there, and flung at him the same questions: "Do you believe in the coming of a personal Messiah? Do you believe in the resurrection of the body?" The earliest sources assert that Wise answered with an emphatic but single "No!" In his later recollections Wise wrote that he had replied: "No, no, no! The Talmud is no authority for me in questions of doctrine." This elaboration—to judge from many sources—might have been what he meant to say, but at the time it is probable that he contented himself with a single, perhaps shouted, negative.[20]

This put the quietus on the entire affair. We have to try to imagine why this was so. It is certain that Raphall was deeply, irreparably outraged. He discerned that he was in the enemy's camp. These were not Jews; they were unbelievers. They were *koferim b'ikor*, heretics, deniers of an essential dogma. Discussion had become worse than useless. He packed his books hurriedly and, saying "Then I can no longer discuss with these people," left the hall, his friends behind him, "all," writes Wise, "as foolish as before."[21] This incident became historic. It was bruited about the country. Pros and cons were debated in many communities. Wise himself wrote:

> There was no definition but a fanaticism was roused which did not come to rest for years after—as we shall see further on.[22]

After the next Sabbath, Wise left Charleston by steamer, happy in the belief that he had made many new friends. Before he left, he wrote, he had gone back to his hotel deep in meditation. Was it possible that Raphall had been in the right, and that he, Wise, was really destroying old beliefs? He felt very lonely, solitary and weak. Poznanski had come to see him the next morning and had suddenly asked him whether he could read Latin and Greek. The congregation in Charleston wanted a preacher with classical attainments and Poznanski had made up his mind to resign. Exactly why he had decided to leave the place at this very moment it is impossible to determine. But Wise informed him that he could read neither of the great classical tongues and that he did not think he would make a good rabbi for Charleston.[23]

On the way back he bought his wife a new silk dress, and some new clothes for himself, so that he looked quite "handsome." Upon his return to Albany, from what must have been an extended trip for those days, he was tendered a banquet by his friends. Greatly to his amazement a telegram arrived from Charleston, informing him that he had been elected rabbi of congregation *Beth Elohim* at a proposed salary of $1,000 a year, and that the congregation would also furnish him with a home. His first reaction was of great joy. Here of a sudden was a prospect of living at peace among people who shared his own convictions, who were not newcomers but men and women of culture and refinement. He talked it over carefully with his wife. She agreed with him. He sent to Charleston his acceptance of the call by wire and simultaneously submitted his resignation to the trustees of Beth El. This latter was to take effect on April 15, 1850. A letter followed the telegram from Charleston, confirming the offer and adding relevant details.[24]

Things began to boil in Albany. "It raised a storm of indignation in that community and a volley of protests from all sides." His house was invested by committees for weeks, begging him to alter his purpose. Even his opponents, Wise asserts, joined in the chorus and promises were piled up as to what they would do for him, if he would stay. Some of his friends thought that he had resolved upon the right course, that after the treatment he had had in Albany he was under no obligation to the congregation. Things went so far that the position in Albany was advertised for a successor and candidates began to make their appearance.[25]

But Wise himself began to waver. Certainly he could not have had any serious belief that great troubles were so near in Albany. Were not all these men, even those who had opposed his "moderate" reforms, now beseeching him to stay as their leader? Possibly he was leaving a task half done! The news that he was to leave Albany and to go to Charleston appeared in the *Asmonean* on April 15, 1850. Even in his *Reminiscences* Wise does not make quite clear why he changed his mind, why he decided to remain in Albany. He went about it by telling his wife that yellow-fever was frequent in Charleston. This alarmed her and she and his children begged him not to go. He permitted himself to be re-elected as rabbi in Albany for three years at the same salary, but with an additional sum of two hundred dollars to be subscribed privately by some members. At the same congregational meeting a new president, Louis Spanier, was elected.[26]

Great manifestations of joy, feasts of reconciliation, and costly gifts followed. Wise himself was not free of inner doubt. He was far from certain that he had acted wisely or rightly. He wrote a letter to Charleston, telling them of his altered decision. This they took in ill part. An anonymous letter appeared in the *Asmonean*, attacking him for his change of mind about Charleston and claiming that he had decided to stay in Albany because of the increase in his salary; that, in short, he had "sold out" Reform Judaism. This Wise answered with restraint.

Of Spanier, the new president, Wise wrote later that "he was not considered sound on the reform question." But it had been Spanier who had presided over the meeting that had re-elected Wise unanimously and, to judge by all words and appearances, Spanier had himself been heartily in favor of the action taken.

One further note needs to be added before we move on. In the *Occident* in the middle of 1850 Wise was writing a series entitled "Letters on Christianity." The third of these was directed to Rev. Miller, to whom we have referred previously, and who had become Wise's good friend. Wise wrote that Jews reject the canonical gospels for the same reasons Christians reject the "apocryphal gospels." The gospels are too inconsistent with human reason, and abound with superstitions and historical errors. He referred again to the conversionist frenzy:

> I must call the plan to "pervert" the Jews very ridiculous. . . . But be assured of my fraternal feelings towards you, and towards every good man, whatever he may believe or disbelieve."[27]

12

Crisis at Albany, First Period *(Concluded)*

In the latter part of 1850 the themes and dramatis personae that were inimical to Isaac M. Wise converged toward the last act. Sixteen years later in an editorial in the *Israelite* called "Dogmatism" he himself summarized the entire experience from his own point of view in these words:

> It may be improper to mention here that in the year 1850 the humble writer of these lines was persecuted like a mad dog, because he would not subscribe to the prayer-book dogmas of a personal Messiah and the resurrection of the body, as the worshipers of words understood them; although he acknowledged his belief in redemption and immortality.[1]

At the time, as we shall see, he ascribed the trouble sometimes to this and again to another cause, which might have reflected more credit upon himself. The contemporary documents make it probable that both causes were there and that both played a part in the action of certain officials and in the sentiments aroused against him by a party of his own members.

Certainly the Charleston affair had an especial role in initiating the final culmination. Much later in the *American Israelite* Wise put on record that Raphall, whom we have observed leaving the hall and probably the city of Charleston in deep chagrin and resentment, began at once to traduce him. Exactly in what organs or to what persons Raphall did this, we are unable to ascertain. Here again is the way Wise put it:

> "The president (of Beth El in Albany) was captivated by Raphall's charges and vilifications. He took up the hue and cry, as did the denominational press, both Christian and Jewish." The latter contended that Wise had rejected beliefs which were important to Christianity too, and which it had derived from Judaism. "Still both Jew and Gentile were equally hostile to Wise and raised at his heels the mad-dog cry of heresy." This, he says, served to advertise him all over the land, but undermined his position in Albany. The "aristocratic and wealthy" president influenced certain classes of members. Hostile, factional feeling was engendered. There was much "bitter and relentless" hatred, until the final act in the synagogue on New Year's Day.[2]

When he had been prevailed upon to reverse his acceptance of the pulpit of Beth Elohim in Charleston, Wise had thought that he was firmly entrenched in Albany. Even those who had seemed most hostile to him, and certainly the president, Louis Spanier, had joined in the action taken in re-electing him for three years with every assurance of confidence and support. But it became evident only too soon that all of this had meant little, that it had in actuality been only a glossing over of the real issues, that no one had been genuinely reconciled. Wise saw that with the best of motives he had made a serious blunder in remaining in Albany. But it was too late to reverse his course.

The man who now led the faction determined to have his head was the president, Spanier. Wise himself had regarded Spanier as a friend, in fact, as he says in several places, a "close friend." Spanier had now shifted to implacable enmity. Various reasons have been given for this, some by Spanier, others by Wise. Spanier himself contended that it was the events in Charleston, plus a "Bull" of excommunication against Wise published by Raphall, together with extended articles retailing Wise's heretical statements in Charleston, that brought about his change of heart. At times Wise and others attributed Spanier's hatred to Spanier's desire to get the Albany pulpit for a relative, or again to Wise's procedure against a board member for Sabbath-violation. Wherever the truth may lie—and the evidence indicates that Spanier was motivated chiefly by his feeling of outrage at Wise's supposed doctrinal heresies—Spanier embarked almost at once upon a course of action calculated to drive Wise out of the pulpit, figuratively and literally. Petty annoyances accumulated. Charges and counter-charges were flung back and forth between the two divisions, reform and orthodox, within the congregation. For four months the congregation and the Jewish community were in a state of constant excitement, exacerbation and turmoil.

In the beginning Wise regarded the charges of Raphall and his "excommunication" as ludicrous, not deserving his attention, as "presumptuous and mediaeval." It was not long however before he perceived that he had been wrong. The "Bull" had been published in the *Occident,* and it represented a number of orthodox congregations, as well as Raphall himself. It declared Wise unfit to be a rabbi or teacher of religion, because of his denial of the verity of the belief in a Messiah and in bodily resurrection. It suggested that Wise be removed from his pulpit. Nor was this confined to the *Occident.* In the new periodical, the *Asmonean,* which had recently begun publication in New York, Raphall abused Wise week after week. Happily—Wise wrote—the *Asmonean* was not widely read at the time. But no one had come forward to defend him. For the moment the orthodox seemed to have the public eye and ear. Wise felt deeply hurt by Leeser's tolerance of this situation, his willingness to harbor Raphall's extremism. Leeser defended himself—or so Wise contended—by claiming that to oppose Raphall would have jeopardized the *Occident*'s existence.[3]

And now we must return to Spanier. Wise asserted that Spanier had originally belonged to another congregation in Albany and had joined Beth El out of sympathy for the reforms Wise had introduced. This is of course possible, for a man may later change his mind. But it seems inherently improbable. Spanier—Wise admits—was a man of culture and of imposing presence, and—as the sequel will show—a man of some wealth. Wise mentioned too, as though it were germane to the issue and to Spanier's personality, that he was a "Hanoverian."[4]

Suddenly then, it seemed, Spanier was his mortal enemy. Spanier's animus was not only against Wise, but against Reform in general. He began by creating a compact party in Albany, by cementing into an alliance all those who disliked Wise or disapproved of his religious direction. The primary purpose of this group, Wise asserted, was to undo all that had been done, to cancel all his reforms and to return to complete ritual and credal conformity. Obviously this could not be achieved with Wise in the pulpit, with his strong allies in the community and with his indomitable and forthright personality in action. Hence it must have been agreed to remove Wise from office and to silence him forever so far as Albany was concerned. Spanier had, too, Wise wrote, a brother-in-law in Charleston, from whom he had had a detailed—and perhaps one-sided—account of the famous debate between Raphall and Poznanski and of its *dénouement* when Raphall interrogated Wise.[5]

Petty annoyances were the first intimations of what was to come. Wise complained to the president about conduct on the part of the *Hazan* unbecoming to his office. It was certainly Wise's conviction that thereupon the *Hazan* would be discharged. Instead Spanier contented himself with a mild reprimand. The *Hazan*, according to Wise, had been frequenting saloons. Perhaps he had been misled by bad companions. Wise wanted him removed at least until he could and would mend his ways. After Spanier's reprimand nothing changed, and the *Hazan* comported himself as before.[6]

At Confirmation on *Shabuoth* Wise had had the boys and girls recite a confession of faith. This was a formulation of what Wise regarded as the essential doctrines of Judaism. Spanier disliked this, regarded it as heterodox, and informed Wise of his distaste and opposition.[7]

There was a letter in the *Asmonean*, signed "Israelite," attacking Wise; and another by a Rev. A. Rice of Baltimore (an orthodox rabbi). On May 3, 1850 Wise published a reply—also in the *Asmonean*—treating Rice with patent contempt. Attacks continued in the *Occident* too, all concentrated upon Wise's replies to Raphall's categorical questions in Charleston.[8]

The following Sabbath, Wise came to his synagogue to find his "regalia" (his cap and gown, and probably his *Tallis*, his prayer-shawl) gone. He preached in "mufti." This was a petty and scurvy trick.[9]

Then followed what Wise himself regarded as one of the central episodes of the whole sorry history. From many sources it is clear that Wise thought that this incident was the sufficient cause of what came after. Nor is his opinion without contemporary backing, for one of the editorials in the *Occident*, to which we shall come later, seemed to bear him out. Wise was then, and remained throughout his career, a strong advocate of and worker for the sanctity of the Sabbath. He had had the congregation adopt a rule that especially no member of the Board of the congregation might desecrate it by working, or by keeping his place of business open. One of the Board-members defied this rule and opened his store. Isaac M. Wise heard of it, went to him personally and begged him to put an end to this violation, not only for himself, but because it was setting the community a bad example. The Board-member refused to listen to him and informed Wise stubbornly of his intention to continue to do as he had been doing. Wise asked him to resign from the Board. This may have been going beyond Wise's rights and privileges, but it is understandable under the emotional stress of the interview. He received a curt, negative answer. Discerning no other recourse Wise then proposed to ventilate the whole matter from the pulpit. Obviously this was not the first time he had threatened to take or had taken similar action, as the documents indicate unmistakably. And certainly this was no violation of Jewish precedent. Historically the synagogue was the place for just such ethical reproof, for appeals not only by the rabbi, but by any layman who might wish to rise and speak.

When Wise's purpose became known, he received a message "from the orthodox group," he wrote, signed by Spanier and delivered by the *Shammash*. This constituted an official command not to mention the subject in the pulpit. Wise retorted *viva voce* that he would not be deterred. When the time for the service came, the *Parnass* rose in the pulpit and warned Wise not to speak. Wise paid no attention to this piece of effrontery and began to speak in a loud voice, drowning Spanier out. Whereupon Spanier and some of his adherents rose and walked out of the synagogue. One must try here to imagine the bustle of whispering and excitement in the midst of which all this must have happened.[10]

But the real crisis toward which all this had been tending came in July 1850. At the instance of Spanier two sets of charges were preferred against Wise. The first asserted that Wise had denied the doctrines of resurrection and the coming of the Messiah. Hence he had demonstrated himself to be an "apostate." The second petition contained six charges: that in a sermon Wise had declared Hebrew to be a dead language, and ceremonies like the laying of *Tephillim* and the wearing of *Tsitsis* superfluous and unnecessary; that Wise had discarded old and beautiful prayers and replaced them with new-fangled and un-Jewish ones; that it could be inferred from his willingness to accept the pulpit in Charleston that he stood for Reform, which connoted—according to the document—that "he can be a Jew no longer"; that he had been seen writing on *Rosh Ha'shono* in the Odd Fellows' Lodge; that he had been observed on the Sabbath swinging himself in the Mineral Spring Garden; that in public he had ridiculed the *Mikveh* (the orthodox ritual bath for women). All this is to be found in the History of Beth Emeth Congregation of Albany. These charges were signed by twelve members of the congregation who petitioned the Board to investigate them and, if they were found to be true, to dismiss Wise.[11]

The charges mingle serious and ludicrous matters and testify to the *naïveté* of some of their signers. They remind forcefully of similar indictments brought against the orthodoxy of rabbis in that period. A specimen from the history of the congregation in Cincinnati which Wise was to serve from 1854 onward may be read with profit.[12]

A copy of these charges was placed in Isaac M. Wise's hands and he was asked to submit his "defense in writing," to be given to the president of the congregation not later than July 14 at ten in the morning!

Wise did not delay until that date. He sent a reply on July 12. In it he informed the president and the Board that he was aware of no law, no reasonable provision, that required a man to defend himself in writing. He stood upon his right to be confronted by his accusers in person and to defend himself orally in their presence, and with the possibility of displaying the truth or untruth of these indictments. He asked that a time and place for such a hearing be fixed.[13]

A meeting was held, but certainly not of the kind Wise had asked. No notice was given of it. It was held on July 24 and was attended by a bare majority of the members of the Board. The meeting was a long and tumultuous one. The charges were read and elaborated upon by Spanier. Wise was given no chance of defending himself. A resolution was introduced that Wise's salary for July should not be paid until a general congregational meeting should decide whether he was to continue as rabbi or not. Usually the congregational annual meeting was held the night after the second day of *Rosh Ha-shono*. In this proposal the meeting was to be advanced to September 5, two days before the Holy Day, and for reasons which the sequel will make clear.[14]

The news of this meeting, and of the plan to be followed, spread like wildfire through the community. Spanier called upon Wise to resign, though why he should have thought this necessary after he had been a party to deposing Wise with or without his consent, it is difficult to perceive. Some of Wise's friends wanted to bring an action in the police-court against Spanier for disturbing the services at the time of Wise's public reprimand of a Board-member. But Wise wanted at all costs to keep this out of non-Jewish hands, and therefore attempted to dissuade them.[15]

Another harassment that added to Wise's worries—an action

doubtless fomented by the president and his friends—was that the parents of children at his school, who belonged to the *Parnass*'s group, stopped paying tuition-fees, though the children went right on attending school. A few of Wise's friends suggested that peace-negotiations be attempted, that the opposing sides should sit down together and try to adjust their differences. This did not prove possible. Wise wrote that he continued in all his duties, not neglecting a single one. But everything conduced to show that the air was growing darker and thicker, and that the outbreak of the final storm could not long be delayed.[16]

Wise contended later that Spanier was receiving many letters from New York, Philadelphia and other communities. This Wise heard from an official at the Albany post office. Nor was the president's correspondence limited to the United States. The conflict, the news of which was being spread by the *Occident* and the *Asmonean*, was arousing much interest and partisanship abroad too. Spanier had letters from London and from Hamburg. Wise said that he saw the addresses, the stamps, and the seals.[17]

It should also be noted here that Wise had regarded the charges made against him—where they had to do with specific actions rather than with opinions—as completely and patently ludicrous. He had never said anything against the Hebrew language that would have lent color to the silly charge quoted. He had never of course mocked at religion, and the petty parts about "writing" and "swinging" he did not deign to dignify with a reply. He paid the *Hazan* and dismissed him, though whether he had the right to do this we do not know. In his reply to the president he added these words: "Who appointed thee prince and judge?" (Exodus, chapter 2, verse 14.)[18]

A meeting of the five members of the Board was held, at what date the record does not inform us. All members were present. Spanier asked satisfaction for Wise's insults, perhaps especially the last pointed, impertinent verse from Exodus. He demanded that Wise be suspended until the matter could be settled. A vote was taken. Only one member of the Board voted with Spanier, and three against him. The vice-president moved that the charges against Wise be repudiated and not entered upon the minutes. This was carried by a vote of three to two.[19] Wise contended that after this defeat Spanier would probably have resigned and matters might have blown over, had it not been for two things: One, which Wise recounted, is nearly unintelligible. Here are his words:

> Some young people hired a cart with a mule, and placed it in

front of the synagogue for the use of the president. Upon his coming out of the meeting, the driver invited him to take a seat in the cart.

The only sense that can be made of this is that it was intended as an insult, as a somewhat childish jest, to bring ridicule upon Spanier; the mule may have been meant as a symbol for his stupidity and obstinacy. The second incident was another "bull of excommunication," which appeared in the *Asmonean* the following Friday. This leveled against Wise the awesome charge—for that time—of being a "deist," and again asked for his "deposition."[20]

The summer was upon the community. Not very much was happening, but there was no visible improvement of feeling. With the approach of the *Yomim Noro'im*, the fall Holy Days, Wise himself knew that hostilities would be resumed and perhaps arrive at an arbitrament of arms.[21]

Two days before *Rosh Ha-shono*, and in defiance of the constitutional provision for annual meetings of the congregation, Spanier convoked such an assembly. No notices were sent in advance to members and no specific reasons were given. But the word passed about swiftly that there would be trouble. And, after all, this had been the chief topic of conversation in Albany for months.[22]

The meeting was packed. Almost every member of the congregation was in attendance. Spanier opened the meeting and went over the same charges that had been sent to Wise in writing. Then the entire question was thrown open for debate. It is to be deplored that we do not possess any record of this discussion. It would be intensely interesting in many ways, both as to issues and attitudes, and as to the judgment about Isaac M. Wise in the minds of those for him and against him. The discussion lasted from three in the afternoon until eleven o'clock at night, eight long hours. Neither side would yield. Spanier refused to put a motion for adjournment. The vice-president, Joseph Sporberg, rose and put the motion in place of the president. This, Spanier argued, was not according to parliamentary law. The majority of the members left. A minority remained and went on with the meeting. First they discharged the *Shammash*, because he was regarded as a friend and adherent of Wise; then they voted to sustain the charges against Wise, to depose him and not to pay his back-salary.[23]

Wise's friends were outraged. They declared that they would not brook this high-handed and illegal action. They held a caucus among themselves and decided to have recourse to the law. The case was taken to the Attorney General of the State of New York, who decided that—in spite of the above-mentioned action by a minority-meeting—Isaac M. Wise must appear in the synagogue at the usual hour for services and in his official garb. If any violence was attempted against him, he was to withdraw and either to call the police or to institute suit. This is in Wise's account and it reads convincingly. The reason for this counsel was probably that no legal action would be possible until some overt and actionable offense would have been committed.[24]

A copy of the resolutions adopted at the rump meeting was sent to Wise. He answered at once, notifying the president that in his opinion the action taken was illegal and that he would remain in office and continue to perform his duties. At this point Wise called attention to the fact that all this was taking place only five months after the congregation, unanimously, had used every possible means to keep him in Albany, when he had been elected in Charleston and had indicated his acceptance of the new post.[25]

The stage had been set. The actors had conned their parts. Wild emotions were arrayed in hearts and perhaps in hands. Yet it is still hard, at this remove of time, to imagine the tension that had been engendered, the unrestrained violence of partisanship. But by this time Wise himself knew it. There was some doubt as to whether there would be trouble at the services. Wise entered the synagogue on *Rosh Ha-shono* morning. He found his usual seat on the pulpit occupied by a friend of Spanier, who had been instructed to preempt it ahead of time. Wise took a seat in the body of the hall among the members of the congregation not far from the Ark. As the Attorney General had counseled, he was clad in full regalia. From here on it would be well to let him describe what ensued in his own words:

> Excitement ruled the hour. Everything was quiet as the grave. Finally the choir sings Sulzer's great *En Komocho* ("There is none like unto Thee!"). At the conclusion of the song I step before the Ark in order to take out the scrolls of the law as usual, and to offer prayer. Spanier steps in my way, and, without saying a word, smites me with his fist so that my cap falls from my head. This was the terrible signal for an uproar the like of which I have never experienced. The people acted like furies. It was as though the synagogue had suddenly burst forth into a flaming conflagration. The Poles and Hungarians, who thought only of me, struck out like wild men. The young people jumped down from the choir-gallery to protect me, and had to fight their way through the surging crowd. Within two minutes the whole assembly was a struggling mass. The sheriff and his posse, who

> were summoned, were belabored and forced out until finally the whole assembly surged out of the house into Herkimer Street. "Louis Spanier," said I to him, "there is the law to which I can appeal." "I have a hundred thousand dollars more than you. I do not fear the law. I will ruin you." I finally reached home, bowed with pain and inexpressible grief. The constable came and arrested me as the ringleader of a rebellious mob at a public service. Naturally, this had all been arranged beforehand; for this constable who arrested me was the gruffest and roughest in the city. He seized me by the coat, and thus led me to the police station through the streets of Albany. Upon our arrival there, the whole rabble was present in order to feast their eyes on the sight of their rabbi appearing before court on New Year's Day; but their hopes were disappointed, for the police judge went into an adjoining room and received me there. My friends had informed him of what had taken place, and he dismissed me on my word of honor. . . . Who can describe that terrible day? Not I! It was agonizing, hellish torture. This victory of orthodoxy proved its grave wherein it was buried.[26]

It will be well to insert, as we go along, some of the sources of the time. The *Albany Evening Atlas* of September 7, 1850, had an article under the heading: "Great Excitement in the Jewish Church." The important parts of this read:

> During the last two or three days the members of the Hebrew Congregation worshiping in Fulton Street have been in great excitement. It seems that they are not all united in love for the Rev. Dr. Wise, their spiritual adviser, and one portion have labored with great zeal to remove him from his pastoral station; while the other portion have been equally zealous in maintaining him in his position.
>
> On Thursday, it seems, an election was held to test the question, when, we understand, there were other feelings than those of brotherly love strongly manifested. This morning, being the Jewish Sabbath, the congregation assembled early, when a strife arose between the two sections as to whether the Rev. Mr. Wise should, or should not, officiate. It seems that as soon as the attempt was made by Dr. Wise to conduct the ceremonies, a general *mêlée* commenced. Argument, persuasion, and conciliation were dispensed with and angry words, threatenings, and even blows were resorted to, and several severe assaults were committed.
>
> The peace of that portion of the city became so alarmingly disturbed, that it became necessary, for the safety of the public, and for the belligerents themselves, to call in the interposition of the police authorities. Sheriff Beardsley repaired promptly

> to the spot, accompanied by a strong force, and soon cleared the synagogue of both parties, locked the doors and took the keys in his possession. This had the desired effect, and the riot and disturbance then terminated.
>
> Several of those who were in the *mêlée* soon afterwards applied to the police for warrants, charging each other with assault and battery. They will have a hearing probably on Monday, if they do not, previous to that time, reconcile matters among themselves, which we hope they may do.

And on Monday, September 9, the same journal contained this paragraph:

> We were misinformed as to the location of the Synagogue in which the Hebrew brethren had their disturbance on Saturday. It occurred at the one in Herkimer and not in Fulton Street, as we were then informed.[27]

In its main outlines this is not incorrect reporting, nor could it have been expected to describe the details, or to assign blame.

Numerous lawsuits grew out of this occasion. Most of them were dismissed. Wise accused Spanier of assault and battery. This did not come up for trial until the following May, 1851. One of the biographies contends that the suit would probably not have been pressed, had not Spanier boasted, as Wise narrated, that he was above the law and that he would ruin Wise. The *Occident* of June, 1851, contained the account of the trial in the mayor's court of May 17 of that year. The Court held that Isaac. M. Wise was doing his bounden duty in preaching on *Rosh Ha-shono,* that only a minority of the congregation had voted to cancel the contract with the rabbi, that this latter action had therefore no legal standing, and that Spanier had no legal or moral right to strike Wise or to interfere with him in the conduct of his duties. It went on:

> That the defendant committed an assault and battery on the minister in the pulpit in the presence of the congregation, and when he was told by the plaintiff that the arm of justice would reach him, he answered that he was too rich to fear the law.

The jury awarded Wise damages of $1000 and costs. These Wise never attempted to collect.[28]

It will be well to bear this factual, contemporary account in mind, in reading Spanier's statements, as we shall cite them somewhat later from the pages of the *Occident.*

On *Rosh Ha-shono* itself, after the violence and the excitement had subsided, Wise went to his home, followed by a number of his devoted friends. The next day he conducted services there, together with the choir who were his ardent adherents. His home was crowded. He preached—he tells us—words of comfort and consolation. There was not a dry eye. Had this come a year earlier, when Wise was depressed and ill, it might have killed him. But now he was well. His trip to Washington and to the South had filled him with confidence and health. He was determined not to be conquered, not to let his enemies, the enemies of all he believed right and good for Judaism, prevail. True, he was burning with fever from the motion of his blood and from the sweeping resentment and wrath that were consuming him. But this too left him after some hours.[29]

When the Holy Day, the second of *Rosh Ha-shono,* was over, Wise went as usual to his school. Nor were the children kept at home. He got to the rooms at eight in the morning. The children flocked about him. One boy delivered an improvised speech, which reflected what all felt. The children embraced him weeping. Wise told them that he would take a vacation of two weeks and kissed them goodbye.[30]

Then he went to the State Library to take counsel with his Gentile friends. One of them, Townsend, offered Wise a position as his agent, to manage his fortune for him. But Wise could not agree "to be the servant of this man's money." Chief Justice Wood said to him of his troubles: "This was necessary. Ordinary insults could not bring you to reason." Wood asked him what he intended to do and advised him to take his legal examination at once, be admitted to the Bar and become Wood's partner. They went to court, appeared before the judges, who said the examination would be only *pro forma.* But final action was postponed until Amos Dean would return to the city. Wise was surrounded by lawyers—he said—who greeted him as their colleague. They left the court and had luncheon and drinks together. There were about twenty in the company and everyone was very cheerful. Wise's wife could not understand his apparent resilience and asked him: "Has the prophet Elijah met you anywhere?" Wise told her that in a free country not even Elijah is needed. She and he assured one another of their trust in God, and in spite of everything they felt happy and uplifted. Wise went alone into his study, where the exultation passed and he was alone with his difficulties. Should he abandon the struggle and leave the ministry? He turned to the deepest sources of his strength and prayed. A voice told him, he related, that he must not "prove false to his holy mission."[31]

The day, however, was not to end with these meditations and resolves. Between eight and nine o'clock in the evening a friend appeared and asked Wise to go with him to a meeting. A number of his friends had come together. Some of the most prominent and the best-spirited members of the congregation were there. The vice-president, Joseph Sporberg, was in the chair, the man who had acted with courage and decision at the congregational general meeting. There was an air of deep earnestness. Wise was told that those who were there had decided that they could no longer remain members of Beth El, that they had resolved unanimously to launch a new congregation—which Wise himself named *Anshe Emeth*, "Men of Truth," on the spur of the moment—on condition that Wise would go along with them. They wished to take steps at once to secure a temporary place of worship, and later either to acquire property and build, or perhaps to remodel a church. Twenty-six of them would undertake these tasks at once. They would also come to an understanding with Beth El. Wise was told that his position in the new congregation, if he would agree to go along, would be as he wished, and that all litigation—except the resolve to bring Spanier to justice—would be avoided. Clearly this was the parting of the ways, suddenly and decisively! Wise was deeply moved, but for a brief time vacillated. He found himself unable to reply at once. One of his friends—probably Dr. Lewi—spoke warmly and sincerely, telling him that they thought they understood his plans and purposes, that they would follow them, and that they regarded him as the "bearer of a new idea." Not only their lives and the lives of their children, but the cause of Judaism, were in the balance. Wise's doubts dissolved "like soap bubbles" he wrote. The very next day Anshe Emeth was incorporated.[32]

Before we go on to the next period in Wise's ministry in Albany, the second, we must append some of the material that is to be found in the pages of the *Occident*, material that may in some part be used as a check on what has gone before in these pages. This is well worth doing, not only because the documents are interesting in themselves, but because they will dispose of the charge that, since most of the facts have been taken from Wise's own account, they may be *ex parte*, not devoid of partisanship, of memory influenced by his own personal point of view, his eagerness to present himself in the best of lights.

In the *Occident* of the fall of 1850 there is a lengthy article entitled "Dr. Wise and His Congregation." Leeser wrote that matters of vital concern in relation to the doctrines of "our faith" were involved. Therefore Leeser had been asked by the president of Beth El, Louis Spanier, to make the facts in the case public. Leeser was not without hope that this:

> may induce our learned correspondent (Wise) to look into the matter more deeply, and to endeavor to trace the glorious doctrines of the coming of the Messiah and the resurrection of the dead to the sacred source whence he has drawn the ideas concerning the good of God and the immortality of the human soul, which we lay before our readers in the present number.

Leeser goes on:

> Dr. Wise, in an unfortunate moment, in the ardour, perhaps, of a new position as a candidate for the ministry of a congregation, some members and the minister of which were supposed unwillingly to receive our creed as it stood and yet stands, was hurried away to answer "No" to a question put to the minister referred to by a learned divine who maintained the side of the *correct faith* [italics in the original]. Would there be any disgrace in Dr. Wise acknowledging in calmer moments that he was mistaken?

Leeser went on to contend that such new doctrines—of repudiation and change—could lead only to disunity and estrangement. Reform like this had always brought strife in its train. He resented Dr. Wise's claim that he—Wise—had had to endure "persecution" at the hands of the *Occident*. Leeser once again offered to Wise the pages of the *Occident* to present his own side of the case. Others might indulge in persecution or in personal defamation. Not he! But Wise had already written something of his own side in the pages of the *Asmonean* and it would be ridiculous for the *Occident* to be silent.[33]

From this it is clear that Leeser regarded the Charleston affair as the nub of the controversy in Albany.

The same issue contained a letter from the hand of Louis Spanier, who was perhaps finding it necessary to present his own plea. Leeser wrote:

> Differences in the congregation threaten to affect alike its character and well-being, and he (Spanier) is forced to make public the subjoined document throughout these United States, whether a man who denies two fundamental articles of the Jewish faith is a fit or proper person to hold the office of Rabbi and preacher in a Jewish congregation.

Then followed a statement, drawn up at Albany on July 22, 1850.

It began with a kind of affidavit. The undersigned were present at the public controversy (this refers to Charleston) between Raphall and Poznanski, where Raphall propounded

> these two questions to the meeting. The first was: 'Do you believe in the coming of the Messiah?' To which question the Rev. Dr. Wise of Albany, who was present, answered foremostly in a loud and defiant voice, 'NO!' The second question was, 'Do you believe in the resurrection of the dead?' The Reverend Dr. Wise was again heard by us to say in a loud and distinct voice 'NO!' Signed by Samuel Hart, Senator, President of Congregation Sheayreet Israel; Jacob Rosenfeld, Minister of the same congregation, and S. Valentino, Secretary and Treasurer.

This account furnished some interesting variants—that Raphall's question was not directed only to Wise but to the entire audience, and if it is true, that Wise chose to shout his own answers. How probable this was we leave to the reader to decide for himself. Spanier's purpose—patently—was to prove Wise guilty of heresy and to drive this in to the hilt with the account of witnesses.[34]

In the same issue Leeser continued to the effect that he has and has had a high regard for Isaac M. Wise, but that he cannot help condemning his views. The Albany congregation is deeply divided between orthodoxy and reform. Wise's friends insist that Spanier and others bear:

> personal ill-will to Dr. Wise, not because he is a reformer, but because he boldly reproved the gross conduct of some men, whom he has thus provoked, and Mr. Spanier wishing the office vacated for some relative of his own. . . .

It would have been far better—wrote Leeser—if Wise had been able to assert that the charges against him on the score of his religious views were untrue. The action of the Albany congregation, immediately after Wise's return from Charleston, proved their deep and genuine attachment to him:

> When, now, in the face of this, a conspiracy is hatched against the rabbi, for such is Dr. Wise to his flock, because he has in the lawful exercise of his authority prohibited the people from eating of the killing of the former *Shochet* [ritual butcher—this is a new element in the picture!], whom he had suspended for causes which he deems sufficient, in which, to confess the truth, if we are correctly informed, we entirely coincide with him; when he is dragged before a court of law on a suit for damages for doing his duty in the premises boldly and fearlessly; we say that those who have been active in such procedures deserve the con-

> demnation of all right-thinking Israelites; for these acts cannot be justified by any plea of heterodoxy, for that must stand on its own ground. If, in addition, it be true, as reported to us, that a man in authority attempted to stop Dr. Wise in his functions, by merely informing him that he had been suspended, and then to prevent him from delivering a sermon as is his custom, we must unhesitatingly pronounce our utter abhorrence of such unauthorized acts. The minister, whatever he be, is not a hired servant to be dismissed at a moment's warning, to be browbeaten and ordered about by the civil officers of the congregation. What business has a President, in a common-sense view, with the pulpit or the reading-desk?

Leeser continued by saying forthrightly that no charges of theological error on Wise's part could condone outrages like these. The very worst had been the appeal to the law of the land. And the court, to our shame, asked: "Is it customary with the Jews to abuse their ministers in such a manner?" But, thank God, this degrading course is not general.[35]

Other charges against Wise, of a trivial nature, and chiefly gossip, follow. It is not worthwhile reviewing these. Leeser then went on to a long disquisition to prove that the concepts of a personal Messiah and of resurrection stem from the Bible itself. It might seem to some venturesome for him to attempt this, but he would try to prove the ancient lineage of these doctrines "against the whole school of neologists." He promised however once again to give space to Wise for his reply.

Leeser—a thoroughly decent man—added that he did not want to be accused—as by some he had been—of helping destroy "one of the few men of intellect of our nation in this country." This he feared some might think he had tried to do by publishing Spanier's letter and by the remainder of his article. Had the matter been purely personal, he would not have given space to it in the *Occident.* But this was in essence doctrinal, and it was important that clear and right opinion should prevail. He trusted too that through discussion the truth would appear.[36]

This was not the end of the matter in the *Occident.* In the same year and under the heading "The Beth El Congregation of Albany" Leeser recorded that he had been waited upon by Spanier, who had come especially to reply to the charge that all of his actions in Albany had derived from his desire to put a relative of his own into the Albany pulpit. Spanier asserted that those of his kin "who happen to be rabbis" already occupied better pulpits (in Hanover and in London). Spanier's way of putting what happened on the pulpit on *Rosh Ha-shono* differed quite naturally from Wise's account. Spanier claimed that he had "interrupted" Wise, when the latter "had attempted to preach." This action, Spanier said, was "owing to the fear he had that it would create unpleasant scenes in case Dr. Wise should carry out his threat, addressed to a member of the Board, to allude to him in his sermon relative to his (the trustee's) violation of the Sabbath." This refers, of course, not to *Rosh Ha-shono*, when Spanier did quite a bit more than "interrupt." It has to do with Wise's other contention, that Spanier had prevented Wise from carrying out what he conceived to be his duty in public reproof for Sabbath-violation. It is an interesting and valuable admission. Spanier contended that Wise had been in the wrong in the suspension of the *Shochet*. Spanier appended the assertion that Wise had preached a sermon on July 1, of that summer, "in which, as people understood him, he spoke against the propriety of observing the ceremonies as opposed to the devotion of our approaching in spirit to God." This reads more than a little obscurely, and, if it means what it seems to say, is completely absurd as a charge. A number of persons, Spanier continued, had advocated formal impeachment. Wise had refused to answer the charges in writing. This had of course been his right. It is not easy to determine whether what follows is still Spanier's statement, or Leeser's comment:

> Thus affairs stood until the 5th of September, when Dr. Wise was deposed in his absence by a majority of votes at a regular meeting of the congregation, in consequence of which he was notified that his contract was declared void and that he could not be allowed to officiate any longer.

This Dr. Wise and his friends regarded as illegal, and there followed on the New Year the terrible scene of which we know. Spanier made the sheriff turn the people out of the house of worship. On *Succoth* the key was returned and the synagogue reopened, but only those who had not seceded together with Wise attended services. Since that time there have been two separate congregations, and Wise was given eight hundred dollars by Beth El "for his past services." All lawsuits have been dropped by both parties (this is of course not quite correct). Things would not have gone to such lengths:

> . . . if there had been laws to define the duties and privileges of the minister, and if there had been a *central board of reference* [italics in the original] for all American congregations.

The latter part is evidently all Leeser's.[37]

The last record that should be added comes from the *American Israelite* of nine years later. It appears to have been a reply to an editorial in the *Occident* attacking Wise for his opposition to the observance of a second day of the holidays:

> . . . we have to remark that our contemporary of the *Occident* ought to be well aware, that in 1846, when we arrived in Albany, N.Y., two of our members had their business houses closed on the Sabbath; in 1847 not one of our members had his store open on the Sabbath, and those very same men do now as they did then. He ought to know that the Albany quarrel in 1850 was started by the orthodox *Parnass* whose organ and defender the *Occident* was, because a Trustee of the congregation opened his business on a Sabbath and we notified him either to keep his Sabbath or to resign his office in the Congregation, or we must take public notice of it. The trustee went to the thickly orthodox *Parnass,* showed him our notice, said he feared we would mention it in our next sermon, and the orthodox *Parnass* came to the Synagogue next Sabbath, sent the Sexton to prohibit us to preach. We took no notice of it, commenced to preach in good time, the orthodox *Parnass* prohibited again, spoke, threatened, etc., and not being heard he and the orthodox party left the Synagogue. The matter was brought before the police judge; the orthodox *Parnass* was reprimanded, his wrath was kindled and the consequences were the rupture and division of that congregation in the fall of 1850 (the above happened about midsummer).[38]

Thus, after the passage of some years, nine, to be exact, Wise had become certain that the chief cause of the disgraceful actions of Spanier and of the disruption of the congregation lay in Wise's valiant attempt to secure Sabbath observance, and to the fact that he was no "respecter of persons." But this is surely a distortion. It cannot be entirely incorrect, nor can it be only an excuse thought up after the first clash, that Spanier and some of his sympathizers were, or believed themselves to be, outraged by Wise's supposed repudiation of essential Jewish doctrines. While Spanier had admitted that he had tried to prevent Wise from preaching against the trustee in question, Spanier had contended also that it was primarily what Wise was reported to have said in Charleston—for which he supplied the statement of witnesses—that was responsible for the final fracas and disintegration. To judge from the record the probability is that behind all these causes and events lay months of growing discord, of deep-seated dissatisfaction. This was the era when German-Jewish congregations were sharply divided in their attitude toward Reform. The record of many others will reveal a similar situation, though no other—as far as we know—broke into such open and disastrous violence.

Thus ended the first period of Wise's incumbency in Albany. These had been four years of swiftly accumulated experience in regard to America; in the extent and clarity of Wise's perceptions concerning the status and future of American Judaism; and in Wise's knowledge of himself. They were still years of vacillation as to his own course in life, for there is every evidence that he was not uninfluenced by some of his friends who were urging him to adopt the profession of teaching or of the law. His inner adjustment was testified to by his emergence from psychogenic ill-health into the magnificent vigor and energy he displayed thereafter. Certainly in these years he began to see the direction in which his own life's work would lie, to bring into being a Judaism indigenous to America, calculated in its universalism to appeal to all reasonable men, but still true to the great principles of its own heritage. He became convinced that this could be done only by cooperative labor, by good-will among various groups, and by the creation of institutions having to do with education, rabbinical leadership, defense, liturgy, etc.

It should however be borne in mind constantly that Wise's own point of view, at which in its main outlines he arrived during these four years, was far from being that usually ascribed to Reform by its opponents, or to Wise himself by those who would misrepresent him out of prejudice. Only some of the peripheral aspects of his own system of belief have become evident thus far in these pages, aspects which had to do with decorum, aesthetic appropriateness in the synagogue, the place of women, the education of children, and the discarding of certain articles of belief which had already been repudiated by rabbinical conferences in Germany. In his "The Reform Movement in Judaism" Philipson gives an extended résumé of the discussions of most of these very points at the Frankfort Conference of 1845, which—as we have seen—Wise attended.[39] For those interested in the exact course of the thinking of various leaders, both pro and con, it would be thoroughly worth-while to review these pages. It was there that Wise had probably arrived at his own point of view, and to this he was consistently faithful. To the remainder of his theology—not to its separate features but to its central form and concept—we shall come in the third section of this book, especially when we consider his specific writings in the field of Jewish Theology on the contrasts between Judaism and Christianity, as he conceived them, and so forth.

There is evidence that this controversy in Albany and the accounts of it in the *Occident* and the *Asmonean* carried Wise's name all over the American Jewish community. From then on his was the name in the forefront in regard to the adaptation of Judaism to the United States. The events of the years that followed and of his activities in them bear this out in every detail.

In conning over the record of these four decisive years, it is hard to bear firmly in mind that Wise was then quite a young man. He came to Albany when he was twenty-seven years old, and this struggle with Spanier and his adherents took place when Wise was only thirty-one. His impetuosity—a personal quality even when he was older—accounts for many things. To leave one's homeland, to pull oneself and one's family out by the roots, to make the long and difficult journey to the New World, to find oneself amidst strange surroundings and unknown men and women, to be in doubt for a space whether one could continue as a rabbi or not, to launch oneself into a new community, to acclimatize one's life to America, absorb its spirit—then so distraught with the gathering issues of slavery—, to strive to pursue the course at least a fraction of which one had decided upon in Radnitz, at Frankfort and in the early days in New York, to find here in America too the stubbornness, what seemed to him the utter lack of realism and vision of the "orthodox": all this crowded into these four years and all of this conduced toward their climax. Out of them Wise emerged much more mature as a man, surer of himself and of his opinions and purposes. This we shall discover more and more unmistakably as we proceed!

13

Calm in Albany, Second Period

WISE MUST HAVE BEEN LEFT VERY WEARY AND DEPRESSED AFTER the final act at Beth El in the fall of 1850. Though his health had improved materially after his visit to Washington in the early months of that year, and despite his own conviction that he had followed the only possible way and that the violence and the bitterness were to be ascribed to his opponents alone and to their reactionism and intransigence, it is obvious from many things that he was discouraged and down-hearted. Much later on, looking backward over his shoulder at this period, he wrote that circumstances had conduced to keep him a "preacher, teacher and writer," that it had not been easy for him to limit himself to Jewish problems, "with my universal and cosmic outlook," but that he could not escape the duty of trying to found a liberal movement in Judaism and to win adherents for what he calls here "The Science of Judaism." Constantly in the background were his Gentile friends who were telling him what a serious mistake it was for him to continue in the ministry and with the new congregation. But his certainty of the rightness—for him—of his course, grew with the days. He was deeply touched by the loyalty of those who had acted so decisively and so affirmatively after *Rosh Ha-shono* and he felt it his high duty to work among this congenial and loyal group of men and women.[1]

A place for worship was speedily found, on the corner of Lydius (now Madison) Ave. and South Pearl Street, on the upper floor.[2] Debate about "Albany" was still stirring up febrile interest all over the country among Jews. Wise himself came to feel—again in later years—that it had proved to be a great victory for Reform Judaism:

> The heretic rabbi had become a sort of martyr and gained in the sympathy of the community, which in fact was the grain [a curious word! is it "*gravamen*?"] of the cause much more than the person.[3]

His friends feared however that his health might again have been impaired. They prevailed upon him to go away for a month, to travel and to collect funds for the new congregation. This was not an unusual procedure in those days, nor did it cease to be a practice for many decades after this.[4]

On his journey from Albany to New York Wise traveled with Horace Greeley and recounted to him the story of his troubles. Greeley proved thoroughly sympathetic and inquired of Wise why he had not answered his opponents in print. Wise replied that he possessed no organ in which this might be done. The *Occident*—he said—was strongly and hostilely orthodox and the new *Asmonean* was also espousing the cause of the same "Party." Wise felt keenly that he had no place in which to set forth the deeper reasons, the impersonal ones, that had prompted his course of action, to enter his plea on the broader levels of scholarship, history, and need. Most generously Greeley offered him the columns of the *New York Tribune*. This offer Wise accepted gratefully, but did not take advantage of until later on. Greeley himself did publish an account of his conversation with Wise and of his intense interest in it.[5]

Wise had the hope that on his trip he would find Jews, especially leaders, who would go along with his own standpoint and who would build up a solid foundation of support for his ideas. Some he did discover, but not many. In the main—he said—he found that he stood alone. In New York, to which he came first, he was received quite coldly. Only Lilienthal grasped his hand warmly. In the main he was denounced as a disturber of the peace. He visited Merzbacher who was then at Temple Emanu-El. Here he met a man named Lehmayer, who promised to aid him in collecting funds for Anshe Emeth in Albany. Lehmayer called on Wise the following day and they went to work. Lehmayer himself headed the list of subscribers. They got together a sum which for that time, and in spite of Wise's apprehensions, was not too bad. On the list—it is interesting to note—was the name of August Belmont with a subscription for ten dollars.[6]

The next day Wise moved on to Philadelphia. All of this was just after *Sukkoth*, 1850. Wise did not care to visit Leeser. Adler, the *Parnass* of Congregation Rodef Shalom, came to see him. Adler must have been convinced that Wise had something of great value to say, and perhaps that his own congregation was not so united in opposition to the new ideas of Reform, for he invited Wise to preach in the pulpit of Rodef Shalom the following Sabbath. Again it is worth remarking that it was the president—not the rabbi or even the *Hazan*—who invited him. Wise inquired of Adler: "Who will listen to me?" He feared he might have become so discredited that people would stay away.[7]

His fears proved baseless. Notices of the service were inserted in the daily papers. Adler received threats from the orthodox of the city, chastising him for his temerity, and threatening—says Wise—"to devour him." But apparently Adler was made of unyielding stuff and did not appear to be visibly disturbed. Gradually on the Sabbath the temple filled. There was not an empty seat. Even the aisles were crowded. Some of Wise's opponents came, at least to do him the courtesy of hearing his side of matters. Leeser, together with some of the members of his recent congregation, the Portuguese synagogue, Mikveh Israel, were also there. Wise looked about him, as he sat on the pulpit, and wondered whether they had come to listen, or to create another serious disturbance. He resolved to be "moderate and calm," but to suppress nothing of the truth he felt within himself. He preached on the "religion of humanity," and based it on the life of "our father, Abraham." He spoke for a full hour. After the service there was much handshaking and much gratulation. Even Leeser came up and clasped his hand.[8]

Here we insert Leeser's own comment upon this sermon in the *Occident*:

> Dr. Wise's style is highly figurative and ornate, perhaps too much so for an English or American audience, but to a German ear accustomed to poetical illustrations he handles his matter delightfully. We may freely say that Dr. Wise has made a favourable impression as an orator, and, if he would only be a little more energetic, that all could feel the earnestness which compels him to speak, he would no doubt reach a high eminence as a preacher among us, and he is young yet to acquire the requisite manner he now lacks.[9]

This is not ungenerous and may have been quite just, though it is not easy to imagine Wise lacking in "energy." It must also be borne in mind that ornateness was the quality of almost all public speaking in the middle of the last century—rounded periods, rhetorical flourishes and much poetical quotation. In general, this does describe Wise's style at the time quite adequately.

After the service Adler took Wise to his home. Both of them were happy. The venturesome experiment had come off without untoward incident. Adler was especially delighted, for it was his hope that his congregation would move steadily toward Reform. Five years later this end was achieved. Between them Adler and Wise decided that Wise was to return to Philadelphia two weeks later, this time to collect money for his own congregation in Albany. Adler had tickets prepared for this second occasion, which would attempt to capitalize on the splendid impression Wise had made at the first.[10]

In his *Reminiscences* Wise found it interesting to note that, when he was in Philadelphia in this fall, it was remarkable that there was not one Jewish preacher in the pulpit in the entire city. Leeser had lost his position, probably as a result of his frequent brushes with the *Parnass*. In the recent past Rodef Shalom had had in the pulpit "a tramp named Kohn," who fell in love with a Gentile, eloped with her and apostatized. The community was disgusted with rabbis. Yet Wise found much loyal Jewishness there. Only a learned, devoted and effective leader was needed in order to speed progress toward Reform and toward the revival and strengthening of Jewish life.[11]

Wise's next stop was Baltimore on the Wednesday of that week. Two of the rabbis, Guenzberg and Hochheimer, his fellow-countrymen, gave him a most cordial reception. Also Braun, who was rabbi of Congregation Har Sinai, came to see him. This latter congregation was the second Reform congregation in the country, the first actually organized for that specific purpose, in April, 1842. It was to be expected, therefore, that they would sympathize with Wise and be eager to hear him. He was invited to preach in the pulpit of Har Sinai the following Saturday morning and again the afternoon of the next day. This he did, setting forth "the principles of the reform movement."

> I embellished my thoughts with flowery expressions, threw bombshells into the camp of orthodoxy, and held aloft the standard of constructive reform.

On Tuesday he spoke again, appealing for funds for Albany. A wire came to him from Adler in Philadelphia, telling him that the people were very insistent upon hearing him again and asking him to return at once instead of two weeks later. This Wise replied he was unable to do. He would come later on, when he would have completed his trip by going to Washington. In Baltimore there was a rabbi, Abraham Reiss, who asked permission to preach after Wise had left the city, so that he might answer him and disprove what he had said. He wished—Wise wrote—"to make *Weiss* black." But he was refused the privilege. Shortly after this time another Reform synagogue was organized in Baltimore, and had its temple on Hanover Street (this was probably Oheb Shalom, later the "Eutaw Place Synagogue").[12]

Wise had completed his work in Baltimore and went on to Washington. There, he recounted, he found many changes since his trip in the early part of the year. Zachary Taylor had died and Millard Fillmore had become President. Daniel Webster had become Secretary of State in July, 1850. Congress was not in session and he had to deny himself the pleasure of listening to more stirring and instructive debate in the Senate. Wise sent in his card to Webster and met him in the vestibule of the Treasury Building, Webster's hand outstretched. Two strangers were also present in Webster's private office to which he took Wise, Judah P. Benjamin, who, Wise wrote —mistakenly—, was then Senator from Louisiana, and a Lieutenant Maury, an authority on "trade-winds," says Wise. Maury was in fact the famous hydrographer, authority on navigation, on winds and currents, recognized in all parts of the world as a pioneer in these fields before the Civil War. Later Maury threw in his lot with the South, invented the electric torpedo and had other colorful chapters in his remarkable career before he died in 1873 at the age of sixty-seven.[13] Judah P. Benjamin, whose name ought to be familiar to all our readers, was born in the British West Indies, reared in South Carolina and educated at Yale. Finally he followed the career of law in New Orleans. He was not elected Senator until 1852 and this part of Wise's *Reminiscences* is incorrect. Benjamin had, however, been admitted to plead before the Supreme Court in 1848 and might well have been in Washington in the fall of 1850. This we shall discuss in greater detail in a footnote. Benjamin was an ardent partisan of the South, became first Attorney General of the Confederate government and later Secretary of State. After Appomatox he fled and settled in England, where he re-entered the practice of law, had a splendid career and wrote one of the great text-books of law. In 1882 he retired to Paris and died two years later. He was a most amazingly gifted person in various fields, but certainly neither a loyal nor an observant Jew.[14]

In his *Reminiscences* Wise gave the details of his discussion with Webster and Benjamin. He contended that Webster and Maury made the "droll confession" that they were not far from being Jews, at least of Wise's kind. But Benjamin, Wise asserted, did not agree and asserted that he had no coreligionists other than Jews. It hurt Wise, he says, that, while Webster was very conversant with the Bible and could quote it readily, Benjamin had no acquaintance with a single Jewish source.[15]

Here occurred Wise's first meeting with the mysterious "Mrs. F.," whose name he was "not at liberty to give." This pseudonym, or initial, to conceal her identity, will reappear often in the later pages of this book. We have been told who the lady was, but discern no purpose in destroying the anonymity Wise wished for her.[16]

Webster had heard from Amos Dean the whole story of Wise's experiences in Albany. He congratulated Wise upon his courage and his liberalism. He said to Wise that he, Wise, had more feeling for Judaism and more willingness to serve it at great personal sacrifice than did the "ministers of our church." Wise replied that he was following a great and noble tradition, which was in the "blood of Jews," which had come to them from a long line of prophets and martyrs. Webster thought this sublime, Wise said, and was moved to tears. When they parted, Wise reported Webster to have said: "One spark of enthusiasm is worth more than a whole conflagration of reason."[17]

In the afternoon Wise called on President Fillmore—a good man, Wise says, but not a brilliant one. He found Fillmore to have an engaging personality, with the delightful informality so characteristic of American public figures at that time. The account of this interview in the *Reminiscences* deserves reproduction:

> I was introduced without further ceremony and cordially received. Fillmore inquired for his friends and acquaintances in Albany, where he had lived shortly before for several years as State Comptroller. I gave him the desired information and congratulated him on his unexpected rise to the Presidency. I asked him further if I could attend to anything for him in Albany, and was on the point of leaving. This seemed to puzzle him, and he said to me: "Washington is a costly place to linger in. If you desire anything from me, out with it at once." When I assured him that I had come for the sole purpose of congratulating him, he seemed astounded and asked me: "Do you know

> anything of the petition?" "Your Excellency, I know of no petition."
>
> He now informed me that he had received a petition from Albany, signed by Dr. Beck and others, in which he was requested to appoint me to a position in the Library of Congress and that he had provided for my entering upon the position the following New Year's Day.

Wise thanked him and refused the generous offer. He himself believed that this refusal was at least in part due to the conversation he had just had with Webster, which had buoyed him up in his belief in himself and in his cause. The President treated his refusal generously and graciously, and told him that, if he needed or wanted such a post in the future, he should come and see him.[18]

During this trip Wise paid a visit to the Patent Office. Here he was shown some of the inventions that were in process. This seemed to him an evidence of the inventive genius that flourishes under freedom. Another interesting experience was a visit in Maury's company to an astronomical observatory, where he listened to a lecture, probably by Maury—among whose accomplishments was much knowledge of the stars too—until after midnight.[19]

He was ready to return to Philadelphia now, as he had been asked by Adler to do. Here Mrs. F. comes in. She had been waiting for him at the hotel, the Willard. She told Wise that she had followed him to Baltimore from Philadelphia, where she had heard him speak, and from Baltimore to Washington. She was, wrote Wise, a respectable and happy wife and mother, who had studied painting. Her home was a temple of the arts. She had a character of tact, culture, and nobility. She returned to Philadelphia on the same train as did Wise and catechized him at some length. He himself wrote that he was "like a schoolboy in her hands." She was ten years older than he, but in her knowledge of human nature fifty years his senior. She had written a poem inspired by what she had heard from Wise and what she thought of him. This she read to him. Its essential figure of speech was one comparing him to a morning-star that announced the break of day for American Judaism. The poem predicted that he would never enjoy true happiness, for he was possessed by three "Furies," reason, intelligence and sympathy, and that he would remain forever young. This poem Wise said he kept for many years as a "sacred relic." From this distance, and to judge from his description, it must have been more than a little maudlin. But that Mrs. F. was deeply interested in him, that she followed every incident of his career, and that she was often of great help to him, all the sequel will show. It is hard to judge precisely what her relation to him was, but there is no good reason for believing that she was ever more than an Egeria to him, sometimes deeply needed and deeply heeded, and at other times, as the tenor of his account implies, a nuisance in her hovering and in her counsel.[20]

Back in Philadelphia, Wise again lectured before Rodef Shalom, on "The Origin of Reform." There was an even larger number of people present than the first time. He learned too that steps were under way to elect him rabbi of the congregation. After a lecture which he gave on Sunday he was visited by a committee of gentlemen, who informed him that they wanted to propose him for rabbi of Rodef Shalom. He listened to them, told them of his appreciation, then explained in detail how his new congregation in Albany had come into being and the reasons because of which this constituted a very special relation between him and it and induced in him an inescapable feeling of obligation. His accepting the pulpit in Philadelphia was therefore out of the question.[21]

In his Sunday lecture, tracing the genesis of Reform, he had covered a very wide span of Jewish history, beginning with Saadia Gaon and coming down to the year 1850. He had also spoken of the contributions to modern Judaism of Spinoza, using some of the studies and even the language of Moses Mendelssohn, and with especial reference to Spinoza's *Tractatus Theologico Politicus* (for which work among others Spinoza was excommunicated in Amsterdam). The next number of the *Occident* had a word of cordial praise for the clarity and scholarliness of this address. Mrs. F. was also there, when he spoke, and sent him a most flattering letter.[22]

Exactly how, when he was in Philadelphia, Wise came to meet a sea captain, we do not know. But meet him he did. The captain invited Wise to sail to New York with him. In his *Reminiscences* Wise notes that he had acquired much valuable instruction from this trip to Philadelphia and Baltimore; beyond all else that the masses of Jews in these cities were not hostile to Reform, that on the contrary they had proved quite receptive, if it were presented to them "clearly and eloquently." For himself it had meant new encouragement, a new spur to work. On board the steamer he pondered on this and on other matters.[23]

In New York his first act was again to pay a visit to his dear friend, Max Lilienthal. A certain Dr. Moritz Mayer prevailed upon Wise to join the Independent Order of B'nai Brith. At that time, he remarked, the organization seemed to him colorless and full of "tomfoolery." But little by little he perceived that it had great possibilities, and plans for its widening and deepening began to come to him. In later years he was very active in its counsels and in its labors. The files of the *Israelite* contain many accounts of the Order's conventions, plans, and point of view.[24]

A trip in those days—even a trip from Albany to Washington and back—that now would seem little more than a suburban jaunt—was a considerable venture in the middle of the nineteenth century, in point of time consumed and effort expended. Wise returned to Albany to find that all was well. Quarters had been rented for the new synagogue at the location mentioned previously. With the exception of that against Spanier for assault and battery, all suits had been settled out of court. He himself received some money from Beth El, probably in compensation for the back-salary that had been withheld. This he gave to the new congregation to aid them in purchasing property. The officers of Anshe Emeth had not been idle. Its organization and its finances were in good order and activities were in full swing. In Beth El itself all the reforms Wise had instituted had been abrogated. The orthodox were in full control and completely jubilant at what they regarded as a sweeping victory.[25]

At this time Wise organized in Albany a sewing society to make clothes for the poor. This proved to be a very popular venture and existed for a considerable time. In Albany the two congregations became the *foci* for bitterly opposed factions in the community. There was little or no contact between them. However, as a result of this silence there was peace and quietude. In Anshe Emeth itself, Wise says, there was brotherly love and cooperation upon all its tasks.[26]

Wise had not forgotten that he had had a generous invitation from Greeley to contribute articles to the *New York Tribune*. For several weeks he worked hard at these. Their purpose was to demonstrate that in America there was no future for orthodoxy as such.[27]

An interesting sidelight on this very time is in a document, a copy of which exists in the Hebrew Union College Archives, the certificate of naturalization of Isaac M. Wise. It is in fact a certified copy of the original in photostat. The certificate was issued on May 31, 1851, and the witnesses whose names are signed were: Daniel M. Prior, Edw. H. Seiberling and Geo. Reilly. It would appear from this that three of Wise's Gentile friends stood by his side when be became a citizen of the United States of America. Nor had he lost any time in enfranchising himself. The country which he had envisaged from afar, and which he had now learned to love with such ardor, was now his own.[28]

His time was taken up now with all his regular duties: conducting a school, pursuing his pastoral rounds, and preaching every week. The harmony and the liberal sympathy of his new congregation seemed to loosen his tongue. In his *Reminiscences* he wrote that he had never preached as well as he did on *Yom Kippur* in 1851. Something of the boundless gratitude he felt to God shone through. The passage that follows deserves to be reprinted here for the light it sheds on his own methods and for its instructiveness about preaching in general:

> My feelings found expression in a flow of words the like of which I have never been able to utter since. I tried to write down the sermon on the following day; but I did not succeed. The enthusiasm born of the moment can not be committed to paper later. I could retain the shadow only; the spirit had flown. The power of the living word is wrongly called the magnet of the speaker. This is not true. When the spirit rises aloft, when feelings master the heart, words are spoken or written for which the orator is not really responsible. The best productions of mouth or pen to which I have given utterance have been, not the result of careful contemplation, but the flashes of momentary inspiration. In such moments I have spoken and written thoughts which I scarcely recognized as my own in calmer moments. . . .[29]

In 1851 the *Occident* carried a paragraph about the new congregation, noting that the synagogue had formerly been a Baptist Church and that it had been bought by Anshe Emeth for $8100, "certainly a great sum for them." While the congregation had been in existence for but one year, it was said to number about eighty families, "each family occupying a pew." There were one hundred and thirty-six pews. "Our readers will easily recognize in this another reform of the Doctor's, one by no means to be commended." The building was on South Pearl Street at the head of Herkimer. The clergyman of the Baptist Church, which the congregation had purchased, had been the very young man who had spoken so fanatically against Jews in 1847. Judging from other accounts, that of the *Occident* errs on the side of caution, for the likelihood is that the church-synagogue seated one thousand people at services. The building was well furnished in all necessary ways. Some remodeling had been done to convert it into a synagogue.[30]

The "reform," to which Leeser referred, was that known as "family pews." Such pews were in the church, when Anshe Emeth took it over. Wise liked the arrangement he found. He had always disapproved of seating women in the balcony, and, as the foregoing pages show, had made some attempts to get them downstairs. The traditional method, the general discrimination against women in Judaism, appeared to imply that they were second-class citizens religiously, that it was shameful or distracting to have them seen at worship. The new system of seating, which Wise instituted, having whole families sit together, commended itself to him—and to the congregation—for two reasons: negatively, because it would at a stroke do away with what he regarded as one of the purely peripheral but ancient injustices of Jewish custom; and positively, in that it would enable families to worship together and to have the warmth of togetherness. If it was said in the Psalms: "Behold, how good and how pleasant it is for brethren to dwell together in unity," then *a fortiori* this applied even more patently and strongly to the uniting of a family in the deepest and most sacred of moments. Since then this change has become universal in Reform congregations. It has also been adopted in a not inconsiderable number of Conservative and even Orthodox synagogues.[31] Wise contended that this was one of the steps he took which brought women into fuller participation in synagogal life and that the later history of Reform Judaism proved the wisdom of the step.

The new synagogue was dedicated on October 3, 1851. The "oration" in German was delivered by Lilienthal, and that in English by Wise. The latter used for text the lovely verses from Psalm 84:

> How lovely are Thy tabernacles, O Lord of Hosts!
> My soul yearneth, yea, even pineth for the courts of the Lord;
> My heart and my flesh sing for joy unto the living God.
> Yea, the sparrow hath found a house, and the swallow a nest for
> herself,
> Where she may lay her young;
> Thine altars, O Lord of Hosts,
> My King and my God—.
> Happy are they that dwell in Thy house,
> They are ever praising Thee, Selah! (verses 1 to 5)

A most appropriate and moving text![32]

We might pause here to note that the congregation met in this building for nearly thirty-five years. In 1875 the structure was somewhat enlarged. At that time there was in the congregation an agitation for a new building, but no decision was made. In 1884 Anshe Emeth was without a rabbi. After all these years of divorce a reunion was agreed upon with Beth El. Time had served to heal the breach. A new congregation called Beth Emeth, a name which symbolized the union, was formed. This was incorporated on May 23, 1889. Isaac M. Wise dedicated a new temple for them on Lancaster, Severn and Jay Streets the same year, his own seventy-first. Almost forty years earlier he had been the rock on which Beth El had split. It must have been a great satisfaction to him to witness and to be part of the reuniting.[33]

The winter of 1851 was devoted not only to his regular duties, but also to a prolonged study of philosophy and history in the Middle Ages. Several times he had considered writing a work on this difficult period with the primary purpose of correcting the injustice done to Arabs and Jews as to their contributions to the history of human culture.[34]

The beginning of the year 1852 witnessed an event of interest and importance, especially in the light of the prejudices of that period. At least part of Wise's vigorous account of it must be reproduced here:

> In January 2, 1852, a resolution was passed in both Houses of the Legislature of the State of New York to the effect that the clergymen of the city of Albany be asked to hold a meeting to prepare a list of all the ministers stationed in the city, and submit it to the Senate, in order that chaplains for both Houses might be elected. The resolution was printed and a copy sent to every minister; hence also to me. On the following day I read to my astonishment in the evening paper that a meeting of ministers had taken place. The list that had been prepared by them was appended. It was to be submitted to the Senate on the morrow. My name was not on the list.
>
> Ye miserable hypocrites, I will teach you a lesson, mused I. I went to the clerk of the Senate, and acquainted him with the proceeding. "Very well, write a short protest, and hand it to me," said he. I wrote the protest and gave it to him. The next morning the report of the clergy accompanied by my protest, was read in the Senate chamber, and was rejected on the ground that it did not comply with the law. The ministers ought to have called a second meeting, and to have invited me to be present. Instead of that, they prepared a protest against the action of the Senate on the ground that I was not one of their number, saying that I was a Jewish rabbi and not a Christian minister. Dr. Wykoff objected, was outvoted, left the meeting, came straight to my house, and informed me of the action. The protest had to be printed; so I went to the different newspaper offices, found the document, read it through, wrote a reply, had it printed at

> once, and on the following morning the protest and my reply were lying on each desk. This caused no end of merriment. One of the senators said that I must be a prophet since I had answered a document point for point even before it had appeared. Upon the opening of the session the clerk announced the receipt of the two documents, but they were not read nor filed since the Senate did not wish to lend official notice to the protest prepared by the clergy. After this was disposed of, my friend, Senator Thayer, arose and moved that I be appointed chaplain of the Senate temporarily until the clergy should have obeyed the law. This motion was carried unanimously without debate. The clergymen made wry faces; but I was chaplain of the Senate until such a time as they would act in accordance with the law and place the name of the terrible rabbi upon the list, a step which they could not make up their minds to take for a long time. Thus I became the first Jewish chaplain of a legislative body. I held the position as long as I was in Albany.

This does not signify that Wise was the first rabbi to open a legislature with prayer. That honor belongs to a Rev. Eckman of Richmond, Va. in the Virginia Legislature in 1850. Here is the prayer which Wise gave before the Senate of the State of New York:

> Lord of Hosts, Rock of Salvation, whose unlimited power, wisdom, and love are revealed in the innumerable millions of creatures that populate the universe, whose providence, special care, and benignity is revealed in every page of the history of nations, hear our supplications, listen graciously to our petitions that we offer up unto Thee in behalf of our beloved country and her faithful legislators who have assembled again to give us laws and regulations to the promotion of liberty, prosperity, justice, and humanity. O Lord, Thou hast inspired and assisted our ancestors when they arose lion-hearted against their oppressors and bought for the warm blood of their hearts the liberty and independence of these United States. Inspire, our Father, O, inspire our legislature with the same spirit of truth and justice, with the same love of liberty and independence, with the same desire to promote happiness and prosperity among their fellow-citizens; remove prejudice, partiality, and factional endeavours from every mind; give unto them the same spirit as the venerable fathers of this republic manifested, let them be freely united in the discharge of the sacred duty to their country that she may bloom and prosper before Thee; that she may be an example of liberty, equity, and humanity; that she may be imitated by those nations that still suffer and sigh under

> the iron rod of despotism, that the citizens be united before Thee to do Thy sacred will, to proclaim Thy holy name. Blessed be the name of the Lord from sunrise to sunset, from now to evermore. Amen![35]

Wise's studies and his inclination to write began to burgeon in 1851 due to an arrangement he made with the editor of the *Occident.* In spite of past differences Leeser invited him to contribute a series of articles to his journal. In the light of his precise knowledge of Wise's religious point of view, this was perhaps foolhardy. It was bound to lead in the end to conflict and misunderstanding. It must have been done by Leeser partly out of regret for some of the things he had written in 1850, from his personal feeling of friendliness toward Wise, and also doubtless from Leeser's own essential gentleness and fairness. Wise indited a remarkable group of articles, under the general heading, "The Principles of Judaism."[36] In them he attempted to lay down the fundamentals of Judaism from the reform point of view. This proved in reality to be the germ of a future work, "The Essence of Judaism," intended as a text-book and published in Cincinnati in 1861. Later he revised this too under the title of "Judaism—Its Doctrines and Duties," and this was published in Cincinnati in 1872. The argument of these essays is primarily directed against the contentions: 1) that the Bible forbids Reform; 2) that the prophets teach the doctrines of bodily resurrection or of a personal Messiah; 3) that every Jew is obliged to believe these dogmas. Here are a few passages from Wise's arguments:

> If the expounders of the Bible teach doctrines incompatible with the laws of nature which are the works of One Eternal God, or to the experience of history, which is the realized will of the same benign Providence, I am bound to reject them in order not to be forced to doubt the authenticity of the Bible, or to suppose that Infinite Wisdom contradicts itself in the Bible, nature and history. I consider everything which is of human origin liable to mistakes. And though I have found many doctrines and opinions in the works of antiquity to which I am opposed, I nevertheless venerate these incomparable treasures for their great value as a whole. But when the Talmud comes into conflict with the facts of natural philosophy, or events as expressed in history, and their natural results, I am fearless on the side of truth, hence when the Talmud imposes upon us doctrines or observances of ceremonies which are foreign to the Bible and which infected us for many centuries with the spirit of intolerance and separation, which degraded religion into a compendium of blind and insignificant rites, which depressed the youthful

> spirit of Judaism and drove thousands from our community, or when the Talmud comes into conflict with the demands of our age, which, if listened to, will bring distraction and ruin in its train, then I am fearless on the side of reform; and if thousands of learned or not learned doctors say "The Talmud is Divine" I must a thousand times pity them that they do not look deeper into the matter, or that they lack the moral courage to speak the truth.[37]

In the February issue of the *Occident* he continued to expound the leading ideas of Judaism. In the third article he wrote about spiritual immortality as contrasted with the doctrine of bodily resurrection; and in the fifth and last in July, 1851, he reiterated much of the contention with which he had begun. He "abandons the dispute," because Leeser had expressed open hostility and disagreement:

> I can easily forgive you (the editor of the *Occident*) for the injuries you have done me, and I pity you, and I hope the day is not far distant when the *Occident* will advocate the doctrines of reform. I will remain an honest friend of Isaac Leeser, but with the editor of the *Occident* I am done. Wherefore I bid a hearty farewell to the reader.[38]

This last resounding shot resulted from a note by Leeser on the third article:

> We do not know that in our editorial career we have given publication to an article with more pain and unwillingness than in laying the above letter "On the Resurrection" before our readers. Dr. Wise speaks plainly enough that he does not believe in it, and that he is satisfied with the philosophical immortality of the soul as all-sufficient in Judaism.[39]

This was a partial return to the spirit and matter of the Charleston-Beth El bitterness.

To Wise's final words in the issue of July 1851 Leeser appends another note. After all, by unalterable law, the last word belongs to the editor:

> We acknowledge boldly that we meant to convey the idea that those who deny the two doctrines (the coming of a personal Messiah and the bodily resurrection of the dead) in question are not fit to be Jewish ministers, and why? Because they have no right to employ the Prayer Book and read the Scriptures to the people in a sense different from what the ostensible words seem to convey. It is not necessary to follow Dr. Wise step by step. But we may say that we do not insinuate that our epistle has

> caused Dr. Wise to retract. We only wish that he had done so and thus aided us to heal the breach which German reformers have produced in four congregations in this country (Charleston, New York, Baltimore and Albany).[40]

The echoes of the battle did not die away for some time. As late as November of the same year (the letter is dated November 13, 5611) Wise returned to his defense in the pages of the *Occident*, this time in the form of a letter, and in spite of his published resolve to say no more in this medium. In the main he repeated what he had said earlier under "The Principles of Judaism." His chief point was that the Talmud and other rabbinical sources are human and fallible, and that they must be subjected to sound criticism. Everything in these sources is true "only as far as they can stand a trial, if weighed against the facts of natural philosophy and history." He promised to go farther in another communication.[41]

It may be amusing to go back to one of Wise's arguments in discussing the dogma of resurrection. He calculated that the probable population of the world in 1851 was 1,120,000,000. This he took to mean that human beings live 720 to the square mile. The figures are hopelessly wrong, but that does not detract from the force of the reasoning. This means that, taking human population on the earth over the course of all the ages, it follows that when the resurrection occurs, people will have to eat, drink, dress and dwell in houses. But how? How is it physically conceivable? There is another view, Wise wrote, that they will then live in a "supernatural" state. But all this is foolish and self-contradictory. Wise also inquired whether the resurrected will die again.[42] Leeser had printed an extensive article by Eckmann, with hypothetical Scriptural proofs of the doctrine. Eckmann referred to the twelfth chapter of Daniel and added:

> Dr. Wise's mode of reasoning would destroy all faith, and would open the door to infidelity of the worst kind; and we regret that he has laid himself open to the charge of advocating dangerous errors, knowing as we do his great fund of information and true eloquence.[43]

To this Wise had replied in Article Number Five on July 9. He took up his pen against Leeser with indignation. "You turned a philosophical dispute into personal invectives of the most abusive kind."[44] This is hardly fair and is certainly a resounding exaggeration. Wise feared that Leeser would continue to append to every article a voluminous note and that another attempt at excommunicating him would be made. Wise contended that the great majority of "Israelites" in America did not agree with Leeser, though how he knew this—except in his most recent experiences in Philadelphia and Baltimore—it would be hard to say. Within the purviews of his own conscience Wise was satisfied. He was especially wroth at the charge that he was "destroying all faith," and "opening the door to infidelity."

> It strikes me that it is the mode of not reasoning which destroys all faith and opens the door to infidelity of the worst kind. This ruinous mode of imposing principles and doctrines upon the Israelite,—imposing them with the special recommendation of being truly Jewish, inseparable from the system of Judaism,—is the horrible cause of infidelity of the 'worst kind.' A whole generation will leave us, if we persist in this course. . . . I think it is my sacred mission to teach an enlightened and pure Judaism, to remove as much mysticism as possible from the system of our faith, to give as much rational evidence as I can bring forward for it. . . .[45]

The last word is Leeser's, who wrote that he had no wish to make Wise out a heretic, "but we fear that he covets the distinction of being made a martyr of." Henceforth Leeser would be compelled to go ahead without Wise's contributions to the *Occident*.[46]

For the general discussion of Wise's mature point of view, not only on the Messiah and on resurrection, but on the whole theological context of Judaism: on the Bible and its authority, on the place of the Talmud in the system of a liberal Judaism, we shall have to delay until the third part of this book and for those works of his later years in which he developed and extended his philosophy of Judaism. We shall then see exactly what he meant by Reform, that, in fact, he stood not far from midway between the extremes.

14

Calm in Albany, Second Period *(Concluded)*

IN THE WINTER OF 1851 TO '52 WISE WAS HARD AT WORK STUDYING and writing. He felt keenly that his education was full of *lacunae*, left by his early years. To the task of filling them in he devoted himself.[1] Occasionally he attended the Literary Society which he had helped found. But, he tells us, less and less. Once in a while he made a trip to New York, but invariably took his work with him on the road and on the steamer.

We have seen that Spanier was convicted, when the trial came up, and told he must pay Wise $1000 as compensation and damages. Spanier retired as president of Beth-El, left Albany and died but a few years later. The bitter struggle, and perhaps especially this adverse legal decision, had broken him. It had not broken Wise. But it must not be forgotten that Spanier was a much older man.[2]

At this time another chapter in Wise's life opened. The *Asmonean*, published by Robert Lyon in New York, had seemed to represent orthodoxy. It had been especially hospitable for a time to Raphall, his arguments and his attacks upon Wise. Unexpectedly, Wise received a letter from Lyon, offering him a "department" in the columns of the *Asmonean*, to be called "Theology and Philosophy." This offer Wise decided to accept eagerly. After some consideration he found himself glad to have a medium in which to air his views, to defend himself and to make propaganda for Reform, as he conceived it. He himself wrote of this time that it was thus that he began to come before the public with a program concerning "what Judaism is and what must be done to restore its original luster." Many years later, in 1895, he wrote that "the logic of events had ripened in him the conviction that the worst enemy Judaism had in this country was ignorance, ignorance of the substance, essence and history of Judaism, among preachers and laymen, Jews and Gentiles." In another place he said that in the *Asmonean* he had written "simply, democratically, popularly and thoughtfully."[3]

In the letter Wise had received from Lyon, the publisher had told him that it was Wise's great friend, Mrs. F. who had convinced Lyon that Wise represented the future, and that it was wrong to oppose him. Wise did not find the decision, whether to accept the offer or not, easy to make. In some ways this seemed to him to represent a parting of the ways. What did it signify? Had Lyon decided to make a radical shift in policy? Surely Lyon must have known that Wise was completely opposed to the pathway which the *Asmonean* had followed until then. Was it perhaps because being a theological echo of the *Occident* kept Lyon from making much progress? Wise sought his wife's counsel. She was as staunch as ever and advised him to devote himself to humanity and to his coreligionists with the same fearlessness he had always shown. He took her advice and wrote to Lyon that he would begin.[4]

The fun was not long in starting. One week the *Asmonean* appeared with the "name of the traduced of all traducers" as a fellow-editor at the masthead. The orthodox party were dismayed, Wise wrote. Hot shot flew week after week. Letters flooded into the *Asmonean*, letters of protest and letters of rejoinder. Wise himself commented that thus it was that he became an editor. And an editor he remained, chiefly for the many years from the founding of the *Israelite* in Cincinnati in 1854, until his death in 1900. He had many occasions to regret it, he claimed, for from then on he was never without the "shackles" of this pressing duty. And it made all else difficult. The announcement of Wise's editorship is in the *Asmonean* in the following words:

> According to an agreement made between the editor of the *Asmonean* and my humble self [Wise], I have taken charge of the theological and philosophical department of this paper, and I deem it my duty to inform the public of the leading principles which will guide me in my task.
>
> Judaism has to struggle against two adversaries, viz. Ignorance

> and Prejudice. The Jew who is ignorant of the principles and doctrines of Judaism and its history cannot be a pious Jew. The non-Jew who does not possess a correct knowledge of our religion is our fiercest opponent. It will be my endeavour in the first place to promulgate correct information on Jewish learning. I shall attempt to remove the veil from the sources of Jewish literature and to open the fountains of our history so that its pure waters may spout forth and satisfy the calm and reasoning readers. I am a republican and consequently an independent man, and acknowledge every man's right to his own opinion, and I am not vexed if my views are gainsaid by others, wherefore I shall utter truth boldly and only notice arguments of opponents for refutation. Especial care will be bestowed upon the history of our nation about which the German Jews have written so much and so well.

To this the editor of the *Asmonean* added:

> The liberal sentiments of Dr. Wise and his open, fearless method of discussing questions having placed him in the front rank of reformers, it becomes necessary to say and repeat in order that there should be no misunderstanding on this point that Dr. Wise's position will not interfere with the management or control of the paper. It will still continue "open to all and influenced by none."

Wise was associated with the *Asmonean* for eighteen fruitful months, almost until he left Albany and founded his own journal in Cincinnati.[5]

Many of the articles Wise contributed to the *Asmonean* are notable for their careful preparatory study, and for their interest and timeliness. Among them was a longer essay on *The Bath Kol* (a voice supposed to descend from heaven and intervene or reveal at critical moments). This was later incorporated in a book, "The Origin of Christianity," published in Cincinnati in 1868. There followed a well-written biography of the sage Hillel; an article on "the Jewish Constitution" and its relation to the Code of Maimonides; a translation of one of the most significant chapters of Zunz's *Gottesdienstliche Vortraege* (a huge master-work on the sermon in Jewish history); from Geiger's *Divan des Jehuda Halevi;* from Zechariah Frankel's *Der Gerichtliche Beweis;* and also from the writings of Rappaport, Luzzatto, Krochmal, Holdheim, Jost, and Graetz. These Wise looked upon as the real progenitors of Reform. Another of his valuable contributions to the *Asmonean*, in pursuit of a policy which he continued for many years in the *Israelite*, was to translate and publish almost every week a rabbinical legend from the Talmud or from the Midrash. He instituted a department of foreign Jewish news, which doubtless he himself extracted from the European publications that came to his desk. There are many other articles devoted to more immediate and practical problems: on "The American Synagogue as It Is"; on "Congregational Schools"; and on "Parties in Israel." In the last-named Wise deplored the fact that realistic and calm discussion was for the present impossible. It was necessary to go slowly. He advocated the improvement of "divine worship," the abolition of the "antiquated chants," and much better instruction of the young in Judaism. He was writing constantly about the imperative need for trained ministers. He wrote, for example, in January 1853, under the title: "The Necessity for a Collegiate Institution." Judaism was being "reduced to a mere shadow." American Jewry had to cease being dependent upon Germany and Poland, train clergymen who will be Americans, and who will be thorough Jewish scholars. Later still he wrote again on this topic on August 19, 1853, "Plan for a Hebrew College." This was twenty years and more before the Hebrew Union College was founded. Here he said:

> Such a college must be located in the city which is in possession of good libraries, hence where a good university, or college, or academy, exists, so that the students by an arrangement with the directors are enabled to study there all the branches of mathematics, physical sciences, and the general branches of *belles lettres*, the commercial sciences, and the classical studies. All the remaining professorships would be these: 1) One of the Bible, its commentaries and Hebrew language; 2) One for the Mishna, Talmud and Aramaic language; 3) One for history of the Israelitish people and its literature; 4) One for rhetoric, logic, and moral philosophy; 5) One for Pedagogics, etc. More than five or six professors would not be required for the commencement.

Wise believed that the necessary funds for a main building and a library should not be too difficult to raise. He asked for help and himself offered to travel. Some of this is astonishingly prophetic, but equally some of it appears to indicate—what we shall later discover to be a fact—that Wise did not then conceive of such an institution as primarily or exclusively a theological seminary.

For some time he corresponded with European scholars whose works he was translating; for example, with Zechariah Frankel, though later Wise conceded that the actual translation in this case was by a talented lady who taught German.[6]

Another experience of this period was interesting both in itself and as a presage of much to come later in his life. Now a century later it is hard to believe that Jews were seriously discriminated against in some of the cantons of free Switzerland. According to contemporary material these were chiefly those sections of the mountainous little land where the Catholic church was in the ascendant. Wise issued a call in the *Asmonean* of May 28, 1852. It was headed "A Call to the American Israelites," and displayed his eminently practical organizing talent, which was to be clearly in evidence in ensuing years. He called on Jews to meet in their synagogues, to appoint delegates to meet in New York, to prepare a suitable petition to present to Congress "against the illegal, inhuman and degrading laws which have been thrust upon our brethren." Signatures of fellow-citizens of other creeds should also be sought. If a congregation is unable to send delegates to New York, it should appoint a representative for itself in that city. Five years later such a protest was made and Wise took a prominent part in it. It ought to be remarked that the foregoing implied a bold concept of the duty and role of the United States. The Swiss Jews had no claim upon this country other than upon the score of its humanity, its sense of fair play, its general concern for justice and liberty throughout the world.[7]

The controversies in which he had been engaged during the preceding summer and autumn had aroused in him the conviction that his grounding in philosophical matters was not as firm as he would have liked. With him the wish did not need a period of gestation to be father to the thought. He dived once again into a study—for he had begun this in Bohemia—of the great Jewish philosophers. First he got his hands upon the books already in the libraries of Albany. These were far from enough. He ordered many more from dealers in New York. Nor did he limit himself to the representatives of Jewish thought in the Middle Ages. He went on at once to those of Christianity and Islam. It was very clear to him again, as he had believed before, that Jewish thought had had a far-reaching influence upon some of the greatest thinkers of the Middle Ages, even upon Thomas Aquinas. He was fired with enthusiasm by this discovery and resolved to write a History of the Middle Ages. He did not worry too greatly about his own competence. Patience and perseverance, he felt, would overcome all obstacles. Upon this project however he never really began, for other plans and other events intervened.[8]

His connection with the *Asmonean* ended on April 12, 1854. A leading editorial announced the termination of Wise's editorship of his department. This, Lyon wrote, did not prove that the *Asmonean* was the "organ of the opposition party." The conclusion of the arrangement came "reciprocally, with the highest respect and friendship."[9]

Wise had been hearing from Mrs. F. with a fair degree of regularity. In one of her missives this doting lady had called him "Hamlet in the Pulpit." This is more than a little silly, but Wise found it deserving of quotation.[10]

The church which Anshe Emeth had bought had an organ. This had been used without question for Sabbath services. But some of the members—with a vestige of their traditional upbringing—questioned whether it might be used for Yom Kippur. An old conservative member commented that the organ would be of little use, if it could not be used on the holiest day of the year. That was enough to settle the matter.[11]

Wise became excited and aroused by a visit from the great Hungarian patriot, Lajos Kossuth, who had suffered defeat at the hands of the Hapsburg monarchy, but who in the eyes of many Europeans and Americans was the great hero of the 1848 revolution. Kossuth came to America in 1851, after he had fled to Turkey. Wise became secretary of the Albany Kossuth Society and delivered addresses on its behalf. Some criticized him for this, saying that it was improper for a clergyman to discuss political topics. Wise replied thus:

> Had I the eloquence of Demosthenes, of Cicero, of Kossuth, the power of Caesar, of Napoleon, of Francis Joseph, had I the wealth of Croesus, of the Rothschilds, I would gladly devote them to the cause which Louis Kossuth pleads before us, for it is the liberty of Hungary, of Italy, of Germany, of Europe, of the whole globe, and liberty is the germ of morals, the mother of revealed religion, the muse of virtue, the requisite of prosperity, the fairest and loveliest daughter of heaven.[12]

This is more than a little grandiloquent. On the central issue—of the relation between the pulpit and politics—Wise adopted very different opinions later on, opinions—incidentally—to which he was far from adhering consistently.

To the dedication of his new synagogue had come Mrs. F. and with her Miss G., unquestionably Rebecca Gratz. Wise repeats the baseless rumor that Rebecca Gratz was the "sweetheart of the celebrated author, Washington Irving." Philipson, the editor of the *Reminiscences*, points out in a footnote that this is an error, for Miss Gratz was a friend of Irving's fiancée and later of the author himself.[13] But no more! As is well known, Walter Scott came to his character of Rebecca in "Ivanhoe" as a result of Irving's letters describing Miss Gratz. Certainly Miss Gratz was a charming and very gifted Jewess, one interested all her life in the welfare of her people. She importuned Wise to write a history of the Jews. Wise was deeply impressed, he wrote, with the pride of ancestry of Portuguese Jewesses like Rebecca Gratz. They "feel the blood of princes in their veins." The whip and the knout have beaten this out of German and Polish Jews. To Miss Gratz Wise replied that he doubted his ability to accomplish what she suggested. But the idea became fixed in his consciousness. Probably it had been there even before he chatted with her.[14]

Thus it was that Wise launched into the studies that were to lead to his *History of the Israelitish Nation*, to a whole new world of bitter controversy, to the venture and the experience that occupied him all the last months of his tenure in Albany.

Another fairly amusing episode that occurred around this time must be introduced before we proceed. Some young Jews in New York had organized a literary society and had invited Wise to lecture to them. This he did in "The Chinese Assembly Rooms" and to a large audience. The next evening he was asked to speak on "Education" before a society of Jewish natives of Posen. In advance someone had told him that this group was belligerently orthodox and that they had been foolish and discourteous enough to invite Wise for the purpose of pillorying him. But Wise was not to be intimidated thus, and he prepared himself for the fray. His resources of debate and of humor were growing, as an incident near the beginning of his Cincinnati career will display.[15]

The tale of this evening is related at some length in the *Reminiscences* and we must abbreviate it. Wise went to a Jewish dealer in antiquities, purchased a *Sefer Hachayim* (a memorial volume) printed in Posen and containing copies of some of the principal epitaphs in the cemetery of that city. A dozen or so of these he memorized. At the banquet he met Illowy, Raphall, and Isaacs. At the conclusion of the meal first Illowy attacked Wise and Reform. Loud applause! Then Raphall took up the word. With him the severity of the attack rose in pitch, as it did still further with Isaacs who came next. Finally it was Wise's turn. It proved to be a blunder to have put him last. But, when he rose to speak on education, the "fun began": noise with glasses, feet, hands, and dishes. In vain the presiding officer tried, perhaps not too vigorously, to get order. Wise bade him sit down and shouted over the tumult, asking whether anyone present had been in the *Beth Hachayim* (the cemetery) in Posen. This caught and commanded attention. Then he began to recite the texts of tombstones to them. These men—whose epitaphs he intoned were honored, he said, because of their Jewish learning. This opened the way to launch into his own ideas on Jewish education in America. He concluded with a powerful peroration against "obscurantists and night-owls who obstructed the progress of humanity." He had won the crowd. Someone shouted, he says, "that fellow has a thousand devils in him." His opponents repented of their attack upon him, and he had won many new friends among the "Poseners."[16]

In the spring of 1853 Leeser published an article in the *Occident* calling for a conference of the "Jewish clergy." To this Wise was opposed. Not that on principle he disliked the idea. On the contrary! He had gone to the meeting of the *Beth Din* in 1846. And all his life —until success crowned his efforts—he comprehended that nothing could be achieved without uniting some or all of the rabbis. But then, in 1853, he felt it was premature, as previous experiences had proved. He wrote in the *Asmonean*:

> You must first have ministers, before you can have a conference. . . . The Conference might have the effect of instituting an ecclesiastical authority of one or more men. That is exactly the thing we hate to see or have proposed under existing circumstances.

Again it is necessary to remark that Wise was not inherently worried about creating such an authority. Once and again he favored the creation of a "Synod." But not until it could have a responsible membership, and not until its place and function could be clearly defined.[17]

We come now to Isaac M. Wise's final activity in Albany. Even this will be dealt with more thoroughly in the third part of this book. Here it will be advisable only to give the circumstances of his writing of "The History of the Israelitish Nation, Vol. I," the part it played in Wise's life, and the excitement it stirred up in the American Jewish community.

It has already been noted several times that Wise had considered various major projects for literary work. He vacillated for some time in regard to a number of them, but at last decided to put in the preparatory work—and a tremendous task it was—upon a History, as first he conceived of it, in two parts, the first to the destruction of the Second Temple, and a second volume until modern times. It was upon the first of these that he got to work. From many words at the time of its early reception one would think that Wise had intended it as a blast in favor of "rationalism" in religion, as propaganda for his own "democratic" philosophy. Only partly was this true. First and foremost he wrote it for educational purposes, because there did not then exist even a passable history of the Jews in the English language. The particular way in which Wise interpreted Biblical history was incidental to his main purpose. He had also the very great advantage of being able to utilize the splendid histories that had already appeared, or were appearing, in German, and there is abundant evidence that he did so use them.

Many years later, writing of this time and of his own purpose, Wise asserted that he wrote the history, "from the rational and democratic standpoint, proving the identity of free thought, democratic liberty, rational religion, and Judaism liberated from the chains of superstition and the fetters of legalism." In this same account many years later he claimed that it was his original purpose to write four volumes: I, to the destruction of the First Temple; II, to the end of the Second Temple; III, to the discovery of America; and IV, up to 1850. The first volume, which he completed in Albany, is entitled in full:

> History of the Israelitish Nation, from Abraham to the Present Time. Derived from the Original Sources, by Isaac M. Wise.[18]

It is numbered as Volume I, and was published at Albany, by J. Munsell, 78 State Street, in 1854. The title page bears in Hebrew a verse from Deuteronomy, chapter thirty-two, verse 7:

> Remember the days of old,
> Consider the years of many generations.

In the document mentioned earlier Wise admitted that the volume was too bulky, that he had made the mistake of beginning with Abraham and of adding too much from exegetical literature. The pattern he followed in the main was derived from Rotteck's "History of the World."[19] Wise prefaced the work with a general introduction, intended for the whole series, and a special introduction to Volume One. This explains much about his studies and sources, and also the point of view from which the work was written:

> The difficulty which he encountered at the threshold in the writing of this volume was this: The facts preserved in scriptures are surrounded by doctrines and miracles so that it often becomes difficult to say which belong to the province of history. The

> facts are sometimes but touched upon by the inspired speakers and often narrated in two or three different ways, so that it is difficult to choose. We have proceeded on the following principle: History is distinguished from religion and theology as the ideas of *knowing* and *believing* (italics his). History records what is established by the criteria of criticism to be fact, while the dogmas and doctrines of religion are based upon faith, not admitting of the rigid application of criticism. Rational theology itself cannot proceed beyond a reconciliation of faith and reason. This however is insufficient for history, where evidences are required that things actually took place, where, when, and how they occurred.
>
> The next distinction between history and religion is this: that the former treats of man, the latter of God. If this be admitted, it must necessarily follow that miracles do not belong to the province of history. Miracles can be wrought by God only, and history records what men have done. The historian may believe the miracles, but he has no right to incorporate them in history. As a general thing man is always the agent on the subject of miracles; consequently the action itself may be historical and can be adopted as history, if it can be ascribed to common rational causes, while the miracle itself belongs to the province of theology. We have adopted only such facts as are able to stand the test of criticism, miracles for which we could not find common and rational reasons were not recorded by us; still we have attempted to find such reasons wherever we could. We did not contradict or deny the rest; neither did we deem ourselves entitled to consider them a part of history.[20]

Wise recorded that he completed this work in the spring of 1853, that he had worked at it steadily, while continuing his editorial labors for the *Asmonean*, building a new congregation, and pursuing his accustomed tasks. This is one of the first evidences of his truly daemonic energy, his immense capacity for work, upon the evidences of which we shall come all through the remainder of this biography. The total work upon the History occupied him for two years, from 1851 onward.[21]

We shall not discuss the essential philosophy of history which Wise set forth above, its logical or religious validity. In the third part of this work we shall come to this, when we shall expound the totality of his final concept of Jewish history, of Jewish theology, of his particular amalgam of rationalism and revelation. There would be no good purpose in pursuing this now.

When the book was finished, Wise took the manuscript and tried to find a publisher for it. With him he carried letters of commendation from Greeley and Seward. No publisher was willing to accept it. Whether this was because of their fear of its "radical" slant, or because they could not believe that it would find a large reading-public, which would justify the investment, we are unable to say. Wise himself wrote: "No one would buy such a godless book."[22]

Wise was not so easily discouraged. Never in all his life! He returned to Albany determined to publish the book himself. He arranged to have two thousand copies struck off and bound. The proofs were read by his devoted wife and himself in the summer of 1853. He had a meeting with his best friends in Albany and told them of his dilemma. The friends rallied to his aid and lent him enough money to satisfy the printer. Wise was despondent at the coldness and hostility of the world, as he believed it to be. His good friend, Amos Dean, liked the book, though he too thought it would "shock the world." Whatever his weariness and his depression Wise went ahead. And, being a man with practical ideas, he engaged traveling agents to secure subscriptions, even before the book was off the press. Proof-sheets were sent to prominent newspapers. At length the work came out, in 1854, and the storm broke. We shall select only a few among the multitudinous comments upon it, most of them wild with fury and vibrant with condemnation. There were, however, some few who agreed with him, praised him and shared his attitude.[23]

He was called a heretic, an utterly un-Jewish rabbi and writer. Comments upon the book covered the whole gamut of excess. Nor was the invective confined to Jews. Some Christians took notice of it and were at least as bitter. But, claimed Wise, none of them could back up their rage by citing any actual errors of fact he had made. There was a letter from Theodore Parker, an eminent Unitarian divine, who praised the work highly, but contended that, if anything, it was too orthodox in tone. Illowy, a fellow-rabbi, published in the *Occident* another bull of excommunication. By this time Wise had amassed quite a collection of such documents! An article in the *Occident* by one Dr. Arnold, a physician of Baltimore, sympathized with Wise, and quoted from Judges, chapter 16, verse 9: "The Philistines are upon thee, Samson!"[24]

To some of this Wise published a rejoinder in the *Asmonean*. Partly he defended himself by a reiteration of all he had written before, but also partly by pointing out that, as in the case of the revelation at Mount Sinai—the heart of his theological system, as we shall see—he had described it "according to the sources . . . and added that the event was thus described in the Bible, but made no further comment. He returned to his argument now well-known that the Messianic belief is without real basis in Judaism, and that the Israelites should have pinned their faith to prophets, not to kings. Illowy's letter in the *Occident* had been in Hebrew. It was in the same language that Wise replied to it. He had some regard for Illowy, moreover, for he was a friend and fellow-countryman.[25]

Greeley wrote that *The Tribune* in New York was still at Wise's disposal, if he elected to use it for his defense. Greeley added that he found himself in complete agreement with Wise, and appended some warm compliments on the work. This pleased and calmed Wise, for it was his opinion that Greeley was the only American of his acquaintance who was familiar with German philosophical literature.[26] On August 4, 1854 he received a very flattering letter from Harriet Beecher Stowe, to whom he had presented a copy of the History. In her letter, in addition to thanks and praises, she added the usual statement that the world owes much to the Jews.[27]

One of the numbers of the *Occident* in that year, 1854, contained a letter signed S. Solis, and headed "Remarks on Dr. Wise's History of the Israelitish Nation." This, wrote Solis, is not a history; it is a tendentious and prejudiced work. Wise, wrote Solis, cited no genuine authority for his basic assumptions except himself. "If the Bible is true, Dr. Wise's history is a farce. . . . It would be useless to point out the discrepancies of a work that contains but few just conclusions."[28]

One of the rare words of defense was also to be found in the *Occident* under the date of January 16, 1854, and came from a Dr. Rothenstein, who wrote that the History "stands unrivaled in English literture, and will remain so for a long time to come." Wise "does not deny miracles, only explains them." To this, as was his habit, Leeser appended a note by way of rebuttal.[29]

Obviously one of the results of this entire record was a sharpening of feeling between Wise and Leeser. One of Leeser's footnotes showed that this was certainly so with Leeser, who admitted that he was both angry and hurt at Wise's charges against him:

> He speaks over and over again of Isaac Leeser. Well, the name is at least an honourable one; and it can be pronounced by my friends without shame, that the one who bears it is their friend. I am not called *Doctor* or Rabbi, it is true; but I would like to see the diploma which constitutes Dr. Wise a doctor of divinity.

Leeser argued acridly that Wise boasted of so much learning, but frequently misquoted the words of the learned. For himself henceforward he will remain impervious to Wise's opinion. It would be interesting to find the words that evoked this reply, but they are not at hand. It is to be doubted that Leeser intended to assert that Wise was not an ordained rabbi, for he had admitted the contrary too often in the *Occident*. In all likelihood he meant only that Wise had no academic degree in divinity.[30]

The *Occident* of another date contained a letter on the History by a certain Sendro Melfonsi of Philadelphia. His point of view is that the History is replete with negations of religion, with a "soulless rationalism." This—he wrote—is neither progress nor Reform of the kind Judaism requires. Wise is led astray. He is—and Melfonsi misquotes "Faust," *ein Geist der verneint* (the original is *Der Geist, der stets verneint!*).[31] ("A spirit that denies in vain!")

The last of these reactions we shall cite is also from the *Occident* and is signed "An Impartial Critic." It reviewed the sorry record of anathemas hurled at Wise, and leaped to his defense. "Doubtless the book has imperfections; but it certainly has many undoubted merits."[32]

With all this hue and cry one would have thought that many would have bought the book to ascertain for themselves what it was all about. Perhaps the reverberations of all this theological disputation, of charge and counter-charge, ring much more loudly more than a century later; and most Jews, or Christians much more for that matter, were going their way without knowledge of all this. Wise himself recorded that his agents were selling hardly enough copies of the book to make expenses and that many lay in stores unsold. He found himself in dire straits. His debts were piling up like those of a typical "Austrian officer." He could descry no chance of paying them. He was unable even to turn over to the publisher the "advances" he had promised. He had had no word from Mrs. F., who had helped him on other occasions, for unfortunately she was away in Scotland. One letter had come from her, enclosing one hundred pounds sterling and some words of pity. He had sent both back, he said.[33]

Theresa Wise could not help noticing the constant look of harassment on her husband's face. She began to worry too, but said nothing about it. Wise sank into his habitual rumination as to whether he had been right to take so many risks, to place himself in jeopardy for a cause that did not seem even moderately appreciative. Ought he not once and for all learn to take care of himself? He thought and thought upon how he could extricate himself from his difficulties. What could he do to meet his debts and to lead a life that itself would conform to his tenet of "rationalism"?[34]

As though by divine intervention destiny chose this very moment to put into his hands a letter from K.K.B'nai Yeshurun of Cincinnati, inviting him to come to them as their rabbi.

It is tempting to interrupt the narrative here and to assess his entire experience in Albany, covering these eight years. But we believe that we have already reviewed its meaning for him, for his experience of his profession, his people, and himself. They had been years of rapid learning, of acute conflict, of extensive contact with American life and some of its best public figures. These had been years in which Wise had discovered his own powers in speaking and in writing, and in some of his first tentatives at organization. He now knew the American Jewish community not from afar, not from any *schema* he had brought with him from Bohemia, but as it was with all its crying wants and hypothetical possibilities. He had certainly arrived at a grasp of the main outlines of the vast task of uniting it and strengthening it. And certainly by this time he could no longer underestimate its looming difficulties.

This was just the moment when it was good for him to leave Albany, to find a wider field; and one—as we shall learn—in a congregation and community uniquely ready for him, uniquely congenial to his ideas and his methods. This was to be the last shift he would make, for in Cincinnati he remained for the last forty-six years of his life. Here he worked; here he dreamed; and here he achieved!

15

Call to Cincinnati

EITHER AT THE END OF AUGUST[1] OR THE BEGINNING OF SEPTEMBER, 1853,[2] Wise received a letter from Jacob H. Goodheart, secretary *pro tempore* of K.K.B'nai Yeshurun of Cincinnati, inquiring on what conditions Wise would agree to come to the congregation as their rabbi. The letter stated that, if mutually agreeable conditions could be arrived at, Wise would be "unanimously elected." The letter arrived in Albany, while Wise was in the midst of his worries about the publication of his *History*. This call, he wrote, roused him from his lethargy:

> It was a streak of lightning, rushing through a dingy atmosphere, clearing and vivifying it. He felt his energy, with all its impulses and yearnings, its thirst for deeds, for practical usefulness, roused afresh.[3]

In some deep inner region of himself he felt a need of the "broad, healthful and youthful West."

Wise knew something of Cincinnati and of its Jewish community. He recalled that this congregation had been one of the first to respond to his summons for a Union and that he had met three gentlemen from Cincinnati at Lilienthal's home in New York. The call to Cincinnati could not have come at a more opportune moment psychologically. The human psyche has strange ebb—and flood—tides. At the time of his violent experiences in Beth El, after the initial shock, he was buoyed up by the indignation and the prompt action of his friends, by the creation of the new congregation, and by his trip to New York, Philadelphia, Baltimore, and Washington. But little by little he had fallen once again into depression. The largest factor contributing to this was the reaction to his *History*, in which for a space he thought he had written his "death-sentence."[4] The Cincinnati call indicated to him that not everyone condemned him, or regarded him as totally outside the pale. Later on he wrote of his feeling at the time: "It seems, then, that the heresy hunt has failed."

In Albany he thought he had come to the limit of his, and perhaps of its, possibilities. His mission there seemed to him accomplished. In the East in general he had found a notable dearth of support for his ideas. This continued to be so through almost all his life. Orthodoxy was too firmly entrenched. All the voices speaking to and for Jews were under its dictation. There seemed no genuine chance of making headway on behalf of a Union or of a College, the two projects which Wise had known for years were the minimum necessary for a start upon raising the level of American Judaism. He himself was fairly deep in debt owing to the expedients he had had to adopt to get out his *History*. He had a wife and three young children and they were not rocked in the lap of luxury.

When he received Goodheart's communication, Wise sat down first in the quiet of his own mind to consider. His faith was neither casual nor shallow. He asked himself what God wanted of him. Was it His will that he remain or that he depart? The community in Cincinnati was likely to be young, aspiring, eager to follow constructive leadership. It might furnish him with a forum for his ideas and with aid in advancing his practical plans. Perhaps he might be able to establish a periodical of his own, which would be the first clear advocate of progressive Judaism in this country. This might become a fulcrum, an entering wedge, to move the intractable mass, to overcome its apparent inertia. A new and powerful impetus might be given to American Jewish life. Since after all Wise was an intense and very normal human being, he could not help thinking too that from Cincinnati he might be able to avenge himself upon the bigots who had been flinging opprobrious epithets at him, who had been trying to read him out of Jewish life.[5]

It is not improbable that even at a distance he felt an affinity with the West. In those days it seemed the "far West," not the Middle West. Though California had had a flood of settlers five years before, most of them had reached it by sea. The overland route was still incredibly dangerous and difficult. And even the journey to Cincinnati could be made most readily by the rivers beyond the Alleghenies and after a journey of no mean hardship. Here, as an instance of his feeling and of the way men in general at that time thought of Ohio, are Wise's own words:

> Do the people of the Far West not read the papers? Do they not know how discredited I am?

For a while he was inclined to look upon the letter as a sorry jest. At this point in his *Reminiscences* he claimed that he had not been entirely unfamiliar with the reputation of K.K.B'nai Yeshurun. He had met: "Abraham Aub, the deceased Griebel, Elias Mayer, and Lewis Abraham; and through them I had become quite familiar with Jewish conditions in Cincinnati."[6]

He strove to secure more knowledge from two friends, both of whom told him that Jacob Goodheart was an "honorable gentleman," a "merchant in good standing." He recalled that he had met Goodheart at Lehmayer's in New York. And to himself he pondered:

> What does Providence wish me to do? The temple and the congregation here are built up and firmly established. My mission here is ended. Anyone else can finish the work. I have three children, and am burdened with debts. Cincinnati lies in the center of the country. There in the West is a new world that comes into but little contact with the East. The people there are young and aspiring and not yet cast into a fixed mold.[7]

His mind was made up at last. He told his wife all about it. It was his habit to do nothing without her knowledge and participation. In Radnitz, and amidst the hazards of the New World, she had abundantly deserved his confidence as well as his love. She agreed, and at once comprehended his reasons and his hopes. Wise replied to Goodheart's letter and laid down the following interesting conditions: that he must be unanimously elected "for life"; that there must be no trial-sermon; that he must be paid a salary sufficient to make him "independent of any gifts from rich or poor members"; and finally that he was to enter upon his new duties six months after he would be notified of his election. If these conditions proved acceptable to K.K.B'nai Yeshurun, it would demonstrate to Wise that they were sincere in wanting him as their rabbi, despite his "failures, stupidity, and bad reputation."[8]

Some of his friends in Albany tried to dissuade him. One of his intimates said to him:

> Hardly anyone in Cincinnati knows you personally; they take you to be that harmless, mild and suasive gentleman as you appear in your writings. The whole West and Cincinnati is staunchly orthodox. If you come among them, you will find yourself out of place and they may shortly consider you the man they do not want. . . . Some even cautioned prominent Cincinnatians to this effect. But he (Wise) thought: they knew him from his writings. He himself knew them as Germans, who had come from places where Rosenfeld, Gutmann, and Leopold Stein (leaders of Reform) preached . . . they must be prepared to support the man whom they know from his writings to stand quite near to them. We were raised in the same school.[9]

The reason for one of his conditions—that an interval of six months was to elapse—was, Wise later wrote, so that either he or they might have time to change their minds. And on the visit to Cincinnati, to which we shall come shortly, he "artlessly" repeated this provision and his reasons for it.

No counsels of caution, or of possible misunderstanding, could deter him now. He was convinced that his intuition about the Cincinnati community and congregation was right, and the opinions volunteered by some of his good friends wrong. And, as we shall see, circumstances from the very beginning substantiated his feeling fully.

Five days after Wise's reply and the conditions he had set forth, he received a telegram from Goodheart, informing him that the congregation had voted unanimously to accept his terms.[10] He could scarcely believe his own eyes. He had known that the conditions were not light. But no objection had been made to them, no attempt to water them down. Was this not clear evidence of the eagerness of B'nai Yeshurun to have him, of their readiness for him and his message? When he told his wife, she said that his reputation could not be as awful as he had thought it to be. Wise was happy as a king. The auspices looked enchantingly favorable. This was a noble way in which to tender a call, generous and open-hearted. Nor was this only his own interpretation of the formal communication from Goodheart on behalf of his congregation. Soon after the telegram came letters from Goodheart, Henry Mack and others, telling Wise that his election signified a victory for Reform Judaism, that the orthodox element were in mourning and prophesying disaster.[11] Another letter came, signed by Moritz Fischel, secretary of B'nai Yeshurun, and by Lehmann Hollstein, secretary of the Talmud Yelodim Institute (the parochial school the congregation had established in 1849), apprising Wise in more detail than had been possible in the telegram that he had been elected—unanimously—head of both congregation and school, that his salary had been fixed at $1500 a year, and transmitting to him an advance of money. For the sake of accuracy it should be noted that the congregation had met on October 27, 1853, and resolved unanimously "that this congregation elect the Rev. Dr. Isaac M. Wise during good behavior as our minister and at a salary of $1500 per annum."[12]

Before we proceed, we must remark that Wise's request for election for life, and the congregation's accession to this wish, were entirely unprecedented at the time. Action like this had neither been proposed nor pursued thitherto.[13] Wise's reason for it was obvious. He wished to get to work and not to have to worry about periodic re-election. He rested upon a new and deeper concept of the relation that should obtain between rabbi and congregation. Nor does this interpretation hinge only upon our own surmise. Twenty-five years later, at a celebration of his anniversary at K.K.B'nai Yeshurun, Wise's dear friend and co-worker in Cincinnati, Max Lilienthal, said:

> Jacob Goodheart said to me in New York, "We have engaged the services of the rabbi of Albany for life." Thanks to your noble congregation, who first uttered these words, thanks to the rabbi who first insisted on this condition! Ministers were elected but for one year, and like politicians had to flatter and humble themselves before every ignoramus who had a right to vote at the annual election. And whenever a man dared to show his self-respect, his superior knowledge, and the will to maintain the dignity of his clerical office, there arose Hydra-like contentions and bitter animosities. We, the elder rabbis of this country, can tell the story of our sadder experiences. But the spell was broken when this congregation first of all said: "I have betrothed thee unto me forever," (Hosea, chapter 2, verse 21) and when the rabbi and the congregation repeated the words of the Song of Songs.[14]

What verse or verses of the Song of Songs were referred to here was not stated.

Wise wrote at once informing K.K.B'nai Yeshurun of his acceptance of the election, and used these words:

> I am a friend of bold plans and grand schemes, therefore I entertain the hope that the Talmud Yelodim Institute will in a few years realize my fervent wishes for a Hebrew college in which our national literature may flourish alongside of a classical and commercial education.[15]

In the booklet (written by Isaac M. Wise and his grandson, Max

B. May) for the Fiftieth Anniversary of the congregation in 1892, it was said:

> Heretofore the congregation was like a company of brave and daring men, each longing to do some noble and heroic deed, but unable, because there was no true and capable leader, and just as every member of a company of soldiers hails with shouts his captain's arrival, and anxiously awaits his commands, so the young congregation, which had been spending its strength in trying various leaders, having at last found one in whom it could put implicit faith, readily submitted itself to his wise, daring and honorable leadership, and marched forward bearing the glorious banner, "Reform."[16]

The congregation, said the booklet, and the record testified, never had cause to regret its action. But we are hastening beyond the progress of events.

Wise now submitted his resignation from the pulpit of Anshe Emeth in Albany to take effect in six months, and begged his friends not to try further to dissuade him. He assured them that he had come to the conclusion that in going to Cincinnati he would be serving his God and advancing the cause of Reform Judaism. Regretfully the congregation accepted his resignation and began to advertise for a successor. The advertisements were placed chiefly in Germany, from which at that time almost all rabbis who were serving congregations had come to America. Whatever candidate applied—they specified—must have the recommendation of Ludwig Philippson and of Leopold Stein.[17]

Naturally the news of all this could not be kept secret. When the general community in Albany learned of it, his old opponents in Beth El and in the community at large did not fail to denounce him once again, and in their imprecations now they included the Cincinnati congregation, which was apparently so blind to its Jewish loyalty as to invite to its pulpit a "heretic," a man who scorned central Jewish doctrines, who planned openly to organize what he called a "liberal" Jewish movement in America.[18] None of this was unexpected to Wise, and by this time he had learned enough to discount these fulminations and to go ahead with some degree of calmness. He resigned his position with the *Asmonean*. This—he wrote—was only to "sharpen his weapons." By which doubtless he meant his plan for a new journal of Reform Judaism which he intended to establish in Cincinnati. His own book, the *History*, began to sell better. His agents were not as idle as they had been. Money began to come in and he could liquidate some of the debts he had contracted in the course of its publication, especially those that he owed to his good friends. Invitations began to flow in from Cincinnati, asking him to attend anniversary celebrations upon his forthcoming trip to the Middle West at the time of *Chanuccah*. It had been agreed that Wise was to come to Cincinnati so that he and the congregation as well as the community might come to know one another. This was not a trial-sermon, nor was it ever intended to be that. Before his trip he had been elected and all the conditions of his service as rabbi—and of the time when his tenure was to begin—had been agreed upon.[19]

At last the time was at hand. Wise set forth from Albany in the company of a physician, Rosenfeld, and of a rabbi, Isidor Kalisch, then serving in Cleveland. The trip was far from easy. It was bitterly cold and there was deep snow all over New York State. Not far from Erie, Pa. the tracks of the railroad had been torn up by an enraged mob. What had roused the mob the *Reminiscences* do not tell us. The extreme weather and the hardships affected Wise's health and he paused briefly in Erie, where he was ministered to by Rosenfeld. Fortunately he recovered quickly and the next afternoon they left for Cleveland, where Wise spent the night at Kalisch's home. The very next morning, a Thursday, he resumed his journey and arrived in Cincinnati. He remained in the city for three weeks, as we shall see.[20]

At this point, Wise's first experience of the city and of its Jewish community, his future congregation, we shall pause to give to the reader a rather hasty sketch of Cincinnati as it then was, and of the birth and character of K.K.B'nai Yeshurun. This was to be the place and these the people where Wise would labor for the remaining forty-six years of his life. All that had gone before—in a certain sense—was prelude. Here his life's work was to be done. Here almost all of his ideas were to be matured and expressed. During these forty-six years he left Cincinnati for meetings, and for the periodic and extended trips he took to other Jewish communities; to dedicate synagogues, to make propaganda for his own pet ideas, to secure or to strengthen support, and in general to keep in touch with the status and progress of Jewish life in America. But even these journeys, numerous and fruitful as they were, took him out of Cincinnati only a small proportion of the time. Cincinnati became his home. He cemented the deepest bonds of friendship and of joint labor with its Jews. It is therefore imperative that we have before us a picture of what manner of city it was, and of what kind of Jews had settled in it.

Cincinnati began as a grant sold to Judge John Cleves Symmes, a veteran of the Revolutionary War. It was part of the opening-up of the Middle West that followed that conflict, and also the result of the daring of the hardy pioneers who had crossed the Alleghenies and lived in the forests of Ohio, and of Kentucky and Tennessee. The new grant that was made to Symmes was called the Miami Purchase and the actual settlement began with his arrival, accompanied by a group of men and women, on December 8, 1788. The new city was christened "Losantiville," because—in bad Latin and French—it was "the city opposite the mouth of the river," in this case the Licking River flowing into the Ohio from Kentucky at this point. Each pioneer was given a house-lot, and also an "out-lot" for purposes of cultivation. The first church was Presbyterian and was built in 1792.[21]

The city grew rapidly. By 1840, fifty-two years later, it had a population of more than 46,000. Those who had come with Symmes were of the old Anglo-Saxon stock that had colonized the Eastern Seaboard. But in the 1830's German immigration drawn chiefly from Bavaria began in the city. Already by 1841 an authority asserted that about one-third of the city's people were German. Cincinnati lived in those early days chiefly on the exchange of commodities and as a merchandising center. It dealt in sugar, cotton, rice, and molasses from the South, and furs and grains from the West. Next to the Ohio River the main artery of commerce into the city was the Miami Canal, which bore barges down from Lake Erie. Already in the fourth decade of the nineteenth century there were newspapers and religious publications, a system of public education—general but not yet adequate—and two colleges, Cincinnati College, and Woodward College. A theological seminary, Lane, had been founded in 1833, and a Medical College as well as the Ohio Mechanics' Institute.

The river was a very busy place and passengers and freight from up and down stream made an exciting area of the Ohio River front. A railroad was begun in 1841 and by 1846 had been completed as far as Springfield, Ohio. Another was constructed and finished by 1850 to Hamilton and Dayton.[22]

The city was built largely of brick. The streets were wide for that day, but not paved. Water accumulated in the streets after a heavy rain. That section of the city which was across the Canal was known as "Over the Rhine," because of its large German-speaking population. There was a German theater, and German was taught as part of the regular curriculum of the public schools. The city had many "coffee-houses," though apparently this was often a euphemism for saloons. For a time Cincinnati was the center of a grape-growing, wine industry. Gradually the region settled down to its normal crop of corn.

We possess a number of picturesque accounts of the city in these early days, by all odds the most astringent being that of Mrs. Trollope, the mother of the novelist, Anthony Trollope, in her "The Domestic Manners of the Americans."[23] She found Cincinnati deficient in almost all the facilities of convenience and sanitation. Refuse was thrown into the middle of the street and the pigs disposed of it. She could discover little beauty in the city. In 1828, when she came to it, Cincinnati had a population of 20,000. Some Negroes had already escaped from the South and lived in a section known as "Little Africa." The city was bounded to the north by somewhat "rugged" hills, but she thought the river itself very beautiful.

Mrs. Trollope considered the city and its people utterly uncouth, bent solely—according to her—on making money. She leveled some of her sharpest shafts against the absurd delusion of the people that "all men were created free and equal." The chief influence in the community, "as in Spain," was that of the clergy, and religion of the most frenetic, revivalist kind prevailed.

Twenty years before the Civil War, and therefore certainly at the time when Wise came there, Cincinnati was a battleground of forces for and against slavery. The Abolitionists had set up shop there. One terminus of the "Underground Railway" was there, begun in 1835. An Abolitionist paper, called *The Philanthropist*, was founded. A year later a pro-slavery mob of citizens smashed its press. But it began all over again. The publisher was besought at a mass-meeting not to continue to sow dissension. Again his presses were torn to pieces and thrown into the river. Some years later Negroes' houses were stoned and the militia had to be called out.[24]

Another traveler in 1840 described the city in such terms that it is evident that it must have changed considerably for the better since Mrs. Trollope's visit:

> It may be doubted whether there is any city in the Union in which there is a more general diffusion of competency in means and comfort, in enjoyments, than in Cincinnati.[25]

Still another journal deemed Cincinnati well-named "The Queen of the West."

Its most interesting visitor was Charles Dickens in April, 1842. He found the city "beautiful, cheerful, thriving and animated." Nor did it become "less prepossessing on a closer acquaintance." He described a temperance convention and procession somewhat humorously, and complimented the city on its free schools. He thought it justifiably proud of these, especially in the light of the fact that only fifty-two years before it "was a wildwood and its citizens were but a handful of dwellers in scattered log-huts upon the river's shore."[26]

The city was fifty-four years old when K.K.B'nai Yeshurun was organized. Cincinnati had made amazing strides in population, culture, sanitation, and industry. Its business and residential districts were then only in the valley along the river, and no one—with the exception of farmers—had climbed the hills to the north to live. Here it may be appropriate to introduce a paragraph which we wrote about the city some twenty years ago:

> The spirit of the young community was patently optimistic, believing ardently in its own future, and full of that legacy of freedom and brotherhood which was deep in the tradition of America and in the silt the frontier left behind as it flowed westward. The atmosphere must have conduced toward large enterprises, great venturesomeness, and a certain expansiveness of mood. The city was fortunate in comprising many families that looked ahead and built firmly and well. They wanted good schools for their children, a university to enable them to scale the higher levels of learning, galleries of art, the instrumentalities of music.[27]

Jews found little or no prejudice to overcome. A local writer in 1845 commented upon the Jewish love of home and kindred:

> Such is the nature of their affection; it is the fruit of their religion, which abounds with love of kindred.[28]

Thus the city itself was progressive, and propitious for a liberal interpretation of Judaism.

The Jewish community of Cincinnati was the oldest west of the Allegheny Mountains. The first Jew—from England—arrived there in 1817. His friends had tried to dissuade him from going into "the wilds," but he went nonetheless. In 1819 he was joined by three others also from England, and that fall the first Jewish service was conducted. Newcomers continued to arrive, mostly still from England. A cemetery was acquired in 1821. There were not, however, enough to form a congregation until 1824, and on January 18 of that year K.K.B'nai Israel (now the Rockdale Ave. Temple) was organized. It did not receive a charter until January 8, 1830. With contributions from other Jewish communities it became possible to build a synagogue, which was dedicated in September, 1836. A benevolent association and a religious school were launched not long after.[29]

The community was still relatively small when German Jews began to arrive. There was not then any Reform congregation, nor in fact—as far as can be discerned—was there any thought of one at the time. K.K.B'nai Israel used the *Polish Minhag* and was strictly orthodox. In all likelihood by 1840 or 1841 there were not more than 1600 Jewish citizens, but this number increased to 2500 by 1845. The Jews were congregated in the central part of the city and engaged almost exclusively in commerce. It was in the early forties, or perhaps in the late thirties, that a group of young, energetic German Jews began to arrive. Many of them had fled from their native lands for exactly the same reason that had driven Isaac M. Wise out of Bohemia. Almost all of them came from Bavaria, many from rather small towns from which their names were derived, and they spoke German with the accent of the region. But among them were many men and women of culture, who were not without acquaintance with classical German literature. It seems exceedingly probable—judging by the record of the next dozen years—that, as Wise is quoted as having written, some of them had been under the influence of Leopold Stein, or of other lights of Reform Judaism in Bavaria. Most of them made the transition from peddling to little businesses with amazing speed, and prospered apace.[30]

In the beginning the German Jewish newcomers joined the "English Congregation," but disagreements were not long in coming. The difference in language, perhaps the typical snobbishness of earlier toward later arrivals, and the use of a form of the liturgy to which many German Jews were not accustomed: these were the probable factors of disagreement. Thus the first Constitution of K.K.B'nai Yeshurun used words which we have previously quoted:

> . . . And whereas, also, the mode of worship in the established synagogue of our beloved brethren, K.K.B. Israel, in this city, is not in accordance with the rites and customs of the said German Jews.

Whatever the specific reasons, these German Jews came together in the year 1840 and organized themselves into a new congregation. They acquired a cemetery, adopted a constitution on September

19, 1841, which testified not only to their unfamiliarity with the language, but also to their essential good sense and ability.[31]

The congregation received its charter on February 28, 1842, met on Fourth Street between Main and Sycamore, and had a *Hazan*, Simon Bamberger, until 1844. The new congregation was active in charitable works. In 1845 it was invited to amalgamate with B'nai Israel, but rejected the proposal.[32]

The congregation then took a step which appeared to indicate two things: first, that it must already have begun to develop in the direction of Reform; and secondly, that it was not yet quite ready for the transition. A remarkable man, James K. Gutheim, a rabbi already widely known for his liberal tendencies, came to them in September, 1847.[33] Shortly thereafter a new synagogue was built and dedicated, on October 14, 1847. Gutheim was elected "lecturer and reader," at a salary of $500 *per annum*. Gutheim soon indicated that he wanted to move toward Reform:

> But, if the Synagogue shall realize this object [to bring blessing and peace], devotion, order and dignity must prevail therein. Our mode of worship must be constituted and celebrated in such a manner that, while participating therein, our mind may be truly elevated and edified. . . . It is thus only that the Synagogue will realize its objects; thus only will blessing and peace gush forth from its heavenly foundations; thus only may you salute the pilgrim to the source of life: "Blessed be he that cometh in the name of the Lord." (Psalm 118, verse 26.)[34]

Gutheim prevailed upon the congregation to introduce a choir. A committee to formulate a permanent ritual, or "order of worship," was appointed. This came in with a report on January 20, 1848, proposing changes in decorum, the omission of certain sections of the liturgy, and changes in the method of distributing the reading of the *Torah*. There was a violent controversy, but Gutheim was authorized to organize and drill a choir.[35]

Wise himself commented in the Fiftieth Anniversary booklet of the congregation that these reforms were of a purely external character. Gutheim's tentative efforts at Reform failed. The congregation at that time was rather bitterly divided, just as Beth El in Albany had been. Immediately after Gutheim gave up the attempt and left, in the spring of 1849, the congregation appeared to return to complete orthodoxy. But doubtless within it the processes were germinating, and the party favoring Reform was slowly but steadily gaining ground, as the sequel will prove.[36]

A new synagogue on Lodge Street was dedicated in the fall of

1848. The congregation had grown to include one hundred and thirty-four members. The annual dues were six dollars. It was also at this time that the congregation received Wise's call (of December, 1848), for a national congregational meeting to achieve a union and decided to send delegates to Philadelphia.[37]

When Gutheim left in the spring of 1849, the congregation elected as his successor the Rev. H. A. Henry, of an avowedly orthodox bent, but a worthy man, a scholar and an author. For what reasons we cannot discover, he was with them for only a little more than two years and resigned on July 11, 1851. That fall the Rev. A. L. Rosenfeld came to them from Charleston, S. C. He too was quite orthodox and left them in Passover, 1853. There was a letter in the *Occident* (of July, 1852) from Henry Mack of Cincinnati, complaining that the congregation "had never had a minister who could gain sufficiently the confidence of the people, by combining learning, oratorical powers, and other talents with a dignified conduct, true piety, energy, zeal and independence, and labour effectually in the promotion of true religion." Rosenfeld got into some trouble with a member of B'nai Israel on the score of his orthodoxy, but this proved to be a tempest in a tea-pot.[38]

It was after Rosenfeld's departure in 1853 that the congregation—without a rabbi from then until Isaac M. Wise's coming—considered what it should do, and hit upon the bold project of inviting Wise from Albany. Unquestionably this decision could have been arrived at only as a result of profound changes in the congregation itself. The record does not enable us to trace the details of this transition. But it is evident that the group favoring reform had gained the ascendancy, that by that time it must have constituted an overwhelming majority of the congregation. For not only was Wise elected unanimously, but during the entire period of his rabbinate in Cincinnati—and even in the earliest days—he had no organized opposition to encounter. He was never called upon to face the situation that had brought him such bitterness and harassment in Albany.[39]

Before we proceed, a few generalizations may seem in order. Not all of Wise's achievements should be credited to him alone. Had he not come into a city that was uniquely propitious for him and in which he swiftly felt himself at home, an integral part of its life and work; had he not found a congregation eager for his guidance, in agreement with him as to the meaning and vision of Judaism; had he not discovered a group of laymen, in his own congregation and in B'nai Israel as well, full of enthusiasm, among them many men of culture and capacity, enjoying then and later a truly unique position in their city: all that he projected and all that he accomplished would have been utterly out of the question. From the moment of his coming he and the congregation were one. They gave him, says its history, every possible "liberty and latitude." They had no wish to restrict "the ambition and the influence of their spiritual leader." This was breadth and generosity rare among congregations of that day. The same history goes on to say:

> Congregation B'nai Yeshurun was spared the turmoil through which other congregations had to pass, largely because the character of its Rabbi was a guarantee that what he said and proposed to do was genuine. Thus it came that the abrogation of customs which had lost meaning was not accompanied by any disturbance of the congregational peace, and the innovations Wise made offended nobody. It will be difficult to find a parallel in this respect. Starting with the current orthodoxy of the old days, Congregation B'nai Yeshurun has gone through all the phases of the Reform Movement into a religious status, which is the highest and most vital. B'nai Yeshurun has uniformly reflected the spirit of the day.[40]

This is not lacking in self-glorification, but it may be taken as shadowing forth a large measure of truth.

The reader should have at least a relative idea of the city and of the congregation to which Isaac M. Wise came on his visit near the end of 1853. He stayed in the city for three weeks, delivered sermons in several pulpits, spoke at the Lodge of the B'nai Brith, set forth his views on Reform, met hosts of people and made many friends, who remained his close intimates and associates. There is a delightful description of these first experiences of his in the *Reminiscences*, a section in which he goes into considerable detail about persons and occasions. We can reproduce only part of it.[41]

He came to Cincinnati late at night and took a room at the old Woodruff House, opposite the National Theater. No one as yet knew of his arrival. The trip had been tiring and he desired to avoid all excitement at the beginning. The next morning he sent his card to the officers of the congregation, especially to Marcus Fechheimer and Jacob L. Miller, also to the president of the Talmud Yelodim Institute, Solomon Friedmann. At nine o'clock in the morning a reception committee came to call upon him and took him to Fechheimer's home, which was at the corner of Longworth (then Center) and Race Streets. He was given the heartiest of receptions and writes that he felt at home at once. The evening of the same day he had visits from all the prominent members of the congregation and each and all grasped his hand and welcomed him.

He wrote in the *Reminiscences* that it was hard to imagine what impression he was making upon them. He was then thin, pale, and with deep rings under his eyes. His hair was long, and his glance "fiery." His figure was bent and he was of insignificant stature. He thought the people might take him for a *Schlemiehl* (a man who knows and can do little). The following Sunday a very frank woman was reported to him to have said: "He is not the same man in the pulpit and outside it." The name of this woman was Lena Stix, and they were friends until her death. A noble woman, said Wise![42]

Wise was pleased with everything. He liked the city, its newness, the air of freedom it seemed to breathe. He liked the people he met. They were of his kind. Their cordiality and their sympathy moved him. With all the tact he could summon he strove to find out what they thought, what their Jewish point of view was. But he did not hasten or press. He went about it discreetly.[43]

Then came the Sabbath. Everyone was in the synagogue on Lodge Street. The service was conducted by Solomon Levi, who was an old-fashioned but exceedingly dignified Jew. The congregation still had some of the practices Wise had abolished in Albany, *Schnodering* and *Misheberachs* (Cf. Glossary). He spoke, but not yet about his "principles." What he said was put with ease and with conviction, and his reputation as a speaker was well on the way to being established. The congregation looked at one another with satisfaction. They had made no mistake. This was the man they had hoped to have. They felt in him many of the things they were to know with clarity in the years to follow: decision, vision, inspiration, and leadership. They wanted a preacher in both German and English, and Wise commanded both tongues. He had made an excellent beginning, and they and he were overjoyed.[44]

Wise would perhaps have waited until after this visit to go into controversial issues. But this was not to be. As throughout his life, he was forced to defend himself and his cause; and in this case on the spur of the moment. Though he had not sought the occasion, neither did he avoid it. The story is both significant and amusing, especially for its display of the same quickwittedness and resourcefulness he had shown before the "Poseners" in New York. It deserves telling in detail. We shall set it down in his own words:

The benevolent society celebrated its anniversary on Sunday

evening. Covers were laid for about two hundred people at Bernheimer's. The members of the various congregations were present in goodly numbers. Food and drink were good, and at the close of the meal the traditional *nevorech lelohenu* (blessing after the meal) was recited. Immediately thereafter the business of the evening was broached. A number of toasts had been officially announced. I was to speak on charity, and the donations were to be collected after my address. Two speakers were to precede and two to follow me. The second toast was "Our Country," responded to by an ultra-orthodox Englishman and a practiced speaker. He said not one word on the subject assigned to him, but devoted his remarks altogether to a scathing denunciation of the progressionists [sic!] and the world-improvers, of the desire for novelty and sensation, so that all eyes were directed towards me. The English element was very prominent in Cincinnati at that time, and was well represented at the banquet.

After he had taken his seat triumphantly, the toast on charity was announced, and I was introduced. I began as follows, without one prefatory word: "Once upon a time the frogs complained that they could find no rest nor peace; nay, more, that they could not sleep, for the earth revolved unceasingly. Some wise frogs interested themselves in the matter, and a general meeting of the frogs was called. The complaints grew louder and louder, until finally all the frogs were convinced of the justice of the same, and thereupon the weeping and wailing became universal. A wise old frog now took the floor and said: 'Wherefore wail and complain? Let us try to think of some remedy whereby we may remove the evil!' The frogs became silent and hearkened. The wise frog continued 'Let us devise ways and means to bring our complaint before the throne of the God of justice, and ask him for relief.' 'But how can we reach the throne of the God of justice that is so high and far away?' asked an humble little frog. 'We can not leap high into the air; for we are only frogs.' This called forth renewed wailing and weeping. The wise old frog arose once again and ordered the assembly to keep quiet. The frogs obeyed and he spoke: 'At night, after the scorching sun has sunk behind the mountains and the peaceful evening refreshes all creatures with its cooling breezes, all hearts beat kindly and glow with love. At such a time truly the all-just God will be merciful to us frogs, His creation. Let us be united, and we can accomplish anything. Let us unanimously and unitedly croak loudly and continuously after sunset in this fashion: "All-just God, we pray Thee to let the earth stand still for six hours after revolving for eighteen hours, in order that Thy harassed and troubled frogs may enjoy

> rest, quiet, and sleep".' The glorious suggestion was greeted with jubilant shouts. All frogdom took an oath of fealty and jumped about comically. The frogs scattered in all directions, and kept their oath faithfully. As soon as after a hot summer day the evening, with its soft breezes and its balmy zephyrs, descended upon earth and breathed love and mildness into all hearts, the host of frogs came forth from the swamps and croaked and croaked loudly and clearly: 'O Thou all-just Creator of all, let the earth stand still for six hours in order that Thy frogs may sleep undisturbed!' The frogs croak continually, the frogs croak still, and the earth—well, it moves none the less."

This witty sally was greeted with a great salvo of applause. Wise then went on to say that this was neither the time nor the place to expound his principles. He had come to seek money for the poor, and he moved on to his prepared toast on charity. The assembly was moved and contributed in unprecedented measure.[45]

The following Wednesday was another gala occasion, the anniversary of the founding of the Talmud Yelodim Institute. Three hundred persons attended a banquet at "Allemannia Hall." There were a number of excellent speeches. Isaac M. Wise had been asked to respond to the following subject, a rather fulsome one: "Israel, the Prince of God, the Banner-bearer of Eternal Truth and Eternal Progress." He had begun to feel thoroughly at home among people who seemed to like and honor him, and he let himself go. This time, after all, he was speaking to his own future flock. He had decided to tackle the topic he had avoided before—reform and progress in Judaism. He omitted no item in what he had come to regard as an indispensable program for American Judaism. Nor did he present this as though it were a complete or radical departure from the precedents of Jewish history. Part of his concern was to show that there had been many forerunners of Reform, the epochs in which and the great personalities by whom Judaism had been reinterpreted and reformulated. Then followed a voluntary subscription on behalf of the school, and contributions twice as large as ever before poured in. The officers of the institution were elated. Thereafter another toast was given by Nathan Bloom of Louisville, the gist of which was an eloquent description of how the stars were now moving from East to West, doubtless intended as a rhetorical flourish for Wise and his forthcoming transit to Cincinnati. Wise left the banquet deeply happy, full of the warmth and the fine feeling of the occasion, and keenly aware of the many friends he was winning.[46]

The next Sabbath he preached again at Lodge Street for B'nai Yeshurun—this time in German—on the future of Judaism in America. It was again his purpose to discuss the places in belief and in practice where reforms were necessary and in what way they should be introduced.[47]

His next public address was at an open meeting of the B'nai Brith, where he spoke of the concepts that underlay the Order and of its opportunities for service. In the days that intervened between these addresses he was being invited constantly to dinner. Here he had a chance to meet his future congregants more intimately, to know them not in the mass, and not through their corporate attitudes, but as warm-hearted, individual men and women. One of Wise's possessions was a direct and friendly way with people, a capacity for easy and natural relations, and this stood him in excellent stead.[48]

After all these occasions and the inevitable strain they involved, he wanted to return to Albany. But his hosts were not yet satisfied. There were other things he ought to do, other organizations and associations who ought to hear him. He was visited by a committee representing K.K.B'nai Israel, the sister-congregation, and in fact the grandmother—Wise himself writes—of all the congregations in the West. It was then "strictly orthodox, English and aristocratic." But there was a large German element that had joined it, and that was beginning to make its influence felt. The committee invited Wise to preach on the following Sabbath. This was rather extraordinary evidence of good-will and of interest. He felt bound to accept, and this kept him in Cincinnati a week longer. He spoke in B'nai Israel on the last Sabbath of the year 1853. His topic was "The Teleology of Genesis." He himself described it as an effort to show that the author of Genesis had had as his purpose to develop moral ideas as an introduction—later in the Pentateutch—to the revelation at Sinai. The patriarchs and others whose stories are told in Genesis were consistently represented as human beings, not sinless, not perfect. Genesis "portrays the whole development of morality." Its emphasis however is on the individual, until in later books it comes to Moses, who is the embodiment of "national morality." The thesis, toward which Wise was aiming, was: "Reason is the final court of appeal in the matter of morals. . . ." He pointed out that this was strictly in line with some of the tortured differences then embroiling Orthodoxy and Reform, for it was his real point that the authority of "reason" is higher than "that which is written." But this is not the place to wrestle with this expression of his ideas.[49]

On Sunday afternoon he met with the members of K.K.B'nai Yeshurun. He told them how delighted he had been and was with Cincinnati. He thanked them with all his heart. They must by now have come to a clear understanding of his convictions and opinions. He informed them that he had no intention of interfering with congregational affairs, but that he conceived it to be his function to teach, and to convince. If even at this late date anyone of them thought that it was better for him not to come as their friend and leader, let him speak, for he could and would stay in Albany. Not a voice was raised. By every possible evidence of word and gesture they told him that they wanted him and that he should come.[50]

Wise left Cincinnati on Monday morning early in 1854. Arrived in Albany he told his wife everything, all the fascinating details of his experiences in the city and among the people where they were to live. Shortly after his return to Albany he received a set of resolutions sent him by his future congregation endorsing the contract and expressing the hope that he would find it possible to come to his post soon.[51] There were also numerous letters, full of praise, telling him how eagerly they looked forward to his coming.

The die was cast. He began making preparations for leaving Albany in the spring. Transporting a wife and family in those days was no light or easy thing and had to be carefully thought out in advance. Moreover, his wife was expecting another child.

Wise recorded that around this time he had met Salmon P. Chase,[52] who had asked him in what school he had been educated. "In the school of life, like father Jacob. This was the school I attended eight long years in the city of Albany." "And you have rescued so much enthusiasm out of that school?" said Chase, "I congratulate you."

One of Wise's cherished hopes, as we have already written, was that, when he would settle in Cincinnati, he would be able promptly to start a paper. He was acutely aware of his need for such an organ. And not his need alone, but that of the "progressive" forces in American Judaism! Under Leeser's direction the *Occident* had remained unalterably conservative. The *Asmonean* seemed to waver from time to time. Wise could find no publisher willing to back such a risky venture. Once more he would have to do it himself. He visited some of his friends in New York, told them of his plan, and from them secured encouraging promises, but no actual money. His debts in Albany—as we have noted—were diminishing, because the *History* was doing better. There too some of his friends engaged to subscribe to and to support a Reform weekly, if he would found and conduct it. And on the way to Cincinnati he did not waste his time, but got other commitments in Syracuse, Rochester and Buffalo. All these, Wise wrote later, were honored and constituted a large part of his first support for the *Israelite*.[53] Meanwhile he was continuing to write for the *Asmonean.* One of his last contributions was entitled "Reflections of Bohemia," which we have used *in extenso* in the third chapter of the background material of this book. He never got to the sequel of this—which he had intended writing—on life in Prague and the Jewish community there.[54] He wrote also concerning another subject that was one of his constant preoccupations, the position of woman in Judaism. This article was on "The Confirmation and Bar Mitzvah." His attitude was that Confirmation was greatly to be preferred, for in it girls and boys would have equal rights and opportunities:

> We leave it to the reader to decide whether this reform [Confirmation] was right and good, or uncalled for, at the same time we can not restrain ourselves from entering our complaints on behalf of our female friends. Is it not insolence that men say in their morning prayers, "Blessed art Thou, etc. that Thou hast not made me a woman?" Is it not an offence to their mothers, wives, sisters, and daughters, and, if it should not be said, why should it be printed? Is it not a rudeness of the meanest kind that a female should be considered as a nobody in respect to person in religious affairs, not only in the synagogue, but in the family circle? This is one of the "established" absurdities, this is evidently the mildest name we can find for it.[55]

In the winter of 1854 his *History* was still being bitterly attacked. Wise thought that all this onslaught might be worrying his new friends in Cincinnati. He offered to release them from the contract. But he was wrong. They were staunch and clearsighted enough to know that both he and they must learn to endure abuse and yet to go ahead.[56]

In January of 1854 his fourth child, their second daughter, Ida, was born, later to become Mrs. Henry Bernheim of Cincinnati.[57]

On the last day of Passover, April 19, 1854, Wise delivered his farewell address to Anshe Emeth. Here are the words he used to describe this in his *Reminiscences:*

> I will not attempt to describe the scene. It was a day of mourning; I was attached to Albany with all the fibres of my heart. It was my first home in the new world. I had so many true and tried friends in the old city on the Hudson. Every child, every tree was dear to me, but my school-days were over,

> I had to go out into the world. I had attended two schools in Albany for nearly eight years; the school of experience, of bitter struggles and brilliant triumphs, and the school of learning, whose lessons I had learned with tireless industry. I had four children, much self-reliance, and a firm faith in God and the truth. A dreaming optimist, an idealist such as I always was, requires no more than this to be happy.[58]

Resolutions of farewell and of praise were presented to him by Anshe Emeth. These were printed in the *Asmonean* of March 24, 1854, and also in the *Occident*. His last regular contribution to the *Asmonean* was a letter in the April 28 issue. Here is a single sentence from it:

> The last sounds of my friends in Albany still re-echo in my heart, and if I was able to give utterance to my sentiment I could write you a touching and beautiful letter.

The letter also pleads for circuit preachers, an idea to which he returned many times.[59]

He had also received from the "Scholars, literati, etc. of the library" a farewell scroll on parchment which had said: "Farewell! May God protect you! Our love goes with you." Another testimonial had been signed by all hundred and thirty-four members of the congregation.[60]

Wise left Albany on April 20 and journeyed to Syracuse and Rochester, using the time to make contacts for the paper he proposed to publish. He claims that in all—before he came to Cincinnati—he had procured about two hundred advance subscriptions.[61] His family joined him in Rochester on April 24 and together they continued westward. Wise was charmed by the countryside that moved past the train windows. Here are a few of his words:

> All the peach, plum, and cherry trees were in full blossom, displaying their pageantry of rich colors in the mild spring sunshine. The fields were full of life and bustle, dotted everywhere with flocks of sheep and playful lambs. It was a charming picture. My children shouted with glee. My wife was most happy, and chatted on a hundred subjects. . . .[62]

He himself was meditating on this new chapter that was opening in his and their life. What would it hold for him? More conflict? More struggle? What lay hidden in the lap of the future? As he pondered, it seemed to him the end of one life and the beginning of another. By a natural association of ideas this reminded him of the Memorial Service on *Yom Kippur*. Thoughts about life and immortality—in which he was a lifelong believer—began to flood his mind. He sat down in the station at Columbus at noon and began to compose a service, his *Seelenfeier*, his Memorial Service, the principal passages of which he wrote on the train between Columbus and Cincinnati that April, 1854. This service is still used on *Kol Nidre* eve in K. K. B'nai Yeshurun in Cincinnati. It was originally written by Wise in German and later translated into English by Bernhard Bettmann. It is also the basis of the Memorial Service for the afternoon of *Yom Kippur* in the Union Prayerbook. It reflects many of his views on life, and of the logical and emotional grounds for a belief in life after death.[63]

Wise and his family reached Cincinnati that night and were established in temporary quarters which had been prepared for them. A meeting of the Board of Trustees was convened on April 26 by Marcus Fechheimer, and Wise was formally introduced to them as their rabbi. He was taken to the Talmud Yelodim Institute by Solomon Friedmann and presented as superintendent.[64]

This was his formal arrival in the city and his formal assumption of his duties. Later on—in fact forty years later—he himself reviewed this time, and the months and years that followed. He dominated the spirit of his people in Cincinnati, he wrote, in moving toward "progressive American Judaism." His success was great from the beginning. In fact, he was in his element. He could work without discouragement and without opposition. He could employ his energies, his enthusiasm, and develop his charitable schemes and projects. He saw himself surrounded by a host of dear friends and zealous co-laborers, a "noble band of men and brethren, such as would gladden the heart of any prince or potentate." His sermons were "explicitly patriotic and American," advocating the abandonment of the concepts of king and Messiah, of Palestine and priesthood, of exclusiveness and extravagances, "and all around him and about him became enthusiastic Americans."[65] All this had the effect of taking him out of his library, "freeing him from his lethargy, and impressing him into the active service of the people."

> . . . All the projects, plans and schemes with which he had crossed the ocean, notwithstanding all the disappointments, reverses, defeats and mortifications, turned up again in his mind with indomitable force, seeking realization. In a very short time he reorganized the synagogue service, backed by the entire congregation, who went with him like a well-organized band of old and tried friends.[66]

To the remainder of his plans and his experiences we shall now come. With his arrival in Cincinnati, Wise was in the place and among the people where he could dream and work, where he would move from strength to strength. He was thirty-five years of age when he began, vigorous in mind and body, capable of incredibly sustained and diverse work, full of a sense of mission, in love with America, deeply confident that Judaism was the only faith for modern man, the only religion compatible with universal reason and destined to become the possession of all civilized men within a brief future. The Cincinnati period is the time of his flowering into full maturity, of his progress through many defeats to final achievement, of his becoming the head and front of liberal Judaism in America.

16

First Years in Cincinnati

ARRIVED IN CINCINNATI, ISAAC M. WISE LOST LITTLE TIME IN plunging into the many tasks—in Cincinnati and in the American Jewish community—which he had been envisaging more and more clearly since his coming to America.

His new congregation, K. K. B'nai Yeshurun, was only twelve years old, but by this time it was vigorous, clearly "liberal" in its bent, and among its members were many men of ability and of culture. Wise himself had asserted that most of its members had migrated from Bavaria, and had there been under the tutelage of Rabbis Levy, Rosenfeld, Aub, Leopold Stein and Gutmann. Some had come from Wurtemberg and had sat at the feet of Mayer and Frankfurter.[1] Wise soon came to feel that he was among friends, in two senses: these were people very close to him in their background of German literature and in their convictions concerning Judaism; they were also approachable, ambitious, and warm. It would be pleasant to pause here and to mention those families in Cincinnati with whom Wise was especially intimate in these early years. Above all—and with remarkably few exceptions—even in those early days the congregation was homogeneous. Hardly any genuine struggle was required to weld them together into an effective working unit, to win their support for plans of action—for Cincinnati and for the country—and to mobilize money and cooperative labor. The earliest biography of Wise commented on this and said:

> Historical justice awards to Congregation B'nai Yeshurun a position of honor in American Judaism, by reason of its record as a "Mother in Israel."[2]

Wise himself had deepened and ripened, but he was not essentially different in 1854 from the person he had been eight years before when he had left Bohemia and had landed in New York. By nature he was a fighter and an optimist. This he wrote of himself later on. He was impatient of delays and of opposition. It was always hard to persuade him that not everything could be achieved in a day. He thought of himself as a "child of destiny," come into the world to achieve something not inconsiderable on behalf of Jews and of mankind. It was with constant exacerbation and difficulty that he discovered that he must reckon with people and with the possible.[3] For some time he was the only Jewish preacher in the entire West. From the very beginning he addressed large audiences, who came to hear him not only from the entire community of Cincinnati, but also from near and distant towns. It appears also—which was much more remarkable for those days—that there was a constant sprinkling of non-Jews at his services, drawn by his eloquence and the weighty, timely themes upon which he spoke. Twenty-five years later in the *Israelite* Wise wrote of those early years:[4]

> We had no trouble in Cincinnati where most all were our friends, and those very few, very few indeed, who were not our friends, did not speak loud enough to be heard. . . . We had little trouble with the Orthodox side of the house. Our troubles were abroad and with the reformers.[5]

Later on we shall come to the episodes and causes which prompted this last comment.

In his school and in his pulpit he was never timorous. From the beginning the instruction of the young was in his charge. Here he could put into effect his bold, clear ideas and convictions on Jewish and general education. The entire record—to some chapters and incidents of which we shall come later—displays his independence, his courage, and his chafing at interference. It had become his conviction that the enlightenment of the people and the creation of instruments and methods for their spiritual nutrition were the very heart of the task. This must begin with the children. A strong foundation must be laid. And to this he dedicated himself in a number of directions: in the Talmud Yelodim Institute, the parochial school the congregation had founded five years earlier, in Zion College which was soon to follow, in the books he wrote, and in the addresses he delivered. As we proceed, we shall list the titles of some of these latter and give examples of them as to style and content. In general in reading them one cannot avoid a start of surprise at their theological and philosophical intricacy, their length, the close reasoning they display and demand. He himself wrote that he preached "in rationalistic style." It was his custom to propound theses and then to devote himself to the arduous task of proving them. His general attitude was that neither his own bare word, nor his or their faith, was sufficient to establish the validity of the ideas he was considering. This must be done by reason, and by reason alone! The very spirit which had animated his *History of the Israelitish Nation* dictated his choice of subjects and his manner of handling them. Sometimes his "opponents," he claimed, called him the "jurist in the pulpit." In passing it must be noted again that, as one reads these addresses, as they appeared in the *Israelite* and when some of them were reissued in book-form, it is both difficult and disturbing for us today to think that congregations in those days could and would listen and comprehend![6]

His inaugural sermon was delivered in Cincinnati on April 26, 1854.[7] It was devoted to a protracted statement of his own Jewish standpoint; it was a combined pronunciamento and program. His friend and perpetual counselor, Mrs. F., was sitting in the balcony. Wise noticed her presence. He had had a card from her in the afternoon, telling him of her arrival in Cincinnati. Doubtless she had come out of the intensity of her personal interest, to see for herself how he would make a beginning. She was on her way from New Orleans to Philadelphia. Her two daughters were with her, and, when Wise called on Monday, he was introduced to them. Mrs. F. reproached Wise for having returned to her, while she was abroad, the loan she had sent him. She declared herself a little hurt, and then went on to predict that if Wise would go on as he had begun the previous week-end, he would continue to amass enemies. It appears consistently to have been her self-conceived role to advise and admonish him. She told him that he was too violent and by all odds too outspoken, that his acquaintance with "the world" was deficient. If he hoped to move toward his goals, it would be far better to use more discretion. Wise himself wrote that her earnestness and his own confidence in her "knowledge of human nature" caused him to listen carefully and to shrink back for a moment. But quickly he assured her that it was unthinkable for him to alter either his temperament or his convictions. The issue was with God! Instead of tempering what he would say, it was his purpose—he told her—

to speak weekly on controversial subjects having to do with Judaism and with religion in general. Perhaps he would start a "conflagration!" He declared himself equal to all his enemies. Mrs. F., who was not unlearned in the Bible, nor unequal in repartee, warned him: "My dear Samson, you will bring down the Temple of Dagon." No fighter—she said oracularly—is ever beloved. All this must have left some precipitate of worry in Wise, for he declared that he went home, wrote down what Mrs. F. had said, and confessed that in many ways the years had discovered to him its truth.[8]

Within a few weeks of Isaac M. Wise's assumption of his task in Cincinnati, the president of the congregation, Marcus Fechheimer, a man of tact and force, announced that the congregation would no longer use the *Piutim* in the ritual, and that the sale of *Mitzvoth* would be abolished. In Albany, Wise had had a long and arduous struggle for both these steps. In Cincinnati they were taken almost at once and apparently without vocal opposition. We shall come shortly to the other "reforms" Wise initiated in these early years, and follow them through consecutively before proceeding.[9]

Not many months after Wise's work had begun, he must already have made a unique impression upon the community. B'nai Yeshurun had become the focus of Jewish interest in Cincinnati. Wise had little tolerance for the prejudices in regard to *Landsmannschaft* (national derivation) or *Minhag* of the congregations of the city. While K.K.B'nai Israel of Cincinnati had been too orthodox and too different for the group of German Jews who had organized K.K.B'nai Yeshurun and chartered it in 1842, it is certain that within the former too there were parties and differences. Wise's coming and the early months of his impact upon the community must have precipitated the conflict, must have convinced the liberal element that there was no future for them in mere dissent and mere obstinacy. They took a remarkable step. The president of K. K. B'nai Israel called a general meeting of the congregation on November 5, 1854, which by a vote of ninety-three to twelve adopted the following resolution:

> That the rabbi of Bene Yeshurun congregation is hereby elected for life rabbi of Bene Israel congregation with the understanding that he is to preach alternately in both synagogues, and to discharge rabbinical functions in both congregations.
>
> That the Bene Israel congregation proceed at once to build a school, and said rabbi is elected superintendent of this school.
>
> That the Bene Israel congregation contribute as much as the Bene Yeshurun congregation toward the salary of the rabbi.[10]

This was certainly an astonishing step. One wishes that more material were available concerning it. It is difficult to imagine that this could have been done without previous consultation with Wise, without preliminary exploration of the feasibility of such a proposal. Or perhaps it was possible that representative members of K.K.B'nai Israel had discussed it with the officers or leaders of K.K.B'nai Yeshurun. But neither seems to have been the case. Nor was there ever a proposal—which would have seemed both logical and natural—to amalgamate the two congregations under Wise's leadership.

On the midnight of November 5, after the adoption of the foregoing resolution, a committee of fifty representatives of B'nai Israel waited upon Wise and informed him of the decision taken. There was much joy. It was felt that this would unite the entire community. Wise wrote that he did not close his eyes that night.[11]

But K.K.B'nai Yeshurun showed no disposition whatever to consider this proposal. From the very beginning they rejected it. Perhaps the old animosity, that had some twelve years earlier led to their leaving B'nai Israel and launching their own congregation, had not diminished or disappeared. All they would concede was that, inasmuch as B'nai Israel was then without a rabbi, Wise might take on the functions described on a purely temporary basis. He preached in B'nai Yeshurun on Saturday morning, and at B'nai Israel on Saturday afternoon. A school was opened, called *Noyoth*, and four teachers were employed. The officers of B'nai Israel and he were on the best of terms. All this tended to strengthen the reform group in B'nai Israel and to discomfit and reduce the number of the orthodox. But B'nai Yeshurun did not budge from the decision it had made.[12] The arrangement lasted until May, 1855, that is, for about six months. There is every evidence that during all this time Wise's cordial relations with Lilienthal had continued. It will be recalled that almost three years earlier Lilienthal had become utterly discouraged with the three German orthodox congregations of which he had been rabbi in New York, had left the pulpit, and was devoting himself to Jewish education. Wise knew what a loss this was for the rabbinate. Lilienthal enjoyed his boundless regard and his warm friendship. Feeling doubtless that the arrangement with B'nai Israel was a mere expedient, that it could not and should not long be continued, and certainly that Judaism would be greatly the gainer if Lilienthal returned to the pulpit and became his co-worker in Cincinnati, Wise recommended to B'nai Israel that they elect Lilienthal. This was done, and the latter came to Cincinnati in the late spring of 1855. The episode came to its end with a set of laudatory resolutions presented to Wise by the officers and members of B'nai Israel, and a handsome silver fruit-basket.[13]

Wise was active in many directions in Cincinnati, and we shall come upon many of them as we forge ahead. He organized a Lodge for the B'nai Brith, the third in Cincinnati. It took the name of Mt. Carmel. It was the twentieth in the United States. Wise himself was made vice-president of it and succeeded in making it a force in the community.[14] He joined the Odd Fellows, through M.J. Mack, and later the Hanselman Lodge of the Masons. In his *Reminiscences* he declared that he had found the "secrets" of those orders childish, and that he was attracted to them and remained in them solely because of their charitable work.[15] He was elected an honorary member of the "Allemannia," and of other societies. Cincinnati had a Benevolent Society, one of the many forerunners of our Federations. Wise served for a time as its president.[16] His own reputation for personal benevolence was great, and he was constantly being sought out by poor people. Thus there exists an article by one Henry Frank of New Orleans, formerly of Cincinnati, who wrote of some of his own recollections of Wise, and said in part:

> He endeared himself to the community by his many charitable deeds; often, when going to the market to purchase the needed supplies for the day, if he chanced to meet a poor woman asking for help, he would give her all the money he had in his pocket, even though it amounted to five dollars.[17]

The family had a tradition, too, that it was almost impossible to keep Isaac M. Wise in overcoats, for he would strip them off and give them to beggars.

Apparently his relations with Leeser were far from improving. No sooner had Wise started the *Israelite*—to the origin and early experiences of which we shall come soon—than he was caught up in the usual round of polemics. The *Occident* began sniping at him. In November, 1854, Wise declared he would not "defile the columns of the *Israelite* by quarreling with the *Occident*. . . ."[18] He proceeded thereupon to contradict what he had just written by asserting that he could debate only with "scientific men," that clearly the editor of the *Occident* could not be placed in that category: Leeser had accused Wise of perverting the intent of Saadya and of Maimonides by claiming them as reformers in their respective days. How, Wise inquired arrogantly, could Leeser make such statements, when he—Leeser—could not read a single word of the writings of either of these great men? Wise requested him to name their books.

It was, Wise declared, "insolent" for Leeser to write thus, for Leeser had had to send to Baltimore to have a "passage of the Morah (sic!) translated for him,—and now he is our judge." Why would not Leeser simply let him alone? In place of argument there was only "slander, gross personalities, and calumniation."

This was the general tone of the *odium theologicum* at this period, and could be paralleled with thousands of similar instances, from articles and from pamphlets.

At the same time Wise was writing in the *Israelite* that he had been succeeding far beyond his expectations in Cincinnati. He had "won over" B'nai Israel, "despite the calumnies of our opponents in the East."

> Our sojourn of six months among our brethren of this city has had the effect to unmask our opponents and to judge our humble self by the light of simple truth.[19]

He wrote that he and his friends wanted only union in the city, to be able to work singlemindedly for the institutions, local and national, that must be born. Soon the entire West would be united. This in turn would lead to the "union of our brethren in this country for great and national purposes."

We have noted that Wise joined a number of fraternal, charitable, and cultural societies. It must be borne in mind that communities and persons depended in those days—more than a century ago—on themselves for instruction and for entertainment, to an extent so far beyond our day that it is not easy to conjure up. The *Israelite* of the fall of the same year gave an enchanting picture of the simple but by no means inactive life of the Jewish community. We shall content ourselves with a single, rather amusing example. Wise had joined the Allemannia, a Jewish social and literary society. These were the lectures the Allemannia sponsored that season:

1. "The Benefit of Literary Associations," by Isaac M. Wise.
2. "The History of the Roman Republic," by Dr. Jacob Auerbach.
3. "The Life and Works of Schiller," by Newburgh and Rosenfeld.
4. "Natural Sciences and Their Influence on Our Age."
5. "The Life and Works of Shakespeare."
6. "The Revolution of 1848."
7. "Cromwell and His Age."
8. "The Jurisprudence of the United States," by Isaac M. Wise.
9. "The Commerce of the United States and Its Influence on

Civilization," by M. J. Mack.
10. "The Fine Arts and Their Influence on Society."
11. "Woman."
12. "The American Revolution," by Lewis Heinsheimer and I. M. Wise.[20]

There was another incident in relation to Leeser in the fall of 1854. Unfortunately we can retail it only from Wise's account, which is patently far from impartial. The progress of events in Cincinnati had alarmed the "orthodox party in the East." According to Wise, this prompted Leeser to make a trip to the West, to try to "save the *Occident*," and to help change public opinion. Again according to Wise, reports came to him that Leeser was attacking him bitterly. Finally Leeser came to Cincinnati. Wise was asked whether Leeser should be invited to preach in the pulpit of B'nai Israel. To this he voiced no objection. Wise sent a committee also to invite Leeser to a banquet to commemorate the anniversary of the "Relief Society," of a Sunday evening. Leeser was to respond to the toast, "Our Guests." At the affair Wise reached out his hand to shake Leeser's, but declared that Leeser had "refused to take it." He did his utmost—he contended—to conciliate Leeser, by offering him the privilege of "making *motzi*," (the prayer before breaking bread) and also giving the blessing after the meal. Wise continued:

> Nothing, however, could mollify his wrath, and when he arose to respond to his toast he overwhelmed me with bitter reproaches and insults in the name of Judaism, which, as he claimed, I wished to undermine and destroy.

There was indignation among those present and cries heard to the effect that Wise should reply. But Wise refused to rejoin, and "Leeser and his friends hurried from the hall."[21] Wise declared that thereafter he was left in peace, and that Taylor, the proprietor and editor of the *Times*, "presented" him "with a gold pen in recognition of" his "Christian humility and pagan stoicism."[22] Naturally this was a highly *ex parte* description, nor have we any check on it for accuracy.

Not very long after he had come to Cincinnati, Wise began a long series of journeys upon which he went during the years of his incumbency. We have already described the purposes he had for making these trips. Most of them are recorded in detail in the columns of the *Israelite*, in the form of long communications Wise sent back from the road. These constitute not only a vivid, vigorous, and usually quite chatty account of what he saw and heard in many

American communities, but also of the changing status of Judaism and Jews in them, and of his own invariable propaganda and progress in regard to his pet schemes; they are also a kind of chronicle of Jewish life in the United States in the latter half of the nineteenth century. Some one should take the trouble to garner from them the characteristics glimpses of places and of people with which they abound.[23]

Such a trip Wise took in the latter months of 1855, and the detailed record of it is in his *Reminiscences*. We can here do no more than give the main outlines and conclusions.

He began by saying that he did not look or feel well. A physician advised him to leave the city. He went first to Louisville and then to Indianapolis. Thereafter, he stopped in Terre Haute and Vincennes, Ind. Next he visited St. Louis and there he had dealings with the officers of two congregations. He found Judaism in a sorry plight. Thence he went up the Mississippi by steamer, stopping at Quincy, Illinois, Keokuk, Iowa, Davenport, and Rock Island. Various other cities on the way to Chicago tempted him to stop and investigate. Finally he arrived in Chicago. He was, he wrote, the first man to preach Reform Judaism in that city. He tried also to make some propaganda for his plan for a College. His next stop was Milwaukee, to which he went by a lake steamer. There was a little synagogue in which he preached, but here he found much hostility to Judaism in general. In Detroit, his next stop, there was only the feeble beginning of a congregation.

This was one trip. It served him for education. It won him friends all along the road. It enhanced his reputation in Cincinnati. The people in his own congregation, Wise wrote, were convinced that they had the greatest rabbi in the universe. This was laughable to him in its extravagance, but he could not talk them out of it. His journeys were instructive but, in these early years, expensive and devoid of practical result.[24]

17

The Israelite and the College

In considering Isaac M. Wise's projects and activities during these first four years in Cincinnati, we shall abandon our practice hitherto of a more or less strict chronological narrative, and assemble the material under one head for the sake of consecutiveness and clarity.

In the earlier pages of this book, especially in Chapter Fourteen, we told of Wise's growing awareness of his need for a journal of his own, and of his first attempts to secure backing for it in Albany, in New York, and on his way to Cincinnati in the fall of 1853.

After his first days in Cincinnati he lost no time in getting started. His inaugural sermon was near the end of April, 1854. By June he had already written and sent out a prospectus for the new paper. It was brief and to the point. The purpose of the new journal was to interest the progressive Jews of the United States. He was helped in his planning by Lewis Abraham and by his brother-in-law, Edward Bloch. A Dr. Schmidt, publisher of a paper called *The Republican*, was induced to take the new journal under his wing for its first year. By the latter part of June there had been enough responses to the prospectus to justify getting out the first number. This appeared on July 6, 1854. It was called *The Israelite*, and only after the passage of some years was its name changed to *The American Israelite*. At its masthead in Hebrew and in English Wise placed his own favorite text from the Bible, the same text which in 1866 he set in the windows at the eastern end of the Plum St. Temple: "Let there be light" (Genesis 1:3). The new periodical—to be published weekly—found a friendly reception in cities west, east, and south. Its birth was heralded by the *Occident* with a dire prediction that it would never survive its infancy. Others ridiculed both it and Wise.[1]

For Wise, the appearance of the *Israelite* was the beginning of a new era. The influence of the paper on Jewish life in the United States was very great, and remained great over the course of a number of decades. For Wise it involved a tremendous additional burden. Every week, by a dead-line, he was obligated to deliver a certain amount of material to the type-setter. He was also in constant debt to its first two printers, Gutenberg—an appropriate name—and Dr. Faust. Like the *Asmonean*—the pattern of which Wise followed in some respects—the *Israelite* had leaders each week on Reform. It carried national and international news about Jewish affairs, poetry, much of which Wise wrote himself, continued novels, and short stories. Wise either wrote or edited almost everything.[2]

Rather significantly the *Israelite* was never called a Reform organ. In a much later series Wise wrote:

> To me, Reform was never an end in itself; I considered it only as a necessary means to clarify the teachings of Judaism, and to transfigure, exalt, and spread these teachings. . . . It was an organ of Judaism.[3]

It was his purpose—he wrote—to instruct rather than to moralize. Among the activities which Wise undertook—and which proved to be astonishingly popular—was that of writing novels. He called himself "The American Jewish Novelist." Some of these fictional adventures bore the following titles: *The First of the Maccabees*; *The Combat of the People, or Hillel and Herod; The Convert; The Catastrophe of Eger; Fidelity, or Life and Romance; Romance, Philosophy and Cabalah, or the Conflagration in Frankfort-on-the-Main; The Last Struggle of the Nation.* German novels appeared serially in *Die Deborah* (cf. later as to character and time of founding) under such titles as these: *Die Juden von Landshuth; Der Rothkopf, oder des Schulmeisters Tochter; Baruch und sein Ideal.* He wrote and published two rather light-hearted plays, *Der maskierte Liebhaber*, and *Das Glueck Reich zu Sein.*[4]

Each week—Wise tells us—he dashed off a chapter or two, just enough to fill the necessary space in either journal. It came red hot from his pen and was sent post-haste to the press. He had no chance to check or to outline in advance. Often he forgot "the name of the sweet heroine and gave her a different one the following week." Once he got two heroines into one novel by mistake. One had to go by some sudden and drastic means. He had the supernumerary burned in the Frankfort fire. This, he asserted, spoiled the appetite of his lady-readers for their Sabbath fish.[5]

The first year he lost $600 on the *Israelite* and paid Dr. Schmidt out of his own pocket.[6]

The pages of the *Israelite* served quite naturally to air his own views, to give them wide circulation, to make propaganda for a Union and a College, and for all the other plans that were brewing in his fertile mind. Thus one of its early numbers printed this:

> We have endeavored in three former articles under this caption [What Should Be Done?] to convince our readers, that we stand in need of many an institution, which can be built up only by the united efforts of our American congregations.

There was no English Bible for Jews; there were no good text-books for Jewish children; there was no good short history of the Jewish people. Wise proposed the translation and reissuance of texts by Elkan and Mannheim in Germany.[7]

At the time of the genesis of the *Israelite* a local orthodox paper had written:

> A weekly paper, falsely called *The Israelite*, edited by the eccentric Isaac M. Wise, of Albany, has made its appearance in Cincinnati. It will be short lived.[8]

Its birth was also cheerfully greeted by a Christian organ, which wrote:

> An anomalous sheet is being published in Cincinnati called the *Israelite*, which is more rationalistic than Jewish, an exotic plant that will hardly flourish in this climate.[9]

One of Wise's difficulties inhered in the fact that not too many Jews in his part of the country could read English. Moreover his risk was augmented by the fact that he was publishing his paper weekly, whereas the *Occident* was a monthly, and the *Asmonean* but a small paper.[10]

For a long time as it proved the *Israelite* was the chief journal for all Jews. It sprang valorously to their defense at home and abroad. As we proceed, we shall give details of many of the causes of Jewish civil and religious rights which Wise championed in and out of the *Israelite*. He insisted again and again on the fundamental truth of the Declaration of Independence. He believed ardently in the American principle of the separation of church and state, and was bold enough to demand that this be applied all along the line, in cases that have since been passed over habitually even by Jewish organizations. He was never willing to take peaceably the oft-reiterated statement that this is a "Christian nation." He was vocal and vigorous on such subjects as Thanksgiving Day proclamations, the Swiss Treaty, the reading of the Bible in the public schools, Christian holidays as public and legal days of rest, and addresses made here and there by politicians. There was never any hesitation or delay. The *Israelite* leaped into the fray; it demanded redress and fair treatment. In the very first volume, Wise inaugurated his criticism of the Thanksgiving Day proclamations and their sectarian verbiage and tone. He reviewed such proclamations by the governors of New York, Massachusetts, New Hampshire, Vermont, and Maine. He singled them out because of their Christian tone and their narrow and illiberal views.[11]

This was still the time—such as he had already witnessed and fought in Albany—when Christian pulpits were raining verbal blows on the Talmud and on Jews, their beliefs, their history, and their character. Every cheap novel contained a rascally Jew, in the pattern of "Oliver Twist." The press and even public addresses had as their stock in trade stale jokes about Jews. No one had the courage to characterize all this as it deserved, or to condemn and oppose it. But this was not Wise's way. He started at once to write articles full of fire and brimstone. He struck out right and left. His Egeria, Mrs. F., begged him to write more gently. This he could not do, for his whole soul cried out against these slanders, these manifest and vile injustices. In the end his rough-and-ready tactics, his courage and his willingness to carry the fight into the "enemy's" camp, proved effective. He silenced the New York conversionists and their magazine. He encouraged cowards to throw off their disguises and not be ashamed of being Jews—on the contrary, to glory in it.[12] In the beginning he was forever receiving letters which would read something like this:

> We are not Jews. We do not need a Jewish paper. We do not wish to be known as Jews. There is no honor in being a Jew.[13]

And a host of other pleas of the same general order! Worst of all—said Wise—was the company of converted Jews, sent to the United States by a London society for the purpose of persuading their fellow-Jews to go over to Christianity. Many of these used the most scurrilous sources of anti-Jewish slander, like the infamous treatise of Eisenmenger, entitled "*Entdecktes Judenthum*" (Judaism Exposed). All these Wise strove to strip bare in all their malice and ignorance.[14]

Some years later—writing of the early years of the *Israelite*—Wise recorded that some of his contributors from the beginning were still alive: Lewis Abraham of Washington, who wrote under the *nom de plume* of "Talmid Americus." There were early stories by Dr. Nathan Mayer of Hartford, Conn. and by H. S. Moos of Cincinnati. By the time he wrote this—in 1892—the *Israelite* had become the oldest periodical of the synagogue in America, for the others had gone out of existence. In the earliest years Wise was assisted by only three rabbis: Merzbacher, Lilienthal, and Kalisch.[15]

We do not know just what his list of subscribers was, but it cannot have been large. The time came when Dr. Schmidt had to tell Wise that he could not go on. The losses were getting too heavy for him to bear. Then Wise took a bold step. He and Edward Bloch bought type, presses, and so on. They were able to get credit for six months. In July of 1855 they founded the firm of Bloch and Co., with debts of $3000. Not satisfied with losing money on the *Israelite*, Wise soon brought the *Deborah* into being, and bought Hebrew type for the first Jewish printing-press in the West. At the end of June, 1855, he moved to the corner of Third and Sycamore Streets and was ready for business early in July.[16]

Nor did this mean the end of his troubles. There was a national financial crisis in 1857. Bloch had been going too fast and too far. The press had got out the first edition of the *Minhag America*, plus two other books. The position of the publishing house was precarious. The question was whether it would be possible to continue further with the *Israelite* or the *Deborah*. Wise could find no friends in Cincinnati who had money to advance. From a Mrs. B., another of the anonymous characters who spring up in his record, he borrowed $1000, and this saved the two journals. By December they had weathered the storm sufficiently to enable him to repay the loan.[17] Wise wrote that around this period he found life more than a little hard. He was reading and writing day and night. He was constantly being scolded and criticized. He was poor as a church mouse. Sometimes it must have seemed to him senseless to continue the struggle. But could he give his enemies the boundless satisfaction of seeing him retire from the arena in defeat? For three months his wife agreed to a drastic reduction of expenses at home. For his part Isaac M. Wise gave up smoking cigars, and this must have been a fearful hardship. He drank but one glass of beer a day, another very real deprivation. Little by little the two papers moved out of troubled into calmer waters. The subscription lists grew apace. Their ability to finance themselves became a reality.

It was at this very time and in the midst of all these doubts and difficulties that Wise determined upon adding a German to his English publication. The announcement of this was in the *Israelite* in the spring of 1855, only eight months after he had begun to publish the *Israelite*. The latter contained a brief paragraph in German to the effect that the *Deborah* will be *ein regelmaessiges deutsches Beiblatt* (a regular German supplement). It will have special reading for ladies, including novels, biographies, poems, reports from the old country, etc. It will come with the *Israelite* to subscribers at an additional cost of one dollar a year. The first number is to appear as soon as the editor will have received 500 subscriptions.[18] This did not take long, for after the passing of four months the first number of the *Deborah* was out, in July, 1855. The paper was greeted joyously. It was the first German paper for American Jews. A similar attempt had been made in 1849 by Isidor Busch of New York, but it had failed within a short time. The *Deborah* was in simpler and more popular style than the *Israelite*. Rothenheim wrote poetry for it and Lilienthal, prose. Wise served as the general utility man. At the outset, 800 copies were struck off.[19]

Wise himself claimed—though this may have been evoked somewhat by his continuous experience of enmity—that his "opponents" were constantly striving to bring about the demise of the *Israelite* and of the *Deborah*. If this was so, then they did not succeed, for both publications grew not weaker but stronger, more and more firmly established in the interest and affection of an increasing roster of readers.[20]

As the pages of the *Israelite* reveal, Wise's struggles were not only or even primarily with those who had a different interpretation of Judaism from his own. In the early years he got into a bitter fight with the "atheists" in Cincinnati. It was these—he claimed—who drove him out of the Republican Party which was being organized just then. Wise wrote that—at least in Ohio—he was present at the "round table" where the party was "born and baptized." But he could not remain within it, and—as we shall see later in detail—identified himself with the Democrats during and after the Civil War. Whatever his protestations anent the duty of religion to stay out of politics, his own political views and activities were an important element in his life, especially during the ten years that now follow. We shall look into these somewhat farther on.[21]

Nothing disturbed and motivated Wise as constantly as one of the central impressions he had acquired shortly after his arrival in America: the almost complete dearth of trained rabbis, the emptiness and ineffectiveness of Jewish leadership, and the consequent low level of Jewish knowledge and Jewish cooperation. We have seen that in his very earliest pronunciamento—in the *Occident* in 1848—he had dwelt upon all this as the chief point and aim of Union. There must be an institute of higher learning. The Jews of the country must educate their sons and daughters, both those who would find their profession in the pulpit, and those who would need a general background of theoretical and practical knowledge and culture. But, if some precedence had to be given, then the need in the very first instance was for competent Jewish leaders.

After his coming to Cincinnati, Wise lost no time in making a start upon all this. The very first volume of the *Israelite* agitated again and again for the founding of a college and for the pursuit of Jewish learning. Fortunately, there were a number of Cincinnatians who understood and were eager to help. In September, 1854, the *Israelite* contained a "Call" for a general meeting issued by a committee consisting of Isaac M. Wise, Jacob Wolff, Bernhard Bettmann, M. J. Mack, and Isaac E. Hackenberg:

> . . . that the Israelites of this country should establish a college on the pattern of German universities, connected with a theological seminary, and a seminary for teachers, in order to promulgate science and the interests of Judaism among our fellow-citizens.

They urged the Jews of Cincinnati to take the lead. An initial meeting was announced for Sunday, October 8, 1854, in the hall of the Allemannia. The members of the committee enumerated above would speak. The call was signed by twenty-three persons, including Isaac M. Wise.[22]

Before we go ahead with the account of the attempt to establish this institution, and its fate, it would be well to dwell for a moment upon one fact concerning it, which the reader should bear in mind. It was not then, nor for a long time thereafter, Wise's intention to call into being solely a school for rabbis. He conceived this as a "Jewish university," for training teachers, scientists, business-men, women, etc. In his mind it was a meeting-place for Jewish and universal Western culture, a contribution of the Jews of America to their own and to general cultural enrichment. Long experience with the attempt to attain this end, bitter disappointments, and the development through which the American Jewish community went after that time, forced him to contract his ambitious aim and to be content with a theological seminary. But certainly he had not come to this at the time of which we are now writing!

He himself backed up this call by the committee with his own appeal:

> The scheme is both grand and honorable, deserving the consideration and hearty cooperation of every intelligent man. . . .

He elaborated the point that there was a great need for "Jewish theology," but that much perseverance would be required to move from appeal to accomplishment.[23]

The name chosen for the new enterprise was "The Zion Collegiate Association." Membership in it was to be ten dollars *per annum.* Similar associations, or chapters, were to be organized in the larger Jewish centers. Unitedly they were to found a Jewish Academy or College. Three hundred members were enrolled in Cincinnati and there was an excellent response in Louisville. Wise himself claimed that, had he understood conditions better and spent more time visiting the West and the South in 1855, Zion College would have come into existence and remained open. But he had not learned enough; he was—he said—still hoping for too much from the East.[24]

On a trip that he made to the East in 1855 he was encouraged by the interest he thought he found in his plan. While he was in Philadelphia, where once again he saw Mrs. F., he spoke in public chiefly to arouse enthusiasm for this plan. Leeser and some of his followers were there. Wise claimed that it was actually this occasion that spurred Leeser on to try his hand at a similar project, the founding of Maimonides College. This school was intended for the orthodox, and its instruction rested firmly upon the *Shulchan Aruch.* The Reform party, Wise asserted, was as yet weak in Philadelphia. Its spirit and its strength were being diverted into other channels. Nonetheless—and mistakenly—Wise returned to Cincinnati, hugging to his breast the belief that he was not far from success.[25]

On the same trip he and his wife revisited Albany for the first time. He preached also at Temple Emanu-El in New York as the guest of Merzbacher. Mrs. F. was present on all these occasions and warned Wise—with her apparently habitual mimicry of Cassandra—that his hopes rested on no sure or solid base:

> You will never be forgiven for obtaining public favor so completely as you have.

It was in these words that she tried to restrain his enthusiasm.[26]

Back in Cincinnati, he went to work with a will. Before long he himself discovered that he was going too fast. The leaders of the community favored his plan. But the majority of Jews had no genuine interest in it. At the time he did not know this and his own passionate purpose seemed to carry the mass along. From the outset it was his plan that Zion College should be completely independent of the congregation. In August 1855 he submitted to the Society a careful plan of organization. He estimated the yearly expenditures for the College at $7000. This proposal was referred to a committee consisting of Henry Mack, Solomon Friedmann, Ferdinand Milius, M. Eskales, and Victor H. Loewenstein. The officers of Zion College at this time were: Moses Ezekiel, president; Henry Mack, vice-president; Ferdinand Milius, secretary; Isaac M. Wise and Isaac E. Hackenberg, secretaries; J. H. Heinsheimer, Solomon Friedmann, M. Eskales, and Victor H. Loewenstein, directors. It was resolved to call a general meeting for the middle of September and to open classes as soon thereafter as possible.[27]

Zion College actually opened in the fall of 1856 and had fourteen students, two of whom were Christians. There were five professors. The paid teachers were Rothenheim for Hebrew and German; Cohn (a young lawyer from Charleston, S. C.) as instructor in English; Junkerman for Talmud and mathematics. Lilienthal was to teach Latin and French, and Isaac M. Wise history, geography and archaeology, the last two *gratis*. The beginnings were not unencouraging. The opening was celebrated with a banquet at Masonic Hall. The élite of the city—Wise wrote—were present; the Governor of the State and later Chief Justice of the United States, Salmon P. Chase, and others. About eight hundred dollars was subscribed. Had American Jews been ready, the school could have achieved much during the next twenty years. Wise wrote of this two decades later. It would have been possible to send out into American Jewish communities educated preachers and teachers, who might have accelerated all the processes of American Jewish life. But it was not to be.[28]

After the College had been opened but a few weeks, a protest was published in the *Asmonean*, and the chapter of the Association in New York was dissolved. There were other acrimonious attacks in the cities of the East. It was impossible to discover what specific offense had provoked all this, unless it rested upon no more than continued suspicion and dislike of Wise for his supposed heresy. Wise himself was consumed with indignation. But he swallowed his wrath and went on working. At times—he asserted—it seemed to him that American Judaism must be nearing dissolution. What hope could there be for so disunited, so cantankerous, a community.[29]

In passing it should be remarked that Salmon P. Chase, who was the chief speaker at the banquet for the Zion Collegiate Association, and who was then serving his first term as Governor of Ohio, was the one who advised Wise to attach himself to the young Republican Party, which in his opinion was that of reform and progress. This, coupled with Wise's admiration and friendliness for Chase, did not, however, prevent Wise from his chronic objection to Chase's Thanksgiving Proclamation in the fall of 1856:

> In conformity with a custom sanctioned by Legislative Resolves, commended by the practice of my predecessors in the executive office, and in itself highly becoming a Christian people, I, Salmon P. Chase . . . etc.[30]

Wise wrote of this:

> The Governor addresses himself to a Christian people, but he ought to know that the people of Ohio are neither Christian nor Jewish; they are a free and independent people.
>
> Next the Governor desires us to thank God "for the mercies of redemption and the hopes of immortality." Fall on your knees, Jews, deists, infidels, and atheists, and thank God that Jesus of Nazareth died on the cross to redeem the people of Ohio, as His Excellency, the Governor, decrees. On the whole, we do not see by what right the Governor of Ohio assumes the prerogative of exercising a religious authority. This is, to say the least, unrepublican and inconsistent with the constitution of the State. . . .
>
> In conclusion, however, we must say, in justice to the Governor, that we do not believe this document to have been examined closely by him. He considered it immaterial and unimportant and cared little for what his secretary wrote. So do we care little about the whole matter. We merely dislike to see sectarian views grafted on the people.[31]

This is a highly characteristic fulmination by Wise, characteristic of his forthrightness and courage, be the offender who he might be.

But we must return to Zion College! Already, in the second issue of the Israelite, Wise had begun to make propaganda for it under the heading "What Should Be Done?" In the first article he called attention to the lack of schools and texts:

> All these difficulties could be overcome by a Union of the American Judaic Congregations.[32]

In the following issue he continued:

> We ought to be American Israelites, *i.e.*, American as men and citizens, and Israelites in our religion. . . . The Israelite is an American who enjoys the privileges which our Constitution guarantees to the citizen. . . . Let us educate our ministers here in our own college, and we will soon have American ministers, American congregations, and an American Union of Israelites for religious and charitable institutions. Let us have American trained leaders, and they will educate for us American citizens.[33]

It was in October, 1854, that he had come forward with his plan for Zion College. In the spring of 1856 the *Asmonean* backed him up to this extent:

> We hope that our children will at no distant day see an Israelite College in every state of the Union.[34]

This was too vague, and perhaps too foolishly ambitious, for Wise, and he replied cogently in the *Israelite*:

> We hope we shall see at no great distant day one grand and complete Israelite college for all states of the Union. Many petty institutions might flourish in this country, but a university worthy of the talents, lofty conceptions, and practical sense of the Jewish mind requires the support of all. As long as we have no ground to shout glory for the privileged of New York, we go in for Cincinnati, on account of its central location, and the readiness of our brethren to make great sacrifices for this national cause, and whenever we shall be convinced that New York is the place for it, we shall advocate such a conviction.[35]

It is important also to have in precise form the resolution adopted at a general meeting in Cincinnati, at seven P.M., and presided over by Henry Mack. The resolution was as follows:

> Whereas the spirit of the age, the interest of Judaism, and the sentiment of the generality of the Jewish community of this city, and of the whole Union require that a seat of learning be established in order to promulgate science, enlightenment, and true religion amongst our fellow-citizens; and Whereas, it becomes expedient, to form societies, to pursue this great and noble cause; therefore be it
>
> *Resolved*, That we organize ourselves into an association to be known and styled as the *Zion Collegiate Association.*
>
> *Resolved*, That this association shall have for its object, the establishment of a university in the city of Cincinnati, the theological faculty of which shall be that of Judaism.

> *Resolved*, That this association shall also have for its object, the improvement of the intellect of its members by literary endeavors, readings of essays, lectures, etc.
>
> Resolved, That in order that it may be in the power of every man to become a subscriber, the admission fee be one dollar, and the subscription two dollars per annum.

This was followed by a discussion and the preamble and resolution were unanimously adopted. One hundred and thirty signed both on the spot. The officers of the meeting were made permanent. To them Wise was added to draw up a plan of action.[36]

Wise commented upon this meeting the following week in the *Israelite*. He was convinced that all right-minded men would join and would help. He regarded it as an excellent meeting, animated by a harmonious spirit and including many younger men. Some of the older citizens of Cincinnati and some of the rich merchants had been absent. Wise asked the reason for this, but did not come up with an adequate answer. He ended with the somewhat trite tag: "United we stand, divided we fall"; and in Hebrew, "If there is no peace, there is nothing."[37]

In an editorial, in December, he noted that the number then associated with the project for Zion College had grown to more than two hundred, and he predicted that the list would soon double. This was not in fact very many, but those who had joined were deeply convinced of the need for such an institution. He hoped that similar societies would be founded in other cities, which were to be accorded one representative for every twenty-five members. And with each representative there would have to be a fee of fifty dollars. He would like to enlist ten thousand men. He asked also for the support of the ladies, especially because:

> . . . it will be one of the first and most sacred duties of the societies to establish a female seminary for the education of our daughters and sisters. "Come and let us go up to the house of the Lord."[38]

A letter appearing early in December in the *Israelite* made plain that one of the very real circumstances with which Wise had to contend was the jealousy and competition between East and West. The writers of this letter announced the constitution of a "Jewish Theological Seminary and Scientific Institution," that its incorporation had in fact been in 1842, and that it was intended "to preserve the ancient and orthodox Jewish faith, its customs, rites and ceremonies." They had acquired five acres in Yonkers, N. Y., and urged that gifts and bequests be sent them. This letter was signed by nine men. Wise wished them every success. He trusted that the two plans would be merged into one.[39]

A circular for the Zion Collegiate Association was printed and broadcast early in 1855, under the date of January 1. This announced to all and sundry that a seat of learning had been organized, that it was to be on the model of a German university, to have a theological faculty, and that it must be backed up by "thorough knowledge of natural, historical, and mental sciences." But equally, "scientific education without religious knowledge is dangerous to the cause of true religion." Good ministers should be good scholars, and *vice versa*. The college was to be in Cincinnati, where there exist four excellent congregations. Here live the largest number of Israelites next to New York (a rather astonishing bit of information!). A plan was outlined by which associations could and should be established in all communities. Jews were urged to correspond. The circular was signed by Isaac M. Wise, Joseph Jonas, and M. Hellman, the Committee.[40]

In the *Israelite* Wise was constantly harping upon this subject. In the spring of the same year, 1855, he inserted an "Outline of a Plan for the Zion College." He did not wish the reader to regard this outline as authoritative. It represented only his own ideas. Again he reiterated that the College must be like a German university, with four faculties, coupled with a preparatory school. There must be in it classical, scientific, and practical faculties, and a department of the arts. Under the first, the "classical," he would have Bible and Rabbinic Literature, Greek and Latin, and modern languages. Under the second, the "scientific," he would include mathematics, natural philosophy, and history. Under practical education he included agriculture, horticulture, pomeology (!),[41] mercantile arithmetic, correspondence and book-keeping, community statistics, and laws. This outline is intensely interesting for its inclusions and omissions, and its very terminology—which has much to do with the state of education at that time. Both sexes were to be admitted. There was to be physical exercise for leisure hours: gymnastics and dancing. What would such an institution cost, and how raise the money? By then he could rely on an income of $2000 a year, chiefly from Louisville and Cincinnati.[42]

A week later he continued with another editorial, again on the plan for Zion College. He estimated what he would need for buildings of instruction, a library, etc. He wanted subscriptions of twenty-five dollars from each member. He planned to sell shares under a "Board of Security" (this is quite unclear). Annual expenses would begin at about $5000 a year and would go up to $15,000. If it proved possible to get one hundred pupils, each paying an annual tuition of sixty dollars, he would be able to begin. He believed he could enroll one thousand members of the Association in Cincinnati and Louisville. The professors could help themselves by giving outside lectures. There could also be benefit affairs for the College, a practice then constant as a method of eking out the budget of congregations and charitable institutions. Poor students would be taken in free.[43]

In the summer of the same year Wise printed a long missive which he sent to the Board of Directors of the Zion Collegiate Association. Many had already promised support to aid in establishing a "university."

> The preparatory college must not only be a Jewish religious, classical and scientific school, but also a technical and mercantile institute, wherein the young man is prepared for the university, as well as for the ordinary vocations of life, requiring a scholastic preparation.

He asked that a start be made. Lilienthal would become professor of classical languages and literature without compensation. He offered his own services *gratis*. In the same article, he submitted a proposed resolution for the government of the institution by a Board of Directors. Tuition was to be from fifty to eighty dollars. He listed—once again—the subjects to be taught. Professors were to be engaged by the Board. The Faculty would come together and elect a "Superintendent." This would be the only institution of its kind on the continent. The building, library, and "apparatus" would cost "no less than $12,000." He urged speedy action, and printed a report of the meeting of the Board of Directors.[44]

The following month he recorded the adoption of his plan, a resolve to undertake the expense involved. He called on the sister-congregations of B'nai Yeshurun to go along with these steps and to help.[45]

In the fall Wise wrote with considerably more optimism than the situation actually justified. He saw his two great schemes approaching realization: Zion College and the "Conference" (to which we shall come in the next chapter). It had been decided that the former would open on November 1, 1855:

> The day when this college will be opened is for us the most sacred and most joyous day of our life, the greatest *gaudium* we have ever celebrated.

He was still awaiting news of support from all over the land. It was also his expectation that the Conference, which had taken place in Cleveland in October, would support both the idea and the practical plan for Zion College. A paragraph followed, inviting pupils to come and notifying them that lodgings would be found for them by Lilienthal and Dessauer. He had been accorded the right to grant eighteen free scholarships.[46]

It was at this time that a banquet to celebrate the opening of Zion College was held. The toasts were: "The Zion Collegiate Association," by Lilienthal; "The President of the United States," by Bellamy Storer, a Judge; "Ohio," by Salmon P. Chase, Governor of the State; "Zion College," by Isaac M. Wise; "The City of Cincinnati, her grapes are delicious, her enterprises are gigantic, but her schools are her proudest ornament," by Judge Carter; "Civil and Religious Liberty"; "Our Invited Guests," by C. Burckhardt; "Our Brethren All Over the World," by Rothenheim; "The Press"; and—as usual—"The Ladies, the only prize for which the brave sells his liberty," by M. M. Cohen.[47]

Examinations for entering pupils were held on November 23. This was recorded in the *Israelite*, together with the plan of instruction, not unlike that of a Prussian *Gymnasium* with Hebrew and commercial subjects added.[48]

Wise noted then that the College had been duly opened on November 26, that there was still bitter opposition in the East, and complete indifference to it by the orthodox of Cincinnati. It was his intention to create in time: (1) a College in place of a German Gymnasium and a *Handelsschule;* (2) a female department; (3) a department to take care of the children of indigent parents; (4) a boarding-house for free scholars. He solicited contributions for all this.[49]

By the summer of 1856 the first year had been completed, and Wise inaugurated the practice—which later he followed religiously at the Hebrew Union College—of a public examination of the students. Without question this was intended to demonstrate that good, solid work was being done, and to win additional support. The examination was in Mathematics, Bookkeeping, French, German, Ancient History, Geography, Introduction to Universal History, and Hebrew. Many friends were present. The showing was very good for so young an institution.[50]

It was certainly Wise's intention to go on. In the summer of 1856 the *Israelite* carried an announcement, "To the Friends and Patrons of Zion College":

I take this method to inform the friends and patrons of Zion

> College, that its next sessions will positively begin August 25th, when all students should be present. There will be two classes the next term, a senior and a junior class. The programme will be published as soon as the professors and directors meet.[51]

Everything seemed hopeful. But the attempt dwindled into failure. We do not possess exact data upon the length of the existence of the institution after the fall of 1856. But in an editorial in the *Israelite* in November, 1858, Wise wrote:

> The experiment made with Zion College Association proves practically that the scheme was impracticable, hence the basis of that scheme can not be tried a second time. We wish those of our friends who are better financiers than we are (this is our weakest point) would propose a plan to carry the above design into practice. . . .[52]

The likelihood is that the College petered out in the fall of 1856, and became the first of Wise's valiant attempts at a school, attempts which continued until twenty years later he attained his objective.

18

The Cleveland Conference and Minhag America

FROM THE EXPERIENCES OF THESE FOUR YEARS—FROM ISAAC M. Wise's coming to Cincinnati to the year 1858—we now single out two special projects: the Cleveland Conference of 1855, and the writing of the English and German versions of the liturgy known as *Minhag America.* This we do, to repeat, for the sake of continuity and clarity.

There would be no purpose in dwelling once again upon the fact that Wise had cherished—almost from the moment of his arrival in America in 1846—the hope for a union of American Jewish congregations. As we have learned from his proclamation in the *Occident* in 1848, this was for him the key undertaking on behalf of American Judaism, the one from which all others were to spring, the one which was to serve—as it were—as a radiating center, a germinating cell, in organization, in influence, in regard to religion, education, defense, and in all the rest. The years that had followed—now more than eight of them—had not served to weaken his enthusiasm for this plan, or his perception of its central importance, but to sharpen and to intensify them. In the beginning he had been defeated by indifference and disharmony.

He had hardly been able to make a start. After his occupancy of the pulpit in Cincinnati he began almost at once to pursue the same end, and this time with what seemed a much greater possibility of success. The story is one that deserves telling in detail for many reasons. At the conclusion of the events themselves we shall pause to draw inferences that seem to us implicit in the whole fairly long series of actions and reactions.[1]

It was mainly in the spring and summer of 1855 that Wise advocated the convoking of a conference of rabbis and laymen. As a matter of fact, he had begun quite early in 1855 in the *Israelite* under the heading: "Let Us Have a Conference." Here he had contended that there were two central problems before the American Jewish community, a College and an Orphan Asylum. One of the latter institutions had already been founded in New Orleans, and Wise welcomed its birth. The Jews of Philadelphia had secured a charter for a College, and some individuals in New York had at least made a beginning in this direction. The heart of the problem, as Wise thought, was the bringing together of these various endeavors. Nor did this exhaust the number of essential tasks that lay before American Jews. There was a crying need for text-books and for numerous other instruments of education and worship. He proposed a conference, therefore (the time, the method of convoking and organizing it, and the place, to be discussed later). He invited communications from interested persons to be directed to the *Israelite*.[2]

A month later and through the same medium he continued his propaganda in an editorial headed "The Conference." He had been using the columns of the *Israelite* to describe the conferences of German rabbis, which had been valiant and fascinating attempts at joint deliberation on liturgy, on the principles of a modern Judaism, and on the cementing of a union. He was eager to induce his readers to reflect on similar needs in the United States:

> Consider the vast responsibility resting upon us. We are the pioneers of Judaism in this land of free thought and the free word among a nation susceptible of philosophical and divine truth. . . . From the blood of our ancestors, shed on European soil, here will revive giant cedars, pillars of eternal truth. . . . Confess that it is our sacred duty to meet and take counsel how to act unitedly on behalf of our sacred cause; how to cement a union of all our energies.

He asked for a regular annual conference "to cement a union of actions and sentiments."[3]

Again three weeks later under the same title he contended that there was no Jew in the United States strictly observing the rabbinical law. On the other hand, if the reformers throw off

> . . . the rabbinical and cabbalistical literature, we either cease altogether to be a community; . . . or we represent mummies remaining from the Mosaic age, as the Karaites do.[4]

This utterance is highly significant from his point of view at the time, both for its negative and its positive implications. It will be well to bear it in mind, as things progress. Judaism must, he wrote, rest firmly upon tradition. But how are we to remedy the many evils that now exist?

> We say BY A REGULAR TRIENNIAL SYNOD [capitals in the original], and such a synod should be prepared by a conference of all competent Israelites of this country.

We shall learn what Wise meant by a "synod," though in later years—toward the end of his life—he came to intend by the term something far different. Progress in Judaism—he claimed—stopped in the Middle Ages. There was, he contended, a deep breach between religion and society. There was a duty now to return to the principle and practice of progress:

> We maintain, and we will prove it, the Rabbis of old, well aware of the principle of progress being vital to Judaism, and of the danger of leaving this principle at the disposition of every individual, acknowledged the religious powers and rights of a synod to make, amend, and repeal laws, customs, ceremonies and usages, and in accordance with the spirit of the Mosaic dispensation.
>
> We must have a conference to organize a synod, for this alone will settle the difficulties and open a bright future for our religion and our religious institutions in this country.[5]

Not very much later Wise was groping his way toward a program for such a synod and such a gathering. He thought that the following might be its main aspects:

1. A regular synod, to meet at least once in three years.
2. Officers and standing committees to carry out its decisions.
3. No decisions to be made contrary to the Bible, the Talmud, and the Laws and Constitution of the United States.

Of this general approach he wrote:

> We expect that these articles of peace must satisfy even the ultra-orthodox, and, we were going to say, every one who reasons on the subject of Judaism.[6]

He followed this with an extended argument based on Jewish legal tradition. He reminded his readers that there had been a body in Poland (The "Council of the Three Lands"), and he ended with an enumeration of the powers of the Sanhedrin as described in the Talmud. We shall not pause at this point to analyze the very astonishing character of these proposals and Wise's probable reasons for making them. This we shall reserve for somewhat later, when the decisions of the Conference will be before us.

Wise took note of the fact that he was receiving many responses from various parts of the country relative to the proposed Conference. A call was to be issued for Cleveland for July 10, 1855, which was *Chamisha Asar B'Shvat.*[7] The call would be published later. He requested congregations to make it possible for their rabbis to attend.[8]

Some inkling, some premonitory fear, may also have been stirring in him, for he appealed to leaders throughout the country not to let differences of opinion concerning reform, the degrees of reform, or the divergences between reform and orthodoxy, divide them:

> The proposed conference in this country will, if properly carried out, and managed in the spirit it ought to be, tend to do much good in setting to rest matters of dispute, and we hope to see all congregations and all classes of Hebrews so represented there, that no party or form of belief shall have preponderance over the other.

He expressed the hope that the strictly orthodox, the moderate reformers, and the "liberal" (by which he certainly meant the "radical" reformers—of whom more anon), would come together. He thought it might be sensible to have some Europeans participate, though exactly how this was to be done he did not investigate.[9]

A warning voice was heard in the columns of the *Israelite* during that summer of 1855, reminding Wise of the abortive conference that had taken place in Philadelphia fourteen years earlier.[10]

The actual Call for the conference appeared in the *Israelite* on August 17. It was headed by a Hebrew text, which Wise used all during this time, and which lay close to his own heart and hopes: *SHALOM AL YISRAEL* (Peace be upon Israel):

In the name of Israel's God and Israel's Religion, the ministers and delegates of the Israelitish congregations are respectfully requested to assemble in a conference to take place the 17th day of October, 5616 A.M., in the city of Cleveland, to deliberate on the following points:

Firstly. The articles of Union of American Israel in theory and practice.

Secondly. A plan to organize a regular synod, consisting of delegates chosen by the congregations and societies, whose powers, privileges and duties shall be defined, to be sent to the several congregations for their approbation.

Thirdly. To discuss and refer to a committee a plan for a *Minhag America* to be reported to the synod at its first session.

Fourthly. A plan for scholastic education in the lower and higher branches of learning.

Fifthly. Other propositions either sent in by congregations, or made by the ministers or delegates at the conference.

By order of the American rabbis,
Rev. Doctors, Cohn of Albany,
Guenzburg of Baltimore,
Hochheimer of Baltimore,
Illowy of St. Louis,
Kalisch of Cleveland,
Lilienthal of Cincinnati,
Merzbacher of New York,
Rothenheim of Cincinnati,
Isaac M. Wise of Cincinnati.[11]

In the meantime, between the issuance of this Call and the conference which was to take place two months later, Wise did not relax or desist from his appeals. He termed the idea "grand and noble," urged congregations to elect delegates, and was forever trying to prevail upon all rabbis to attend.[12]

In September, 1855, K. K. B'nai Yeshurun of Cincinnati, Wise's own congregation, elected two delegates to attend the Cleveland Conference.[13]

Writing in the *Israelite*, Lilienthal appealed to future delegates in an editorial; headed, "Do Not Come Prejudiced to the Convention in Cleveland." He pleaded that the meeting should represent all divergent groups in American Judaism. It was his hope that a personal coming-together would tend to mollify differences. It was not that he wanted anyone to surrender his principles. But he feared that they might be carried away in the heat of polemics and begged them to be on guard against this.[14]

As the time for the conference approached, Wise became more and more specific in his feeling concerning it, and in his hope that it might prove to be epochal in character. He besought the delegates not to become disheartened if not all differences could be ironed out at once:

> What we have to do is:
> 1. To fix regulations for the proceedings.
> 2. To find a platform, on which most diverging opinions can meet.
> 3. To appoint committees for the different questions to be brought forward, which, in the course of the next year, will prepare the propositions for their final solution to be fixed next year, please God, by the synod for final decision and adoption.

He concluded again with his motto: *SHALOM AL YISRAEL.*[15]

Shortly before the time when the conference was actually to meet, the *Israelite* reproduced some comment from the *New York Express*:

> This idea of uniting the Jews in this form (for Zion College) towards a common object originated with the talented and liberal-minded Dr. Wise of Cincinnati, editor of the *Israelite.* This gentleman is deemed by orthodox Jews, strict followers of the Rabbis, as rather latitudinarian in his principles, but he is remarkable for his strong devotion to the cause of his religion and to the elevation of the moral condition of his people.[16]

At last the Conference met. It will be better, in our opinion, to abstract the account of it from the contemporary numbers of the *Israelite* rather than from Wise's *Reminiscences* published some twenty years later, though we shall hereafter append some of his comments.

Rabbis and representatives were present in Cleveland from the following communities: Albany, Chicago, Cincinnati, Cleveland, Detroit, Louisville, New York, and Philadelphia. Nor was this only a rather broad cross-section geographically of the Jews of the country for that time. It was also fairly representative of the various "parties" and interpretations of Judaism. For example—Wise wrote—there was present a Mr. Levy of Cleveland, a staunch "rabbinist" in principle. The Conference convened on Wednesday, October 17, 1855, in the hall of the Medical College. Salutations were delivered. The Rev. Isidor Kalisch of Cleveland was in the chair and began with a Hebrew prayer. Lilienthal was acting as secretary. The account stated also that those who came seated themselves—more or less spontaneously—by "parties." Wise noticed that the suspiciousness of the orthodox was not allayed when the following were elected as officers: Isaac M. Wise, president; Rev. E. Cohn of Albany, vice-president; Lilienthal, secretary. Though some of the orthodox voted for them, they tended to feel that the conference might prove to be in the control of the "reformers."[17]

It was not long, however, before the entire atmosphere of the Conference changed "as by magic." Its primary business was to "cement a platform." A preliminary committee was appointed. Wise asked permission first to lay before the delegates a proposed platform. This was the sketch he read:

1. That all Israelites agree upon the divinity of the Bible, and
2. That the Talmud is acknowledged by all as the legal and obligatory commentary of the Bible.[18]

It will have been remarked that in effect Wise had already proposed something similar to this in the pages of the *Israelite*. But perhaps it had not been sufficiently noticed, or taken very seriously. At any rate, at the conference this proposal produced an immense effect. Leeser was present and—while Wise was speaking and presenting this proposal—left the back of the hall, where he had been sitting, and walked up to the front. The orthodox—Wise said in the *Israelite*—were taken by surprise. Lilienthal—who had certainly been apprised in advance of the content of this proposal—rose and spoke in its favor, claiming that "men of progress always based their measures and decisions on the biblical-talmudical laws." Then Leeser took the floor. His apprehensions had vanished. He prophesied that October 17, 1855 would become a great Jewish holiday.[19] The platform was discussed, then referred to a committee to bring in to the conference in complete form. This was the text the committee hammered out:

> The conference of the rabbis and congregational delegates assembled in Cleveland, actuated by the earnest desire to preserve the union of Israel and its religion by a mutual understanding and union, and convinced that the organization of a Synod is the most efficient means to attain this sacred aim, and whose legality and utility is taught in the Bible, Talmud and history—consider it their duty:
>
> To convene a synod, and call upon the American Jewish

congregations in an extra circular, to send their ministers and delegates to the said synod.

The Conference also feels obliged to give utterance to the following points which they unanimously agree to be the leading principles of the future synods:

1. The Bible as delivered to us by our fathers and as now in our possession is of immediate divine origin and the standard of our religion.
2. The Talmud contains the traditional, legal and logical exposition of the Biblical laws which must be expounded and practised according to the comments of the Talmud.
3. The resolutions of the Synod in accordance with the above principles are legally valid.
4. Statutes and ordinances contrary to the laws of the land are invalid.[20]

This was debated point by point, and then adopted. Wise wrote of the Conference:

> This conference is a moment of historical importance. Every name of the men assembled in Cleveland will be inscribed in the records of history. None can predict or even imagine the influence which this body will exercise upon our institutions, our position in society, and the development of our religion on this American soil.[21]

He ended again with the motto he had chosen, *SHALOM AL YISRAEL*, now with a triumphant ring. A meeting was also held in Cleveland on behalf of Zion College. The proclamation of the Conference was signed by eighty. In the *Israelite* he reproduced the document also in German.[22] In a November issue he reprinted his words calling for a Synod on March 9, 1856. Now all would understand that he was no rebel. Even Hirsch of Frankfort (Samson Raphael Hirsch), Zechariah Frankel, Rappaport (his teacher in Prague), and Leopold Zunz would endorse this declaration. He feared that the "progressives" might be tempted to believe that he had betrayed his own—and their own—cause. He trusted this would not be so, for this—in his opinion—would be a misinterpretation. He had not abandoned his belief in progress or in reform:

> But every attempt at improvement or progress must be based upon our laws.

The main question was: what good could the proposed Synod do? Its chief function would be to listen to different views and parties, and to prevent schisms. Decisions would then no longer depend upon an individual rabbi.

Whatever reforms are desirable and required, let them be legal, general, or not at all. This can be done by a Synod only.

He declared himself not afraid to put his own programs before seventy elders, like the Sanhedrin of old. Even if they should disagree with him, he would bow to their decision. Above all else he desired "peace and union."[23]

At the Conference the declaration agreed upon was obviously a compromise. In the preliminary discussions the orthodox present had wanted the conference to come out for the "divinity of the Talmud." In the opinion of the reformers this was extreme, and seemed to make union out of the question. Finally the committee referred to had been appointed—consisting of Merzbacher, Wise, and Leeser. They had met and talked from eleven o'clock at night until four in the morning. It was they who had agreed upon the text, which proved satisfactory to both sides. It was read at the Conference to the delegates, lay and rabbinic, on October 18, and received with much applause. In his *Reminiscences* Wise called it a "peaceful solution." He contended also that it was clearly understood by all parties that it did not lay down any prescribed rules or dogmas for individuals or congregations, that—in fact—it was to serve only as a general basis for religious practice and procedure. It was assumed that the Synod—which this resolution proposed to create—would go forward and not backward in religious matters. All were willing that the Synod should introduce reforms. Or at least this was Wise's interpretation of what lay behind the words themselves. The orthodox—he wrote—demanded only that the reforms be legal and consistent, that is, that they could be arrived at within the Law, and that they should not be mutually incompatible or contradictory.[24]

It is difficult to judge this meeting without bearing in mind what happened immediately afterward. But we should be careful to recognize that at the time this compromise was regarded by those present as a complete reconciliation of the two points of view, and as laying the basis for a genuine unification of all Jews in the United States. Each group regarded it as a victory.

A committee—consisting of Lilienthal, Merzbacher, and Greenebaum of Chicago, was then appointed to bring in concrete and detailed plans for a Synod. All other problems, to consider which the Conference had come together, were discussed somewhat hastily and referred to other committees. The plan for a *Minhag America* was put in the hands of Wise, Rothenheim, Merzbacher, and Kalisch. The organization and furthering of schools was assigned to Lilienthal, Kalisch, and Gotthelf of Louisville.[25]

The following day, October 19th, 1855, the Committee on Synod reported. Its proposal was that most of the members of the Synod were to be rabbis, and that all "preachers" were to be members *ex officio*. In addition each congregation was to have one delegate and one additional representative for each hundred members. The Synod was to have as its task the founding and supervising of all national Jewish institutions. The Conference—which was of course to continue—was to have all religious questions under its jurisdiction. Wise and Miller were appointed as a committee to convoke the next Conference. Wise wrote that the debates had been good, warm but fruitful, and that the sessions had begun with mutual suspicion but concluded with every evidence of agreement and fraternity. On the evening of the 18th of August, Zion College Association Number Three was formed in Cleveland (the second had been organized in New York).[26]

Wise himself was strongly of the opinion that at Cleveland the battle for a united American Israel had been fought and won. At the beginning no idea entered his mind that this meeting would prove utterly futile and that the association would not survive more than a few months. He expected the Synod to serve as an instrument for lawful progress, to which the orthodox could not object. The next Synod was to provide for the establishment of a college, of congregational schools, and the adoption of a common ritual. He remarked that it had been only eight years since Merzbacher and he had been the only leaders in the United States on the side of Reform, and that they had been denounced as disturbers of the peace. It seemed to him at this meeting that the orthodox had been defeated and had been clutching at a few concessions. In his imagination he envisioned American Judaism united, progressing toward a glorious future. Of this he was so certain that he composed triumphal hymns. Mrs. F.—somewhere in the background as usual—warned him to hold his optimism in check. He listened to her and withheld the publication of these "inspirations." Instead, later on, he put them into a novel, "The Conflagration." His idea was:

> American Judaism, free, progressive, enlightened, united and respected.[27]

Here we must pause to interject some observations on Wise's—and others'—hopes, and the prematureness of their optimism. It is easy to be sage after the event. Nonetheless it is not easy to read the details of this Conference, to study the text of the resolution adopted, and to comprehend why Wise—and Leeser—regarded this as affording a common platform upon which all American Jews could stand. One thing it does demonstrate, nevertheless: that Wise and his friends were quite willing to make compromises for the sake of unity. Wise at least put two things in some rational relation to each other: reform and the unity of American Jews. The latter seemed more important to him than the former, though it was obviously his conviction that effective union could be attained while making what he called "reasonable progress" within Judaism. The formula enacted at Cleveland is so equivocal that it was certainly no miracle, first, that it was immediately attacked; and, secondly, that it could not serve as a basis for united belief and action. It abounds in dubious phrases and expressions.

Just what does it mean? That the Bible is literally inspired in every page and letter, and that therefore all of its laws must be observed? The section on the Talmud is even hazier. Is this intended to connote that all the decisions of the Talmud are binding upon all Jews? And who or what is to be the authority on what the decisions of the Talmud are? Maimonides, the *Shulchan Aruch*, or one of the other codes? The language falls between two stools, stating and yet not stating that the Talmud is a binding authority. The word "exposition" is the most misleading of all. To sum up, it is very hard to see how wise leaders could have regarded this as a workable basis for a united American Israel.

Certainly then—and on many other occasions—Wise was of the opinion that all the reforms he proposed could be justified on a Biblical basis and in relation to the development and character of the rabbinic law. As we shall see later on, he himself wavered more than a little in his estimate of the Talmud and its religious authority. In his general attitude toward Reform he did not differ greatly from the more moderate group in Germany, men like Abraham Geiger, who believed that progress had always been the rule in Judaism, and that change was no less valid or imperative in our day than it had been under the *Tanaim* or *Amoraim* (the rabbinical generations of Mishna and Talmud). This is not the place to enter deeply into Wise's concept of Reform, to which we shall come, when we consider his whole theological system.

Nor was this the only time he favored the creation of a Synod. *Mutatis mutandis* he agitated for such a body almost to the end of his career, though his concept of its character and function developed considerably. But in general he conceived it as a modern continuation of the Sanhedrin, which within the framework of the Law would have the right to interpret and alter it, always by legal methods, by the devices of development set up in ancient days. This need not be regarded as far-fetched, nor childishly confiding, as might appear on the surface, for in our own day there is a strong Orthodox party who contend that, now that Israel has been reborn in the ancient land, a Sanhedrin ought to be reconstituted as a final authority, possessing the divine power to make supreme decisions, at least for traditional Jews.

In some ways it is even more astonishing that Leeser regarded this formulation as a possible one and went along with it, at least for a time. The likelihood is that each group was interpreting the equivocal language according to its own prejudices and its own hopes, and that Leeser looked upon it—for his part—as a surrender by the reform group to the doctrine of the binding character of Torah and Talmud.

Also, one cannot help speculating what would have happened to Jewish religious life in America if the work of this Conference had stood. It is not beyond all historic possibility that even within this flimsy structure some kind of framework might have been built, and that though differences of approach and interpretation would have developed (as when have they not in Jewish life, even when it was most monolithic?) the Jews of America would have possessed *one* organism for religion, charity, education, and defense. Certainly Wise—and others—thought this entirely feasible. For a while, later on, his own Union, established in 1873, did actually have within its fold the majority of American Jewish congregations. It was only in the last two decades of the nineteenth century, and from then on, that three parties appeared and began to go their separate ways. But we can go no farther; it is futile to speculate upon what might have happened. For it was not to be! This Conference did not, in actuality, build a platform upon which all the Jews of America could stand.

That this was so became obvious in short order. Hardly were the minutes of the Conference published and the text of its central resolution available, than bitter attacks began. In "Some Unpublished Letters of Ethical Importance," by David Philipson, there exists one concerning this Conference. David Einhorn and Samuel Adler, both recently arrived in the United States and both much more extreme "reformers" than Wise, launched vitriolic attacks. This, Philipson declared, was the beginning of the unfortunate division between the so-called "Cincinnati school" and the Eastern reformers, which lasted until Wise's death. Wise was the leader of the former, Einhorn of the latter.[28]

Somewhat later under the date of December 1, 1857 Wise wrote to Samuel Adler. He still wanted a meeting of rabbis to discuss these points:

1. A basis for establishing a seminary for rabbis, teachers and cantors; and
2. The founding of a Jewish Library.

Turning to the "reformers," of whom Adler was one, Wise wrote that he did not "agree with the following views":

a. The morality of the Talmud is narrow;
b. Judaism consists of the axioms of the human mind;
c. Revelation is the intensified potency of the human mind;
d. The Bible is symbolical;
e. Reform is the essential matter; Judaism is secondary.[29]

This is, of course, a highly *ex parte* statement of Adler's views, but it does indicate strongly that Wise was not willing to abandon the historic, traditional character of Judaism, nor to acknowledge that it could rest upon a purely rational, "natural" basis without some doctrine of revelation. Wise declared that he could not abrogate those things that have Biblical authority, that this could be done only by a Synod (even this is rather strange and dubious!):

> Reform has up to this time brought about only disruption (I plead guilty for myself also); it has nowhere united its own forces, it has not permeated the people because it has lacked authority, viz. the pronouncement of a synod.[30]

Men might differ on theological problems, but that should not stop them "from cooperating energetically for general and common interests." A most revealing letter, one that underlines many of the comments we have made on Wise's own hopes at the Cleveland Conference!

Protests against the Conference were rushed into print in Baltimore, Charleston, S. C., and New York. These administered mortal blows to the proposed unity. Rather amazingly they seemed to Wise like "lightning from a clear sky." And most unexpectedly of all they came in the first instance not from orthodox leaders, but from the Reform camp. This was—to Wise—a schism especially painful in character and apparently fraught with misfortune. He was plunged into profound dejection. If no agreement was possible within the reform group and among reform leaders, how was a progressive movement possible in America? Like Jeremiah—he wrote—he sat upon the ruins. In his diary he set down these somber reflections:

> Dispossessed of the holy land, we are swaying in mid-air, as it were, without support. Strife, contention, and disunion are rife among us.[31]

He reproached himself for his failure to go at once to other cities and try to persuade and convince his brethren. But this he could not bring himself to do, for Einhorn in his new periodical, *Sinai*, and Lyon in the *Asmonean*, had been writing what seemed to him most insulting and abusive articles. An aversion against public activity took hold upon him. Some of his friends and he were being treated like "adventurous tramps," like self-seeking parvenus. Everything that was written revealed endless rage and fanaticism. The brunt of this was not his alone. Lilienthal, Rothenheim, and Kalisch were included in the slanders and misrepresentations, as he termed them. But Wise was regarded as the ring-leader, and therefore became the chief butt of the arrows.[32]

Wise declared that he had fought for so many years, refusing to enter other professional occupations, only to be abused as though he were a street gamin. The battle was not soon over. It lasted for some years. Nor, in Wise's opinion, did any individual or any group gain by it. Judaism and possible progress were the sole sufferers. The real purpose of the Conference was overlooked. It was the Talmud that was the chief target. The cry—especially of Einhorn—was that the Conference had written itself down as believing in the authority of the Talmud. Nor was Einhorn without able assistance. Ludwig Philippson and Leopold Stein—for the latter of whom especially Wise had had a long and deep affection and regard—entered the lists and excoriated him and the Conference. In his *Reminiscences* Wise repeated several times that either they, or he, failed to understand. Later on, according to him, the opposition admitted that all problems of reform could have been solved on the basis proposed—though precisely where these admissions were made, and in what way those who made them imagined this possible, we are not told. In 1874 and '75, again in the *Reminiscences*, Wise wrote that real Reform had advanced no farther twenty years later, and that some Talmudic basis was being sought even for radical reforms. But in 1855 the Talmud—as had in fact been the case in Germany too—was denounced in unmeasured fashion and called immoral, in articles and sermons. And orthodox Judaism was represented as an offense against reason and morality.[33]

All this Wise could not bring himself to stomach. He had shown no hesitation in fighting Christian missionaries on their own ground. Now he gathered his forces to oppose these intemperate and untrue assaults upon the Talmud and upon orthodoxy. In the beginning Lilienthal wrote most of the articles in the *Israelite*, and Rothenheim in the *Deborah*. But Wise followed with a series in the *Israelite*. Naturally all this did not assuage the bitterness of his opponents. Far from doing that, all of this served only to intensify and perpetuate it.[34]

These have been general observations drawn almost entirely from Wise's own reactions to the sequels of the Conference. It will be valuable now to follow in the *Israelite* the comments that are contemporary and therefore more to be relied upon.

About a month after the Conference, Wise recorded that he had received a letter from Einhorn protesting against an alleged mutilation of a sermon Einhorn had delivered in Baltimore, presumably attacking the Conference and Wise. In the course of this Einhorn had referred to

> . . . the foul peace of Cleveland, according to which all Israelites —also the Rev. Dr. Wise formerly of Albany and now of Cincinnati—must believe in the infallible exegese of the Talmud.

Wise rejoined that he would pay no attention to this undignified attack. But to this fine resolution he was unable to adhere, for shortly thereafter he was marshaling arguments against it.[35]

His dislike of the "East," and of the reform leaders there, was being born and intensified during this period. The *Israelite* contained an editorial entitled "The Little Big-Men of New York." Wise alluded to their ignorance and their indifference. New York had then 600,000 people and was an "ocean of villages." No one was as intolerant toward the rest of the country as they:

> Either all the little big-men must be sent to Salt Lake, and their schemes thrown overboard, or there will, in a few years, be no more miserable place for Judaism than New York City with its little big-men.[36]

Soon thereafter he was thundering against the "ultra-parties which would attack every word and syllable." There must be some middle ground. Israel has a mission and must be true to it. According to the ultra-reformers: "we need no forms, no outward signs to unite Israel." Spirit and doctrines will suffice. But this is neither true nor wise. "We need forms and uniformity." These men in their bitterness would dispose of all Jewish history summarily.[37]

He defended himself against the charge that he was a traitor to the cause of Reform and progress, that he had altered his convictions to suit his convenience, and that he "contradicts himself." Is this for money? You cannot bribe him! He is as poor as ever. Is it for honor? Ambition? He does not need either. Is it right or wrong to try to unite Israel?

> Is it right or wrong that the Cleveland Conference refused to depart from the historical basis of Judaism, pointed out by three thousand years of history?

The men at Cleveland understood just as well as these venomous attackers the "demands of the age," and the immemorial doctrines of Judaism.[38]

He hammered away at his essential objectives: "We must have union, at any risk and any sacrifice, principles excepted." We must have a position, public institutions, a University, a theological seminary:

> The different parties represent different theories, and must recognize each other as Jews, upon a firm basis; must have confidence in each other, must view each other with a brother's eyes and constitute one house of Israel.[39]

But by the early months of 1856 the sad truth was inescapable. The Cleveland Conference was dead. The storm was over. This effort had suffered the same fate as the *Rabbinerversammlungen* in Germany. Both orthodox and reform repudiated it. In the *Asmonean* the orthodox were heaping abuse upon it. Nor were the extreme reformers less sweeping or vindictive in their condemnation.[40]

At last—in February 1856—Wise was stung into utterance by the unrestrained opprobriousness of Einhorn's attacks. He published a "Protest Against Dr. Einhorn's Calumny," which began thus:

> Ever since Dr. Einhorn had publicly declared his secession from the religion of his fathers, and heralded himself to the community as the apostle of deistical rationalism. . . .

In *Sinai* Einhorn had written against the Talmud, which—Wise wrote—he had slandered as "total thoughtlessness." Wise called this "malicious and slanderous calumny." Wise reminded Einhorn of the wonderful sections of the Talmud, like *Pirke Aboth* (The Sayings of the Fathers), of the originals of the Sermon on the Mount, and of works on the Talmud by many great modern scholars. Einhorn—Wise wrote—would underwrite and underline Eisenmenger's libels and slanders:

> You should not thus have given the sword of lies into the hands of our opponents! . . . As long as you remain an enemy of the Jews and of Judaism, I am your opponent, but shall not enter in a public controversy with you.[41]

This reply he continued in a second installment. He declared Einhorn's conduct "highly improper, offensive and arrogant." In *Sinai* Einhorn had written:

> Its [the Talmud's] morals are narrow-minded; the sublime, world-embracing spirit of the Bible is foreign to it. . . . It elevates the principle of the sanctity of the external and for itself dead work (all this section is more than a little obscure), so far as to the prohibition of self-reflection on the causes of religious laws, yea, even to the controversy whether religious observances lose their validity by a *total thoughtlessness* [italics in the *Israelite*].

Wise declared that he would be willing to defend the contrary thesis before any tribunal. There is not one word of truth to this passage, he wrote:

> It is either a malicious and slanderous calumny, or it is the product of deranged brains.

Wise cited works on the Talmud by Zipser, De Sola, and Nork, tracing the principles of Christianity to rabbinic writings:

> Sir, you should not have thrown this lie in our face!

Einhorn, he reiterated, was libeling his own fathers.

Wise felt himself not only under the necessities of defense, but also of explaining "scientifically" (a key-word of that era!) why he had helped draft and had fully endorsed the resolution at Cleveland. He advanced four propositions:

1. The Talmud amends biblical laws.
2. The Talmud has rescinded biblical laws.
3. The Talmud has made new laws.
4. The Talmud has rescinded many of its own laws.

He presented a considerable mass of material to document all four of these theses. It followed that there was nothing strange or wrong in approaching Reform from a Talmudic standpoint. He noted too that—in spite of all this hubbub—there continued to be peace in his own congregation in Cincinnati. A meeting had adopted a resolution voicing confidence in their rabbi. To some extent he withdrew again into his study. He was driven back into intensive Talmudic studies. From these he learned, he said, "a heroic but effective remedy. . . . If you have a headache, study in the law."[42]

The controversy went on unabated, and Wise continued to comment upon it in the *Israelite*. In an issue in the early spring of 1856 he wrote, contrasting his own purposes with those of his "opponents." He claimed that all he had been attempting to do was to create and to unite. But all that he had received was obloquy. Those who hate him had even written to Germany, and seen to it that a condemnation of the Cleveland Conference had found its way into the *Allgemeine Zeitung des Judenthums*. Various communications were being published in the *Asmonean*, as though they stemmed from Ludwig Philippson. But Wise declared that he was not discouraged, and that he would "always go on in the name of God and Israel."[43]

Even after all this Lilienthal did not feel that the Cleveland Conference had been completely futile, that it had served no purpose other than to arouse animosity and to bring incipient divisiveness into the open. He believed that it had "brought life and motion into the stagnant waters of the inertness, tedious inactivity, and despicable indifference, that prevailed throughout our congregations." American Judaism was still desperately in need of "impartiality," earnestness, truth and decorum; also, he added, of "deep scientific researches and investigations."[44] And a few weeks later the same writer proclaimed his intention of helping convene a second Conference. The storm of passions might succeed in preventing this. But he still did not doubt the honesty of his opponents.[45]

Almost a year passed. The small Jewish press of America was still writing about it, and doubtless a host of sermons was delivered about it. Wise was concerned that his own point of view should be clear and that it should be made intelligible to the average Jew. Thus he wrote "Defending the Cleveland Conference":

> The orthodox of this or any other country have not one word to say against these articles [he is referring to the pronouncement of principles of the Conference from a scientific basis]; they say, because we thus wrested from their hands the arms with which they fought against the reform party, we silenced their mad dog cry of infidelity. We show them that the party of progress rests upon the solid basis of orthodoxy, historical and scientific principles. . . . Some ultra-radicals cry "No Talmud!"

Wise contended—in strong terms—that this last cry, if carried to its logical conclusion, meant "No Bible!":

> . . . they reduce this sacred volume to the AXIOMS [capitals in the original] of the mind. . . .[46]

In the same article he continued:

> Let us, first, repeat the premises, from which we start in our reasoning on this subject. There can be no Judaism without the observation of the biblical laws. None has a right to dispense with them. The biblical laws are impractical unless they are expounded. . . .

But there is also an inherent right—and duty—to correct the decisions of the Talmud, in accordance with the changed conditions and needs of a different time. A Synod has these rights:

> 1. To suspend a biblical command for the time being, if it intends to preserve the rest.
> 2. To abolish rabbinic ordinances which are not practised. . . .
> 3. To make such regulations and establish such customs as are subservient to maintain the unity, forward the prosperity, or elevate the dignity of Israel, not, however, in contradiction to the Law or its legal consequences.

All of this, he said, must be in accordance with Jewish law. All reforms proposed and made must be both legal and necessary. To be sure that this shall be so, there must be a Synod.[47]

Sixteen months after the Conference we find him remarking that there had been little or no progress during that period, that most men had been intimidated by the extremism of personal attacks. Most of the committees appointed at the Conference had remained inactive. Only one—that on liturgy—of which he had been serving as chairman, was meeting or working. It was out of the question to call another meeting of the Synod. The *Occident*, Leeser's paper, had been calling for a Union. The *Israelite* would be glad to follow. Neither Wise, nor Leeser, was willing to abandon the hope toward which they had looked and for which they had labored so long.[48]

It is sad that the good will that was engendered between Leeser and Wise at Cleveland did not endure. Wise noted that he was being attacked in the *Occident* on the Cleveland Conference, and especially on the matter of the forthcoming *Minhag America* (the genesis of which we shall describe soon):

> At any and every occasion he [Leeser] has raised the mad dog cry of heresy at our heels, with the avowed intention not only to defame the products of our pen, but to ruin us in the Jewish community. He always did so with a fanaticism, recklessness and malice, which would do honor to a Peter de Amiens, or even to any Pope preaching a crusade against the infidels. The violence of his passions, the conspicuity of envy and avarice, and his frequent confessions of ignorance in Jewish matters, rendered his attacks ridiculous and obnoxious to every sensible man, and, with every attack of his, he increased our popularity; therefore we abstained often from replying to any of his slanderous assaults, leaving him altogether to the contempt of other people.

It appears that Lesser was accusing those who were at the Conference of perpetrating a fraud, of being willing to affix their signatures to principles in which they did not believe and upon which they would not act. Leeser was especially exercised about the forthcoming *Minhag America*, which—he was sure—would omit the orthodox doctrines of a personal Messiah, the old Temple sacrificial worship, and the restoration of Israel to Palestine.[49]

There was only one lasting result of the Cleveland Conference. We have noted earlier that among the committees appointed was one which went back in Wise's mind to the *Beth Din* Lilienthal had summoned in 1847 and which had proved immediately and completely abortive. Wise had never abandoned the project of a liturgy, which he had brought there, and probably still had the sketch and the text he had drawn up then. At Cleveland four were appointed, Wise as chairman, plus Rothenheim, Merzbacher and Kalisch. The committee was thus composed exclusively of the "moderate" reformers and could be expected to agree upon purposes and methods. Unfortunately, Merzbacher[50] died in the following winter. The other three took up the task, chiefly in the winter of 1856 to 1857. They prepared the first part of a new prayer-book, that is, the one to be used for week-days, Sabbaths, and the three Festivals, but not for the High Holy Days. They adopted the following principles—as Wise described them in the *Israelite:*

1. No one man is authorized to make a prayer-book for the congregations;
2. The ancient form of the service is to be preserved;
3. Individual congregations are to decide how much English or Hebrew they will use;
4. Whatever is against the concepts of Biblical Judaism, American Israel, or the wants and demands of the time, is to be

> omitted. The service was not to be beyond a reasonable length, and there was to be provision in it for the use of choir and organ.[51]

In his *Reminiscences* Wise listed also those sections of the traditional liturgy which he thought should be eliminated:

> It was out of the question to retain the old prayers unchanged, because the belief in the coming of a personal Messiah descended from the house of David had disappeared from among the people. The return to Palestine, the restoration of the Davidic dynasty, of the sacrificial cult, and the accompanying priestly caste, were neither articles of faith nor commandments of Judaism, while the lamentations over oppression, persecution, and the accompanying cry for vengeance were untrue and immoral so far as American Jews were concerned. The cabalistical portions which had crept into the prayer-book, and the obstinate adherence to the doctrine of the bodily resurrection were regarded as unjustified. We also agreed that the Sabbath service including the sermon should not last longer than two hours. . . . We resolved to publish an English and German, as well as a Hebrew version, of the prayers, and that it should be left to each congregation to decide what language it wished to use. . . .

Wise was the referee, Kalisch and Rothenheim the critics. Whatever was not adopted unanimously was rejected. Wise prepared the English version for which Nathan Meyer furnished metrical translations. Kalisch and Rothenheim composed the metrical portions of the German version. The prose German translations were divided among the three.

> The commission met in my library, and finished the work in thirty-eight sessions. They adhered anxiously to tradition; they had no desire to found a new religion, nor institute a new cult; they wished to recast the old and traditional prayers reverently so they might be brought into accord with the religious consciousness of the time and the democratic principles of the new fatherland. After the work had been finished, Bloch and Company had to defray the cost of publication. . . . Before the last leaf had left the press, it had been derided and decried throughout the land, although only the first part (without services for New Year's Day, and Day of Atonement) had appeared. The name, Minhag America was popular; but not the book, which was attacked savagely in both camps (orthodox and reform) in the East and rejected. My congregation was the first to adopt the book, but not without objections being raised. . . . The old

> prayer-book was deeply rooted in home, school, and synagogue.
> It was in the summer of 1857 that the Minhag America finally appeared. For eleven years I had cherished the idea, and now it was consummated, but it was attacked with all the weapons possible immediately upon its appearance, and yet it is the only monument of the first Cleveland conference and is now [written in 1875] used in at least one-third of all American Jewish congregations. . . .[52]

Part of the opposition arose also from the fact that congregations in the East were wedded to a German prayer-book. They could not yet adjust themselves to the idea—Wise contended—of an English text in addition to, or instead of, the German. It should be added that *Minhag America* became the most widely used prayer-book in American Jewish congregations (Wise claimed later that about one hundred congregations had adopted it), until the creation of the Central Conference of American Rabbis in 1889, and the consequent labor upon and publication of the first volume of the Union Prayer-book in 1894. Other formulations by Einhorn, Jastrow, and others, enjoyed some popularity, but not compared with *Minhag America.* Later on, in the third part of this volume, and the second part as well, we shall examine the book in greater detail. Here it needs only to be remarked that Leeser was right, that the book did omit the doctrines which Wise had opposed consistently, and about which he had never concealed his opinion; but also, in fairness it should be added, that in its arrangement, in its close following of the rubrics of the Hebrew, and in its general spirit, the book was much closer to traditional practice than other books of other men, or than many that followed later, and not in Reform Judaism alone.[53]

The book also followed the principle, which Wise had initiated in Albany, of omitting almost all the *Piutim.* It claimed to have discarded "narrow nationalism" in favor of "universalism," especially in the "Eighteen Benedictions." Later we shall come to the publication of the second volume for the holy days, and also to a volume of hymns, psalms and prayers which Wise prepared at the request of his congregation.

The *Israelite* of September 11, 1857, contained the first announcement of the publication of *Minhag America,* and offered it for sale. The Hebrew text was to cost seventy-five cents; with the German translation, $1.25; and with both English and German, $2.00.[54]

Early in October K.K.B'nai Yeshurun, Wise's own congregation, adopted Minhag America by a vote of one hundred to eighteen, and thereupon the eighteen agreed to make it unanimous. Oheb Shalom congregation in Baltimore adopted it at a general meeting of members in the summer of 1858.[55] Louisville was next, apparently, but on condition that Wise preach in their pulpit once a month and superintend the religious school. They offered him a stipend of $500 a year. To this arrangement, as four years earlier to a somewhat similar one from B'nai Israel of Cincinnati, Wise's congregation would not agree. To compensate Wise, B'nai Yeshurun increased his salary by the $500 in question. Wise had found the offer flattering, but quite impractical.[56]

The reader should be made aware of the fact that at this precise point, and most abruptly, the *Reminiscences* end. Why it was that Wise in 1857, or later on, found no time to continue, or perhaps no inclination, we cannot say. But from now on we shall depend upon his general writing, upon the biographies that came out after his death, and especially upon the pages of the *Israelite* and of the *Deborah.*

Near the end of the period with which we are dealing, in 1858, Wise set forth his considered opposition to the prayer-books which had Hebrew and German only. He wrote:

> 1. that he can discern no reason why the synagogue should be identified with the German element;
> 2. that he dislikes the linguistic separation from the community this practice tends to perpetuate; if there is anything beyond the Hebrew, it should be English;
> 3. why perpetuate the language of a country where Jews were and are denied their rights?
> 4. the entire youth in the United States is ignorant of German;
> 5. it is dangerous to introduce a book, use it for ten years or so, and then get rid of it;
> 6. the object of a prayer-book is solely and exclusively to maintain the union of synagogues. A German prayer-book only destroys union.
>
> Strange, indeed is the fact of radical reformers insisting upon Germanizing our synagogues in the heart of America; still against every sound principle they attempt to impose a German prayer-book on the synagogue just to impede the course of reform.[57]

All of these experiences which we have been describing in some detail were of great importance in Wise's later career. They did not dampen his enthusiasm for Union and for a college. They did not convince him that he was wrong in believing that only thus could Jews be united, only thus could the level of knowledge and of cooperative action be raised. But his comprehension of the difficulties that lay in his way, in the opposition of the "East," of the "radical reformers," and of the unappeasable orthodox (as they seemed to him), became clear and constant. His own point of view, his belief that a compromise was possible by which *all* American Jews could be brought together, had to be reconsidered. This did not entail an abandonment of his fundamental premises about the nature and validity of Reform. Only his hope that this point of view—the same point of view held by most of the leaders in the middle of the nineteenth century in Germany and Austria—could become that of the whole American Jewish community, vanished never to return.

19

Politics and Reform till 1858

It will be necessary, as we go ahead, to take note of some of Wise's political leanings, opinions and activities. Despite many pronouncements concerning the wisdom of keeping the pulpit clear of politics, Wise evinced a deep concern for and interest in his adopted country. It proved therefore impossible for him to be consistent in holding to his self-declared principle. Not infrequently he spoke and wrote on political matters, especially when in his opinion they had to do with vital ethical problems. How could one remain silent at such a time? How could one fail to range oneself either against some of the wild and wayward political movements of that momentous period just before the Civil War, or with some of those that seemed to him to preserve the great historic ideals of America? Not all his attitudes or decisions will be easy to understand. We shall let them speak for themselves, and permit the reader to judge for himself their internal consistency, and often their wisdom.

Quite early during the time of his residence in Cincinnati Wise became disturbed about the "Know-Nothing" Party. In general the reader might do well to consult an excellent chapter headed "The Know-Nothing Movement and the Jews" in Dr. Bertram Korn's book, *Eventful Years and Experiences.*[1]

The Know-Nothing movement, a strange but usually ephemeral phenomenon in American political life, was founded in 1849 as a secret patriotic society, based largely on xenophobia. As an effective political group it lasted only until about 1858, but for these nine years attracted to its ranks many who had been left stranded after the falling-apart of the Whig Party, and who could not yet align themselves with the new Republican Party and that party's concentration upon the issue of slavery. The Know-Nothing Party rested mostly upon anti-Catholic prejudice, and on the fear of Irish and German immigration. It was one of the ancestors of the "white, Protestant, nativist" tendencies and appeals of much later days.

For the most part the Know-Nothing Party let Jews alone. The main outlines of its record will be found in Dr. Korn's excellent and careful chapter. Wise was deeply disturbed by its appearance and its avowed policies. He thought that it tended to lump all foreigners together, Jews included. Already on July 4, 1855, in an address at K. K. B'nai Israel in Cincinnati—an address that was extensively copied—Wise directed his attention to this movement.[2] He was—he wrote—bitterly attacked for this pronouncement by a number of Jews. This action of his also caused some misunderstanding with Mrs. F. who favored the bestowal of citizenship only after twenty years of residence. She advised Wise to let political issues alone. He found this attitude on the part of "so noble-hearted a woman" incomprehensible. He wrote her a long and appealing letter, the text of which is given in the *Reminiscences*. Her answer indicated that he had persuaded her.[3]

Wise felt certain that the Know-Nothing movement was bound to turn its attention to Jews and to harm them. In the *Cincinnati Commercial* in 1854 he wrote:

> The Hebrew vote is thrown almost unanimously in favor of Know-Nothing candidates and the Know-Nothing leaders entertain strong hopes that they have attached the Hebrews permanently to their party.[4]

This is astonishing information. Its correctness may well be doubted. On other occasions Wise was accustomed to insist that there was no "Jewish vote," that the strength of the Jewish position in America lay in splitting their allegiance among the various political parties.

Wise continued to comment on the Know-Nothing Party on other occasions, claiming that, although some Jews were being admitted to its "lodges," the likelihood was that its leaders were prejudiced against Jews. He thought that there was more here than met the eye, that Jews had best beware, since most of them were "foreigners," and inasmuch as the avowed intent of the Party was to curtail their rights.[5]

But his opposition to the Know-Nothing movement did not derive solely or mainly from his concern for Jewish rights. He disliked it, first and foremost, because to him it was a direct and flagrant repudiation of everything to which the United States was consecrated:

> . . . Even if there were actually anything to fear from the Romish Church, we would still abhor the very idea of religious intolerance. Is our republic so weak, so unsatisfactory, that we must fear its downfall by those who enjoy its benefits, then it is high time that the politicians remedy those deficiencies, instead of persecuting those who are dissatisfied. If the idea of Romanism is dangerous to the republic, are the Catholics not a small minority? have we not a free press, liberty of speech? are these powerful instruments not strong enough to guard our republican institutions? where is your host of hired missionaries and book-peddlers? We beg you, in the name of common sense, do not so badly slander and outrage republicanism, as to tell us the lowest and most despicable passions of man, religious fanaticism and intolerance, are necessary to guard republicanism. Do not, in the face of all history, past and present, endeavor to make us belief [sic!] Protestant fanaticism is any better than Roman fanaticism, or that a republic with exceptional laws, with a system of proscription for religious opinions is anything like a republic. . . .[6]

So much for his opinions on Know-Nothingism. We shall return somewhat later in this chapter to another of his political ideas and proposals.

Looking back on the first year of his tenure in Cincinnati, Wise put on record that its most important events were the decision to found Zion College, with results that seemed to him to indicate "the speedy realization of its object." He noted too that he had revised the "prayer-book of Merzbacher," that Lilienthal had been elected in Cincinnati, and that major improvements had been made in the Lodge St. Synagogue. He remarked too upon the steady progress of the *Israelite*. He believed that the *Occident* was losing a major part of its readers. He referred to the election of Einhorn in Baltimore, little suspecting what his relations were to be with that notable; and he commented finally on the progress of congregations in Cincinnati, in Louisville, and also in Germany.[7]

What reforms was Wise sponsoring in Cincinnati, and how did he go about advocating them and instituting them?

It is unmistakable from the record that from his experiences in Albany he had learned this at least: that he must not press, must not do too much at once, that—in fact—his motto must be *festina lente*, "make haste slowly." He began with several easier things: the excision of the *Piutim*, and the abolition of the custom of selling *Mitzvoth* in the synagogue. His next step had to do with the creation of a mixed choir. This he began in the very first months of his leadership in Cincinnati.[8]

In the *Reminiscences* Wise himself asserted that it did not take him long to size up and to "master" the situation. Whatever was left of orthodoxy in his own congregation began swiftly to disappear. The *Beth Din* of the city dissolved. He was asked to follow the orthodox custom of studying a portion of the Talmud (a *Shiur*) and commenting upon it, after the death of his father. This he refused to do and preached against the custom, claiming that it was in reality a Jewish substitute for the Mass. He met a superstitious Jew who thought that ghosts came out of an unclean *Mezuzzah*. He showed that he was just as capable as his opponents of holding a Talmudic discussion, but that he intended to use his learning to enlighten, not to keep in ignorance.[9]

He claimed that his word was becoming law to the four local congregations. Most of the orthodox respected him, though occasionally an insult was directed at him. He knew how to defend himself and how to get an apology. He went often to restaurants, occasionally drank with people, and went to the theater, the opera, and dances. The only thing he never permitted himself was card-playing, for this—he thought—would bring about undue familiarity.[10]

There is an article by Henry Frank of New Orleans, formerly of Cincinnati, written to Dena Wilansky, when she was preparing her book *From Sinai to Cincinnati* in April, 1928. Frank wrote that Wise had already organized a choir in 1854 and that he taught it himself, using his violin to help the voices:

> He was a great lover of music and he succeeded in inducing young people to volunteer gladly to become members of the Choir.[11]

In March, 1855, the congregation decided to enlarge the seating capacity of the synagogue, to add a choir gallery, and to install an organ. This touched upon a moot point of reform at this time. At the congregational meeting the orthodox members opposed installing an organ, but were outvoted by an "overwhelming majority." The renovated and enlarged building was rededicated on August 24, 1855.[12]

With three exceptions the choir consisted of volunteers. In 1856 two non-Jewish professionals were added, probably to bolster up the amateurs and to fill out the harmonies. This was an innovation, not only in B'nai Yeshurun, but in the country, and caused more or less of a sensation, for until then Christians had not assisted at a Jewish service.[13]

Wise entered into a more detailed description of how he went about the organization of his first choir. The *Parnass* of the congregation favored it. Wise managed to get together a remarkable group, among whom were: A. J. Friedlander, Frederick Eichberg, L. Loeb, David Wise, Ludwig Brandeis, Gideon, "and others." They formed a society, and young girls were included. Their singing teacher was a musician named Junkermann. There was intense enthusiasm. At that time the *Hazan* was Marx Moses, who—Wise wrote—had a good voice and some musical training. He persuaded Moses to study the Sulzer Evening Service for the Sabbath. This the *Hazan* did. He sang it, and no one objected.[14]

When the choir was ready for its first participation in the service, it was a notable Friday evening. Members of the congregation flocked to Lodge Street to hear. The "harmonious strains of Sulzer's music resounded." It proved to be a brilliant success. The young people in the choir were in transports. By the autumn of 1855 they had learned the service for Sabbath morning also. Wise contended that it was hard later on to imagine what a victory this had been, and that no real reform was possible "until the Jewish ear had again become accustomed to harmony and beauty." In this respect Wise was a breaker of new paths for the Jews in the West.[15]

In the meantime other reforms were gradually and peaceably being introduced in B'nai Yeshurun. Ways and means were sought to get an organ. The president, Jacob Miller, declared himself in favor of it. The Board of the congregation were unanimously for it. When Lodge Street was remodeled, the *Bimah*, the central altar was removed, and there were sixty more seats for women. The cost of the remodeling was between ten and twelve thousand dollars, and this money was brought in by selling the seats. The president and Wise also called on members and got pledges of money for the organ, to be repaid in three years without interest. All this was done just after Passover in 1855.[16]

In May, 1855, the *Israelite* carried an announcement that the organ was being installed. It commented on the fact that a few years earlier this would have been deemed a heresy. Wise had pleaded for this step, contending that the organ was a "Jewish instrument," already used in many synagogues in Germany. He quoted from

Leopold Zunz (doubtless from the *Gottesdienstliche Vortraege*) and from the *Shulchan Aruch*,[17] concerning the phrase *Zecher l'Churban* (a "memorial for the destruction"—of the Temple).[18]

As had been the case in Albany, Wise spent much time and effort striving to maintain observance of the Sabbath. He spoke to owners and operators of businesses, and persuaded them to keep their shops and offices closed.[19]

The organ was played for the first time on August 24, 1855, and all rejoiced in it.[20]

Missionaries were visiting Cincinnati as they had Albany. Wise fought them with all his energy, especially in the new pages of the *Israelite*. He claimed that he had had the pleasure of seeing the "Mission to Jews" close its enterprises in Cincinnati.[21]

Nor was he idle in regard to his own intellectual development during these first years. He became interested in comparative mythology, in law, in Jewish philosophy—once more—and in history. Mrs. F. advised him to read the Zendavesta (the sacred books of Zoroaster, the classical Persian religion), the Vedas (the oldest literature of Hinduism in India), and the Chinese "King" books (the writings of Confucius). He plunged again into the "sea" of the Talmud, and before his eyes the giants among the rabbis, the *Amoraim*, came to life. He wrote of himself that by this time he had acquired a "corrosive analytical method," and that he found the sharp insights and the logical reasoning of the Talmud wondrously attractive. Occasionally he would turn aside from Jewish and comparative religious sources and read Heinrich Heine, from whom he learned the fine art of self-ridicule, of a wry smile at life's annoyances. Or so he says![22]

All this time he was acting as superintendent of the Talmud Yelodim Institute. An examination was conducted publicly at the beginning of the summer of 1856. The subjects were Hebrew—the Pentateuch, Psalms, and biblical history—and some catechism. One girl, he reported, twelve years of age, read the first twenty Psalms without a single mistake. There was also an examination in English, Geography, the history of the United States, Mathematics, and German:

> This institute is so organized that it fully prepares the pupils for the Zion College.[23]

We have already noted that Merzbacher died in October, 1856. Wise regarded him as one of the few learned and progressive rabbis of the country and as his very dear friend. In the *Israelite* he wrote of his death and of some of the meditations it induced in him:

> We have no school to educate the champions of Israel, and no desire to establish one. We have plenty of money to spend for any and every article of luxury. We are rich, very rich, make plenty of money. But Judaism, the Synagogue, the future of our great cause, our mission among the nations, the honour and position of Israel's religion,—let us be silent, dumb with shame and blush. . . . With pain-stricken heart we look into future days and see angels weeping around the coffin of American Judaism, because none consoled her of all her friends. The indifferent look on with indifference; I cannot. Had I the power of thunder, I would cry my pain in every heart until they awake and act in behalf of God and Israel.[24]

In other words, where were the men to come from who would replace Merzbacher?

Wise's use of Heine as recreation and escape was timely, for a letter reached him from Paris, March 14, 1856, telling him that Heine had passed away almost a month earlier. Wise wrote concerning how hard the last years of Heine's life had been.[25]

A considerable part of his interest during this period was devoted to an attempt to move away from his own German background and interests. He wanted to fill himself to the brim with the consciousness of a free-born man. He wanted to become an American through and through. Some of those who already disliked him found their aversion sharpened by all this, for—as was the habit of some German Jews—they clung tenaciously to their old-world background.[26]

While he was in the midst of this striving, Wise himself could not help asking himself searching questions. If the Jew should succeed in identifying himself completely with America, would not Judaism disappear? This was and is the immemorial problem of assimilation, the practicability of a vital Judaism coupled with complete absorption in the American milieu. Perhaps—Wise thought—the dilemma could be solved by more general knowledge of Jewish history, of Jewish sources in general. Jews must not only be Americans, but they must also have "Jewish patriotism," a rather curious phrase! The way to complete Americanization was not difficult to discover, but that to an integral Jewishness was not nearly so apparent. Wise came to the conclusion that it should be the aim of Jewish leaders:

1. To emphasize the historical mission of Israel.

2. To bring before the public the bright side of Jewish character.
3. To popularize, by the written and spoken word, Jewish learning and Jewish literature.
4. To familiarize the public with brilliant periods in Jewish history in fictional form.

Upon some parts of this task he began at once. He continued to study the Talmud and Jewish history. He cut down on his own public speaking and entrusted some of the work in the *Israelite* to his co-workers.[27]

Two events happened in October, 1856, which moved and stirred Wise deeply. The first was the coming to America of Gabriel Riesser of Hamburg, concerning whom and whose influence upon the young Wise we have written in a much earlier chapter. Riesser, the outstanding champion of the rights of the Jews of Germany, visited Cincinnati as part of a lecture tour. Wise called to mind how he had read Riesser's journal in a distant village in Bohemia; how he had learned that Jews possessed inborn rights, which ought to be respected; how he had had to endure a severe scolding from his teacher of Talmud for reading a German book or a magazine. He had got his hands on everything Riesser had written—every article, every leaflet—and had wept in solitude at what these had revealed. The mighty castigating language awoke him. How then could he help greeting Riesser with excitement? Nothing was left undone to honor him. A banquet was given at Allemannia Hall. The prominent citizens of Cincinnati, Gentiles and Jews, were there. Riesser was lauded in toast after toast. Yet he had hardly left the city, when a German weekly attacked him savagely as an "apostle of the Jews."[28]

Some of the English missionaries who were appearing in Cincinnati had the effrontery to declare that Reform Judaism was a half-way station to Christianity. No one else did anything to thrust this calumny down their throats. Wise found a novel means of discrediting them. He got his hands—how, he does not say—on the last will and testament of a "Faithful Missionary in Berlin." This was the work of a baptized Jew, by name Hoga. In it on his death-bed Hoga revealed the impostures and hypocrisies of some of his former comrades. The document had been suppressed in England and was until then unknown in the United States. Wise published it in its entirety in the columns of the *Israelite*. It asserted that Jews were "bought" by the missionaries—but at an exorbitant price. Some of these very "bought" Jews came to see Wise, begging for readmission into Judaism. One of these cases he described in detail—that of a Jew who had taken this money and who came to him for reconversion.[29]

An interesting sidelight on his emotional state at that time was given by an editorial in the *Israelite,* entitled "Swimming Against the Current":

> Swimming against the current is hard and dangerous work; therefore, only the expert swimmer, gifted with a powerful energy, a potent buoyancy, and a strong volition, can and will venture the difficult task.[30]

Minute-books were kept in the Talmud Yelodim Institute. There were almost constant troubles with discipline. One of the teachers resigned because he could not maintain order. It is interesting to note in the pages of these books how much better Wise's English was than the broken, badly spelled entries of the lay committee-members. Some of Wise's comments, in his script, show that occasionally he resented the interference of laymen in the ordinary conduct of the school. A general meeting was called on October 31, 1857, to listen to complaints against him, and accusations that he was neglecting his duty. A resolution was transmitted to the board of B'nai Yeshurun, asking them to bid the rabbi "attend better in the future to his duties." Wise paid no attention to this whatsoever.[31]

The membership of the congregation—recorded in an annual report of the secretary in the fall of 1858—was 207.[32]

We have left untouched and unconsidered the numerous trips Wise was making during this period either to the Middle West or to the East. Their purposes we have already discussed.

Now began Wise's active championship of Jewish rights, an activity in which he was engaged strenuously at various times in his life from now on. He was one of those who pioneered in this field, who did not believe Jews should sit idly by, while their co-religionists were being maltreated or discriminated against, either in the United States or anywhere in the world. Nor did he ever hesitate to use all the media of propaganda available to him. He believed ardently in the right of Jews as American citizens to petition their own government, all the way up to the President, and he was completely outspoken in regarding it as part of the interest and historic duty of the United States to be a champion of liberty and of civil rights everywhere.

Already in November, 1854, Wise had learned that Jews were not being given equal treatment in some of the cantons of Switzerland. This will seem astonishing today to many in the light of the splendid democracy of that little mountainous enclave, its own experience of oppression under the Austrian Empire, and its gallant attainment of liberty. Reciprocal rights of domicile in Switzerland were available only to "Christian Americans." Wise wrote:

> Could it be imagined that a government like ours would sanction a discrimination so odious, while another, the very opposite in character, has intimated its displeasure that such a blot should appear in the history of Switzerland, in the nineteenth century?[33]

The precise cause of this fulmination is explained by Dr. Korn in the work previously referred to:

> The Swiss cantons which would not allow Jews to take up residence within their borders insisted that each canton be permitted to determine whether non-Christian Americans should or should not be exempted from such restrictions. There was much debate in the daily press and in the Senate on this question of discrimination against American citizens by a foreign power.[34]

The Secretary of State, Lewis Cass, had taken a strong position, and American statesmen—among them Webster, Clay, and President Fillmore—had made clear their sense of outrage.

Wise expressed the hope that the Supreme Court would set this treaty aside, inasmuch as it seemed in clear violation of the Constitution.[35]

The matter remained in abeyance for some three years. Then in 1857 Wise started putting an appeal at the masthead of the *Israelite*, suggesting that meetings be called through the country to protest against this treaty, or rather against its continuation in force. He recommended that Jews should try to influence the President:

> Slaves and cowards only will submit to such an outrage; we are men, and must be treated as such. . . .[36]

He followed with a series of articles on "The Treaty of the United States with the Swiss Confederation." Thus two weeks later he wrote as follows:

> We hope that the unanimous voice of the press will cause the President and General Cass, to set aside a treaty which was made in violation of the fundamental laws of our country. They must consider it their duty to do justice to their fellow-citizens, and erase a disgraceful transaction from the laws of our country.[37]

Six more weeks passed and Wise wrote that there had been enough of propaganda. The time had come to act. A meeting was called, to consist of representatives of Jewish communities. The time was to be October 28:

> . . . to proceed to Washington, and lay our grievances before the President, and we entertain no doubt redress will be had.

A preliminary gathering was held in Cincinnati at the Y.M.H.A. with Wise in the chair, to draw up a memorial to the President. The memorial referred in detail to the objectionable paragraph in the Swiss Treaty, the construction which the Swiss authorities had been putting on it, and its patent disadvantages to citizens of the United States "of Hebrew persuasion." The President was petitioned to communicate to the Swiss government a request for the alteration of this section of the treaty. Wise was to go to Washington to try to arrange an interview with the President.[38]

A few days later he reproduced a long communication drawn up in Baltimore on October 29, signed by three Baltimore gentlemen, by himself, and by Jewish citizens of Kentucky, Illinois and Ohio. Wise later reported that the mission to the President—which took place on October 31—had proved completely successful:

> The President today received the delegation in the most friendly manner. His response to our address was direct and decisive.

The Secretary of State pledged himself to use his influence to induce the Swiss to agree to a fair settlement. Wise promised to give more particulars later on.[39] There is somewhat more detail in the *Israelite* of November 13:

> The General [Cass] assured us, if any one of the senators had known the pernicious nature of the treaty, it would not have passed the Senate.

Cass promised to make "strong representations" to the Swiss. Wise ended with the comment that this interview and its result could have happened only in America.[40] An interview with Cass was held by Col. Cohen of Baltimore, F. Leopold of Cleveland and Wise in 1858. The purpose of this was doubtless to see to it that the action pledged would be taken. Cass informed them that he had been in touch with the American legation in Bern, the chief of which was named Fay, and that he expected prompt results. The committee derived the same impression from a conversation they then had with William Hunter, chief clerk of the State Department. They were provided with all relevant documents by Cass and went over them thoroughly. These showed that negotiations had been pending between the United States and Switzerland, that the cantons in question had been asked why they insisted on imposing restrictions on Jews. The papers described the conditions that obtained in all cantons, some of which were called guilty of "mediaeval doctrines and views."[41]

The plea attained its object. Switzerland saw to it that American Jews had equal rights. This case is especially interesting from several angles: first, as one of the earliest, perhaps *the* earliest, of direct application by American Jews to their own government for redress; secondly, as the establishment of a technique, a method of appeal, which became customary; and thirdly, as a precedent for similar actions, notably later in regard to Rumania and Russia. Wise's part in all this was not inconsiderable, as it was in others to which we shall come later on.

We shall end this chapter with two rather strange letters which Wise wrote to Stephen A. Douglas, then Senator from Illinois, Lincoln's adversary in the famous debates in 1858, which had in fact concluded on October 15. It must be borne in mind that by this time Wise was a Democrat and that he regarded himself as having a vital interest in the success of the Party in Ohio and nationally. Nonetheless, even with these prefatory remarks, the letters cannot but seem curious, coming from a rabbi. The only plausible explanation seems to be: first, that he hoped to win Douglas' help with the matter of the Swiss Treaty; and secondly, that he hoped to get additional circulation for the *Israelite* and the *Deborah*. Here are the letters, which we reproduce without abbreviation or alteration:[42]

The first is under date of November 3, 1858:

> Honorable Sir,
> I take pleasure to congratulate you to the triumph you and your principle achieved in your own State. I hope the Democrats will shape their future policy in accordance with the lessons they have lately received in almost all the northern states.
>
> By referring to a paper of mine, which I hereby send you, you will see that I fought with the democracy in favor of your policy in regard to slavery and territories. Had not Groesbeck [?] voted for the English bill and were he not decried here, because the English organ is pledged to the administration and the German organ to the Catholic Church, which the people well know, the victory would have been ours.
>
> It is well understood now, that you have the first claim and best chance to the presidency in 1860, but the papers dare not say so. I did because I am fully independent. I think you should have an organ in this central city, which now as a weekly runs over this entire West and South West, and after a year or so as a daily works in your favor.
>
> To this purpose I can offer you these advantages; 5000 directions [addresses, subscribers, presumably!] in all parts of the

United States; which we have in our book and an established reputation as a journalist.

Such a paper should be edited with special reference to the German population, in a style as they like to read, but with German; for the educated portion of the Germans read English and they lead. I know their taste and have for years given them satisfaction.

If you think this proposition worth while, consider about it and let me know the result.

As regards influence, my Chicago correspondents, Greenebaum especially, can inform you, if you think it worth while to inquire.

Most respectfully,
Isaac M. Wise.[2]

The second letter is dated December 9 of the same year:

Dear Sir,

Your not having acknowledged the receipt of my first note should discourage me to address you again, but I ascribe your silence to pressure of business, still I must impose upon you some more.

The matter to which I wish to call your attention is this: The Democratic Party is too much identified with Jesuitism and Catholicism, a fact which estranges to her the liberal class of the northern population. The Israelites especially have lately been frightened away from the Democracy [by this he means the Democratic Party] by the Swiss Treaty, in which nothing has been done yet by the cabinet to alter the matter, and the Mortara case in Rome, against which simply to protest in behalf of justice and humanity, in the name of liberty of conscience, General Cass refused. It is indispensably necessary that Congress do something to improve the feelings of the multitude toward the Democracy.

I request you, for your own interests' sake, to bring these two affairs before the Senate, in any shape best suiting yourself, and press them to a favorable result, at your earliest convenience. The documents are in the Department of State, but if you wish I can send you all the papers relating thereto. Mr. Valendigham of Dayton, Ohio, called for the papers in the Swiss affair, and thinks to bring it up in the House. But if you think improper to take these matters in your hand, let me know it, and I will write to some Senators of my acquaintance.

Please let me have a decisive answer at your earliest convenience.

Respectfully,
Your Obedient Servant,
Isaac M. Wise.

Wise enclosed in this second letter some materials about the Mortara Case.

As far as it is possible to ascertain Douglas replied to neither of these letters.

20

Before the Storm

DURING THE FIRST FOUR YEARS OF HIS INCUMBENCY AT B'NAI Yeshurun in Cincinnati Wise had found the main lines of his life-work. He had begun the process of reform within his congregation. He had welded it together into effective unity of thought and action, into a group of men and women who believed in his leadership and who were eager to follow him in the adventures on behalf of Judaism upon which he embarked. He had come to know the Jews of the Middle West well; and those of the East too, though never as closely nor on as friendly a basis. Thus he had prepared the ground for a support for his schemes that would not be exclusively local. He had founded and was exceedingly busy editing the *Israelite* and the *Deborah*, which were the most widely read Jewish periodicals of the time in the United States and which served to carry his ideas and his plans to most Jewish communities. He maintained contact with these latter also by the voluminous correspondence he printed from men or women who represented him locally. He had participated in the Cleveland Conference, and at it and in its consequences had become certain that it was not then possible to unite all the Jews of America, chiefly—it seemed to him—because of the partisanship and the extremism of both "radical Reformers" and intractable orthodox. He had made his first attempt at calling into being a "university," which among other things was to be a theological seminary. He had acquired a technique for defending Jewish rights at home and abroad, and had improvised a method of action by which Jewish communities could bring their collective influence to bear. He had not found time to continue the writing of books, though some of his hasty writing in fictional form had appeared in *Israelite* and *Deborah* and had later been bound and sold. He had been the prime mover in the only achievement that had come out of the Cleveland Conference, the *Minhag America*, one of the first and most interesting attempts at a liturgy which, while adhering to the form of the *Siddur*, had added to it English and German translations and eliminated what Wise regarded as outmoded theological sections and "cabalistical poems and prayers."

All of this constituted no mean record of effort and of accomplishment for four years. Behind this façade of external events and activities lay much in his own inner development. Everything that one can read—chiefly in his editorials in the *Israelite*—indicates that he had been finding himself more and more surely, coming to a mature estimate of his own powers and faculties. That estimate would probably not have coincided with the opinion of him held by later generations enjoying the advantage of the perspective given by the passing of a century. While Wise regarded his main purpose as the bringing together of the Jews of the United States, the raising of their level of Jewish culture and knowledge, of their Americanization and the esteem they enjoyed among their fellow-citizens; he conceived of himself also—and consistently—as a philosopher, a scholar, an exponent of the classical Jewish tradition to Jews and Gentiles. His books may now be little read, translated, reprinted, or even referred to. In his time they were widely distributed and widely perused. Of this there is every possible evidence. We shall describe these books as they appear, and much later on—when we come to arrange, analyze, and systematize his thought—we shall devote some time to each, to the part it played in his own inner evolution, and to what it contributed to his final, rounded view of Judaism, its history and its theology. We shall not here or hereafter belabor the degree of Wise's scholarship, or enter into a detailed discussion of his access to sources and his accuracy of memory or reference. Two things do, however, need to be stated. In the sense of his knowledge of Jewish sources, and later of a relatively good command of the great classical works of philosophy and history, he was a better scholar than he is now generally given credit for having been. He understood clearly some of the pressing needs of scholarship in relation to the New Testament and the origins of Christianity in general and he did some pioneering work in these fields. After these two things have been said, it is necessary to add—what is sufficiently obvious—that he was not to be numbered among the creative Jewish scholars of the nineteenth century.

The years between 1858 and the beginning of the Civil War were devoted chiefly to his own congregation, to his editorship of *Israelite* and *Deborah*, and to his usual travels. A few incidents that may contribute somewhat to our familiarity with him happened in this time. But most of the important matters: his attitude toward slavery, his own personal opinions and utterances on the crucial political and ethical problems antecedent to the election of Lincoln and the outbreak of the conflict, we shall reserve for treatment under one continuous heading in the following chapters. It must be borne in mind constantly that these years, three years before the firing on Fort Sumter, were years of tremendous excitement in the United States: the years of the Dred Scott decision, the outlawing of slavery by Minnesota, and the tragedy of John Brown at Harper's Ferry. They were also years in which Wise was coming to his own convictions on "Union," "secession," the prospect of war, etc. The circumstance of his living in Cincinnati must have had a ponderable influence upon him. The community was poised—as it were—between North and South. Its trade was largely with the South, for which it was a distributing center via the rivers. It had served as a terminus for the "Underground Railway," and as the residence of Lyman Beecher, Harriet Beecher Stowe, and others. It had indulged in anti-Negro riots and in outrages against the Abolitionists and their publications. Many of the members of Wise's congregation, and he himself, had close ties with the South, commercially and personally. His political affiliations and preferences, which turned him more and more into an ardent member of the Democratic Party, were crystallizing at this time.

These must be seen as "years between," after the arduous first four years in Cincinnati, and before the years of tragic climax, of pain, and—to some extent—of silence, during the Civil War.

The congregation was growing steadily between 1854 and 1860. Members were attracted by the vigor of Wise's leadership, the warmth of his personality, and the splendid laymen who led the congregation and supported their rabbi. Services had been held since 1848 in Lodge Street.[1] To judge from an old picture of the synagogue, it must have resembled an old central European Jewish house of worship, rigid and unattractive, and not generous in its accommodations. During these very years it was rapidly getting to be too small for the congregation, and its neighborhood had been deteriorating. At an annual meeting of the congregation in the fall of 1860, at which officers and trustees were elected:

> A committee was appointed to furnish the congregation with a suitable plan to build a new temple of large dimensions, the present synagogue on Lodge Street being too small and not properly located.[2]

The chairman of the committee was our old friend, Marcus Fechheimer.[3] Unfortunately it proved impossible even to make a beginning upon this project. The rumblings of the coming war put a stop to all else. Wise himself wrote of this time in these words:

> I will not leave congregation B'nai Yeshurun. The honour of Judaism in Cincinnati and throughout the West requires that B'nai Yeshurun, hitherto the banner-bearer of reform and progress on this side of the Alleghenies, should come out of Lodge Street into the broad daylight of a better locality. Still, if the congregation believes that the time has not yet come for such an enterprise, I will patiently wait with you. If some of our wealthy members leave us, I will stay with you even if my salary must be reduced one-half.[4]

Though these lines were written somewhat later—in 1863—when a proposition was being considered for B'nai Israel and B'nai Yeshurun jointly to build a Temple and to have Wise and Lilienthal lecture alternately, the former in English and the latter in German, the proposal had to do primarily with the inadequacy of Lodge Street and the economic difficulties the war was bringing to the leading members of both congregations.

Wise also continued as head of the Talmud Yelodim Institute, in the rooms of Lodge Street. Around this time he wrote that this institution must be better than the public schools, that it must follow the biblical injunction: "And thou shalt teach them diligently to thy children" (Deut. 6:7). Pupils at the school between the ages of ten and twelve must—he wrote—have English, German, and Hebrew grammar; geography, the history of the United States, and arithmetic. They had to know Hebrew "etymology" and be able to translate anywhere in the Pentateuch and in the Historical Books. They must be given moral and religious instruction. At that time Wise reported that the school had about 150 pupils. They were not orthodox and attended classes with uncovered heads. No religion was taught except that of the Bible. Some children of "indigent orthodox parents" were among them.[5]

In 1859 the *Deborah* was placed entirely under Lilienthal's direction. The *Israelite*, which Wise was still editing, was, however, the "main arm of Judaism in America."[6]

He continued to appeal for the founding of a College, chiefly in editorials appearing in the *Israelite*:[7]

> We have one national literature. This is the basis and cause of our oneness. Therefore, the knowledge of this, our literature, and the united desire to inquire after the truth, is not only our private duty and satisfaction, is not only for us and our children, for us and our neighbors, it is the glorious bond of Israel's union all over the earth, the earthly representative of God enthroned among Israel.
>
> If Israel's sacred inheritance should be preserved intact, we must unitedly, and all of us, support and preserve our synagogue, schools, and literature, and truth must be the main object of these institutions.[8]

In the same year he wrote that, though the scheme for Zion College "exploded," the central idea "sits firmly," and is still being discussed in many places. In the same issue he announced that all necessary arrangements were being made to open a "Hebrew College" by the first of September, 1861. Professors had already been engaged. Prospective pupils might first go through the Talmud Yelodim Institute and then to the new College, which was to consist of three departments:

1. The Hebrew Department.
2. The Classical Department.
3. The Commercial Department.

Wise outlined a probable course of studies. The plan was elaborate, more or less along the same general lines as had been that for Zion College. Sessions were to be held from September 1 to July 4. The tuition fee was to be $85 *per annum*, but now plus $285 for board and lodging. The course, he guaranteed, would prepare those who would complete it for a profession. "The faculty consists of the very best professors. Their names will be published in due time."[9]

Around the same time he had suggested that every congregation collect half a dollar *per capita* from its members, to go toward the creation of a fund to enable young American Jewish scholars to pursue theological studies abroad.[10] But clearly he must have regarded this only as a stop-gap, for his consistent attitude was that American rabbis should be educated in an American institution.

An editorial, entitled "We Have No Literature," was published in the *Israelite*, deploring the fact—referring naturally only to American Jewish literature—that we are without such a literature, and suggesting reasons for this deficiency. Anyone—like himself—who would try to remedy the defect would lose much, and would be fiercely attacked. Jews—he said—do not read books about and for themselves, a complaint still being made in our own day:

> We have no literature and none to expect under the present awkward circumstances.[11]

Shortly before that he had proposed the creation of a society for tracts. This was one of his many germinal suggestions, which later years took up and carried into effect. Judaism—he wrote—is in great need of exposition and of defense:

> We emphatically deny the truth of the New Testament; but there are no books in the hands of our people to prove their assertions in this respect. . . . If we have principles to defend, why do we not do it?[12]

Questions kept pouring in from Christians concerning the nature and meaning of Reform Judaism. But nothing existed in English with which to answer them. Wise commented upon the incredible poverty of apologetic literature among Jews. Nothing was available except the *Israelite* and some English sermons. Some of his opponents were accusing him of wishing to destroy Judaism. On the contrary, all he was striving to do was to explain and to defend it more effectively. He had written an outline of a work of exposition and apologetics. No one else would touch it. He had no choice but to go to work himself. He wrote a short booklet in which each and every statement rested solidly and solely upon Biblical support. No quotations from the Talmud were utilized. This must not be taken to mean that Wise had abandoned the attitude toward the Talmud which he had elaborated at the time of the Cleveland Conference, but simply that this book was intended also for Christians, who would acknowledge only Biblical authority.

It was in this little book for the first time that Reform Judaism was presented as resting basically upon the Bible:

> Our orthodox friends thought that the doctrinal theology was strictly orthodox, the moral theology and ceremonial teachings ultra-radical.

The book was called *The Essence of Judaism*, and was published in Cincinnati in 1861. Many thousands of copies were sold. It was employed in Jewish schools and by Christians also. No catechism—Wise declared—ever replaced it.[13] Later on, the book was remodeled and republished under the title *Judaism: Its Doctrines and Duties.* We shall review both these as part of Wise's general system of ideas on Judaism.

From the beginning Wise had intended to continue his *History of the Israelitish Nation.* The *Israelite* began the publication of a chapter to serve as a beginning for a second part. It was on the Babylonian Captivity. Wise announced this in his periodical in March, 1860. In memory he went back to the appearance of the first part in 1854 and to the flood of hostile criticism that had rushed over him:

> We wrote with the blood of our heart . . . but then came envy, passion, selfishness.

Partly as a result of this experience Wise contented himself for some time thereafter with writing historical romances: *The Last Struggle of the Nation, The Combat of the People, The First of the Maccabees,* etc. But these, he declared, were only sparks from the anvil of his enthusiasm for Jewish history.[14]

Around the same time an event took place which was to engage his interest and his concern for a number of years. He learned that a "Board of Delegates" was being formed. This was in the East, where most of his "opponents" lived and were active against him. His first comment upon it was that it was a plot against Reform, and he asked his friends in Cincinnati and elsewhere to stay clear of it. The Board of Delegates claimed that it was to be a "champion of the Jew." The Jew, Wise declared, did not need such a champion. Jews could take care of themselves.[15] It will become evident as we proceed that in the beginning the Board of Delegates was itself not clear as to its own purposes. Partly it was conceived of as a union of congregational representatives, partly for the purpose of founding a theological institution, and only partly for the defense of Jewish rights. Its history will be pursued in later chapters.

In 1859 the war of Italy's independence and unity was beginning. The work of Cavour, Mazzini, and the gallant leadership of Garibaldi were moving toward a climax, which culminated in May, 1860, when Garibaldi landed with the "Thousand "in Sicily. A consistent lover of freedom, and excitedly interested in it all over the world, Wise followed this news keenly. In the *Israelite* he published a letter from a "friend" who had left the Austrian army, and had then joined the forces of Victor Emanuel in Sardinia.[16]

The Mortara Case has appeared in our record once before, in the second letter Wise wrote to Stephen A. Douglas. At that time we did not pause to explain its background. The main facts are given in Dr. Bertram L. Korn's book on "American Jewry and the Civil War":

> On June 23, 1858, Edgar Mortara, an Italian Jewish child of six years, was seized by the Papal guard on the grounds that, during an illness some years before, he had been secretly baptized by his Catholic nurse. All efforts to restore him to his family were fruitless. News of the incident reached Jewish communities all over the world; a fever-pitch of indignation was the natural result. Had mediaeval experiences come back again to plague the harried Jews? . . .[17]

It was as a result of this case—Dr. Korn writes—and of the excitement it aroused, that the Board of Delegates was formed by nine congregations of New York plus thirteen from outside New York responding to the call of Samuel M. Isaacs in the *Messenger*. Calamities have not infrequently stimulated the creation of important Jewish bodies. It was the Kishineff massacre that prompted Jacob Schiff to organize the American Jewish Committee.

Wise was as aroused by the "Mortara Case" as everyone else. His first comment appeared at the end of 1858. To him the Mortara Case exposed the true aim of Christianity, a bitter remark: "The old serpent is as venomous now as centuries ago." All that has changed is its potency for evil.[18]

A few weeks earlier he had tried to get the Catholic press of the United States to protest. This had proved a forlorn hope. Nonetheless, Wise felt mortified and embittered by the absence of any response. He wrote that all of this demonstrated what would happen, if Catholics ever got the upper hand in this country: "Where is our security of person, family, religion, house, and home?"[19] Very soon he reverted to the method he had found so successful in regard to Swiss treatment of Jews. Quite often he asked the readers of the *Israelite* to send petitions about the Mortara Case to President and Congress.

He expressed his own personal belief that Edgar Mortara had never really been baptized, that this was all a ruse. However, he admitted that the reaction of the world to this Catholic action had been helpful to Jews, whose position "might have become worse":

> Mortara is the savior of many a Jew in continental Europe. . . . The eyes of the world are open and you can not close them.[20]

He printed in his columns a letter to President Buchanan and to

General Cass. With his own Democratic Party he found the matter hard to take up, for he believed it to be overwhelmingly Catholic. The government itself—he declared—had taken a weak and negative stand. This should be radically altered, and Congress prevailed upon to express its horror.[21]

Three months later Wise put on record that Moses Montefiore, the great British Jewish philanthropist and defender of Jewish rights, had journeyed to Rome to try to get a hearing on the Mortara Case.[22] On a visit Montefiore had made to Damascus, where an accusation of ritual murder had been brought against Jews in 1840, and another murderous charge in 1860, he had had a wonderful success. In 1860 Montefiore had appeared in Damascus together with Abraham Camondo of Constantinople and Shemaya Angel of Damascus itself. But in Rome Montefiore was treated with contempt and discourtesy. From the Pope he was unable even to get an audience. Wise commented that it had to be understood that behind the Pope was the power of Austria.[23]

It must not be forgotten that all during this period, and increasingly in the years to follow, Wise was fully aware of the tragic position of Jews in Russia. He was always severely and openly critical of Russian policy. As early as November 16, 1855,[24] he condemned the severity and inhumanity of the Czar. Near the end of the same year[25] he rejoiced at the defeat of Russia in the Crimean War:

> Russia, the arch enemy of civilization and enlightenment, of equal rights and liberty, the powerful and relentless defender of privileges and exclusive laws, this taskmaster of thirty-four millions of serfs, Russia, the gigantic scarecrow of the friends of liberty, was chastised and humiliated by the allied powers in the year 1855.[26]

And at long last Wise witnessed the fruition of his efforts on behalf of Swiss Jewry, and of American Jewish citizens in Switzerland. This was largely the work of Theodore S. Fay, the United States Minister at Berne. In the decade following the interview with the President and with Cass, all restrictions had been removed. By 1874 full religious liberty was written into the Swiss Constitution. Thereafter, the treatment of aliens became a federal, and not a cantonal, question.[27]

This concludes the record of these years. We shall now attempt to chronicle one of the most difficult and momentous periods in Wise's career, and in that of our country: the time immediately before and during the Civil War. We shall place before the reader all the material available, commenting only when it may be necessary for the sake of clarity, and leaving it to the reader to form his own judgment. A time of trial by fire for the nation and for the men in it!

21

Wise on the Civil War

Now we have come to the very eve of the conflict. Since this cannot be a history of the United States during Wise's lifetime, we shall have to content ourselves by placing Wise's life and his opinions and actions in relation to what any moderately well-informed reader should already know. We must assume that vividly before the imagination of anyone who peruses these pages is a picture of the charges and countercharges; the irreconcilable differences of opinion; the political, religious and ethical disputations resounding in all the States, North and South; the rumble of the distant, approaching thunder of armed conflict; the many subsidiary issues that had to do with States' Rights; the legality and morality of "secession"; the fate of slaves who "ran away" up North; the wild reports as to French and British sympathies for the South; the bewildering multiplicity of parties and political panaceas: those who thought that slavery and States' Rights were paramount to all else; those who believed that slavery was a disease that cried to heaven for abolition, and who filled pulpits and political platforms with their extremist sermons and speeches; and those who believed that time would solve and heal all this and make feasible a gradual transition from slavery, yet preserve the Union unimpaired.

In his recent great book, *America as a Civilization*, Max Lerner gives this brief pen-sketch of the time:

> The division of a nation into economies and two ways of life, the

> tyranny of King Cotton over the mind of the Old South, the Confederate dream of a Greek Republic founded on slavery on the shores of the Gulf, the shadow of slaves' chains falling across the American soul. The slave revolts and the massacres on both sides, the underground railroad, the knock in the rainy night; the heroism of Frederick Douglass and Harriet Tubman, John Brown at the arsenal at Harpers Ferry. The days of the great Senate debates, a gangling boy growing up in Illinois, "a house divided against itself cannot stand," the Presidential car transferred from one station to another at Baltimore in the quiet of the early hours. The freeing of the slaves, the draft riots, Lincoln passing long lines of hospital cots with rough jokes to rid the heart's sorrow. . . .[1]

But we are moving faster than the event. As yet it was the time of the lowering prelude to war, not war itself; the crystallization of opinions in the swirling crucible, the confused processes by which a great nation moves toward decision in its legislative halls or on the field of battle, as America's tragic destiny at that time had ordained it to be.

As the record now will reveal, Wise found himself to be of an opinion and in a Party, that were and are difficult to understand. We shall review all that he thought, said, and wrote about the issues that led to Civil War, about the Abolitionists, about Lincoln, about Jewish rights, and the anti-Semitism that—perhaps for the first time—reared its head in America, and finally about the ethics of slavery. This will best be done by letting him speak for himself. What were the inner wrestlings his words evidence? How did he comport himself during these five strife and hatred-filled years?

That he was opposed to slavery there can be no serious doubt. But it is equally certain that he did not regard this issue as great enough to risk breaking the Union. He opposed secession,[2] and up to the last minute continued to hope for some compromise proposal similar to those that had been fashioned by the men he had met in the Senate in 1850 and 1851, men like Clay, Calhoun, and Webster, who had debated hotly, but who had kept the country together. Wise was deeply and even desperately opposed to war. He could not bring himself to agree with Lincoln that there was no real choice, if the Union was to go on, but to force the South back into its loyalties. As a political and moral attitude this of Wise was not as uncommon as one might think. The country was far from united, not only obviously as between North and South, but within the South and within the North. Events were hurrying men along, forcing moderates into radicalism, sharpening opinions toward extremes of expression and conduct. Behind the tumult there must have been many thousands who took no part in this, who pleaded and hoped for moderation, for "gradualism." One writer[3] asserts that Wise was chronically unable to take a "radical" position on any issue, that he was "passionate and vehement," but not extreme. This estimate is borne out, as we have seen, in his willingness to take a middle-of-the-road position on orthodoxy and reform at the Cleveland Conference. Before the war, Wise published an editorial in the *Israelite*, in which this paragraph occurs:

> The present state of political affairs should convince every sober-minded and well-informed man that radicalism will not do in any province of human activity. There are no leaps in human history. . . . Radicalism will not do in politics, because there are historical rights, inveterate views and habits, thousands of interests connected with the existing state of affairs which will not yield to theories. It is easy for agitators to excite the passions of the populace, make friends and arm defenders for any theory; but it is impossible to revolutionize radically all historical rights.[4]

This general principle Wise was perfectly willing to see applied to religion also:

> Let us be reasonable in piety and pious in our reasoning. Let us be progressive in improvements and conservative in principles.[5]

Again and again Wise gave expression to this general attitude toward the central issues at stake in the United States. He declared himself in favor of "peace and union" at any cost, even if it had to be the "everlasting legalization of slavery." In the *Israelite*, in the months just before the outbreak of war, he published no sermons except those for peace, no letters except those favoring Union. Doubtless he received many others, but they were not permitted to appear. Letters from Szold, De Cordova, Hochheimer, fellow-rabbis of his own frame of mind, and even advertisements by M. Loth, a prominent member of B'nai Yeshurun, later to be the first president of the Union of American Hebrew Congregations, were inserted in the pages of the periodical. Wise thought that a counsel of moderation had a fair chance of success, that "the second sober thought of the people will decide in favor of union at any risk."[6] The full text of this section of his editorial, eloquent and affecting, read thus:

> Destroy not this temple of freedom that humanity weep not over its fall, and coming generations condemn not your rashness.

> Pause and consider! Providence reserved this sea-girt continent for the last and highest triumphs of humanity; no power on earth can change this manifest destiny. . . .[7]

Only two weeks later he wrote an editorial on the proposals of Secession that were already audible in the South. It should be borne in mind that this was a month and a half before Lincoln's election, which the South interpreted as a sure signal for adverse action against them in Washington. Wise wrote:

> The fanatics in both sections of the country succeeded in destroying the most admirable fabric of government.

He referred to the "demagogues who sought office at any price." But by this he did not mean Lincoln.

> Must the Southern states stay in the Union with the conviction that none of their men can ever be elected President, or Vice-President, of the United States? . . . By what means will you coerce eight or ten states to obey your mandates? . . . No free state has a right to force another free state to adopt repugnant measures.[8]

Though he loved and believed in the Union, Wise appeared to indicate here that he accepted the contention of South Carolina and of other southern states that the right to create the Union in 1789 had implied the right to secede, that the "sovereignty" of the states, the concept woven into every part of the Constitution, signified also that that sovereignty included the last resort of any genuine individual —to make his own choice as to allegiances and associations. It must not be thought that Wise welcomed the threat of secession. By every word of his at this time it was obvious that he came to the above conclusion only with the greatest reluctance. When South Carolina did in fact secede, Wise gave up hope of preserving the Union. Nor in the beginning could he bring himself to admit that the resort to arms was the only logical rejoinder to secession:

> Force will not hold together this Union; it was cemented by liberty and can stand only by the affections of the people.[9]

Earlier than this he gave evidence of his belief that the Republican victory in the fall of 1860 would be a "national calamity," that it would tear the country apart:

> Here is the house divided against itself, the irrepressible conflict. . . . Either the Republican party must be killed off forever by constitutional guarantees to the South, to make an end forever to this vexing slavery question, or the Union must be dissolved.[10]

This opinion he reiterated more or less in an editorial at the beginning of the year 1861:

> The year 1861 must witness either the end of the Republican party or the dissolution of the Union.

Wise contended that the Republicans cared no more for the Union than did the "fire-eaters" of the South:

> This is the most terrible blow the cause of humanity is likely to sustain in the year 1861.[11]

At last war had begun! Secession and the firing on Fort Sumter meant that the South had come to the conclusion that there was no other choice. Wise was now face to face with what was certainly the most difficult decision of his career. He withdrew into the quiet of his own soul, reviewed all that he had felt and said in the pulpit and in the *Israelite,* and tried to decide upon his stand henceforth. His conclusion was not long in crystallizing. Whether his decision was wise or good is a much more difficult question. Certainly now, almost a century later, it seems to us to have been neither, especially coming from a great religious leader, a lover of liberty, a man of insight and learning. We have the incalculable advantage of knowing the sequel, of knowing Lincoln, not as he seemed to some in 1860 and 1861, but as he has come to be in the memory of the American people and of the world; the advantage also of knowing what happened to the country after the war and after the travail of Reconstruction. Wise had to decide what he would do, based upon his repudiation of force as a means of solving social and political problems, based upon his confused and hesitant attitude toward the institution of slavery—to which we shall come before long, based on his chronic views on "religion and politics." Whatever the inner processes that were stirring in his soul, it was with this that he came forth:

> We are the servant of peace, not of war. Hitherto we saw fit to say something on public affairs, and it was our ardent hope to assist those who wished to prevent civil war; but we wasted our words.
>
> They say civil war is commenced. What can we say now? Shall we lament and weep like Jeremiah over a state of things too sad and too threatening to be looked on with indifference? We would only be laughed at. . . . Or should we choose sides with one of the parties? We cannot, not only because we have dear friends and near relatives, beloved brethren and kinsmen in either section of the country, that our heart bleeds in thinking of their distress, of the misery that might befall them. Therefore, silence

> must henceforth be our policy, silence on all questions of the day until conciliation shall move the hearts of millions to a better understanding of the blessings of peace.[12]

With the exception of Wise's writing and acting about Grant's Order No. 11, he was faithful to this self-imposed policy. Whether this meant his consistent adoption of a genuine "neutrality," it is not easy to decide. Like many in the border states Wise was a "Peace Democrat." This was the group for whom Henry Ward Beecher found the scornful expression "Border-state eunuchs," men opposed both to the extreme abolitionists and to the extreme secessionists.[13]

It is more than a little astonishing to look through the pages of the *Israelite* for the next four years, to receive the impression that there was little awareness of the war, of its wavering balance of advantage, of all the moving and dramatic scenes being enacted. That Wise was not stirred and disquieted by these, that he did not follow the conflict from day to day, is utterly unthinkable. But he remained true to this resolve, his avowed principle that it was not the concern of religion to mix in these matters.[14]

Later on we shall adduce some evidence that—as for many others—the beginning of the Civil War brought with it many special difficulties and problems for Wise: the possibility that he would not be able to go on with the publication of the *Israelite* and the *Deborah*, that the Talmud Yelodim Institute might have to be closed, and that it would affect his own congregation, at the very least in its hope of erecting a new house of worship.[15]

During the war, Wise continued to regard Southerners as friends, an attitude that was exceedingly difficult and even dangerous in the midst of the waxing hatred such an intestine conflict was bound to engender. He could not be brought to call them enemies. After the war he appealed again and again for an end to hostility and fratricidal hatred, again and again for a "soft" peace. During the war he supported the war loans of the North, as was the duty of every good citizen, and also the charitable campaigns; he printed much news also of soldiers and officers. Outside of this the pages of the *Israelite* were consistently "non-partisan," exhibiting neither rancor nor resentment, and continuing to express friendliness and concern for the Jews of the South.[16] Wise published the casualty figures, took note of the issuance of the Emancipation Proclamation, the election of 1864, and of other great events. But usually he was insisting that the salvation of the individual soul was of more moment than anything that could happen in the world outside. He was thoroughly familiar with the classical Jewish literature of Europe, with the books in which lie enshrined Jewish reactions to wars, pestilences and persecutions. It was perhaps as a result of perusing these that at times he would write that the war was a punishment by God to purify the soul of America:

> Would to God the calamity of civil war that has befallen us would lead us to investigate closely the national sins that exist among us, and rouse us to extinguish them forever. . . . If this war costs us ten thousand professed politicians, it will turn out a blessing at last, a blessing to the whole land. . . . We cannot enumerate the ten thousand national vices that exist among us, vices which directly or indirectly brought on us the national calamity under which we now suffer. Let these suffice to establish the fact, that this storm deservedly came upon us, that it will purify the atmosphere, and we shall go forth purified and improved to a great extent. . . . All the standing armies, navies, national guards, armories, forts and fortresses, can not save this republic from ultimate destruction, if the nation comes not to the conclusion that there are more precious objects, holier and more lasting interests, to be attended to than the one and ever annoying object of making money.[17]

There were many similar utterances. For example:

> Think of all the human lives lost and to be lost yet in this civil war till peace will be restored to the country; think that the main cause of this lamentable struggle is materialism; then tell us, can all the money in creation pay for the lives lost? . . . We have seen enough to know that the everlasting portion of man must not be mixed with the perishable. This war will last but a short time; but our religion will last forever. This war is for our country, our religion is for mankind. This war is for the temporary and perishable things, our religion is for life eternal. Therefore these two subjects must not be mingled.[18]

Sometimes Southern Jews would find their way through the lines to Cincinnati. Wise was eager to ascertain what was happening to his friends in various Southern cities. In 1862 he reported that all was well with Jews in various communities: "Our informant tells us wonders of the material prosperity of our friends in the far South."[19]

His fundamental attitude and opinion continued to whisper through the interstices of his silence. Even as late as 1863 he wrote an editorial in the *Israelite* under the caption: "The Revolutionary Object of Extremists." Its gist was in these lines:

> Every dispassionate man acquainted with the history of the last

> decennium, at least every one who is capable and willing to trace back effects to the causes thereof, will admit that the present rebellion originated in the fanaticism of extremists. "Slavery is a divine institution," is a phrase no older than the anti-slavery preaching from the pulpit.

He went on to contend that extremes met in the arguments advanced by the Abolitionists in the North and many ministers in Southern pulpits. Jefferson had argued for and established a wise separation of Church and State. For more than a century this policy had been observed. Then preachers turned politicians and precipitated the strife.[20]

Later in 1863—in connection with *Rosh Ha-shono*—Wise reviewed the events of the preceding year. The terrible war was still going on. Grant's infamous order (treated in detail later) had been revoked. Three Jewish chaplains had been appointed in the Union Army, by name, Gottheld, Sarner, and Frenkel, and this—it was to be recorded—against the insensate opposition of some. He still hoped for peace.[21]

Even in the summer of 1864, when it must have become unmistakable that the end of the war could not be distant and that the South was to receive a humiliating and final defeat, Wise was still clinging to his policy of "neutrality," phrased at times in rather querulous tones:

> Either [a man] must rejoice over the defeat of our armies and pray for their destruction, or he must blindly admire the blunders of our military leaders and shout Hosannah to Abe Lincoln and his thousand and one demonstrations of imbecility, in order to gratify one or the other faction. Either one must believe the Negro was created to be a beast of burden to others, or you must say he is just as good as you are. . . .[22]

In this already appeared two items, to which we shall come later in greater detail: Wise's feelings about Lincoln and about slavery. In essence the passage is—though in somewhat unintelligible terms—a refusal to range himself with either "faction," to be forced to choose either extreme.

During the war, Wise attempted—in 1863 and 1864—to obtain the release of some Confederate Jewish prisoners at Fort Delaware. These had written to him for aid. It is remarkable that the letters had reached him. He appealed to the readers of the *Israelite* to send them food, and he published their names.[23]

The total picture of Wise and the Civil War is one of a suspension of judgment, a resolve to remain aloof, a conviction that right and wrong were not clearly aligned but confused and hopelessly divided. Certainly this course of action is far removed from Wise's customary forthrightness, boldness, and especially from his profound love for and gratitude towards America. Two factors were probably responsible for his refusal to place himself clearly and unmistakably on the side of the "Union": his deep detestation of and opposition to the Abolitionists; and his equivocal attitude toward slavery. To these we shall now come.

22

Wise on the Abolitionists and on Slavery

MORE THAN ONCE WE HAVE REPEATED WISE'S UTTERANCES ON THE duty of keeping the pulpit out of politics. He was certain that a rabbi, or a clergyman, had no ethical right to use his pulpit, or a religious periodical, to further a political purpose. Clearly the Abolitionists—men who used every medium and every place to voice their opinions about slavery and their tireless propaganda for outlawing it—were men whom he would detest and of whom he would disapprove with all the force of his soul. In his opinion they degraded religion, used it as a tool, and proved themselves unscrupulous and intemperate. He did not regard them as sincere bigots, but hypocrites, self-seeking, fanatical hypocrites. And yet after the Civil War—though somewhat tardily and ungraciously—Wise admitted that the abolition of slavery had been a step necessary to the moral well-being of the United States. This did not, even then, bring with it his admission that slavery had been a good or sufficient reason for going to war with the South. Nor did he ever indicate that some of the Abolitionists—men like Wendell Philipps or William Lloyd Garrison—were more than wild and irresponsible praters, bringing disgrace upon the fair name of religion.[1] He lumped them all together as "fanatics, demagogues":

> Red republicans and habitual revolutionaries, who feed on excite-

> ment and delight in civil wars, German atheists coupled with American puritans who know of no limits to their fanaticism, visionary philanthropists and wicked preachers who have that religion which is most suitable to their congregations.

If he had had to select one essential cause that beyond all others had brought on the Civil War, he would have placed his finger on the Abolitionists:

> They would rather see this country crushed and crippled than discard their fanaticism, or give up their political influence.[2]

A controversy was in progress for some time in regard to chaplains in the Union army. Up to that time these could be Christians only. Wise quoted with pleasure the words of a Presbyterian journal that "two thirds of the chaplains in the army are unfit for their place."[3] Lincoln himself was reported to have uttered harsh words about them.[4] It is not possible here to follow the details of this record, which are set forth clearly and ably in an entire chapter of *American Jewry and the Civil War* by Dr. Bertram W. Korn.[5] The only point that needs be made here is that in this case also Wise believed that the Abolitionists were in some considerable measure responsible for barring Jews from the chaplaincy.[6]

In his invariable bitterness against the Abolitionists Wise appeared to forget that his own attitude was not unanimous among rabbis, that in fact some rabbis were themselves Abolitionists. Certainly this was true of David Einhorn, with whom Wise had been at odds on most questions ever since Einhorn had come to the United States in 1855.[7] In 1860 Wise had paid a visit to Baltimore and had written back to the *Israelite* that Einhorn's congregation "is half radical in practice and entirely so in theory." This did not refer to their stand on the war, but to religious beliefs and practices. Benjamin Szold, another Baltimore rabbi and the father of Henrietta Szold, was a man much nearer his own opinions, midway between extremists of both sides. In January 1861 in the *Israelite* Wise reproduced a sermon by Szold pleading for peace at any price.[8] Yet, as far as it is possible to discover in the sources available, Wise never attacked Einhorn directly on the issue of slavery. Doubtless he intended to include Einhorn in his many scorching statements about Abolitionists in general.[9]

It was not only for their intransigent stand on slavery, or even because they had dived headlong into politics in violation of his own avowed principle of the duty of the pulpit to stay clear, that Wise hated the Abolitionists. He hated them even more because he believed that they had no concern for other minority-groups, that, after they had wept for the Negro, they had no pity left for others. In 1850, for example, the Massachusetts Legislature had adopted an anti-alien law, which denied to foreigners the right to vote or to hold office until after a residence of seven years and the completion of the process of naturalization. Lincoln too thought badly of this law.[10] The failure of the Abolitionists to express their indignation and to utilize their eloquence in this case, to pay any attention to the straits of other men discriminated against in America, convinced Isaac M. Wise that they were not sincere lovers of man, but politicians with few scruples to moderate their hunger for power:

> Do you think the Israelites of the South must be your white slaves, as you in your naturalization laws treat the foreigner, placing him below the Negro? . . . Too often . . . those who faint away at hearing of a Negro thousands of miles distant having been abused, are always ready to wrong their next neighbor.[11]

The most important point is that Wise accused the Abolitionists again and again of being the primary cause of the Civil War. There is, however, a reservation implicit in his charges, remarkable as they are for their intemperateness. It is hard to believe that Wise meant to say that there were no other causes for the conflict between brothers; that slavery itself, political claims and interests, economic differences, the host of other views and rhetorical outbursts of South and North, played little or no part in the eventual outbreak of hostilities. What he was trying to say, without question, was that all of this might have been allayed by compromise, in the present as it had been in the past; that slavery might have been held within limits, had it not been for the tension, the hatred, the wild provocation, cast into the national arena by the Abolitionists. That he believed precisely this his words indicate unmistakably:

> Who in the world could act worse, more extravagant and reckless in this crisis than Protestant priests did? From the very start of the unfortunate difficulties the consequences of which we now suffer so severely, the Protestant priests threw the firebrand of abolitionism into the very heart of this country. . . . There was not a Protestant paper in existence that had not weekly an abolitionist's tirade. There was scarcely a sermon preached without a touch at least of the "existing evil." You know who made Jefferson Davis and the rebellion? The priests did, and their whiners and howlers in the press. The whole host of priests would rather see this country crushed and crippled than discard their fanaticism or give up their political influence.[12]

The term which Wise employed here, and which he used in many other paragraphs of a similar nature, "Protestant priests," was in itself calculated to arouse scorn and antagonism. It was a clear symptom of his own acute feeling.

The same clergymen who were battering at the nation concerning the Negro were—according to Wise—trying to have the United States called a "Christian nation." To this every sinew and cell of Wise was unalterably opposed. Concerning this we have already cited a number of instances: his words about Chase's Thanksgiving Proclamation, and others. In 1861 such a proposal was actually placed before Congress by the Pennsylvania Synod of Presbyterian Christians. Of this Wise wrote:

> O ye hypocrites and pharisees! You would trample under your impious feet the rights of the Israelites and millions of intelligent citizens who believe not in Christ—you would cast the firebrand of civil war in our midst to slay the innocent women and children. . . [you] embrace the distant Negro and rebuke the distant slave-holder whom you fear not, who can not come and join your church, increase your salaries, or praise your superlative wisdom."[13]

Wise contended a number of times that such a "priest," "abuses the place and misuses the trust placed in him." If his conscience bids him speak, now that the Union is in danger, let him speak to save it from bloodshed and war. Let him be—as he ought—a man of peace! Instead, it is he who is goading the nation into war!

Later we shall come to Wise's position in regard to Jews in the South, the whole grievous problem of anti-Jewish prejudice that was a concomitant of the dislocations of civil war. Apparently the Abolitionists expected the Jews of the South to take the same stand as their own against slavery. To this Wise rejoined:

> . . . You abolitionists, with the grandiloquent and bombastic declamations of philanthropy, freedom and attachment to the government, why do you not go down South and expound your doctrines to the community, and, if you dare not do it, why do you expect the Jews there to stand in opposition to the masses of the people?[14]

Wise claimed that at times Abraham Lincoln seemed to agree with him as to who "started the war." Lincoln was reported to have said to a visitor in 1863, "Sir . . . the parsons and the women made this war."[15]

The Abolitionists did not lift a finger to defend Jews against the rising intolerance of the time:

> If so many Negroes had been injured as were Hebrews by the order of General Grant, the bottomless absurdities of Parson Brownlow, and the heartless agent of the Associated Press, you would have cried as loudly as the people of Sodom and Gomorrah; but for the white Hebrew who gave you a God and a religion, you had not a word to say.[16]

So much for Wise's furious charges against the Abolitionists, his accusations of their direct responsibility for plunging the country into war, for a reckless and "political" attitude toward slavery!

This leads logically to the next question: what was Wise's own point of view in regard to slavery? Was it clearly expressed? Did he take the trouble to formulate it, to ground it firmly in his general religious and ethical system? Was it an ethical stand that would commend itself to us by reason of its resolute humanity, its far-seeing moral courage, its clarity and insight? Sadly it must be confessed that we can answer none of these questions in the affirmative. Let us adduce the evidence and let the reader judge for himself. But it is fair to say in advance that Wise was neither "pro" nor "contra" slavery in the full sense, that in this respect too his point of view suffered from the same ill that characterized his general attitude toward the Civil War. It was a "middle-of-the-road" stand, pleasing to neither side. Perhaps as a natural result Wise was accused of both extremes: of being pro-slavery, and sometimes—though not as frequently—of being opposed to the institution. He did not leave his opinion forever in doubt. Somewhat later he set himself, in the *Israelite*, to a fairly long study of the Biblical—the "Mosaic"—attitude toward slavery. After the available material will be in the reader's possession, we shall return briefly to draw the necessary conclusions.

One writer on Wise asserts:

> For all his theoretical objections to the inhumanity of slavery he was more hostile to the war-mongers in the North than to the evils of slavery and became, in effect, a defender of the South.[17]

This is too forthright and summary a judgment to be valid. It oversteps the mark. Certainly, as the same work contends, it is true that Wise would have agreed to the continuation of slavery forever, if that would have called a halt to, or would have prevented, bloodshed.[18]

Later on we shall come to the fact that Morris J. Raphall, the very rabbi with whom Wise had fallen out in Charleston, S. C. in 1850 on the dogmas of a personal Messiah and of bodily resurrection, was a defender of slavery, and claimed that it rested on divine sanction in the Bible. At that time we shall review the charge that Wise agreed with Raphall and was therefore himself "pro-slavery."

Fairly early in the day Wise denied that the Bible placed Negroes in a separate category as the accursed descendants of Ham, the wicked son of Noah:

> Among all the nonsense imposed on the Bible the greatest is to suppose the Negroes are the descendants of Ham, and the curse of Noah is applicable to them. . . . Canaanites are never mentioned in the Bible as men of color (and they *are* listed as descendants of Ham; Genesis, Chapter nine, verse 18, etc.) . . . Besides we can not see how the curse of Noah could take effect on the unborn generations of Canaan . . . when the Bible teaches that God visits the iniquity of parents to the third and fourth generations only and [upon] those who hate Him.[19]

Certainly Wise was not among those who thought that slavery was a genuine good or that it was the duty of Americans to perpetuate it. He declared himself horrified when in 1861 it seemed to be the intention of some Southerners to reopen the slave-trade. This was reported shortly before it had become obvious that the conflict was unavoidable, and when actual hostilities were about to be precipitated. Wise was fearful that France and Spain might make an alliance with the South and invade Mexico, which in fact France did when it placed Maximilian on the throne there. Nothing could be calculated to alarm Wise more than the prospect that the autocracy which he had seen in his childhood and young manhood in Austria might be transplanted to the Western hemisphere. It had always been his hope that the reverse would happen, that America would bring the blessings of democracy to Europe. He wrote:

> Spain is the only slave-holding power in Europe . . . the only power that has not prohibited the slave-trade.

The possibility that Spain, or France, might come in through Mexico and effect a junction of forces, that the slave-trade with all its horrors might begin anew, terrified him.[20]

Near the end of the war he wrote an editorial, called "The Situation," on the utter irreconcilability of those for and those against slavery:

> There is no medium way, the factions, the extremes, are as mad

> today as they ever were, the voice of moderate and considerate men is cried down. God alone can heal us of our madness.[21]

We shall see—somewhat later—that he had rather curious ideas on the advantages savages enjoyed in being brought to a civilized country and to slavery. Even in 1864 he was unable or unwilling to come to grips with the ethical problems of slavery, or with the economic conditions in the South which had for long tended to perpetuate and even to extend the evil. He said a good word for an American Colonization Society, which since 1821 had been taking Negroes and colonizing them in Liberia.[22]

In the same year the *Israelite* carried an article by Lewis N. Dembitz of Louisville, "On Slavery and Polygamy Tolerated by the Bible." This Wise had clipped from the Louisville newspapers, and its conclusions were quite similar to his own.[23]

The promulgation of the Emancipation Proclamation (January 1, 1863) prompted Wise to publish an extended exposition of his views on slavery, as it was provided for in the Bible. These articles were not, however, published until 1864. As we shall see, their conclusion was that Moses attempted to abolish slavery "by indirect-direct laws which rendered its existence impossible."[24] The title of the articles was: "On the Provisional Portion of the Mosaic Code with Special Reference to Polygamy and Slavery." In this he wrote:

> It is evident that Moses was opposed to slavery from the facts:
> 1. He prohibited to enslave a Hebrew, male or female, adult or child.
> 2. He legislated to a people just emerging from bondage and slavery.
> 3. He legislated for an agricultural community with whom labor was honorable.
> 4. He legislated not only to humanize the condition of the alien laborers, but to render the acquisition and retention of bondmen contrary to their will a matter of impossibility.[25]

And the long article concluded with this passage:

> We are not prepared, nobody is, to maintain it is absolutely unjust to purchase savages, or rather their labor, place them under the protection of law, and secure them the benefit of civilized society and their sustenance for their labor. Man in a savage state is not free; the alien servant under the Mosaic laws was a free man, excepting only the fruits of his labor. . . . Negro slavery, if it could have been brought under the control of the Mosaic or similar laws, must have tended to the blessing of the Negro race by frequent emigration of civilized

> Negroes back to the interior of Africa; and even now that race might reap the benefit of its enslaved members, if the latter or the best instructed among them were sent back to the interior of Africa.[26]

This rests on grounds that are more than a little astonishing: first, it repudiates by implication the whole concept of the inherent rights of man, of the dignity of the human being *per se*; and, secondly, it propounds the thesis that slavery is preferable to savagery.

With all this, Wise denied constantly and consistently that he was pro-slavery. And this he did as late as 1897, many, many years after the Civil War. An article was written by Max J. Kohler, "The Jews and the Anti-Slavery Movement."[27] In the course of this Kohler charged Wise with sanctioning slavery. He wrote:

> Dr. Raphall's remarks were most apologetic, but he took the square stand that Judaism sanctioned slavery and that that institution was morally right. Extreme as his position was, it cannot be regarded as original, nor did it lack approval, for Dr. Wise, in the American Israelite, and Isaac Leeser in the Occident (January 24, 1861, p. 268, and January 31, 1861, p. 274), expressed their approbation of his stand.

One of the books about Wise waxes very indignant at this accusation, and declares that there is not a "scintilla of evidence" to bear it out:

> Why Mr. Kohler misinterpreted these articles in so sweeping, false and unjust a manner it is difficult to understand.[28]

Kohler's allegation was repeated in another book, by Philip S. Foner, *The Jews in American History, 1854-1855*.[29] He too asserted that Wise endorsed slavery and the sermon by Raphall.[30]

It will be well to have before us precisely what Raphall said. This was in a discourse on "The Bible View of Slavery," delivered on January 4, 1861, on a National Fast Day, which President Buchanan had announced "to mobilize national sentiment against the impending break-up of the Union."[31] Raphall put Judaism squarely in opposition to the philosophy of Abolitionism. The sermon was intended as a counterblast against Henry Ward Beecher, who—Raphall contended—perverted Biblical texts to justify his own standpoint:

> I would therefore ask the reverend gentleman from Brooklyn and his compeers—How dare you . . . denounce slaveholding as a sin? When you remember that Abraham, Isaac, Jacob, Job

> —the men with whom the Almighty conversed, with whose names he emphatically connects his own most holy name . . . that all these men were slaveholders, does it not strike you that you are guilty of something very little short of blasphemy? And if you answer me, "Oh, in their time slaveholding was lawful, but now it has become a sin," I in my turn ask you, "When and by what authority you draw the line? Tell us the precise time when slaveholding ceased to be permitted, and became sinful?"

The sermon as a whole was not as uncompromising as this passage reads, for Raphall tried later to draw a distinction between Biblical slavery and that which obtained in the South. Whether this was his purpose or not, the sermon was given a tremendous amount of publicity as an outright plea for slavery.[32] Raphall, however, was fully aware of the fact that the Biblical concept of a slave "as a person in whom the dignity of human nature is to be respected," and the Roman view, adopted by many in the South, which made a slave a mere "thing," were worlds apart. Thus one writer concluded that while Raphall was a defender of slavery, it was not Southern slavery of which he was speaking.[33]

Wise did not share this view. His own opinions about the place of slavery in the Bible were much clearer, much more carefully drawn from the sources, written with much more awareness of the humane intent of the Mosaic Code. Therefore, throughout his life Wise continued to deny that he had shared Raphall's opinion and scornfully repudiated the claim that he had ever regarded slavery as a "divine institution," sanctioned by the "Old Testament Scriptures," or that

> there is a single paragraph on record to show that the said Isaac M. Wise ever was a pro-slavery man or favored the institution of slavery at any time.[34]

Some years before, in 1868, when Raphall died, Wise wrote that Raphall had attempted to find sanction for "an inhuman institution," and that "this was a great blunder." But with his customary generosity he tried to clear Raphall's name by placing on record the fact that Raphall himself had striven to right his error, but that it was too late.[35]

Conclusions are not easy to draw from the evidence we have placed before the reader in this chapter. In this case, as in relation to the Civil War itself, Wise placed himself squarely neither on one side or the other. He hoped that the country could remain one, even at the cost of permitting slavery to continue. He regarded slavery as an evil, but not as an unmitigated evil. He believed that it brought some benefits to the "savages" who were captured, or sold themselves, out of Africa. He seemed to have in mind that the South, had it been given a chance, might have adopted the inner purpose of the Bible in discouraging slavery, and in moving toward a system where slavery would become undesirable humanly and economically. He could not bring himself to echo the extremism of the Abolitionists, to denounce the institution of slavery as a stench in the nostrils of God and man. Nonetheless he was glad that the institution had been abolished, and hoped that the breaches of war could be healed and that the South could go on under a new dispensation. In sum, these appear to have been the main facets of his thinking. It is evident that he expressed himself with reluctance and only when the matter of Biblical sanction came to the fore; that in this regard too he would rather have kept silent. It must be said also that it cannot have been easy for him to adhere—in regard to this problem—to the contention that "religion" and "politics" must be kept separate and distinct, to maintain consistently the position that slavery was not a religious, an ethical issue, of the first order of magnitude, penetrating very deeply into all the concerns and imperatives of faith!

23

The Jews and the Civil War

In this chapter we shall consider two further phases of Isaac M. Wise's life and thought during the Civil War. We shall first review the facts relating to his connection with the famous, or infamous, order issued by General Ulysses S. Grant on December 17, 1862. This cannot include a complete treatment of this case, which will be found elsewhere.[1] And secondly we shall add to this some specific items having to do with the general position of Jews during the war and Wise's view thereupon.

On the date just mentioned Grant issued the following order at his Headquarters at Holly Springs, Miss.

> The Jews as a class violating every regulation of trade established by the Treasury Department and also department orders, are hereby expelled from the department within twenty-four hours from the receipt of this order.
>
> Post commanders will see that all of this class of people be furnished passes and required to leave, and any one returning after such notification will be arrested and held in confinement until an opportunity occurs of sending them out as prisoners, unless furnished with permit from Headquarters.
>
> No passes will be given these people to visit headquarters for the purpose of making personal application for trade permits.
>
> By order of Major General U. S. Grant:
>
> JNO. A. Rawlins,
>
> Assistant Adjutant General.[2]

Before long the news of this document had spread not only throughout the South, but via the border states into the North, where it created consternation and indignation in Jewish communities. Later on the *Israelite* recorded that one of the most remarkable facts about this Order was that two non-Jewish houses (the names are not given) were not included in the order. It was claimed that these knew of the issuance of the order in advance and were thus enabled to gain a monopoly of the cotton trade. To this item of information Wise added a tirade against military rule in general, and printed a Washington despatch uncovering a huge fraud by high-ranking officers in Washington involving millions. The religion of these officers, Wise remarked, was of course not mentioned.[3]

Another order was issued, also at Holly Springs, by Colonel John W. Dubois, using the following language, the insolence of which is certainly intentional:

> On account of the scarcity of provisions all cotton speculators, Jews, and other vagrants, etc. . . . having no permission from the Commanding General, will leave town within twenty-four hours.[4]

On this further insult the *Israelite* commented:

> It is not the Jew, it is the American whom that order disgraces. In us it is not the Jew but the man and American citizen who feels outraged by such proceedings. As a Jew we feel ourselves in our religious conviction far, far beyond the slanderous jargon of anybody, far beyond the reach of general orders, stump speeches, or other ephemeral pieces of paper. . . . As a man and citizen, however, we feel outraged and demand justice from the hands of the chief magistrate of the country. We send this paper to the President, Mr. Stanton, Generals Halleck, Grant, Rosencrans, and others, and hope they will bestow proper attention on the subject. At the same time, however, we request our friends to collect all orders and affidavits on this point, to be brought before the President, and to be placed on record for future reference, for the information of the historian who will render an impartial verdict.

Shortly thereafter[5] Wise brought to the attention of his readers the fact that the Dubois order had followed Grant's instructions, and that at least one Jew who could not prevail upon himself to credit all this had been arrested. On this latter act Wise wrote:

> Need we comment on this handsome piece of military despotism? We trust not. . . . But we do not care for causes. The

> orders above mentioned do exist, and this suffices to alarm every honest friend of the Republic. Are we to be slaves of military chieftains? Are we playthings in the hands of presumptuous men to abuse and maltreat us at pleasure? Are we frogs and mice to be trampled under anybody's feet, or are we men who stand by their rights? Is there no law in the land, no authority higher than bayonets? If we stand this, then we are unworthy of being citizens of a free country. If we do stand all this, we must not wonder if one day anybody will treat us as pariahs and outcasts of society. Israelites, citizens of the United States, you have been outraged. Your rights as men and citizens trampled in the dust, your honour disgraced as a class, you have officially been degraded. It is your duty, your duty of self-defence, your duty first to bring this matter directly before the President of the United States and demand redress and satisfaction due to the citizens thus mortified and offended. It is not only the business of the Jew to look to these matters, it is everybody's affair. . . . If the Jews, as a religious community, are handled thus, how will the Catholics, Unitarians, Universalists, or any other religious denomination be treated, if a general or provost officer sees fit to come down on one or the other?[6]

It was chiefly the Jews of Louisville, Paducah, and Cincinnati, who heard of these documents from their coreligionists within the lines. Meetings were called immediately. The meeting held in Cincinnati appointed Wise, Lilienthal, and Edgar M. Johnson to meet with similar committees from Paducah and Louisville. A resolution on the matter was introduced in Congress by Senator Powell of Kentucky and by Congressman George H. Pendleton of Cincinnati.[7] This resolution was tabled in the House by a vote of 56 to 53, and in the Senate by a vote of 30 to 5. This was a most depressing result, but it was far from being the end of the matter.

From further reports it appeared that Grant's order was being enforced with much inhumanity. Wise tried at once to get in touch with the President. He despatched a wire. The probability is that this message never reached Lincoln, for Wise had no answer. Before the committees from various communities could assemble, discuss, and get to Washington, a Mr. Kaskel of Paducah went to the capital and was introduced to President Lincoln by Congressman Gurley of Cincinnati. As soon as Lincoln learned from Kaskel and from the documents he had with him that Order No. 11 of Grant had veritably been issued in the form given above, he directed General Halleck, the Commander, to revoke it. Wise recorded however that

Halleck's transmittal of this revocation was half-hearted and that at the time Grant made no public apology.[8]

It may be inferred that, while Wise was glad that Lincoln had at once understood and acted, he was still seriously alarmed. We shall see later that this incident must be placed in its setting, in its relation to the startling rise of anti-Jewish feeling during the Civil War. Wise had written[9] that Americans and Jews had to determine:

> Whether a general may with impunity deprive people of their rights, which to protect he is sworn and paid for.

Wise was also offended by the silence of most of the Cincinnati press, though later the *Enquirer* wrote that no offenses by individuals could justify such a general act. Wise accused some of the military officers of having themselves seized a monopoly of the cotton trade. in the occupied areas. The Order lumped together the good and the bad. It was guilty of the condemnation and maltreatment of a "class." Jews were not "mischief-makers"; they were not dishonest. He ended with these characteristic words:

> Politically, we are sorry to say, they [Jews] are mostly of the party that has Lincoln for its leader, having voted for him for President.

Whether this assertion corresponded with the facts, it is now impossible to determine. Wise wanted a withdrawal of the order and an apology from those responsible for it.

Naturally the air was full of charges, countercharges, and explanations, veracious or imagined. Quite interestingly, Wise wrote in the *Israelite* three weeks later:

> It is claimed that Grant was following an order from Washington. This could only have come from Chase[10] since the President and Halleck deny knowledge of it. Perhaps in the general confusion it is impossible for anyone to know. The President should at once inquire into the matter. The whole thing begins in a lie and ends in tragic discrimination. . . . If there is justice in Washington, and that there is Abraham Lincoln assured us, let it be found out who dared issue an order of so revolting and absurd a nature to a commanding general, without the knowledge of the commander-in-chief.
>
> For the sake of General Grant, for the sake of the President himself, let the matter be investigated and duly exposed.[11]

It was while the two rabbis and Mr. Johnson were on the way to Washington that they learned of Kaskel's interview with Lincoln and of the revocation of Grant's order. They decided nonetheless to continue their journey and to try to speak with the President. This they did and Wise wrote of their meeting with Lincoln as follows:

> The interview was of an informal and friendly nature. We had but little chance to say anything, the President having been so splendidly eloquent on this occasion. He assured us in every possible form that neither he nor General Halleck believed that Grant issued so absurd an order, until the official document dispelled every doubt. Furthermore that he entertained no prejudice of any kind against any nationality, and especially against Israelites, to whom he manifested a particular attachment. He spoke like a simple, plain-spoken citizen, and tried in various forms to convince us of the sincerity of his words in this matter.[12]

This impression of Lincoln, and others which we shall introduce later, should be placed side by side with the bitter and undiscerning words Wise wrote when Lincoln was nominated and elected in 1860, and when he made his First Inaugural. These will follow in a later chapter. It should also be noted that together with Wise and Lilienthal were Martin Bijur of Louisville and Moses Strauss of Baltimore.[13]

Though some other events having to do with Grant will be reserved for later treatment, it is only fair to insert a note here. Grant was nominated for the presidency by the Republican Party in 1868. To his candidacy Jews voiced strenuous objection and opposition,[14] because of his conduct more than five years earlier. Nonetheless Grant was nominated and the *Israelite* was silent until after his election. It published then a letter by Grant to J. N. Norris of Galena, Ohio. In this missive Grant claimed that the famous order had been issued because he had been incensed at the time by reprimands he had received from Washington, referring to the alleged acts of Jews within his lines. He claimed that he himself had never been prejudiced against Jews, either as a "sect" or "as a race." As a matter of justice the *Israelite*[15] appended to this the admission that under Grant the Jews had had a record in the cotton trade that was none too good; but also—rather inconsistently and illogically—that this was a slander and did not justify the order. Grant asserted that on December 17, 1862 he had had a communication from Washington, in which this was said:

> We are reliably informed that the Jews in various cities are buying up the gold to take South and invest in cotton that will

> place in the hands of the rebels increased means to carry on the war. That should be prevented. You will, therefore, take measures to prevent it in your department.

From whom this order came—certainly without Lincoln's knowledge—our sources do not reveal. In part Wise commented on this:[16]

> With the advent of our armies in the southwest, the cotton trade began to claim the attention of cotton traders. Some prominent gentlemen in Washington, Senators and high officials whose names we know, but do not wish to mention, were the first and most extensive cotton dealers at the time, and realized vast profits from the trade. Some Jewish houses in the West discovered the opportunity and went into the cotton trade. This was an unpleasant opposition to the Washington operators, for the Jews paid higher prices, bought cotton up, and brought the speculators down on them. . . . Nothing was easier at that time than to play chicaneries on the Jews. It was given out that the Jews smuggled gold across the lines to purchase cotton of the rebels, and everybody was ready to believe and to add in explanation, "All the Jews buy all the cotton, and all of them smuggle all the gold." This was a master-stroke, for it led to secret instructions from headquarters to all commanders in the West to look after the Jews. . . . All these chicaneries and outrages did not terrify Jewish traders along the line especially in Grant's Department, where most of the cotton was. . . .

Wise had taken a strong position, one which he shared with other Jewish leaders and Jewish communities. Lincoln had acted, as one would have expected of that great figure, and at least one central principle of American democracy had been vindicated.

As we have asserted previously, all of this must be understood in its general setting of excitement, of bitterness, and of that *crescendo* of prejudice that seems to be an inevitable concomitant of danger and fear. Wise adhered to his decision of silence and neutrality. It was very rarely that he referred to the war at all in the columns of either of his publications. In fact, it may be laid down as a rule he had obviously adopted, that it was only when there was some charge against Jews, or when some fundamental right of Jews was at stake, that he broke his self-imposed policy.

In an excellent general work[17] it is said that all of the available sources appear to indicate that there had been relatively little anti-Jewish prejudice before the Civil War, and that this had been almost entirely on the part of Christian Fundamentalists, evangelists, revivalists, and missionaries.[18] But hardly had the war begun when all this changed for the worse. Economic and political stresses, the anxieties and fears on both sides of the line—but especially in the North—brought on a veritable epidemic of slander, of whispering and writing, of speech and action. It is not improbable that it was this very period in which anti-Jewishness as a movement began in the United States, assumed organized forms, and discovered some of its classical methods and accusations. On November 22, 1864, Simon Wolf wrote to the editor of the *New York Evening Post*:

> The war now raging has developed an intensity of malice that borders upon the darkest days of superstition and the Spanish Inquisition.[19]

One year before this Wise had written:

> As Israelites we were more mortified and outraged during this war than we were in Austria under the Metternich regime, in Russia under Nesselrode, in Bavaria under Mounteufel. . . . we feel sorely afflicted, and disgusted, and wish nothing more earnestly than peace.[20]

Wise reprinted in the *Israelite* a large number of anti-Jewish articles from other sources, paragraphs from speeches of politicians and of clergymen. He answered each and every one of them with a rising level of temperature. He was, however, guarded in his treatment, and careful not to distort the facts. Wherever there were pro-Jewish statements to be used as counterweights, whenever someone spoke intrepidly against the bigotry of the time, Wise quoted these too. Instances other than Grant's and Dubois' orders abound: e.g. that of Major General S. A. Hurlbut of November 30, 1863, prohibiting fourteen Jewish houses in Memphis from selling military apparel, despite the fact that all the record proved that they were doing nothing illegal,[21] and that—curiously enough—the order itself contained no stated cause for its severity.

Charges of this kind were far from uncommon. Wise contended that many of them were a smoke-screen to divert popular attention from the real malefactors, from the real traffickers in corruption and bribery. As all through their history, Jews were being assigned the role of scape-goats. Thus the *Cincinnati Enquirer* of October 20, 1861, had claimed that:

> A combination of Jewish clothing houses in this city was organized to take advantage of the pressing necessity of our Western soldiers for blankets.

The Jews of Cincinnati were sorely offended and angrily aroused.

The accused businessmen went to the editors and demanded that their business records be examined, the slander disproved, and detailed retractions published. As indeed they were![22]

The matter of chaplains was also making constant trouble. A Presbyterian journal asserted that two-thirds of the Christian chaplains, then the only ones permitted in the Union Army, were unfit for service, and Wise himself claimed that he knew of two "professional atheists" who were chaplains.[23] He urged his readers to send petitions to Congress to rescind the iniquitous and un-American law which was preventing Jews from serving as chaplains. Many other editors followed him in this:

> Petition that body from all parts of the United States. Wherever Israelites live, draw up a petition to abolish that unconstitutional law; have it signed by every neighbor you find disposed to do so, and send it to your representative or senator in Congress. Let the petition be written by one who understands the business, have it printed and circulate it as much as possible; do not spare your time or save a few cents; it is your duty to protect your rights. This is the only way to remedy the evil; do not neglect it.[24]

Quite a few years later, in reviewing his own activities at this time and later, Wise wrote thus:

> We have protested fifteen years since against the insolence of politicians and their violations of constitutional provisions. When Congress excluded the Jews and the Catholics from the chaplaincy in the United States army, we protested, although none in the Congress would listen except Mr. Vallandigham of Ohio. When General Grant's insolent order No. 11 appeared, expelling the Jews from his department, we protested, although none in Congress except Mr. Pendleton, of Ohio, and Senator Powell of Kentucky, would give us any assistance. When the late Vice-President Wilson (Henry Wilson, Grant's second term, March 4, 1873 to his death, November 22, 1875) publicly insulted the Jews in the Senate of the United States and it had become fashionable in Washington among speakers and correspondents to insult some Jew or throw suspicion on some Catholic, we protested, although demagogues and idiots decried us as a traitor, a secessionist, a sympathizer with treason. When Generals Wright, Butler, and a number of post commanders, provost marshals, spies, and clandestine traders insulted and slandered the Jew, we protested again, and if it had not been for Abraham Lincoln and Salmon P. Chase there would have been none in Washington to listen. . . .

> . . . This is a Democratic Republic and must be governed by honest men without hypocrisy or insolence, without religious lines and imposition, and also without Blue laws, Sunday laws, Puritan holidays, God's special police hereabouts, Bible fanatics or other fanatics.[25]

It was on July 12, 1861, that an Ohio Congressman—probably Vallandigham—moved in the house to strike out the provision that chaplains in the Federal army must be Christians. The same man was later a leader of the Copperhead Democrats. At that time he said a brave and just word about Jews, and denounced the claim that the United States was a "Christian country." The amendment was rejected. Wise applauded Vallandigham, deplored the failure of his motion, but had no additional constructive suggestion to offer at the time.[26]

Wise continued to blast away at the Republican Party, claiming that it was penalizing rabbis for not supporting abolition. In addition to this charge of discrimination, Wise complicated his case more than a little by asserting that the whole institution of the chaplaincy was wrong, that it violated the American principle of the separation of Church and State. Among other charges, he accused the army of appointing chaplains from among those ministers who had helped bring on the war. If there were to be any chaplains at all, then all religions had to be accorded equal rights. Jews paid taxes like anyone else, and were dying in battle. How could they—when they were serving in the field—be denied the ministration of rabbis?[27]

Another attitude of Isaac M. Wise during these tumultous years was his consistent refusal to condemn Southern Jews, or to cease having friendly relations with them. This was quite consistent with his entire relation to the war, but, in the midst of the fever throbbing in all veins, it must have been an exceedingly difficult stand to maintain and justify, and it brought down upon him a whole arsenal of charges. Wise contended that Southern Jews had as much right to support the Confederacy, as those of the North the Union. Einhorn and Felsenthal both disowned and repudiated the Jews of the South. Wise never! Whatever tidings of them filtered through the lines Wise published in the *Israelite*. At one time he put in an advertisement for a rabbi for Charleston, S. C. Nor in the text of the journal was there any indication that this rabbi was to minister to the "enemy." Wise looked upon these Jews as his friends and nothing could move him from this.[28]

There were bitter articles in some Northern newspapers demanding the extermination of Southern Jews. Wise replied to this, urging that these Jews be regarded and treated like any other individuals. He wrote of the Jews who had given their lives for the Union, and adduced many evidences of Jewish patriotism.[29] His general plea on behalf of his brothers on the other side of the line, combined with his detestation of the Abolitionists, was best expressed in these words from the *Israelite*:

> If the largest proportion of the Jewish people of Richmond, Charleston, and New Orleans give "aid and comfort to rebellion," as our opponents maintain, they do exactly as others do in the same localities. . . . You abolitionists with the grand eloquent and bombastic declamations of philanthropy, freedom and attachment to the government, why do you not go down South and expound your doctrines to the community, and, if you dare not do it, why do you expect the Jews there to stand in opposition to the masses of the people?[30]

Two years later Wise published a letter of General Benj. J. Butler about five Jews who tried to run the blockade. In this connection Butler had called Jews "a nation without a land." Wise replied sarcastically and indignantly.[31]

It would be possible to mulitply instances, to add many similar expressions of his point of view. But Wise's personal opinion and the action he took indicate clearly that his neutrality in regard to the war did not extend to cases where Jews were attacked as Jews, where the fundamental American principle of religious equality seemed to him imperiled or swept aside. In such cases, he was fearlessly and utterly outspoken.

24

Politics and Religion

IN THE BEGINNING, WISE HAD NO MORE COMPREHENSION OF THE greatness of Abraham Lincoln, no more ability to see behind the uncouth exterior, the homely speech, the frequent recourse to rather rough humor, than did many other hundreds of thousands in the United States. That this was the case in the very early years of Lincoln's appearance upon the political scene in Illinois is not astonishing. But it is much more so after the debates Lincoln had with Stephen A. Douglas, of which Wise wrote in his two letters to Douglas in 1858. Wise's vision was doubtless blurred by his own political prejudices, his ardent espousal of what he called the "Democracy," his hatred of the Abolitionists, and his conviction that a compromise might have been found which would have saved the Union.

When Wise learned that Lincoln had been elected President of the United States, he was plunged into deep depression. He wrote:

> The people of the United States just committed one of the greatest blunders a nation can commit, for which we must pay at once. . . .[1]

A few months passed, and Lincoln stopped in Cincinnati on his way to Washington to deliver his first Inaugural Address. Wise wrote of him, as he saw him in Cincinnati, in words that are painful in their condescension and lack of insight:

> Poor old Abe Lincoln, who had the queer life of a country lawyer, having been elected President of this country, and now going to be inaugurated in his office, the Philistines from all corners of the land congregate around their Dagon and worship him. . . . Why all this noise? . . . Wait until he has done something. . . . Some of our friends might like to know how the president looks, and we can tell them: he looks like *Der Landjunker das erste Mal in Stadt,* "like a country squire for the first time in the city." He wept on leaving Springfield and invited his friends to pray for him; that is exactly the picture of his looks. We have no doubt he is an honest man, and, as much as we can learn, also quite an intelligent man; but he will look queer in the White House, with his primitive manner.[2]

When Lincoln arrived in Washington and delivered his memorable address, Wise printed a letter in the *Israelite* criticizing him for winding up with these words: "the Patriotism and Christianity of the country." And to the strictures of his correspondent Wise added this:

> We have only to say for Mr. Lincoln that his style of writing is so careless and without any successful attempt at either correctness or elegance that he must not be criticized on using this or that word to express an idea.

Wise went on to claim that Lincoln had had the heaviest vote of "infidels" in the history of the country, and concluded:

> By and by he will learn the precise use and aspect of terms. He takes domestic words, as used in Springfield and vicinity, to express familiar ideas. In Springfield religion is called Christianity, because people there do not think of any other form of worship, hence Mr. Lincoln uses the same word to express the same sentiment. We do not believe there is a German infidel, American eccentric, spiritual rapper or atheist in the Northern states who did not vote for Mr. Lincoln. Let us see how much benefit he will derive from their Christianity, or how he will settle the political troubles with such piety. . . .[3]

That Wise should have reacted in his habitual way to Lincoln's use of the term "Christian" is not to be wondered at; but this scorn leveled at Lincoln's use of the language and the whole *de haut en bas* tone are indeed regrettable. Which of us, however, would relish having all his words reread a century later, words written in so precarious and controversial a time?

In the next four years Wise's attitude toward Lincoln went from one pole to the other, from mockery to deep veneration. He did not see at first, it is true, but at last he came to see. The turning-point was probably the visit he and the committee paid to Lincoln on the matter of Grant's order, described in the *Israelite* on January 8, 1863.[4] In the following chapter we shall come to the time of Lincoln's assassination in April, 1865, and what Wise said and wrote of him then.

Meanwhile Wise was continuing to maintain that politics should be kept out of the pulpit. His key-utterance on this was that in the *Israelite* early in 1861:

> Not one single word have we, as yet, said in the pulpit on the politics of the day . . . because it is a settled principle with us —the pulpit is for higher than a political object.

He accused seekers after public office of being often for themselves and not for the weal of the community.

> Politics is a business. . . . Preachers may now earn short-lived laurels by defending this or that side of the political question, but no fame, no glory must be grand enough to be purchased at so dear a price as the sacrifice of duty. Therefore we never spoke one word on politics in the pulpit. . . . Preach the word of God, that is your vocation.[5]

This principle Wise interpreted rather narrowly. As the record shows, he took it to mean that the pulpit itself, the actual machinery of worship, the sermon, must not be diverted to political purposes. But he thought he was able to dissociate from this limitation his own life outside. For he was active at various times in political meetings and causes. We have already referred to the fact that he was present at the Ohio organization meeting of the Republican Party, and said that he withdrew because of its identification with leading non-Jewish German "atheists" in Cincinnati.[6] He then joined the Democratic Party and was an active member in good standing, wrote that he had voted for Douglas in 1860, and later penned a long and somewhat fulsome eulogy of the same statesman in the *Israelite*.[7] The record of his political life is to be found in detail in the pamphlet, "The Americanization of Isaac M. Wise," by Dr. Jacob R. Marcus.[8]

But by all odds the most interesting chapter in relation to his politics occurred in 1863, when on September 5 the Democratic State Convention meeting at Carthage, Ohio—just outside Cincinnati—nominated him for the State Senate on the first ballot. The meeting was held on the Jewish Sabbath and Wise could not be present. His friend, Israel Brown, apologized for his absence and transmitted to the Convention the information that "the Doctor would accept the nomination." The *Cincinnati Enquirer* of September 6, 1863, recorded that this announcement was greeted with cheers. The *Enquirer* was then a Democratic paper and wrote thus:

> Dr. Wise . . . a gentleman of learning and accomplishment, well-known as an estimable Hebrew rabbi of this city . . . would make an excellent State Senator.[9]

Wise consulted his congregation at once, informed them of his nomination, and tried to ascertain what their opinion of this step was. It is fair to assume that he had believed in advance that they would entertain no serious objection. If this was the case, he was due for a rather astonishing few days. For they asked him at once to decline the nomination, because he could not be absent from his pulpit, and because he was indispensable to them and to the cause of Judaism in many other ways. From the officials of the Talmud Yelodim Institute he had a letter in precisely the same vein.[10]

We have more details than this. The Board of Trustees of B'nai Yeshurun called a meeting two days after Wise had been nominated and decided to "instruct" him to decline. Here are their words:

> The Board feels greatly honoured by this demonstration of confidence bestowed upon you; they are also well aware of your sincere attachment to our common country; nevertheless as it is an established fact with us that our minister should be present in the synagogue whenever divine service is held, and also, your services otherwise being indispensably necessary in our congregation, as well as in the scholastic department, you are hereby politely, but most emphatically, requested to decline said nomination at once. . . .[11]

The language was courteous, but firm. Perhaps even somewhat peremptory! The majority of his board and of his congregation were not Democrats. This was in the middle of the war, during one of its most doubtful periods. The congregation may well have felt appalled by the prospect of having him in the State Senate with his views on "secession," "slavery," etc.

On his side, Wise might have contested the essential point that was made in the resolution transmitted to him. The board had never tried to restrain him before. They had always followed a most generous interpretation of their mutual relationship. He had traveled often and long. He had been out of his pulpit not for one but for many Sabbaths, laying cornerstones, dedicating synagogues, installing rabbis, making propaganda for Union and College.

The reason for this swift and decisive action by his Board of Trustees was certainly to be sought elsewhere: in their own political allegiance, in their fear that Wise, who enjoyed a wide reputation, might increase the Democratic vote in so critical a time. The Democratic candidate for Governor of Ohio was an old friend, Clement H. Vallandigham, who had returned from a mission to Canada, a long-time leader of the anti-Lincoln Copperheads and a hateful symbol to all those who were heart and soul with the cause of the North. It is probable that the heads of the Jewish community would have gone to any length to prevent Wise's following through with this action. All the signs point to the fact that the pressure upon Wise to decline was much greater than mere resolutions, that it was expressed in a host of personal approaches and declarations. It is not inconceivable—though this is mere conjecture—that Wise might have been offered as an alternative to his declination his dismissal from the pulpit. On the surface there was dignity, politeness, respect; but beneath were resentment, fear and anger. This—as we shall see—the reports in the Cincinnati dailies indicated unmistakably.[12]

Wise had to take prompt action. It would be excellent, if we had his *Reminiscences* up to this point, and could know what he was thinking. We have to surmise that he reviewed the entire situation, weighed the pros and cons, and came to the conclusion that it was not worth fighting for, that he would be sacrificing far too much, were he to defy the resolution of the board. This could not have been a contingency beyond his imagination, for on other occasions he had done just that. We do know that he submitted, and that he answered the board in these words:

> As you maintain you cannot dispense with my humble services for the time I might be obliged to spend at the Capital of the State, and the law of the congregation specifically ordains it so, I certainly feel obliged to decline a nomination so honorably tendered, notwithstanding my private opinion, that I might render some services to my country, not altogether unessential, especially as those who nominated me know well my sincere attachment to this country and government. God will save the Union and the Constitution; liberty and justice for all, without my active cooperation, being after all without any political aspirations—only an humble individual.[13]

Most of the Jewish papers did not comment on Wise's nomination, or upon his declination. Only the *Jewish Record* expressed the opinion that the stand taken by Cincinnati Jews was completely unpatriotic. "While this country is in danger, everbody must put his shoulder to the wheel, and do his utmost to save it." It called Isaac M. Wise "a bright ornament—among the wilderness of stupidity and ignorance out West," and believed that he would have brought honor to American Judaism. His congregation, the journal concluded, had performed a grave disservice to the nation and to American Judaism.[14]

Wise himself failed to comment upon the entire incident in the columns of the *Israelite*. He contented himself with publishing the correspondence. The *Cincinnati Enquirer*—as we have noted above—was not as taciturn. These are its words, revealing, if true:

> The Rev. Dr. Wise has been forced, by outside pressure, to decline the Democratic nomination for State Senator. Had his name been on the other ticket, the shoddy contractors who have been so busy pulling the wires to produce this result would have been contented to let it remain. The names of these shoddy contractors do not appear on the record, but they are known nevertheless.[15]

The other side was represented by the *Cincinnati Daily Gazette*, a Republican sheet, which wrote sarcastically about clergymen and politics, and made a ribald and quite unintelligible statement about "the possible relationship of circumcision to the biblical attitude toward slavery."[16] The comment of the *Enquirer* is thick with innuendo, with implied charges that members of Wise's congregation were pursuing their economic interest in their Republicanism and in their refusal to permit Wise to accept a Democratic political office. Whatever the basic causes, and whatever the genuine meaning of this episode, it ended in silence and inaction. It is not unlikely that Wise carried from this one more cicatrix to add to the many the war years had inflicted upon him.

To the rather extensive record we have set down in these four chapters on Wise's life and opinions during the Civil War, only a few additional facts need to be added, which have to do mainly with his own professional and personal life.

The disruption of the life of the whole country precipitated by the war affected every plan and every enterprise. For a time Cincinnati, being on the border, was under martial law. Wise's debts accumulated rapidly. He wrote that he might be compelled to suspend the publication of both his papers. His employees had left him to "join the ranks of the country's defenders."[17] By 1861 the *Israelite* was the oldest Jewish periodical in America. Its influence was especially strong in the Middle West and in the South.[18] Even earlier than this Wise had expressed the fear that he might not find it possible to continue.[19] Half his subscribers had been in the South. The cost of printing and paper rose steeply. Money, even money to borrow, was very scarce. A proportion of his Northern subscribers also canceled their subscriptions. Not all of this was due to economic difficulties. Some of the latter group were outraged at what they interpreted as Wise's "secessionist" policy.[20] But he found expedients and never stopped publication.

We have noted earlier that the Board of Delegates had come into existence in 1858, as a result of the abduction of Edgar Mortara, for the proclaimed purpose of securing and maintaining Jewish civil and religious rights at home and abroad.[21] Though Wise opposed this organization most of the time and regarded it as unrepresentative, he did try to induce it to undertake steps to launch a Jewish College. In this he was unsuccessful. During the war a protest was drawn up, signed by Lilienthal, Wise, Samuel Adler, Hochheimer, Felsenthal and Einhorn, against the creation and existence of the Board of Delegates. This document was published early in January, 1862. The text of the "Protest" denied that the Board of Delegates represented the Jews in the United States. The Board had petitioned Congress to repeal the clause of a bill, or bills, about chaplains, confining that service to Christians. The rabbis who signed the protest set themselves a difficult and somewhat unpalatable task, to inform Congress that it favored the same action, but that no one had ever "delegated" to the "Board of Delegates" the right to represent them, or Jews in general. The document is not one that sheds great credit upon those who signed it. It was only one more evidence of the inability of Jewish leaders to unite at that time, and of the great acerbity they showed toward one another.[22]

In the *Israelite* in 1862, Wise devoted himself to a review of the genesis and character of the *Minhag America.* He referred to the second volume, for the holy days, which he had written together with Lilienthal. The volume was ready, and Wise asked for suggestions and criticism.[23]

Nor, even in the midst of this apocalyptic time, had Wise abandoned his hope for a united American Jewry, or for the creation of effective agencies for education. In March, 1866, he published an article by one A. Cohen of Chicago suggesting that every Israelite in America over twenty-one years of age contribute annually one dollar for the purpose of establishing a College. This appealed to Wise, and in the issues that followed he published various concrete suggestions concerning how this could be carried into effect.[24] He continued to write about congregational union, but by this time he had come to the conclusion that a college to train rabbis could be created only after calling into being a union of congregations to found and support it. This was and is an interesting development, a significant milestone along the road to his achievement in 1873 and 1875. His editorial is headed, "To the Israelites of the West":

> In the East reform is an object *per se*, with us it is secondary; we want reform in order to endear and preserve our religion, therefore we ask the question, what benefit is this or that reform to our sacred cause; they want reform *per se*, and ask only the question how will this or that reform be liked. Here is a principle of which practical results speak. The Eastern reformers are theoretical, we are practical; they are negative, we are positive; they consider themselves wiser and more learned and more respectable than we are, that is, the bulk of the people, and keep aloof; we are democratic in our religious feelings. Nothing can be more desirable than a union of synagogues. The future greatness of Judaism in America depends upon a union of congregations. We must be united in a form of worship in order to have no element of discord among us. . . . Hitherto all attempts at union were frustrated by the reform leaders in the East. The proposition of having one college for all of us was defeated in the East.
>
> The attempt to establish a synod, the surer safeguard of union, was killed in the East. The humble essay of one prayer-book for all was denounced, attacked, condemned, and everything else, in the East again. Therefore, we have come to the conclusion that it is impossible almost to effect a union with our Eastern contemporaries. But a union we must have, based upon the progressive principles of reform. We must unite the congregations of the Mississippi valley in order to do the work here, if we can not do it all over the country. . . .
>
> We must have a college . . . . our strength lies in union and progress. . . . You have established congregations and support them well. Now is the time to unite them for grand purposes.

And he predicted—correctly—that a Union would come into being within a quarter of a century.[25]

By this time K.K.B'nai Yeshurun had 220 members, as a report of April 21, 1859, revealed.[26] A meeting of the board of the congregation was called for a Sunday afternoon in April, 1863, to discuss the possibility of erecting a new synagogue. The inadequacy of Lodge Street was dwelt upon. The only question was whether the congregation during the war could collect enough money to erect a temple "as large and costly as required."[27] Some time earlier the congregation had also considered enlarging the Talmud Yelodim Institute so that it would be able to serve all the Jewish children of Cincinnati, which then had between nine and ten thousand Jews. Lilienthal and Wise were to occupy coordinate positions as superintendents; there were to be three primary schools in different parts of the city. But this ambitious, unifying plan never went beyond hope.[28] Nor was the congregation able to build then. It was found necessary to delay the attempt until after the war. Then the project was pursued vigorously and successfully.

One final item having to do with Wise's personal life needs to be appended. Early in the war Wise found that his work, and the world, were "too much with" him. He longed for more quietude. He bought a farm in College Hill on December 20, 1861. This farm in Springfield township, which was sold by John Cleves to Gershner Gard, went through various hands and was later divided into farms and lots. The section was known as "College Hill" because somewhere along the course of its history it had had the reputation of having housed several colleges. It was on the turnpike between Cincinnati and Hamilton now known as Hamilton Ave. Here Wise and his family lived when the weather moderated, and here he and they found peace and the soothing beauty of nature. The house had an interesting history, and is still a kind of museum of Wise and of his family.[29]

The four years of the Civil War were without question one of the most difficult periods of Isaac M. Wise's life. Had he been able to identify himself with the Federal cause, had he shared the general sentiment about slavery, about the necessity of preventing secession, of preserving the Union by force, he could have thrown himself into many causes and spoken many stirring words. Instead he withdrew into silence and rarely wrote a syllable that revealed what was passing in his soul. He devoted himself to his congregation and school, preached on subjects that ranged a much wider gamut than the contemporary exigency, and maintained his contacts with his coreligionists in other communities, especially in the Middle West. Though there must have been more than a few differences of opinion between himself and his own people in Cincinnati, as far as it is possible to judge there was no impairment in their feeling for one another. The congregation continued to grow, as did the school. It was a time of waiting, of the suspension of many things Wise wanted passionately to do. It was a time of boundless concern on his part for America, for this republic that had drawn him from distant Bohemia, the destiny of which he was wont to conceive and to describe in such glowing, Messianic terms. It was a time when he found the hateful virus of anti-Jewishness revealing its pathological symptoms. And this in a land which for him was dedicated to the extermination of these diseases of the old world.

The sequel will show that he came out of all this with powers undiminished, with his eagerness to serve his faith and people unimpaired; that he had retained the admiration, the loyalty, and the eager cooperation of his own congregation. He was not old. The end of the Civil War found him but forty-six years of age and at the zenith of his powers. The cessation of the conflict, the slow and painful settling of the country into the years of Reconstruction, enabled him to return to the tasks he had set himself from the first years of his coming to America. That which follows, the thirty-five years left to his full life, are the time of the ingathering, the harvest long after the fan-wise casting of the seed, and the last years of mellow wisdom and of the presence about him of disciples, friends and family.

25

The Task Resumed

Events were moving fast in 1865. In January both houses of Congress had concurred in the amendment to the Constitution prohibiting slavery in the United States. Richmond was taken near the beginning of April. It was clear that the end was near and that the South could hold out no longer. At the beginning of April, Lee surrendered what was left of his army at Appomattox Court House. Just one week later, on the night of Friday, April 14, Lincoln was shot in the head in his box in Ford's Theater by John Wilkes Booth, and died the following day. Wise was as appalled and as overwhelmed with horror and sadness as were almost all other Americans at this tragic, devastating news. He called Booth a "mad villain,"[1] and on the many occasions that gave him an opportunity, proceeded to express the deep admiration, no! the veneration, he had acquired for Lincoln. With whatever mistaken picture of the man he had begun, however much he had been swayed by partisan prejudices and myopic distortions in the beginning, at the time of Lincoln's debates with Douglas and his election to the presidency in 1860, Wise had found his way at last through to the truth. That Sabbath he spoke of Lincoln as "the brightest jewel, the greatest hero, and noblest son of the nation."[2] Every synagogue in Cincinnati held a service of mourning for Lincoln, of eulogy of the martyred president.

B'nai Yeshurun had its service at Lodge Street. Wise thought of

Lincoln as a modern Abraham going forth from his father's house, with the promise that he and his people would "be a blessing," and he quoted *in extenso* the moving and significant verses from the beginning of Genesis, Chapter Twelve. He went on to say that it was a time for grievous lamentation and repentance for our sins, and that the only way to honor Lincoln would be to unite for the building of a great nation:

> He was kind, charitable, and lenient toward the enemies of his country, long-suffering and hoped for peace.

In his memory the union must be perpetuated. His soul, the great soul of a truly great man, would be with us forever:

> Brethren, the lamented Abraham Lincoln, believed to be bone of our bone, and flesh of our flesh. He was supposed to be a descendant of Hebrew parentage. He said so in my presence. And, indeed, he preserved numerous features of the Hebrew race, both in countenance and in character.[3]

It would be pleasant, if there were a jot of evidence to substantiate this. But at the time Wise had met Lincoln, when he had gone with a committee to ask that Grant's order be revoked, not a word of this had appeared in the *Israelite*, nor in any recorded address of his. It is possible, says Dr. Korn,[4] that Lincoln may have uttered some characteristic remark about the descent of all men from Adam. Wise did say something to Rabbi Henry Vidaver of St. Louis, to the effect that Lincoln had mentioned his "Jewish descent." But there is no discoverable evidence that Lincoln had ever said anything resembling this to any other human being, or that there was any trace of Jewish ancestry anywhere along his mother's or his father's lineage. That he, Wise, saw something Jewish in Lincoln's face meant little, for each saw there whatever nobility was his own!

In the *Israelite* Wise printed as soon as he could a heavily black-bordered column headed "Lincoln is Dead," some of which read:

> The noblest, best, and truest friend of our country has died a martyr to the cause of liberty . . . but still the Republic lives —shall live forever. . . . His image shall live forever. . . . His image shall ever live in the hearts of his countrymen. If the good are great, Old Honest Abe was the greatest man that ever sprung from mortal loins.

Wise wrote that all wept when they learned the news:

> Attired in the garb of simplicity and good humor, his modest worth lay concealed under a rough and uncouth exterior. He

> was an upright, honest, unassuming man, possessing the extraordinary skill of hiding his individuality behind the mighty deeds planned in his great intellect, and executed with a firmness worthy of the man who controlled, to the greatest extent, the destiny of the only free nation in the world, at a time when traitors at home and abroad attempted its life. . . . He was forgiving in his nature, gentle as a child, and above the low machinations of his foes. . . . May his soul rest in peace.[5]

Wise tried also to grasp Lincoln's meaning as a human being, and wrote of:

> The passions, feelings, struggles, victories, motives and thoughts of . . . the man who stood at the head of affairs during this gigantic struggle, his cares and troubles, his sleepless nights and days of anxiety, his thoughts and schemes, his triumphs and mortifications, his hopes and fears, and ten thousand more sentiments, feelings and thoughts. . . .

To describe Lincoln in words was not possible. What the citizens of the United States should strive for was to emulate him, to see to it that he would not have died in vain:

> Let us carry into effect and perpetuate the great desires which heaved the breast of Abraham Lincoln; let us be one people, one, free, just and enlightened; let us be the chosen people to perpetuate and promulgate liberty and righteousness, the union and freedom of the human family; let us break asunder, wherever we can, the chains of the bondsman, the fetters of the slave, the iron rod of despotism, the oppressive yoke of tyranny; let us banish strife, discord, hatred, injustice, oppression from the domain of man. . . . and we set him the most durable monument in the hearts of the human family. . . .[6]

Wise would not put Booth and his fellow-conspirators on the plane even of regicides, or of others who had slain heads of state. He wrote:

> Caesar was slain to restore the Roman Republic; Lincoln and Seward fell victims of revenge to crushed slavery. Liberty or slavery, patriotism or revenge—here is the difference between Brutus and the assassins of Lincoln and Seward.

Forgotten, banished into oblivion, were all Wise's early carping words and all his own half-heartedness about slavery. At last, perhaps at long last, but nonetheless generously and whole-heartedly, Wise had come to comprehend the unique greatness of Lincoln, his meaning for America and for mankind, his integral relation to that dream of liberty and equality which was so deep in Wise's own heart.

The war was at an end. The time had come to shape the peace, to heal wounds, bind up the breaches, lay the foundations of a newly reconstituted nation. Wise was optimistic as to what was coming. He believed that a genuine peace had been won and that it would prove lasting:

> As long as the question was war, civil war, with all its horrors, or slavery, the people submitted to the latter in order to escape the terrors of the former. But when the question was changed into liberty and union, or secession and slavery, the people, of course, decided in favor of liberty and union.
>
> Those who had slaves, in a few short years, will be glad to be free of their burdens, thank Heaven that they enjoy the fruits of their own labor, and will confess with us that a free nation only is mighty, a free man only is happy, and liberty means the freedom of all.[7]

It is good to know that at the end Wise had realized that the issue was between slavery and union, between secession and liberty. His quick and characteristic hope that even the South would find the liberation of the slaves good, and that a united and reconciled nation would rise from the ashes of tragedy and the sacrifices of war, was not destined to survive the days that followed, though he continued to express it and to print plea after plea for it. In a victory sermon which he delivered on April 14, 1865,[8] he asked for mercy for the vanquished, a welcome back into the Union for the rebellious states, and the repudiation of a policy or practice of revenge. Even after the assassination of Lincoln he rebuked those clergymen who were asking for reprisals against the defeated South, and accused them of being utterly without "Christian" spirit. He greeted the Amnesty Proclamation of 1865 with "joyous satisfaction," and called it a "blessing and honor to our country." He asked that all Southern prisoners of war be freed and permitted to return to their homes:[9]

> That we should and must remain one nation is evident and clear to every mind; therefore, whatever restores feelings of fraternity among us, is to our blessing, and whatever excites sectional prejudices, ill feelings and dissatisfactions, is a curse, nugatory to our best interests.[10]

Not infrequently he was found wondering whether the virulent anti-Jewish prejudices that had arisen and manifested themselves during the war would go on, or whether they would end with the conflict. He counseled various precautionary measures, especially that of making permanent the fine record of Jews in the war; and in almost every issue of the *Israelite* he was defending Jews against the accumulated calumnies of the latest months and years. In Washington, Simon Wolf was gathering statistics from the war records which would enshrine enduringly the names, numbers, and services of Jews in the Civil War.[11]

Wise had resumed his custom of traveling and visiting Jewish communities, for specific occasions and for general contact and work. In 1866 he went with Leeser, with whom he must meanwhile have re-established friendly relations, to visit Richmond, Va. He was greatly grieved at what he found in this once proud and wealthy Jewish community.[12] Wise's impressions were quite direct and natural. He wrote bitterly of the domination of the city by Negroes. It seemed to him that this was unendurable and that, if it went on, white men and women would be compelled to leave the South.[13]

Wise noted that, as Judah P. Benjamin had been the chief target for prejudice both in South and North, so August Belmont had enjoyed that privilege in the North. Wise wrote of a libel against Belmont:

> Since the outbreak of the late rebellion we have been used to the outpourings of such persons.[14]

Near the end of 1866 Wise sat down to estimate what was happening to the world, in pursuance of the old Jewish custom of review and reckoning on the New Year. He wrote of the state of affairs in Europe, of the revolution that—in his opinion—seemed inescapable in Spain, and of the division of Turkey. Europe—he believed—was sleeping on the crater of a volcano. His own country was by that time in the throes of reconstruction. It was his opinion that people in general in the United States would have liked a display of generosity to the vanquished, but that party interests had served to foment political passions and to make a quiet, peaceful sequel to the war impossible. He set himself to define the measures that would bring about a true peace. The Southern states should be required to enfranchise the Negro within five years. And all Jews, who had an inherent and immemorial interest in liberty, should take a great interest in the conception and execution of this plan.[15]

Somewhat later, when Andrew Johnson had completed his term as President, Wise was violently opposed to the nomination of Grant, putting aside for that occasion his frequently proclaimed principle against mixing religion and politics. He thought Grant "morally and intellectually unfit" for the office by his inability to understand the "theories and principles of personal liberty which vitalize our government." But—he declared—he would not make Grant's attitude toward Jews the sole issue in the campaign. To this we shall come again somewhat later.[16]

In former chapters we have told of Wise's conviction that the congregation had outgrown the Lodge St. Synagogue, both in dimensions and in dignity, and of the necessity of postponing the building of a new temple because of the exigencies caused by the Civil War. We come now to the time after the war when the project could be undertaken and completed. For the sake of continuity we shall set down the main facts concerning the new temple from the beginning.

As early as 1860 a committee had been appointed to consider plans for a new temple. The members of this committee were: Marcus Fechheimer, B. Simon, Jacob Netter, Solomon Friedmann, Henry Mack, Lewis Eichberg, Philip Stromberg, Aaron Stix, William Kraus, Daniel Wolf, and Isaac M. Wise. On December 7, 1860, there was an article in the *Israelite*, which described the panic that was almost everywhere, because of the feeling of certainty that Civil War was about to begin. Wise declared that the new temple would have to wait. But even during the war events looking toward a new house of worship were progressing. The congregation held a meeting and unanimously decided to build. The resolution was adopted with a great display of enthusiasm. This was on April 5, 1863. Subscriptions were initiated at the meeting toward a building fund. Marcus Fechheimer and Jacob Elsas were first, with pledges of $2000 each. In a short time the total had grown to $21,000;[17] and, when other members of the congregation were approached, it rose to $40,000. Two committees were then appointed: one on Finance, consisting of Jacob Elsas, B. Simon, and Simon Mack; and one on Propositions (probably meaning property), the members of which were: Henry Mack, Jacob L. Miller, Solomon Levi, Solomon Friedman, M. J. Mack, A. J. Friedlander, Max Mack, and Simon Shohl.[18] It was announced that on May 8, 1863 a site had been found, a piece of property one hundred by one hundred and thirty-two feet, at the corner of Plum and Eighth Streets, and that it had been purchased at a cost of $35,000. It was then estimated that the cost for the building to be erected upon it would be about $55,000. Some years later this proved to be only about $170,000 off, for the total cost was $263,525. The difference was due not only to inexperience, but also to rapidly rising costs during and after the Civil War. Ground was broken in July, 1863, and the foundation begun in August. It took two years to make much progress with the work, and three years to complete the edifice.[19]

The plans were described in the *Israelite* of May 6, 1864:

> It is in the byzantine style, with two steeples and several minor towers, which was preferred. The building, according to the plan, will be truly grand, both in design and dimensions.

It was to seat 2,000, 1,400 without the galleries, and would be an "ornament" to the city. The architect who had been chosen was J. K. Wilson. Later on the booklet issued for the congregation's fiftieth anniversary in 1892 described the temple as follows:

> It is an Alhambra temple, with slender pillars and thirteen domes (perhaps to correspond to the "thirteen attributes of God" in the famous passage in Exodus, 34:6-7).

An organ was ordered from Koehnken and Co., a Cincinnati firm. The instrument was to cost $9,000 without the "case."

The *Israelite* then described the laying of the cornerstone on May 12, 1865. This account was amplified also in the Fiftieth Anniversary booklet. We combine both, as in the account written in "As Yesterday When It Is Past":[20]

> The procession, which was to march to the site of the new Temple, assembled at the Lodge St. Synagogue. The daily papers devoted lengthy descriptions to the occasion. The Israelite commented on the spiritual connotation of the event, the downtrodden children of Israel who had found refuge in this new land, and the magnificent showing they made in this impressive ceremonial. Those who met at Lodge St., included the children and teachers of the Talmud Yelodim Institute, representatives of four sister-congregations of the city, the Mayor of the city, Charles F. Wilstach, the members of the City Council, judges, clergymen and other guests, and, of course, the rabbi, officers and many of the members of K.K.B'nai Yeshurun. Dr. Lilienthal made an address at Lodge St., and then the procession began. It was preceded by music and banners. In addition there were the five oldest members of the congregation. They carried three silver goblets, containing oil, wine and corn. Others in the procession bore objects which were to be placed in the cornerstone: an open Bible, an American flag, and so forth. The procession wound its way from Fifth to Vine Streets, north to Sixth, on Sixth to Race, on Race to Seventh, on Seventh to Plum, and thence to the lot on Eighth and Plum. Arrived there, they launched into the ceremony for the dedica-

tion of the cornerstone. Two hymns were sung by a men's chorus, under Prof. Barus. A history of the congregation was read by Henry Mack. This recapitulated the main events in its life: that it was the first reform congregation west of the Alleghenies, that it was first organized "in 1839," but that no records existed before September, 1841; that its first property was a burial-ground, acquired in the year 1840, near Brighton House; that at the outset services were conducted by a member of the congregation, and that the first Reader of the congregation was Simon Bamberger, who received a salary of $75 a year.

The cornerstone was then laid by Henry Mack with the assistance of the five elders. Dr. Wise delivered an oration, "which," says the Fiftieth Anniversary Booklet, "expounded the principles upon which American Judaism was based. It was the Judaism of American citizens, the religion of One God, one human family, giving freedom, equality, justice and salvation to all!"

But we do not depend solely upon this account. The *Israelite* contained the full address. In it Dr. Wise referred to the City Hall, diagonally across the corner, and the Catholic cathedral, immediately across Plum St. Later on he said: "Our place of worship shall be a *temple* in which the Psalms of Israel, the praise and glory of the Most High, shall be sung by melodious voices, as in days of yore the chorus of Levites proclaimed the Eternal One by song and psalmody. The Harp of Judah shall resound again, the organ and trumpet, the harp and the flute announce again the King of Glory, as the sons of Aaron did in the Temple on Mt. Moriah. The daughter of Israel shall no longer be excluded from the house of the Lord, and none shall be a stranger in the tabernacle of the Lord of Hosts, 'for my house shall be called the house of prayer to all nations,' saith the Lord; truth, salvation and God's divine presence shall abide therein, happiness and gladness, and every pious soul shall exclaim over it, 'Here I will dwell, for I have desired it.' It shall not be a house of mourning or weeping; it shall be a *temple*, a permanent resting-place; such as the heart desires, as the soul yearns to dwell in it forevermore; where God rejoices over His people, and righteous children sing His praise. 'This is my resting-place forevermore; here will I dwell, for I have desired it.' This shall be the motto engraved on the keystone of this divine structure, and announce to the world and to coming generations, why this congregation, *B'nai Yeshurun,* laid the cornerstone to the *First Temple* in this city.

The procession then marched back to Lodge St. in the same order.[21]

Some months before Wise had inserted in the *Israelite* a review of the history of the congregation. He wrote that the work of the congregation had gone forward steadily since his coming to it in 1854. He enumerated the changes he had introduced: a Choir, *Minhag America*, and the continuation of the Talmud Yelodim Institute and its improvement. He wrote proudly that B'nai Yeshurun stood at the head of all the congregations of the West in numbers and in "progressive measures." Into the cornerstone—he wrote—were placed: the history and records of the congregation; copies of daily and of denominational papers; the Constitution of the United States; a list of the Executive officers of the United States and of the State of Ohio; coins and currency of the day. Corn, oil, and wine were poured over the stone. He declared that it was good to lay the cornerstone, now that victory had come to the nation. Some of the passages, here given from his address, were as follows:

> As long as the dispersed sons of Israel suffered persecution and had no actual home among the various nations, it was quite natural for them to pray for redemption and look back upon Palestine as the only secure haven for the shipwrecked and oppressed ones. . . . Things have changed; thank God they have! The progress of science and art, philosophy and criticism, invention and practical application, revolutionized all the departments of humanity, especially politics and religion. Doctrines inconsistent with reason are no longer tenable. . . . No wonder, then, that the house of Israel felt and feels the vigorous effects of progress, and underwent a revolution of sentiment in regard also to doctrines and observances. The redeemed crave no redemption, so much is certain. The house of Israel, being politically redeemed, here, and all over the civilized world, cannot consistently wait and pray for a political redeemer. . . . Again, he who has a home, and is at home, can not feel homesick.

The children of Israel look back with veneration upon the home of their ancestors, the "beauteous land of Zion," but:

> We do not wish to return to Palestine, nor do we pray for the coming of a Messiah.

Not one land, but the whole world, is God's chosen abode.

> We are American citizens and Israelites by religion.

In the cornerstone were placed also copies of *Minhag America* and of *The Essence of Judaism*. This was called a "temple," because Israel shall "weep no longer." The time had come to rejoice:

> The laws, precepts, and doctrines of Israel have become the beacon-light to suffering humanity.[22]

In the latter part of the summer of 1865 the *Israelite* announced the forthcoming dedication of the new Temple, to take place on August 24.[23] A day before the dedication the Temple was opened for inspection. A daily paper wrote of it: "Cincinnati never before has seen so much grandeur pressed into so small a space."[24]

The dedication was at hand. One of Wise's early biographers wrote:

> The writer will never forget the fervor with which Isaac M. Wise once pointed up to the great dome of the Temple and asked that the sons, for whom the fathers built it, turn their eyes heavenward with equal piety.

And to the congregation at the time of the dedication, he had said:

> Judaism welcomes the light of day and decks itself with becoming pride.[25]

On the Sunday before the dedication the remainder of the cost of the building was met by selling pews. A total of $90,000 was realized. This was the last amount needed, and the congregation owed nothing. The first pew was bought by B. Simon for the sum of $4,600 and Abraham Aub the next for the same amount.

The account of the dedication we take again complete from the same source as that we drew upon in regard to the cornerstone:

> The Marshals for the occasion were M. J. Mack, Nathaniel Newburgh, L. Schloss, and Leopold Fechheimer. Services began again at the Lodge St. Synagogue at three in the afternoon (Friday afternoon). The evening service was read by Solomon Levi, president of the congregation, and a closing prayer delivered by Dr. Wise. Then followed a procession, quite similar to that organized for the laying of the cornerstone, and again including city officials, members of other congregations and societies, and clergymen of Christian churches. Arrived at the Plum St. Temple, they began the second service. Henry Mack, who had served as chairman of the building committee, received the key to the new building from the hands of his daughter, Henriette, and spoke a few words. The organ pealed forth. The services were read by the Rev. Mr. Rubin, of Temple Emanu-El, New York City. Next came a number of circuits of the temple (*Hakofoth*). The oldest members of the congregation carried scrolls of the law, young boys the curtains of the ark, the covers and mantles, and girls flowers and decorations. The Perpetual Lamp (*Ner Tamid*) was kindled by boys especially selected for this sacred task.

A preliminary discourse was delivered by Dr. Lilienthal. We quote some words from the *Israelite's* account:

"It seems to me as if we were now concluding a new covenant of a new brotherhood; as if we were assembled to verify the words of the Prophet: 'Every people may walk in the name of his God, and we in the name of our God'; but let us not desecrate the covenant of our forefathers, for 'have we not all but one Father; has not one God created us all?' . . . Let the light of love and brotherly understanding shine brightly and lustily throughout the land. Let link by link be added to the chain of love that unites us so harmoniously in our growing, gigantic West. Let us leave this house, impressed with the sacred words of this consecration. 'Let there be light,' light that enlightens our mind, warms our hearts, fosters our affections. Yes, the Lord said there shall be light, and it will be light to His glory and to our good, forever and ever. Amen!"

The choir then sang a "Hymn on the Law," written by Isaac M. Wise, on one of his favorite words from Holy Writ. We print it in its entirety, and comment that we are fortunate enough to possess still the original program of the dedication ceremonies:

"Let there be light," a second time
  The Lord of Hosts proclaimed;
Let error yield to truth sublime!
  And justice reign supreme!
The sun then rose on Sinai's height;
And poured on thee a flood of light.

A flood of light, these words and laws;
  Which Moses taught thy sires;
The banner of thy holy cause,
  Which truth and love inspires;
It is the sun from Sinai's height,
Which poured on thee a flood of light.

This Word of God, this "law of fire,"
  The queen of truth and grace,
Is Isr'el's pride, his sole desire,
  His heaven's golden rays.
Lift up on high this book of light,
Which God revealed on Sinai's height.

This Law of Laws, so dearly bought
  With sighs, and tears, and blood—
The blood of saints, who bravely fought

A world in error's flood;
Let's cling to it, the book of light,
Which God revealed on Sinai's height.

We cling to thee with holy glee,
The Law of God is ours!
The God who rules o'er land and sea,
On worlds his blessings show'rs—
Revealed the Law on Sinai's height,
He poured on thee a flood of light.

The First Circuit had been after an Introductory Prayer, and to the accompaniment of the Hundredth Psalm. After the Second Circuit there had been the reading of passages from Sacred Scriptures, drawn from First Kings and from Isaiah. The Third Circuit, after the above Hymn, was composed of men bearing the Scrolls of the Law. "Boys dress the scrolls with the new mantillas and the jewels; the damsels decorate them with their flowers and wreaths; then they are deposited in the tabernacle; the boys spread the covers on pulpit and desk; the Bible and the Prayer-book are deposited thereon, and the damsels decorate both with flowers and wreaths."

Thereafter followed the Dedication Sermon, delivered by Isaac M. Wise. He began by expounding the principles of Reform Judaism, and dwelt on the distinction between a synagogue and a temple. The worship, which is to be conducted in the latter, is to be in gladness, not in perpetual mourning. "Let happy hearts be united into one grand chorus, and worship the God of our Fathers with solemn hymns and exulting psalms. Let each soul rise on the golden wings of faith and confidence to the throne of light and truth, and return cleansed of all earthly dross, purified of all that is dark, small or narrow, sanctified with the divine and eternal, pervaded of heavenly goodness and wisdom, and return to weeping humanity an angel of consolation, a harbinger of glad tidings from the throne of grace, strong in virtue, mighty in goodness, and great in love—this is our object of divine worship, the first object of this temple, and a leading principle of modern Israelites." Wise then continued with the second principle: All nations are enjoined to worship God. The religion of the future will be universal and after the pattern of the faith of Israel. To spread this faith, destined soon to become that of all men, is the second object of this temple. Thirdly, Dr. Wise enumerated the signs and symbols of God's grace and of His promises to Israel. Fourthly, he took his stand upon the Word of God, as it is in the Bible, and declared that no new religion is needed, but only a rational

> and spiritual interpretation of it. "These are the leading points of American Judaism, the new school in Israel, which, in the name of God, shall be expounded in this temple, to the salvation of man, the glory of God, and the final triumph of truth. Holy and eternal truth shall be our aim, God's grace our shield, song and psalmody our divine worship, gladness and happiness our portion before God. In this spirit, brethren, let us dedicate this gorgeous temple to the only true God."
>
> The program noted, rather distressingly, that *during* the Dedication Sermon, Minister and Choir sang in Hebrew, Psalm 127, "Praise God, all ye nations!" The Invocation came next. The congregation rose, and together with the Choir responded, "Amen. Hallelujah!" to each sentence. Next the Dedication Hymn was sung. We shall reproduce only the first stanza:
>
> Resound, ye domes, with holy hymns,
>   Break forth in joyous lays,
> To Him whose glory suns bedims,
>   Whose love outlasts all days;
> Ye gorgeous pillars sing
> The praise of Israel's King!
>
> From the evidence of the words we judge this too to have been a composition of Wise's.
>
> Next came an Organ Symphony, and then the service for Sabbath eve. Services were also held the following morning, and a German sermon was delivered.[26]

One touch is recounted in the *Israelite* which must have been extraordinarily impressive. The congregation rose. Wise pronounced the benediction and asked God to consecrate the new Temple. This the *Cincinnati Commercial* described as "the most solemn part of the service." God's blessing was invoked seven times, after each an Amen! The faces of the multitude (seats were at a great premium, selling in advance for $25) were uplifted toward the pulpit, under the dim light that lay over the new shrine. It was "never to be forgotten."[27]

The edifice which the congregation had built, for which Wise had prayed and worked for years, was worthy of his spirit and adequate for the needs of the congregation. It was in an accessible part of the city, for then most of Cincinnati's Jews lived on Fourth or Eighth Streets within easy walking distance. Its seating capacity would care for the congregation for a generation or two to come. It was beautiful and inspiring in its oriental richness. Perhaps a patina was added to it, as the years passed, by the dreams, the sorrows and the prayers that made its walls resonant. It stands still in the same place and is still used by the congregation.

The building was not "byzantine," but Moorish, as Wise's second descriptive term for it, "Alhambra," indicated much more correctly. It had two minarets on the Plum St. side and its ground plan was that of a "T," with the cross-arm at the eastern, or pulpit, end of the building. The choir was in a gallery at the other end of the auditorium. It had many domes, larger and smaller, and the lower space was made intricate with arches and slender columns. Several temples, more or less resembling it, were built around the same period, especially two in New York: that of the Central Synagogue at 55th Street and Lexington Ave., and the old one of Temple Emanu-El, now gone, which was at 43rd Street and Fifth Avenue.

To complete the story, though it means leaping ahead, the interior decoration of the Temple, which adds so greatly to its warmth and beauty, was not painted on its walls until the fall of 1874, eight years later. A German artist of Cincinnati, by name Thien, was employed, and designed and applied the arabesques in color that cover the entire interior. At the same time numerous inscriptions in Hebrew were placed over the Ark, above the arches, and along the cornices. These Dr. Wise had selected, and they "represented in full the main principles of Jewish theology." It took three months to do all this, and the Temple was closed for that period.[28]

This is now one of the oldest Jewish houses of worship in continuous use in our country; it remains just as it was in Wise's lifetime. The years have added depth and solemnity to it. It is a monument to him and to the troubled time just after which it was built.

Meanwhile the congregation was becoming not less but more active, not less but more devoted to its many tasks. Shortly after the dedication of the new Temple Wise initiated one of his most interesting ventures, an idea which was quite original with him, and which —as we shall see—was widely copied. He wrote of this many years later:

> There was danger of the Sabbath being forgotten; working-men and business-men could no longer attend services. This was one of the reasons why we in 1865 started and advocated a Sabbath with sermons and an instructive lecture at a convenient hour on Friday evening, primarily for those people who claim not to be in condition to attend divine services on the Sabbath day. This innovation crossed the ocean and was introduced in Berlin, Vienna, and elsewhere, after it had been adopted by a hundred or more congregations in America, and saved the

> Sabbath in most of them. . . . It is a reassurance that the true Sabbath day will not be forgotten in Israel.[29]

This innovation proved very successful; it enabled Wise also to take up from the pulpit many of the theological, philosophical, and polemical subjects which he wished to develop, and which he felt needed investigation and thought. Many of these lectures-series were published in book form. The most noteworthy were: *The Cosmic God; Judaism and Christianity, Their Agreements and Disagreements;* and *Jesus, the Apostles and Paul.*[30] These lectures served a negative as well as a positive purpose. Much later we shall come to consider Wise's attitude toward the Sabbath, and his consistent and indignant opposition to a "Sunday Sabbath." Later on Lilienthal wrote a letter to *The New York Times*[31] on the effect of Wise's lectures on Christianity. He called them bold and ingenious. They were usually heard by Christians, even by some Protestant ministers, who—in spite of their dogmatic dissent—were greatly interested in Wise's treatment, and frequently aided by the material he expounded, with most of which they were quite unfamiliar.[32]

Wise had not become reconciled to the existence or to the declared purposes of the "Board of Delegates." Shortly after the war he attacked it once again in the *Israelite*. They were proposing—he wrote—to establish a College for Rabbis. Wise was certain that this would be far from the institution he had in mind, that it was likely to be quite conservative and unprogressive in character. He ridiculed the claim of the "Board of Delegates" to "defend" Jews. If Jews were to wait for the defense of this group, Wise wrote, their liberties would be in serious jeopardy. The whole thing was a "farce." A real meeting of all congregations in the United States, *that* would be one thing; but to have ten congregations out of the forty in New York, and the New York congregations all together a small fraction of those of the entire country, venture to speak for all; this was insufferable.[33]

That fall on *Succoth* he spoke on "The Means to Preserve Judaism." The outlook for the Jews of Europe he found dark. Apathy was the chief characteristic of the Jewish communities across the Atlantic. They seemed to have lost their capacity to advance:

> If you ask me, what progresses not in either nature or history, in the physical or mental realms of existence, I can only answer, that which is not, for whatever is progresses.

This—Wise asserted—was the standpoint of the prophets, and of the rabbis of *Mishna* and *Talmud*. Judaism must lay aside "obsolete forms and obnoxious peculiarities. . . ."

> Spiritless forms can exercise a nugatory influence only.

We must go to any limit to accomplish this objective. He advocated, first of all, "Union":

> It must be clear, almost self-evident, that no Israelites and no body of Israelites can detach themselves from the congregation of Israel and remain Israelites in religion; for the mission of Israel is an integral and important part, a fundamental directive of our religion, and this mission belongs to the whole congregation of Israel. . . . The union of Israel is as inseparable from our creed as the doctrine of revelation, immortality, reward and punishment, or any other cardinal doctrine."

He declared that, as time went on, he was finding more and more allies in his striving toward union:

> The progressive reforms of one Israelite, or of a body thereof, must never go so far as to separate the same from the congregation of Israel.

But one must not despise Gentile allies and associates:

> Hence a close union of American Jewish congregations should be cemented and for no other except religious purposes.
>
> Each of our congregations is a republic upon some isolated island, and has no connection with the other. This can lead only to impious results.

He proposed once again the holding of an annual "synod":

> A conference or whatever a body of representatives from all the congregations might be called, the chief end and aim of which should be in the first instance to cement a close union of all American congregations, and keep us in union with Israel, in union also with the progressive intellect of the world.

But this was not to exist as an end in itself. It had as a primary duty to foster "intellectual culture":

> If you wish to preserve Judaism, use the means placed at your command by God himself, cultivate your intellect, walk in the light of the Lord. If you wish to preserve mental culture among our offspring, encourage, support and cheer gifted students. This is and always was our main force, our fortress and armory among the nations.

> Every American congregation should have a separate fund for the purpose of encouraging mental culture.[34]

In the spring of 1866 the trustees of K.K.B'nai Yeshurun were considering some further advances in relation to the prayer-book. For some years they had already been using the first volume of *Minhag America.* They now wanted a second volume, along the same lines, for the *Yomim Noro'im*, that is, for *Rosh Ha-shono* and *Yom Kippur.* They proposed that with very few exceptions, and as Wise had already done in Albany, the *Piutim* and the *S'lichoth* should be omitted and replaced by selected passages from Scriptures, a treatment still followed on *Yom Kippur* in the Union Prayer Book. It was moreover specified by the committee that services for *Rosh Hashono* should be not longer than three hours, *Yom Kippur* Eve two and a half hours, and for the day of *Yom Kippur* ten hours. Rather curiously they recommended that the Shofar should be blown from the choir-gallery. Wise was asked to compile and translate a book for use along these lines, the final work to be submitted to this committee on religious rules and regulations. He was asked to have it ready for use the following fall. Five hundred copies were to be printed, and the book was to be sold for three dollars a copy.[35]

Occasionally—as we have noted earlier—Wise was having trouble at the Talmud Yelodim Institute. The Board of the school reprimanded him for his conduct toward a teacher whom he was examining for a prospective post. What the exact complaint was the record does not state. The meeting at which the Board passed this resolution must have been an exceptionally acrimonious one, for the president, Nathan Menderson, resigned, because he considered "himself insulted by the attacks on the Rev. Dr. Wise at the last general meeting." And once again Wise paid little or no attention to the matter.[36] There were periodic public exhibitions of the work of the school; one such had been in June at Melodeon Hall. All subjects—the account said—were as in the public schools, with the addition of Hebrew, German, French, penmanship and drawing. A new principal had been selected for the school, a Dr. Mayer of Gladenbach in Germany, a fine Hebrew and German scholar.[37]

During these post-bellum years the spiritual atmosphere of the country must have been exceedingly troubled. Wise had appealed for leniency toward the South, and this was the policy of Andrew Johnson. But vengeful groups were in the saddle, tried to impeach the President, and initiated the steps that led to the whole sorry story of Reconstruction. From time to time Wise took notice of this in the *Israelite*. He wrote that "The North is crying for revenge against the South, and Christianity seems to play no part." He was inspired by this unhappy situation, and by the sad reflections it induced in him, to indite a poem, the first stanza of which was as follows:

> If happy thou intend'st to be,
> On life's meand'ring path,
> Then learn, unmov'd, to hear and see
> The wicked man in wrath.
> Let justice mourn and virtue weep,
> Let innocence succumb
> To tyrant's sword; in dust do creep,
> And let thy mouth be dumb.[38]

In the summer of 1867 Wise made one of his usual trips, this time to the East. He sent back to the *Israelite* extensive and chatty accounts of what he was seeing. In one of these missives he commented upon the fact that twenty-five of the thirty congregations in New York "offer up prayers daily to the throne of mercy for the restoration of Israel to Palestine." He told his readers what Temple Emanu-El was like under Samuel Adler, and of the congregation then led by David Einhorn:

> There is great prejudice in New York against your humble writer. In the Emanu-El congregation many think I am too orthodox, so they do in Dr. Einhorn's congregation, while others can not forgive me the supposed sin, to have made reform to a common good among American Israelites, when they claimed it as an aristocratic privilege.

He spent some time also in Newark and Rochester, and commented on the announcement by the "Board of Delegates" of their purpose to open a "Maimonides College," which was however still only on paper.[39]

Whatever his experiences during the Civil War, and whatever the reactions to his brand of Reform, Wise was in constant and great demand by congregations all over the country. No other man spoke so often in so many cities as did he. And, despite the letter of their objection to his accepting the nomination to the State Senate of Ohio, the board of his own congregation adopted and consistently adhered to a most liberal attitude toward these absences and activities on the part of their rabbi. They might have resented the frequent interruptions of his local duties. But they were well-advised in giving him much latitude. They had no real wish to restrict his ambition, or to circumscribe his influence. They were—in fact—

very proud of him and of his name in the country. This was a breadth of relationship rare among congregations at that time, and rare even now. Wise was away lecturing, dedicating synagogues, traveling, but there is no single record of protest by K.K.B'nai Yeshurun, and there are many resolutions of approval and encouragement.[40]

Wise dedicated every house of worship west of the Alleghenies and many in the East as well. Nor did this tend to harm his own flock. In the fall of 1866 the secretary of the congregation reported upon the condition of their finances after the dedication of the Plum St. Temple. Wise's salary was raised from three to four thousand dollars a year, "in appreciation." The congregation was also carrying a life-insurance policy for him. A *Hazan*, Dr. Mayer of Hesse, was engaged at a salary of $1000 *per annum*. The text of the new prayer-book for the Holy Days was adopted at a general meeting of the congregation on April 1, 1866. The congregation then had 244 families in it.[41]

In general, the tensions of the Civil War were relaxing. A new sanctuary, and a very beautiful one, had been built. The congregation was prospering. Wise's circle of influence was constantly expanding. He had not ceased to agitate and to hope for progress toward union, and toward an adequate system of education, in American Israel. In the meantime he was carrying on all his multitudinous tasks: the Talmud Yelodim Institute, his pulpit now with extended and carefully prepared Friday evening lectures, his editorship of *Israelite* and *Deborah*, for both of which he was continuing to write a large proportion of the material, his pastoral duties, and his interest in many civic activities in Cincinnati itself.

26

Conferences and Progress Toward Union

THE EMPHASIS OF THE NEXT FEW YEARS WAS LARGELY UPON VARIOUS tentatives that were made toward united action on the part of rabbis and on the part of Jewish congregations. It was obvious that the time could not be very distant when some method of cooperation would be attained, despite the anarchy, the ill-will, the contention on unessentials, the immaturity, that had been afflicting the American Jewish community for so many years. Wise himself had been at work at one or another of these objectives now for more than twenty years. Doubtless also, as time was elapsing, the German Jews, who were newcomers to America when he himself had arrived, had been acquiring American ways, adjusting more integrally into their respective cities, building up their own congregations, and comprehending more clearly the needs that made united action advisable. The experience of the next few years displays clearly, however, that there were still sharp differences among rabbis, that is, between certain parties of rabbis; and that there was still more than enough fuel for theological fulminations and controversies. But behind it must also be read the fact that there were more than a few spiritual leaders who did not spring so readily into postures of attack or defense, who wanted to work with their colleagues, who felt the need for congregational unity. And behind them was a growing body of laymen who wanted union, who were willing to aid in progressing toward it, and who in some instances furnished intelligent and vigorous leadership for it.

Wise's primary awareness—perhaps—was still of the intemperate opposition of rabbis in the "East." In his travels, in his correspondence in the *Israelite*, in the responses that came to some of his proposals for joint thought and action, he had learned that in the Middle West and in the South Jews largely were ready for some form of congregational union. He did not cease striving for some *modus vivendi* with his colleagues in New York, Philadelphia, and so forth; nor did he desist from proposing plan after plan to his friends west of the Alleghenies and south of the Mason-Dixon line. These years from 1869 to 1872 were converging toward the certain realization of his central idea; they were also years that elicited his own two consistent qualities of resourcefulness and of pertinacity. Opposition angered him, but never to the point of rendering him incapable of action. Failures daunted him, but never to the extent of causing him to relinquish his purpose.

One of his ideas—as we have written before—was for the creation of a publication society. He understood, and had understood for two decades, that the unproductiveness and the cultural illiteracy of American Jews must be remedied. This was one of the means by which he proposed to do it. It was his idea that such a society for the publication of Jewish books should be initiated and carried on by a conference of congregations. Even if the Jews of America continued to be unable to agree on doctrinal points, on a "synod," or on a prayer-book, at least they ought to be able to go ahead with this undertaking.[1]

By all odds the most important event of these years after the close of the Civil War was a rabbinical conference called in Philadelphia. The initiative for it came directly from those who had berated Wise for his part in the Cleveland Conference of 1855, who had declared themselves uncompromisingly opposed to his concepts and practices. Primarily two men, Samuel Adler of Temple Emanu-El, New York, and David Einhorn of Temple Adath Yeshurun, also of New York, sent out a notice to a select list of rabbis, asking them to come together to discuss the principles of a new form of public worship and to consider other weighty questions, like those having to do with marriage and divorce. Despite the fact that Wise had made repeated attempts in New York to conciliate these men, especially Einhorn, despite the fact that he could not have been unaware that they—and their sympathizers—were still violently and perhaps irreconcilably incensed against him and were still publishing protests against him, in some of which they had said publicly that they would have nothing more to do with him, Wise went to the meeting. He himself did not regard their respective views and positions as irreconcilable. He was an inveterate believer in the possibility of compromise.[2] That his hopefulness was not utterly unjustified is shown by the fact that at the closing meeting of the conference he acted as chairman. He preached also in Rodeph Shalom on the Sabbath morning after adjournment.[3] We shall shortly review the work of the Conference and of Wise's part in it. In sum, however, it may be remarked that there was nothing startlingly new except a proposal:

> Whereas circumcision is not a necessary condition for entrance into Judaism, and the omission of the rite does not exclude any Israelite from the community of Israel, and does not absolve him of his duties as such, Resolved, that the circumcision of proselytes be not required as an "act of initiation."[4]

This was Wise's own proposal, already put forward at German conferences of rabbis.[5] The proposal was propounded and substantiated by many references to rabbinic law; but it was still too advanced for the Philadelphia Conference, and was not adopted until 1895 by the Central Conference of American Rabbis.[6]

But we are hastening before the event. The Conference itself, consisting of rabbis only, was held at the home of Samuel Hirsch, rabbi of Keneseth Israel, Philadelphia, from November 3 to 6, 1869. Attending it were: Samuel Adler of New York, Chronik of Chicago, Deutsch of Baltimore, Einhorn of New York, Felsenthal of Chicago, Gutheim—then in New York, Moses Mielziner of New York, Kaufmann Kohler, then in New York, Schlesinger of Albany, Sonnenschein of St. Louis, and Isaac M. Wise. The Conference adopted a set of principles.[7] These we reprint entire, for their intrinsic interest, for their bearing on the development of rabbinic points of view, and for their contrast with the Cleveland Conference of 1855. It was in fact the first thoroughgoing attempt to formulate a credo for liberal Judaism in America:

1. The Messianic aim of Israel is not the restoration of the old Jewish state under a descendant of David, involving a second separation from the nations of the earth, but the union of all the children of God in the confession of the unity of God, so as to realize the unity of all rational crea-

tures and their call to moral sanctification.

2. We look upon the destruction of the second Jewish commonwealth not as a divine punishment for the sinfulness of Israel, but as a result of the divine purpose revealed to Abraham, which, as has become ever clearer in the course of the world's history, consists in the dispersion of the Jews to all parts of the earth, for the realization of their high priestly mission, to lead the nations to the true knowledge and worship of God.
3. The Aaronic priesthood and the Mosaic sacrificial cult were preparatory steps to the real priesthood of the whole people, which began with the dispersion of the Jews, and to the sacrifices of sincere devotion and moral sanctification, which alone are pleasing and acceptable to the Most Holy. These institutions, preparatory to higher religiosity, were consigned to the past, once for all, with the destruction of the second temple, and only in this sense—as educational influences in the past—are they to be mentioned in our prayers.
4. Every distinction between Aaronides and non-Aaronides, as far as religious rites and duties are concerned, is consequently inadmissible, both in the religious cult and in life.
5. The selection of Israel as the people of religion, as the bearers of the highest idea of humanity, is still, as ever, to be strongly emphasized and for this very reason, whenever this is mentioned it shall be done with full emphasis laid on the world-embracing mission of Israel and the love of God for all His children.
6. The belief in the bodily resurrection has no religious foundation, and the doctrine of immortality refers to the after-existence of the soul only.
7. Urgently as the cultivation of the Hebrew language, in which the treasures of divine revelation are given and the immortal remains of a literature that influences all civilized nations are preserved, must be always desired by us in fulfillment of a sacred duty, yet has it become unintelligible to the vast majority of our coreligionists; therefore it must make way, as is advisable under existing circumstances, to intelligible language in prayer, which, if not understood, is a soulless form.[8]

The Conference made some attempts also to adapt matrimonial practice to the law of the land. The text of the resolution to this was given later in the *Israelite*. It legislated against polygamy, in accordance with the procedure of Western Jewry over the course of centuries, declared once again for the religious equality of women with men, and acknowledged the sole applicability of the law of the land in regard to divorce. It contended that the *Get* (the decree of divorce) had never had a religious, but only a civil, character. It asked all Jews to follow the spirit of the pronouncements of the Conference. "All rabbis must be governed by them or refute them."[9]

Wise himself followed the Conference with a number of articles in the *Israelite*, commenting upon it. It had been planned at Philadelphia to hold a second session in November, 1870, in Cincinnati. Wise found himself in agreement with the spirit of the pronouncements of the Conference, though whether he went along completely with paragraph seven, concerning the use of Hebrew, is an open question. But the remainder, with its typical "universalistic" outlook in regard to the dispersion of Israel, the abolition of the "Aaronic priesthood," its implicit rejection of the doctrine of a personal Messiah, its preference for the doctrine of immortality in place of the dogma of resurrection, was entirely in accord with the principles to which he himself had been giving expression ever since he had come to America. Wise expressed the hope that the Conference would become a permanent American Jewish institution, and serve the many purposes he had always had in mind for such a coming together of rabbis.[10]

Some months later he was still explaining the articles adopted, and his attitude toward them. He had his doubts about the single word "Mosaic" in Article Three of the declaration, which seemed to imply that Moses himself instituted the sacrificial cult, here declared outworn. In the third section of this book we shall see that this was quite far from Wise's own idea about the authority and derivation of such sections of the Torah. The section on Hebrew he declared too involved and vague. Each congregation should choose for itself how much of the Hebrew text of the liturgy, and how much of the vernacular, it would use in its services. The sixth article he regarded as "tautological," repeating the substance of the first. He recorded also that Kohler had proposed an eighth paragraph on Bible-reading at public worship, though precisely what changes Kohler had in mind Wise did not describe. At any rate, the suggestion was tabled.[11]

Meanwhile he was hammering away at one of his favorite themes, which we have written of twice before, that progress in American Jewish congregations was bound up with doing away with the use of German. Both services and sermons ought to be in English, and, he declared, "progress and liberalism" were bound up with this step.[12]

A month later he went into a somewhat protracted exposition

of the fate of his own resolution about the circumcision of proselytes. Einhorn had introduced a motion that children, that is children of Jews, should be regarded as Jews though not circumcised. Wise had introduced an amendment to the effect that this should apply to proselytes. This latter had been referred to a committee which was to report the following year. Wise's comment in the *Israelite* was to the effect that, while Einhorn was "casuistically correct," nonetheless to neglect circumcision makes one an impious Jew. The action to adopt Einhorn's proposal and postpone decision on Wise's was most inconsistent. He himself had voted for the former in the expectation that his own amendment would be adopted. The disappointment of this expectation had already brought some bitter misunderstandings. He himself regarded circumcision as an essential Jewish practice, not to be discarded or minimized. He set down too the fact that four committees had been appointed at Philadelphia: on liturgy and marriage laws; on the Sabbath; on school and congregational matters; and on ritual. A proposal had been made—probably by him—that the rabbis should summon a congregational conference, but this had not been adopted. The Philadelphia Conference—Wise concluded—had been distinguished for learning and zeal, and would lead to much good.[13]

This good-will on Wise's part, and his prediction that the Conference would have some beneficial results, proved mistaken. There were no consequences of the Philadelphia Conference. It led to no second meeting. In fact, it led to nothing. Neither, as far as can be discerned, did it serve to mitigate the antagonism toward him that had been so strong on the part of Einhorn, Adler, Hirsch, and Kohler. A later meeting in Pittsburgh in 1885 did, in effect, continue, in large part reiterate, and make more explicit some of the principles adopted at the Philadelphia Conference. But this was an independent meeting of a much later date and after conditions had altered materially.

Wise went on trying. He himself summoned a meeting of all rabbis, whose congregations were using his *Minhag America*, for Cleveland, July 11 of the following summer, 1870. The purpose of the meeting would be to "preserve and further promulgate, to revise and re-edit." He invited all to attend.[14] Later on he reported that this meeting had been arranged by Lilienthal, Kleeberg, Mayer and himself. The rabbis who attended were: Adler of Chicago, Cohen of Cleveland, Kleeberg of Louisville, Lilienthal of Cincinnati, Mayer of Cleveland, Mayer of Richmond, Sonnenschein of St. Louis, Tuska of Memphis, and Wise. They met in Tiphereth Israel Temple and began by laying down specific principles for the completion of the work: the Sabbath was to be maintained without substitute; Hebrew was to continue as the essential of the liturgy; passages relating to a personal Messiah, the restoration of a political Israel or a return to Palestine, to sacrifices and the Levitical priesthood, were to be excised; the text would speak of immortality and not of resurrection. Ample margin was to be left for prayers in the vernacular and for hymns as well. The conference decided also to publish its minutes so that all might be able to follow their reasoning. There was nothing startlingly new in the "principles" adopted. With few exceptions they had become the stock in trade of the reform rabbis at that time. The work was begun, but not completed. The heat in Cleveland—Wise wrote—was very oppressive. Finally, without finishing the task, the conference adjourned until October 24 to meet in New York, and Wise concluded in the *Israelite* with the proud prediction that the *Minhag America* "will be the liturgy of American Israelites in spite of all private interests and private whims." He fully expected this to become the "cornerstone to a complete union of American Israel."[15]

The adjourned meeting was duly continued in New York from October 24 to 30. There were nine rabbis in attendance. A resolution was passed at the beginning to invite all New York rabbis to be present. Two more came the next day. Rules were adopted. Wise followed his customary procedure, and introduced a resolution that a congregational union should be formed. Again this was "indefinitely postponed." Then a resolution was moved to found a "College." Lilienthal proposed that they do away with the "second day" of *Rosh Ha-shono*. The meeting proceeded next to a review of the Hebrew text of the *Siddur*, and adopted the portion for Sabbath eve. A discussion ensued whether Hebrew or the vernacular should preponderate at the services. A committee on college was appointed, to report at the next meeting. This far at least Wise had got. At this point in the meeting Wise became alarmed. Exactly why this happened to him, his own article does not indicate. But he had the strong feeling that the intention of the meeting was to drop his *Minhag America*, and substitute another prayer-book for it. He rose and announced that he could no longer meet with the conference. He claimed that this conference had been convoked only to revise the book, and that in the light of this he would not himself have attended. He would not and could not assist at the "abolition" of *Minhag America*, for a large number of congregations were using it, and had adopted it at his suggestion. He went on to assert that the very name, *Minhag America*, had "been identified with the principle of union and progress of the masses of our coreligionists." A new book would have to encounter many obstacles. A proposal was then made that, unless there was a unanimous agreement to publish a substitute for *Minhag America*, it would be retained. To this moderate motion Wise agreed and returned to the meeting.[16]

In a later copy of the *Israelite* there were further details about the work of this meeting. The prayers for the evenings of the three festivals (*Sukkoth*, *Pesach*, and *Shabuoth*) were read and adopted. There was a resolution to convert the conference into a permanent and general union of rabbis. The meeting also took a moderate stand on another controversial topic; it declared that it could discover no prohibition against worshiping in synagogue with uncovered head. The conference adjourned, to meet again on June 5, 1871, in Cincinnati. Its task in the future was to be to revise the evening prayers for *Yom Kippur*. Another question was referred to a committee: whether the presence of ten men would continue to be regarded as essential for the conduct of a public service (a *Minyan*). Committees were appointed to go over the German and English translations of the Hebrew text.[17]

Wise contended that the total purport of the first two meetings was that *Minhag America* would become the ritual for all the Jews of the United States:

> Much has been gained, and in unity of sentiment. We must have patience and not try to hurry processes.[18]

The third session was held, beginning on June 5, 1871. One of the early biographies asserted that the "radicals" stayed away from this, as they had from the first two. At this time the question was current as to belief in a "personal God." The discussion had actually originated and was carried on chiefly among Christians. At one of the sessions in Cincinnati someone expressed himself hastily and perhaps unguardedly on this topic. This was deemed sufficiently important for a violent protest, issued by Samuel Hirsch of Philadelphia, who "as author of an Hegelian philosophy of the Jewish religion," cannot have meant seriously to defend the proposition that God is "personal, real, and substantiated." Again from this controversy Wise learned the old lesson:

> In the East the incident showed that the Rabbis are not leaders, and it induced me to abandon the hope of ever finding sympathy with them. I stopped bothering about them, and I resolved I would appeal to the people.[19]

The number of rabbis attending these meetings was increasing, for there were twenty-seven in Cincinnati. Officers were elected. There was an introductory address by Lilienthal. Wise had brought with him proposals in regard to the services for *Yom Kippur*, and these were referred to a committee. Wise moved again that the Conference be made permanent; that all rabbis should have the right to join; that it meet annually; that a committee be appointed to formulate a code of laws for the government of the conference; that it favor and attempt to organize a "Hebrew Congregational Union," also a Synod; and lastly that it should find ways and means to solicit support for all these projects. A congregational union was to come into existence when thirty congregations would agree to join, with a total membership of not less than three thousand. These suggestions were all referred to a committee on "seminary."[20]

Rabbi Tuska of Memphis had died, and memorial resolutions were read. It was decided to reprint *Minhag America*, when the work of the conference would have been completed; to substitute a one-year cycle of readings from the Torah in place of the three-year one; and to draw up plans for a seminary. Attempts had been made to persuade the "stand-outs," the rabbis who still refused to attend with their colleagues, to join, but this had not met with success. There were recommendations from a committee on "circuit-preaching." At forthcoming conferences a "lecture was to be given," presumably by a member, and this was to be assigned in advance. There was a committee on synagogal music. Sonnenschein proposed that the name of the congregational union to be formed should be changed to "The Union of Israelite Congregations of America." This was adopted. The number of congregations and members Wise had suggested be regarded as adequate for a beginning was reduced. A vote of thanks to Wise was passed. It was proposed that the next conference convene in Washington, that it meet annually, and that it discuss the whole problem of *Shechita* (ritual slaughtering). Some committees were appointed, including an Executive Committee.[21]

In general, and coupled with other events which we shall chronicle in the remainder of this chapter, one cannot avoid the feeling that events were moving swiftly and surely toward congregational and rabbinical union. This Wise himself felt, and doubtless the conviction brought him profound satisfaction. In an editorial entitled "The Importance of the Conference," Wise contended that it had been the most momentous of all those held by the rabbis and that it would prove to be an epochal chapter of Jewish history in America. He asserted that half of the rabbis of the land had been present, that an excellent spirit had prevailed, that much learning had been exhibited, and that its accomplishments had not been paltry. Above all, it was necessary to form a congregational union. The place of the next meeting had been transferred from Washington to Chicago.[22] Wise made record also of the fact that among other objectives the conference had resolved: to unite on behalf of Judaism for the creation of a scholastic institution, and for the education of preachers and teachers; to publish cheap editions of the Bible and of religious-school texts; to support weak congregations; and to inaugurate a Synod which was to meet every third year. Wise did not seem at this time to conceive of the Synod as a modern Sanhedrin, but probably as a new name for the rabbinical conference itself.[23] And last of all Wise commented sadly upon the fact that Jastrow and Hirsch, both of Philadelphia, were still issuing protests against the Conference.[24]

Wise's progress toward his long-time objective of a congregational union was evident in more ways than at these rabbinical meetings. After all, the central motive-force would have to come from the congregations, from leading laymen who would be convinced that this was an imperative step and who would cooperate with him in bringing it about. The entire record shows that he was making appreciable progress in this direction. It is unfortunate that our material is inadequate at this point. It would be helpful to have the correspondence, doubtless voluminous, which he was carrying on with men in congregations outside Cincinnati, especially in the Middle West and South, and to know exactly what he said in pulpits and in parlor-meetings on his numerous trips. For him the whole plan was of a piece. He wanted a seminary, but he had come to realize that there was but one method of getting this, through the previous creation of a congregational union, which would furnish the necessary power and the necessary funds.

In February, 1870, he wrote an editorial, on "Education for the Pulpit," in which he used these prophetic words:

> If we want a seminary we must have a convention to establish and support it. . . . As long as the congregations do not meet in convention and adopt measures and have them carried out by their executive committees, the community at large will take no interest in the matter.[25]

At the end of July, in the previous year, he had called attention to the fact that thirteen congregations had already voted in favor of calling together a "conference of congregations." He assured his readers that, as soon as seven more would join these thirteen, this meeting would be called.[26] He had coupled this a little later with an appeal for the establishment of a theological seminary, and had asked that as soon as possible practical plans should be drawn.[27] The growing use of *Minhag America* was excellent, but it was not enough. It was his intention—he wrote—to organize:

1. A Seminary Association, to establish such an institution "somewhere in this country."
2. A publication society.
3. A Hebrew School Union.
4. A perpetual union of congregations.[28]

Every few weeks Wise was calling attention to the steps that were being taken to achieve one or the other of his main objectives. Among the congregations that had indicated their willingness to join a national union were some of the oldest and largest in the land. Wise himself was of the opinion that, though the time was approaching, it was still premature to call a national meeting, for this would tend to create disunity. It was his hope that, after the rabbinical meeting (which we have described) to be held in Cincinnati in the summer of 1871, perhaps a hundred congregations would then be willing to make a beginning.[29]

A few weeks later he wrote an editorial, "The Seminary Again and the New York Circular," which latter was addressed to the rabbis and officers of all reform congregations in the name of the Emanuel Theological Seminary Association of New York. "Men of dignity" had signed the circular. The purpose of the institution to be created was to educate rabbis and to found a home for Hebrew literature. The circular asserted that capital of between six and seven thousand dollars would be needed. Up to that time no wealthy man had come forward in New York. Wise contended that it would be a mistake to place confidence in the generosity of the masses. He was certainly not opposed to this undertaking, wished it well, hoped that it would find a prompt and favorable response, and ended with these characteristic words:

> Tell them to thank heaven that Isaac M. Wise is in Cincinnati, and not in New York.[30]

That summer, in an editorial on "The New Scheme," he announced that he was serving as chairman of a committee which had been appointed at a meeting in reference to the "Board of Delegates" to submit a plan for a theological seminary. In the future he would publish plans and would like them discussed. His estimate for expenses was far above that of the New York circular, for here he said that $300,000 would be "indispensably necessary." Who would subscribe the first $5,000 and "render his name immortal in the history of American Judaism?"[31]

Once again he was writing of *Minhag America* as a way-point on the path to congregational unity. He noted that for a time Einhorn himself had agreed to go along, but only with the English part of the liturgy:

> The liturgical question settled, and there is nothing in our way to cement a lasting union.[32]

Soon thereafter, under the heading "Let Us Be One," he was appealing for the firm establishment of an annual conference of rabbis to discuss theological questions, and of a Board of Delegates to do the business of the community. Upon the latter every congregation was to be represented.[33] On September 9, he wrote another editorial with an even stronger title: "We Must Be One." Whatever sacrifices would be found necessary to achieve unity must be made. The air was full of violence and bitter words, but they would soon be forgotten. He proposed that the rabbis unite in a conference, and the congregations under an expanded and reorganized "Board of Delegates." It was to be the principle of differentiation that rabbis would deal with all theological questions and make proposals to the Board of Delegates, which in its turn was to endow "colleges," especially a theological seminary, to provide "traveling preachers," to furnish classical Jewish literature, to assist poor congregations, to erect synagogues, and to correspond with similar bodies in Europe. "All this without disadvantage to any individual or congregation."[34] Wise was groping for a form, a method, which would utilize existing machinery and transform it into broader purposes of unity and of creation.

He claimed once again that the need for a seminary was especially acute, and that this need was best demonstrated by the prevailing ignorance, and by the venom of men now in the pulpit.[35]

His own congregation was following his progress closely and was giving him all the support within its power, in liberty of action, in its own espousal of his aims, and in the active cooperation of some able laymen. In the fall of 1871 B'nai Yeshurun adopted a resolution favoring the creation of a Synod, and of a Union and a Seminary.[36] And later Moritz Loth, the first president of the Union when it did come into existence, and one of its strongest and ablest advocates, dispatched an "address" to the congregations of the Middle West and South, proposing to them the formation of a Union and of a rabbinical seminary.[37] In that same month, again at the suggestion of Mr. Loth, B'nai Yeshurun requested its sister-congregations in Cincinnati to go along with it in summoning a meeting of congregations.[38]

In April, 1871, doubtless with Wise in the background, Lilienthal and Cohen had issued a call to congregations. Huebsch of New York presided, and there were nineteen rabbis present. Congregations from Ohio, Pennsylvania, Virginia, New York, Kentucky, Missouri, Louisiana, Illinois, Kansas and Indiana, were represented. Those present adopted a resolution proposed by Isaac M. Wise, to form a "Hebrew Congregational Union":

> With the purpose to advance the union of Israel, to establish a scholastic institution and a library, appertaining thereto for the education of rabbis, preachers and teachers of religion, to provide a cheap edition of English Bibles. . . . And provided that a meeting should be held whenever twenty congregations, representing 2000 members, appointed delegates.

This was the meeting, referred to above, at which Mayer of Cleveland said that he did not believe in a "personal God." All the members, Wise declared, were aware of Mayer's "radicalism," and took no notice of this declaration. But the second day the papers appeared with a sensational account, headed: "Rabbis do not believe in a Personal God." This incident was again seized upon, especially by Einhorn and Hirsch, to discredit Wise and the effort to establish a union and a college. A protest appeared in the *Jewish Times* of New York, signed by almost all Eastern rabbis.[39] This included much abuse of Wise, who was entirely innocent in relation to this incident. Again Eastern support was alienated and the breach between Einhorn and Wise widened. Wise wrote:

> This attack forced me to the conclusion, that the rabbis will never build a union, they will never be able to construct an American Judaism.[40]

Through opposition, against vituperation, despite indifference, Wise forged ahead. He was on the very eve of success, and all the hatred and the contrariety would not suffice to stop him.

Meanwhile Wise was living his life, carrying on the manifold activities and interests which flowed along from year to year. Despite his concentration upon his chief goals, his life was not pre-empted by them. He found time for contact with a host of friends, for pastoral duties, for his carefully prepared discourses, and for some participation in public life.

He and his wife, Theresa, celebrated the silver anniversary of their marriage on June 6, 1869. His congregation had had a large and warm "demonstration" for it. He had been given a check for five thousand dollars, a considerable amount at that time. There was an address by their good friend, Lilienthal. Good wishes from the board of his congregation, and from many, many others, had been transmitted to them. The teachers of the Talmud Yelodim Institute had their place in the celebration. It was a memorable day and was noted in the Cincinnati newspapers.[41] The celebration had been at Floral House in College Hill. Wise was there with his wife and children by his side. The choir of the Temple sang under the direction of Carl Barus. There was an address also by Henry Mack, the president of the congregation, who presented not only the gift mentioned, but also a long scroll signed by members and trustees. A youth of fifteen years of age, Joseph Friedman, presented Wise with an "easy chair." There was a poem by Minna Kleeberg, the wife of the rabbi of Louisville, and resolutions from B'nai Israel, read by Lilienthal. Wise responded to all this. There was even a grandson present, the son of the Benjamin Mays. Many Christian ministers and journalists were also present. All in all, it was a very warming and happy occasion.[42]

Wise was continuing his original policy of series of lectures on late Friday evenings, his device that had been copied in many lands and which—he claimed often—kept the Sabbath eve alive. Near the end of 1869 he announced that soon after the beginning of the year he would inaugurate a course of lectures on "The Talmud and the Gospels, A Historical Inquiry into the Origins of Christianity." This proved to be the basis for a book which he published later on.[43] At this time the Friday evening services at the Plum St. Temple were beginning at seven o'clock.[44]

An important event in his life was an invitation to open the Senate of the United States with prayer.[45] The prayer was delivered on May 20, 1870, and read as follows:

> O Lord, who art power, wisdom and justice, absolute and infinite, who lookest upon the earth and it trembles, who touchest the mountains and they smoke, and yet, in thy boundless grace hast girded man with might from thy might, hast enlightened his mind with wisdom from thy wisdom, and hast

impressed his conscience with justice from thy justice, who hast mercifully granted us the sacred boons of freedom and government, and hast appointed this land to a home of righteousness, an Eden of liberated humanity, a rock of hope and banner of consolation to struggling nations; we beseech thee to vouchsafe thy gracious blessings to this body of our chosen men, that they deliberate wisely, resolve justly, and far from selfishness and vain ambition wield the power vested in them to the prosperity of our country, the realization of justice, the progress of freedom, the triumph of humanity, and the elevation of human nature; that prosperity and justice, freedom and peace, righteousness and wisdom be forever the united gems in the diadem of our country, the banner of victory unfurled to all nations and tongues. And mayest thou pour out upon these favored sons of the nation the spirit of wisdom and intelligence, the spirit of counsel and might, the spirit of knowledge and the fear of the Lord. So may it be thy will, Father of the universe, now and forever. Amen!

This was not the first time that a Jew had opened one of the Houses of Congress with prayer. The entire record is given by Dr. Bertram W. Korn in a chapter entitled "The First Jewish Prayer in Congress."[46] That honor was given to Rabbi Morris J. Raphall, before the House of Representatives, on February 1, 1860.

In 1870, Wise made a long tour of the eastern part of the country, delivering three lectures which he had previously given in his own pulpit: "On the Origin of Christianity (Jesus, the Apostles, and Paul)." He went from New York to New Orleans. In New York the lectures were given at Steinway Hall.[47]

In the same year reports of massacres of Jews in Rumania reached the United States. Great excitement pervaded the communities, and meetings of protest and appeal were held. Resolutions were despatched to Congress. Senator Sumner asked the State Department for information on these barbarities. Wise got up a meeting in Cincinnati which demanded that the Rumanian government apprehend and punish the criminals responsible for these inhumanities, a forlorn hope, indeed![48]

Toward the end of the year Wise left Cincinnati and paid a fairly extended visit to New York, in the course of which he was present at the cornerstone-laying of Congregation Ahavath Chesed, Lexington Ave. and 55th Street, the present Central Synagogue, of which the rabbi then was Adolph Huebsch. The cornerstone was laid on December 14, 1870.[49]

In the summer of the following year Wise sent a letter to the

Augsburg Synod, which was read by Abraham Geiger. Wise said:

> I intended to visit the synod, but I am unfortunately "*Eved Olom*" (a perpetual slave).

He went on to describe the interest manifested in the synod by American Jews, and closed, "May God bless you."[50]

Late in 1871 Wise inaugurated another series of lectures on post-biblical history.[51] His next was on rabbinical literature, and without question these were intended to supplement each other.[52]

On a visit to Rochester, N. Y., he had lectured at the Athenaeum on "Our Country's Place in History."[53] In the fall of 1872 he began a series on Hebrew philosophy and philosophers.[54]

In the *Israelite* there was an occasional paragraph or sentence about his health to the effect that he was not too well and would have to diminish the pace and extent of his activities, especially that he must give up traveling so much "and enjoy more regular night rests."[55] It would have been astonishing if the number and tension of his bewildering activities had not occasionally told on him. But there is no evidence at any of these times that he cut down, or that he stopped rushing about the country.

And, finally, for this chapter, we shall note that in the fall of 1872 Wise announced the publication of *Judaism, Its Doctrines and Duties*, to which we have referred above, a catechism intended for the instruction of the young, a reworking of his earlier *The Essence of Judaism*.[56]

27

The Crowning Years

BY EVERY INDICATION THE TIME WAS VERY NEAR AT HAND WHEN Isaac M. Wise would attain some of his chosen goals, when he would succeed in calling into being a Union and a College. Announcements, efforts in diverse directions, the growing response, and behind all these the feeling that a consciousness of the inevitability of these steps was broadspread, the discussions at several rabbinical conferences, some of the correspondence in the pages of the *Israelite;* all these were indications of the converging of possibilities. The opposition to Wise was as intense and as vituperative as ever, but it had little effect on congregations outside the Eastern seaboard. His own activity was incessant. He was writing and speaking on behalf of a Union all the time. Between 1855 and 1873 he had visited almost every Jewish community, large or small, from Missouri to the Atlantic, and from New Orleans to New York. He had lectured to large and attentive audiences, had laid the cornerstones of numerous synagogues, and then usually dedicated them upon their completion. He had been active in the councils of the B'nai Brith, and had gone to various cities to install new lodges. His name had become a household word in American Israel, certainly far beyond that of any other rabbi or Jewish leader of that time in America. Wherever he went, whatever he did, he never failed to speak of the one central, imperative necessity for joint action, for brotherly union, for raising the level of knowledge among American Jews, and for training American spiritual leaders. Certainly, in the twenty-five years or more since his coming to America, things had developed markedly. There was no such paucity of well-trained rabbis as there had been. But those that were in American pulpits were without exception men who had been educated, and who had usually begun their careers, in Germany or in Austria. There had been some tentatives at union for defense, for education, for counsel; the Board of Delegates, Maimonides College, etc. But these had been either abortive, or limited—according to Wise—to partisan groups and partisan points of view. Jews were still divided, in accordance with their derivation (*Landsmannschaften*), by the lack of any real unanimity of approach among rabbis and lay leaders, and by specific differences on matters of ritual and creed. Among certain groups and with certain men minor divergences in belief, or in practice, were permitted to inhibit any genuine cooperation on larger issues.

The total picture showed very clearly that Wise did not have in mind the creation of a sectional, or partisan group. Though he was convinced that moderate reform was necessary and that it could be accepted by all on the American scene without doing violence to traditional Judaism, it was not his primary objective to cultivate this approach, to insist that it alone must become the basis of united action. He wanted *one* congregational organization, and *one* school, not only for rabbis, but for teachers, laymen, Christian clergy, and others. For a time, as we shall see, he believed that he was on the very point of attaining this end.

Some of his habitual emphasis was also upon the "American" character of this enterprise. Judaism was *the* religion of the nineteenth century, and in the twentieth it was sure to win a comprehensive victory. It was the religion *par excellence* that went along with the democratic, humanitarian ideas of America. All of this should be signalized by adaptations in creed and verbal form. It should be basic to the method and the character of Jewish associations and Jewish theological institutions. It would, however, be incorrect and unjust to assume that, because of this, Wise was of the opinion that what he regarded as the ageless essentials of Judaism should be modified or abandoned. There was no need for this and there would be no purpose in it. By divine good fortune—as he saw it—the two went together, the rational, philosophic, spiritual purpose of Judaism, and the "liberal," libertarian dedication of America.

He was persistently misunderstood. In and out of season the Jewish press outside Cincinnati berated him. Just at the time of the first meeting of the Union of American Hebrew Congregations, the *New York Jewish Times* contained these sneering words:

> The whole movement which, we are sorry to say, is on a level with all the plans and schemes which were set on foot by Dr. Wise. They can not rise above the commonplace. And this last product of his feeble brain will fare no better; it also will end in dust and smoke. . . .
>
> And it matters little to him [Wise] what the result of these fanfaronades are [sic!]; they help to spread his name and fame; for all we know, if he lives long enough, he will, with such undaunted energy as he possesses, yet succeed in being made the Jewish Archbishop of American Israel. . . . But how does the thing stand in reality? What is accomplished? A sectional division is created which will retard the work of genuine union for years to come. . . . None of the representatives are so unsophisticated as to believe that Eastern congregations will consent to join them in something in which they had no voice, where their advice and co-operation had been rejected by a distant statement that only Southern and Western congregations were asked to attend.
>
> Every one not blinded by prejudice or partisanship must know that the largest number of Israelites are found in the East and North, that the most prominent scientific minds are ministers of Jewish congregations in the East; that the greatest wealth exists there, and that a "union" of American congregations from which the congregations of New York, Philadelphia, Baltimore, and other cities, are left out, is a nonentity, and that such gigantic enterprise as the establishment of a Jewish high school can, if at all, be supported only by the united shoulders of all congregations. . . .
>
> Let us take the most favorable average of one hundred members each [to each congregation that joined] and we have three thousand individual members of the union. They are to pay one dollar a year per member, and we have the magnificent sum of three thousand dollars with which the Wise College is to be maintained.
>
> What a farce! Is it not bringing ridicule upon the effort and upon Judaism by thus exposing ourselves to the eyes of the world? . . . Why, it ($3,000 *per annum*) would not suffice to pay the salary of a single professor.[1]

All this disdain and all this cocksureness were answered by the event. Wise did succeed in just what this paper declared to be impossible. For some time it looked as though his union and his college would unite all American Jews. A non-partisan source concedes that he was the one person in American Jewish history most responsible for the orientation of American Jewish life about the synagogue, a fact that is still one of the central circumstances about our community.[2] Moreover, what he did during these very years with the Union of American Hebrew Congregations, and with the Hebrew Union College, became a pattern that was followed in essential ways by both Conservative and Orthodox Jews when somewhat later they came to organize their own national congregational associations and seminaries. It is impossible to overestimate the pervasive influence of his achievement, in spite of detractors, and in spite of the subsequent drift of American Jewish history. But the time has come to let the record speak for itself. We have already followed some of the preliminary steps, and we shall carry on the narrative from there.

In the fall of 1872 Wise's own congregation appointed a committee of twelve for the purpose of convoking a conference of congregations of the West, South, and Southwest, to form a union of congregations, which should have for its very first purpose: "The establishment of a Jewish Theological Faculty for the education of Jewish ministers and teachers."[3]

This does not seem to have had any immediate results, for early in the following year, following a recommendation of Moritz Loth of B'nai Yeshurun, the congregation got in touch with its sister-congregations in Cincinnati, B'nai Israel, of which Lilienthal was rabbi, and three others, to persuade them to go along in the effort to found a union, and again "to establish a seminary or college for the education of young Americans for the pulpit."[4] The purpose of this step, as the sequel displayed, was to send out a joint appeal, signed by representatives of five Cincinnati congregations, to congregations in the West and South, to meet in Cincinnati in July of that year, 1873, as a preliminary to union.[5] When the delegates from the Cincinnati congregations came together on March 30, 1873, they elected Julius Freiberg, of B'nai Israel, as their chairman, and Lipman Levy as secretary. All of this is recorded in an editorial in the *Israelite* headed: "Is It Coming?"[6] The names of the other congregations represented were: Ahavath Achim, Adath Israel, and Sherith Israel. The meeting was held in the vestry rooms of the Plum St. Temple and was called to order by Henry Mack. They discussed the methods of addressing other congregations, of raising funds, and other relevant questions.[7]

Meanwhile Wise was far from idle. The *Israelite* of this period had a reference in every issue to what was going on. It formulated a tentative plan of organization and proposals for a constitution. About a month later it announced that a general committee had been organized and had made the definite resolve to issue a call to all congregations of the sections mentioned:

> For a congregational convention to form a "Union of Congregations" under whose auspices a "Jewish Theological Institute" shall be established, and other measures adopted, which will advance the prosperity of our religion.[8]

Later in the same month there was an announcement that the first conference to form a Union would be held in July.[9] And once again Wise sketched a possible constitution and outlined the primary purpose of the Union as that of establishing a "Hebrew-American Collegiate Association."[10] This he repeated a week later, except that this time he called the proposed theological institution: "The Hebrew and Rabbinical College."[11]

A very interesting editorial was in the *Israelite* of June 20, under the heading, "The Main Question." It deserves quotation *in extenso:*

> To intelligent men it appeared clearly impossible to build up Judaism in America . . . without passing through a thorough refining process of reform. Here the main trouble began. . . . None of the parties thought it possible to yield. . . . The reformers maintained Judaism could not exist here without going through a renovating reform, and the orthodox maintained reform Judaism is none at all. You must be orthodox or nothing. So the struggle began and was continued with considerable feeling on both sides. . . . Reform and orthodox congregations would not and could not co-operate. In the course of time the cause of reform was triumphant, and especially in the West, North, and South, where the young and rising communities started out at once on reform principles, and the older ones were obliged to follow the example set by congregation Bene Yeshurun, of Cincinnati, so that our orthodox congregations became few and far apart, by no means fanatical. . . .
>
> Thus, the nugatory effect of the reform movement on the united action by the Hebrew congregations would have been overcome long ago, if it had not been for our "great men." History teaches that whenever an old system is set aside by popular movement to bring about a new one, a large number of "great men" are called into existence. . . . These "great men" frequently become a great plague among the community for the time being, because their disputes are the disturbing element. . . . Hitherto American Judaism has not been able to get over the effect of "great men's" disputes and quarrels. . . . How shall we get over them, is a question which has engaged our attention for a long time, and here is the result of our reflection. We have grown from fifty to two hundred congregations in a quarter of a century. . . . Are we or are we not able to take care of our affairs without the lead of "great

> men?" If we are, let us do it in God's name. Let us shelve a few dozen of "great men" till our affairs are settled, and then let them call again. In order to get over them we must do a little while without them.
>
> This is the question now before the congregations, Are we sufficiently advanced to take care of our own affairs? Are we independent and intelligent enough to do it? . . . If we are minors no longer, if the work and combat of a quarter of a century have educated and trained us up to the point of independence and wise judgment, then in God's name let us unite and do our work to the best of our ability. July 8th this question will be decided for the present.
>
> Our confidence in the masses was always strong and invincible. Therefore, we started at the very first conference in Cleveland with the idea of a union of congregations by chosen representatives. But it was defeated in 1855. . . . We reiterated it in the Philadelphia Conference (1869) and it was defeated on the spot. Again we brought it up in the Cincinnati conference (1871) and it failed again, always by the particular work of our "great men." Now the question is before the congregations in an entirely new shape. It comes as a proposition of sixty Cincinnatians representing five congregations. No congregation can ignore it without loading upon itself the blame of many of its members. None can reject it without giving its reasons to the world why this or that body refuses to co-operate with its sister congregations in the great work of union. . . .
>
> Now the question will be decided, Are we ripe for the great work, or are we to remain minors a little while longer until we can pick up courage enough to go and do that which should be done, that which is our duty before God and man? Our confidence is unshaken. We hope. We wait impatiently, because we know on the eighth of July Judaism can open a new era of its history in America, or declare its incompetency, to be dragged along many a year to come.[12]

Seven days later the *Israelite* announced that the organization meeting would be held in a "fine hall," the Melodeon, at Fourth and Walnut Streets, beginning at 10 A.M. on July 8, 1873.[13]

Delegates from thirty-four congregations assembled, and without extended discussion resolved to organize a Union of American Hebrew Congregations, the main purpose of which would be:

> To establish a Hebrew Theological College to preserve Judaism intact, to bequeath it in its purity and sublimity to posterity, to Israel united and fraternized, to establish, sustain, and govern a seat of learning, for Israel's religion and learning.[14]

The thirty-four congregations that met on July 8 represented twenty-eight cities. The historic session was closed by Isaac M. Wise with prayer, and it is not difficult to imagine the fervor and the gratitude that must have infused that prayer.[15] The *Israelite* carried a detailed report of this momentous meeting, which lasted from July 8 to July 10. It contended that not a harsh word had been spoken. Moritz Loth presided. A constitution was adopted. The Union was to meet annually (later its conventions were made biennial). Its first object was the establishment of "The Hebrew College." It discussed methods of raising funds. The members of the first Executive Board were chosen. All the congregations of Ohio were represented, and, besides them, congregations from Texas, Louisiana, Arkansas, Mississippi, Georgia, Tennessee, Kentucky, Missouri, West Virginia, Michigan, Illinois, and Indiana; in all, thirteen states. The next convention was planned for the following summer in Cleveland. It was estimated that the congregations represented in that summer of 1873 had a combined membership in the neighborhood of 2000. The *Israelite* concluded its account with the boast that a new chapter had been written in the history of American Israel, and Wise expressed the fervent hope that before long the new Union would draw in every American Jewish congregation.[16] Wise's spirit and his prayers were well-expressed in some of the closing words of the article:

> The youngest child was born. . . . The child was born in peace, brotherly love, and beautiful harmony. . . . The new chapter in our history begins with peace and sends forth the ancient salutation *Shalom Aleichem*, "Peace to all of you". . . .[17]

A beginning had been made for the first time since Wise had issued his original proclamation in 1848. The Union was genuine. It began with high hopes. But it comprised only a minority of American Jewish congregations, and it was very young. As the *New York Jewish Times*—in the vitriolic article quoted above—had contended, the wealthy Eastern congregations were opposed to this new venture and stayed out of it. Somewhat later, after he had been made president of the newly born Hebrew Union College, Wise wrote some words about himself, a few of which are very much in place here:

> Isaac M. Wise has many and fierce opponents. He has projected and worked too much not to have them. No public spirited man can ever escape them. But he has many more ardent and faithful friends, whose confidence he fully possesses and who are always ready to support him heartily. His opponents who

> were also opponents of the Union of American Hebrew Congregations will, of course, decry his election.
>
> In his official capacity he recognizes no opponents, no enemies, he will work for the benefit of all, and however humble an individual he may be, he will always be guided by the principle, "The disciples of the sages augment the peace of the world." He will have no isms and no schisms to impose, no sophistries to defend, no superstitions to advocate, no prejudices to foster. . . .[18]

It should be noted once again that, as a result of his experience of many years, because of the significance of his failures, Wise had come to realize that the way to a College was through a Union. Already in 1865 he had written:

> We shall never be silent until we have roused the congregations of Israelites to a consciousness of their duty.

The logic to which circumstances had forced him was: first an alliance of congregations; then a college.[19] But this was not the sole end of the Union. It was to work toward the solidarity of the Jews of the United States, to arouse their self-respect, to help them defend themselves, and to raise them in the esteem of the American people.[20] Every matter of doctrine was excluded in the concept of the organization and a specific assurance was written into the constitution of the autonomy of individual congregations who had affiliated or would affiliate with it.[21]

The second meeting of the Union was announced for Cleveland, for July 14, of 1874.[22] This meeting was duly held. Twenty-one more congregations responded, so that the total represented the second year came to fifty-five.[23] An extended report of the second convention was in the *Israelite* of July 17, 1874, and a long resolution enacted by the convention, implementing the opening of the Hebrew Union College was reproduced.[24] Wise followed with an editorial, in which he declared proudly that this had been not a "western," but a truly "national" assembly. Some of its critics might claim that it was insignificant, but:

> This is a national affair of the greatest importance to the House of Israel on this continent.

It had already launched many important tasks: the publication and distribution of a cheap Bible; Sabbath-school education; the Hebrew Union College; and "circuit-preaching":

> We passed those days in a peculiar state between waking and

> sleeping, thinking and dreaming. Is it possible that the phantasms of our youth have resurrected and put on tangible bodies?[25]

In the following year Wise claimed that the Union was now reaching all the way across the country, from Portland, Oregon, to Philadelphia and Charleston, S.C.; from Texas to the Great Lakes.

> It is the youngest and most promising institution of the Israelites in this country. . . .

The next convention was to be in Philadelphia in July, 1875, and, he predicted, it would probably represent two-thirds of the congregations of the country, "to cement a fraternal union of all American Israelites."[26]

Evidently things were moving rapidly, for the following month the *Israelite* recorded that eighty-two congregations had affiliated with the Union.[27] For some unstated reason the place of meeting was changed to Buffalo, where the assembly was held beginning on July 13, 1875. Nor was this an undistinguished body of pedestrian representatives. Wise took pride in listing the eminent men who were already a vital part of the Union, and who would presumably be at Buffalo.[28]

Shortly thereafter he wrote of the Union in words that bear out many of the things we have written heretofore:

> The Union of American Hebrew Congregations is "Israel's new glory," and is destined to bind all the Israelites of this great country into one great union, under whose auspices the greatest glories that Israel has ever achieved will be accomplished.[29]

In the fall of the same year a letter was sent to all congregations not yet affiliated with the Union, over the signatures of Moritz Loth, president, and Lipman Levy, secretary, appealing to them to join at the earliest moment.[30]

We shall not follow the destinies of the Union of American Hebrew Congregations further at this point. In later chapters we shall note those events at its annual, or biennial, meetings which had a bearing on Wise himself. Suffice it to add for the present that in 1876 at its Washington convention the Union adopted a resolution to meet with a committee of the Board of Delegates for the purpose of bringing about the unification of that body with the Union, and so that "all Hebrew congregations of the United States" might thus be enabled to join.[31] We shall come somewhat later to the success of this project.

Let us now turn back and review some of the events and causes that led to the opening of the Hebrew Union College. This too—as we have noted often before—was a consistent purpose of Wise from the beginning of his American career. The first sign that his efforts would bear fruit came in February, 1873, when his oft-reiterated appeals for support, for the coming forward of some wealthy man or men, with enough spirit and understanding to envisage the needs of American Jews, found a response. This was on the part of Henry Adler, of Lawrenceburg, Indiana, who addressed a communication to Congregation B'nai Yeshurun of Cincinnati, of which he was a member, offering to deposit $10,000 as an endowment for a "Jewish Theological Faculty." This gift became the nucleus of a fund that aided the College in its first years.[32]

Shortly thereafter Wise published another editorial on the need for a "Theological Faculty," and claimed that he would be able to get along with a faculty of not more than three men. This proved to be prophetic, as we shall soon discover.[33] As soon as the Union had actually come into existence Wise called on all congregations to join it, and announced that a Board of Governors had been appointed to work out a code of laws and a curriculum for a College.[34] This was in pursuance of one of the decisions of the Union that it would found a College in which "the future advocates of our religion shall be educated."[35] It is interesting to record also that even at this time Wise had not made up his own mind that the institution was to be solely for the purpose of educating rabbis.[36] Many times in previous pages we have remarked that his original idea had been to have a "Jewish university" with various faculties, and with secular as well as religious departments. Obviously he had abandoned this original plan somewhat reluctantly, and came in the end to confine himself to a theological institution.

When the Union came to adopt a curriculum for the Hebrew Union College, it resolved also to found a seminary for Jewish girls, to establish a publication society, and to work toward better observance of the Jewish Sabbath. It promulgated rules for the conduct and aid of "Sabbath schools." Many of these will be recognized as Wise's own objectives over the course of many years.[37]

It was at the Cleveland convention of the Union, in 1874, that a Board of Governors for the College was selected which very soon thereafter had its first meeting. It elected a president of the future institution, Wise himself, and officers of its own.[38] Of the choice of himself Wise wrote in the *Israelite*:

> We deem it our duty to speak a few words for the president-elect, and may say that he considers it the highest honor which

> could have been conferred upon him. Neither a seat in the Senate of the United States, nor the office of Chief Justice appears to him as responsible and honourable a position as the presidency of the Hebrew Union College, where the finest opportunity is offered to contribute largely to the education of the young people of our country; to lay a solid foundation to the future greatness of American Judaism, and to promulgate Hebrew learning, to raise high the moral and intellectual standard of Judaism. . . . An arduous task has been imposed on him with this honour. It is no small enterprise to organize and build up a seat of learning for the education of the rising and coming generations. This will take more work than is commonly supposed, and can be successfully accomplished only by the earnest and unanimous support of the Board of Governors, faculty, and the executive committee of the Union, the confidence and hearty support of our co-religionists in general, upon whom he relies, to all of whom he sends fraternal greetings with the solemn promise always to do his duty fully to the best of his knowledge and ability. It will be the object of his life and happiness to afford the opportunity to the young Israelites of our country to acquire an academical and enlightened education, to take out into practical life the wisdom and truth amassed in the treasures of Israel's rich literature.[39]

The Board of Governors, newly created by the second council of the Union, met in the vestry-rooms of the Plum St. Temple for the final steps in the organization of the Hebrew Union College. It was announced that the Preparatory Department would open on October 3, 1875. Some students had already registered, and would be placed in good homes for board and lodging. It was calculated that the annual expense per student would be between four and five hundred dollars. The original faculty was to consist of Isaac M. Wise as president, and Solomon Eppinger for the D-grade (the lowest class of the Preparatory Department). Wise was to teach history, and the formal opening of the institution was set for October 3 at the Plum St. Temple. This, said Wise, in the *Israelite*, would inaugurate a new chapter in the history of American Israel.[40]

One of the problems was that of the academic training of the students at the College, for from its actual beginning it was realized that the institution could not be both a secular and a rabbinical school. Often before Wise had contended that he wanted to establish such a seminary in the neighborhood of a good university. As early as 1860 it had been proposed to found a University in Cincinnati, but the Civil War, and continued litigation over a bequest made in 1859 by Andrew McMicken, delayed matters. In his will in that year McMicken had left a large estate to the city with the provision that a college for "white boys and girls" was to be built upon it.[41] It was not until 1873 that the University of Cincinnati was opened, and its academic department was McMicken College. To this institution many classes of the Hebrew Union College went, and from it they received their academic degrees. Some came much younger than the age at which they could matriculate in a university, as members of the preparatory department of the College, and these went to Woodward High School, or later to Hughes High School, of the public-school system of the city.

At last all the preparatory decisions and the plans were over, and the formal opening of the College took place. The exercises were held at the Plum St. Temple on October 3, 1875. Addresses were delivered by Bernard Bettmann, Chairman of the Board of Governors, by Rabbi Sonnenschein of St. Louis, by Max Lilienthal, and by Isaac M. Wise. In the course of his own address Wise said:

> Little remains to be said after all the eloquent addresses unless he should speak of the gladness and delight that he felt that at last, after twenty-five years of toil and struggle, this great project of the Hebrew College is being realized, but he feels incapable to do this well; he lacks words to do justice to his feelings.[42]

Later on, in a reminiscential series in the *Deborah*, Wise wrote of the time and of the occasion. The actual sessions of the Hebrew Union College were held in the basement of the Mound Street Temple, B'nai Israel, (8th and Mound Streets, in downtown Cincinnati; the temple still stands and is used by a Negro church). Fourteen "noisy boys" constituted the student-body. Four of them—Wise wrote—wanted to study, and ten solely to create a disturbance. The place could not be run by Eppinger alone and Wise had to help. Thus once again he became a schoolmaster. The class was originally divided into two sections. It was, he confessed, a little "hole-in-the-wall" school, located in a rather damp and dark cellar. Every night the books had to be locked up as a precaution against mice.[43] They had no English text-books, for at that time none existed. Most of the students did not understand German. Wise set himself to dictate a Hebrew grammar. For a history text he used Josephus. One of his greatest difficulties was with instruction in Talmud and Maimonides. To use his own words, the only texts available were in "Polish-German Jargon." He used some of his "spare" time to translate *haggadic* sections of the Talmud, and some selections from Maimonides' *Sefer Hammada* (that part of the Code which Maimonides made of the rabbinic law which deals with religious beliefs), and parts of the *Moreh Nevuchim* (*The Guide to the Perplexed,* Maimonides' great Aristotelian-Jewish philosophic work). These products of his own labor he printed in the *Israelite,* and then had them reproduced for class use.

But Wise was full of hope and of joy in the task. A year later[44] he wrote modestly of himself:

> I thank the Almighty that I am deemed worthy of cooperation in this work of Israel's resurrection.

There were at the beginning three departments planned for the College: a preparatory, a Hebrew classical or collegiate, and a rabbinical or graduate. The first of the three was open to students who were attending or had completed high school or college. The Collegiate was open only to those who had gone through the preparatory department; and the rabbinical was open to graduates of the collegiate. The institution was also available for study by other than Jews, though—as far as the record goes—there were no non-Jews at the College in its earliest days.[45]

In 1876, one year after the opening of the College, Lilienthal was added to Wise and Eppinger as a member of the faculty. Neither Wise nor Lilienthal received any compensation for their services at the time, and Eppinger was paid only a very meager salary.[46]

A later account claimed that there were seventeen, not fourteen, pupils at the opening. Four of these completed the course in 1883: Israel Aaron, of Fort Wayne and then Buffalo; Henry Berkowitz, of Mobile, Kansas City, and then Philadelphia, where he succeeded Jastrow; David Philipson, of Baltimore (Har Sinai), and then Cincinnati, where he followed Lilienthal and Benjamin; and Joseph Krauskopf, of Kansas City and Philadelphia, where he succeeded Samuel Hirsch. The second class, which graduated in 1884, consisted of: Louis Grossmann, of Detroit, then assistant to Wise in 1898 and his successor; Max Heller, first with Felsenthal in Chicago, then at Beth Israel in Houston, and at Temple Sinai, New Orleans; Joseph Stolz, of Little Rock and Chicago; and Joseph Silverman, of Dallas, Galveston, and Temple Emanu-El, New York.[47] The record is still not quite straight, for the *Israelite* of the same period, in its account of the actual opening of the College, numbered only thirteen students, twelve regular who were in high school, and one in University. Five of them were Cincinnatians, and eight were from other cities.

Some of this discrepancy may have been the result of the fact that among the first students Wise enrolled were sons of his very good friends in Cincinnati who never had any genuine intention of going into the rabbinate, but who would surely not be harmed by being subjected to a little Hebrew education. Wise himself contended—again in the *Israelite*—that, had more funds been at hand, he could have begun with twenty-five students. He needed money to assist those who came from "abroad." He appealed for the creation of a sinking-fund, and also for money and books in general.[48]

For years it had been Wise's hope, and the hope of some of his best collaborators in his congregation, that the Talmud Yelodim Institute would train boys who would enter the rabbinate, and that from among them some of his disciples at the College might be recruited. A. J. Friedlander, chairman of the Talmud Yelodim Institute, wrote:

> May we live to see the Israel Theological College a reality, and the first scholars to enter the same be graduates of the Talmud Yelodim Institute.

Toward this end the directors of the Institute formed a preparatory class, intended to induce young men to enter the College. This was on October 18, 1874.[49] Eppinger also had been teaching there: *Mechilta*, Psalms, and Deuteronomy. The following year Mr. Friedlander reported:

> I am proud to say that the scholars of this class were among the first to enter the Hebrew Union College, the glorious opening of which we have witnessed a few weeks ago. May our young sons and daughters grow up with the College in honor to ourselves, and to Judaism at large.[50]

The actual beginning of the Union, and the opening of the College in 1873 and in 1875, did not bring to an end the insensate opposition of some leaders and some congregations. There were still efforts to organize a Hebrew Theological Seminary in the East. This did not appear to worry Wise unduly, for he bade his readers in the *Israelite* not to concern themselves with all this, and declared that it "will do no harm to anybody." Perhaps the New York congregations would stay out of the Union for a year or two more, but no longer![51]

Though it involves leaping ahead somewhat, it seems advisable to describe some relevant facts about the College at this point, and of Wise's relationship to it.

Every year Wise welcomed the new students who were entering the institution, with an appropriate address. Speaking once on the importance of scholarship, he said:

> There can be no victory without combat, no triumph without struggle, and the value of the one is measured by the intensity of the other. The student's combat is in his studies, and his triumphs in his learning. . . . Young men, the mystery of success lies in your acquisition of knowledge first, and an enthusiastic persistence in your work. Your knowledge is your capital. There is nothing profane in learning, and what is usually called profane learning is an important department of your studies. . . . Judaism must be studied in the products of the Hebrew mind, and these are preserved in Israel's great literature.[52]

He insisted constantly with his disciples that they must cultivate religious zeal. This was for him the *conditio sine qua non* of the rabbinate:

> The morality of the rabbinical student who seeks rabbinical honours from his Alma Mater, includes the possession of genuine religious zeal and enthusiasm. Without this he may become an actor in the pulpit, a polished elocutionist, a sensationalist, a seeker of plaudits, but no rabbi. I consider it my duty to admonish all present to leave this college, if they lack religious zeal and enthusiasm, for they never will be honest rabbis; their whole life would be criminal. If you do not possess this excellent quality, you must cultivate it assiduously, so that it may become permanent in your character; you must be conscientious in your religious practices as in your studies. . . .[53]

These were no idle words with him. They were intended with the utmost earnestness. Nor were they mere admonition; they rested upon his shining example and upon the warmth and charm of his own personal influence. By all accounts he was a splendid teacher who won at once the love and the confidence of his students. None of them could ever forget the kindness with which he had treated them, and they returned his love many fold. To the boys he was "Master," the original flavor of the word "Rabbi." He did not treat his work at the College in a cavalier mood. He prepared with the utmost care, and many of his later books were the direct result of his labors for the College; especially the second volume of his history, *The History of the Hebrews' Second Commonwealth*, published in 1880; and his *Pronaos to Holy Writ*, in 1891.[54] The anniversary of his death is commemorated at the College as Founder's Day.

The annual reports of the College, incorporated in the volumes of the Union of American Hebrew Congregations, give constant evidence of Wise's painstaking labors as head of the institution. He had a remarkable group of laymen on his Board of Governors, especially its chairman, Bernhard Bettmann, from 1875 until his retirement in 1911. In his last official report, on February 27, 1900, Wise told his co-workers that the College had reached the very zenith of its glory, after a quarter of a century of work. There was a faculty of nine distinguished men; the institution had graduated sixty-four rabbis, bestowed many honorary degrees, and at that time had a roster of seventy-three students.[55]

The course of the College in its earliest period consisted of eight years of instruction, four in the preparatory department, and four in the collegiate. The College remained in the vestry-rooms at Mound Street until 1877, when it removed to larger quarters at Plum Street. Later on, as we shall note, it had a building of its own on Sixth Street.[56]

Often Wise thought it might be sensible of him to retire. His burdens continued to be heavy. Perhaps, too, the institution might benefit financially. Then it would occur to him that an endowment of at least $150,000 would be needed to replace him, to compensate someone, or several people, to do his tasks. From 1875 to 1879 he received no money from the College, either as president, or as professor of theology and philosophy.[57] In December, 1879, he was voted by the Board of Governors the sum of $83.33 a month, until September, 1880, as an allowance toward his house rent. The reason for this was that it was his work at the College that compelled him to maintain a residence in the city in addition to his farm at College Hill.[58] From September, 1880, to March, 1900, the time of his death, he received an allowance of $50 a month for the expenses of his presidential office. In twenty years he received thus a total of $12,000, almost all of which he used to aid needy students, and not for himself.[59]

Every year his "boys" gathered about him, celebrated his birthday with him, and regarded him as a "venerable sage, a wise counsellor, a kind father."[60] His home and his table were always open to them. At the Seder meal on the Passover it was his practice to invite the whole student-body to his home, and it was always an occasion of great joy as well as of deep religious sentiment.[61]

One of his ideas which has been forgotten was to set up a preparatory department in New York. The Fifth Council of the Union, at Milwaukee, in July of 1878,[62] planned that Temple Emanu-El of

New York should run such a school; and the Sixth Council voted an appropriation for its maintenance. Later on—in February, 1887—it was reported that the "Board of Delegates of American Israelites" and a committee representing the Union of American Hebrew Congregations, had come to an agreement to establish a preparatory school for the College in New York.

Thus within two years two of Wise's dreams were translated from the realm of hope to that of actuality. In order to set before the reader a consecutive and consistent picture, we have concentrated upon these two sequences of events in relation to Union and College, and have passed over other important things that were happening in his life as a rabbi and as a man.

Certainly the most astonishing of these was a decision that he made, apparently with some degree of precipitateness in 1873. Even with all the material before us, the entire episode is not easy to understand. Wise seemed wedded to Cincinnati. The congregation loved him, revered him, and followed his leadership loyally. They had given him much latitude, and mobilized an astonishing group of laymen, astonishing both in number and ability, who stood by his side. Very rarely was there disagreement: over the Talmud Yelodim Institute, and in regard to his nomination for the State Senate in 1863. But these were not enough to have made any serious difference in his relation to the congregation, or theirs to him. He had come to them "for life." This provision had—in fact—been his own idea. In exactly what terms he thought of this as it applied to himself, it is not easy to decide. But the facts appear to indicate that, except in the case of "moral turpitude," this involved, as he thought of it, a permanent obligation on the part of the congregation; but that also it left him freedom to depart, if he thought it wise or necessary, for the good of American Israel, to terminate his arrangement with them and go elsewhere. Any other interpretation is hard to apply to what happened in 1873. Wise was fifty-four years old. He was at the height of his powers. His name was honorably and favorably known throughout the country. Suddenly he was offered the pulpit of Anshe Chesed in New York. He was informed of the terms of his election. In the Fiftieth Anniversary Booklet of the congregation, in the writing of which he had a large part, in 1892, the event was described thus:

> In August, 1873, Dr. Wise, thinking that he had been neglected somewhat by his congregation, and believing that he could

> extend his field of usefulness and more easily carry out his project for a union and a rabbinical college in the East, accepted a call from Congregation Anshe Chesed of New York City, which had elected him for life at an annual salary of $8000, house, rent, etc. The rabbi thereupon placed his resignation in the hands of the board, to take effect on the 26th of September, following. The Congregation refused to accept the resignation, and appointed a committee to wait on him.[63]

One of the most curious and inexplicable aspects of all this is that Wise had resolved to accept this election as rabbi of Anshe Chesed just one month after the epochal meeting at Melodeon Hall of thirty-four congregations, to organize the Union, and to proceed to the founding of the College. In spite of the language of the paragraph above, Wise's reasons for leaving Cincinnati, or wishing to leave, at this time, remain obscure. He had written and spoken countless times on the "little big men" of New York, on the unhealthy character of the Jewish community there, and on the arrogance and uncooperativeness of its rabbinical leaders. He had again and again written of Cincinnati as the ideal place for the headquarters of the Union, and for the founding of the College. How then could he suddenly decide to accept this offer, and to prepare to remove to New York?

More accuracy is possible from the minute-books of the congregation. Under date of August 19, 1873, there is the record of a special general meeting that was called:

> As the object of the meeting, the President stated that in behalf of the Board of Trustees he was instructed to present to the Congregation the following Document of Rev. Dr. Wise, received a few days previous, which contained his Resignation as Rabbi of this Congregation.[64]

Then follows a copy of the letter itself:

> Cincinnati, August 11, 1873.
>
> M. Loth, Esq., President of K.K.B.Y.
>
> Dear Sir:
>
> Having accepted a call of the Congregation Anshe Chesed of New York, although with deep regret and after a long and prayerful struggle, I must hereby tender my Resignation to K.K.B'nai Yeshurun, to take effect on the twenty-sixth day of September, 1873. I will at once confess that I love the Congregation, with whom I must part, but circumstances are of such a nature, that I think it is for the best of Israel and the Congregation B'nai Yeshurun especially, that such a change take

place. My attachment to the Congregation B'nai Yeshurun will not decrease by distance of locality, and I beg leave to consider you, personally, dear Sir, and all Members of the Congregation personal friends forever,

Yours,

Isaac M. Wise.[65]

In the *Israelite* he wrote of the offer in words that must have rung ominously and oddly in the ears of his friends in Cincinnati:

> It is the first time in the annals of Jewish history in America that such an offer has been made to a rabbi. This brings the *Minhag America* permanently to New York, and decides forever the value of all the protests and newspaper quarrels which were spread so profusely during the past two years.[66]

In reading these two paragraphs, his letter, and that from the *Israelite*, one is set wondering. What lay behind this sudden decision? Was it genuine dissatisfaction with some situation, or some fancied slight, in Cincinnati? Did Wise genuinely think it to the advantage of B'nai Yeshurun for him to leave? Deep down, was he attracted by this munificent offer from the very city where he had been most bitterly excoriated, flattered that behind all the vituperation was at least one congregation that wanted him, and that would go along with his ideas and his concepts of Reform? Had he given it careful thought, and come to the conclusion that at this strange moment, just after the meeting in Cincinnati in July, after the refusal of the Eastern congregations to attend, he would gain, or rather that the causes to which he was so intensely devoted would gain by his removal into the very midst of the theological maelstrom? No sufficient answer to any of these questions is possible, and no action of his life is more equivocal and more difficult to square with the remainder of it.

In K.K.B'nai Yeshurun there was the utmost consternation. One has to picture to oneself meetings hurriedly called, whispered conferences, chagrin and astonishment. The whole matter was at once referred to a special committee, consisting of Wise's most intimate friends: Bernhard Bettmann as chairman, and the other members, Henry Mack, Moritz Loth, B. Simon, Solomon Friedmann, Solomon Levi, and W. Rosenfeld. Five ex-presidents of the congregation were among these. At the annual meeting of the congregation, on September 28, B. Bettmann reported for the committee.[67] They had telegraphed to New York asking Anshe Chesed to release Wise from his engagement. A recess of ten minutes was taken at the annual meeting, while the committee spoke with their rabbi. Wise came into the meeting then, to the accompaniment of frantic applause. And, rather quietly, he told the meeting that he had agreed to reconsider, and that, if the New York congregation would release him, he would prefer to remain in Cincinnati.

At the outset of its deliberations the committee had drawn up a resolution which it had without question put into Wise's hands at once. It was B. Bettmann who was responsible, in the first instance, for its form:

> We hold that as no congregation has a right to remove from office for a trivial cause a Rabbi who has faithfully and consciously performed his duties, so no Rabbi, except for the promotion of a great principle, has a right to leave his congregation, so long as it unanimously claims his services, insists upon his continuance in office for life, and provides properly for him and his family.

The resolution continued with a charge against Anshe Chesed, that it "had made several efforts to induce Wise to accept a call," and that all this had been done without notification to B'nai Yeshurun, "thereby violating the comity which should mark the course of one congregation toward another." The resolution continued:

> Whereas, we have nevertheless without prejudice and actuated by an earnest desire to do justice to all parties concerned carefully examined all the facts in this case and can sincerely and honestly declare that we should consider the loss of our rabbi a sad bereavement, yet we should not hesitate one moment to sacrifice our personal feelings on the altar of our common cause, were we fully convinced that the interests of Judaism or the reverend gentleman, himself, could be promoted by the proposed change; and,
>
> Whereas, from a full knowledge of all the circumstances we are satisfied that such is not the case, and that on the contrary the departure of Dr. Wise at this time would especially be a great loss and perhaps a permanent injury to the young and rising congregations of the West, many of which sprang into existence through his influence, and almost all of which look upon him as their guide and teacher, demanding a closer proximity to them than this removal would make possible, and consequently his remaining with his congregation which for nearly a quarter of a century has stood by him as one man, and has invariably and joyfully supported him in his successful endeavors to elevate the cause of Judaism in this country, and may therefore justly claim for itself a little more than ordinary consideration at his hands;

> Be It Therefore Resolved, That reminding the Rev. Dr. Wise of his solemn promise given to us twenty years ago that he would devote the rest of his life to the furtherance of the holy cause of Israel as our rabbi and in our midst, a promise of which under the present circumstances we cannot and will not absolve him, we respectfully but firmly decline to accept his resignation;
>
> Resolved, That we respectfully and earnestly request Congregation Anshe Chesed to yield for the above reasons what they consider their newly acquired rights to our older and more firmly established ones."[68]

The gist of the resolutions was exceedingly simple, namely: that, in the estimation of his congregation, election for life was not a unilateral but a reciprocal obligation. At any rate, Anshe Chesed agreed to release Wise, and Wise agreed—not reluctantly—to remain in Cincinnati.[69]

Into Wise's life at this time came a very deep sorrow. The wife whom he had married when he was a young man of twenty-five, and while both of them were still in Bohemia; the wife whom he had come to know and love in the Bloch household in Grafenried while he was yet a student and was tutoring her two brothers; the wife who had left her home, fled across the border into Saxony, and crossed the stormy seas with him; who had shared all his hopes and fears, all his triumphs and defeats, came to her last days in 1874. By her bedside, when Theresa passed away on December 10, were eight children, four sons and four daughters. She was little more than fifty years of age, for she had been born on March 15, 1823. The last decade of her life had been of almost uninterrupted sickness and suffering. None of our sources mentions the nature of her illness, but all agree that for her last two years her mind was hopelessly clouded. This, Wise's own words which we shall cite in a moment, indicate.

Theresa Wise was deeply beloved by her husband, by her children, and by a host of friends. She was a gentle woman, especially kind to the poor. She shared her husband's love of music. In the end she had to be watched day and night, for in the autumn of 1874 she had fallen out of a window.

The *Israelite* announced that the funeral would be held at the Plum St. Temple and the funeral sermon delivered by her and Wise's dear friend, Lilienthal, who said, in part:

> She was a wife in the noblest sense of the word; but she was still more. She had some of those qualities which distinguish her husband. She was inspired by that indomitable courage

> which is not bowed down by the threatening struggles of life. She was blessed with that spirit of invincible hope which never despairs in the gloomiest hours of man's life. . . .[70]

To her memory Wise dedicated one of his finest books, *The Cosmic God.* He himself said that he had written this work to divert his mind during her long illness and to find the "consolations of philosophy." The words of its dedication read thus:

> To her, my beloved wife, who in life possessed my heart with its best affections, I dedicate in eternity my best thoughts.

And in the preface he wrote:

> This book, conceived in sorrow, composed in grief, and constructed at the brink of despair, contains my mind's best thoughts and my soul's triumph over the powers of darkness. My wife, my dearly beloved companion in this eventful life, the mother of my children, the faithful partner of my joys and sufferings, was prostrated with an incurable disease. For nearly two years she lived the life of a shadow, without affection or clear consciousness, no more herself than the ruin is the castle. I prayed, I wept, I mourned, I despaired; and yet my cup of woe was not full. . . . Ruthless attacks upon my character, of restless assailants, from the camp of implacable foes, embittered my joyless days. My energies failed. Insanity or suicide appeared inevitable. In this state of mind, the Satan of Doubt persecuted me with all his furious demons. . . . I plunged headlong into the whirlpool of philosophy. . . .[71]

For two years he was alone and, in the early months, deeply stricken. But his was a resilient spirit. It was not possible for him to remain forever in the valley of the shadow. He met another woman in New York. Exactly when and how the meeting took place we do not know. But Wise fell in love again, deeply and happily. The recipient of his affections was Miss Selma Bondi, daughter of the late Rev. Jonas Bondi, of a good rabbinical family, and herself a woman of great intelligence, culture, and strength. We possess the letters Wise wrote to her early in 1876.[72] Both are dead, now for many years, and it can do no harm to set down here some of his words to her, for they reveal him in a new light, as a passionate, poetical, and sometimes whimsical lover. These letters are in the Archives of the Hebrew Union College, and were originally in German. They were translated into English by Mrs. Bertha Lauter.

Cincinnati, April 6, 1876, 10 o'clock at night.

My dearest, beloved, sweetest Selma:

I arrived just an hour ago and I wired you. Before going to bed I send you a thousand kisses with all my love.

*S*elma dear, my sweetest bride,
*E*den's charms illume thy face;
*L*ovely is thy noble pride,
*M*atchless thy enchanting grace,
*A*ngel-like thy fairy sight,—etc.

Yours totally crazy,
Wise

April 9.

My Sweet, only Selma:

I just received your heartfelt letter which is my Selma complete with all the beauty of her soul and clearness of her spirit so that I think I am near you. . . . Whatever I write to you is a shadow, a weak echo of my love which is yours forever and ever. You want me to excuse your possible lack of logic, darling? My sweet, there is no logic in love. It whirls and storms without rule and without law. I cannot love you according to rules, I love you from the bottom of my heart, and so I feel your love which makes me more than happy. I, as your minister, will not give you absolution for one crime: if you do not love me enough. Everything else will be pardoned.

On the same day he wrote to her that, "The secret of our love is well known around here." It was a matter of fairly general information that they were engaged to be married, and his children were well satisfied.

On April 11 he wrote to her about their wedding day, which was to be on the following Monday. He was about to return to Cincinnati *via* Philadelphia, Washington, and Cumberland. On May 2 he would go to visit his mother in Peoria, Ill. He asked whether she needed money, for he was a "merchant" as well as a rabbi. He would arrive in New York about ten o'clock at night:

My wonderful Selma:

My confidence in your brains is as unlimited as my love, and I love you with all the mighty emotions of an incorrigible "*Weltschmerzler*" (one accustomed to bear all the sorrow of the world!) and reformer. . . .

April 12.

My darling Selma, my dearest wife:

In your darling letter of Monday I have found my Selma completely, my Selma in love, my dreaming, best Selma, that I pressed the letter to my heart and kissed it. I have read out of it thousands and thousands of kisses and I am sending you in exchange my heart, full of love, totally crazy and mad. . . . If you had thought you had selected a quiet, settled man who is a philosopher, with whom you can go through life easy-going, you are mistaken, my sweet Selma. I can think for days, I can think about problems for weeks, but my heart does not have anything to do with my head, in my heart I am just as youthful an enthusiast as I am a settled thinker with my brains. I love you so much because I have discovered in your heart the same warmth, the same fire, the same high feelings, because you are quite my "alter ego."

April 12.

My sweet dreamer:

I cannot love you a little, I cannot remember you a little, I cannot long for you a little. I love you wholeheartedly, and that's how I think of you and how I long for you.

Concerning the bad jokes: I'll make a bargain with you, that you won't even have to praise my verses and I won't divorce you anyhow. I solemnly swear that I won't reproach you as long as you love me sincerely. . . . Since yesterday my imagination is busy figuring out how you will look in your artful and tasteful bridal gown. I paint you in all colours, see you in all your attractiveness pour out your loveliness about you. . . .

April 14.

Now I have my regular hours in which to write to you. I write to you in the afternoon and immediately after dinner. . . .

Your letters, my wonderful Selma, are really perfect. They show the highness of your soul and the nobleness of your heart. whoever knows how to love as you do and knows how to express herself as you do must be a noble human being.

You have made an agreement with the gods of Olympus, I feel you will be everything for me: wife, friend, adviser, guardian angel, the good genius on the path of life. In your young love I become young again, my dearest wife. . . .

At home, my dear Selma, you will be the matron of my house and the queen of my heart. . . .

April 18.

. . . because when I am away from you, my biggest pleasure is to write to you.

Our wealth, my darling, is love and it will remain a well of happiness forever.

I have discovered a new doctrine which I formulate as follows: love augments the perceptibility [he probably means perceptiveness]: that's why lovers see the latent but possible preferences which stay hidden to cold eyes. This sounds paradoxical but it is true. Otherwise, there is a proverb that love is blind; but that is not so; it looks more precise and deeper. . . .

April 20.

On Saturday we will write the introduction to the second volume of our novel and it will be beautiful how many volumes and copies might follow. . . . so we will go on spinning the novel into eternity and each chapter shall contain a share of joy.

You will be like a queen in your bridal gown, made by your own hands, and the majesty of virtue and nobleness of your soul will emphasize the charms of the loving bride. . . .

They were married on Monday, April 24, 1876, in New York, in the presence of one of Wise's oldest friends, Dr. Joseph Lewi of Albany, "and lady," and of some other guests. The ceremony was performed by another old friend, Rabbi Adolph Huebsch of New York. The *Israelite* announced that the new Mrs. Wise would direct household affairs at 126 Dayton Street, in Cincinnati. Wise would deliver sermons and lectures at the temple, and she would deliver them at home. He invited his friends to call and to inspect the new establishment.[73]

Various changes were being made in the observances of the congregation, always with its preliminary discussion and consent. In 1871 Wise had abandoned the triennial cycle of readings from the *Torah*. Originally he had himself advocated and adopted the former, for the purpose of shortening the service. In 1873 the congregation finally and officially discontinued the observance of the second day of *Rosh Ha-shono*. The second day of the "three festivals" had been dispensed with years earlier. In the same year the congregation took the rather negative, and certainly guarded, action, that it was "not unlawful" to attend divine services with uncovered head. A few of the older members continued to wear hats, as certainly under this rule was entirely permissible. It is interesting to make note of the fact that the congregation, as far as its records show, never went beyond this rule, which is permissive, but not mandatory.

During this period Wise decided to change the name of the *Israelite* to the *American Israelite,* "to distinguish it from similar publications of the same name in other countries."[74] He wrote too that the paper had never been a financial success. "The main fault, however, as regards the finances may be in the carelessness of Isaac M. Wise about money affairs, we will admit this at once."[75]

Even as late as 1873 Wise was still concerned about the treatment that was being meted out to the South. From the end of the Civil War he had favored leniency, and not the rigors and revenges of reconstruction. He wrote:

> As long as the South is interfered with, any way molested, or denied any rights or privileges which others enjoy anywhere, we will be found to stand with the South.[76]

In 1874 Wise went to Nashville to speak at the dedication of the synagogue. President Andrew Johnson was also a guest, and the rabbi of the congregation, Kalisch, together with Wise and Johnson, rode in the same carriage. Johnson—Wise reported—said some flattering but trite things.[77]

He had not weakened in his dislike of the habitual kind of Thanksgiving Proclamation issued by the Presidents. Grant sent one out in 1876, and Wise objected with especial vigor to the phrase, "the day of our Lord." But his dislike of the practice went beyond the verbiage employed:

> What right has any President of the United States, any Congress or Supreme Court to interfere with the religious affairs of the people?

This case—doubtless with some relish—he blamed on the Republican Party.[78]

In April, 1879, the congregation had a splendid celebration of the conclusion of his twenty-fifth year of service as their rabbi. An artist was commissioned to paint a life-size portrait of him, and, by motion of the trustees of the congregation on April 29, 1881, the portrait was presented to the Hebrew Union College, where it hangs till today. Also in the same year, K.K.B'nai Israel united with B'nai Yeshurun to celebrate Wise's sixtieth birthday, at the Plum St. Temple.[79]

We conclude this lengthy chapter with a record of some of the series of lectures he was giving on Friday evenings. In 1873 there was a notice, near the beginning of the year, in the *Cincinnati Enquirer* and in the *American Israelite*, that on the previous Friday he had begun a series on the philosophers and philosophies of Israel.[80] In the summer of the same year he initiated a long series on "The Origin of Christianity."[81] This was followed, late in the same year, with a supplementary series on "The Martyrdom of Jesus of Nazareth, a Historic-Critical Treatise on the Last Chapters of the Gospels."[82]

Toward the end of the next year he lectured on what he called "*Soph Davar*" (The End, or Gist, of the Matter), on some philosophical and theological problems of modern times.[83] As a matter of fact, these were the addresses to which he referred in connection with the death of his first wife, and which were published soon thereafter under the title, *The Cosmic God*.[84] To it he had also added a sub-title: *A Philosophic Conciliator of Science and Religion.* It consisted of 250 pages, in octavo size, and was sold for fifty cents.[85]

Thus ended these remarkable years in his life, years which witnessed the birth of the Union of American Hebrew Congregations and of the Hebrew Union College; years during which he thought of leaving Cincinnati for New York; years that saw him bereft and married again. Those that followed were to prove years of fulfillment, of consummation, of creative leadership, of the ingathering of the fruit of the trees that had been planted in these decades of the seventies. The country was upon the verge of a great change, the beginning of Eastern European migration to America, the alteration of the very face of the Jewish community, a multitude of new problems, and of problems in a form Wise had never envisaged. We shall see how he met these challenges, and what he thought of the later years of his life.

28

Three Years of Peace

THE NEXT THREE YEARS IN ISAAC M. WISE'S LIFE—FROM 1877 TO 1880—were not eventful. They witnessed the expansion of the Union and the College and the overcoming of some of the obstacles and difficulties that had dogged his steps for more than two decades. Primarily and simply they were marked by the continuance of what he had been doing, by concentration upon the tasks to which at last his own persistence had permitted him to come. He must be imagined at the height of his powers, believing with all his soul that the Union of American Hebrew Congregations was to be the one instrument for a new era in the life of Judaism, and that the Hebrew Union College would rear a new generation of scholars and leaders, just as Jochanan ben Zacchai had reared them in the first century. It was because of his consistent devotion to these organizations and these activities that his life seemed for this period to lack motion and outward incident.

In the middle of these three years he celebrated the twenty-fifth anniversary of his service as rabbi of K.K.B'nai Yeshurun of Cincinnati. This was on May 2, 1879.[1] The Temple was beautifully decorated for the occasion. Services were held on Sabbath morning at half-past nine. An orchestra aided with the music. There was an "oration" by Lilienthal. A resolution was read on behalf of the trustees of the congregation. Some of the pupils of the Talmud Yelodim Institute participated. The resolutions were read by

Nathaniel Newburgh, then president of the congregation. The service ended with a prayer and a benediction. The *American Israelite* printed the speeches and resolutions, as well as the response Wise made to all these laudatory, warm-hearted tributes.

But more important perhaps than this formal occasion was the review Wise wrote for the *Israelite* in its issue just before the event.[2] Although this recapitulates some of the material in foregoing pages, it is so interesting in its revelation of his own motivation and his own interpretation of events, attitudes, and persons, that we venture to print it entire:

> It was twenty-five years ago today that the editor of the *American Israelite* preached his introductory sermon in the Lodge Street synagogue before K.K.B.Y. and numerous outsiders and visitors. What a change has come over American Israel since that time. There was then no Hebrew congregation west of the Mississippi; none west of Cincinnati except St. Louis; none west or north of Chicago except a nucleus of a congregation in Milwaukee; none south of Louisville except New Orleans; none in all the South except Richmond, Va., Charleston, Savannah, and Augusta, Ga. Judaism was limited to the few cities of Albany, Syracuse, Rochester, Buffalo, New York, Philadelphia, Baltimore; small congregations in Washington, Boston, New Haven and Hartford, Connecticut; then there were also congregations in Cleveland, Cincinnati, Louisville, St. Louis, Chicago, Milwaukee, New Orleans, with a beginning at Mobile. There was no synagogue and no congregation outside of these cities. . . . With a change of principle in Bene Yeshurun congregation of Cincinnati a new era commenced in the American Judaism—the era of synagogal reform all over the land, with the establishment of the Union of American Hebrew Congregations and Hebrew Union College, the second chapter of our history begins.
>
> What we had personally to do with these epochs and the intermediate transitions we leave to the future historian and the all-seeing eye of God. We know that about two hundred of our sermons, lectures, and addresses have appeared in print, have been delivered in all parts of the United States between New York and San Francisco, and were circulated in hundreds of public journals as no other rabbi's were in any country. The influence which this may have exercised together with the weekly exertions of the *American Israelite* and the books we have written, we have no means of ascertaining.
>
> The position of American Israel has changed entirely in the past twenty-five years. The Jewish religion stands now before

the enlightened portion of the community as the most intelligent and the most liberal religious system. . . . We are no longer pitied, hunted, or converted by bigoted sectarians; all the new-fangled creeds pass by us unnoticed; atheism, nihilism, and the so-called free religionism make no impression in our ranks; we are as solid a line here and now as we have been in the days of hard-shell orthodoxy; simply because Judaism has been reformed in form and essence as its spirit demands to correspond with the spirit and tastes of this age and this country so that the religious Jew can also be a citizen of a free country, a member of society, and a reasoner upon the very height of modern thought. This is the field in which we have done some work in the last twenty-five years, because God has given us both the pen and the pulpit, the English language and a boundless enthusiasm and a congregation to back us and support us under all circumstances and to encourage us in all possible ways and manners.

The last, however, was this: When the Personal God question had been agitated we sided with the philosophical standpoint. Some of our very godly colleagues were aroused against us in the wrath of the righteous. The president of our congregation was rather inclined to orthodoxy in general and it was known that he was orthodox. He happened to be in New York when one of our most prominent opponents (Einhorn) came to him and tried to impress him with the benevolent idea that we ought to be removed from rabbinical office on account of our ungodly theology. He tried rather hard, and the president came home to tell the story (not to us), which had the effect of crowding our place of worship Sabbath after Sabbath with men and women who came merely to make a demonstration (as we were afterwards told). When *The Jewish Times* [of New York] made the most damaging attacks on us, we were most popular at home and abroad. When *The Jewish Messenger* [a New York *Weekly*] most fiercely decried us as a heretic and innovator, we possessed unlimited confidence at home and abroad as an enthusiastic defender and expounder of Judaism. Nobody will believe that this was a personal favour on the part of our friends and patrons; it was the spirit of self-reflection, progress, and generosity, which nothing could arrest, nothing could turn against him who treasured and cultivated it. It is an acknowledged fact now that the lofty standpoint taken where faith and reason, religion and science do not collide has secured to Judaism the high position which it now occupies in the estimation of the most advanced thinkers of our country, and that the keynotes struck on our part concerning Jesus, the Apostles, and Paul have overcome a vast amount of prejudices and hostile feelings which did exist between Jews and Gentiles. We look upon each other in quite a different light from what we did twenty-five years ago.

We had no trouble in Cincinnati where most all were our friends, and those few, very few indeed, who were not, did not speak loud enough to be heard.

With the introduction of the Minhag America we considered the question of synagogue reform closed. We knew very well that all other necessary reforms would follow without trouble, as they actually did, and that there must remain a balance of orthodox people to have things their own way until their children will change it. The Friday evening service and lecture, now an institution all over the country, was at once adopted by many congregations as an antidote against Sunday services on the one hand and as a substitute for Sabbath morning services, which many could not attend, on the other hand. We had little trouble with the orthodox side of the house. Our troubles were abroad and with the reformers. First there was a party which had a peculiar idol, viz. the apotheosis of reform. They made of Judaism a reform and were continually negative. To abolish this and that was religion, to scold the orthodox was called preaching. We had great trouble with that party to convince it that reform is a handmaid and must serve the purpose of elevating Judaism and endearing it to its votaries; that the preacher must be positive, must teach and edify, win and give satisfaction to the yearnings of the heart. Then came hostility to Hebrew and the Talmud which were bound to be overcome in behalf of Judaism which must have and preserve its literature or go under in the vast majority of its opponents. Then came the attempt to Germanize the American synagogue, which we could not support as young America would speak English in spite of all theology and the synagogue must be no foreigner in this country. Then came the personal attacks for which we never cared. We looked upon it as a funny article. Then came the bitter denunciations of the union and the college schemes, and a dozen other episodes all of which are overcome, thank heaven, and the whole aspect has been changed. This is another and better time than it was twenty-five years ago. The Jew is proud of his history, faith, and position in society. The synagogue is modernized and respected. Judaism is a badge of honour, its teachers, organs, and votaries command attention and respect. Things have changed, and we thank God that we have lived to see it.

This is a new country. Everything therein is young, energetic, and thriving. This is a free country in which intellectual fruits ripen fast. In a few years when forty or fifty graduates

> of the Hebrew Union College will stand at the head of the synagogues Judaism will be an American institution, its spirit and influence will be widely felt, and its future will be different from its past. It will be furnished within and will be prepared in spirit far outside its own boundaries. It will be perpetually the reformatory element, the harbinger of truth and light, and its votaries will increase by the thousands among the most intelligent portions of the country. The foundation is laid, the house must be built. The artisans are preparing themselves for the rebuilding of Israel's sanctuary on the American soil."

Though the exact details are not available, it is clear that again in 1879 the Democratic Party of Ohio had wished to nominate Isaac M. Wise for the State Senate. This time, however, in contrast with 1863, he himself did not regard it as either possible or desirable to accept and to serve. He wrote of it in the *Israelite:*

> The reason why the editor of this journal refused to be nominated as State Senator by the Democratic Convention, is simply the utter impossibility to devote any time to study of political questions and the work required by a senator who has the ambition of filling his position well. If one has under his care a weekly paper, a large congregation and Sabbath school and the Hebrew Union College, he can hardly afford to enter upon new obligations. This is the sole reason for declining the honor.[3]

In the spring of 1880 services were held at the Plum St. Temple in memory of Adolphe Crémieux. At the service both Lilienthal and Wise spoke. Previously Wise had delivered an extended lecture on Crémieux's life and work. Isaac Adolphe Crémieux was a Jew, who became Minister of Justice of France, a brave defender of his coreligionists and a man of great nobility of character.[4] We had referred to him briefly in Chapter Two, Part One.

Near the end of this period his beloved mother, Regina Wise, a description of whom we reproduced in pages much earlier than these, born in Steingrub, Bohemia, in 1794, died at the age of 86 years. Her passing occurred on June 11, 1880. Wise went to Peoria to bury her and thanked the many friends there who had been so kind to her, especially at the end.[5]

In the same summer Theodore Thomas, who was teaching in Cincinnati and conducting the orchestra, must have proposed bringing Richard Wagner to Cincinnati. Wise had conceived a violent hatred of Wagner, doubtless because of the German composer's anti-Semitism, and this hatred Wise carried over to his music. In the latter half of this book we shall reprint some amusing paragraphs, which occasionally Wise inserted in the *Israelite* about Wagner and the "Music of the Future." This time he contented himself with asking Thomas to desist, and as the reason he adduced that it is we and not our grandchildren who would have to listen to Wagner's music.[6]

In the *Israelite* he published a long and recondite series of articles on the *Massorah*, the chain of rabbis who established the precise text of the Hebrew Scriptures. Some of his readers complained—he recorded—about the unreadability and—for them—the unintelligibility of this material.[7] Parallel to this Wise was working hard at the second volume of his History, which he said that he intended primarily as a text. He conceded that in preparing for it he had used the work of many German authorities, though precisely which authorities he used he did not say. He did not, however, depend only upon the work of other men, for to his reading he added some extensive research of his own, especially concerning the origins of Christianity. All of this latter he condensed into short paragraphs. When it was completed, he had no idea whether the work would be bought or read. Some critics took notice of it and tried to blast it with their scorn. But they did not succeed. It was widely purchased and perused. Wise himself—he said—had learned to despise reviews.[8]

Having completed this major work, he took a short period of rest. It was just at this time in 1880 that he became aroused on the entire subject of Biblical criticism. To this topic he returned on many occasions, not only in numerous paragraphs and articles in the *Israelite*, but also in some of his larger works, like the *Pronaos to Holy Writ*. To his attitude toward the "lower" and "higher" criticism we shall come in the third part of this book. But he wrote of his interest at this time:

> When the scholars and half-scholars had gone so far as to portray the Books of Moses as a late creation and as a patchwork, stitched together by deceitful priests, and as to deny the existence of Moses, and to explain all Biblical history down to David, or even later, as a myth, and to declare all of Biblical Judaism to be a product of the Babylonians and Aryans (Persians), I was seized with fear for historical Judaism on the one hand, and on the other hand I had to speak against this to the students of the College.[9]

If these strictures and destructive analyses could be proved, everything went to the ground. He was forced to the very margin of despair. For some time he went carefully through the chief works of Biblical criticism and attempted to lay the foundations of a system of his own. This resulted in the *Pronaos*, published in 1891, and which—at the time he was writing these articles in the *Israelite* in 1897—was still used as a text at the College.[10]

Previously we have described the time when the Board of Delegates came into being, the purposes it was intended to serve, and the small number of congregations that had affiliated with it. Nonetheless, the newly created Union of American Hebrew Congregations quite rightly regarded it as a form of fruitless and destructive competition and soon began to make the attempt to arrive at some agreement, some form of amalgamation. Wise announced early in 1877 that at the forthcoming convention of the Union in July of 1877 it was quite probable that the Board of Delegates would become merged with the Union, and also that one of the conditions of the agreement was to be the creation of a preparatory section of the College in some eastern city.[11] He himself was opposed to taking them in. He thought the Union would gain little or nothing. It had always been his opinion that the Board of Delegates represented no more than a small and unimportant segment of New York congregations.[12]

His counsel was not followed. In the judgment of the leaders of the Union at the Philadelphia convention it was better to effect a conjunction of forces. The Board of Delegates was to be taken in on condition that it would prevail upon most of the eastern congregations to join the Union. If this proved successful, the constitution of the Union was to be changed, to make provision for the Board of Delegates within its framework.[13]

In 1878 Wise wrote—repeating a summation he had made in some previous year—that four measures were necessary for the Jews of the United States:

1. The formation of the Union of American Hebrew Congregations;
2. The establishment of a Hebrew Young Ladies' Seminary;
3. Circuit-preaching for smaller communities;
4. The entry of "Israelites into agricultural pursuits."

He declared the life of the farmer to be greatly preferable to that of the city dweller. Later on we shall come upon much evidence that, increasingly in the later years of his life, this conviction grew upon him and affected his estimate of many problems of Jewish life and Jewish settlement.[14]

Of the eastern congregations, no large one joined the Union until 1878, when Temple Emanu-El of New York (Gottheil, rabbi), and Temple Beth El (Einhorn) came in. Both were represented at the Milwaukee Council in 1878. It was a curious fact also that at this same assemblage the editor of the *New York Jewish Times* (M. Ellinger) represented Einhorn's congregation, met Wise, shook his hand, and buried the hatchet.[15]

It was at this same convention in Milwaukee that Wise declared one united American Israel had come into being. The Board of Delegates had been amalgamated and the East was no longer standing apart. In the place of the Board of Delegates the Union created a Committee on Civil and Religious Rights. It is worth noting that this committee continued to act for some years, maintained an office in Washington, and regarded as its chief task—as Wise had indeed regarded it in his own life—the defense of Jews in the enjoyment of their rights, at home and abroad. In the *Israelite* Wise remarked also that by this time most of the opposition to him had melted away. Sabato Morais—later the organizer of the Jewish Theological Seminary (in 1886)—had accepted Wise's invitation to aid at a "public examination" at the Hebrew Union College. The eastern congregations were joining the Union. One of the new projects was the organization of an American Rabbinical Association, to be called the Rabbinical Literary Association, which was to complete its plans and meet in July, 1879, in New York.[16]

Wise was still urging that the Union undertake the creation of a Jewish Publication Society.[17] Two years later he recorded the fact that the Union then had a roster of 121 congregations, a truly remarkable proportion of those then in existence in the United States. But—with some sadness he noted—in spite of his hopes, many of the great congregations of the East were still not registered.[18]

For this period we possess an interesting document, which throws light upon some of its incidents. This is in the form of a memoir of Dr. Joseph Lewi, in the Archives of the Hebrew Union College. It will be recalled that Dr. Lewi was one of Wise's closest friends in Albany. His profession was that of "podiatry." The two families had lived in the same house on Ferry Street, and there to the Wises were born their eldest son, Leo, their daughter, Ida (Mrs. Henry Bernheim), and later on Isidor and Wilhelmine. When Wise came to the time of his violent troubles in Albany, Lewi was one of his chief aides. When a large number of members seceded from his first congregation and formed a new congregation, Wise had presided at a table, which later he gave to Lewi as a souvenir, and which Lewi later sent to the Board of Governors of the College.

The memoir reverted to the time of which we have been writing, when Wise was having constant difficulties with the eastern congregations. Lewi played a notable role in the events of this period in what he called the "Surrender at Saratoga." A memorandum of Isidor Lewi (under date of March 27, 1919) narrated that Wise had come to Albany in the summer of 1878 and that his friend had invited him to go to Saratoga with him for a while for rest and relaxation. By chance, while they were at the resort, they met Lewis May, Jesse Seligman, Moses Schloss, and others who were officers and board members of Temple Emanu-El of New York. Until then Wise had been unable even to arrange a conversation with them, much less to win them for the Union. This was a heaven-sent opportunity, foreseen by Lewi. They met, and talked for many hours. Wise pled with them to move past their inveterate prejudices for the sake of Judaism in America. Success crowned his efforts. Later Wise said that "the last barrier in the path of the Union's success had been razed." "And he always believed that, though the victory might have been achieved without it, the work done on a day which had been planned by two busy men as a day of idleness, hastened the event." At the next Council of the Union in New York, July 6, 1879, these very men were present as delegates and Temple Emanu-El was a member. It was followed by other eastern congregations, where "a quarter of a century earlier Dr. Wise had begun his reform campaign."[19]

Slowly but surely the College too was forging ahead. From very humble beginnings in a cellar, and with but two men teaching, it was gathering momentum, expanding, gaining students, and defining its own methods and purposes. At Wise's death in 1900 the faculty had increased from two to nine.[20] In preparing its curriculum Wise had consulted prominent rabbis, though he did not bind himself in advance to be guided uncritically by their counsel. The curriculum was being considered even before the opening of the institution, at the Cleveland convention of the Union, in July, 1874. Of this Dr. S. Wolfenstein, Superintendent of the Cleveland Jewish Orphan Asylum, wrote:

> At the second council of the Union of American Hebrew Congregations, held in July, 1874, at Cleveland, Ohio, Drs. Lilienthal and Wise and myself were appointed to prepare a curriculum of studies for the new rabbinical college. We met a consecutive number of Sundays at Cincinnati. . . . Our meetings were very animated as a rule. Lilienthal and myself agreeing

> and Wise opposing us. . . . It was on one of these occasions when Lilienthal, lighting a fresh cigar, broke out in a laugh, in which he liked to indulge so heartily, and turning to me exclaimed: "Wolfenstein, you are a fool and I am another. We quarrel with Wise, and, nevertheless, he will do as he pleases." He certainly was right. When I attended the College examination in May or June, 1878, Rabbis Morais and Zirndorf (then in Detroit, later on the faculty) were my colleagues. I did not find much of the program we had prepared carried out. Wise had cut down the scientific and theoretic subjects, laying stress upon matters touching and pertaining to practical life. Most probably he was right.[21]

During the early years of College and Union Wise was traveling constantly as far as California and later to the cities of the East. His purpose was to convince Jews of the necessity of the two new institutions, to win friends and gain support. He hit upon an interesting device, namely, to invite prominent rabbis yearly, to serve as a board of examiners of the students of the College. This was to prove a master-stroke. Many of those who had been his bitter enemies accepted his invitation, came, and were won over. He invited not only men of the "radical" reform wing, but also leaders of orthodoxy. Here is a list of those who served in the first seven years:

1877, Sonnenschein of St. Louis and Mayer of Pittsburgh.
1878, Morais of Philadelphia, Wolfenstein of Cleveland, and Zirndorf of Detroit.
1879, Huebsch of New York, Felsenthal of Chicago, and Hahn of Cleveland.
1880, F. De Sola Mendes of New York, Adler of Chicago, and again Sonnenschein of St. Louis.
1881, Samuel Hirsch of Philadelphia, Goldammer of Nashville, and Samfield of Memphis.
1882, Adolph Moses of Louisville, Emil G. Hirsch of Chicago, and Isaacs of New York.
1883, (the year of the first graduation), Kaufmann Kohler of New York, Benjamin Szold of Baltimore, and Jacobs of Philadelphia.

The reports of these examiners are to be found in the proceedings of the Union of American Hebrew Congregations. They certified as to the excellent preparation of the students, and praised their work and that of the College itself.[22]

Wise was constantly trying to improve the quality of instruction. He realized how heavy a burden Lilienthal, Eppinger, and he were carrying. A German letter of his exists, written to Rabbi Bernard

Felsenthal of Chicago on March 21, 1879. In it he offered Felsenthal the professorship of Bible and Exegesis with a salary of not less than $2000. He urged Felsenthal to consider the post. His task would be to teach Bible—Hebrew "style"—Exegesis, and Literature; Hebrew Grammar, Rashi, and *Targumim* (the Aramaic translations of the text); also to instruct the students in the Septuagint (the first Greek translation), and the *Peschitta* (the oldest Syriac translation).[23]

In 1879 Moses Mielziner joined the faculty. His field was Talmud. He was a splendid scholar and a greatly beloved teacher, a man of great sweetness and mildness of character, like Hillel of Babylon. After Wise's death he acted as president of the College for a brief time.[24]

Wise knew that he would have to begin building up a library. No institution of learning can prosper without books. Much less one among Jews! In 1876, a year after the founding of the College, there were only 276 volumes in its library and these were mostly prayer-books. Wise had appealed for books through the *Israelite*, but in response got mainly those for which some Jews had no space on their shelves.[25]

Wise's purpose with the College was strikingly manifested in some of his words in his opening address in September, 1879:

> I, for my part, declare that this shall be an orthodox Jewish Academy, in spirit like that of Rabbi Jochanan ben Zaccai, Abba Areka, or Mar Samuel, in which Jewish learning for its own sake shall be earnestly fostered, and the Jewish spirit as it is manifested in our literature shall have the control over all exotic and original ideas, from whatever source or age they may come.[26]

In that very year the College had thirty students registered. Wise was looking forward to the time, four years thence, "when Americans will preach Judaism to Americans." The difference will soon be perceptible.[27]

In the following year (1880), the Union decided that it would undertake the effort to secure money for a building for the College. It was time the institution moved out of the basements of the Mound St. and the Plum St. Temples and had a home of its own. A committee was appointed to raise funds and a plan was adopted.[28] Their efforts were crowned with success, and on April 24, 1881, the College moved into a large double stone house on West Sixth Street in Cincinnati. At its dedication Wise said:

> This is the first time in the history of our country that any

> house has been dedicated as this to higher Jewish learning in the double sense of the term by communication from teacher to students.[29]

A page or two earlier we have referred to the plan to organize a Rabbinical Literary Association. Wise had regretted greatly the failure of the Philadelphia Conference to meet again, the impermanence of the rabbinical meetings he had called thereafter in regard to *Minhag America*. Then and later on he perceived clearly that there must be a body of rabbis, either a Synod with specific legal authority, or at least some conference to deal with theological and ritual problems with which, in his opinion, laymen could not and should not deal. It was at the Sixth Council of the Union that the constitution of such a group of rabbis was drafted, not by the Council itself, but by the rabbis who were present. Lilienthal was chosen as president, and it was decided to invite rabbis from abroad to join.[30]

There were periodic meetings of this body, devoted mostly to reading papers on crucial problems in the realm of theory or of practice. It was decided to publish a quarterly and to strive to bring together all the "Jewish ministers of our country."[31] In 1880 the *Israelite* published an account of a meeting of the Rabbinical Literary Association in Detroit, from July 13 to July 15. There were essays and debates. This was the first actual meeting of the body:

> We may congratulate the Rabbinical Literary Association on the success achieved at its first public meeting, and also congratulate the Jewish congregations on the happy morning dawn of peace and concerted action among its teachers. The beginning is quite promising, may the future be as bright as our hopes.[32]

The plan to issue a quarterly was carried through, and the committees to gather material for it were appointed and began to function.[33]

Although a number of excellent and promising meetings were held, this association too failed to fulfill Wise's hopes. It went the way of all the other rabbinical meetings and conferences. It was not possible to establish a permanent, organic group of rabbis, until Wise had graduated a sufficient alumni group of his College and in 1889 he could create the Central Conference of American Rabbis.

Thus these were years of hard labor, of hovering in constant concern over infant institutions, of gaining friends and money for them, and of speeding them on the way toward the great service Wise had envisaged for them.

29

First Fruits

THE DEVELOPMENT OF WISE'S LONG-AWAITED INSTITUTIONS, AND HIS concentration upon them, continued for the next several years. The record was being written in the growing number of congregations affiliating with the Union of American Hebrew Congregations, the increase of support for the Hebrew Union College, the expansion of its faculty and of its library, and the entry into the American rabbinate of its first graduates. To all this we shall now come. But first let us review a few things that were happening in Wise's personal life and in his labors in his own congregation.

In the Archives of the Hebrew Union College there is a letter, written by the Grand Consistory of Masons to Isaac M. Wise Jr., on May 19, 1936, giving the record of his father's progress in that Order. Wise petitioned the Consistory on January 3, 1882, for affiliation with the Union Lodge of Perfection in Louisville. He was elected, made a Knight Rose Croix, a Knight Kadosh, and had bestowed upon him the thirtieth degree on January 24 of the same year. On the same date at the same place he was made Master of the Royal Secret. All these terms are meaningless to us, but of a certainty signify that Wise had been a Mason for some time and had risen in its ranks. He was a member of the Scottish Rite until his death.[1]

James A. Garfield, twentieth president of the United States, was shot by Charles J. Guiteau on July 2, 1881, survived for two months, but died on September 19. In the *Israelite* of September 23 Wise published a black-bordered column with the news of the President's death from an assassin's bullet. A service of mourning and memorial was held at the Plum St. Temple. The memorial address was delivered by Wise; resolutions were read by M. J. Mack. The congregation recited the Kaddish, and Lilienthal spoke at exercises that were held at Hauck's Opera House.[2]

But far closer to Wise himself, having to do with the oldest and dearest of his personal memories which began immediately after his landing in New York in 1846, was the death of Max Lilienthal in the spring of 1882. Between them there had been a friendship as of David and Jonathan. Into it, in all its years, there had never entered an element of discord or of envy. Their goals and beliefs were identical, and, though they differed greatly one from the other in personality, in drive, and in other qualities, they maintained the same ideals of Judaism, were completely at one in what they were convinced had to be done to further the cause of Judaism, and worked side by side for all the years of their association. Rarely in the history of the American rabbinate has there been so close, so complete, and so fruitful a friendship. Lilienthal's death signified a profound and acute personal loss for Wise. Services were held to mourn for Lilienthal. To the announcment of these in the *Israelite* Wise added these words: "You have lost a father and a guide, and we a teacher and a sage in Israel." And he concluded: "And yet I cannot speak, for my soul mourns within me. *Alai libee davoy*." ("My heart is faint within me." Jeremiah, 8:18).[3]

The *Israelite* must have been doing well in these years, for in 1883 Wise found it advisable to enlarge it, to increase the size of the pages upon which it was printed, and at the same time to use smaller type. Thus it became possible to include a considerably larger amount of material in its columns.[4]

Early in the next year there was an impressive ceremony at the Plum St. Temple. A German Jew of Cincinnati had for some years been married to a Catholic woman, and a single daughter had been born to them. Wise had instructed mother and daughter in Judaism, and they were converted at a joint ceremony. In addition to the formal part of the ceremony, the questions directed to both about their knowledge and acceptance of the historic faith, Wise delivered an impressive address. Mother and daughter had been conducted to the altar by some of the officers of the congregation. Wise read the Eighty-fourth Psalm and at the conclusion of the ceremony blessed them both. To the mother he gave another name, that of Hannah.[5]

In the summer of the same year (1884) he delivered the Baccalaureate Address at the University of Cincinnati.[6]

Another death that came very close to him occurred on October 10, 1884, that of Adolph Huebsch, rabbi of Congregation Ahavath Chesed in New York. In the preceding pages we have chronicled the numerous occasions when these two had met, the friendly and cooperative relations that obtained between them, and Huebsch's officiation at Wise's second marriage. The *Israelite* carried a black-bordered column and a long eulogy of Huebsch, written by Wise.[7]

Again and again Wise referred to the excellent attendance at his Friday evening services. It did not cease to be astonishing to him—as it would be to us today—that large audiences came week after week, that they gave every apparent evidence of their interest in the often recondite and philosophical series of lectures he was delivering. He remarked upon the fact that they listened closely even to his series on "The Cosmic God." He deprecated his feeling of amazement and gratitude by noting that of course only a "small percentage of the 250,000 people inhabiting this city ever took any notice of these lectures." But the number of those who did come inspired him, and he enjoyed lecturing to them.[8]

It was just around this time that Felix Adler had embarked upon his career as founder and leader of the Ethical Culture Society, which—according to Wise—rested upon the proclaimed principle that the beliefs of religions were irrelevant and often untrue, and that it was only ethical values that needed cultivation. Wise took notice of him and of the society quite often in polemics directed against them in the pages of the *Israelite*. He had not a jot of sympathy with Adler's point of view. In 1882, in some lectures, Wise accused Adler of preaching atheism, and contended that, while Adler was against both Judaism and Christianity as revealed religions, he had a secret admiration for Jesus of Nazareth. He begged Robert Ingersoll's pardon for appropriating the famous form of his apothegm, and wrote: "There is no God, and Felix Adler is his prophet."[9]

He continued to proclaim the great success of the Friday evening service and the contribution it had made toward Jewish religious life. He claimed that it:

> Has done away with the craving appetite of our ultra-radicals for the Sunday service, that most sickly of all morbid whims of fashion.[10]

No house of worship in America could boast of a better attendance, of more devotion, or of better order and decorum than could B'nai Yeshurun, and nowhere else were divine services conducted more impressively:

> In a grander and more appropriate style corresponding to the demands of this age and country.

He noted again that his was the first congregation to use the *Minhag America*, and incidentally that his congregation did not approve of frequent or irresponsible shifts in liturgy.[11] The following year he noted that the congregation then numbered 301 members, and that the sister-congregation, B'nai Israel, had exactly the same number.[12] In the fall of 1883 he began a series of lectures entitled "Judaism and Christianity, Their Agreements and Disagreements." This was—in fact—the second part of such a series. The first had already appeared in book form.[13] His congregation must have had the feeling that Wise, or some of his friends, were contemplating further changes in the ritual, for they adopted a motion forbidding any further alterations, and especially that the amount of English and German in the service must not be increased. Wise commented that all this was done without any influence on his part, and that the congregation wanted the Hebrew to remain just as it had been.[14]

In the following year (1885) Wise was asked to contribute an article to the *American Jews' Annual*. He wrote a "Sketch of Judaism in America, 1884-5." This is of a great deal of intrinsic interest, throwing light not only upon the American Jewish community as it was then—more than seventy years ago—but also, and in many important respects, upon his own point of view. We reproduce the most pertinent and interesting sections of the article:

> It is unscientific to speak of a Jewish race. . . . but chiefly because the descendants of immigrant Jews in this country are typically Americans, according to the section of the country in which they live.
>
> Speaking therefore of American Jews as a distinct class of the population, you can refer to but one characteristic criterion, distinguishing them from the others, and that is the Jews' religion, which is called "Judaism"; you can only speak of a religious denomination and the characteristics of such a denomination in consequence of the peculiar workings of the mind, prompted by such particular religious tenets, or inherited of ancestors whose minds were influenced in like manner. . . .

Wise then inserted an estimate that there was about a third of a million then in the country, or about one-half of one percentum of the population. Among them there were very few Jews who took no interest in their religion or in Jewish organizations.

The Reform movement was started in 1845, first in introducing choirs in the synogogues, then mixed choirs, consisting of ladies and gentlemen, then the organ, or at least a melodeon; next came family pews and seating the women in the body of the synagogue with their husbands or fathers, which was followed by the introduction of classical music into divine service, the engagement of choristers independent of their religion, and finally culminated in the men sitting with uncovered heads in the Temple during divine service. Every one of these steps was hotly contested by men claiming to represent orthodox Judaism, still it was gradually accomplished, so that today the old-style worshipers are decidedly in the minority, and all large congregations all over the land worship in reform temples, while every new congregation established anywhere, excepting only the Russian-Polish, start with a Reformed Ritual and discipline.

First there had been reforms in ritual, then in ideas; the doctrine of the coming Messiah, "returning of Israelites to Palestine," the re-establishment of the Jewish monarchy, the restoration of the sacrificial polity, the resurrection of the body, "and various Kabbalistical notions and formulas imposed upon Judaism from and after the 16th century," "Still the reformatory side prevailed with the majority."

Even then, in 1884 and 1885 there was very little uniformity among Jews, due chiefly to differences in language. Some have the retention of Hebrew, with little of English, and German. "A minority favors reduction of Hebrew to a minimum." All of this is still in play. The rabbis were not yet in agreement: "Take for instance the doctrine of revelation, the authenticity of the Pentateuch, the universal character of the Sinaitic revelation, and similar doctrines which must necessarily be clearly expressed in a Jewish liturgy."

Congregations themselves are capable of unity even less than the rabbis. "It is the opinion of prominent men that anarchy is preferable to hierarchy and free development leads to more desirable results than stereotyped dogmas and imposed enactments. Therefore they advocate the autonomy of the congregations and the freedom of every officiating Rabbi. . . . The question of the legality of every innovation is to be decided by the congregation and its Rabbi. . . . The development and reformation of Judaism has been accomplished on this very principle, and yet the congregations always abide within the pale of pure monotheism which is after all the life and substance of Judaism."

Wise went on, once again, to advocate the establishment of a Synod, since "no individual congregation is the *Keneseth Israel* (the entire congregation of Israel), united only are they, the *Keneseth Israel,* as no faction of a congregation is the congregation. The Synod means unification, union and rejuvenation; the Synod means uniformity in ritual, liturgy, catechism in the Temple and the Sabbath-school. We do not speak of a hierarchical Synod, we speak of a democratic Synod in harmony with the spirit of Judaism and our country, in which none loses his independence and freedom, and all are guided by instruction, advice, and convincing evidence."

He referred then to the attack made upon him in a "memorial by Rodeph Shalom of Philadelphia" (to which we shall come), charging that paragraphs in the *American Israelite* were offensive to certain "anonymous individuals," and asking that the President of the Hebrew Union College be asked to resign, or be deposed. If this would not be done, the congregation threatened to leave the Union. Wise had been defended by a Committee of Five of the Union. Once again he reviewed here the principle, eternality, and truth of the Sinaic revelation: "All laws, except those of the Sinaic revelation, wherever and by whomsoever they were enacted or ordained, are authorized verbal applications of precepts or doctrines, to regulate and govern emergencies and circumstances for the benefit of the community or any individuals thereof. . . . If the precepts underlying such laws are of Sinaic origin, they are divine and eternal, while the law in its verbal incarnation is neither, and is therefore subject to amendment or abrogation." To this doctrine the orthodox were, of course, opposed. Some on the other hand, adhere only to reason and reject revelation altogether. On this Wise had given lectures at the Plum St. Temple, before audiences of Jews and Christians, and published them in a book, *Judaism and Christianity, Their Agreements and Disagreements* (Cincinnati, 1883). He had continued in 1883 to 1884 on Proselytism. Anyone who accepts the Sinaic revelation is "*de jure* one of the congregation of Israel." Felsenthal had earlier proposed the abrogation of the circumcision of proselytes. Then came the problem of intermarriage. This Moses had prohibited only with idolaters. "Therefore it must be correct (based on historical study) to maintain that there exists no Jewish law interdicting marriage among Jews, Christians, and Mohammedans, or any other non-Heathens, unless you place yourself upon the purely orthodox standpoint and maintain, a law once is a law forever. And yet such intermarriages are by no means desirable, as long as the Christian looks upon every non-Christian as an outcast here and to be damned hereafter. . . ."

The Dietary Laws Wise found obligatory only in so far as they are "sanitary" in character. The whole matter ought to come before a Synod. These three lectures of his had been terribly abused, had led to much controversy. But the masses are "faithful guardians of Judaism."

This article abounded with controversial material. It would not be advisable to discuss this here, or to place it in its setting of Wise's system of ideas. All this will be considered in its proper place in the third part of this book, in relation to his concept of Reform, of revelation, of the Mosaic law, of the processes and validity of tradition and authority in Judaism, of Hebrew, intermarriage, etc. We shall also put down in order Wise's reactions to the coming of the great tide of Eastern European immigration, to which he referred here with the rather unpleasant words "excepting only Russian-Polish," and to the new forms of orthodoxy they brought with them.

The *Israelite* announced in the spring of 1881 that the following Sunday the building purchased by the Union of American Hebrew Congregations would be turned over to the Board of Governors of the Hebrew Union College, and would in due time be dedicated. The building was at 484 West Sixth Street in downtown Cincinnati. At the dedication, when it was held, there was a prayer by Lilienthal, the presentation of the building by Moritz Loth; a response on behalf of the Board of Governors by Bernhard Bettmann; an address by Wise, and addresses also by Thomas Vickers, Rector of the University of Cincinnati, and by J. D. Cox, Governor of the State of Ohio. The benediction was given by Sonnenschein of St. Louis.[15]

Even before the first graduation the Seniors of the first class of the College were in demand. In the *Israelite* Wise recorded the fact that two had been elected to pulpits in the spring of 1883: Krauskopf to Kansas City, and Israel Aaron to Fort Wayne, Indiana.[16] In that summer Berkowitz was chosen for the pulpit of Mobile, Alabama.[17]

In July, 1883, ten years after its organization, the Union met in Cincinnati for the purpose of celebrating its decennial and, at the same time, the first ordination of rabbis. There were then 128 congregations in it, the largest representative body of Israelites until then ever assembled in America.[18]

The first graduation was held at Plum St. Temple on Wednesday,

June 20, 1883, in the afternoon. There was a procession in which were Wise, Solomon Eppinger, Moses Mielziner, M. Loth, B. Bettmann, and Rabbis Huebsch, Kohler, Mayer and Gottheil. The four candidates for the rabbinate followed. The program consisted of an introduction by B. Bettmann and an address and prayer by Benjamin Szold; the laureate address by Gustav Gottheil; an address on "Judaism and Science" by Israel Aaron; and an address by Rabbi George Jacobs of Philadelphia. The degrees were bestowed by Wise, and the response and valedictory were by David Philipson. There was a declaration on behalf of the Union by M. Loth, and a closing address by Kohler. A banquet was given later on at which Julius Freiberg was the master of ceremonies, and at which many toasts were given.[19]

To leap forward a bit, the second commencement exercises were at the end of June, 1884. An address was delivered by B. Bettmann, president of the Board of Governors; a prayer, by Rabbi Schlesinger of Albany; an address, by Rabbi Landsberg of Rochester; the laureate address, by James K. Gutheim of New Orleans; an address, by Louis Grossmann of the graduating class; the valedictory, by Joseph Silverman; and the closing address and prayer, again by Sonnenschein.[20]

In the *Israelite* in the same summer Wise made record of the fact that the Faculty of the College then consisted of: M. Mannheimer, Hebrew and Bible; Solomon Eppinger, Talmud and Aramaic; H. Zirndorf (who had just been added to the Faculty), history and literature; M. Mielziner, Talmud and Rabbinic Disciplines; and Wise.[21]

During this period of which we have been writing, the Rabbinical Literary Association had continued to meet once a year. When the Council of the Union had met in Chicago, just after the Rabbinical Literary Association, from July 12 to 14, 1881, the *Israelite* noted:

> The Union, as far as the congregations which joined it are concerned, is a cordial one. With the exception of five or six Eastern rabbis, who are at best but half in America, their other halves being yet somewhere in Europe, all are united and work for the Union.[22]

The year previous the Rabbinical Literary Association had had a bitter discussion on "The God of Judaism and the God of Science." This had attracted much public attention. Wise had maintained that the traditional law should be recognized only to the extent that it reflected the Mosaic spirit. He contended that it should be reducible to the simple principles of the Decalogue.[23] It was in 1881 that Wise submitted to the rabbis a motion advocating the establishment of a Synod, an attempt he had made any number of times before.[24] About thirty rabbis were present. Lilienthal was still president. Wise delivered a paper which was violently attacked by Samuel Hirsch of Philadelphia, who, as Wise wrote in the *Israelite:*

> drifted into bitter, vulgar, and inexcusable personalities, derogatory alike to his own dignity, and to that of the Association.

Wise appealed to the chairman to stem this abuse. This the chairman attempted to do, but without success. Thereupon Wise withdrew from the hall. On the third day, July 12, Zirndorf read a paper on "An Encyclopedia of the Science of Judaism." It was decided to meet in Cincinnati the following year.[25]

But—like several of its predecessors—the Rabbinical Literary Association did not enjoy a long, or perhaps even a vigorous, life. Wise noted that by 1884 it was dead. No attempts were being made to call another meeting, nor was there as yet any substitute for it that might bring rabbis together for mutual counsel.[26]

The Union of American Hebrew Congregations carried through the agreement it had made with the Board of Delegates by which the latter had decided to become amalgamated with it. The Union thereupon appointed a Committee to Defend Jews' Civil Rights, to work against the evils of discrimination, and to do something about cases where clauses prejudicial to Jews were discovered in treaties proposed or made with other countries.[27]

Then ensued an episode which has become notorious in the history of Reform Judaism in America, trivial and ridiculous though it was. A banquet had been served to the delegates of the Union of American Hebrew Congregations in Cincinnati, at Highland House. Wise wrote that "misfortune befell some of our very eminent colleagues of the Jewish press." Oysters, and other seafood, were served them. Wise expressed his regret, admitted it had been a blunder, but pleaded—for himself—that it had not been his duty to supervise the *Kashruth* (ritual purity) of meals; that he had more important business to attend to.[28] Comments upon this incident were whispered about the country, and rang angrily in the Jewish press.

Whether this was the specific cause that triggered action by Congregation Rodeph Shalom of Philadelphia, whose rabbi was

Marcus Jastrow, a most excellent scholar and the author of a great Talmudic dictionary, but a man of belligerently orthodox learnings, it is not easy to tell. The evidence appears to indicate that Jastrow had for some time disliked some of Wise's utterances as president of the Hebrew Union College, and that it was primarily these that prompted the decision of Rodeph Shalom. Wise wrote in the *Israelite* of May 9, 1884, replying to some of Jastrow's strictures, and he submitted proof that the latter had five years before tried to oust Lilienthal and himself from the College. Wise was sorry he could not oblige the gentleman and return to orthodoxy.[29]

In addition to this, the Archives of the College possess these notes from a history of Congregation Rodeph Shalom:[30]

> On April 20, 1884, a resolution was adopted calling for the appointment of a committee to inquire into the propriety of withdrawing from the Union of American Hebrew Congregations. The Committee consisted of Isaac Nusbaum, B.F. Teller, Mayer Frank, and Simon Fleisher. They met and submitted their report on June 15, 1884. The report considered carefully the entire question. It called attention to the fact that the congregation had joined the Union of American Hebrew Congregations; that it desired to share in the support and control of the Hebrew Union College at Cincinnati, with a hope that a standard of religious education and life for Jewish institutions might be established; and that the Jewish youth of America might be properly prepared for the Ministry. The report states that the committee views with alarm the utterances of the President of the Hebrew Union College. It laid stress upon the necessity of a certain tone of reverence for ancient institutions and traditions; and emphasized the necessity of respect for the opinions and beliefs of others. In particular it complained of certain controversial phrases by Isaac M. Wise, President of the College, in the *American Israelite*, such as: "Men of purely Jewish stomachs and unadulterated tastes." "Nobody has appointed those very orthodox critics, overseers of the kitchen or taskmasters of the stomach." . . . "The *American Israelite* does not deal in victuals."
>
> We object to the statement made by Rev. Dr. Wise that "No Israelite in this country has written more than I have and no man's books and essays were read by more Jews and Gentiles, from which no man was more abused or more ignored, my best literary efforts as well as my lighter essays."
>
> The committee recommended that the Congregation Rodeph Shalom withdraw from the Union of American Hebrew Congregations until such time as a better state of affairs may make it appear advisable to re-enter it.

This resolution was adopted by the board of the congregation and the Union was notified of its withdrawal. It did not affiliate with the Union again for eleven years, re-entering it in October, 1895.[31]

Wise's life was liberally spiced with such controversies and such actions. In general, he had learned to ignore them and go ahead. This course he pursued in respect to the College, the Union, and the *Israelite* as well. Three years before Congregation Rodeph Shalom decided to come back into the Union, one of the College's graduates, Henry Berkowitz, was in its pulpit as successor to Jastrow.

30

Chiefly of the Pittsburgh Conference

THE UNION WAS GROWING STEADILY IN STRENGTH. THE YOUNG RABBIS who had been ordained at the Hebrew Union College were having no difficulty in finding pulpits, and before long they were in the most influential congregations in the country. They were spreading loyalty to and an organic interest in both the Union and the College. In these years, however, the attention and much of the labor of American Jewry were preoccupied with the needs of the hordes of new immigrants who were pouring into the country, the pressure of relief work, and the various schemes for aiding them and settling them that were being discussed by all organizations.[1]

Wise was constantly publishing appeals in the *Israelite* to the effect that all congregations should desist from their attitude of doubt and separatism, and should at last make up their minds to join the Union, "to perfect the unity of American Israel."[2] When the Union convened at St. Louis in 1885, it resolved to form a Jewish Literary Union, "to unite and set to work all literary capacities together with all friends of Jewish English literature." Probably the chief purpose of this was to create some substitute for the Rabbinical Literary Association, which had ceased to function. Gutheim of New Orleans acted as chairman of the committee that created the "Jewish Literary Union." Wise was elected its first president, and at the beginning there were about forty rabbis in it. Its first project—it announced—would be to publish an English translation of the Bible. It is sad to record, however, that this project was never realized, was never—as far as the record reveals—even begun.[3]

Two years later, in the columns of the *Israelite*, Wise set himself the task of reviewing the "History of the Union." From the three articles, as they appeared, it was obvious that his chief purpose was to explain for the benefit of his readers why the Union had not made greater progress than in point of fact it had. Many times he had promised that before many years would have elapsed the Union would have within its fold all the synagogues of the United States. It will be worth-while to follow his account in these three articles.

In the first of them he went back to the time—forty years before—when dissension was the rule, when attempt after attempt had failed to make a beginning toward cooperation. Rabbinical conferences were consistently followed by "protests, dissensions and desertions." This was true of the New York meeting of 1848, that in Cleveland in 1855, and the Cincinnati gathering of 1871. All of them passed resolutions to establish a union, but side-issues always combined to make this impossible of realization. The work of the Cincinnati conference was swallowed up in "bitter and reckless discussion" of the foolish utterance of one man about a "personal God." Wise expressed his own belief that many of the attacks—like this—had in reality another purpose, to destroy the conference and the possibility of union. He had become convinced that nothing could be accomplished by working initially or solely with rabbis, and that he had to learn how to get the congregations themselves together. The result was the formation of the Union of American Hebrew Congregations in 1873. But the birth of this once again evoked a storm of acrimony. Though retarded by local prejudices and general "indifferentism," the Union grew. But not enough money was forthcoming for the maintenance of the Union and the College, so that they might pursue their tasks vigorously, and so that they might "turn their attention to other necessary institutions." "The Union began crippled." The Council of 1877 in Philadelphia adopted a resolution to take in the Board of Delegates, which represented a number of congregations of New York, Philadelphia, and neighboring communities. It was hoped and believed that the congregations of these cities would come in together with the Board of Delegates. In a report—adopted at Milwaukee in 1878—it had been planned that the Board of Delegates was to become "a committee on foreign correspondence and cooperation with similar bodies abroad, and watching over civil and religious rights at home." At the Sixth Council in New York in 1879 it had been felt that the Union had been fully established. But—Wise contended—various mistakes had been made: the meetings were changed from annual to biennial, which "kept it out of sight too long"; the Board of the Union and of the College were made sectional bodies, half of their members being from the East and half from the West; the Board of Delegates should have been a Committee of the Union, instead of which it was separately incorporated. [This is somewhat unintelligible and contradictory, compared with what has gone before!] Thus the Union was ignored in Europe, and the Board of Delegates "was accepted as the representative body of American Israelites." The Emanuel Theological Institute of New York was utilized as a preparatory department for the College. This served to increase the cost of operation, but added nothing in strength or influence to the service of the College. The New York school chose a man from a small Portuguese congregation in Philadelphia as its president. Nor had all this succeeded in eliminating the antagonisms of the past. "The antagonists of peace and union, harmony and cooperation, never gave up their arms." Two recent events appeared to indicate that that antagonism still existed. The Union had launched a project for agricultural settlement of "Russian refugees." But the enterprise was crippled from the start. "Today the only agricultural colony of Russian refugees that has a real existence is the Beersheba colony in Kansas," established by the Union. The second instance was the centenary of Moses Montefiore, to be used to establish a chair in his name for "sacred literature." Opponents proposed a dozen other schemes. The chair was established, but no funds had been forthcoming. Wise had also been trying to search out money to help poor students at the Hebrew Union College, again without success. All these circumstances tended to show why the Union had not done more in the fifteen years of its existence. But—he concluded—the majority of American Jews were for it, and the opposition would be silenced.[4]

In the second article Wise went on to describe the antagonism he had constantly endured from those who came from lands where democracy was unknown, who—according to him—did not understand Jewish life: "The majority rules, and where intelligence is at a low ebb in the body," some individual rules. Congregations would drop out for trivial reasons. He cited some examples. It was the habit in the East to refer to the "Western" Union, and the "Cincinnati" College. Wise himself was called incompetent. Both institutions were frequently urged to remove him from leadership. Nevertheless, at the tenth anniversary of the Union, in Cincinnati, July 10-12, 1883, out of the 128 congregations then affiliated, 114 had had delegates present. This was the "largest body of representative Israelites from all parts of the country ever assembled on this Western continent." The graduation of the first class of rabbis in 1883 was a glorious triumph. There was a banquet. Among other dishes were oysters, shrimps and crabs. This mistake was seized upon by some veteran opponents, and became a *casus belli.* Again was heard "the mad dog cry of heresy." Everything about Wise and his movement was *T'rephah* (ritually unfit). It was true, however—Wise continued—that no one believed in the *kosher* practices of those indulging in all this shouting. But congregations were hurt by the wild charges. A number of them in Boston, Hartford, New York, and Philadelphia left the ranks. This weakened the cause. "The future historian will admire the consistency, self-denial and inspiration for Israel's cause in those men and congregations who did stand by their flag. . . ." He inquired whether all this had been honest. "God knows!" Everything essential was dropped for the cry of heresy against Wise, "the reformer, the radical, the restless innovator, the ambitious, stupendous, destructive and impious Dr. Wise."

A new chapter had begun, and all of this had been written to explain why the Union had not done more in its first fourteen years of existence.[5]

The third article continued with reference to a matter which we have already described, the defection of Congregation Rodeph Shalom of Philadelphia. This did not prevent the Council of 1885 from being a very enthusiastic one. One rabbi in the East (Morais) had started another seminary. Many charges were made against the College; one of them was that the University of Cincinnati was not able to furnish a first-class secular education. The reform group felt the need of defending themselves. Therefore Kohler had convoked the Pittsburgh Conference (described later in this chapter). Wise debated with himself whether he should go, or "should he not maintain a kind of armed neutrality in the face of the combating parties? Could he keep aloof?" He went, for he decided that "silence would be a crime," and a "token of weakness." This did not connote that he was going "to Canossa." He "went to Pittsburgh to fall as a man rather than to rise as a renegade."

In Pittsburgh—he wrote—there were men with a diversity of approaches, that is to reform; but they were honest. Many of them were also men of genuine learning. It was better to take them by the hand as friends, to try to remain united. He had also to think of the Union and the College. The orthodox and the conservatives were constantly denouncing and persecuting him. To fail to go to this meeting would only have served to alienate the "reform element." "If no peace can be made with Eastern conspirators, let us have peace, union, and good fellowship among ouselves."

Nothing practical was done at Pittsburgh [the reader should keep clearly in mind that these are still Wise's opinions we are quoting]. It was an attempt to find peace on fundamental principles. But, as soon as it was over, false reports began to appear: that it had abolished the Sinaitic Sabbath and circumcision; that it had denied the verity of revelation, of prophecy, miracles, the "divinity of the Bible." In all this there was not one word of truth. The same charges were raised against the Union and the College. The old sophistry was in incessant circulation: that Isaac M. Wise *was* the College, and the College was Isaac M. Wise. And once again the Union was weakened. With the aid of two Portuguese congregations it was decided to organize a Seminary, like the Jews' College in London, like Padua for the Portuguese, and Breslau for the Germans. "Up to the date of this writing it is an advanced Sabbath-school, and none can tell yet, what it will be later on."

The Tenth Council of the Union held at Pittsburgh was attended by a large body of representatives. It had outlived the storm. Its future seemed very bright. Dr. Solis-Cohen of Philadelphia had appealed to the Jews of America to provide half a million dollars for the Seminary and to force the closing of the Hebrew Union College. Again the cry of heresy! Wise called this a "medical man's arrogance." Solis-Cohen had been answered by Gustav Gottheil, who said with some scorn that a medical man had now become the judge of Jewish questions. But all this—Wise felt—would do no real harm to Union or College. His only purpose had been in all this to review and to explain why many things had conspired to retard the development of the Union and the College, and to circumscribe their areas of service.[6]

Earlier Wise had printed a detailed account of the Pittsburgh Convention of the Union of American Hebrew Congregations, held July 12 to 15, 1887. This meeting had resolved: to collect an endowment fund for the College; to discontinue the Committee of Examiners; to begin the creation of a Sabbath School Union; and to transfer the seat of the Board of Delegates to Washington (the Chairman was Simon Wolf).[7]

We turn next to various matters affecting the Hebrew Union

College during these years from 1885 to 1889. It was hard for Wise to forget that not only were the New York rabbis failing to help him, to send students, or to collect funds; they were usually striving to harm him and the College. He remarked—ironically—that they were "reliable men."[8] In the same summer he submitted his annual report as President. At that time the College had graduated fourteen rabbis. Its faculty consisted of Wise, Mielziner, Zirndorf, David Davidson (Talmud), S. Mannheimer, Eph. Feldman (who taught Hebrew in the lower grades, and was himself then in the Senior Class), M. Goldstein (literature and music), and Aaron Hahn (who gave some lectures). The College had a roster of thirty-five students.[9]

In his report the following summer—in 1888—Wise reviewed the origin of the College, resolved upon by the First Council of the Union, on July 8, 1873, in Cincinnati; the decision had also been reiterated in Cleveland on July 4, 1874, where the name "Hebrew Union College" had been adopted. The laws to govern the institution were also formulated and adopted there. At the meeting in Buffalo on July 13, 1875, the work had been completed, and the beginning of the Preparatory Department provided for. The College opened on October 3, 1875, with seventeen students and two teachers. Later on Lilienthal volunteered to serve on the faculty. The principles governing the institution—Wise wrote here—were: "No test would be required as to age, sex, domicile, or religion, color or previous condition." There would be no fees, and stipends would be found for needy students. Later students were helped to go to High School and to the University of Cincinnati. Now a mansion has been bought, at a cost of $30,000, and the College has a regular theological faculty and a library. Wise listed forty-two graduates, and enumerated the members of the faculty at this time: Mielziner (Talmud), Davidson (Talmud and Commentaries), Zirndorf (History, Exegesis and Homiletics), Mannheimer (Hebrew and Aramaic, Bible and Mishna), Eph. Feldman and Isaac L. Rypins (assistants in Bible and Mishna), and Wise (Professor of Philosophy and Theology).[10]

Within a year of the Pittsburgh Conference of the Union the *American Hebrew* of New York, then an organ of orthodox Judaism, attacked Wise as a heretic, in its issue of February 25, 1886.[11] This was in an editorial entitled "The Need of the Seminary." The *American Hebrew* asserted that it had originally supported the Union and the College, but had come to the conclusion that no real Judaism was being taught. Therefore, it believed that a new institution should be started, "free from the shadow of baneful influences which have perverted the Cincinnati institution."[12]

It was shortly after this pronouncement that the Seminary was begun. Upon this sequence of events Wise had an occasional bitter comment. For example, in May, 1886, he wrote an account of a ministerial association meeting in New York:

> We have not the slightest idea how these different elements can establish a Sabbath School Union, unless the Eastern colleagues, like Dr. Gottheil and others, embrace the reformatory cause. . . . they have the intention of establishing an orthodox or conservative seminary in New York.[13]

Two years later Wise was calling Sabato Morais to task, because of what he called a "diatribe" which Morais had published, in which Morais had asserted that the Seminary would be the only means of "salvation," and in which he had excoriated everyone who disagreed with him. Wise called Morais a "good Hebrew, a hoary and good man." But he expressed the forlorn wish that Morais would be more brotherly and more tolerant. In another paragraph he asked that reform Jews stop supporting the Seminary and Morais.[14]

We come now to the meeting, which we have placed as the title for this chapter, the famous conference held in Pittsburgh in 1885, which set a norm for Reform Judaism for many years to come, and about which very much has been written and spoken. It will not be our purpose to evaluate it or to discuss it, either as to its genesis, the background of its "Principles," or its specific or general influence upon liberal Judaism in America. None of these enters into the intent of this work, which is exclusively to set forth the elements that contributed to Wise's life, work, and thought. We shall, therefore, consider the Pittsburgh Conference solely in its bearing upon him: his initial feelings concerning it (some of which we have already reported), his part in it, and his comments upon it after it was over. That all this may be set clearly before the reader we shall also set down at the proper moment the paragraphs adopted at the Conference.

We have seen that Wise had tried repeatedly to call together meetings of rabbis, and had himself participated in many of them. But none of them endured. The reasons may have been that there was too small a number of rabbis then in the United States, and that they were not homogeneous enough in attitude and in education. In the *Israelite* Wise wrote prophetically: "The graduates of the Hebrew Union College established an alumnal association and elected their officers. The first meeting will take place in St. Louis in July, 1885. Here you have the nucleus for a permanent rabbinical association."[15]

In 1885 Kaufmann Kohler of New York invited all the reform rabbis of the country to come to a conference in Pittsburgh. We have already put down Wise's debate with himself as to whether or not he should go.[16] In another issue of the *Israelite* Wise commented upon Kohler's purpose in calling the conference, and wrote: "We are the vast majority of the Jews of the United States; and we are pronounced reformers."[17] Later on—in the fall of the year—he published the call itself. The meeting was to be held November 16 and 17, for:

> All such American rabbis as favor reform and progress and are in favor of *united action* in all matters pertaining to the welfare of American Judaism.[19]

A number of rabbis convened in Pittsburgh in response to Kohler's call. The actual number of days of the meeting were more than Wise had announced, for the rabbis remained in session from November 16 to November 19. Wise wrote of it:

> The attendance was small, eighteen rabbis being present and among them the ministers of the most respected reform congregations of this section of the country. . . .

Permanent officers were elected: Wise as President, Joseph Krauskopf as Vice-President, and Philipson and Gutman as secretaries. The meeting:

> Declared itself the continuation of the Philadelphia Conference of 1869, which was the continuation of the German Conferences of 1841 to 1846. Dr. Kohler read a paper in which the principles were discussed on which the conference might unite.

This document was referred to a special committee for the purpose of formulating it into a "declaration." The committee met, completed its task, and brought it before the rabbis. It was amended and then adopted. It was hailed with delight and approbation (all this in Wise's report in the *Israelite*):

> Many lauded it as a resurrection of the spirit of ancient Judaism in the fullness of its humanizing power and its educational force.

It was acclaimed in much of Europe. The only objections heard were from the orthodox. There were rumors that the Conference had abolished circumcision, the Jewish Sabbath, and the belief in a personal God.

It is evident, however, that the Pittsburgh Conference had

found the means and standpoint to unite the reformatory elements within the pale of American Judaism.

Wise added a footnote to the effect that he adhered to this platform. Propaganda was being spread to induce congregations to withdraw from the Union because of the Pittsburgh Platform. But this was—Wise declared—to no avail. "No orthodox seminary exists yet, and none will ever be established."[20]

The declaration of principles adopted by the Pittsburgh Conference reads as follows:

1. We recognize in every religion an attempt to grasp the Infinite, and in every mode, source, or book of revelation held sacred in any religious system the consciousness of the indwelling of God in man. We hold that Judaism presents the highest conception of the God-idea as taught in our Holy Scriptures and developed and spiritualized by the Jewish teachers, in accordance with the moral and philosophical progress of their respective ages. We maintain that Judaism preserved and defended midst continual struggles and trials and under enforced isolation, this God-idea as the central religious truth for the human race.
2. We recognize in the Bible the record of the consecration of the Jewish people to its mission as the priest of the one God, and value it as the most potent instrument of religious and moral instruction. We hold that the modern discoveries of scientific researches in the domain of nature and history are not antagonistic to the doctrines of Judaism, the Bible reflecting the primitive ideas of its own age, and at times clothing its conception of divine Providence and Justice dealing with men in miraculous narratives.
3. We recognize in the Mosaic legislation a system of training the Jewish people for its mission during its national life in Palestine, and today we accept as binding only its moral laws, and maintain only such ceremonies as elevate and sanctify our lives, but reject all such as are not adapted to the views and habits of modern civilization.
4. We hold that all such Mosaic and rabbinical laws as regulate diet, priestly purity, and dress originated in ages and under the influence of ideas entirely foreign to our present mental and spiritual state. They fail to impress the modern Jew with a spirit of priestly holiness; their observance in our days is apt rather to obstruct than to further modern spiritual elevation.
5. We recognize, in the modern era of universal culture of heart and intellect, the approaching of the realization of Israel's great Messianic hope for the establishment of the kingdom of truth, justice, and peace among all men. We consider ourselves no

longer a nation, but a religious community, and therefore expect neither a return to Palestine, nor a sacrificial worship under the sons of Aaron, nor the restoration of any of the laws concerning the Jewish state.

6. We recognize in Judaism a progressive religion, ever striving to be in accord with the postulates of reason. We are convinced of the utmost necessity of preserving the historical identity with our great past. Christianity and Islam, being daughter religions of Judaism, we appreciate their providential mission to aid in the spreading of monotheistic and moral truth. We acknowledge that the spirit of broad humanity of our age is our ally in the fulfillment of our mission, and therefore we extend the hand of fellowship to all who cooperate with us in the establishment of the reign of truth and righteousness among men.

7. We reassert the doctrine of Judaism that the soul is immortal, grounding this belief on the divine nature of the human spirit, which forever finds bliss in righteousness and misery in wickedness. We reject as ideas not rooted in Judaism, the beliefs both in bodily resurrection and in Gehenna and Eden (Hell and Paradise) as abodes for everlasting punishment and reward.

8. In full accordance with the spirit of the Mosaic legislation, which strives to regulate the relations between rich and poor, we deem it our duty to participate in the great task of modern times, to solve, on the basis of justice and righteousness, the problems presented by the contrasts and evils of the present organization of society.[21]

A resolution was also adopted in regard to circumcision, as follows:

> Inasmuch as the so-called Abrahamitic rite is by many, and the most competent, rabbis no longer considered as a *conditio sine qua non* of receiving male gentiles into the fold of Judaism, and inasmuch as a new legislation on this and kindred subjects is one of the most imperative and practical demands of our reform movement, be it
>
> Resolved, that a committee of five, one of them to be the president of this conference, be entrusted with framing a full report to be submitted for final action to the next conference.[22]

At the session of November 18 a further resolution was unanimously adopted:

> Whereas we recognize the importance of maintaining the historical Sabbath as a bond with our great past and a symbol of the unity of Judaism the world over; and whereas, on the other hand, it cannot be denied that there is a vast number of workingmen and others who, from some cause or other, are

> not able to attend the services on the sacred day of rest; be it resolved that there is nothing in the spirit of Judaism or its laws to prevent the introduction of Sunday services in localities where the necessity for such services appears or is felt.[23]

One of the early biographies of Wise declared that there was nothing in the general tenor of these resolution to arouse Wise's enthusiasm; that they did not do justice to the uniqueness and genuineness of Judaism; that they were too "universalistic"; and that they did not avow the truth of revelation. In the *Deborah*[24] Wise wrote:

> The Conference at Pittsburgh did not intend to restore genuine unanimity. The prime motive in calling it together was to give support to the reformers of the East against the Rabbinists of the East.[25]

It may be well to pause here and ask a few pertinent questions. Wise had declared that "nothing practical had been done at Pittsburgh," and that there was no truth in the charges, which began to be spread, that the Pittsburgh Conference had abolished the "Sinaic Sabbath and circumcision," or had denied the verity of revelation, or the "divinity of the Bible." And yet, as one reads its declarations, one finds it far from easy to understand why Wise went along with it so completely and so enthusiastically. We shall refer in a moment to the things he wrote of the Conference in the weeks and months that followed it. But it is strange to note that apparently he took no umbrage at the resolution on a Sunday Sabbath, which did violence to all he had been saying and writing for many years—and with great passion. He did not argue about the second paragraph of the Platform, which could have been the words of a "higher critic," and which in the most cavalier fashion passed over the whole issue of the revelation of Scriptures. Some of the qualities and opinions that made the Platform a point either of rallying or of dispute for almost fifty years presented no difficulty for him, as far as it is possible to judge by what he wrote: the denial of the nationhood of Israel; the discarding of all hope of a return to Palestine, the sacrificial cult, etc. But it cannot have been so pleasant for him to have gone along with the specific language in the earlier paragraphs, with their reading out of consideration of the whole doctrine of the uniqueness of Judaism, and calling the Mosaic law only a "system of training."

Wise's whole course of action—at the Conference itself and in the period that ensued—is far from easy to comprehend. The only explanation that offers any degree of credibility is what he himself said, that he was once again willing to go very far in compromise for the sake of unity, in the hope that, by not insisting overmuch upon his own convictions, by not insisting upon issues, he might pave the way for complete rabbinic cooperation in the country.

At any rate, he was soon at work defending the Conference. A week after it had adjourned, he was denying in the *Israelite* that it had either discussed or done anything about "the Sinaitic Sabbath and the Abrahamitic sign of the covenant. . . . Nor were revelation and inspiration denied . . . or the Talmud in any way attacked. . . ." "All reports to the contrary are false." Whatever individual opinions may have been expressed in these directions were no more than individual. Those declarations that were finally made were "well founded in historical Judaism."[26]

The following week he indited a more extended article on the Pittsburgh Conference, which—according to him—"opens a new chapter in the history of American Judaism." He asserted that the Conference and its results were brought about by the unity in the idea of progress among progressive rabbis. Once again he claimed that there was nothing startlingly new in the "principles," but that they placed Judaism in the vanguard of liberal faiths. Rather curiously, and paradoxically, he asserted that the results of the Conference showed that "we are the orthodox Jews of America," and they (his opponents) "were the orthodox of former days in other countries." It was his opinion that certain direct consequences would flow from the Conference: the end of rabbinical opposition to the Union and the College; a Sabbath School Union; the discussion and decision of all future issues in conference and not by journalistic controversy. At the next meeting there would be reports on marriage, the liturgy for burial, family worship, the manner of admission of proselytes into Judaism, etc. He declared his own gratitude to Kohler, the "efficient cause" of the meeting. At the masthead of the *Israelite* he placed a complete text of the Platform. And this he continued to do in seven issues of the journal, evidently so that his readers might be brought to familiarize themselves with the text thoroughly. He continued by saying that the Eastern papers were furiously incensed by the Pittsburgh Platform, but, inasmuch as they had opposed Reform violently from the beginning, this could not be called anything new, and nothing was to be feared from them. He referred finally to what he called a "premature and therefore unjust" sermon by Benjamin Szold, who—according to him—had by then been captured by the enemies of the Union:

> The future of American Judaism belongs to the men of those very principles which were announced in the Pittsburgh Conference.[27]

Shortly after this, early in 1886, there was a conference of Southern rabbis in New Orleans, presided over by James K. Gutheim. It adopted the Pittsburgh Platform, but declared itself against Sunday instead of Sabbath services.[28]

It had clearly been the intention that the men who met in Pittsburgh were to come together again. Various tasks had been delegated to committees, and various proposals were still to be debated, and adopted or rejected. Wise announced in February that the next conference would be in Cincinnati in May.[29] It seemed to him still that at Pittsburgh the "foundation has been laid down for a union of American rabbis, and this is a victory for American Judaism." The date of the conference was postponed to June, but still in Cincinnati.[30]

In the same month he wrote that nothing in the history of American Judaism had elicited as much controversy as the Pittsburgh Conference. Nor was this true only of America, for many of the European journals had taken it up and commented upon it. But its results seemed to meet with the approbation—he said—of forward-looking elements everywhere.[31]

Information as to the next conference was becoming more precise. It was to be in Cincinnati, beginning on Monday, June 28, at the Plum St. Temple, and it was being called by a committee consisting of Wise, Adolph Moses, and Emil G. Hirsch. Immediately after it would have concluded its deliberations there was to be a meeting of the Jewish Literary Union.[32] Members of the Southern Conference of Rabbis would attend, and an invitation to them had been sent out by Gutheim and Voorsanger (then in Houston).[33] Wise anticipated that men would come from all over the country, and that they would act in behalf of the progressive men and societies of American Judaism, "to which the vast majority of American Jews belong. Opponents will doubtless keep aloof."[34]

One of the problems to be discussed at the forthcoming Cincinnati Conference was that of *Milath Gerim* (the circumcision of proselytes), originally taken up by Wise at the Philadelphia Conference and referred to a special committee at Pittsburgh. At the time of the Philadelphia Conference the matter had been discussed by Geiger in the *Juedische Zeitschrift*.[35] Wise himself had quoted at length from Leon da Modena of the 16th century. It had also been discussed by Felsenthal in a publication of the year 1878. Wise expressed the hope that the committee to deal with this would bring in a report, and that his point of view would be accepted.[36]

But all these hopes were doomed to disappointment. By the middle of the summer it was clear that nothing would be done. Wise then expressed the belief that most of the work to be accomplished would have to go to the future Sabbath School Union. The Jewish Literary Union did meet, and had five members present. Wise regarded the postponement of the sequel to the Pittsburgh Conference as temporary. He was convinced that the "group" would meet again in 1887, perhaps again in Pittsburgh.[37] In spite of his optimism, this was the last of the Pittsburgh Conference. and there were no large or important rabbinical assemblies until the organization of the Central Conference of American Rabbis in 1889.

For some time Wise continued to comment upon the declarations of the Pittsburgh Conference, answering what he termed the "ridiculous charges" made against them. Thus in September of 1886 he was denying that they were intended to "form a new religion":

> It expounded Judaism from the reformatory standpoint, not for the congregation, but for the only purpose of finding a basis of union for the rabbis of the reformatory school, to unite them to common work and usefulness for the benefit of Israel.

Moreover, he concluded, the Union and the College had and have had nothing to do with the Conference, with its declarations, or its results.[38]

The importance of the Pittsburgh Conference did not inhere in any organizational results, as Wise had hoped. It proved—in this respect—to be as abortive as had been its predecessors. Nor did it succeed in eliminating the deep differences of opinion in regard to the interpretation of Reform that had been raging between "East" and "West." Its only service was that of drawing up a formulation of beliefs, which for most reformers was regarded as authoritative and definitive for many years to come, and which was not thoroughly or officially reconsidered or altered for half a century.

A few odds and ends, having to do with Wise's life and activities, will round off this chapter.

In February, 1885, he announced that he would begin publishing an edition of the *American Israelite* in Chicago, and he hoped that this would not hurt the *Occident*. Chicago ought to be large enough for both.[39] That same year he wrote that the circulation of the *Israelite* was larger than the combined circulations of "all the Jewish papers published between the Atlantic Coast and the Rocky Mts."[40]

In the fall of 1886 he published a review of the events of the past year (under the title of "American Judaism"):

> There was no lack of attempts at unification and cooperation, and no deficiency of enthusiasm during the past year among American Israelites, notwithstanding all the petty dissension and small jealousies, the lack of fidelity, the forgetfulness of promises, the neglect of duty, the spites and grudges of individuals and bodies, whose perfidy is Albion-like. The principle of unification advances. It has taken hold upon the hearts of the public. It has taken root in the convictions of the intelligent. It will prevail. . . .

His mother-in-law, Rosalia Jonas Bondi, passed away in New York. Her husband, his wife's father, had been a banker in Dresden, had had four daughters. He had lost his fortune, migrated to America in 1863, and was made rabbi of Ahavath Chesed Congregation in New York. He founded a journal, *The Jewish Leader*, which appeared until his death, March 11, 1873. His wife, Rosalia was buried by Kaufmann Kohler.[41]

Wise made a trip to Kansas City early in the fall of 1885 to dedicate a new synagogue which was then being served by Joseph Krauskopf as rabbi.[42]

A few weeks earlier U.S. Grant had died. Despite the mixed quality of his feelings about Grant, Wise arranged a memorial service at the Plum St. Temple and delivered an oration in which he declared Grant to have been a great general, but not as able or as distinguished in other ways. Nonetheless, he praised him as a great American.[43]

That same autumn he was urged by the officers of his congregation to turn his attention to a subject which had been concerning them more than a little. Therefore he announced and delivered a series of lectures "For Infidels," intended to take up the bases of doubt and of faith.[44]

And, last of all, it is noteworthy that for some years he had been serving as a trustee of the University of Cincinnati. A paragraph in the *Israelite* announced that F. Wilson and he had been reappointed, that he would accept the honor once more, and that this was the only political office he would take.[45]

31

Chiefly of the Central Conference of American Rabbis

THE THIRD OF THE NATIONAL ORGANIZATIONS FOR WHICH ISAAC M. Wise was directly responsible, and which flowed inevitably from many years of striving and from the preceding creation of the Union of American Hebrew Congregations and the Hebrew Union College, was the Central Conference of American Rabbis, born at Detroit in the summer of 1889. From the very beginning Wise had been certain that one of the most important elements in shaping a united Jewish community in America, in raising its intellectual and spiritual level, in giving it effective leadership, was some form of rabbinic cooperation on a national scale. On every occasion when rabbis came together, whether for the purpose of considering special theological problems, as at Cleveland and Philadelphia, or for some specific practical task, like the meetings held for the revision of *Minhag America*, Wise had never failed to try to make the association more than temporary. He had urged this, year in, year out, in the *American Israelite*. He had varied somewhat in his concept of the purpose and function of such a rabbinical union. A large part of the time he spoke or wrote of it as a kind of modern Sanhedrin, a Synod, which would have the right to legislate on problems not only of ritual and practice, but even of some vexed theological, or credal, issues. Always in his mind there was a careful distinction between the duties and rights of a congregational association, and one to consist of rabbis. The first, while safeguarding the autonomy of individual congregations, should unite them for the creation of a theological institution, primarily—though not exclusively—for training rabbis; for a seminary for young Jewish women; for a Sabbath School Union; for a common liturgy; for text-books; for the defense of Jewish civil and religious rights here and abroad; and for additional purposes which he outlined from time to time. But it was never his concept that such a congregational union should include within its purview the discussion of, or decision upon, basic theological questions. For this such a gathering would not be equipped; nor would it be wise for it to hazard concern with such problems requiring theoretical [what he and his time called "scientific"] knowledge and a historic sense in regard to Judaism. It will, however, appear that he was not of the opinion that all wisdom was of the rabbis. He was well aware that in his own time there were some laymen—though certainly not many—who possessed sufficient interest and sufficient discipline to participate in these tasks.

It is significant that the order of the creation of the three bodies of Reform Judaism was as it was: a congregational union, a theological institution, and—last of the three—a rabbinical association. This corresponded roughly to the levels of opposition, the varieties of disunity, which he had found upon his arrival in America. All the literature of the time—especially the multitudinous and often vituperative pamphlets of that era—testifies to the fact that it was the rabbis who were especially inclined to polemics and to world-shaking differences, based often upon what might be regarded as minor points of belief or practice. Congregations often followed the lead of their spiritual preceptors. But the events showed that most of the congregations were quite capable of coming to the point of union and of concentrating upon the much more central needs their cooperation would aid them in filling, rather than upon the bitterness and partisanship that too often had characterized them in the middle of the nineteenth century. The College was obviously the most momentous activity congregations had to foster, for all else depended upon an American—and a well-disciplined—spiritual leadership. In a very direct sense progress in regard to liturgy, education, defense, and many other things, was contingent upon the presence in the United States of rabbis, not from across the seas, and not schooled under conditions and in a realm of ideas far from consonant with the concepts or the needs of the American Jewish community. And finally, as the sequence of events had demonstrated amply, there could be no regular, permanent, association of rabbis until the Hebrew Union College, six years after it had begun to ordain rabbis, had amassed a sufficient roster of alumni to serve as the nucleus for such an association. Whatever may be the opinion of the reader about Reform Judaism, or at whatever judgment of the life and work of Isaac M. Wise he may have arrived after reading this complete record (and of his system of thought after reading the third part of this book), it cannot be denied that Reform set the pattern for congregational cooperation, for rabbinical training, and for the many services and achievements of rabbinical union. More or less, *mutatis mutandis*, all Jewish movements in America have followed these leads. It is worth remarking that in the United States these three organizations have become the pattern for all, and remain the oldest in point of service in the cause of Judaism. It was largely Wise's unswerving resolution and dedication from the very outset to all this, his indomitability, his vision, which were responsible for the transformation of chaos into cosmos, of controversy into joint labor.

A few weeks before the convention of the Union of American Hebrew Congregations, to be held in Detroit, in the summer of 1889, Wise wrote:

> "Will you call a conference?" said one of our friends in a sort of admonishing tone. We will not, is our reply, although we are willing at any time to call the continuation of the Pittsburgh conference, if the majority of its members authorize us to convene it, or if, in July next at Detroit at the meeting of the council of the Union of American Hebrew Congregations the rabbis present want it so, or, to establish some new rabbinical connection. At the same time we admit, as we always did, that a close union and cooperation of the rabbis in this country would be a great blessing to the cause of Judaism and a great benefit to the rabbis themselves.
>
> We are in a state of primitive anarchy in all matters appertaining to the synagogue, and the lawful relation of the rabbi and the congregation, and by the way of self-deception we call it personal freedom or free development, or by any other optimistic name, which is the mantle of charity thrown over the frail limbs of our disintegrating self-conceit. If you want a change, you must do it, we are tied down to the Pittsburgh Conference.[1]

Later on, five years after the organization of the Conference, Wise gave as the reason for naming it the "Central Conference of American Rabbis," that there had already been one in the South and another in the East. He had supposed that the members of the new organization would come, aside from the alumni and faculty-members of the Hebrew Union College, from the Central States, from Ohio, and from the Mississippi Valley. But he had been wrong. By that time there were more than one hundred rabbis, and the organization had become truly national. But—he wrote—"it does not include Polish, Russian, and other so-called orthodox congregations."[2]

Shortly before the meeting in Detroit the *Israelite* contained a notice:

> We think that the best that can be done by the present generation for the future of Judaism in this country must be done by a solid union of its most promising intelligence, the closest cooperation of all watching and guarding each individual factor.[3]

The *Israelite* commented also that this convention of rabbis "shall be the continuation historically of former conferences," a theme that was frequently reiterated.[4]

It will be best, however, to take the account of the organization meeting from the records of the Conference itself. More than thirty rabbis met at the call of the Chairman of the Union. A printed proposal looking to the formation of a rabbinical conference had been circulated in advance by David Philipson. Berkowitz was elected secretary. The discussion as to the need for and the method of organizing such a conference was participated in by: Isaac M. Wise, Joseph Silverman, Davidson, Samfield, L. Mayer (of Pittsburgh), Wolfenstein, Hecht (Milwaukee), Aaron, Birkenthal (Hamilton, Ont.), Samuel Sale, and others. The motion thereupon adopted read as follows:

> We, the rabbis assembled to organize ourselves into a Central Conference of American Rabbis, have appointed a committee of five to report a plan of organization.

The committee consisted of: Mayer, Berkowitz, Mielziner, Aaron, and Sale. The rabbis reconvened the following day at Russell House in Detroit, and the report of the committee was submitted and adopted. It was resolved to call such an organization into existence, with the usual officers. The basis of its work was to be—as Wise wrote later—that of the previous rabbinical conferences in Germany, from Braunschweig in 1844 and onward. Any rabbi in a congregation might join, provided he did so before the following Passover. After that day these would be eligible for membership:

all possessors of a Doctorate of Philosophy or Philology who would also have a rabbinical diploma; "all autodidactic preachers and teachers of religion who have been for at least three successive years discharging those duties in any one congregation"; all authors of eminent books on any subject appertaining to Jewish theology or literature; and "all who have rendered important practical help to the cause of Judaism." These were much more liberal and inclusive provisions than obtained later on. The annual dues were set at five dollars. The Honorary President was Dr. Samuel Adler, who had been unable to come. The Conference was to meet annually, immediately before the sessions of the Union and at the same place. It resolved to publish an annual yearbook. To the first of these Yearbooks was added a section containing the proceedings of the previous rabbinical conferences in Germany and America. Half the dues were to be set aside for a relief fund for indigent colleagues. The first officers of the Central Conference were: Isaac M. Wise, President (over his "strenuous protests," but unanimously nonetheless); Sale, Vice-President; Berkowitz, Recording Secretary; Philipson, Corresponding Secretary; A. Hahn (Cleveland), Treasurer; and the members of the Executive Committee: Mayer, Mielziner, Samfield, Sonnenschein, Jos. Stolz, Max Heller, and Adolph Moses.[5]

In opening the Conference Wise declared that it must consist of "men of national conceptions; without local prejudices, without sectionalism; also without selfish ambition or private interests."[6]

Wise was in his seventy-first year when he assumed this additional responsibility.[7] Somewhat later—in the *Deborah*—Wise looked back over this time. In his own draft for the organization he had provided that Samuel Adler—then eighty years old and rabbi-emeritus of Temple Emanu-El of New York—was to be president. But despite this Adler had been made Honorary President, and he himself was compelled by a unanimous vote to become president. He "could not escape." But—he wrote—he made things easy for himself and let the members do the work.[8]

In the original draft of the Constitution of the Central Conference these words were used:

> The object is to lay the foundation of a central authority of American Judaism on democratic principles, the autonomy of the congregations, the personal and the official right of every Rabbi in office. . . .[9]

The Conference met for a second time in Cleveland, July 13-15, 1890, at the Young Men's Hebrew Association. In his presidential address Wise took note of the fact that within one year the organization had grown to a membership of ninety. He harked back to the rabbinical conference held in Cleveland in 1855, thirty-five years before. This had resolved to establish a "permanent synod" on democratic principles:

> As a doctrinal basis for the synod the following points were agreed upon: (a) the law of the land is supreme, which meant Judaism must be Americanized and republicanized; and (b) all Biblical law still in practice shall be practiced according to Talmudical interpretation.

This—Wise said—would exclude none of the reforms introduced in American Judaism. The above differs markedly, however, both in order and in statement from the actual text and the usual interpretation given at the time to the decisions of the Cleveland Conference of 1855. The comment is interesting in regard to Wise's own attitude toward it after all those years. He had tried to make progress by organizing Zion College and by preparing *Minhag America*. But he had had to encounter incessant, violent opposition. The Civil War broke out and made the continuation of work impossible. The Philadelphia Conference of 1867-8 had had immediate and disastrous consequences in controversy, "which destroyed every hope of ever reuniting American rabbis." Then came the founding of the Union and the College, "contrary to the will and with the outspoken opposition of the protesting rabbis."

> This was hoped to become a rock of peace, unanimity, and good will, and so it did among the congregations, but not among the rabbis.

There had been much intemperateness and many attempts to destroy the Union and the College. "They did succeed in isolating some congregations, even against the will of their respective members." The purpose of the Central Conference is "to redeem the American rabbinate from the odium of autocratic and quarrelsome disposition. . . ."[10]

Wise had written in the spring of that year—1890—that the Conference had become large enough for a "Great Sanhedrin," since it numbered then more than seventy-two members.[11] As a matter of fact, it was growing rapidly. Even in that year it had become the largest body of rabbis in America or in Western Europe. No lay members had been taken into its fold, as Wise had originally planned, and as the Constitution had provided.[12]

It will be permissible to leap ahead ten years to the time when, at the celebration of his eightieth birthday, Wise referred to the Conference in these words:

> By this God-blessed organization the American rabbis were united in a bond of brotherhood, all feuds, strifes, quarrels and animosities which raged among us for many years vanished like the fog before the sun.[13]

Over the years Wise presided and delivered an annual address. These messages abound with suggestions for building Judaism in America on this central principle:

> Judaism is inviolable as a revelation; it is Mosaic and Sinaitic, or it is nothing.

He would never place in jeopardy the basis of Judaism—as he conceived it—by admitting the validity of Biblical criticism. But it was not his purpose to impose his views on the Conference concerning the authenticity of the Pentateuch, or the revelation on Mount Sinai.[14]

It was not long before it was decided to draw up a liturgy to replace *Minhag America.* With great generosity and understanding Wise approved this project and cooperated to bring it to pass, despite the fact that *Minhag America* had become easily the most popular prayer-book among the Jews of the country. He wrote—for example—an account of a meeting of the committee engaged in the task of revising the ritual, held in New Orleans, January 12 to 15, 1892. Mielziner was in the chair and Isaac S. Moses acted as secretary. They were well on the way to completing the task. Wise wrote much also concerning the delightful hospitality of New Orleans and of his disciple, Max Heller.[15] At last he was ready to announce that the *Union Prayerbook*, as it came to be called, was ready for publication and delivery.[16] This was certainly the most important of the activities of the Conference in its earliest days.

Next we shall come to another momentous task, the assignment and preparation of the papers on Judaism read at the World's Parliament of Religions during the Columbian Exposition in Chicago in August, 1893.[17]

In 1891 the Council of the Union met in Baltimore beginning on July 7. Wise had announced that there would be a report and some proposals from the Board of Delegates. One of these that would be placed before the Union—from what source the *Israelite* does not state—was that the Union should be vested with jurisdiction over religious problems. With this Wise declared he had no sympathy and trusted that it would be defeated.[18] The following year he announced that the forthcoming convention of the Union would be at Washington, to begin on December 1, and to be preceded by sessions of the Central Conference.[19]

The even progress of work at the Hebrew Union College was darkened by the suicide of two of its students in the "A" Grade, by name Salinger and Frauenthal, the former from Philadelphia and the latter from St. Louis. Wise was deeply grieved and could find no reason for this tragedy, except that both boys had probably been suffering from *dementia praecox*.[20]

To the faculty of the College was added in the fall of 1892 a man destined to play a great role in American Jewish life, though not at the College. Max Margolis was then twenty-five years old, had received a Doctorate of Philosophy from Columbia, had studied at Humboldt Gymnasium in Berlin, and had pursued rabbinical studies in Russia. He remained at the College until 1897.[21]

On April 6, 1889, Wise's seventieth birthday was celebrated at a gala affair at the Plum St. Temple. The sister-congregations of the city participated in the happy occasion, as well as representatives of the Union. There were congratulatory addresses by Henry Mack, the president of Wise's congregation; by the children of the Talmud Yelodim Institute; by David Philipson for K.K.B'nai Israel; and by B. Bettmann for the Union. At the end, as a token of affection and regard, Wise was given a deed to the property at 615 Mound St., which had been bought for $14,500, and its library furnished by the alumni of the College. This was to be the home in which he would spend the last decade of his life. Julius Freiberg spoke for the Board of Governors of the Hebrew Union College, and Israel Aaron for its alumni. The President of the University of Cincinnati brought greetings, for Wise was still at that time a member of its Board of Directors, and remained so until 1898. Charles S. Levi spoke for the students of the College. The orator of the day was Joseph Krauskopf of Philadelphia. There were messages by the hundreds from congregations and organizations from all over the land.[22] A cantata, dedicated to Wise and written by Goldstein, the cantor of B'nai Israel and a synagogal composer, was sung. The Hebrew words had been indited by Mielziner. There was a closing-prayer and benediction by Edward N. Calisch, then of Peoria. The *Israelite* printed the texts of almost all these addresses. The program—it commented—was good, but "a trifle lengthy." Wise kissed each pupil from the Institute in turn.[23]

There was also a celebration of this birthday at the College. Here the speakers were members of the Faculty, plus Wolfenstein of Cleveland, David Philipson, Joseph Stolz, E. N. Calisch, and the Preceptor, Feldman.[24]

In 1892 the congregation celebrated its fiftieth anniversary. For this occasion Wise and his grandson, Max B. May, wrote a little booklet detailing most of the history of the congregation.[25] Wise announced the appearance of this booklet, and wrote that it would tell a remarkable and significant story.[26] The *Israelite* contained a long account of the celebration. There was a tremendous assembly at the Plum St. Temple. An orchestra aided with the music. In the procession were fifty pupils of the Sabbath School, the board of the congregation, surviving charter members, etc. The music for the service was sung by a choir of thirty-six voices. Rabbi Charles Levi opened the service with prayer. There was an introductory address by the then president of the congregation, Louis S. Levi. A poem was read by B. Bettmann. And Wise himself spoke:

> What is still more remarkable is that all reforms and changes introduced tended to a steady growth not only in numbers, but in spirituality and genuine piety, in love and admiration of Judaism, and faithful adherence to its eternal dicta. In this temple is yet today Prayer-meeting [*Minyan*] twice every day. Here the Hebrew language is still cultivated in the school and preserved in the temple to a large extent.

The congregation, he said, had introduced Confirmation and the late Friday evening service. M.J. Mack spoke in memory of the officers and members of the congregation who had died during these fifty years. In the evening there was a banquet at which the surviving charter-members and ex-presidents were guests of honor.[27]

Some time before, Wise had had a note from Isidor Lewi, the son of his old friend in Albany. Lewi wrote that on a tour of Europe he had visited Radnitz, the Bohemian city which Wise had served as rabbi until he had left in 1846. Lewi informed Wise that no one there remembered him any longer, for forty-four years had elapsed. But it was recalled that Wise had delivered his last sermon in Radnitz on the last day of Passover.[28]

There was at this time a note in the *Israelite* of some historical interest, to the effect that the Jewish population of the United States in 1891 was about half a million, and that the German Jews were still in the majority, though barely.[29] Toward the latter part of the next year, Wise reviewed the course of events from *Rosh*

Ha-shono to *Rosh Ha-shono*. Very sadly he commented upon the great increase of anti-Semitism in the world and its many distressing manifestations. He himself—he wrote—used to think that Jews were somewhat at fault. But now, as a result of the recrudescence of the blood-accusation, he is sure that it is all a composite of lies, slanders, and libels. How—he asks—can the world retrogress so? Certainly things were changing drastically from the world as it was in his youth, from the millennial atmosphere that prevailed after the American and French revolutions.[30]

Samson Raphael Hirsch had died. Though he differed with him, Wise had—as did hosts of others—a deep regard for him. Wise declared him to have been one of the great formative influences of the century in Jewish life and thought, together with Frankel, Geiger and Holdheim:

> The radical Holdheim; the liberal, scientific Geiger; the conservative, scientific Frankel; and the out-and-out Rabbinic-cabbalistic Hirsch.

But Hirsch, whatever his point of view, was a deeply respected and creative man.[31]

The burdens of office must have begun to hang heavy upon Wise's shoulders. For the first time in all the years of his incumbency he took an assistant, Charles S. Levi, one of the graduates of the College, who preached his inaugural sermon at the Plum St. Temple on August 31, 1889. Wise announced that Levi would deliver sermons during the Holy Days, and would later give his own course of lectures on Friday evenings.[32]

An interesting note is to be found in the *Israelite* in the summer of the following year. It is a brief sentence, indicating that once again that year Wise would take no vacation. Though there had been no specific mention of this earlier, it seems evident that—in contrast with most of his colleagues—he had been unable to find the time to leave the city and to divest himself of his responsibilities.[33] Part of his preoccupation was due to the fact that he was about ready for the appearance in print of his *Pronaos to Holy Writ*.[34]

He appealed to his readers to send petitions and resolutions to Congress against the "Blair Sunday Bill," probably a bill to make Sunday a national day of rest. Wise declared that this would destroy the Constitution itself.[35]

A very happy occasion for him was a journey he made to Albany, on May 24, 1889, to dedicate a new synagogue that had been erected by his old congregation, Beth Emeth, now for some time reunited.[36]

Despite his age and his crowding tasks he was continuing his practice of giving carefully prepared addresses on Friday evening. In the fall of 1891 he gave such a series, on "Israel's Place in World History."[37] The autumn of the next year the subject was "A Review of the Messiahs in Jewish History."[38] And the last one of which we have record in this period was on "Superstitions of Our Age."[39]

He had now reached the age of seventy-three, and there was no sign of weakening in him, either in his capacity for work, or in the vigor and creativeness of his mind. He was still carrying the labor of the *Israelite*, the *Deborah*, his congregation, the Union, the College, the Talmud Yelodim Institute, his public duties, the new Central Conference of American Rabbis, and the thousand-and-one obligations that came his way outside the regular course of his professional life. Surely of him as of Moses could it be said: "his eye was not dim, nor his natural force abated."[40]

32

The Last Years

OCCASIONALLY THE ISRAELITE CONTAINED FACTS BEARING ON THE general character and dimensions of the Jewish community of America. These indicate some things about what that community was when Isaac M. Wise came to Cincinnati in 1854, and what it had become in the latter years of his life. One issue stated that in 1812 Rabbi Gerson Mendes of New York had estimated that there were then approximately 15,000 Jews in the United States. In 1848 M.A. Bert placed the size of the Jewish population at 50,000. The Union of American Hebrew Congregations took a census in 1880 which indicated that the Jewish population of the country then was 230,257. David Sulzberger of Philadelphia—finally—had placed it at 937,-800 in 1898. The editor of the *Israelite* himself thought it likely that it was somewhat over a million.[1]

Several years earlier Wise had again been appointed one of the "regents" of the University of Cincinnati. He had already served in this capacity for twelve years. This election was for six more.[2]

Ex-President Rutherford B. Hayes, nineteenth President of the United States, died in Fremont, Ohio on January 17, 1893. Gov. William McKinley of Ohio had requested that memorial services be held. This Wise did at Plum St., and called Hayes "an honest and unpretentious man."[3] Nor was this his only reference to political life. In the spring of the same year he announced the inauguration of Grover Cleveland, to be held on March 4, and proclaimed this to be a "great day for America."[4]

Wise was still vigilant and vocal in regard to the maltreatment of Jews. The *Israelite* was constantly writing concerning tyranny in Russia, of the varieties and diabolical ingenuities of Jew-hatred and persecution under the Czars. Several years before he had written of the massacres in Rumania. A petition was drawn up, and directed to the Secretary of State, asking that the treaty with Rumania—which must have lapsed about this time—not be renewed. Wise claimed that this petition had been signed by men of all races and creeds, and urged his readers to join in it.[5]

In the years that followed nothing of moment occurred in regard to the civil or religious position of Jews, or in the history of the country itself. But—like everyone else—Wise was shocked deeply and audibly by the blowing up of the Maine. He reported that the people of the country were divided about going to the help of the Cubans then fighting for their independence from Spain.[6] McKinley decided upon war, and for the most part Wise backed him up. Wise wrote that "many wished it, many dreaded it," but he asked nonetheless for patriotic loyalty and unity.[7] From then on—and for some time—he placed an American flag at the masthead of the *Israelite*.[8] During the Spanish-American War a rather strange enterprise was afoot—to collect contributions on behalf of "the American Patriotic League," and to present a battleship to the government of the United States. Wise appealed especially to those of Russian birth, to give to this as testimony of their gratitude to America[9]

He was often commenting upon the Dreyfus case. His reaction to it, however, was neither as clear, nor as extreme, as Theodor Herzl's. It did not appear to Wise a world-shattering event, or one having much to do with the essential status of democracy or liberalism in France. In 1898 he wrote that the issues of the case were becoming more transparent and the innocence of Dreyfus more patent. He wrote, too, that, though the entire tragic story had threatened many things in France, justice would be done. He quoted *in extenso* a long article on the case from the *Cincinnati Commercial-Tribune*.[10] This event, the Dreyfus case, was but one of many things that happened in the later years of Wise's life that might have shaken his pristine belief in "progress," the millennial time of brotherhood and freedom he had thought it to be, in the certain equality Jews would soon win everywhere, and of the future of Judaism as the "universal religion of the West." Occasionally in his writing there were signs of depression; but for the most part he remained to the end unshaken in his optimistic convictions. Wise noted later that Dreyfus had been brought back to Paris from Devil's Island, confessions had at last been made from which the truth had become unmistakable, that a new trial was about to be held, and that certainly Dreyfus would be acquitted. He expressed the hope that thereafter all "scores should be cancelled," and that there would be "no revenge."[11]

It was also during this same time that the Union Prayerbook was completed by the committee of the Central Conference of American Rabbis, of which we have written earlier. Wise hailed this event and declared it the final step in the unification of American Israel, the cessation of strife, and the completion of the process begun by the Union and the College. This had been achieved as soon as the alumni of the College were "numerous enough to form a safe nucleus to spiritual union, a unity of principle and sentiment. . . ."[12] Though it proved true that the great majority of reform congregations soon adopted and used the Union Prayerbook, a number continued to use those of Jastrow, Einhorn, and others for many years thereafter.

It was gradually being impressed upon Wise that his original hope of bringing all American Jews together into one congregational union, one rabbinical association, one theological institution, was never to be realized. After the Milwaukee convention of the Central Conference in 1896 Wise wrote that the organization comprised only reform rabbis, but that its standpoint rested firmly on the history of Judaism in all ages, and not upon one period, one place, or one class.[13] The Union Prayerbook, he wrote:

> comes to you with the sanction of the largest conference of American rabbis that ever met here. . . . We look upon the completion of the Union Prayer Book as the triumph of the cause in which so many good men for the last fifty years were enthusiastically engaged.[14]

It was during these years that the European propaganda for Zionism came to a head, after Pinsker, Hess and Smolenskin, after the publication of Herzl's *Der Judenstaat*, and after the convoking of the First World Zionist Congress in Basel in 1897. To all this Wise referred at some length in his presidential message to the Central Conference at Montreal in the summer of 1897. He had always been opposed to what he thought to be Jewish "particularism," to any concept of a return, religiously or nationally, to Palestine. This rested upon his interpretation of Jewish history and of Judaism as a faith, as well as upon his belief as to God's purpose with Israel, and his intense and ardent Americanism. We shall not here cite either the gist, or some of the typical sentences of this pronouncement, for in the third section of this book we shall attempt to give a consistent and complete account of Wise's views on Jewish colonization in Palestine and elsewhere; on the Jews as nation, race, or religion; and on the appearance of political Zionism.[15]

Charles S. Levi left the congregation and was followed by Louis Grossmann, a graduate of the second class of the College, who had till then been serving in Detroit. It was in 1898 that Grossmann came to Cincinnati to become Wise's assistant, to head the religious school, and to preach on alternate Saturdays. He remained as rabbi of the congregation after Wise's death.[16]

Quite often, especially in these final years, Wise was writing about what a rabbi should be:

> He must first and foremost be a Jew with heart and soul thoroughly and enthusiastically, a man in whom there is no guile; a teacher who never loses his patience, truthful and reliable as a rock, and benevolent as the palm in the wilderness. The audience must be convinced that whatever this man in the pulpit says is certainly true to the best of his knowledge, and that he does as he teaches. This is a man's moral weight, it is the magnet to attract. Men who preach for a salary, live to make money, and see in wealth the object of existence, may be honest, but they are poor preachers, as inefficient as those who preach one thing and do another. . . . A rabbi must be a master of Jewish literature and history or he is a fraud. . . .A rabbi of this age must be a classical and scientific scholar and a pleasant orator, or he is useless to his congregation. . . . The rabbi must speak and preach in the language of the country in which he lives, hence the American rabbi must teach, speak, and preach in English to the young, else they will not understand him. The rabbi must know and feel the wants of his congregation, he must understand old and young, and they must understand him. The rabbi must stand as high, and, if possible, a little higher morally, intellectually, and scholastically than the best of his members; he must be an authority. . . . He must not be made by the office he holds, he must make the office respected and honoured. He must love his office and his congregation and not the wealth of the individual members thereof. "For the lips of the priest must guard knowledge and the Law is asked from his mouth, for he is a messenger of the Lord of Hosts" (Malachi 2:7).[17]

On Sabbath mornings he was himself accustomed to use a text. Near the end of his life he wrote of this, urging it upon his disciples as a practice:

> For the benefit of the young preachers we state here that the text of the sermons—we never preach without a text from the Bible—were mostly taken from the Book of Psalms which is inexhaustible in the richest and most sublime treasures in theology and ethics. . . . Speaking to the young men, we would say, never preach a sermon without a text from the Bible, a text containing the theme which you can elaborate. The text is the best proof in support of your argument. A sermon without a text is an argument without a proof.[18]

Wise served as president of the Hebrew Union College for twenty-five years until his death. Though—as we shall see—he was occasionally disturbed about the possible fate of the institution after his own departure, he had given it more standing and more vitality than he had thought. His reports to the Board of Governors were filled with avowals of his purpose and accounts of its progress. The central goal of the institution he stated quite traditionally: it was to hand on the Law, which had been and must remain sovereign. Learning was the most sacred aspect of the Jewish heritage. He never tired of repeating that the rabbi of the future must continue to be a creative scholar and a leader of his people. He gave lectures, upon which he labored hard, on theology, the immutability of Law, on Jewish philosophy, on Apologetics, and on many other subjects. His influence upon his pupils was limitless. He inspired them with his own love of people and faith and his own dauntless belief in their future. He entered the lives of his disciples, in learning, and in the warmth of love.[19] He was constantly commenting upon the status and growth of the College. Thus in 1894 the *Israelite* (this was eleven years after the graduation of the first class) had a brief paragraph to the effect that by that time the College had ordained forty-three rabbis, and that its student-body numbered forty-six.[20] None of the honors and none of the duties of his life meant as much to him as did the presidency of the Hebrew Union College.[21]

When the Union met in New Orleans in 1894, Wise wrote of it:

> The forerunner of this union was an organization called the Board of Delegates, which existed for a number of years prior to 1873 and was finally merged in the union.

But—he claimed—the Board of Delegates was never more than sectional, and had its origin chiefly in antagonism toward reform:

> The call for the Union of American Hebrew Congregations came direct from the reformatory side of the community. . . .

> but the congregation remains the representative body of Israel's cause, and the Union of American Hebrew Congregations remains the *Keneseth Israel* ("the congregation of Israel," that is, the whole house of Israel), from which none is excluded.[22]

At this biennial convention there was an address by Leo N. Levi, a prominent and thoughtful layman. This address teemed with strictures upon Reform and upon rabbis in general. Wise declared it a futile and unjust pronouncement, based upon an outmoded kind of "*Rabbinerhetze*" (baiting of rabbis). The Central Conference called an emergency meeting in New Orleans and at once adopted resolutions protesting against the content and manner of Mr. Levi's paper, its untruth and unfairness. Discussion of this raged over the country for some months.[23] At the same time Wise participated in services at the Touro Synagogue. He commented upon their form:

> The divine service as a whole is somewhat antiquated, not for me, however, to whom the Hebrew has yet all the charms of a mother-tongue. You say *Shema Yisroel* and I feel what you say; you say "Hear, O Israel," and I can only hear.[24]

In the last three or four years of the century there were signs that his strength was beginning to wane. What he wrote may have been evidence of no more than fatigue, for he was still carrying disproportionate burdens. He was indeed entitled to the conviction that old age was upon him, and that a time of rest was at hand. Thus—in a letter written to Julia Richman, Mrs. Rebekah Kohut and Prof. Gottheil, May 31, 1898, he used these deprecatory words:

> I have become a dried-up, old and pedantic schoolmaster dipped in some particular subjects as the *Moror* [the bitter herb at the Seder meal, the first night of the Passover] is dipped in *Charoses* [apples and nuts, supposed to represent the mortar of the bricks Israelites made in Egypt]. I could not possibly write anything to amuse, entertain, or interest the general public of "Helpful Thoughts." I beg to be excused.[25]

Nor was he too sanguine about the fate of his creations. In a holograph letter to Simon Wolf, November 1, 1898, he claimed that, since the retirement of Moritz Loth, the first president of the Union, nothing was being done in the Union to bring in new congregations, though the then heads of the body "are men of honor and the highest integrity, men of noble intentions and sincere Israelites." Nothing can be done, "and this it is that makes me sick." The worst enemy of the cause is "cold indifference." "To meet this foe I am too old." He was deeply satisfied with the work of the College. He asserted that he had confidence in the congregations—the orthodox, of course, excepted. The College had fifty-eight graduates and their presence in the American pulpit had changed it radically. There were seventy-eight students at the beginning of the academic year:

> What chagrins me is, that I had to do the whole work unaided, and I am now nearly eighty years old, and have no security before me that this college will not after my death go down as fast as it was built up, when I have before me the fact that in the last fifteen years nothing was done to enlarge the Union or replenish its treasury. . . . We look like a bankrupt concern. . . . I discovered too late that perhaps Napoleon was right after all, money and victory are synonymous.

He urged that an alliance be made with the B'nai Brith:

> You certainly did understand the policy in establishing a Central Conference of American Rabbis, which was to free the Union of theological bias.

As to the Conference, "it is responsible for all reforms."[26]

There was great excitement during these years over a most exceptional event—the Columbian Exposition, commemorating four hundred years since the discovery of America. This was held in Chicago in 1893. Arrangements were made for a World Parliament of Religions, at which each faith was to elucidate its own principles. Such a convention was unprecedented—and thus far since then without any successor. Judaism was to be represented by the Central Conference of American Rabbis. In some of the issues of the *Israelite* Wise discussed the role Judaism was to play, and how its part could best be planned.[27] It was important not to present "a hybrid," an unorganized and unrelated series of papers. Themes were assigned well in advance. All of these were published subsequently in a book, *Judaism at the World's Parliament of Religions.* Wise himself was assigned three subjects: "The Theology of Judaism," "The Ethics of Judaism," and a "Bibliography of the Jewish Periodical Press." Louis Grosmann aided him with the last of these. He himself felt the task to be one of supreme importance. In fact—he wrote—he felt like the High Priest on Atonement Day. After much meditation he decided to tell the simple truth.[28] He wrote of the Parliament that it would be "perhaps the last opportunity to expound and defend Judaism under the eyes of the whole religious world," though just why he felt so ominously about it is hard to understand.[29] The Jewish section of the Congress was from August 10 to 31, 1893.[30] In one of Wise's own holograph letters, written to a lifelong friend, William Stix of St. Louis,[31] he wrote:

Cincinnati, Sept. 22, 1893.

My dear friend, Wm. Stix:

I am much obliged to you for your kind congratulations on my second speech ["The Ethics of Judaism"] delivered before the Parliament of Religions in Chicago. You are the only man outside the hall where it was delivered, that did send me kind words of recognition.

According to the official critics in Chicago, my first speech in the Parliament on the Theology of Judaism was my masterpiece, but I could not publish it in full; it is too long and too abstruse. It will appear in full in the book in which all will be collected in one volume [published eventually by the Union in Cincinnati, 1894].

However, I do not glory in any of my literary productions, nor am I greedy for applause, although like others I am glad to hear a pleasant word from my friends and do highly value your kind letter. What I do glory in and consider the most triumphant moment of my life is, that I could and did proclaim the God of Israel and His ethical law in that august assembly, before the eyes of the world's scholarship, and I did do it intensely Jewish, without reference to any other creed, belief, or literature, simply our own from our own sources; and have thus published to the world boldly and fully the sap, flower and fruit of Judaism, and yet commanded the respect of the assembled representatives of all religions. This is the great triumph in which I glory, for which I praise the Almighty, that He has preserved me to celebrate that most gratifying moment of my life. . . .

Yours, as ever,
Isaac M. Wise.[32]

A second edition of the *Pronaos to Holy Writ* was published in 1893, appearing to indicate that it was being used in various parts of the country.[33]

Various celebrations of anniversaries occurred in the last years of his life. We shall review these, but without including the wealth of speeches that accompanied them.

The fiftieth anniversary of Wise's ordination as a rabbi was celebrated on October 21, 1893 at the Plum St. Temple. There was a speech by Charles S. Levi, who said: "The history of reformed Judaism in America is the history of Isaac M. Wise's fifty years. . . .";

and an address by Wise. He thanked the many who had arranged the celebration, and those who had helped him throughout his career. He went back to his opening sermon in Radnitz, and preached on Isaiah, Chapter 51, verses 1 to 3 as a text. About Albany he spoke somewhat optimistically in retrospect:

> Although I announced at once and without restraints my reformatory ideas and projects, all went well in peace, harmony, and mutual satisfaction.

His inaugural sermon in Cincinnati had been on April 26, 1854 at Lodge Street. The first number of the *Israelite* had appeared four months later, "the first English organ of reformed Judaism." Again he spoke of the wonderful relationship that had obtained between his congregation and himself. The closing prayer and the reading of the service were by Rabbi Samuel Hirschberg, then of Fort Wayne, Indiana. The entire congregation filed past to shake the hand of their venerable preceptor. In the next issue of the *Israelite* Wise thanked all and sundry and remarked that for fifteen years he had made it a habit to read only the foreign press, thus ignoring the many attacks made upon him.[34]

During these last years the congregation and the institutions he had founded lost no opportunity of coming together to express to Wise their gratitude and affection. Nor, in reading the accounts of these occasions, does one have the feeling that they were perfunctory or formal. In every line they evidenced the remarkable position Wise had won among his people, perhaps too their awareness of the fact that he was not to be with them much longer.

Wise's seventy-ninth birthday was celebrated at a Friday evening service at the Plum St. Temple arranged by the ladies of the congregation. The dark, colorful synagogue was gay with flowers. On the platform sat Jacob Ottenheimer, president of the congregation, David Philipson, Wise, and Louis Goldman, vice-president of the congregation; also Charles S. Levi, and an augmented choir and orchestra. All on the podium made speeches. A silver loving cup was presented by Leah Rosenthal, and Isaac M. Wise responded. Then in the evening a banquet was held at the St. Clair Hotel by the students of the College. This lasted until after midnight. Abraham Hirschberg of the Senior Class was toastmaster. There were songs by the College Glee Club, and toasts by Mielziner, Philipson, Leo Wise, E. L. Heinsheimer, Charles S. Levi, and Joseph S. Kornfeld.[35]

Then one year later came the much more important occasion of

Wise's eightieth birthday. The Central Conference of American Rabbis timed its convention for Cincinnati to correspond with that date. On the program[36] there was a note to the effect that Wise's birthday had been "on the third of Nissan, 5579." The Board of the Talmud Yelodim Institute had met on February 10 and resolved to participate. They gave Wise a *Sepher Torah* (Scroll of the Law) "with a proper inscription."[37] By this Wise and the congregation were deeply moved. A special banquet was held after the service at the Plum St. Temple. On the platform at the Temple were: Rabbi M. Samfield of Memphis; Rev. Howard Henderson, Louis Grossmann, Charles S. Levi of Peoria, Joseph Silverman of New York, Max Heller of New Orleans, David Philipson of Cincinnati, and Messrs. Louis Goldman, Julius Freiberg, Nathan Drucker, Jacob Ottenheimer, B. Bettmann, and Frederick Rauh. The children of the Talmud Yelodim Institute marched in at eight o'clock in the evening. There was an invocation by Charles S. Levi, and a floral offering by the children; an address by Louis Goldman, then president of B'nai Yeshurun; a presentation on behalf of the congregation by Nathan Drucker; for the Talmud Yelodim Institute by Jacob Ottenheimer; for the College by B. Bettmann; an address for the Central Conference by Samfield; for the alumni association by Max Heller; for "our sister congregations" by David Philipson; also a paper by Henderson, a representative of the Methodist Conference:

> We come as citizens of Cincinnati to acknowledge your many services rendered to our city during your forty-five useful years of residence.

The address was reported to have been very "flowery." For the congregation Wise was given a bronze bust made by Sir Moses Ezekiel; Philipson presented him with a silver loving-cup; Silverman with a silver vase. Wise closed with a "few simple and touching sentences."[38] There were also many gifts and messages from congregations and individuals from all over the land.

Then in the evening there was once again a banquet, given by the students of the College. There were present Wise's family, the Faculty, and the Board of Governors. The master of ceremonies was Simon Cohn. Rabbi Adolph Moses spoke for the Board of Governors, Mielziner for the Faculty, Rabbi Abram Simon (then of Sacramento, Calif.) on "The Alumni"; Louis Grossmann for B'nai Yeshurun; Israel Klein on the students; and Dr. Julius Wise on "The Family." A special number of the Hebrew Union College

Journal was published. This contained: a sonnet to Wise by Jacob S. Raisin; "A Renaissance of American Judaism," by Louis Grossmann; "What's In a Name?" by Mielziner; "Modern Paganism," by Maurice Harris; "A Much Needed Reform," by William Rosenau; "An Acrostic to Isaac M. Wise," by Prof. S. Mannheimer; "Dr. Wise as a German," by Max Heller; and other articles, including one on "Wise as a Journalist," by Louis Grossman, and a poem dedicated to him by Harry Weiss.[39] The banquet was held at the Phoenix Club. Wise himself was not reached until midnight. He rose to say that he had done and said many foolish things in his life, but one of them had never been to make a speech after eleven o'clock at night. But he ventured on the prophecy that within a short time the whole world would recognize Judaism and the truth of its doctrines.[40]

There was something fitting about all this: that during these years there should have been so many occasions at which disciples, friends, fellow-workers, and congregants could gather to speak to and of Isaac M. Wise. He must have looked old and bent then, as his pictures of this last year reveal him. Eight decades had passed over him. The way from Steingrub to Cincinnati had been a long and often a hard one. No man had given himself so without stint. No man had pursued his aims more steadfastly, undeterred by scorn or antagonism. All that remains to be told is of how the end came to him, and a few of the things—among the innumerable series of addresses and articles, poems and tributes—that were said of him. To this we shall devote the last chapter of this part of our book.

33

"At the Call of Thy Messenger"

MANY YEARS BEFORE, ON HIS WAY TO CINCINNATI IN THE FALL OF 1853, Isaac M. Wise had written a special *Seelenfeier* service for *Yom Kippur*. In this he had dwelt on the pathos and the beauty of human life, the longings for justice, truth and love that stir the human heart, and the intimations of immortality life reveals. In one paragraph he wrote:

> At the call of Thy messenger, the king descends from his seat of gold and purple, his staff and pallet of straw are left behind by the beggar. The strong and the weak, the rich and the poor, the sage and the fool, the just and the wicked, all bend their steps toward that final goal that awaits every one born of woman, and the places that knew them will know them no more forever.[1]

Thus we come to the time in the spring of 1900 when Wise's last day was upon him. He had lived a long, vigorous, and useful life. Despite some periods when nervous tension had made him think he was ill, he had enjoyed superb health all his life. But he had worked at a pace and to an extent far beyond those of the ordinary man. The burdens he had carried had always been heavy. Four-score years had moved over him, from the time of his difficult and chequered youth, from the many years of his wandering and studying, from his chafing at the tyranny and the confinement of his world in Austria, from his bold cutting of his ties to his home-land and his journeying to America, from his struggles in finding a place for himself in the young, scattered American Jewish community, from his battles for more freedom and more modernism in Judaism, and through all the years in which he had fixed his eyes upon the goal of Jewish unity and Jewish knowledge, and had striven with might and main and against contumely and antagonism to attain these ends. That he could pursue this way so long was a result of his extraordinary resilience of mind, his refusal to be paralyzed by defeat.

But the years had been taking their toll. The strong frame was weakening. Weariness had been creeping into that indomitable spirit. At last the time had come when he must answer the "call of Thy messenger." It is good to know that he heard it in the fullness of years, not like Moses looking down from the heights of Moab upon the Promised Land beyond the Jordan, but in the midst of his people, surrounded by his victories. It is good to know, too, that he died in peace, with the kiss of God on his lips, perhaps even as he had sometimes prayed to die.

There is some discrepancy of detail among the accounts of his death: in a chapter by David Philipson, in the biography of his grandson, Max B. May, and in the contemporary accounts immediately after his death in the *Israelite*. We shall note the discrepancies in passing, but adopt the principle that the account of the *Israelite* is the most correct.

On Saturday morning, March 24, 1900, Wise went to services at the Plum St. Temple. He preached on one of his favorite texts, one that could hardly have been more appropriate as his last. It was on the beautiful passage in Numbers, Chapter Six, verses twenty-two to twenty-seven, which we shall reproduce here, though it is well-known:

> And the Lord spoke unto Moses, saying: Speak unto Aaron and unto his sons, saying: On this wise ye shall bless the children of Israel; ye shall say unto them:
>
> The Lord bless thee, and keep thee;
>
> The Lord make His face to shine upon thee, and be gracious unto thee;
>
> The Lord lift up His countenance upon thee, and give thee peace.
>
> So shall they put My name upon the children of Israel, and I will bless them.

He spoke on the efficacy of prayer. The sermon was delivered to a large congregation, and in his delivery of it there was no sign of an abatement of his mental or physical powers. At the conclusion of the services, and in accordance with his wont, he descended from the pulpit, and many came forward to grasp his hand and to say "*Gut Shabbos.*" (A good Sabbath!). There was no intimation of trouble, no sign of the swiftly approaching end. He had a genial word for each of those who spoke to him.[2]

From the Temple he went to his home on Mound Street and had his mid-day meal with his family. Here too he seemed in excellent spirits. Several people at the Temple had told him that they had been especially instructed and moved by the content of his sermon, and he had promised them to write it out and to send them a copy.[3]

Again as was his habit he left his home and walked to the College. At that time there was an afternoon service held by and for the boys, but Wise did not attend it. He gave an hour of instruction, beginning at two in the afternoon. Here enters a slight discrepancy. The time just given is in one source;[4] but another, probably more accurately, wrote that he had gone at 2:30 P.M. to the Hebrew Union College, and had then taught. Philipson, thereafter, has him returning to his office, where the blow fell.[5] But the other accounts agree that it was at the end of his hour of teaching that he felt faint and knew that something was wrong with him. The most dramatic of the accounts then describes him as falling to the floor, while he was in the class-room with his pupils, and being picked up by the boys and carried to his couch in the president's office.[6] But the article in the *Israelite* said merely that he had felt faint, and had been assisted by his son, Jonah, through the corridor and to a sofa in his private office.[7] It was, however, obvious that something was seriously wrong, and first Dr. Hillkowitz, and then Dr. Joseph Ransohoff, were called. In the meantime, in a semi-coma, he had been taken from the College to his home. Here again the accounts differ. One of them has him already past help at this time, unconscious and without movement.[8] But the contemporary record indicated that, when the doctors came, they found him fully conscious and in excellent humor.[9] The likelihood is that it was during that night, the night of March 24, between Saturday and Sunday, in the hours after the outgoing of the Sabbath, that the final stroke came upon him, and that he sank into almost complete unconsciousness, an unconsciousness from which he never rallied. Thus it continued for many weary hours, all day Sunday and into Monday, March 26. During the first night, the night of Saturday the 24th, he tried to speak several times, but his words were either inaudible or unintelligible. He tried to write, and a pen was placed between his fingers. But he was unable to hold it, and it fell to the bed.[10]

He was in no pain. His tender and beloved wife sat by his bedside patiently and hopelessly. His children, and hers, were about her and by him. Colleagues of the city, members of the faculty of the College, and pupils, came to inquire, and to ascertain whether they could be of help. Many friends from among the members of his congregation came to the lower floor of the house, at 615 Mound St., to make anxious enquiries. But in the room there was no sound except that of his labored and faltering breath, softer and softer, weaker and weaker, as the day advanced. Naturally the account from which we rephrase this was informed with much sentiment. It said that he was "sleeping like a child," that his wife had her arms about him, "peering into his beloved face." The afternoon passed, and, as the sun was setting, he ceased to breathe. His soul had fled. An older colleague, who was in the room, repeated the time-honored words of Job: "The Lord hath given, the Lord hath taken away, the name of the Lord be blessed." (Job 1:21).[11] According to the *Israelite*, he passed away at six in the evening.[12] He would have been eighty-one years old on March 29, but three days later.

His body was taken to the Plum St. Temple, where on the morning of the 29th, it lay in state. Thousands of his fellow-citizens, and hosts of his congregants and friends, came to take a last look at his mortal remains. He lay in a plain pine-box, as he himself had specified. It was lined with white muslin, and a black pall had been thrown over the rude coffin. There was but one token of flowers upon it, of smilax and violets. The funeral services were set for ten o'clock on the morning of Thursday, March 29, his birthday. At the home, before leaving for the Temple, prayers were read by Moses Mielziner, his friend, a scholar, and a gentle, loving soul.[13] It was a raw and rainy day, but the Temple was filled, every seat taken, and many who could not get in were standing outside under the rain. There was a perceptible smile on Wise's face as his body lay in the coffin. Nearly all the wholesale and retail houses of business in the city had been closed to honor him. Superintendent Boone excused the children from school.[14]

The order of services at the funeral was: an opening prayer by David Philipson; a hymn written by Isaac M. Wise and always used at the Plum St. Temple for *Kol Nidre* at the Memorial Service, "*Es leben unsere Toten*" ("Our dead live"); and the funeral oration, for forty minutes, by his assistant and successor, Louis Grossman, who took his text from Psalm twenty-five, verses 12 to 13:

> What man is he that feareth the Lord? Him will He Instruct in the way that He should choose. His soul shall abide in prosperity; And his seed shall inherit the land.

Thirty years before Wise had indicated that he wished these verses used as the text at his funeral. They were moving and fitting.[15]

There was a great procession that followed his remains to the United Jewish Cemetery (maintained jointly by B'nai Yeshurun and B'nai Israel) in Walnut Hills. The cortege arrived there at 1:30 in the afternoon. The commitment prayer was given by Rabbi Charles S. Levi, who had been his assistant in former years, and at the graveside the last simple words of tradition were spoken by Louis Grossmann. The grave was filled in by the family and friends.[16] The active pallbearers were eleven students from the Senior Class of the Hebrew Union College.[17]

After the passage of a year his congregation caused a marble obelisk to be erected over the grave, where it still stands, and a headstone placed, on which the inscription is as follows:

ISAAC M. WISE

Born in Steingrub, Bohemia, March 29, 1819
Died March 26, 1900
Rabbi of K.K. Bene Yeshurun
Founder of
The Union of American Hebrew Congregations
The Hebrew Union College
The Central Conference of American Rabbis

In the memorial number of the *Israelite* on April 5 there were poems by George Kohut, Annette Kohn, Ida Goldsmith Morris of Glasgow, Kentucky, and Hoke Heidler of Elkhart, Indiana. The Mound Street Temple devoted its entire Sabbath morning service to memorial. Many congregations throughout the land had a special service in Wise's honor. There was a memorial meeting of the printers at the New York Times, and a resolution of sympathy for its publisher, Adolph S. Ochs, Wise's son-in-law. To the funeral had come many rabbis from the entire country, not only graduates of the College, but many friends and co-workers also. Almost every Jewish paper had a memorial edition. There were many public tributes in a great diversity of places, especially in the regular daily press of the country. The *Israelite* cited especially a service that was held at Temple Sinai in New Orleans, served by his disciple, Max Heller, and reprinted some of his words:

> It is here we must understand the personality, if we would account for the tremendous influence it wielded. At its foundation was the principle of work, of the supremacy and para-

> mountcy of duty. His powerful mentality was absorbed in the duty of each hour to the defiance of every physical hardship; in inexorable loyalty to his purpose he could outstay every younger strength. His calm, unquestioning, self-centered purpose, absolutely superior to every selfish or material consideration, set him upon a pedestal above all the swaying contentions of men who might be his superiors in talent, but who had to bow down before his single-mindedness and elevation of aim. Withal, the most resisting were drawn to him by the kindliness and geniality of temperament, which lighted up his weighty seriousness of manner.[18]

A Memorial Service was held at Plum Street on Sabbath afternoon, May 5. On the platform were Frederick Rauh, vice-president of the congregation, and Julius Freiberg, president of the Union. There was an address by Louis Goldman, president of the congregation, a memorial oration by Louis Grossmann, and speeches by Bernard Bettmann for the College, Jacob Ottenheimer for the Talmud Yelodim Institute, Philipson for B'nai Israel, and the final address by Max Heller of New Orleans for the alumni of the College. The service closed with a prayer and benediction by Moses Mielziner. There had also been a prayer by Judah L. Magnes, then a student at the College, on behalf of the students.[19]

On March 31, the Saturday after Wise's death, there was a special service in the Chapel of the College. At it Moses Meilziner delivered an address entitled "An Appreciation." This deserves quotation at some length. Meilziner began with a text taken from II Samuel, chapter three, verse 38:

> And the king said unto his servants: "Know ye not that there is a prince and a great man fallen this day in Israel?"

Such a prince and a great man was Isaac M. Wise, and therefore his death is felt by all. No one had more cause to do him honor than the Hebrew Union College, to which he devoted the best of himself. The students loved and revered him, and say: "We are now orphaned, for our spiritual father is no more."

Mielziner then proceeded to make an extended comparison of Wise with Jochanan ben Zacchai, the great Jewish scholar and leader, who founded the rabbinic academy at Jabneh in the first century of the era. Ben Zacchai, when he was about to die, gathered his disciples about him. They asked him for a last admonition and blessing, and said to him: "Thou art a light for Israel, the right-hand pillar, the powerful hammer."[20] These are significant epithets. They apply equally to Isaac M. Wise. Like Ben Zacchai he too was a light in darkness. Ben Zacchai proclaimed that Judaism was not indissolubly bound to the sacrificial cult of the ancient Temple. Israel's true sanctuary is the divine law of truth and justice. To this faith he gave new life and new energy. All this was equally true of our American Jochanan ben Zacchai. He found Jewish affairs in the United States in a sad state of disorder. To these shores Jews had brought diverse customs and practices and many of the ideas of the ghetto. These could not be in harmony with the air of a land of liberty. Isaac M. Wise devoted his efforts to bring light and order. His favorite motto was "Let there be light." His journal and his many addresses stirred hosts of people. He rejuvenated Judaism, freed it from the notions and practices of the ghetto, and brought Jewish worship into harmony with modern thought and modern culture.

Wise—Mielziner went on—was the author of several important works on Jewish history and theology. Among many he spread a knowledge of the glories of our past and of our sublime mission. This was true for non-Jews as well as for Jews.

In the second place, Jochanan ben Zacchai was "the right-hand pillar." This was intended as a reference to King Solomon's Temple, before which the right-hand pillar was called "*Jachin*" (He establishes). And this was a reference to Ben Zacchai's inestimable service in establishing an institution which proved to be the mighty pillar of the temple of Judaism. The Roman general [by tradition, Vespasian], who gave Ben Zacchai permission to found an academy at Jabneh, could not have suspected that this would prove to be the means for the salvation of Judaism. Thus Isaac M. Wise also established institutions which saved Judaism in America, especially the College, for the salvation of Hebrew knowledge and for the education of rabbis and spiritual leaders. To his foresight, his wisdom, and his labors the College owes its existence. Even Wise's enemies and antagonists now admit the usefulness of the Hebrew Union College, especially since its graduates have gone forth to occupy the pulpits of the largest congregations. Of this Wise was not only the founder, but until his death he was its president and one of its very best professors. The students were "daily witnesses" of his devotion and his fatherly care, in spite of his age and in spite of his arduous labors in other fields. He was also rabbi of a large congregation, and editor of two religious papers.

Thirdly, Ben Zacchai was a "strong, powerful hammer." True, he was a gentle person, greeting all men with kindliness. But he was also a "hammer," to combat the Sadduccean principles, and to refute the arguments of those who were opposed to his spiritual and liberal interpretation of the Law according to the exigencies of changed times. Clearly Ben Zacchai was the prototype of Wise, who himself was gentle, kind, almost childlike, yet who wielded a mighty pen, combating antagonistic opinions, repelling assaults; not personal attacks, for these he ignored, but attacks upon what he regarded as right and holy.

The rabbis said: "Where wise men destroy, it is for the purpose of building up." Isaac M. Wise used the hammer to destroy, so that he might build anew. The Talmud says: "A sage who dies cannot be replaced." Jochanan ben Zacchai gave as his last blessing these deeply significant words: "May the fear of God influence all your actions." Wise left a similar blessing in the verse from Psalms, which he selected as his life's motto, the text used by Grossmann in his funeral oration, from Psalm 25, verses 12 and 13.

This entire analogy is fitting and instructive, and it is for this reason that we reproduce the larger part of it in substance.[21]

There would be no purpose in appending here the tremendous number of articles and addresses which followed Wise's death. We have adduced the spirit and the progress of his life, so that those who have read might judge for themselves, without resort to summations and appraisals.

What needs to be added in conclusion is merely that which was done by the Central Conference of American Rabbis in his memory. The alumni of the College appointed a committee, of which Moses Gries of Cleveland was chairman, to collect a fund to put the College on a permanent basis and to see to it that Wise's fear that the College would die with him would not be borne out by the event. A Sabbath in the spring of 1900 was to be dedicated to this purpose all over the country.[22] The Acting President of the Conference, Joseph Silverman, sent out to its members news of Wise's death, and in the letter said that the loss of no American rabbi had ever created so universal a sorrow:

> Dr. Wise was the pathfinder of American Israel and American Judaism. I do not ignore or belittle what other men have done for Judaism, but I verily believe that Dr. Wise was original, independent and fearless in breaking the way through the intricate confusion caused by the conflict of a traditional religion with modern life.[23]

A Memorial Service was held at the convention of the Conference in Buffalo, and addresses were made by M. Landsberg, Isaac S.

Moses, L. Mayer, Samuel Sale, and Schlesinger. Thus Mayer spoke on Wise as a theologian:

> Most men are keenly susceptible to the influence of current thought. Always self-centered without being selfish, Dr. Wise was an exception to this rule. The theories of the modern school of higher critics met with strong opposition from him. The Sinaitic revelation he regarded as historically unassailable. . . . His defense of his views concerning the authenticity and authority of the Bible, which from first to last underwent no change, made him the subject of many an attack from his opponents.[24]

Wise's life was ended. But the institutions he had called into being with so much travail did not die with him. His own fears as to their fate proved unjustified. Nor have the reminiscences of his own life and spirit disappeared from among American Jews. A life so valiant, so devoted to high ends, forging its way from frustration to victory, filled to its brim with abounding faith in God and in His revelation through His people and their faith, is not blotted out by its *finis* upon earth. The validity of his personal theology, the contribution made by the kind of Reform Judaism he advocated and its destiny, these we leave to others. This was his life and these were his works. They are written as part of the record of man, to be read and judged by God and by the generations to come!

Part III

Isaac M. Wise
His Thought

Foreword to Part Three

THE PURPOSE OF THE THIRD PART OF THIS BOOK IS TO SET FORTH a systematic outline of Isaac M. Wise's thinking on the various subjects that most interested and concerned him. His writing and speaking covered many years, in his books, in articles in the *Israelite* and in the *Deborah*, and in many of his published addresses. Obviously it was not probable that they would be completely consistent. No man writes for so many years without maturing, without occasionally—or even often—changing his point of view, shifting in the emphasis he himself tends to give to various aspects of his opinions. In some cases we shall indicate these variations. But for the most part we shall consider his literary remains as a whole.

It is not intended to compile an anthology, to throw together passages in his own words. This would prove too lengthy and too dull. This must not, however, be taken to mean that we shall not include many statements of opinion as he himself wrote them, for otherwise these pages would seem too abstract, would do too little toward setting before us the man as he was—not only with his habits of mind, but also with his characteristic way of phrasing his views. At the outset it should be obvious that the systematization of his thoughts—in this Part Three—will make them more schematic than in fact they were, more logical and consecutive in their order and expression.

To the more general sections dealing with his opinions concerning religion in general, Judaism, Zionism, etc., we shall also append a chapter entitled "Curiosa," consisting of out-of-the-way paragraphs, sparks struck off his anvil, dealing with a great diversity of topics, often amusing, colorful, indicative of the variety and vitality of his interests, sometimes of their whimsicality, and then again of his stepping in where angels fear to tread. But these too may contribute toward our visualization of the man.

As was noted in the Preface to the whole, this entire section was planned for a specific reason: chiefly because in the opinion of the author there has been a rather startling amount of misconception and even misrepresentation of Wise's opinions, his concept of Reform Judaism, his attitude toward Hebrew, etc. While the purpose of this Part is not primarily polemical, it should be corrective. It is my hope that, with this complete outline of his opinions, and with the careful documentation the notes afford, these distortions or fantasies will be exposed.

Parenthetically it is necessary to call the reader's attention to the fact that we have already included much material on his opinions, as they fitted into the framework of his life in Part Two. These can be found, and appended to the remainder, by use of the Index.

The general plan of Part Three will—again somewhat schematically—be as follows:

FOREWORD

Chapter I. *On Religion in General*

Chapter II. *On Judaism*
- A. Judaism and the Jew
- B. On the Theology of Judaism

Chapter III. *On Judaism (continued)*
- C. On Biblical Criticism
- D. On Miracles
- E. On the Messiah and the Messianic Hope
- F. On the Mission of Israel

Chapter IV. *On Judaism (concluded)*
- G. On the Talmud
- H. On Hebrew
- I. On the Rabbi

Chapter V. *On Reform Judaism*
- A. On Reform in General, its Concepts and Practices

Chapter VI. *On Reform Judaism (concluded)*
- B. On the Position of Women
- C. On a Synod

In general our method will be to utilize only one statement, or one formulation of an idea; but in the notes we shall refer to all the places where this and others like it—in some cases very many—are to be found, so that the reader who may wish to do research on some aspect or other of Wise's thinking may be able to find the passages without too much difficulty.

It is our feeling that this last section of our book will bear out the statement made frequently in its biographical pages: that Wise had a vigorous and sometimes subtle mind; that he was—while not a great creative scholar—far from unacquainted with classical Jewish sources; that the diversity of his interests—Jewishly and humanly—was amazing; and—finally—that he was much less "radical" in his approach to the great central issues of Judaism than were many others in Europe or in America. It was his own claim, made again and again, that his kind of Reform was in the mainstream of Jewish tradition, that it could be accepted without doing violence to any of the great constants of Jewish belief or of Jewish practice. Doubtless he deluded himself somewhat in this, and in his belief as to the probability that his particular approach would soon find universal acceptance and lead to complete Jewish unity of opinion and of organization. But this very conviction on his part exerted a great influence upon his own methods of thought, his own instinctive or reasoned reaction to many aspects of Jewish theology, of the forms of Jewish life.

In a word, it is our hope that we shall contribute to a greater understanding of the man, not only through the incidents of his life, but also through the manifestations of his own mind. It is a truism that a man, especially a man like Wise, lives at least as much in what he thinks as in what he does.

1

I. On Religion in General

CONCERNING WISE'S VIEWS ON RELIGION, AND ON THE MANY IDEAS and problems associated with it—especially in his own day, there is one chief source: a series of addresses he delivered in the fall and winter of 1874 to 1875, later published in book-form under the title, "The Cosmic God." To this we have already referred in the Second Part of this work.[1] But we shall review the circumstances of its origin again briefly, before giving to the reader a rather rapid résumé of the work, with the occasional quotation of Wise's own words.

The book was dedicated to the memory of his first wife, Theresa Bloch, who died on December 10, 1874 at the age of fifty-one. The book—Wise wrote—was conceived in sorrow. The two years of her suffering and decline before her death were filled with anguish for him. Doubts assailed him. One night he opened the Bible and happened upon Psalm 119, verse 92:

> Unless Thy law had been my delight, I should long since have been lost in my affliction.[2]

This initiated his process of recovery. He plunged into philosophy, and through this hard method found himself again.

The work is a rather far-reaching consideration of the fundamental problems of philosophy, science, metaphysics, and religion; full of the evidences of his own reading and thinking, intended to allay his own doubts, to answer his questionings of himself and his people, containing some rather remarkable *aperçus*, and also some naïve and thoroughly dated ideas. We shall set its main contentions before the reader, but we shall not be able to help him with the terminology, history, or adequate exposition of many of the points made. The work must speak for itself as to its own merits and failings.

As we have said, "The Cosmic God" was in reality an attempt by Wise to find himself, to defend the cause of religion, to make what use he could of philosophy.[3] It was his belief that he would be able to arrive at a God-concept by strictly "causal reasoning." The book is therefore "in the main a new evidence of the existence of Deity."

First of all, it is necessary to enter into the problem of truth and its criteria. He proposes to go over all essential problems concerning the religion, philosophy, and science of the 19th century, and to search out what may be thought by intelligent men. Truth is complete in God, but partial in man.[4] Its chief test is self-consistency. Knowledge comes to man only in part through the senses. It has another source as well—from the mind. The latter is superior to the former. There is also the entire realm of meaning to be taken into account. Even a materialist, by believing in order, demonstrates his acceptance of the reality of the mind.[5] Fascinatingly, may the writer remark, this is to be compared to one of the main points made in a splendid book by Alfred North Whitehead, "Science and the Modern World."

What are the criteria of truth in the realm of the mind? Mind is the supreme reality even in relation to the senses. Here again the test is in inner consistency. Natural science is in essence the harmonization of the sensual elements of experience.[6] These two (that is, science and philosophy) cannot be left as contradictory, or disparate, disciplines. They in their turn must be brought into agreement.

Wise declared himself on the side of Immanuel Kant, and against Bishop Berkeley. He accepted the reality of the "*Ding'-an-sich*" (the "thing in itself")—that is, the actuality of material things outside the mind. Man has been given the capability of finding full truth, if he will but seek it.[7]

What are the methods of knowledge [the field of "epistemology" in philosophy]? We come to know, first, by "receptivity and spontaneity." Wise devotes himself here to a recapitulation of the views of John Locke and Immanuel Kant. He accepts Kant's addition to the thought of Locke, namely, that "ideas are in the mind prior to sensual intuition."[8] The mind begins with *a priori* ideas. These may seem complex, but are really simple. The transformation of sounds into meaning is a spontaneous process. All percepts are thus transposed by the mind. But the mind has other functions which are independent of sense, the perception of ideas.[9]

He turns next to the relation of mind to brain. The translation of physical into psychical terms is unimaginable. "You are the thing that puzzles me." . . . "You cannot satisfy the human understanding in its demand for logical continuity between molecular processes and the phenomena of consciousness." [Here again, let the editor remark, we find in Wise a fairly remarkable shadowing forth of some very recent discussions by scientists.]" "This is the rock on which materialism must inevitably split, whenever it pretends to be a complete philosophy of life." [This is the central point made with great brilliance in Lange's "History of Materialism."][10]

Man is thus both a physical and a spiritual entity. He has mental and moral qualities. Among other things, materialism cannot account for our "knowledge of our knowledge." Materialists harp on the physiology of the brain, as the seat and organ of thought. But the mind is the cause, the brain the effect. How can one conceive of a brain contemplating itself? No elaboration of physics or chemistry, no writing about the phosphorus content of the brain, can help us to comprehend how matter can think.[11] Where in the brain is the seat of judgment, of truth, or of error? It is the mind that controls the brain, that criticizes and corrects. If this were not so, all science would have been impossible, and would be unsound.[12]

Where are to be found the evidences of the human mind? Chiefly in its products: in language, history, art, science, religion and philosophy. Wise sets himself to enumerate and review the number and diversity of the achievements of man in language. History is the mind actualized, crystallized in deeds. But the unifying force here and in all else is mind.[13] The same essential reality reveals itself in art, which is the evocation of unity out of disparate parts by the subordination of matter to the uses of the mind. Science too is patently an activity of the mind, discovering the laws of nature, adding to the wealth of the human spirit, constructing and applying laws. "Man understands nature, but it does not understand him."[14] Most wonderful of all is self-consciousness, self-knowledge. When guided by spontaneous inspiration, this self-knowledge is religion.[15] When it applies discursive reason, it produces philosophy. It is not the function of philosophy to prove anything, but rather only to systematize it. The mind has many methods of procedure, some inductive, and some deductive. It follows the process from cause to cause, and through His attributes to God. In all the stages of his growth religion abides in man. The spirit must first know itself, and then it comes to learn of the reality of spirit without.[16]

Man is unique in moving from the finite to the infinite.[17] One of his most mysterious and wonderful activities is philosophy, in which he sifts and compares. Each philosophy is another step forward and inward. It is a vulgar error to term all of it subjective. Science is—in fact—impossible without philosophy. Philosophy is the focus of the ideas of an age.[18]

Having striven to establish the contention that mind exists, that it is central, the author can proceed to reason from that starting-point on many other matters.

Wise turns next to one of the thorniest and most polemical problems of his time, Darwinism, which here he calls "Homo-Brutalism."[19] He regards the entire thesis of Evolution as, at the very least, uncertain, incapable of explaining the genesis of life or of man. Evolution would make man a child of Fate, and would repudiate freedom and reason.[20] The word "freedom" leads him to an excursus, eloquent but digressive, on the struggle for that spiritual commodity in the eighteenth and nineteenth centuries. Darwinism itself is a pernicious doctrine, robbing man of dignity, making might right, and "war to the knife" a law of nature. Darwinism also gives aid and comfort to the effete aristocracies of Europe.[21]

Wise turns next to a rather confused discussion of "race." He claims that the Bible does not teach the unity of the human race[22] [in this he is at odds with the rabbis]. Not all men are descended from Adam and Noah [this was discussed in detail in the "History of the Israelitish Nation," pp. 42-45]. Nor is it possible to move biologically from race to race. Finally, Wise resents the assertion that man is descended from animals.[23]

Man is unique. Wise admires Darwin, but thinks he has failed to make out a case. The truth is rather that apes are fallen men. No good purpose is served by the theory that man is descended from simians. This serves only to degrade man. The theory of evolution displays inexplicable dissimilarities between species. This is true especially as between man and the primates. Man must have appeared on earth with some of his physical and psychological possessions, his posture, and the human larynx. Psychic dissimilarities are even greater and more striking. It is fallacious to reason that, because some psychic traits exist in animals, therefore man represents a difference only in degree. Mind is not a question of quantity, but of quality. All animals are mere machines. Mental traits are ascribed to them by men. In general, Evolution

> . . . is not based on any known fact and explains none. It is useless in all departments of human knowledge and practice. It is nugatory to morals, robs man of the consciousness of his dignity and pre-eminence, and brutalizes him. . . .[24]

Next Wise turns to Ontology, the realm of being. His mind is overwhelmed by the idea of space and its immensities, by the effort to grasp the universe. But one must try! . . . First of all, what is matter? Is it, or is mind, the essence?[25] He continues with a consideration of the atomic theory in ancient and modern times. The fundamental error—to which he had adverted earlier—lay in thinking that a greater degree of reality inheres in matter than in the intelligence of man.[26] The world is only an image. Everything exists in the intellect (Berkeley); there is nothing real outside. Just the contrary of this is argued by the atomist. But, since we know nothing of the real nature of the atom, how can this help us, or bring to us any explanation of life or mind?

By the nature of his work and its method the scientist must be a materialist. But he must not arrogate to himself the claim that this is all knowledge, all truth. Wise begins then a review of philosophic materialism; with the physicists of Greece, in the Middle Ages, thereafter in the cases of Gassendi and Hobbes. Again he inserts a digression, this time about the fate of liberalism in Germany and at the time of Metternich.[27] Christianity was undermined by men like Haeckel, who disposed summarily of the idea of God. Two new dogmas appeared: that the world is a blind machine, and that experiment is the only path to truth. And, secondly, that only that which exists in the senses exists. It is Wise's hope that the nineteenth century will correct these tendencies, and that materialism will die out with the causes that produced it.[28]

He proceeds to describe the current state of knowledge about the atom. Atoms are "inert, passive, and imperceptible." But in reality science deals only with forces, not with matter as such. Atomists assert that there is no matter without force, and no force without matter. To Wise "the atomistic standpoint is erroneous."[29] He pursues an argument—which we need not follow here—and which is now archaic, that force is separable from matter, and that all we know of the world without comes through the impinging upon us of forces.

The real world which we know is, therefore, not that of matter, but of force.[30]

Next he takes up the world of biology—chiefly to ask the old, unanswered and perhaps unanswerable question: What is Life? "Life," he writes, "is the differentiation of vital force which produces and develops individual organisms and preserves its identity."[31] This rests upon the postulate that there is a vital force having separate existence in the universe which is the original cause and the driving force of all life. Life bears no resemblance to any other natural force. Even the crystal has no freedom of growth or of movement. Life cannot be banished from the material universe. As to its origin, science must admit its ignorance. The oldest rocks exhibit no trace of life. Life must have had a beginning. Scientists are wont to evade the problem by saying—like Agassiz, "All life is from the egg"—that the generation of life took place in an unknown manner. The truth is that the explanation of organisms is in themselves. The vital force is free, universal, but also individualized. Everything proceeds from an organism. "This universe is no piece of dead mechanism. There is vital force, there is life in it."[32]

Wise continues with the enumeration of theories as to the origin of species, with especial emphasis naturally upon Darwin's. None of them accounts for the origin of life. As far as can be seen, there is no continuous, systematic chain of organisms, and we lack many transitional forms. He denies the theory of the recapitulation of evolution in the embryo. His own conjecture is: that soul came into the world, overcoming and governing inert matter. Progressive forms reveal its victories. But each form is permanent. And the process was finally harmonized and perfected in man. Before it could realize itself in man, the vital force had to move through these phases.[33]

What is the aim of the world? From it Spinoza would have excluded all cause, all aim. There are two extreme points of view: of those who see purpose in everything, and of those who see it in nothing. To the materialist, teleology—that is, that the universe has a purpose and a goal—is ruled out. For him spirit is imperceptible; therefore it does not exist. Yet who can deny its existence?[34] The truth is that we have only an indirect perception of physical force, but of intellect a direct one. The idea of causality comes only from the mind. But we also discern it in the universe, into which it comes from an intelligence in nature. Everything in the world has a final cause.

Can we discover will and intelligence in nature by strictly inductive methods? The answer is in the affirmative. The higher the vital force, the more it tends to create individuality. Life has freedom, even the freedom to deviate. "Freedom is the actualization of an inherent will." This will exists in the world. Will and intellect are attributes of life. The thesis is that freedom, will, life, all exist in nature, and therefore end and aim also exist.[35]

But there are other approaches. History reveals causality. It is not blind and aimless. Behind each stage in its progress are those stages that have gone before. Without reason history is unthinkable. Man makes history by his mind, but it must be in harmony with that law "which is superior to man's will."[36] Both exist, universal necessity and individual freedom. This is the Logos of history. There is and must be perpetual progress, but it is not continuous. Human nature is the same forever. The Logos preserves the good and neutralizes the evil.[37] He gives many examples from history: the movement toward freedom; the punishment of sin, etc. The First Cause uses human means to attain the ends. "*Die Welgeschichte ist das Weltgericht.*" ["World history is world judgment."] Genius too reveals the divine plan. Like a flash of lightning it makes its appearance. Talent wills; genius must. It breaks through forms and creates. It is not inherited [*contra* Francis Galton]. All great geniuses stood alone. "It is a special commission from the Logos of History to advance the human family to higher conditions of existence."[38] Genius is not happy; it is always at war with itself and with the world. But geniuses are the leaven of history.

What is the force in nature that is life, freedom, and also government and justice in history? What can we know of God's nature? Here we enter into the realm of metaphysics, which cannot be inductive. We move beyond the limits of causality. But there are other methods of knowing—outside philosophy and science.[39] There must be a governing force which binds together all forces. The mind is incapable of thinking of a causeless effect. There must be one universal, consecutive chain. "There can be nothing in the effect which is not also in its cause."[40] Forces are not exclusively physical, but also psychical. And the Force behind all others must be above inorganic nature, and also physical nature and history. The First Cause is One. Any division would be unreal and self-contradictory. All dualism is false. The same force is everywhere. The process culminates in man, "the primary force become self-conscious again."[41] Man works on to accomplish the subjugation of matter, the resurrection of the self-conscious spirit, the triumph of life over death, of light over darkness.[42] Thus everything, *sub specie aeternitatis* [under the aspect of eternity], is one. "He is the Cosmic God, for He is the cause of all causes, the first principle of all things, the only substance whose attributes are life, will, and intellect. God appears to none and to all. He resides nowhere and everywhere. He does not change. This God is to be commended to philosophers and scientists; also to the simple-minded, and to everyone. God has given to man the power to look into the mysteries of His creation."

Nature is a combination of force and matter. It is a "continual birth."[43] Time is only a category *a priori.* Time is only a relative concept. There is only one real substance, the psychical. Causality is universal. God regulates all. The laws of nature are abstractions of the mind.[44] God is the organism of all organisms. Is God conscious? Dematerialized intelligence [by which he appears to mean "immaterial spirit"] is always conscious. God is not incarnated in Nature. He is beyond and above it. God is in the universe, but outside material nature. Time is an illusion.

Nature recognizes itself in man. His consciousness is its final cause. God's purpose works toward an end. Man is both subject and object. Within him exist all things. In his self-consciousness is to be found also the categorical imperative, the moral law. All this is dependent upon his being a free agent. Degrees of self-consciousness go, therefore, with degrees of morality. For all this—the origin and character of ethics—the materialist has no possible explanation. But this is made possible only by the very nature of the intellect. Inorganic nature is not moral. Only one conclusion is possible: the moral nature of man comes from the First Cause, which becomes itself again. Man's history is progression from a low to a high degree of self-consciousness. This then—man's knowing himself—is the veritable "*Ding-an-sich.*" Man is the connecting link between God and Nature;[45] he is "partner in the work of creation." Man fulfills his destiny and becomes immortal by progressing in self-consciousness. History too moves toward an appointed end. Society is the repository of all experience. The end toward which history progresses is one encompassing self-consciousness of the whole human family.[46]

Wise ends—much as he began—with words which again indicate under what circumstances he wrote this work of thought and of faith:

> None will ever learn under what painful and truly distressing influences these lectures were conceived, written and delivered. . . . In the darkest hours of my existence. . . .[47]

Under this general heading of Religion a number of additional topics, or topics partially covered hitherto, need to be taken up, none of them of central importance, but all nonetheless throwing interesting side-lights on Wise's opinions.

In the columns of the *Israelite,* Wise referred quite frequently to Darwinism, which was of course, for some decades in the nineteenth century, a matter of bitter contention, occasioning a flood of pamphlets, books, and sermons. As we have seen from "The Cosmic God," Wise would—in general—have none of the doctrine of evolution. In one passage he quoted the investigations of a certain professor of Berne, Switzerland, and commented: "Thus the gorilla theory is a dream without a foundation in science."[48] Years later he linked evolution with another of his pet dislikes, biblical criticism:

> This is also the case with the wonderful conglomeration of a number of unfounded hypotheses into the system of Darwinism, and that other conglomeration of unverified hypotheses into a sort of system or rather an apparatus with which to overthrow the historical veracity of the Old Testament Scriptures.[49]

Yet, when Darwin died on April 20, 1882, Wise wrote of him somewhat more gently:

> German naturalists, historians and philologians built up that Darwinism, which in its last sequences is nugatory to religion and ethics and even absurd in many instances. Darwin's own theory of evolution is not incompatible with religion and ethics, and we are told that he remained a Christian. . . . He remained a specialist but as such he certainly was one of the most distinguished of our century.[50]

Occasionally Wise continued to write about the role of reason and of faith in religion, an old and difficult problem, which played a great role in the theological discussions of the Middle Ages, and culminated in the great work of Thomas Aquinas. In general—like most religious leaders—he thought that skepticism, while it might play a useful part in the burgeoning of the mind, was self-defeating:

> But skepticism refutes itself; for the skeptic must either know or doubt that he doubts. If he doubt that he doubts, then doubt is not an established principle from which one might start to reason on the knowledge of man, because its existence is doubtful. . . . He has to admit that there is one who doubts. . . . The universality and sameness of the elements of religion and reason are facts which upset skepticism.[51]

This type of logical trap was a commonplace in dealing with this subject, and Wise was merely rephrasing it in his own words.

Several years later he spoke on "Reason and Religion" in a Christian church in Cincinnati. In this lecture his main point was that reason is of great value in philosophy, but that it cannot furnish the data upon which it works, for these must come either from direct experience, or from tradition. Religion errs when it excludes or ignores reason. But reason—in its turn—must reckon with the facts adduced by religion.[52] Considerably later, in commenting on Hartmann's "*Philosophie des Unbewussten*" ["Philosophy of the Unconscious"], he wrote that it was interesting in that it demonstrated—*contra* the scientists—that one must come back to the First Cause. By inductive reasoning alone one cannot get to the "God of Israel."[53]

Wise was a great believer in immortality. Again and again he wrote of it. He contended that no religion could be regarded as satisfying or complete without it. He did not agree with the contention that it was not one of the religious principles taught by the Bible, except perhaps in a few of its latest passages. He contended that Moses himself taught it, and found substantiation for this rather ingeniously [we shall come to this later in these pages]. Again and again he insisted upon his point that man is a dual being, body and soul, the traditional Jewish point of view. To this he came from a great diversity of directions. He wrote—for example—on "The Moral Aspect of Memory," of which a typical and significant sentence is the following:

> Hence memory is the function of a non-material substance, which we call soul. . . . Memory is an attribute of the immortal soul and remains in it eternally.[54]

He regarded immortality not only as an essential part of the religious credo, but as indispensable in its meaning for the average man:—

> If you want to enkindle religious zeal, establish the immortality doctrine in the consciousness of your congregations.[55]

In later years it was his habit to publish little sparks from the anvil of his meditations in the *Israelite* under the title of "Aphorisms." Here are two of them, the first from June 2, 1876:

> With the birth of an organic being, it begins not its existence, it merely opens its mundane existence; so with death it does not close its existence, it simply closes this cycle of its sublunar career.[56]

Or again, under date of April 28, 1876:

> What we call the human body, is transient matter kept momentarily in this form. The soul is the man, the efficient and ever active cause of the body's existence and motion.[57]

2

II. *On Judaism*

A. JUDAISM AND THE JEW

Like all who write often and much about Judaism, Wise was occasionally prompted to try to define it, to compress into a small compass the entire experience and teaching of Judaism and the Jew. Sometimes his definitions approximated the classical formulations of Hillel, or of Akiba, in laying their entire emphasis upon the moral law as the essence and the heart of the religion. But often again, driven by his own convictions about Judaism as a revealed religion, he tended to define it in more formal terms. Thus—under the first heading—he wrote:

> Legalism is not Judaism, nor is mysticism religion; the belief in fiction is superstition; Judaism is the fear of the Lord, and the love of man, in harmony with the dicta of reason.[1]

He declared the three "theological dogmas" of Judaism to be: "creation, revelation, and life eternal."[2] On another occasion in somewhat different terms he asserted that Judaism rests upon three pillars: "The Covenant, the Revelation, and the Promise."[3]

Most often, however, he approached Judaism from the aspect of revelation. The idea was central to him. With all his heart he believed that no true religion could exist without a basis in revelation. The unchanging center of Judaism was—for him—the revelation on Mount Sinai, and this played the greatest part in most of his attempts to state the essence of Judaism. Thus he wrote in an editorial in 1866:

> Judaism revolved perpetually on the indestructible and unimprovable axis of everlasting verities which Israel inherited of the patriarchs and was taught by Moses. . . .[4]

While it is part of the task of modern Judaism to find "the correct norm between legalism and rationalism"—a habitual concern of Reform leaders in that period[5]—this must not be taken to signify an abandonment of historical facts that go beyond reason. Thus, in 1860, he wrote a "Letter to a Gentleman Who with his Family Wishes to Embrace Judaism."[6] This purported to be a brief summation of Judaism, in these terms . . . . . . First must come belief in one, invisible God, who is just and merciful, who is absolutely good. One must repudiate the Christian teaching of universal depravity. Man is made in the image of God. Sin comes, not from the devil, but from ignorance and error. Judaism commands neighborly love and obedience to the laws of God, as revealed in His words. Man is given free-will to obey or to disobey. Sin sullies the soul and estranges from God. One must make atonement, and also believe that for all men a time of justice and peace is to come.

> There is but one truth and this was revealed to Israel; therefore, Israel is the mountain of the Lord, which all nations must finally ascend, there to learn of God's ways and to walk in His paths.

This age of perfect justice and peace is to be that of the Messiah. A Jew must cling to these precepts even against persecution and scorn, and even at the cost of his life. Especially must he—as the crux of the whole—obey the Ten Commandments.

Again he wrote: Some ask, What is Judaism? "We can answer the question in a few words: Judaism is the religion revealed on Mt. Sinai."[7] He had written a statement of principles for his Confirmation Class, and he reprinted in the *Israelite* this section from it:

> Judaism is the religion revealed directly to Israel on Mt. Sinai, and indirectly through Moses and the Prophets. The revealed matter is preserved intact in the twenty-four books of Sacred Scriptures called the Bible, or Old Testament. . . . The principal laws of God are the Ten Commandments, revealed on Mt. Sinai to all Israel, as the law of the covenant between God and His people.[8]

Or later he put this even more strongly and more polemically:

> Judaism is the religion revealed on Mt. Sinai. . . . If God did not command us to be, do and believe so, we are the worst blunder

> in history. Those who cannot believe the former must believe the latter.[9]

God has revealed Himself to man in three ways: in "nature, Sinai, and history." It was upon all three that Moses built up his account of revelation.[10] Wise also followed the lead of Jehuda Halevi in the *Kuzari* and of Maimonides, in contending that:

> All religions go back to Judaism, and it goes back to Moses. He only was a prophet in the proper sense of the term.[11]

Wise followed the general opinion of his time, and that of Moses Mendelssohn's famous thesis, in asserting that Judaism has no dogmas. This was somewhat difficult for Wise in the light of such definitions of Judaism as some of the foregoing. Nonetheless he found an intellectual formulation, which seemed to him to make this logically tenable. He wrote:

> Dogmas have no place in our system. . . . The existence of One God is no dogma; it is a thesis demonstrated by every department of nature, as an invariable necessity. . . .[12]

To a correspondent he wrote at one time that it was true that Maimonides had formulated his famous "Thirteen Articles," but this—Wise contended—Maimonides did when he was a young man. Crescas and Albo agreed in their opinion that Maimonides' formulation was not correct; and even his friend, Don Isaac Abarbanel, wrote that these were principles, not dogmas. Maimonides put them in their now familiar form to counteract the influence of Islam. Later he amended them in his introduction to *Chelek* in the *Mishna*. But the Thirteen Articles were inserted in the liturgy, and:

> Being once there, the common man never thought of investigating the matter. . . . and it became the sole authority of the *Am Ha'aretz.*[13]

Lastly under this heading we shall take up Wise's rather singular feeling about the name "Jew." This appellation he disliked, for reasons which he himself gave. He was not unique in this. This was a general prejudice of the time, having its origin in Germany, where most Jewish societies and organizations carefully eschewed the use of the term. Wise carried this dislike with him to America and found it re-enforced and intensified here. This was clearly shown in the names he proposed for the three organizations he created: The Union of American *Hebrew* Congregations; the *Hebrew* Union College; and the Central Conference of American

Rabbis. His failure to have the name "Jew" in any one of them was no accident; it was intentional and consistent. As a rule he liked to refer to "American Israelites."

> Whatever this or that friend may have to advance in favor of the word Jew, it will always appear to us as an improper and unbecoming appellation for the children of Israel. A better term would be Israelite. The word Jew is a corruption of *Judaeus*, meaning one descended from Judah.[14]

To this topic he returned many times, and with even greater warmth:

> When people speak of the Jews there is—they know not why —an echo of derision or disrespect connected with the sound of the word. When they speak of Israel—and they know why— there is an echo of veneration connected with the ancient term. This alone is sufficient reason to obey the divine command 'Israel shall be thy name' (Genesis, chapter 32, verse 29). A Jew is one born of Jewish parents, but an Israelite is a worshiper of the one God.[15]

Sometimes Wise wrote on the question of whether Jews are a race or not. His own point of view was a rather curious one: namely, that Jews are a race, in the common usage of the term, but that this has little or nothing to do with their character, or even less with their mission in the world. Thus he wrote in 1876:

> A lady writes us that she does not like to see the Jews called a race, a special race, when science knows of only five races, and the Jews are Caucasians. But the common use of words is not always in consonance with the technical terms of science. In common parlance it is used: Jewish Race, as Anglo-Saxon, Teutonic, or Romanic races, without offense to anybody.[16]

Wise believed that Judaism, the religion of "Israel," was destined before long to be the faith of all civilized men. To this thesis he returned again and again. Several expressions to this effect were already reproduced in the Second Part of this book. In an article in the *Israelite*, headed "Ancient and Modern Jews," reiterating that Judaism has no creed, he continued:

> Judaism, its ceremonial part excepted, is not alone the religion of the Jews, but of all intelligent men in the world who have the moral courage to make themselves independent of inherited superstitions and early impressions. But the religious victory which the intelligent of all nations achieve after much struggle,

> we Jews learn in the days of early childhood, and therefore have a considerable advantage.[17]

Toward what goal do the footsteps of the Jew move? Of this Wise wrote—dramatically—in a lecture on "The Wandering Jew":

> He must reappear and wander on to the end of all woe and misery in society, till the habitable earth shall be one holy land. . . . Then the curtain will drop on the grand drama of the Wandering Jew. . . .[18]

To sum up, Wise believed that Judaism should be a balance between legalism and reason; that it is primarily the religion revealed on Mt. Sinai, the sign and seal of which are the Ten Commandments; that it has no dogmas, but rests on revelation and on reason; that the term "Israelite" is preferable to Jew; that Jews are a race in the common usage of the term; and that they must continue to exist until mankind shall have come to the millennial age of justice and of truth.

B. ON THE THEOLOGY OF JUDAISM

The chief sources for a study of Wise's theology are to be found in one large work, the *Pronaos to Holy Writ*; in a smaller work entitled *An Introduction to the Theology of Judaism*; another (from the year 1887) called *The Sources of the Theology of Judaism*; a paper delivered before the Free Religious Association of Boston in 1869, under the title, *The Outlines of Judaism*; and in many articles and addresses reprinted in the *Israelite*.

One common strand runs through all these, one common approach to the theology of Judaism. Over the course of the years there are minor variations in emphasis, or in order, but Wise was quite consistent in his general attitude toward the problems of authority, of the Bible as a revealed book, of the rabbinic law, and of other associated questions. We shall attempt to give the gist of what he wrote, quoting only when his own words seem to add something definite and characteristic.

Throughout his career the essence of his own thinking was that Judaism is a revealed religion, and that the revelation was that on Mt. Sinai. This he would not permit to be rationalized away, or to be obliterated by the skeptical, and—to him—destructive approach of the literary critics. For him the giving of the Ten Commandments, from the hand of God through Moses into the keeping of the children of Israel, was historical and definitive. Thus he wrote:

> Those who want more, vastly more, to be contained in the term 'Judaism' than the substance of the Sinaic revelation, are mistaken. . . . Judaism is the religion revealed on Mt. Sinai.[19]

Or again:

> The Torah is genuine, authentic, Mosaic; all theories, hypotheses and allegations to the contrary are flimsy *a priori* speculations, without any documentary basis or justification in fact. This, he believed, was demonstrated in the pure Hebrew of the Torah; hence it cannot be regarded as an imitation of the Babylonian. . . . Without this belief, there may be a religion, but it is not Judaism. . . . Judaism bases its structure of three thousand years' duration upon the Torah of Moses.[20]

This must not be taken to connote that Wise regarded the five books of Moses as a whole as directly revealed. Even in ancient days the rabbis could discuss the authorship of the last passages of Deuteronomy—whether Moses could have written about his own death, or whether it was Joshua who wrote it. An Abraham Ibn Ezra could introduce hints into his commentary, questioning the Mosaic authorship of certain phrases and sentences. With reference to various passages in rabbinical literature which appeared to take the same position, Wise contended that the veritable revelation was only that of the Ten Commandments. Thus, in an address on "The Law of the Covenant" before K.K. Anshe Ma'arav in Chicago, he asserted that it was only the Ten Commandments of which it was said: "Ye shall not add to the word which I command thee, and ye shall not diminish therefrom" (Deuteronomy 4:2).[21] On occasion he reiterated his contention, given in our review of his ideas on religion in general, that beyond reason lies revelation, and in Judaism this revelation is "The Torah of Moses."[22]

In 1861 he published a little book, called *The Essence of Judaism*, intended primarily for confirmands. Later its title was changed to *Judaism, Its Doctrines and Duties*. This was an exposition of "progressive Judaism." It was strictly Biblical and ignored the Talmud.[23] The catechism stood squarely upon the principle that only the Decalogue was central to Judaism. Wise wrote of it in these interesting and suggestive terms:

> Here the author stands upon the orthodox historical ground as invariably maintained in the post-biblical literature of the

> Hebrews, that whatever is not in Moses, in the Torah, is not canonical material in Judaism. The prophets and prophetesses could neither add thereto nor diminish therefrom. They generalized, rose to the ultimate abstractions, from statutes to categories, but never went beyond Moses. . . . .

Earlier in his life, in contrast with the opinion he came to later—which we have already cited—Wise believed that Judaism had dogmas, and listed them as these: the belief in a Supreme Being, in inspiration and revelation, in Providence, in reward and punishment.[24]

Later on, in *The Sources of the Theology of Judaism* (1887), Wise defined theology as "the science of the conceptions of Deity in the human mind." Theology rests not on reason, not on induction, but on facts that are present before reason can work upon them "analytically or synthetically."[25]

> Judaism relies for its material upon the revelations, in the threefold covenant recorded in the Torah of Moses. . . . The Theology of Judaism is the science of the conceptions of Deity in the human mind and their logical sequences, in conformity with the postulates of reason, as laid down in the Torah of Moses, expounded, expanded, and reduced to practice in different forms, by Moses, the prophets, the hagiographists, the sages and the lawful bodies in the congregation of Israel.[26]

Here he began to make the point—to which we shall refer in detail—that there is a sharp distinction between the original revelation and its subsequent extension and application. The former is unalterable; the latter is "national and temporal."

> Whether all the laws of Moses were written by him in various scrolls or some of them were preserved traditionally and written down at some later date, is in fact of no vital importance. However, we have the authority of the book itself to the effect that Moses wrote it (Deut. 31:9, 11, 24, and 26), although some matter may have been added at a later date, like Deuteronomy, chapter 17, verses 14-20 (etc.) All *a priori* arguments amount to nothing in face of the plain and undeniable records which state *Vayichtav Moshe*, "And Moses wrote."[27]

The ethics of Moses are the highest possible and derive from his theology. Nothing has been added by later generations.

Again, in the paper called *The Outlines of Judaism* (delivered before the convention of the Free Religious Association, Boston, Mass., 1869),[28] Wise contended that the Ten Commandments are the "groundwork" of both doctrine and law in the Bible:

> Moses enlarged upon them in accordance with the needs of his age and country; the prophets expounded and the sages applied them to meet emergencies. . . . The decalogue contains the unchangeable principles of law, but all other biblical laws are subject to modification by proper authority.[29]

We have already told the reader that the most consistent and serious of Wise's expositions of his views on Jewish theology was to be found in the *Pronaos to Holy Writ*, for years used as a textbook at the Hebrew Union College.

Primarily the book was concerned with the theology of Judaism as it is implied and expressed in the Hebrew Bible. Wise began with the same contention as in the foregoing paragraphs—that the substance of Jewish theology is in the *Torah*, and that all else is commentary and expansion:

> It is presumed[30] that the revelations of God's nature and will in the Torah are the ultimate for man's comprehensibility [sic!] and his attainment of happiness in time and eternity. Therefore, the Torah is eternal. This always was universal doctrine among orthodox Israelites.

The book continued with a discussion of the text of the *Torah* and of the speciousness of the reasoning of many Biblical critics. Some parts of the *Torah* Wise regarded as older than Moses, and as included by Moses in the canon.[31]

Wise was fully aware of the doubts so cautiously expressed by Ibn Ezra on the Mosaic authorship of part or of all of the Torah. He took this to mean no more than that a few historical passages in the Pentateuch were of later origin.[32] He entered then into an argument on the evidence for the originality and dependability of the Pentateuch in its present form. It is not necessary to recapitulate these contentions. One of the strangest of them, however, was to the effect that the fact that there is no doctrine of immortality in the Torah [a statement which Wise himself denied in other places] proves its antiquity.[33] The repetitions in the *Torah* do not indicate—according to him—the work of different hands. He follows the rabbis in maintaining that every repetition adds something to the meaning and is for some specific purpose.[34] He ended by summing up the reasons why he insisted upon his own system and would not yield to the "fragmentists":[35]

> 1. There is no documentary evidence whatsoever of the existence of such fragments, but there is much evidence that these are genuinely Mosaic documents.

2. The whole *Torah* is one in spirit, in principle, in doctrine, in precept and in law. Hence it stems from one author.
3. If fragments had existed, the Biblical records, which are so scrupulous about names, would have taken notice of them.
4. The whole "fabric of speculation basing upon the Jahvistic and Elohistic criteria of authorship (that is, contending that the different sources are identifiable with their use of different names for God) is *eo ipso* worthless."[36]

Nor would he have any truck with the claim that Ezra was the final author of the *Torah*:

> What Ezra actually did is reported in the Books of Ezra and Nehemiah. . . . There exists no solid ground on which to base any doubt as to the authenticity of any book of Holy Writ.[37]

Before closing this chapter it will be of help if we go farther on one point: Wise's claim that *the* revelation was the Ten Commandments, and that all else was an attempt—in the light of temporal conditions and needs—to apply its principles. From this he drew the important inference—important for him intellectually and spiritually—that other generations have and have had the right to other applications and other formulations. Thus he arrived at a philosophy of Reform, by which for him it adhered to Judaism as a revealed religion, resting upon immutable theological and ethical doctrines, but permitting and even necessitating change and development. Much that he did in his life becomes intelligible upon this basis: his adherence to the platform of the Cleveland Conference of 1855; his frequent and passionate claim that he was the real "orthodox" Jew, and that what he offered could serve as common ground for all Jews. This was so weighty a point with him, Jewishly and psychologically, that we shall dwell upon it and consider it again, when we take up his attitude toward the Talmud.

Here is a clear and succinct expression of his fundamental principle:

> Those based on the principles expressed in the Decalogue are the eternal laws, time and its revolutions affect them not, the progress of science and enlightenment improves them not, they are immutable like reason and justice themselves. Again, those laws not based upon the principles of the Decalogue are provisional laws which were enacted to suit a certain time and meet certain emergencies, but pass away with them.[38]

Later he wrote:

> . . . The only question can be, how and by whom they should, from time to time, be changed to correspond with the spirit of the age? To this the Bible replies, by the seventy elders, the Talmud replies, by the Sanhedrin and we translate it into a Synod. . . .[39]

Rabbinic literature is "useful and instructive, but not definitive."[40] The rabbis themselves distinguished between commandments (*mitzvoth*) connected with Palestine, and those that applied to any land. All the eternal laws cluster about the Decalogue, "the only platform on which all Israelites can stand and, within the divine covenant, worship the Most High. . . . ."[41] Wise listed some of the laws of the Pentateuch which were to be regarded as temporary: laws about the appointment of judges; all laws about the Temple, the altar, the sacrificial system, gifts, tithes, priests and Levites; laws having to do with cleanliness, animal food, and prohibitions of intermarriage are permanent. These latter are to be deduced from the injunction against killing, and exist for the sake of preserving life and health. The laws, which are here called temporary, were in fact often changed by the rabbis. Such changes may not be made arbitrarily. They must follow some traditional procedure and have behind them a valid authority. Sometimes he put this not in traditional, but in general human terms:[42]

> That much is true then, only that portion of Judaism which will and must become the common good of all men, is religion to us, and only in this respect we are Jews; all other laws, ordinances, customs and usages, wherever and whenever written or practiced, have a secondary importance for us, it is the object and not the means we reflect upon. . . . Only that which is expressed, contained, or implied in the Sinaic revelation is Judaism.[43]

From the foregoing a clear picture of Wise's concept of Jewish theology ought to have emerged. Judaism is a revealed religion which is above reason; the revelation was and is the Decalogue from Mt. Sinai. All attacks upon this, as well as upon the Mosaic authorship of the *Torah*, are invalid. The applications of this revelation vary in several respects. Where these are strict legal inferences, resting upon its spiritual or ethical bases, they are as eternal as it is; but where they are applications to the field of public polity, or of personal or social relations, they are temporary and alterable. This must, however, not be permitted to detract from the fact that all the Bible is a divine work, that it is full of inspiration and instruction, and that the rabbinic literature is a precious heritage for all Jews, setting before them the interpretations and admonitions of great religious geniuses from whom we can and must learn.

A few corollaries must be added to Wise's main thesis about revelation and authority. He carried out in some detail his general contention that laws, which relate to special times and places, to social arrangements, to bodily health, were not eternal, but intended only for a period. Many of the aspects of the actual Mosaic code were intended to bring about unity in a "mixed multitude."

> With all this, however, we know of no scriptural proof that Moses originally intended all that Levitical law and all the Levitical priesthood and institutions to be carried into Canaan and stand there forever. . . . . . We are forced to the conclusion the Levitical laws of Moses were not intended to be eternally obligatory.[44]

In an article on *Shabuoth*, in 1869—in contradiction to an argument given above—Wise claimed that the doctrine of immortality was in the Pentateuch:

> . . . How could Moses proclaim a law which requires of man to subdue this physical world and his own physical passions, lusts and propensities, if he considered him a creature made for this world and this life only?[45]

Or—many years later—he treated this difficult subject once again, and wrote on the doctrine of immortality "as a Mosaic Dogma of Judaism":

> Moses has told us enough about the immortality doctrine to justify the Rabbis of the Mishna in assuming as a dogma revealed from God to Moses that man is an immortal being, as in one form or another it was always believed not only in Israel but also among the Gentiles as far back in antiquity as the records of the languages and the dumb witnesses of inscriptions reach. None can deny it, none can prove it; so did Moses and so ought we to do in submission to common sense and the feelings of man.[46]

His approach to the dietary laws followed the main line of his reasoning about the Mosaic Law in general. But he could not quite bring himself—either in theory or in practice—to regard them as having no force, no meaning for the Jew today. Thus he wrote:

> In explanation of our position in regard to the dietary laws of Moses, we have to say that we certainly consider each and all

> of them well-considered sanitary [hygienic] laws, based upon experience and scientific principle. What Moses forbade as an article of food is injurious to health. This is well known now to scientists. Therefore, as the results of science become popularly known, the Mosaic dietary laws gain general authority among the intelligent portion of the community. But when the zealous orthodox make of those laws a matter of religion, a test of orthodoxy, a touchstone of Judaism, we must protest. It is not religion, it is sanitary advice which every intelligent man should take, especially those who believe in the laws of Moses. A man can be a conscientious believer in Judaism and a religious Israelite without obeying any laws which are not contained, expressed, or implied in the Sinaic revelation.[47]

Many times during his ministry and in his writing he inveighed against the use of pork, which he was wont to call "poisonous flesh." Upon this subject he was invariably vehement.[48]

He favored *Shechita*, the ritual method of slaughter, as the most humane devised by man, intended primarily to prevent cruelty to animals.[49] But he contended that this was not at all a religious matter, and had nothing integral to do with Judaism.

> There are higher duties, and they must not be subjected to this or any other superstition. . . .[50]

He liked to reprint reports that certain people, who had been foolish enough to eat pork, had contracted trichinosis, and he went as far as Germany to find instances. Moses surely knew what he was doing when he forbade *Hazir*.[51]

Even near the end of his life he repeated the substance of all this:

> The facts in our possession are too scanty in favor of either side [as to which animals should be prohibited, and which permitted]; consequently every conscientious man must obey these laws, until it is scientifically established that they were given as a local reform, and timely compromise, and then, even, it would be every man's duty to exclude from his diet the flesh of such animals of which we know for certain that it induces disease in the human organism [swine, rabbit, etc.]. . . . We can arrive at no satisfactory conclusion, therefore we should not eat that which Moses forbids. Others, however, may hold their views on the subject.[52]

At two conferences Wise had tried to get pronouncements from the rabbis in favor of taking in proselytes without demanding circumcision of the males. This was equally so at the Pittsburgh Conference of 1885, where such a resolution was in fact adopted. Doubtless pursuant to that meeting Wise wrote a letter to David Philipson on September 26, 1886, part of which follows:

> Having of late argued the question of *Milath Gerim* [the circumcision of proselytes] so frequently in the *American Israelite* and in the *Deborah*, I can only repeat, that to the best of knowledge and conviction it ought to be abolished in all cases of adult proselytes, especially from our standpoint when we look upon Judaism as the universal and not as a tribal religion. A conference or synod ought to abolish it and establish a form and formula to accept proselytes in the covenant without circumcision. At the same time, however, I think and have said in the *Israelite* that until a conference or synod has so decided it appears to me unlawful and unadvisable to deviate from the established rule in the *Shulchan Aruch*, nor would any congregation acknowledge the uncircumcised convert as a member of the family.[53]

Wise added that in his opinion progress should be made on important points only with the consent of all.

3

II. On Judaism *(Continued)*

C. ON BIBLICAL CRITICISM

Again and again Wise returned to the Biblical critics. If their claims were true, the whole basis of the Pentateuch, of historical Judaism, and of the concept of a revealed religion, fell to the ground. Wise felt himself outraged to the very depths of his soul by the arrogance, and by what he regarded as the fallaciousness of this tremendous literature, centered for him and for most of his contemporaries in the writings of Julius Wellhausen. In these writings—and especially in the wide divergence between their treatment of the Old and of the New Testament—Wise thought to descry more than a trace of anti-Semitism, of an effort to deny to Israel all spiritual originality and all historical veracity.

In the preface to his *Pronaos* he declared that the purpose of the book—a purpose made imperative by the attacks of the critics—was to establish the authority and the authenticity of the holy writings:

> The science commonly called Biblical Criticism, actually Negative Criticism, which maintains, on the strength of unscientific methods, that the Pentateuch is not composed of original Mosaic material, no Psalms are Davidian, no Proverbs Solomonic, the historic books unhistorical, the prophecies were written *post festum*, there was no revelation, inspiration or prophecy, must also maintain that the Bible is a compendium of pious or even impious frauds, willful deceptions, unscrupulous misrepresentations; whence comes the Bible truth of which they speak? . . .[1]

After its appearance (the *Pronaos*) there was an article—by an unnamed author—in *Hebrew Bookland,* which said in part:

> In his lifetime it was customary to throw easy jibes at him as an ignoramus. But the charge was false. The author was struck in reading the book by "Wise's learning and originality." The *Pronaos* "is among the earliest of the reasoned replies to the Higher Criticism." It was striking, the article continued, that the "most orthodox book on the Pentateuch was written by the leader of American reform."

On occasion Wise devoted himself to specific points involved in the so-called critical approach to the Bible. We have already pointed out that he did not accept the contention that Deuteronomy was a product of the sixth century before the Common Era, and had been passed off as being by Moses.[2] He claimed that the critics "draw on fantasy and call it criticism."[3] He was perpetually and vocally outraged by the emphasis upon "*Jahvism*" and "*Elohism,*" to which we have already referred in passing:

> The whole hypothesis of modern critics on JEHOVAH and ELOHIM are whims, caprices, which the Germans call *Schrullen,* which have positively no value, and lead only to an entire misapprehension of Bible texts. . . . So, for instance, is the second chapter of Genesis nothing else than a commentary and supplement to the first [the traditional view], to introduce the history of man, notwithstanding all the quibbling on that subject. These extraordinary theories must be dropped by all who wish to understand the Bible.[4]

He returned again to the charge and wrote:

> As Israelites whose belief in Judaism is genuine, we have nothing to do with these hypotheses; and as critics we can only denounce them as false in every particular, false from the beginning to the end.[5]

One other passage should be included, for its slightly different emphasis:

> We do protest most emphatically against the alleged results of that negative Bible criticism which uproots the veracity and integrity of the inspired writers and reduces the ancient history of Israel to a record of rude barbarism. We do so not because that negative criticism is injurious to Judaism, although we believe it is a death-blow aimed at it and at religion in general, especially if those alleged results are carried into the pulpit or the Sabbath-school, where they can do harm only and no

> good at all; because we firmly believe that truth must take care of itself.[6]

Wise's explanation of the anthropomorphic and anthropopathic passages in the Bible—and especially in the *Torah*—is the customary one, that of Philo and of Maimonides, namely, that they are allegorical. There is no pure approach possible to the nature of God; this must be made solely by analogy.[7]

Wise was especially vigorous in denouncing the claim that most of the material in the Bible, and especially in the Pentateuch, was derived from Egypt, or from Babylon.

> There is no use telling us these laws were taken from any other nation's code, when we know they existed nowhere else.[8]

His objection was not only to the content of Biblical criticism, but to its "apodictic and vindictive tone."[9] The whole description of the history of Israel, which emerged from the errors of the "critics," was "rank nonsense"—especially the assertion that before the Babylonian Captivity the Hebrews were "polytheists and pagans."[10]

We have already referred to his charge that the whole attitude of the critics in relation to the "Old Testament," and toward the "New," was a crystal-clear confession of their prejudice and their blindness:

> So they do as many more dignitaries of the church and Christian professors do; they go to the New Testament blindfolded, and hurl their superlative learning, ingenuity and wit at the Old Testament—so one can be simultaneously orthodox with the church and fashionably radical with the dominant school.[11]

A very good summing-up of his own point of view was to be found some years earlier:

> That which is called Bible criticism, down to Marx and Wellhausen, is actually a shapeless conglomeration of hypotheses, in which there is vastly more error and unwarranted assumption than truth, more philological quibbling and self-fabricated historical items than grains of fact. . . . If all those books written since two centuries would suddenly be swept away by a conflagration, the world would lose nothing in the form of research and science. Nor are Jewish scholars "bomb-proof against the fashion." Moses learned nothing from the Egyptians or from Indo-Germanic tribes. In principle and system Moses is original, entirely averse to and incompatible with any or all known systems of mythology.[12]

Perhaps, instead of proving that Moses borrowed ideas from Egypt, the truth lay the other way around. What is to be found in the Bible is utterly beyond the religion of Egypt and beyond the beliefs and teachings of all the other nations of antiquity.[13]

D. ON MIRACLES.

In the second part of this book—at the time Isaac M. Wise wrote and published his *History of the Israelitish Nation*—we reviewed in some detail his attitude toward miracles as history in the preface to that work, and in the controversy that ensued upon its publication. He had described the principle he would follow, chiefly in these words:

> The next distinction between history and religion is this: the former treats of man, and the latter of God. If this be admitted, it must necessarily follow that miracles do not belong in the province of history. Miracles can be wrought by God only, and history records what men have done. The historian may believe in miracles, but he has no right to incorporate them in history. As a general thing man is always the agent or the subject of miracles, consequently the action itself may be historical, and can be adopted in history if it can be ascribed to common and natural causes, while the miracles as such belongs to the province of theology.[14]

This Wise intended—at the time—to apply to the writing of history; it had nothing to do with the general place of miracles in Jewish theology, or with his own personal acceptance or rejection of them.

In general in Judaism this point of view was not far wide of the mark, for even in the *Torah* there are passages which indicate that a miracle is no test of the truth of a statement, or that it is wise to adduce a miracle as evidence (cf. e.g., Deuteronomy, chapter 13, verses 2-4). The Talmud accepts all Biblical miracles as a revelation of God's omnipotence, but it insists that they are not fundamental to the faith. Some rabbinic passages represent God as pre-ordaining miracles, so that from Creation they are parts of the regular order.[15] As a logical rule the rabbis were of the opinion that miracles might not be utilized as evidence for one verdict as against another ("One may not rely on the miracle"; and cf. especially *Baba Metziah* 59b and *Taanith* 20b). There was also among the mediaeval philosophers—especially in the cases of Saadya Gaon and Maimonides—the tendency to rationalize miracles, or to interpret them metaphorically. Variations of these points of view were to be found in the works of Gersonides and of Crescas.

Wise himself went considerably farther than the stand he took in his History. Even there it seemed clear that he ruled out miracles as history because he had a basically skeptical attitude toward them. Later he wrote that he believed all miracles capable of a natural explanation. He quoted at length from Maimonides' *Yesode Hatorah*, which is not a résumé of the philosopher's own opinions, but—as part of his Code—a summation of the attitude of the rabbis in the Talmud:

> It must be admitted that according to Jewish doctrine miracles prove nothing; hence in regard to orthodoxy there is no difference whether a man believes the Scriptural miracles literally or explains (them) rationalistically, or psychologically, or even believes that they were written only.

But, he conceded, the concept of God's complete omnipotence signifies that He could work miracles, if He willed.[16]

To Wise the entire matter was not a key-point in Jewish belief, as many centuries of tradition had demonstrated:

> If we are not sure the miracles are true, is it not superstitious to believe in them, and, if so, is not this contrary to the whole tenor of the Torah, which declares every superstition a sin or even a crime? We maintain that one may be an orthodox believer in the Theology of Judaism without believing in the literal truth of the miracles recorded in Scriptures, as did many of the ancient teachers of Judaism; and on the other hand, one may firmly believe the miracles literally as recorded in Scriptures, as millions of our ancestors did, without being guilty of the sin of superstition.[17]

The logical effect of this was to make essential Jewish belief independent of the entire matter of miracles:

> What Jewish reasoners and expounders of the Torah do maintain is that the theology of Judaism depends not for evidence on any miracles. Human reason plus revelation is sufficient without anything else. Judaism is the only system in which reason and faith are reconciled, and must necessarily become the fundamental principle of mankind's religion of the future.[18]

The same argument is to be applied to the claim of Christians that the miracles wrought by Jesus in the New Testament are incontrovertible evidence for the truth of Christianity:

> The miracles in the New Testament prove nothing. If you contend that belief in the Torah is also dogma resting upon miracle, we would reply that it is not necessarily so. . . . We believe in the Sinaic revelation on account of the historical evidence which supports it, the like of which can be adduced to a few facts in history, certainly to no miracle aside of the creation of the world. You see, opposite Judaism all arguments basing on miracles are decidedly worthless. . . .[19]

Only once again, as far as we can discover, did Wise take up the subject, and again from a rationalistic approach. He inquired whether reason can accept miracles. And, if not, does this tend to impair the authority of Scriptures? Or, perhaps, were miracles intended as "poetical embellishments of events appearing marvelous?" His general principle—here enunciated—is that "nothing which reason rejects is to be accepted."[20]

In sum—though this is all more than a little vague—what seems clear is that here too Wise applied his general principle of reason as an approach to religion, a special prejudice of his time, except in his case in relation to the final appeal to revelation as the heart and substance of faith. His stand, however, was not personal; it rested solidly upon much of Jewish tradition.

E. ON THE MESSIAH AND THE MESSIANIC HOPE

Many times in the foregoing pages we have come upon Wise's opinion concerning a "personal Messiah." This he had heard discussed at length and with much learning at the Rabbinical Conference at Frankfort in 1845. In Albany in 1850 he had become embroiled with his president, Spanier, on this among other things, as a result of the report of his discussions in Charleston with Raphall.

Wise was not alone in this. This was—and is—the attitude of Reform Judaism in Germany and in America. As part of the entire picture of his theological platform, it will, however, be of value to add some passages on the Messiah and the Messianic Age.

At the Rabbinical Conference in Philadelphia—from November 3 to 6, 1869[21]—these were among the resolutions adopted:

> The Messianic aim of Israel is not the restoration of the old Jewish state under a descendant of David, involving a second separation from the nations of the earth, but the union of all men as children of God in the confession of the unity of God,

> so as to realize the unity of all rational creatures and their call to moral sanctification.
>
> We look upon the destruction of the second Jewish Commonwealth not as a punishment for the sinfulness of Israel, but as a result of the divine purposes revealed to Abraham, which, as has become ever clearer in the course of the world's history, consist in the dispersion of the Jews to all parts of the earth, for the realization of their high priestly mission, to lead the nations to the true knowledge and worship of God.[22]

Wise believed—and said and wrote repeatedly—that the Messianic Age was practically at hand. Thus in 1875:

> Before our very eyes the world moves onward into the golden age of redeemed humanity and the fraternal union of nations, as our prophets thousands of years ago have predicted. We are fast approaching the universal democratic republic with civil and religious liberty, cemented by the world's advanced intelligence. This century settles old accounts. It is progressive.[23]

In 1881 Wise delivered an extended series of Friday evening lectures on the general topic, "The Origin and History of the Messianic Idea."[24] In these he advanced the contention that the idea of a personal Messiah had no warrant in the Mosaic writings. Later on —early in the following year—he supplemented this with two addresses to prove that the concept of a personal Messiah did not become an official Jewish teaching until the time of Rabbi Akiba, and that therefore Jesus was not originally in and of Judea, but came from Egypt.[25] And, in the following week's *Israelite,* he wrote:

> Therefore I maintain that orthodox rabbinic Judaism, which came from Palestine and Persia into Europe, first accepted the idea of a personal Messiah to come from the Graeco-Hebrews. . . . And the belief of a suffering Messiah—as met in the rabbinical Haggadah of the third and succeeding centuries, the Messiah of Ephraim or the Messiah who was to be a son of Joseph, to precede the son of David, was adopted from Christian expounders of Scriptures and history, when the Jews themselves suffered persecutions. . . . The Old Testament Scriptures have nothing to do with these beliefs. . . .[26]

And finally, in the following month, as the last of this series on "The Suffering Messiah Among the Hebrews," he wrote:

> It is evident, therefore, that the suffering Messiah was never adopted among Jews as a religious belief, although in their sor-

> row and affliction some of the rabbis appeared inclined to adopt and Judaize the Christian doctrine. Wise claimed that both, Christians and Jews, had lost sight of the Messianic idea, the unity of the human family on the moral and intellectual basis. It appears that both of them forgot the Bible, and each built up a theology of his own.[27]

Nowhere in his writing is there an adequate treatment of the biblical, especially of the prophetic, concept of the Messiah, either as it is to be found in Isaiah, or—as it is wonderfully and deeply limned—in Deutero-Isaiah.

But that there will be a Messianic Age, in which Judaism will triumph, as the Bible predicted, Wise never doubted:

> The religion of the future will be Judaism in its pure and denationalized form. However the prejudiced world may protest, in theology it must finally become Jewish. There is no other way left to conciliate reason and faith. . . . the hour of redemption for mankind must come, the Messiah must be sent to redeem them. Here in America the salvation of mankind must originate.[28]

F. ON THE MISSION OF ISRAEL

To a certain extent we have already given many of Wise's central views on the mission of Israel: in the paragraphs of the Philadelphia Conference, and in various statements made in the course of his life. These derived directly from his universalistic interpretation of Judaism, and from his concept of the dispersion of Israel. Jews had been spread among the nations to teach the truth, to labor until all men would accept the simple, rational truths of their faith, to serve as a "priest-people" among the races of earth. This he had taught very early during his residence in the United States. In the *Occident* of 1849 he had written:

> The mission of Israel was and still is to promulgate the sacred truth to all nations on earth; to diffuse the bright light that first shone on Sinai's sanctified summit, all over the world.[29]

In defining his interpretation of Reform, both for the *Israelite* and for the *Deborah*, he had inserted these words, all in italics:

> . . . and always starting from the basis, that the essence of Judaism is destined to become the universal religion, while its form must change according to the demands of different ages, and fall away altogether with the final triumph of its essence.[30]

In the same editorial he gave early utterance to a sentiment, a prediction, which he repeated again and again during his life, and which was often quoted by his disciples:

> He [Wise] entertains not the least doubt that, *before this century will close* [italics his], the essence of Judaism will be THE religion of the great majority of intelligent men in this country. This conviction gives him the boldness and fortitude to stand on his own ground notwithstanding the numerous attacks and violent onslaughts made against him, or rather his system. Who stands firmest will be victorious at last.[31]

The same optimistic forecast was made in an article in the *Asmonean* in 1854,[32] concluding with these words:

> The civilized world hastens rapidly to the point, when there will be one shepherd and one flock, when there will be "one God and His name one."

It is important to remark at this point that—as we shall discover more clearly and in greater detail—Wise's violent opposition to the Zionist movement, when it arose, derived in large part from this view of his. Jews were a religion, and not a nation. Under God's providence they had lost their nationhood in 70 C.E., so that they might broaden the scope and meaning of their mission, so that they might interpret and apply it in universal terms. In this he was consistent throughout his career. It was, therefore, not difficult for him to subscribe to that part of the Pittsburgh Platform which declared:

> We recognize, in the modern era of universal culture of heart and intellect, the approaching of the realization of Israel's great Messianic hope for the establishment of the kingdom of truth, justice and peace among all men. We consider ourselves no longer a nation, but a religious community. . . .[33]

He claimed to discern among "advanced Gentiles" a gradual approach to the content of "Israelism."[34] This content he described as the simple, broad doctrine of the Bible, that which was for him the very core of the Jewish message. All the rest was elaboration, sometimes a watering-down. And in time the latter too will go. Jews must cleave to their own heritage, learn it and exemplify it, with especial hopefulness now that it seems clear that many others will flock to it:

> We must wander on till the end of woe and misery has come, till the earth shall be one holy land, every city a Jerusalem, every house a temple, every table an altar, every parent a priest,

and Jehovah the only God; till light and truth shall have dominion over all, every land be a home of the free, every government the guardian of liberty, and mankind one family of equal rights and duties. Then the curtain will drop on the drama of the Wandering Jew. Then a good morning will have risen upon the world.[35]

4

II. On Judaism *(Concluded)*

G. ON THE TALMUD

It should be recalled that at the Cleveland Conference in 1855 Wise had been one of the formulators and signers of a declaration, part of which asserted:

> The Talmud contains the traditional legal and logical exposition of the biblical laws, which must be expounded and practiced according to the comments of the Talmud.[1]

This was intended as a compromise upon which all American Jews could agree. That Wise did not interpret it to mean a recognition of the unalterable authority of the Talmudic interpretation or formulation of the Law, many subsequent pronouncements prove. Even a year or so before this he had written an article in the *Asmonean* under the title of "The Talmud and Progress," which gave expression to his basic stand.

In this article Wise claimed that the inflexibility of the orthodox was at least in part to be ascribed to their ignorance of the Talmud. The Pharisees favored change—for example in regard to capital punishment—though the Bible contains express laws providing for it. It was Wise's point of view—to which he held with a fair degree of consistency—that the Talmud itself advocated change and progress:

> We assume. . . . . that the Talmud contains a progressive code of laws, as developed during centuries, on the principles of the

> Mosaic dispensation. This, in itself, represents the principle of progress.

What according to his view had brought this to an end? Many laws had been made or altered since the close of the period of the Talmud. Maimonides was guilty of an egregious error in codifying the Law and thereby attempting to fix it, as was Joseph Caro somewhat later:

> We may, therefore, safely advance the opinion, that a thorough and scientific investigation of the Talmud and the post-Talmudic literature, in order to ascertain the principles on which our sages proceeded, would be the greatest service that could possibly be rendered to the cause of progress, improvement and salutary reforms; it would show us the proper method of the ancients in this course, a method sanctioned by the history of twenty-five centuries.[2]

In this attitude Wise was taking the same stand as the great scholars of the school of *Die Wissenschaft des Judenthums*, especially Zunz and Geiger.

In defence of the Cleveland Conference he maintained the position that reform is both desirable and possible within the framework of the Talmud. Thus he wrote:

> Know it, therefore, knowledge of the Talmud is required to judge and discriminate which reform is legal, Jewish and admissible, and which is contrary; therefore no reform without the Talmud.
>
> Had we the power of the thunder we would proclaim it throughout the inhabited globe: There is no Judaism without progressive reforms, and there can be no reforms within the pale of Judaism without the Talmud.[3]

Only ignorant men would reject the traditions of Israel which are in the Talmud and the *Massorah*. No genuine Judaism or Christianity, no comprehension of the Bible, is possible

> If the connecting links between our age and three thousand years ago are removed; it is a matter of impossibility to comprehend the meaning of a book then composed. There is religious inconsistency in the cry "No Talmud!"[4]

Wise published a collection of Christian opinions on the value of the Talmud, a collection that stemmed from Rabbi Isidor Kalisch.[5]

All of this was more or less in the heat of controversy. In the following years he set himself occasionally to confront the same difficulty. Thus in the *Israelite* in 1856 he wrote that even Einhorn had admitted some of the validity of his point of view by writing:

> The Talmud is one of the most important movements in the development of Judaism. It has led it safely through the calamitous epoch of Jewish history and has enriched it in many ways. In fact, it must be acknowledged as a high merit of the Talmud that it has broken the inflexibility of the Biblical letter; it has, though unconsciously, reformed the Mosaic law in its most vital aspect, with respect, namely, to the demands of time within and without.[6]

Lilienthal made a fair résumé of the controversy in these words:

> If it is admitted that the Talmud was itself a reform, why should not the principles which justified that reform be searched for?[7]

And Wise restated his own position thus:

> The Sanhedrin was empowered, being instituted by Moses and being maintained by Talmudic authority, to meet emergencies; it could suspend Biblical laws, it could provide for new conditions. It could take care that the letter of the Bible be pervaded by the creative power of life.[8]

In the *Israelite* in 1856 Wise published an editorial, first under the title "Why I am a Jew," and followed by one with the contrasting title, "Why I am a Talmudical Jew."[9] He wrote a lengthy answer to articles that had appeared in European journals by Stein and Philipson, and he attempted to show that the Talmud was not unchanging, but had advocated the progressive alteration of certain laws.[10] Three years later the subject was still preoccupying him, and he wrote that a great service could be rendered by ascertaining precisely the principles upon which the sages of the Talmud proceeded: "it would show us the proper method of the ancients in this course, a method sanctioned by the history of twenty-five centuries."[11]

As the years followed, his attitude became less certain. In 1884 he had been giving a course of lectures on the Talmud, and concluded with these words—which should be read carefully—in contrast to what has gone before:

> The Talmud is advisory; it possesses historical importance and authority, and remains forever subject to Israel's reason and conscience. It is groundless folly to say we reject the Talmud, as none can reject history and the consciousness of the people.

> It is not true that we are or ought to be governed by the Talmud at the expense of our reason and conscience, either as individuals or as the congregation of Israel.[12]

The last—and in some ways the most interesting—of the passages in Wise's life and in his thinking about the Talmud occurs in the record of the sixth annual convention of the Central Conference of American Rabbis, in Rochester, N.Y., from July 10 to 13, 1895. Among the questions that Wise—in his presidential message—proposed should be submitted to special committees for consideration was the following:

> What is our relation in all religious matters to our own post-biblical patristic literature, including Talmud, casuists, responses, and commentaries?[13]

A committee was appointed, consisting of M. Schlesinger, Emil G. Hirsch, and A. Guttman. According to Philipson's *The Reform Movement in Judaism*,[14] most members had left the convention by the time the report was made. Only about twenty remained. A long and rather warm discussion ensued. A number of "radicals" contended that the report did not go far enough, that both biblical and post-biblical works should have been considered together as to the matter of their authority. After amendment, the report of the committee was carried by a bare majority. It read as follows:

> Your Committee, appointed to consider that portion of the President's message which reads, etc. . . . begs leave to report that, from the standpoint of Reform Judaism, the whole post-Biblical and patristic literature, including the Talmud, casuists, responses, and commentaries, is and can be considered as nothing more than 'religious literature.' As such it is of inestimable value. It is the treasure-house, in which the successive ages deposited their conceptions of the great and fundamental principles of Judaism, and their contributions to the never-ceasing endeavor to elucidate the same. Consciously or unconsciously every age has added a wing to this great treasure-house, and the architecture and construction of each wing bears the indelible marks of the peculiar characteristics of the time in which it was erected. Our age is engaged in the same task. We, too, have to contribute to the enlargement of this treasure-house; but we have to do it in our own way, as the spirit of our time directs, without any slavish imitation of the past.
>
> To have awakened the consciousness of this historic fact, is the great merit of Reform Judaism; and the more this consciousness grows upon our mind, the more the conditions and

> environments of our modern life force it upon us, the more persistently we have to assert: *that our relations in all religious matters are in no way authoritatively and finally determined by any portion of our religious literature* [italics in the original].[15]

Philipson moved that the report be adopted. Hirsch suggested that it be accepted, but then given back to the committee for some reshaping and rewording. Max Heller objected to some things in the report in the light of the delicacy of the question, and urged—not on principle but as a matter of "expression"—that the word "religious" be inserted before "literature." At this point Wise asked Vice-President Gottheil to take the chair, for he, Wise, wished to speak on the matter. He reminded the Conference that his question, in his report, had not been inserted except after much thought. The "underlying question is, 'Shall this literature be considered binding authority on Jewish Communities?' " He felt it to be obligatory on the rabbis to speak out, to place themselves on record before the world.[16]

The action of the Conference evoked great excitement. The conservative press—mistakenly—interpreted the large negative vote as expressing the feeling that the Talmud was regarded as still binding. At the next convention—in July, 1896—Wise again referred to the entire matter, in these words:

> The vote of eleven to nine placed the conference on record that nine out of twenty hold the post-biblical or patristic literature as authoritative and final for us in all religious matters. So the vote was generally understood by outsiders, and this placed the conference in a ridiculous position of inconsistency, the same which I. M. Jost charges on German conferences in his time. As this was positively not the import of that vote, it places the nine of the opposition in a false light before the world as being adherents and advocates of orthodox Rabbinism. It will therefore be necessary that a reconsideration of the said vote be moved by some one who voted on it in the affirmative. We must sustain the position we took from the beginning; that this conference consists of the reformatory element only and exclusively, and its standpoint is historical Judaism, that is the Judaism of all ages and not that of one period, place or class of people. We cannot submit to the legalism of the Talmud, the Kabbalism of the Zohar, the literature of the Karaites, or even the rationalism of Maimonides and Mendelssohn, because either of them was a child of his respective age and not of Judaism of all ages; and this only and exclusively is our basis. To us that is true which always was true to all. That is the

> standpoint upon which we based ourselves, and there we must abide, if we wish to maintain the confidence of our co-religionists, and do our duty before God and man.[17]

A new committee was appointed, including two of the nine who had voted against the report at the preceding convention. In their report they made plain that the vote should not have been construed as it had been, and that they did not differ from the majority, or from the original report, in their conviction that the writings mentioned possess no final religious authority for Reform Jews.[18] At the original meeting, also, Wise had protested against the proposal to table the report on the ground that he would not "stultify" himself "before the country and before the whole of Reformed Judaism." It was well understood, he said, that "we do not believe in the Post-Biblical and Patristic literature as religious authority."[19]

The process of Wise's development and the character of his opinions on rabbinical literature ought now to be plain. In general, these derived logically from his entire standpoint on Jewish theology, on revelation, on the role of the Ten Commandments, and of all else in Jewish tradition. He was not to be numbered among those who belabored the Talmud; he was never guilty of the uncontrolled scorn, the frequently extravagant language of many of the Reformers, in Europe, also, who repudiated rabbinic literature out of hand and poured upon it the vials of scorn. There is much evidence, which we shall adduce in connection with other subjects (for example, the origins of Christianity) that Wise was not a tyro in the Talmud, that he knew its text and its spirit quite well. Nor did he underestimate its enormous importance for spiritual and ethical vision, for the interpretation of Judaism in the spirit of the Pharisees, for having saved it alive in one of the most difficult and tragic periods of Jewish history, and for deepening and expanding the Jewish spirit. But this did not connote or imply that he regarded it as an "Oral Law," as a continuation through the Holy Spirit of the revelation on Mt. Sinai, or that he was ever willing to be bound by it as a whole or in part. Even his willingness to go along with the Cleveland formula in 1855 was probably to be explained by his belief that this too intended to say only that the Talmud was of help in understanding and interpreting Scriptures. That Wise was not a mere doctrinaire reformer in relation to all this is best demonstrated by the fact that he spoke and wrote very often in his life about the rabbinic writings, set himself with great diligence to make their wealth and inspiration available to his people, and did not write derogatory or denunciatory words about them.

H. ON HEBREW

On few aspects of Wise's life and mind has he been more misunderstood—by some—and more misrepresented, than on his attitude toward the Hebrew language. It is therefore of much more than passing importance that we set down—as far as possible in his own words—just what he thought about this. In the course of narrating the chapters of his life, we have already included a number of passages which in passing spoke of his love of Hebrew, of his feeling about it in the liturgy, of his treatment of it in composing *Minhag America*. To these must now be added a number of other expressions of his on this topic, which was very near to his own past and to his own heart.

The material is not very extensive, but it is quite significant from a number of aspects. In his early days Wise was very scornful of those who could not read Hebrew and read it well. Thus in his *Reminiscences* he wrote about Isaac Leeser, whether fairly or unfairly we cannot tell:

> Upon perusing this letter, I grew very angry at the thought that a man who could not read unpunctuated Hebrew, presumed to direct Jewish affairs in the role of editor and guardian.[20]

Later on he wrote about the prevalence of instruction in the classics in American schools in the middle of the nineteenth century, and of the fact that Hebrew was taught very rarely. This he found difficult to understand, for the Bible can be appreciated only in its original language, and this ability to read it would be of far more value than would all the so-called "classics":

> We, for our part, believe that there is more poetry and sublimity in the Bible than in the classics. . . . . there is more truth contained in them [the Biblical books] than in all other books of antiquity. Hence, if any ancient language should be studied, it is certainly the Hebrew.[21]

In another paragraph in the *Israelite* he maintained that the rather exceptional capacity of Jews is not due to "phrenology," but to their century-long training in Hebrew:

> Let every one make his children attend to Hebrew studies. It benefits the child in developing his mental capacities, it guards him against religious impositions, and banishes superstitions from his mind.[22]

Among other kinds of prejudicial treatment of Reform which he had to face was that which contended that Reform wished to abolish the use of Hebrew. Wise wrote, "but this it not true, sirs!"

> History tells you that, as soon as the Israelites forgot the Hebrew . . . the schisms began. . . . Take away the Hebrew from synagogue and school and you take the liberty of conscience from the Israelite. . . . You see, Mr. L., this is not the object of reform, as it cannot be its object to choke itself.[23]

He made very clear that by this he meant not only Hebrew in the liturgy, but Hebrew in the religious school as well. What access would a Jewish child have to the treasury of the Jewish past, or of the Jewish present, without Hebrew?

> Your Bible is Hebrew. You have no authorized version. A large portion of your prayers is Hebrew. The preservation of the Hebrew and the purity of the Hebrew doctrine are inseparable. Wherever the Hebrew has been dropped, there sprung up a new religion which was not Judaism, error has been fostered, the Bible has been typified and mystified [a rather obscure combination of words!], an oppressive hierarchy has been established upon the necks of an ignorant people, the simplicity of divine truth has been submerged in artificial dogmas, and confusion has taken hold upon the minds.[24]

It was his habit to subscribe to and to read some of the remarkable Hebrew periodicals of his day. Thus he wrote congratulating *Hamaggid* upon the completion of its thirty-first year of publication, and hoped that it would live long and prosper.[25]

It was his firm belief that every Jew should learn the language of the country in which he dwelt and speak it well. But Hebrew should also be his language and he should know and read it well.[26] It pleased him that there was evidence that "the rising generation of Hebrews in Palestine will speak Hebrew." He could not resist saying too that this would be good in itself, and in addition would "extinguish the jargons."[27]

In one of the papers which he prepared for the World's Parliament of Religions in Chicago, in 1893, "An Introduction to a Bibliography of the Jewish Periodical Press," he wrote also of Hebrew journalism:

> Hebrew journalism has accomplished another wonderful task. It has laid the foundation to the Science of Judaism, i.e., the history and theology of Judaism. . . . And still another, which is, perhaps, the most wonderful. Those journalists rejuvenated

> Hebrew to a language of modern culture, with an abundant terminology for all sciences, industry and commerce, so that the ancient language of the Bible is now expanded to a complete vehicle of modern society.[28]

In the *Israelite*, near the end of his life, he appealed for financial help for Eliezer ben Yehuda, who was at work on a great, complete Hebrew dictionary, and who was in many ways the greatest force in our time for making Hebrew once again a living language.[29]

While, as we shall see, he was opposed to Zionism and all its works, he regarded it as good for Jews to have at least a smattering of Hebrew, but not at the expense of the language of the land where they lived.[30]

Thus it is a slander against Wise to say that he wished either to diminish, or to abolish, the role of Hebrew, in the synagogue, in the school, or in the life of the Jewish people. He himself loved it, occasionally composed a poem or a letter in it; found it closest to his own memories and emotions, when he prayed, or when he sat down to read the Bible; was glad that it was springing into new life toward the end of his own career, in Eastern Europe, in its revival through many writers and some splendid periodicals, and especially in Palestine among Jews who were going there or who were born there.

I. ON THE RABBI

In connection with Wise's work in his later years at the Hebrew Union College, we have already quoted two eloquent passages of his, one on what a rabbi should be, and one on preaching from a Biblical text. Many times during his life he wrote on the profession to which he had given so full and so dedicated a life.

The rabbi in ages past was a judge; but now he has become chiefly a teacher:

> His claim upon the respect of his brethren is based on his intellectual superiority, his purity of character, and his enthusiasm for the cause he serves.[31]

In writing in the *Israelite* of a journey he had made to Chicago in 1856, he was impelled to speak of what a rabbi should be, "a man thoroughly versed in Jewish theology and conversant in our literature." He bemoaned the fact that such men were then so scarce, and declared that this lack was one of the primary causes of "our disunion and want of concert." He continued to protest—as he had protested from his arrival in the country and during his years in Albany—against making rabbis of *Hazanim*, of those whom he calls here "our singing colleagues":

> We want men of knowledge who know our creed and our literature, who know it from its primitive sources, and are capable to expound it.[32]

Quite a few years later he wrote on *Semichah*, or ordination. This was called, as a "German invention," the *Hatarah*, or *Hatarat Horoah*, the diploma authorizing a man to become a Rabbi and bestowing the title upon him. It had also grown to be the custom that any rabbi could ordain men, and this had been greatly abused.[33]

In the Archives of the Hebrew Union College is a letter that Wise wrote to my own father, on September 5, 1886. From its context it is evident that Max Heller was about to try for the pulpit of an Eastern congregation. Wise wrote for the purpose of being helpful, of making suggestions as to how a young candidate should go about it. It is a warm and characteristic letter, and some of it deserves reproduction:

> I must give you some hints. Do not speak from notes of MSS. It is killing among our people to speak from MSS, or even from notes. In your case it is still more disturbing. You must bend down to the MSS, which takes you away from the audience and disturbs the sound of your voice. The speaker must continually eye his audience, there is magic force in the eye, and preserve uninterruptedly a graceful and imposing position which is interrupted by bending. There is some uncertainty and weakness in your voice, as if you would lack conviction and courage, which you must overcome; and you can do that easily by feeling convinced that you know what to say and how to say it, and you know all that better than your audience whom you teach. . . .[34]

Another letter of his in the Archives was directed to Rev. J. L. Mayerberg on May 23, 1888. This constituted advice on "What to read to make you a competent preacher." Here is what Wise recommended:

1. The Bible, and study its peculiar eloquence. Use also the Midrash and the Agadah.
2. Jewish history, regularly and carefully, especially Jost, Graetz, Zunz, Wise, and others.
3. His own little book, *Judaism*, and also *Judaism and Christianity*, The *American Jewish Pulpit*, and others.

This will furnish material enough. In regard to the form of the sermon, read Blair's lectures on Rhetoric, and "any small text-book on pulpit oratory." No teacher is needed. If Mayerberg should tire of this curriculum, Wise said he would suggest another. He was always ready to serve. The best equipment is "enthusiasm, and zeal, firm conviction."[35]

A third letter was directed to Edward N. Kalisch [usually spelled Calisch]. Wise informed his pupil that his own [Wise's] congregation wished to get rid of its cantor and take Calisch as his assistant. Wise requested him not to consider it. He added:

> Never take a second place, when you have held a first one. *Ma'alin b'kodesh* [In sacred things one goes upward not downward!]. Never think of leaving your post, unless you are called to a decidedly higher position, which a secondary post never is.

He closed "with friendship and love." And in regard to another offer Calisch had received, Wise wrote later:[36]

> They must be treated with strict independence and self-reliance, either to bend or break, before you engage yourself to be their Rabbi.[37]

Many more could be added to these rather desultory and disjointed utterances. But it is evident that Wise regarded the rabbi as a scholar, an authority on Jewish literature, a dedicated servant of Israel, a teacher, but above all a man of moral rectitude, of light and leading.

5

III. *On Reform Judaism*

A. ON REFORM IN GENERAL, ITS CONCEPTS AND PRACTICES

A recognizable picture of Isaac M. Wise's concept of Reform Judaism could be drawn from the material that has already been placed before the reader: his beliefs in regard to Jewish theology, the Mosaic law, the processes of change and adaptation in the rabbinic law, etc. But it is important to have before us more precisely and in more consistent form what he thought. One of the main purposes of this entire work was conceived to be that of making clear Wise's own individual stand in regard to the nature and scope of Reform; and this we shall attempt to do largely in his own words.

First, in regard to terminology! In general—as was the habit of most of the founders and leaders in Germany—he utilized the term "Reform." This was taken by him to mean not an ethical remaking, but simply the adoption of the principle of change. Thus, in the *Israelite* in 1886, he wrote an Introduction on the various forms of Judaism, which included these pertinent sentences:

> Orthodox, Heterodox, Conservative, Radical, are the terms which have been invented in the controversies of this century to characterize and name various parties taking part in the process of development within the pale of Judaism.
>
> Speaking of "Reform," it must always be borne in mind that it never touched the principles, doctrines or precepts of Judaism.

> Its object was always and is now to lead the Israelite out of the obsolete and isolating forms forged for him in the past centuries . . . and to give him and his institutions, morally, politically and socially, the modern form of cultivated society.[1]

On the other hand, he was at times quite aware of the misleading character of the word "Reform" in English. Thus some years earlier he had written:

> In Judaism, the term reform is a misnomer, as nobody seriously entertains the idea of re-establishing old forms of worship in their original simplicity. There are conservative and progressive Israelites . . . We do not reform. We abolish antiquated forms, and supersede them by such new ones as correspond with the demands of our age.[2]

As far as we have been able to discover, only a few times did he alter the word to "Reformed," a term characteristically employed by some Protestant sects, and appearing to indicate that the process of change had been completed:

> Reformed Judaism, the subject of this humble essay, acknowledges no necessary stability of the form, and no change of the principle. All forms change, adapting themselves to new conditions, and all changes proceed from the same principle, which is not subject to change. This is the central idea of all Jewish reasoners on Judaism in the 19th century and in civilized countries.[3]

Occasionally he would call Reform by a title which became a favorite of some of his followers in subsequent years. Here are three samples from various years of his preference for "American Judaism." Wise would not have been deterred by having had pointed out to him that orthodoxy, conservatism, were—under the American system—equally "American." He would have conceded their right to their own opinion, but would have maintained nonetheless that Reform, or "American Judaism," comported far better with the freedom and with the intelligence of the land and of American "Israelites":

> Whatever custom, law, doctrine or practice can be justified before the tribunal of reason, if it collides with American sentiments, is doomed to perish; and whatever is left, that is American Judaism, or Judaism transformed to correspond to American sentiments, feelings and thoughts; and that only will be preserved.[4]

In the foreword to the Fiftieth Anniversary Booklet in 1892, he began with these carefully chosen words:

> American Judaism, i.e. Judaism, reformed and reconstructed by the beneficent influence of political liberty and progressive enlightenment, is the youngest offspring of the ancient and venerable faith of Israel. The old soul is found in a new body; that majestic palm tree is but transplanted into a more fertile soil and invigorating clime. . . . It is the American phase of Judaism.[5]

And in 1896 these words occurred in an editorial paragraph:—"Rationalistic Judaism—and this is American Judaism. . . ."[6]

The attentive reader will have noticed in the previous part of this book that in a number of quotations Wise—and others—used another term, namely "reformatory" Judaism. At the time we let this pass without comment. But this form was not exceptional with him. It is evident that he regarded it as simply an adjectival equivalent of the noun "reform," and that he was quite unaware of its penal, or corrective, implications. "Reformative" would have been closer to what he had in mind. Let us add a few examples to clinch the point. He delivered an address in Memphis, Tenn. in 1870, in which he bade the Jews there cling to "Reformation and abhor deformation."[7] Later on he remarked that in the East no one had ever been able to "build up and sustain a reformatory organ."[8] In an editorial paragraph he wrote:

> The reformatory idea which has built up Judaism in America . . . . makes its conquests also in Europe.[9]

In a more extensive article on American Judaism in 1888, he began by claiming that the American environment changes all men and all religions, that orthodox religions become difficult to maintain here, and—once again—that Jews are Jews by religion only:

> He [the American Israelite] is positively not the same believer as his co-religionists elsewhere, or as his grandfathers were. Therefore, speaking of the religion of American Israelites, we can only call it American Judaism. . . . The main mistake, however, is that men, earnest and able, overlook the undeniable fact that American Judaism is progressive and reformatory.[10]

Writing in 1896 about the reasons for the success of the *Israelite*, he named as a principal one: "The reformatory banner upheld with an inflexible consistency."[11] And—finally—at a convention of the Central Conference of American Rabbis in Milwaukee in 1896, his presidential address contained these sentences:

> This is proof positive before all the world, that American Judaism is identical with reformatory Judaism; that conservative, orthodox, or anachronistic parties are the minority sects, whom we ought to respect and treat with fraternal kindness and consideration, but no longer as a *vox populi* or an influential factor in the historical processes of American Judaism. . . .[12]

So much for the diversity, and sometimes the ineptness, of his name for the movement! We turn now to his definitions of Reform. Here there is a genuine *embarras de richesse*. Wise tried again and again to define, to expound, to elucidate. He was well aware of the widely prevalent misunderstanding, of the polemical assertions that Reform was an abandonment of Judaism, a "way out," a perversion of the traditional essence of the faith. It is important that we have as clear and detailed an idea as we can of his own approach to the concept and practice of Reform. We shall therefore have to take the chance of wearying the reader with a multiplication of his own attempts at definition. To this should be added some of his more ambitious attempts at tracing the ancestry of Reform, hard upon the heels of some of his colleagues in Germany and Austria. One of these—to which the assiduous or curious reader may refer, if he be seized by the impulse—is in a protracted series Wise wrote for the *Israelite* in 1871 on the genesis of Reform.[13] In these articles he began with Maimonides and Albo, continued from Abarbanel to Mendelssohn—at some length, turned next to Jost, Zunz, Rappaport and Luzzatto, to Reggio and Krochmal, to Geiger, Fuerst and Graetz, and ended with the problem of the translations of the Bible. Most of these articles were later reproduced in a volume of Wise's Selected Writings, and can be found there.[14] Interesting as they are, it would occupy far too much space even to indulge in a sketch of their contents.[15]

We shall first quote in chronological sequence some of Wise's statements in regard to orthodoxy and reform. Some of these appear to us to be of especial significance, both positively and negatively. From them one can judge what Wise thought Reform was and what it was not.

In an article on "Orthodoxy and Reform," in 1866, occur these sentences:

> We do not wish to mislead our readers to the belief, by too frequent recurrence to the subject, that reform is our main object. Judaism, its elevation and preservation, the proper under-

standing of its precepts, a due appreciation of its benign influence, and the choice of adequate means, to naturalize it on American soil and transmit it to posterity, untarnished and unalloyed—this engages chiefly our attention, and it is this which we wish to impress deeply on the mind of our readers. . . . Reform, thus, is the means, not the end. The entire Anglo-Jewish press [he wrote] stresses orthodoxy. But the press does not understand the spirit of the age. It is an old house in a sad state of disrepair.

The young and the intelligent desert them, the enlightened portion of the community pitied their narrow-mindedness and ridiculed their antiquated notions. Synagogues are deserted, and schools unattended. This has hurt Judaism greatly. The future of Judaism in this country is identical with the cause of progress and reform. The latter is the proper and only means to attain the former. . . . This is an age of inquiry, criticism and philosophy. The time of uninquired faith and symbolic expression closes itself, few and far apart are their votaries among the American Israelites. . . . Dogmatism and mysticism must yield to universal religion, such is the spirit of the age and the essence of Judaism. . . . The triumph of Judaism depends on the success of reform and progress.[16]

Or again, Wise wrote of Reform as a "modernization" of Judaism:

Gradually we are coming out from the rabbinic and casuistical Judaism, in which we were preserved about sixteen centuries, upon the wide field of universal religion, where the prophets left us twenty-three centuries ago. The national forms have been spun out and worked out and worn out to their utmost extent. The idea of [Jewish] political nationality fell with the walls of the Ghettos and with the repeal of exceptional laws. The sublime elements of universal religion . . . are left to us and to the world; the rest is gone, goes, or will go. . . . The idea is breaking the form, that is the pulsation of the age.[17]

It was his contention that orthodoxy was not compatible with the spirit of that time, with the critical, rational, and universal mood that had been transforming western man:

. . . it is the orthodox principle that religion must be in conflict with reason. This is as true of Christianity as of orthodox Judaism. It places religion in conflict with the understanding and consciousness of the nineteenth century, to the prolific increase of infidelity.[18]

On the other hand, Wise himself had never taught or himself believed that on essentials Orthodox and Reform Jews differed:

> They do not differ in their religious beliefs. All religious Jews believe in One God, etc. The orthodox hold that every law of Moses and every Rabbinic law, custom and observance is eternally obligatory upon Israelites, and must practice them conscientiously, to please God and to worship Him.
>
> The reformers hold that all laws, etc. are subject to change; whatever means, etc. have lost their efficiency of leading to piety, righteousness and humanity, have abrogated themselves, and they have changed their observances and mode of living according to the reasonable demands of this age and country, and so also in other countries of advanced civilization, and do admit such changes as the progress of civilization and enlightenment demands.
>
> The conservatives are a class of whom we have no exact knowledge, as they never advance any set of principles or any principle at all. They seem to be occasional growlers, who perhaps are too honest to call themselves orthodox, because they know themselves to be far from it, and yet lack the moral courage, for one reason or another, to side openly and honestly with the reformers, either by reason of superstition, policy, or a natural spirit of opposition.[19]

It was his consistent opinion that there was no future for orthodox Judaism in America, and to this he held even after the great migration of East-European Jews to the United States:

> We give these immigrants ten to fifteen years' time to be fully Americanized, and just as long as their orthodoxy will hold out. . . . Hence American Judaism must be reconstructed, as was proposed long ago. This must not be permitted to go by default or obstinacy.[20]

From these passages it should have become obvious that Wise regarded reform as a change from orthodoxy, not in regard to essentials, not in respect to the great principles of faith and conduct, but only touching the laws, customs, practices, which were—to him—temporal manifestations, which had been altered in the past, and which must be discarded or transformed in his day, so that the religion would appeal to "intelligent" men, so that reason would again become regnant, and so that the center and core of the faith might be cleared of the debris of the ages.

If Wise made clear his attitude toward orthodoxy, his reaction to the "radical" reformers was equally explicit. Again and again he wrote that these were his chief stumbling-block, his most ruthless and irreconcilable opponents and detractors. In one of the early works on Wise there is some useful material bearing on this. Wise contended that the "radicals" were negative, while his approach to Judaism was positive. He claimed that the "radicals" were without any genuine appreciation of what proper laws of growth really are, holding the past together while adapting it to the present. Thus Einhorn had written:

> What has been haunting the mind so long and has had a mere ideal existence has now seized upon hearts, has inflamed them, and the things that have been tolerated no longer, not only in spite of religion, but in the name of religion. . . .[21]

This is more than a bit obscure, but it is intended—we believe—to say that orthodoxy has obscured the true content of Judaism, and has long been a hindrance to its true spiritual development. To this Lilienthal retorted:

> Unnatural leaps are of no avail in history—in history as in nature all things are confined within a process which works by degrees —opposition to this eternal law brings failure.[22]

Einhorn insisted that the ethics of the Talmud was narrow and exclusive (*engherzig*), that rabbinic literature lacked the world-embracing spirit of the Bible. To this Wise retorted:

> Reform will not advance as some radicals may wish, but it will take deeper root and occupy a larger field than a reform restricted to a few and separate congregations."[23]

Wise explained that he had been among the convokers of the Cleveland Conference in 1855—which had been so abusively attacked by Einhorn and others:

> . . . To bring life into all congregations, so that the ones may not remain stagnant while the others, reforming head over heels, break with the history of our people.[24]

The reader should refer back, also, to the pages about the sequels to the Cleveland Conference, and to some of Wise's answers to its detractors (pp. 292-302).

Between these two extremes, between orthodoxy and "radical" reform, Wise stood. This did not mean that he was in all ways a "middle-of-the-road" thinker. By far the best way of seeing this clearly is to turn now to the actual definitions of Reform which he gave in the course of years. While these differ in some details, in emphasis and coloration, there runs beneath them a large degree of consistency, which the thoughtful reader will discern and which we shall sum up at the end. At the peril of spinning out this section on

Reform to too great a length, we shall set before the reader quite a number of Wise's own formulations, from 1854 to 1899. But, since this is one of the central purposes of this work—to bring into focus and clarity Wise's concept of Reform—we cannot permit abbreviation to cause us to run the risk of obscurity.

The first we select was written before Wise went to Cincinnati, for the *Asmonean*, in the spring of 1854. This was primarily an appeal for unity:

> The nineteenth century is the age of dissection and dissolution. The process is affected by the application of light . . . We must either progress or retrograde, there is no standing still. . . . Let the men of all parties and shades express freely their opinions, on the questions now agitating their minds. One will instruct the other, the energies are developed in the struggle only, a question is then only properly understood, if it be stated by two opposite sides. . . . Let our own and our children's prosperity and happiness be the efficient cause, and TRUTH the final aim of our endeavors and discussions.[25]

Hardly had he begun to publish the *Israelite*, when he felt it necessary to define its policy, especially in regard to Reform. Thus, on July 28, he published a lengthy editorial on "Reform," in which are these central sections:

> When we advocate reform, it is not our intention, as our opponents charge us, to abolish Judaism, or its time-sanctioned forms; or to lessen its influence upon the hearts of its votaries. If rulers had been more reasonable, there would have been no revolutions. If priests had modified Christianity, there would now be no deists, no infidels, no atheists. So the "Rabbins" should not have been so intractable, or should have been capable of understanding the powerful change going on under their eyes. There is now a wide schism between life and religion. . . . Intelligent men would yet remain with us, and it would be an honor to be a Jew. . . . Our Rabbins of the last century have done great injury to the synagogue. Some assert that, since rabbinic Judaism has preserved Biblical Judaism for nearly 2000 years, to touch it is to make the whole edifice unstable. But rabbinic Judaism has lost its hold, and except to a few is quite obsolete. Moreover, it is not true any longer that it maintains and preserves religion. . . . the thinking man, standing in the midst of a progressing society, requires much more than this. . . . We were once children, an isolated and persecuted people. . . .
>
> He goes on to contend that it was not rabbinism that was really responsible for the survival of Judaism. It was this

elevating and inspiring consciousness [of a lofty, noble faith], which preserved Judaism and the Jewish nation. But now cardinal principles are lost sight of for the multitude of thoughtless observances. Hence the only choice now is conformity or indifference. The essential spirit of Judaism must be liberated.

The principle of Reform is: All forms, to which no meaning is attached any longer, are an impediment to our religion and must be done away with. . . . Whatever makes us ridiculous before the world as it now is, may safely be and should be abolished. . . . Whatever tends to the elevation of the divine service, to inspire the heart of the worshiper and to attract him, should be done without any unnecessary delay. . . . Whenever religious observances and the just demands of civilized society exclude each other, the former have lost their power. . . . Religion is intended to make man happy, good, just, charitable, active and intelligent.

The article concluded by contending: there is no authority in religion besides the Scriptures and common sense. The Mishna and the Talmud are sound exegesis, but are subject to scientific criticism.[26]

Occasionally Wise devoted himself to the task of replying to various charges made against Reform. Early in his tenure in Cincinnati, he treated these questions: Do reformers wish to abandon the idea of the Unity of God, the practice of circumcision, to deny the authority of the Bible, or to abolish the Sabbath and the holidays?

What the reform party proposes, it proposes for the welfare of the future generations, it wishes to prevent the endless desertions and splits, it wishes to banish the hideous indifference which has taken hold of a large portion of the Jewish community; it wishes to inspire the Jews with a new love for their religion—and with such intentions it does not fear senseless and groundless insinuations, but trusts in Him, who grants His best blessings to every just and sincere undertaking.[27]

One of his clearest treatments of the purposes of Reform was in an editorial in the *Israelite* in 1859, which we shall reproduce at some length:

Reform is distinguished from innovation, in that the former hath purpose and limits, the latter has none. . . . Reform must move within the sphere of Judaism. . . . To extinguish a system signifies not to reform it. This latter term can only mean to expose and abolish errors, misconceptions or malpractices, but always remaining in the main within the given limits of the system. . . . Successful attempts may be made to reconcile reli-

> gion and philosophy, as Maimonides did with Judaism and the peripatetic philosophy; but then as to the reformer of philosophy, philosophy is the basis, so Judaism must be the basis to the reformer of Judaism. Therefore reform has its limits, of which the reformer must be conscious.
>
> The reforms in Judaism, during this century, have a double tendency, a reform of doctrines and theories, and a change of forms. Criticism, this mighty lever of modern learning, seized also upon national literature. Under this heading comes much of modern knowledge, which is in direct contradiction of old concepts of Judaism. This is the first part of Reform, which we style theoretical reform. This . . . proved many an established conception and accepted doctrine as unfounded and untrue, purporting always to guard religion against the incursions of superficial skeptics, and remaining always within the limits of scriptural Judaism. . . .
>
> Practical reform involves a change of forms, new forms for new conceptions. Many customs and practices, intended to keep Jews and Gentiles separate, laws about eating, drinking, dressing, etc. have become obsolete. What shall we do now with these laws, when we are citizens of almost all civilized countries, and by our own free will come in contact with all classes of people? Evidently they exist no more for us.
>
> Next comes the problem of music, of the sermon, of decorum, of forms and ceremonies. . . . Therefore reform stepped in between the extremes, endeavored to draw a distinct line of demarcation between essence and form, idea and symbol, the eternal and the transient parts of Judaism, to stop the violation of essential laws, and reorganize the scattered fragments of conflicting opinions. Wherever reform has not this object in view, it is innovation. Reform, therefore, has its limits, strictly marked by the Bible itself, beyond which the Jewish reformer can not and dare not go. He may explain the Bible, by the aid of ancient and modern researches and obtain results directly contrary to established views, but he can not go beyond it. Thus reform has purpose and limits, and innovation has not.[28]

Quite often he continued to write about the need for Reform, the disorganization and the weakness of the orthodox synagogue, at the time of his coming to America. The choice seemed to be not between orthodoxy and reform, but between survival and disappearance.[29]

Another excellent résumé of his position, entitled "A Challenge," was in the *Israelite* in 1887:

> This is the basis of Reform for him:
>
> 1. It rests on the Bible.

2. "The Bible expounds itself."
3. Rabbinical literature is to be taken as literature, following Rabbi Meir, who said: "I eat the kernel and throw away the shell."
4. All the reforms he proposes are justifiable on Biblical grounds, and even on Talmudic. In themselves they are necessary for the preservation and elevation of Judaism here and now.
5. Changes in the synagogue should be uniform and sanctioned by a conference or synod. But even without the possibility of these, each man must do his duty to the best of his knowledge.
6. Judaism is a universal religion. Israel itself is the Messiah; "And America is THE COUNTRY [capitals in the original] where universal religion will celebrate its first and glorious triumphs."
7. We need colleges and seminaries for our own tradition.
8. Only children are convinced by miracles.[30]

He was compelled to return again and again to those reformers who went far beyond him. The time had come—he wrote—to tell some people that "anarchy is no reform. . . . The Jew must submit to Jewish law and custom, unless he can show good cause against either."[31] In his opinion the creed of the "radical" reformers violated this central canon:

> For the principles of Judaism are axioms of the understanding not based upon dogmas contrary to the postulates of reason; what reason and nature teach or corroborate is indestructible, and must finally be confessed by all intelligent persons.[32]

In his first presidential message to the Central Conference, at Cleveland, in July, 1890, he spoke in part as follows:

> This is the historical standpoint which acknowledged *eo ipso* the rights, claims and wants of time, place and circumstances as important factors in the development and progress of Judaism, without severing the present and future from the glorious and marvelous past of Judaism, the intelligible revelations of Providence in history. American Judaism, seemingly a new creation, in fact but the most recent phase of Israel's ever progressive faith, built itself upon this basis. . . . We cannot afford and do not propose to make any concessions to the advocates of anachronisms or adherents of the immovable *status quo*. . . .
>
> . . . Again, the development of Judaism signifies the liberation of its universal spirit from all antiquated, meaningless, tribal, merely national and merely local paraphernalia, which

> impress it with the appearance of onesidedness and awkwardness, as a stranger in the land of the living, a foreigner in its own home, and provide forms and institutions for the manifestation of the spirit, which are at least approximately universal and nearest to the understanding and feelings, the cogitations and sentiments of the largest community.[33]

Reform—he wrote—is "in fact a separation of the spiritual and ethical contents of Judaism from the concomitant legalism."[34] Even near the end of his life he was still writing about the necessity of this process, justifying it from the Talmud itself, which—he said—evidenced an "opposition to congealed forms."[35] He was also opposing those who would do away with everything, who—in his opinion—were cutting themselves off from the living tree of Judaism:

> When these self-made reformers say, "We Jews made the Bible, the Talmud, and all the commentaries, all being spirit of our spirit, and we can also undo it, if we want it so," they tell a falsehood. Not we Jews, but some very few of us, have done it, and hammered it into the brains and souls of the masses in the hard-fought battles of truth against ignorance and stupidity. It is not spirit of our spirit; it is of the spirit of the few enlightened and God-inspired souls that rose among us by the grace of God. Who are we, what right have we to obliterate the spiritual gifts of these men of God, those princes of peace, those mighty men of righteousness? Evidently none! All that is left for us to do is simply to ascertain what of all that is ordained was intended for all eternity and all mankind, and what was intended originally for a certain age or country. This is all that reformers are permitted to do. You dare not destroy other people's property.[36]

6

III. *On Reform Judaism*

(Concluded)

A. ON REFORM IN GENERAL, ITS CONCEPTS AND PRACTICES (continued)

Before proceeding to a final summary of Wise's interpretation of Reform, it would be well to complete the picture. We shall, therefore, continue with various subsidiary, specific problems, subsumed in the foregoing under the general question of the forms, ceremonies, and practices which are appropriate to Judaism in a given time and at a given place.

Wise felt it necessary to reply to Rabbi H. Pereira Mendes, in 1887, who had offered an explanation as to why his congregation had not affiliated with the Union. Much of the argument—Wise wrote—was based upon misrepresentation. There existed no proof that the Hebrew Union College had ever taught: "the transfer of the Sabbath [to Sunday, evidently]; the abolition of the Abrahamitic covenant; the discarding of the dietary laws; the denial of the divinity of the Bible." It would have been easy—Wise wrote—for any fair-minded man to have ascertained for himself that all this was utterly without foundation.

Rather strangely the *Occident*[1] had had a paragraph to the effect that from Judaism should be purged "every trace of foreign ideas and their consequences." Wise responded to this in the *Israelite* with the suggestion that these things should be eliminated: the second day of holidays; the benedictions over the Shofar; the Lulab; the *Megillah;* Chanuccah lights; *Hallel*; hand-washing, all of which—he contended—are unbiblical; also chanting in favor of choral singing; the reading of the *Torah* every year [the Bible says every seven years]; the practice of "calling-up" to the *Torah* and the *Misheberach,* etc. He advocated also dropping the "foreign admixture" of *Shechitah,* the search for leaven before Passover, making meat *kosher,* the use of four-fold dishes. This was rather a comprehensive list, some of the items of which are not easy to understand [especially, the reading of the Scroll of Esther on Purim, and the lighting of the Chanuccah lights].[2]

In another place he listed three reforms that—according to his way of thinking—were needed in the synagogue: to put female voices in the choir; to institute family-pews; to adopt *Minhag America.* He added to this the Friday evening service and lecture; the *Torah* to be read by young people rather than by the *Hazan;* that all funerals be held from the synagogue; and that there be *Minyan* twice a day for mourners.[3]

We have already explained his attitude toward the dietary laws. This was, however, part of the problem of reform specifically. We add therefore this clear paragraph, which stated his position succinctly:

> In explanation of our position to the dietary laws of Moses, we have to say that we certainly consider each and all of them well considered sanitary laws, based upon experience and scientific principle. What Moses forbade as an article of food is injurious to health. This is well known now to scientists. Therefore, as the results of science become popularly known, the Mosaic dietary laws gain general authority among the intelligent portion of the community. But when the zealous orthodoxy makes of these laws a matter of religion, a test of orthodoxy, a touchstone of Judaism, we must protest. It is not religion, it is sanitary advice, which every intelligent man should take, especially those who believe in the laws of Moses. A man can be a conscientious believer in Judaism and a religious Israelite without obeying any laws which are not contained, expressed or implied in the Sinai revelation. We hope this will suffice; if it should not, we will, as soon as time permits, explain further what we understand, under the dietary laws in Deuteronomy, which is written in the style of *K'lal U'prat* (general and particular), with the verbs always in the subjunctive mood.[4]

Elsewhere Wise declared that the practice of laying *Tephillin* (phylacteries), or of placing the *Mezuzah* (affixed to the doorpost of a Jewish home), had no real Biblical warrant. To this Ibn Ezra agreed. These are literal applications of that which was obviously intended to be taken metaphorically.[5]

As we have seen, he was constantly arguing against Sunday services in favor of Sabbath observance, and in favor of his own innovation on Friday nights.[6]

He had himself introduced the organ into the synagogue. This followed the procedure in Germany, where it was the earliest of all points of controversy in the genesis of Reform (July 17, 1810, Jacobson at Seesen).[7] Wise called the pipe-organ "the sublimest instrument of the world. . . . It is not so much a single instrument as a multitude of them, dwelling together—a cathedral of sounds within a cathedral of service." He thought it especially fit for the expression of religious emotion.[8]

His congregation in Cincinnati abolished the second day of the holidays (the "three festivals") on February 2, 1859, and of *Rosh Ha-shono* fourteen years later, in 1873.[9]

One of his main tasks—from the days when he attended the Frankfort Conference in 1845, and from his rabbinate in Albany—was the revision of the liturgy, the drawing up and publication of *Minhag America*. In 1857 he enumerated some of the reasons why the prayers had to be revised:—to abolish those prayers which referred to the sacrificial system, prayers for the coming of the Messiah, and prayers for a restoration to Palestine. He concluded:

1. Two-thirds of the American Israelites neither expect nor wish the coming of the Messiah-king, and the prayer-book should be the common good of all.
2. It is a deplorable inconsistency or hypocrisy, to be a republican in sentiment and practice, and a royalist in prayer.[10]

His congregation adopted the *Minhag America* on September 24, 1857, unanimously.[11] He had objected also to some of the prayers which date probably from the tenth and the twelfth centuries, which —according to him—abound in superstitious ideas and phrases, especially to the "eighteen benedictions" (*Sh'mone Esreh*), and their emphasis in part on the gathering together of the scattered children of Israel:

> Those who wish to live on this free soil are granted every liberty imaginable, and dare not pray for the restoration of a kingdom, or rather, in fact, would not do it; and those who wish to return to Jerusalem can do so now quite conveniently.[12]

He was consistently opposed to the continued use of German, which was becoming—he said—as strange to Jews as would be Chinese. Why perpetuate the language of a country in which Jews had never enjoyed equal rights? After ten years it will certainly be meaningless and useless. Parenthetically, it was strange that the agitation to continue the use of German should be coming from the "radical" reformers. This never meant that he would either abolish or diminish the use of Hebrew:[13]

> Because, furthermore, our brethren in all parts of the world are conversant with the Hebrew service, and no Israelite should feel himself a stranger in the house of the Lord.

If we abandoned Hebrew, we would be broken up into sects.[14]

Long before he was able to establish the Central Conference of American Rabbis, Wise advocated a Union Prayer Book—in fact, as early as 1881. He listed these prayer-books as then in use: the *Minhag Sephardim*; the *Minhag Ashkenaz*; the *Minhag Polen*; *Minhag America* in seventy or eighty congregations; the Temple Emanu-El *Minhag*; the Einhorn *Minhag*; also books by Szold, Jastrow, and Huebsch, which were used in perhaps less than fifty synagogues. There were no less than eight in use. Eventually—he predicted—one prayer-book will be used by all, but it seemed as yet too early for this.[15]

Wise advocated the elision of the *Kol Nidre* prayer,

> Which has given rise to so many false accusations, and of which there is no mention in the Talmud, as it has no foothold whatever in the Bible. Sensible men ought to know that formulas of that kind are out of date and place, and ought to be dropped.[16]

The last comment by Wise which we possess concerning the prayer-book is in an interesting letter he wrote to Max Heller on November 30, 1896, in regard to a paper he had asked Heller to read at the convention of the Central Conference at Montreal that summer, on "The Theology of the Union Prayer Book." In the letter Wise said that he regarded this as a paper of especial importance for the definition of Reform:

> "None can tell what is and what is not our creed. What is Judaism now in our days?" The two volumes of the Union Prayer Book express the Reform interpretation implicitly. "I think a plain, full statement of the doctrines underlying the prayers and contemplations of these books will tell *our creed*

[italics his] in full without any legislation or without establishing otherwise any dogmas. This is the piece of work I invite you to contribute to the conference and the next following Yearbook. *The Body of Doctrine Expressed and Implied in the Union Prayer Book.* . . . I do verily believe that the prayer-book contains expressed and implied the entire theology and ethics of Judaism, the Biblical God-cognition, the attributes of God as the foundation of ethics, providence and *Die Sittliche Weltanschauung* (the ethical world-philosophy), revelation and inspiration (*Min Hashamayim*, "from God"), the covenant and Israel's mission, Israel's obligation to obey and to promulgate God's law, immortality with future reward and punishment, the perfectibility of man and mankind, and soon the whole theology of Judaism. The paper, I think, will show that aside of legalism the American Rabbinate represents the genuine orthodox Judaism."[17]

We have had several references to Wise's proposal, following various authorities, that *Milath Gerim*, the requirement of orthodox Judaism that adult male proselytes must become circumcised, should be dropped. Henry Berkowitz addressed an inquiry to the rabbis of the country, asking their opinion on this *Sh'elah* ("question"). Among the answers was one from Wise. Papers were read on this problem, which appear in the Yearbook of the Central Conference.[18] The matter was referred to a committee of five, which reported in New York, and a resolution was adopted, canceling the requirement.[19]

Wise himself addressed a letter to Rabbi Julius Mayerberg, who had obviously asked for guidance, to the effect that, to "accept a proselyte" into Judaism, it would be wise to call together two members of the congregation, form a *Beth Din*, and examine the adequacy of the preparation and belief of the prospective proselyte, "if this is not done in the synagogue before the assembled congregation." The proselyte (if a woman) should "go to the *Mikveh* (the ritual bath) with two or three ladies." She ought to "say the *B'rocho* (blessing) which you taught her." He suggested that his book "Judaism, Its Doctrines and Duties" would be excellent for instruction—or other works which he mentioned.[20]

A correspondent had written to him in 1885, inquiring why he favored the abolition of circumcision. To this he answered that, as far as he knew, neither he nor anyone else had advocated this, but only of circumcision for adult male proselytes.[21] His desire to drop the custom with adults derived from his general point of view:

He [the convert] is *de jure* a son or daughter of the divine covenant between God and Israel . . . whether he did, or did not,

> submit to circumcision. This rite ought not longer be permitted to deter the honest believer from joining our ranks.[22]

It is worth recording again that Wise did nothing whatsoever about the wearing of hats in his own synagogue for twenty years after he came to Cincinnati. He had other and more important problems to take up.[23] And then the form the action took was simply that those who wished to do so might remove their hats. Wise's own point of view was a very moderate and reasonable one. He wrote, for example:

> It is a precious small business to allow such an insignificant matter [as wearing or not wearing a hat] to outlaw a Jew from the house of God. . . . The orthodox Jew may look upon it as a violation of his conscience to enter a synagogue bare-headed, but the liberal Jew certainly does not consider it a sin to keep the head covered. . . . If reform does not teach its followers common-sense, toleration and good manners in all things appertaining to religion, there is not much use for its existence.[24]

Earlier he had noted that rabbis, discussing this practice in 1845, had declared there was no real law that one must have his head covered.[25] He called attention to the *Mishna* (*Taharoth*) which spoke of Israelite dignitaries who went bare-headed into the Temple, even up to the altar. Rather whimsically, too, he referred to the story of Elisha (II Kings, Chapter 2, verses 23-25), whom some boys taunted because he was bald-headed. Wise remarked that he must also have been bare-headed, otherwise the boys could not have known.[26]

B. ON THE POSITION OF WOMEN

Throughout his career Isaac M. Wise argued and worked for the improvement of the status of women in Judaism. This he regarded as one of the primary tasks of Reform. Nor, as far as can be told, did he admit any limit to the general principle that he put forward—that there should be absolute religious equality of the sexes within the realm of the faith. This went back to the beginning of his career in Albany, where he introduced various innovations in this direction.

In Cincinnati he continued this process. Nor did he content himself with proposing and instituting various reforms: about the choir, family-pews, etc. He spoke of these, and of their religious significance, on many occasions. Thus in 1855 he published a series of articles entitled "Does the Canon Law Permit Ladies to Sing in the

Synagogue?" It was his contention that only Talmudic casuists could maintain that there existed any serious hindrance to the use of female voices in the synagogue.[27]

Among the specific ventures which he regarded as essential for Judaism in the United States was an academy for women. Certainly in his mind this had as its purpose the equalization of educational opportunities of men and women. Thus he wrote in 1858:

> If we are right in regard to the religious education of woman—and we would like to see the shade of an argument against our position—then it is highly necessary that we should have a female academy, where the daughters of Israel would be offered an opportunity to finish their education and have the benefit of a thorough and enlightened religious instruction.[28]

After the Philadelphia rabbinical conference (in November, 1869), Wise wrote nine articles on marriage and divorce, one of the oldest and most difficult of the problems of Judaism in regard to the position of women. Orthodox Judaism favored regarding both marriage and divorce as primarily problems and responsibilities of religious law. Reform Judaism had long taken the position that this should not apply to divorce, which ought to become a purely civil matter. Fifteen years before this, *Halitzah* [the strange ceremony, when a man would not marry his brother's, childless, widow] had been abandoned. Here, too, Wise believed in complete equalization in the rights of men and women.[29] In the main he was following the carefully argued and documented position of Abraham Geiger:

> It appears to us that the same undeniable religious feeling which craves the religious sanction to the covenant of matrimony, also expects the religious protection of the parties to that covenant.

It was Wise's opinion that no sanction should be given to a second marriage, without due consideration of the moral status of the parties concerned.[30]

In a series on Reform in 1876 Wise enumerated some of the improvements that had been made in regard to woman's place in the synagogue: in the choir, in the attendance of women at worship, in the confirmation together of boys and girls, in the institution of family-pews. He asked also for a liberalization of marriage laws: "if a man may marry his deceased wife's sister, then a woman may marry her deceased husband's brother." Women—he noted—were at congregational meetings, and on the boards of synagogues. The religious sentiment of women "must be given full scope to develop."[31]

In his Collected or Selected Writings there is an article on "Women as Members of Congregations."[32] In this he traced the background of Biblical women: Miriam, Rahab, the mother of Samuel, Deborah, Ruth, etc. The line was continued in some of the great women of the Talmud, especially Beruriah and Yaltha. Wise wrote that, despite rabbinical laws, woman remained "the queen of the hearth and home." But Jewish law had an oriental character, excluding women from the affairs of men. It was regarded as preposterous to think of calling women up to the *Torah*, or of admitting them to public religious honors. Again he enumerated his own innovations, and went on to say that in the synagogue women were greatly needed: on school-boards, and on the choir-committee. But, especially, they ought to be members of synagogues with equal rights and equal opportunities:

> We are ready to appear before any congregation in behalf of any woman wishing to become a member thereof, and to plead her cause. We will debate the question with anyone who will show us in what woman is less entitled to the privileges of the synagogue than man, of where her faith is less important to her salvation than man's is to him. Till then we maintain that women must become active members of the congregation for their own sake, and for the benefit of Israel's sacred cause.[33]

In one passage we have already set down Wise's views on intermarriage, his own personal belief that the interdiction in the *Torah* of marriage with an idolater did not apply to Christianity or Islam; but that, nonetheless, in the light of the attitude of Christianity toward Jews, he could not sanction it even in his own day and even with his own generous views on human relations. On this topic he spoke at length from his own pulpit in 1879, reviewing the history of Jewish law on intermarriage. He said, in part:

> The covenant of matrimony is too sacred to be trifled with. . . . No Jewish minister has a right to sanction the marriage of a Hebrew man or woman to a person outside of the Jewish faith, because the congregation of Israel, by law and custom, prohibits such intermarriages, and the rabbi is the teacher, not the legislator, of the congregation; the priests are the church, the rabbi is not.

He continued in the same vein on another occasion, to the effect that, as long as Jews are regarded as "damned," as long as they—Jews—

continue to think Christianity mistaken, such marriages will be not only wrong but dangerous.[34] Some years later he expressed himself even more strongly upon the same theme:

> If the rabbi believes, as he ought to, that matrimony is a sacred institution, sanctified by the law of the covenant, by the expressed will of the Maker of man, in whose name and by the authority of whose revealed law he unites the couple before him in the holy covenant of matrimoney, and invokes upon them God's blessing; he will not make a comedian of himself to do and say all that for persons who do not believe a word about it. If any one does not believe in the Living God of Israel and the Sinaic revelation, he has no reason whatever to believe in the sanctity of the marriage compact as being instituted by the law of God, and consequently has no cause to be married by a rabbi; who acts by that authority alone. This is certainly higher ground which it might be difficult to controvert.

He ended with the suggestion that the entire problem of intermarriage should be submitted to a Synod. But until it would have met and rendered its decision, no intermarriage should be sanctioned.[35]

His own conviction—frequently expressed—that women should serve on congregational boards had not found acceptance in his day, though now it is commonplace among reform congregations. He continued to argue for it even in his later years.[36]

In regard to the place of women Wise went much farther than the majority of his liberal contemporaries did, and than many of his successors would now go. He believed in the ordination of women as rabbis, something that has not yet been done by any seminary, or by any group of rabbis. Thus he wrote in 1890:

> There are, we maintain, in this country Jewesses who are both able and willing to occupy the pulpit. We have opened for them the Hebrew Union College, because we wish some of them would prepare themselves for the ministry.[37]

Two years later he reported that a Miss Frank of Oakland, Calif. had preached in a pulpit, first in Washington, and later in two in California:

> In the Hebrew Union College, among the different female students, we had one who heartily wished to prepare herself for the pulpit. We discouraged her, because it appeared to us, she had not the requisite oratorical capacities and without them success in the pulpit is not very likely. We can only encourage Miss Ray Frank or any other gifted lady who takes the theologi-

> cal course, to assist the cause of emancipating woman in the synagogue and congregation.[38]

The same attitude which Wise manifested concerning the place of woman in the synagogue, he extended to civic and political life. He was consistently in favor of the extension of the suffrage to women, wrote that he himself had never used the word "obey" in the marriage ceremony, and that of course its employment is not in the traditional formula of Judaism, but only in Christianity. Nor could he find any distinction made between men and women in requiring them to obey the Ten Commandments or the Mosaic legislation in general.[39]

C. ON A SYNOD

Often in the pages of the Second Part of this book we have set down Wise's pleas for the creation of a Synod, and the many attempts he made—at rabbinical conferences and elsewhere—to persuade others to join him in calling one into existence. His concept of the character and function of such a Synod changed somewhat over the course of the years. In the beginning he regarded it as solely a rabinical task, for only rabbis had the authority and the knowledge to compose it. Later he wished to admit learned laymen, representatives of a congregational union. Though he was equally consistent in denying that such a Synod would have a "hierarchical" purpose, it is patent that he thought of it as a method of regularizing change, of giving to reinterpretations of the law a *Halachic* sanction, of pursuing in broad outline the processes of classical rabbinic days. He was very eager that reforms should not be regarded as merely individual, or as the work of a dissident group. He wanted them approved on the basis of Jewish tradition, as a reasonable interpretation of its central principles and its temporal realizations. He had evidently given much thought to the problem of authority in Jewish life, and the Synod was his habitual and primary answer to it.

We shall now come to somewhat closer grips with this question, in the various treatments Wise gave it through the years. These we shall treat chronologically, so that whatever change and development appeared in his own views may become clear.

As early as 1856 he was writing on "The Synod," reviewing arguments as to the need of it and its place in Jewish history.[40] He regarded it as an acutely needed corrective against anarchy:

> Reforms, if they should exercise a salutary influence, must come from the people and must satisfy the demands of the people, they must be legally Jewish, and must not have the tendency of exciting suspicion or disunion among ourselves; they must tend toward elevating Judaism and endearing it to its votaries.

This would conduce also to diminish congregational quarrels about belief and ritual, and make for unity in schools and charities. A Synod alone could correct some of the contemporary evils.[41]

After the Cleveland Conference of 1855 Wise continued "advocating the 'Articles of Union' as adopted" there:

> "Historical Judaism and the Synod" are our watchword, and we shall not stop repeating this to the community until either they yield and act, or we go home to our heavenly Father.[42]

If there are to be "progressive reforms," "which sever not the ties of our nation":

> We want a conservative authority opposed to the nullifying attempts of ignorance and frivolity, the arrogance of self-made Ministers and overbearing *Parnassim,* the money-raising speculations to which congregational officers are now reduced. We must have an authority to form a center of union. . . . This authority is the Synod in every country with its executive committee and the General Synod, consisting of members elected by the several Synods, and of its executive committee.[43]

His point of view became clear and explicit in a holograph letter to Dr. Samuel Adler, in German, written in 1857:

> Turning now to the subject of Reform Judaism, let me say that I do not agree with the following views:
>
> a. The morality of the Talmud is narrow.
> b. Judaism consists of the axioms of the human mind.
> c. Revelation is the intensified potency of the human mind.
> d. The Bible is symbolical.
> e. Reform is the essential matter, Judaism is secondary.
>
> . . . Reform has up to this time brought about only disruption (I plead guilty for myself also); it has nowhere united its own forces, it has not permeated the people because it has lacked authority, viz. the pronouncement of a synod. The synod is *the* [italics his] authority in Judaism and therefore also the center of gravity for the great whole, the central point of unity; it finds its justification in the Talmud. . . .[44]

In 1878 he recommended a Synod again, because reforms then were only by the whim of single rabbis. The Synod should consist of learned men, both laymen and rabbis, should meet once a year, and should publish an "organ."[45]

When the Rabbinic Literary Association came into existence for a few years, it appointed a committee to report on a Synod, which was to consist of expounders of the Law and professors of the Hebrew Union College. No changes were to be proposed except with the consent and approval of this body. Every member was to be bound by the decisions of the Synod. Voting was to be accompanied by adequate explanations. The Synod was to meet every second year and to establish its own rules of procedure. These were Wise's own personal suggestions and he invited discussion on them.[46]

As he came to conceive it, the Synod was not solely a deliberative body. It was to be vested with coercive power:

> A Synod to which its members do not submit is a nonentity, a debating society at best. We have that in the Rabbinic Literary Association to all intents and purposes. Now the question is, are the rabbis willing to submit private opinion to the decisions of a Synod? If they are not, none can be established.[47]

He admitted that the idea of a Synod had not originally been his, but had probably originated with Kohler. The committee appointed by the Rabbinical Literary Association at Detroit consisted of Kohler, Gottheil, Gutheim, and Wise. Wise made suggestions to the committee, and said he would abide by its decisions "as did the *Tana'im* at Jamnia, Usha and elsewhere."[48] In the fall of the same year he printed his paper on the Synod, given at Chicago in July of 1881:

> Every man of practical reason must feel satisfied that the decision of a majority is a safer guide than that of one in all practical matters. Therefore, I am in favor of a Synod, although I have no right to make an official report, and can offer you only a motion of my own.

Not all the members, or perhaps none, of the committee agreed with him, for he had a letter from Gutheim claiming that, at the present juncture of affairs in American Jewish life, a Synod would be "impracticable, inexpedient, and, hence, unavoidable [unattainable, or inadvisable?]"[49]

Two years later, Wise returned to the advocacy of a Synod of "ministers," but deriving its authority by consent from the Union of American Hebrew Congregations. Its members must be Jewish, and recognize Judaism as a "positive religion."[50]

In 1885 he reported on the Union convention in St. Louis:

> There was some lively discussion on the subject of the Synod. Quite a number of the delegates are in favor of establishing a Synod to bring uniformity into our liturgical affairs. It was somewhat difficult to convince those gentlemen that a Synod must have legislative authority or dwindle down to a mere shadow without substance, to a debating society with the only benefit perhaps of mutual information, and that the Council, according to the Constitution of the "Union," had no jurisdiction to authorize such a body (because of its guarantee of autonomy to each congregation). Still the argument of the committee was finally accepted by all, and the report unanimously accepted that the Council could not establish a "Synod."[51]

Shortly thereafter he published an editorial, the purpose of which was to dispel some misunderstandings that might have resulted from the foregoing discussion. A Synod—he wrote—is not a Sanhedrin, but "an ecclesiastical assembly for the purpose of deliberating on doctrinal or disciplinary subjects." It must consist of rabbis and "elders" only. It must arrive at unanimous decisions, which would then become laws. But thus far no congregation had declared its willingness "to submit to the enactments of a Synod." On the contrary, there was an express provision against this in the constitution of the Union. Wise ended with the proposal that those congregations that do agree should constitute a Synod, or wait until such a number would become available.[52]

Again he cited the multiplicity of prayer-books being used in liberal synagogues as an "emblem of anarchy." The need for unity in liturgy was a pressing one, and a Synod should be created to promote it.[53]

A very interesting series of articles appeared in the *Israelite* in 1895, under the rather curious title, "The Difficulty in Defining Judaism." To a certain extent these were personal memoirs, and sometimes very revealing ones, which we have utilized in the biographical section of this work. In the eighth of these Wise turned to some of the problems still prevalent among American Jews. He referred to himself thus:

> He also knew that the reformative current, in order not to precipitate itself, must be led into a legitimate channel. He thought both parties in legitimate cooperation would tend both to advance and to restrict one another and gradually develop an advanced American Judaism without any schism in our own ranks. For with all his progressive ideals he always dreaded the

> idea of producing sects in Judaism. The problem was to discover the proper method of bringing together the two sides of the camp in good will and let them have an organized authority to lead the entire body forward without violence of genuine orthodoxy and without unjust limitation to the progressive spirit.

He thought he might solve this by creating a synod of rabbis and laymen. He reviewed again the unifying influence of the Cleveland Conference, at least in the beginning. "Each party looked upon it as a triumph of its own cause" . . .

> The first point was to convene a synod of rabbis, ministers and laymen, which should constitute the highest authority of the synagogue.

There was some argument about the name: *Beth Din*, Ecclesiastical Court, Sanhedrin, or something else. But the name Synod was adopted. Another debate followed on the qualifications for its members:

> it was proposed to have authorized rabbis and other theological scholars appointed by congregations as delegates. . . .

All agreed on what such a synod should be and do. The real question was what would such a synod not be empowered to do. The first answer was this:

> All laws, ordinances, statutes and customs of Judaism in conflict with the law of the land are no longer obligatory in Israel; hence the Synod could not enact anything in conflict with the law of the land.

To this no one objected:

> Though it did away at once with a considerable portion of legalism, the very stronghold of orthodoxy, by setting up without talmudical authority a new legalism, in opposition to the old, and established the principle that existing law may be replaced.

This went far beyond the rabbinical dictum: *dina d'malchusah dina*, "the law of the government is the law." An argument followed on whether the Talmud should be regarded as enjoying equal authority with the laws of Moses. This seemed about to break up the meeting into two factions. But a compromise was found, which can be read in our account of the Cleveland Conference. Unfortunately the sense of triumph engendered at Cleveland proved abortive, and no real gain had been made.[54]

Nothing came of it, no Synod, no *Minhag*, but more virulent enmities and deeper divisions:

> It resulted in the course of time, in breaking up reformatory Judaism into as many factions as there were makers of prayer-books and catechisms; and drove the orthodox leaders back into their narrow confines.[55]

Suddenly in 1896 Wise appeared to have had a sudden change of heart. He found the idea of a Synod absurd:

> The idea of convening anywhere in Europe a convention or conference of rabbis, conferring on them the authority of reform Judaism is perfectly ridiculous. Who could confer such authority? On whom could that authority be conferred? What could such a conference do with that so-called authority? No man or body of men in Israel possessed any authority in matters of religion not provided for in the Torah, and this gives equal rights, privileges and authority to every Israelite, to all alike.[56]

It might be supposed that it was only the fact that this proposal had to do with "Europe" that caused his rejection of it. But in 1899 Wise declared that the congregations were not prepared for a genuine compromise between reform and orthodoxy. He was not, however, willing to consign the possibility to the limbo of forgotten things. He proposed some kind of voluntary meeting and discussion, ending with a treaty of peace:

> On this plan it might be possible that a majority of our congregations be represented in the first convocation of the synod, to constitute it, define its aims, claims and duties, and prepare the work for the next session of the body.

If only extremists on both sides could be kept apart, it might be possible to put before such a group propositions like these:

> a. it should deal only with congregations, one which enforces the dietary laws of Moses and the Rabbis down to the Shulchan Aruch, provides a Mikveh and a Cheder
> b. which keeps its Sabbath on Saturday [the text says "Sunday," but this is an obvious misprint]
> c. which strictly observes the Biblical holy days in due season, with an additional holy day to four of them

All of this Wise was imagining brought up by "extremists" at a Synod. It would take a whole winter season to discuss these proposals. This served to show that a Synod had become impossible:

> In this country of individual freedom and ingrained rights, which prevail not only in every congregation, but also in almost every individual therefore [thereof?].

There might be a union for administrative and practical purposes, but

> We have no use for ecclesiastical union or for sects in Judaism. It is not our duty to reform the orthodox, nor is it the duty of the orthodox to reclaim the reformers. Let each worship as he thinks proper, and build up Judaism.[57]

Thus, at the end of his life, Wise had abandoned a life-long hope. The time was too much with him, the multiplying and deepening disunities, the disappointments of a whole career.

Later after Wise's death there were a number of years in which the Central Conference of American Rabbis discussed the proposal of a Synod, listened to a majority and a minority report, and finally decided to have none of it.[58]

* * *

The material presented on Reform in these two chapters has been fairly voluminous, and, though it has followed in part a topical and in part a chronological arrangement, it does not in its present form sufficiently set forth a clear, logical exposition of Wise's concept of Reform. Therefore we add here at the end a résumé. We shall put it in the form of successive propositions, which must of necessity be much more apodictic and much more schematic in character than Wise's own thinking. But their purpose is quite simply to enable the reader, within a small compass, to judge Wise's thinking on this all-important aspect of his life, work and thought. Wherever possible, these dicta are put in Wise's own words. We divide them into positive and negative propositions.

I.

Reform is an expression of the "spirit of the age."

Reform is in accord with the spirit of inquiry and of critical intelligence.

Reform is intended to be "universal" in spirit and in content.

Reform holds that all laws are subject to change.

Reform contends that its own limits were marked by the Bible itself.

Reform follows the laws of growth, but without "unnatural leaps."

Reform is a continuation of the practice and tradition of the rabbis and of the Jewish sages.

Reform regards rabbinic literature as literature, but also as useful and often inspiring, and as an exposition of the Bible.

Reform has respect and regard for the work of the Jewish sages, and of the inspired sons of Israel.

Reform is an effort to rescue Judaism from indifferentism, desertion and ignorance, by inspiring Israelites with a love for Judaism and by a return to essentials.

Reform has to do with both doctrines and forms.

Reform must be in accord with American sentiments and must adjust itself to its environment.

Reform believes that the future in America and in the world belongs to it.

Reform would be strengthened by the creation of some central authority, so that changes proposed would not be arrived at capriciously, or by individuals, but in full consonance with Jewish law.

Reform wishes to bestow full religious equality upon women.

II.

Reform is not a "way out" of Judaism.

Reform does not wish to establish a "sect" in Jewish life.

Reform has no intention of "abolishing Judaism," or of lessening its influence.

Reform is not in conflict with reason.

Reform is no mere innovation; it is striving not to destroy a system but to reform it.

Reform does not differ on religious essentials from orthodoxy.

Reform is not "negative" in approach.

Reform recognizes no final authority but Scriptures and common sense.

Reform adopts only such specific changes as it regards as justifiable on biblical grounds.

Reform is not "anti-Talmudic."

The object of Reform is to lead Israelites away from obsolete and isolating forms; to abolish antiquated customs and supersede them by such new ones as correspond to the demands of the age.

Reform does not touch the "principles, doctrines, or precepts" of Judaism.

Reform believes in a "rational" approach to miracles.

Reform has sloughed off "national" ideas: a personal Messiah, the return to Palestine, the Aaronite priesthood, the sacrificial cult, etc.

Reform does not favor intermarriage.

7

IV. *On the Jew in America*

A. GENERAL STATEMENTS

In the course of our pages on Wise's life, especially in the days of his first experiences in America, we described some of the conditions that obtained in the American Jewish community at that time, Wise's own opinions of them, and sometimes his specific reactions to them. To these now need to be added various ideas and views which he entertained in the course of his career.

Early in his life in America he asked Leeser:

> . . . How it happened that of all the Jews who had emigrated to these shores between 1620 and 1829, there were not two hundred families left that belonged to congregations, while the majority had disappeared among the masses, traces of them being clearly recognizable in hundreds of Christian families. Leeser never answered this question, and the orthodox party owes me the answer still.[1]

Wise's own comment and opinions were:

> Many Portuguese families died out, others amalgamated with their Christian neighbors, and again others forgot entirely all about Judaism. Hence it appears that their peculiar orthodoxy was inefficient to preserve Judaism with particular vitality.[2]

Shortly after his coming to Cincinnati Wise reviewed the progress that had been made in Jewish life. Thirty years before there had been very few congregations. Judaism had found no real place in the land and enjoyed no recognition. A great change had taken place since then: fine buildings, rabbis instead of *Hazanim*, much progress in education and in "spiritual enlightenment." This launched him upon one of his favorite themes:

> We must have an educational establishment of a higher order to train up men, who will be able to defend our cause, to expound our law, to inspire our friends.[3]

But conditions were still far from ideal. Even in those days the country was full of Jews whose motto was "Let us alone!" Indifference was rife. A task of very great dimensions lay before him and others: to rouse them, to educate them, to unite them.[4]

It is worth repeating his statement in 1857 that his congregation in Cincinnati was then "the largest in the United States."[5]

In 1859 he contrasted things as they had been in 1846 and as they were thirteen years later. In the earlier year there were only two regular preachers in the whole country: Lilienthal and Merzbacher in New York. Leeser in Philadelphia and Isaacs in New York preached once monthly, "we believe." In 1859 there were twenty-four rabbis. They should meet and try to unite and elevate the synagogue. In 1846 there had been one Jewish monthly, *The Occident*. In 1859 there were five. In 1846 there had been two Hebrew schools, both in New York. Since 1846 about one hundred new congregations had been formed. There had also been great progress by the Jewish community in wealth. America was far ahead of Germany in Reform Judaism. In 1846 there were only Temple Emanu-El in New York and Beth Elohim in Charleston, that were Reform. In 1859—he declared—Reform was triumphant all over the country.[6]

An interesting article on "The State of Judaism" appeared in the *Israelite* in 1865:

> So things have changed, so all old forms are dissolved or decayed and ripe for dissolution. This is the word of the spirit of the age, in the field of religion, which reveals itself through men like Strauss, Wislecenus, Ronge, Renan, Colenso, Buckle, and thousands of minor writers.

Nothing good had been lost, nothing essential:

> The faith in miracles and the belief in established authorities are shaken by the progress of courage, the faith in the true and the good is as firm as the foundations of the earth.[7]

In a second article he wrote that:

> American Judaism is in nearly the same condition as the congregation was that came up from Babel under Zerubbabel.

The change from autocracy in Europe to democracy in America was hard, "like the sudden transition from boyhood to manhood," also the "change from the narrow Ghetto to the broad and long avenues of public life." Thus the American Jew had become an utterly different person "from his countrymen at home."

All this was reflected in the condition of American Jews. There were many signs of health, but also some evils. Jews are Americans at heart, but still foreign in language. The liturgy is foreign, "tinctured with royalty and mediaeval sentiments." Jews must have one language, English, and must be thoroughly Americanized and modernized. Every congregation is today an independent republic, which has nothing to do with any sister-congregation, "and this is not freedom; it is anarchy." Jews are divided into *Landsmannschaften* and into many sub-orders under these:

> Actually we have as many Israels in this country as we have congregations, and all attempts hitherto to remedy this evil, proved a failure.

Formerly Jews were bound together by the *Shulchan Aruch.* But now each is a law unto himself:

> The congregations must come to the conclusion, that as they elect spiritual and secular officers, for their government, so they must elect representatives to the general meetings of American Israel . . . As it is the duty of every member of a congregation to abide by the resolves of the majority of his congregation, so it is the duty of the congregations to abide religiously by the resolves of the majority of the general assembly.
>
> Our mission in this country is precisely the same [as it had been in all Jewish history]: we are the religious monitors of this country, we oppose the follies and errors of sectarianism, and, clinging tenaciously and firmly to the word of God as revealed to common sense, we are of incalculable benefit to the spiritual development of this country.

Jews must avail themselves of the opportunities of freedom, which they enjoy actually for the first time:

> We shall never be silent, until we have roused the congregations of Israel to a full consciousness of their duty, in which God may assist them.[8]

Later he remarked that European Judaism had been "retrograding" and that only American Judaism continued to progress. But—he added rather acidly—"Polish-English" influences for orthodoxy had been hurting us here. "Shall we endure it much longer?"[9]

Jewish "sectionalism" was gradually fading away. Of this prejudice and division Jews should beware. They must remain "indivisibly one."[10]

Quite often he solaced himself with the assurance that he had helped change the whole status of the Jew in America in the esteem of his fellow Americans and in his own eyes:

> Those who now say with just pride, I am an Israelite, where some years ago they carefully concealed the fact, are not aware of the bitter struggles in the combat against friend and foe, which this change has cost, and most likely never will appreciate it.[11]

His opinion about rabbinical controversy, a chronic fact of his experience in America, was wavering. Usually he thought that this tended to bring Judaism into disrepute. But again:

> We live in America with a free press; it can not be stopped, men will disagree, unless we re-enact the synod law of *acharay rabim l'hatos* ("to follow a multitude to do evil"), which could hardly be enforced. We respect the rabbis that disagree more than those who always say amen.[12]

B. ON IMMIGRANTS

One of the great facts of the later years of Wise's life was the vast migration of Jews from Russia after the May Laws of Ignatieff and the wave of pogroms and discriminatory legislation. This circumstance altered the entire configuration of American Jewish life. To this we have called attention several times in earlier sections.

Several things make Wise's reaction understandable. He did not like these newcomers. It is sad to have to record that he was far from free, most of the time, from the prejudice of "Western" against "Eastern" Jews. He found them quite distastefully foreign and quite incurably orthodox. He fell into the habit of calling Yiddish a "jargon" and of sneering at it, as though it were utterly without strength or virtue as a language, as though it were no more than a badge of shame, a symptom of the corroding effects of persecution. Some of this doubtless derived from his own early attempts to rid himself of *Juedisch-Deutsch*, and to acquire "classical" German. This was not the whole story, as we shall see, for Wise believed that Russian Jews could and would be welcomed and aided by their brethren, that the newcomers would soon become Americanized and liberalized. He believed that a large part of the solution lay in settling them upon the land rather than in the great cities. In another section we shall come upon some of his attempts in this latter direction.

Before Herzl, Wise was charging that Zionism was a part of the spirit of "recent immigrants," who had not unlearned foreign ideas, or made a satisfactory adjustment to America. Even in England, after Herzl had gone there, Wise insisted that Zionism was only a "Russian-Polish hobby." On another occasion he asserted that Zionist leaders in America were men who had not acquired American ideals and were perhaps by nature incapable of understanding and appreciating them. Thus he coupled his dislike and disapproval of Zionism with his often negative approach to the Jewish newcomers.[13]

But to return more directly to this way of thinking and feeling about Russian-Jewish immigrants. In the early 80's he wrote:

> We can not help admitting that, momentarily, those newcomers are of disadvantage to the Jews as a class, although those immigrants are certainly no worse than the Italians, Hungarians, or Irishmen who honor us with their presence. . . . But as regards the religious phase of the problem, we have not the least apprehension that they will do us any harm or exercise any influence upon the development of American Judaism. They will come to us, we can never come to them. Let them come by the thousands, we will welcome them as friends and brothers, and are willing to assist them wherever we can.[14]

Later his words became sharper, as he discovered that Reform could get no foothold among the immigrants:

> The question has been raised, ought we any longer to give support to those Russian refugees whom we have housed, fed, clothed these twelve to fourteen years, when they, by their public organs, constantly denounce and coarsely insult us as "Reformers" under which they understand a class of Israelites, who stand far below them and outside the pale of Judaism? Have we not done enough good for those for whom we are not good enough? They maintain that we are not their co-religionists; what other claims have they upon us? Whoever will answer this query will have an impartial hearing before the public in this organ.[15]

Wise had the occasional habit, also, of speaking or writing as though the Russian Jews belonged to a different people and a different faith.

Thus he penned these words: "They are Jews and we are Israelites."[16] and later he elaborated upon this distinction.

He thought that the congregations formed by the newcomers would quite promptly learn, join the Union, and affiliate with the College. He called upon them thus:

> It is high time for them to understand that they live in America, and that the American Hebrews are naturally their friends; that they wish to be recognized as men and Israelites, consequently that they must show their willingness to have friends and assist in bearing the burden. . . .[17]

Wise followed closely the course of affairs in Russia. He printed protest after protest against Czarist inhumanity. This was the cause for the human flood breaking upon the shores of America: "Count Ignatieff ought to be hanged!"[18]

Not all of his words were cold or critical. Some of his paragraphs in the *Israelite* glow with warmth, with the attempt to persuade his fellow-Jews to give the refugees a brotherly welcome and brotherly help. He began to record the many attempts being made to turn the newly arrived immigrants to agricultural pursuits, chiefly under the leadership of the "HIAS."[19]

Nor was he chronically guilty of blaming all Russian Jews for the faults of a few. He reported some violence and some objectionable attitudes, in New York and Cincinnati, but asked his readers not to take these as representative of the many. Naturally there would be some "scamps" among those who had come:

> It is our duty to do good, and, if we occasionally receive abuse in return, or discover that we have assisted unworthy individuals, we must not be discouraged, nor seek an excuse for inactivity.[20]

. . . Not rarely he worried about the Americanism of the immigrants, their building up "among us a semi-Asiatic Hassidism and mediaeval orthodoxy."

> . . . The good reputation of Judaism must naturally suffer materially, which must without fail lower our social status.

The newcomers must be swiftly educated and enlightened. Some should come to the Hebrew Union College, and he asked for funds to make this possible.[21]

One of the fascinating sidelights of the time is a word of his to the effect that English-Jewish journals were "heaping upon American Israelites" abuse with reference to the Russian immigration. American Jews were being called niggardly, penurious, and —Wise claimed—without justification.[22]

For the sake of completeness and accuracy it is sad to have to reprint the worst of his fulminations, and the sharp boundary he drew between him and his, and them and theirs:

> If it were not for the reform congregations of New York and Philadelphia, there would be as much difference between the Hebrew population of those cities and of this great country as between us and the inhabitants of North Africa. It is next to an impossibility to associate or identify ourselves with that half-civilized orthodoxy which constitutes the bulk of population in those cities. We are Americans and they are not. . . . We are Israelites of the nineteenth century and a free country, and they gnaw the dead bones of past centuries. Besides the name we have very little in common with them. For the honor of American Judaism and our defense opposite the enlightened world, we do not want to have even that in common; we let them be Jews and we are the American Israelites. . . .[23]

We had noted earlier that Wise disliked Yiddish and transmitted this dislike to others after him. But it would not be wise to permit this to be a mere assertion. Here are some of his own words:

> So they have now a jargon, without alphabet (they use the Hebrew) and without grammar, an obsolete and corrupt German-Hebrew-Slavonic excuse for a language.

From these harsh words he went on to say that both customs and language keep "them" strangers in the United States. Of course, Christian fanaticism and "absolutism" had made them what they were, but this was only slight consolation.[24] He regarded the Yiddish press, of which there were then three journals in New York with thousands of readers, as doing harm to the Americanization of the immigrants, "ever so many of them can read nothing besides their jargon literature."[25]

8

V. *On Colonization and Zionism*

A. COLONIZATION AND AGRICULTURE IN GENERAL

As we cover some of the aspects of Wise's record, it will appear that he was not opposed—as he would have put it—"*eo ipso*"—to Jewish colonization. On the contrary, he regarded it often as the best solution for the problem of Jewish homelessness. In the later years of his life, perhaps partly because of his own living at the College Hill farm, partly from reading some of the social philosophy of Leo Tolstoi, he inclined more and more to the opinion that the only normal life was that of the tiller of the soil. Jews especially needed this as a corrective for the distortions, the spiritual and sociological warping of the Ghetto. Nor, as we shall come to learn in the next section, did he have any initial prejudice against agricultural colonization in Palestine. It was only his violent antipathy toward Zionism, his feeling that it confuted and would tend to disrupt everything he believed about Jews and Judaism, that later made him reject also the experiments in settling Jews in the Holy Land. But it will be wise to let his own words speak for him, and to let the reader judge for himself the processes of change in his point of view, and the probable inner reasons that motivated them.

Some of his ire at the project for a Jewish state in Palestine did not seem to apply to other similar ventures, for there was a time when Wise expressed approval of a plan to settle Jews in Yemen, in southwestern Arabia, and to make them an independent political entity there.[1] In earlier years he had written about the many advantages of being a farmer, who is a man "in nobody's way." The farmer's occupation is unlike the mill-trades and crafts. He does not invite envy, competition, or contempt. Wise believed in getting "as many Jews as possible out of those God-forsaken countries and to turn their attention from the commercial to agricultural pursuits."[2]

In 1890 Wise declared that, whether persecuted Jews went to Palestine or to North America, if they decided to pursue agriculture, their sufferings would be ended.[3] Again and again, around this period, he was writing to the effect that salvation—not for Jews alone, but for all the persecuted of Europe—lay in becoming farmers. He deplored the fact that very few who came to America went upon the land, but had tended to form "new ghettos," especially in New York and Chicago.[4] What the exiles from Russia needed was:

> physical and moral redemption which a long and intelligent toiling and tilling of the soil, steady association with nature, can only effect.[5]

The last declaration of this kind occurs in the year of the first Zionist Congress.[6] Thereafter we read no more of his faith in the regenerative power of agriculture.[7]

In 1879, probably at Wise's instance, the Union of American Hebrew Congregations resolved to appoint a committee of five to purchase some land to be used for the colonization of Jewish immigrants. Funds were to be solicited, land found and purchased, and divided into freeholds for ten families, each to have eighty acres free, free even from the payment of rental for seven years.[8] A note three years later indicated that this was to be done chiefly in the State of Kansas.[9] In the minutes of the annual meeting of Wise's own congregation in Cincinnati in the same year there was an appeal for funds to be sent to the Union for agricultural colonies—to buy cattle for Vineland, N.J., for some settlers in Louisiana, and for farming colonies in Colorado and in Kansas.[10] The name of this effort was the "Hebrew Union Agricultural Society," under the aegis of the Union.[11] An appeal was made in the following year for five thousand dollars for the "Beersheba Colony," which the Union had established.[12] The colonies that had been set up were said to be "far away on the prairies of the West."[13] There was another colony at Painted Woods, Dakota [whether North or South we cannot tell], which was as yet in a purely experimental state. No news was reported from a dairy-farm set up near Washington, D.C. Vineland, N.J. was still afloat, and a settlement at Cotopaxi, Colo. had been abandoned.[14] The *Israelite* was following these ventures almost from week to week. It had an occasional comment upon the fine progress being made, especially in the Union colony in Kansas. These experiments—the journal said—evidenced the saving power of democracy. Ten years more would see all the settlers thoroughly Americanized.[15]

In the end—with the exception of a very small group of settlements, which were not under the tutelage of the Union—all of it came to naught. As little as in the case of the much more ambitious colonization of Jews in the Argentine by the Baron de Hirsch Fund was it possible to get large masses of Jews on the land, or even to keep upon it the comparatively small groups who were placed there. The echoes began to die away in the last decade of the century, and it was not long before nothing more was heard of them.

B. ON THE RETURN TO PALESTINE

We have planned this chapter so that we shall conclude with a complete record of Wise's reactions to Zionism, and the reasons for them. But he was not consistent in the years that went before: that is, in regard to the return of Jews to Palestine, the beginnings of the Hebrew renaissance there, and many other things. It is interesting and necessary to enter into this, for it will show that, *mutatis mutandis*, Wise too loved the Holy Land, was happy to see Jews go there, and only became indignant and vehement, when other impulses and other convictions seemed to him contravened. Our method will be: first, to cover the material utilized in an essay, "The Attitude of Isaac Mayer Wise toward Zionism and Palestine," by Melvin Weinman, and then to follow the *Israelite* chronologically in its various references to this entire subject. We shall conclude by summing up the total significance of this material.

Wise was quite able to write of the land of Israel with some of the pathos and ecstasy that were habitual in Jewish tradition:

> Democratic Palestine, after a heroic struggle of two hundred years, was vanquished by Rome. Jerusalem was laid in ruins, its temple and palaces were destroyed, and the Jew was buried

> under the ruins of his country. The land once flowing with milk and honey became a waste. The sycamore groves which once re-echoed with the melodies of the harp of Judah, resounded with the cry of the woe-stricken Jew as he went forth from his land. The flower of his youth had perished there. There were the graves of his sires, prophets, heroes, and singers. There were the monuments of his glory, the reminiscences of fifteen hundred years of wonderful history; every spot told a tale of sublime deeds. He left there his independence, his freedom, his rights, his happiness. He went forth an exile to the land of strangers.[16]

In the beginning Wise was a strong supporter of colonization in Palestine. He regarded this as feasible and desirable for small groups, but not for the masses fleeing from Russia and Rumania. The associations of the Holy Land had—for him—become entirely religious and non-political.[17] Wise did not think that any considerable proportion of the refugees would wish to go there. Evidently they regarded America as much more to their liking.[18]

In the beginning, also, before the Basel Congress, Wise thought that, while political Zionism was utterly visionary, colonization in Palestine might be very good, if it could succeed in turning peddlers into farmers. Later he changed his mind about this too. The plans of Laurence Oliphant, a non-Jew, to purchase Gilead and Moab from the Turks, and to improve them and settle them with Jews, elicited from Wise the comment that Oliphant would have great difficulty in finding settlers. He insisted on the political and practical difficulties pioneers in the Holy Land would have to encounter.[19]

In 1891 restrictions that had been initiated by the Turks were increased and intensified. Wise claimed that this was one of the results of Jewish nationalist schemes, which had succeeded—according to him—in alienating Turkish good will.[20]

His record of dislike and disapproval of Zionism was neither as consistent, nor as severe as later appeared to be the case. In 1871 Wise wrote that the two thousand-year-old claim of Jews upon Palestine should be recognized by the Great Powers. But later, in 1886, he found a way to reverse this, by saying that in modern times conquest alone gave title, and that therefore Jews had lost the right to Palestine eighteen hundred years before.[21]

Sometimes he would regale the readers of the *Israelite* with eloquent descriptions of the conditions obtaining among Jews in Palestine, educational, economic, and religious. He pictured the poor state of the land and the hard life of its Jewish community, which then numbered between thirty and forty thousand souls. Sixteen years later he wrote that Jerusalem had a population of twenty thousand Jews and that they were suffering abject poverty.[22] And yet later he reprinted a letter from a traveler who contended that the land was not poor by decree of nature, but only because of an improvident and unjust government.[23]

In 1860, Wise suggested that Jews who were being exiled from Morocco, should be settled as colonists in Palestine, if it and they would be "placed under the protection of European consuls." He advocated that rich Jews should invest in Palestine, because "agriculture will soon be profitable there."[24] He wanted congregations to subscribe funds for these purposes.[25] These things he favored not only positively, but negatively as well, for such measures would relieve beggary in the Holy Land, and turn its Jews toward a healthy and normal life.[26] Baron de Hirsch, the great Jewish philantropist, was settling Jews chiefly in South America. Wise asked him to consider putting a million dollars into buying arable land in Palestine and settling perhaps a million Jews there.[27] One of his most striking utterances was in 1892, when he asserted that, if he were not so taxed with thronging affairs of his own, he would found a society for all Jews in the United States to assist in a broad project of colonization in Palestine. He went so far as to specify that no speculation in land must be permitted. This would "be prevented by making occupation and improvement the only valid titles to the land given to a colonist."[28]

At times Wise appeared to understand that there was an immemorial religious and emotional drive toward Palestine.[29] It was also not impossible that part of his enthusiasm for colonizing Jews in Palestine derived from his dislike of wholesale Jewish immigration to America. This was stated with more than a little clearness in an article in the *Israelite* on April 15, 1887.

In Palestine, Jews—he thought—might become missionaries of civilization to the Arabs.[30] The success of some of the colonies that had begun in his time pleased him. He wrote that this demonstrated "that the Jew can succeed in anything he undertakes."[31] But, as time went on, he came to have a strong distaste for everything about Palestine. All of it had become linked with the idea of a Jewish state, and that banished it from his interest and his sympathy.[32]

During various years Wise kept track of advances in culture and education in the Holy Land. One comes upon paragraph after paragraph which he had clipped from the Jewish press: about plans to publish a *Midrash Rabbah* in Palestine; about Eliezer ben Yehudah

—and always with praise; about A. M. Luncz, a blind writer on the land.[33] He praised the technical school of the *Alliance Israelite Universelle* in Jerusalem, and reprinted the Turkish government's laudatory comments on a school in Jaffa. He supported appeals to raise money for these institutions.[34]

Even in less usual directions Wise was following all that happened in Palestine and commenting upon it—occasionally with humor. Thus, when it appeared that there would be a railroad from Jaffa to Jerusalem, he wrote: "This improvement does away with the ass for the coming Messiah; he can ride in a railroad-car clear into the city of Jerusalem."[35] Jerusalem was being "resurrected from its widowed and forgotten and dilapidated state," and getting modern conveniences and appurtenances.[36] Even in Wise's day there was some talk about a canal from Aqaba to the Mediterranean; he took note of this and its political importance, and wrote also of the visit of the German Kaiser to the Holy Land.[37]

Next we turn to some of his specific references to plans for Palestinian colonization in the columns of the *Israelite*. Like the foregoing these were quite numerous, and we shall select and reproduce only those that add something, that make his comments and reactions more vivid, or that aid in completing the rather confused picture of his feeling toward the land.

At the time when Moroccan Jews were being exiled, in 1860, fairly long before the ideas and plans of Zionism had begun to be known generally in the United States, Wise wrote thus of this proposal:

> If we are allowed to make a proposition in this matter, we would say, improve this opportunity, buy a tract of land in Palestine in the plains of Jericho or Esdraelon, or somewhere near the sea coast, and send those exiles there. . . . Let this colony flourish and it will soon form a nucleus for the oriental Jews. . . . Let them be armed and drilled to defend themselves against the petty bands of Beduines, and be placed under the protection of European consuls. Thus a firm foothold might be gained in Palestine. . . .[38]

At that time he did not seem appalled by the idea of Jewish settlement in Palestine, by the exigencies of self-defense, or by the prospect that many more might come to settle by their side.

Nor did he then hold the opinion that there was anything offensive or impractical about colonization:

> The matter (The Society to Colonize Palestine) certainly deserves consideration, not only because thousands of dollars

> are annually sent to the poor of Palestine, without any permanent improvement of their condition. If anything is to be done, it must be something permanent.
>
> No intelligent mind can feel indifferent toward the land of liberty's birthplace, the cradle of civilization, the everlasting foundation of the temple of justice, the cornerstone of the superstructure of humanity—the land to which now the innumerable pilgrims of the three civilizing religions look with pious awe. . . . All that could and should be done is to bring an industrious population into the country to develop its rich resources. . . . There is certainly nothing visionary in this prospect, nothing impracticable or the least unlikely. . . .[39]

He knew of the constant and annoying importunities of beggars and *Meshulochim* (messengers sent to raise funds) from Palestine:

> If they wish to colonize Palestine, and working men go there to build up homes for themselves and their families, we can say, yes, let us support them; let us give them all the aid we can give. It is the land of our fathers; God has given it them; let us reoccupy as much of it as we can get peaceably and justly.[40]

But in 1880 he wrote that colonization in the Holy Land was not nearly as feasible as in America:

> The land of our fathers of two thousand years ago appears to us no better than that of our own and of our children. The political restoration of Israel can not be accomplished in Palestine, it is too small a country for any grand political purpose. We do not expect or wish that restoration, we wait for the universal republic—the Kingdom of Heaven on earth, predicted by the prophets, to embrace this entire habitable globe and all its population.[41]

It might, however, be advisable—he wrote a year later—to divert some Russian-Jewish migration to Palestine, where they could be "implanted in new homes," and "sit every man under his vine and every man under his fig tree, with none to terrify him" [his translation; Micah, chapter 4, verse 4].[42]

In 1882 he noted that colonies were, in fact, being established:

> The idea of the Jews returning to Palestine is no part of our creed.[43]

What had aroused his ire was the claim that Jews are a nationality, and the plan to make of Palestine "an exclusively Jewish country." He ridiculed such notions even when they had come from Emma Lazarus, or from George Eliot.[44] Yet he was still in favor of settling

Russian and Rumanian Jews there, warning still that the soil was said to be barren, except perhaps "in Galilee, where especially the olive and silk culture is said to be very profitable."[45]

In 1887 he printed a few vivid sentences on the visit of Baron Edmond de Rothschild to *Zichron Ya'akov*, and on the pledge of friendship that had been given him by the Moslems, especially the Bedouin.[46] He predicted that the Baron's aid for immigration into Palestine would be able to settle no more than 100,000, after which the land "will be pretty well filled up. . . ." [47]

One of his most interesting utterances was in the summer of 1891. It was so thoroughly at variance with much that he had said both before and after, that it deserves reproduction here:

> The persecution of the Jews in Rumania and then in Russia, together with the unreasoning anti-Semitism of Germany and Austria, roused in the breasts of numerous orthodox Jews the dormant hope of returning to Palestine.
>
> The more enlightened class began to feel again their dormant attachment to their own nationality. The national and race swindle set in motion by Napoleon III for purely political purposes, infected also the enlightened class of Jews, and they turned their attention to the Hebrew language and to Palestine. There exist now numerous Palestine societies in New York, Philadelphia, London, Paris, Vienna, all over Austria, Poland and elsewhere, whose great object is to settle Palestine with Jews to restore the Hebrew nationality and language.
>
> They have already done a considerable amount of work in this direction, especially with the help of Baron Rothschild who —perhaps with other capitalists—spent large sums of money in the colonization of Palestine. The project is more romantic than practical, but it is not altogether impracticable. It brought quite a little number of Jews to Palestine, and made successful agriculturists of them. Wealthy men purchased land and city property in Palestine and built up Joppa and Jerusalem along with the progressing culture of the soil and the growth of commerce.
>
> It has done an amount of good to that country, to the fugitives and emigrants that have gone there and opened a highway of emigration to the thousands who need a haven of rest. . . . It seems evident that emigration to Palestine will continue and even increase. . . .[48]

The whole spirit of these paragraphs is of an entirely different order than most of Wise's comments, even in its references to "nationality and race." But this mood did not last long with him. Usually, in various connections, he was writing things of this character: "that all that national enthusiasm among those Jews is merely romantic without any practical idea at bottom."[49] Yet he appeared to understand and to sympathize with some of the valiant efforts of the *Chovave Zion* ("Friends of Zion"):

> We go with the *Chovave Zion* any time and anywhere to settle as many as possible of our brethren in agricultural colonies just as much as we glory in Baron Hirsch's Argentine plans and works.[50]

He had some apparent comprehension of the fact that the growth of anti-Semitism in Europe was in part responsible for the rise and spread of Zionism, but he predicted with more confidence than vision:

> The present anti-Semitic craze will be overcome, which will take but a few years—and no European Jew will want to emigrate to Syria or Palestine, as none did before the outbreak of this social pestilence. It is all a momentary furore.[51]

And in 1895 he referred to all that was being done as "fantastic speculation."[52]

He was not of the opinion that Biblical prophecies implied a return to Palestine:—"it is any home 'which thy fathers inherited.' The penitent fugitives will return to their homes, is the sense of that prophecy."[53]

What is the total impression that all these passing comments make? First, Wise—as we have noted—liked the settlement of Jews upon the land, and believed it a corrective for many centuries of city-dwelling. Unless they were complicated by other issues and other beliefs of his, he followed with interest, and had a lively enthusiasm for, reports of Jewish agricultural settlement in Palestine. Secondly, he was not without sentimental attachment to the Holy Land. But he was careful to indicate that this applied only to the past, and had—in his opinion—nothing to do with the destiny of Jews in the present or in the future. Thirdly, he was not initially nearly as incensed at the use of such terms as "nationality," or "race," as we shall see he became later on. Fourthly, he wavered between two opinions: that successful agricultural colonization was possible in Palestine, and that it was out of the question, because of material and political conditions. Fifthly, he tended to regard it as desirable that some Rumanian and Russian "emigration" be diverted to Palestine.

If it is permissible to try to put into words the general *Tendenz* of these many expressions of opinion on events relating to Jews and Palestine, it would appear probable that Wise's opinions crystallized gradually, paralleling the slow accumulation of historic and popular movements and causes that came to their climax in international Zionism. It was only by degrees that Wise came to believe that Zionism was a menace to his own Messianism, his interpretation of the character and destiny of Judaism, that Zionism was more than the fantastic and visionary scheme of a few dreamers, and that his own opinion became sharpened and made definite. This was also—it must be recalled—in the last years of his life, when it was not probable that he could alter fundamentally the convictions he had carried down a long career.

9

V. On Colonization and Zionism (*Concluded*)

C. ON UNIVERSALISM AND PARTICULARISM

The key to a comprehension of Wise's ideas on Zionism is to be found in his approach to the problem of universalism and particularism. As well as any other, he knew that Jews had a national past, and that they had regarded themselves, as the world regards them, as a "people." But, consistently for him, Jews were and are a "religious people," a "religious community." He brooked no compromise upon this. He had faced this dilemma in his early years in regard to some of the specific beliefs of orthodoxy: the return to Palestine, the concept of a personal Messiah, etc. For him Jews were *Jews by religion only*. Nothing should remain in the religion which was not of universal application, which could not readily and rapidly be accepted by all men. The "mission of Israel" involved being dispersed—by the will of God—to carry the truth to the nations, and to labor toward the time when "the knowledge of the Lord would cover the earth, as the waters cover the seas." (Isaiah, chapter 11, verse 9.)

For him Israel was a priest-people, a bearer of divine truth. Before we come to the crux of the problem, his numerous and specific pronouncements upon Zionism, it seems wise to set before the reader a number of characteristic and significant passages from his writings on Israel as nation, and Israel as faith.

As a motto for the whole we select this passage:

> Thus did Moses speak, and thus did he act. He built up the chosen people, the ideal nation, the eternal nation, which is and exists whether it have a land or it have none, a government, or none; the people which has seen the rise, decline and fall of ancient empires, has stood at the cradle of modern nations, has groped its way through the darkness of the Middle Ages; and at the dawn of liberty and justice among the nations, rose with energy to demonstrate its ability to cooperate in the solution of the new problems of resurrecting humanity.[1]

Or again, in more direct reference to the problem with which we are dealing:

> The public expression of Israel's unity rests in its worship. Outside the synagogue we are citizens of the lands of our nativity or adoption, and do not differ from our fellow-men.[2]

As early as 1852 he wrote to the same effect in the *Asmonean:*

> As citizens we must not be distinct from the rest, in religion only are we Jews, in all other respects we are American citizens.[3]

This was strongly phrased in the declaration adopted at Philadelphia in 1869, in which Wise took part:

> The Messianic aim of Israel is not the restoration of the old Jewish state under a descendant of David, involving a second separation from the nations of the earth, but the union of all children of God so as to realize the unity of all rational creatures and their call to moral sanctification.[4]

Wise wrote of this a number of times thereafter, and always in the same vein:

> Outside of the synagogue we are citizens of the land of our nativity or adoption and need not perceptibly differ from any fellow-man. In public-life, in business, in culture, in all worldly aspirations, we have lost our identity, and very few if any wish to restore it. In the synagogue, in the public demonstration of our religious life we must preserve our identity, we must bear Israel's badge of honour conferred on the congregation of Yeshurun by Moses and the prophets, by the hands of Providence manifested in three thousand years of history.[5]

One of his most extended and sharply underlined treatments of this problem appeared in 1879, and was occasioned by a proposal to purchase Palestine:

> If Palestine should be purchased, who is to go there? The American Jew is an American to all intents and purposes. So is the English Jew an Englishman, the French Jew a Frenchman, and the same is the case in Germany, Hungary, Italy, and also in Russia, although they are oppressed, yet they are intensely Russian. It may be put down as a fact, American and European Jews would not immigrate to Palestine, not even if the Messiah himself, riding upon that identical ass upon which Abraham and Moses rode, would come to invite them. Those who pray for their returning to Palestine do not mean it. . . . If one believes that the Jews would go to Palestine, if that country were purchased by the Jewish capitalists and made into a quasi-Jewish country, he is gravely mistaken. The Jews' nationality is endemic; it is not conditioned by space, land, or water. . . . The Jews' nationality had been for centuries before this event (the destruction of Jerusalem in 70 C. E.) independent of every soil; it has been and now is in his blood, in the purity of his race, in his beliefs, in his mode of thinking and feeling, it is all intellectual and moral without any reference to soil, climate, or any other circumstances. The Jewish nationality and his attachment to it has been made portable; he carries it along with him wherever he goes, unites it with the country of his choice, and, if he is a good man, he is patriotic as a citizen no less than as a Jew. The one supports the other. He does not feel the least necessity of returning to Palestine, if the country in which he lives suits his tastes and interests.
>
> This is a point which many of our Gentile neighbors do not seem to understand. The Jew has no king and no country, they say; that is a punishment to him because he has done this or that, or because he does not believe this or that. Has the Jew, Isaac Moses, less a country than the Gentile, John Peter? Does France belong to Pierre more than to Moïse? What a horrible piece of nonsense! Are the Catholics or Methodists less scattered than the Jews? Is any race in the world in possession of any country? Now, we say, the Methodists have no king and no country. They are scattered all over this continent, England, and a large part of the Western continent. They will surely purchase Utah and Wyoming and live there. . . . Perhaps these Jewish capitalists who will buy Palestine will also obtain decrees and enactments of various governments to force Jews to immigrate? . . . But will not religous belief do it? And it is well known that religious belief works miracles. Do you not believe

> the Bible, and does not that book predict the return of the Jews to Palestine? As regards miracles, of course, we have nothing to say, except that in our humble opinion, from and after the year 1879 no miracles will be wrought. Sober people expect none, and the Jew is a very sober man. Whatever the belief of the Jews may be in regard to Palestine and the Messiah, it will hardly have any more influence on them practically than the second advent belief has on Christians, or fatalism has on the Turkish merchant who purchases goods in Vienna or Leipzig for his house in Constantinople.[6]

Three years later Wise repeated that Jews look for no political restoration, because:

> We wait for the Universal Republic, the Kingdom of Heaven on earth. . . . We rather believe it is God's will that the habitable world become one holy land and the human family one chosen people.[7]

One of the commonplaces of the period was the insistence that dispersion was not a punishment of Israel, but a blessing under the Providence of God. This was set forth in unequivocal terms in the Philadelphia Declaration, and many times subsequently in Wise's own words in the *Israelite*.[8] From the *Minhag America* Wise omitted all prayers for the restoration of a Jewish kingdom, even the *Lecho Dodi*, because it referred to a return to Palestine. He himself recommended leaving out of the *Haggadah* for the Passover Seder the words "Next year in Jerusalem!"[9]

For him, without exception and without equivocation, the future lay not in dividing mankind, certainly not in resurrecting nations long disappeared, but in unity against evil, in the creation of one great human family.[10] The prophets—in his opinion—did not foretell the re-establishment of a Jewish state:

> They stated in unmistakable language that the Jewish faith will eventually become the faith of the world and their writings meant nothing else.[11]

And yet Wise was not always so clear concerning the distinction between the concepts of nation and of religion. In the *Occident*, he had written:

> We must adhere to our nation, because God has chosen the whole as His people, and maintain our distinct nationality in a religious respect all over the globe, until all mankind will have received our sacred message.[12]

Though it might be contended that this was quite early in his American career, and that later he changed and developed, that his ideas became more consistent and more definite, yet here he seemed to think of Jews as a nation, true! a nation in dispersion, a nation with a religious mission, but a nation nonetheless.

He loved the Book of Jonah with an especial love, because of its universalism, and regarded it as "very poison" to the orthodox and to intolerance in general.[13]

There can be no question that, as the years progressed, Wise became sharper and more consistent in his espousal of a universalistic interpretation of Jewish entity and Jewish duty. Thus, in a sermon on *Chanuccah*, in 1880:

> The race-proud Jew is a fool, as all race-proud people are. The National Jew is a liar, because there exists no Jewish nation, and he is not a Jew simply because his mother was a Jewess. The Treitschke-Stoecker theory that the German Jew is not a German is a lie. The Jew's pride and distinction is exclusively in his religion and his firm faith in the laws and promises of the Almighty to Israel. . . .[14]

Even on the difficult question, whether a Jew who apostatizes remains a Jew in any real sense, Wise felt no difficulty. For him such a one ceased to be a Jew, and his few racial characteristics disappeared in a single generation. The Jews—he thought—exhibited no real stigmata of race, and ceased to be a nation at the time of Hadrian.[15]

What unites Jews all over the world "is the common fate and the common religion. . . ."[16]

Last of all, in this section, we set down a resolution proposed at the convention of the Central Conference of American Rabbis, in Cleveland, in 1890. It was signed by David Philipson, Max Landsberg, and I. S. Moses, and read as follows:

> Although it has been stated time and again that the Jews are no longer a nation, and they form a religious community only, yet has this thought not been thoroughly appreciated by the community at large; we still hear of the "Jewish nation" and the "Hebrew people," and therefore this Conference feels itself called upon to declare once more that there is no Jewish nation now, only a Jewish religious body, and in accordance with this fact neither the name Hebrew nor Israelite, but the universal appellation Jew is applicable.[17]

A lengthy discussion took place. The resolution lost by a vote of thirteen to twelve, for reasons that do not appear in the minutes as published. A motion was then made for reconsideration, but there is no record that the resolution was taken up again on the following morning. Nor is there any explanation of why this resolution was defeated.

The purpose of this section, on Universalism and Particularism, is clear. With very few exceptions or divagations Wise was a confirmed Universalist. For him Jews were a religion only, and this and this alone constituted the character and the *raison-d'être* of their existence. This principle he applied unswervingly to all credal matters and to all practical proposals in regard to Jewish life. Jewish destiny lay in faithfulness to the message of Israel, in dispersion, so that Jews might become teachers of truth and righteousness, and in faith in the coming of the time of universal brotherhood, justice and truth among men.

D. ON ZIONISM

In this final section of our chapter, "On Colonization and Zionism," we shall reverse our procedure utilized hitherto. First, we shall let Wise speak for himself, especially in the last years of his life, when, after the publication of Herzl's *Der Judenstaat*, political Zionism became a matter of primary interest and concern to almost all Jews. And secondly we shall turn to summations and descriptions of his point of view.

He had begun in 1876 on his approach to Zionism, and most of the substance of an article that appeared in the *Israelite* was repeated and re-phrased a host of times:

> . . . the Jews do not think of going back to Palestine among the Bedouins and sandy deserts, and the nations in power do not want them to go there. No European country today would give permission to the Jews to emigrate with their wealth or even without it; and the European Jews have as little an idea to go as the Rothschilds want to purchase Palestine, or to be kings of the Jews. It is all dream and phantasy. The world goes not backward, its march is onward, and this will expunge the old race prejudices as well as the religious superstitions of the races. We are marching toward Jerusalem, we march toward one God, one law, and one human family, and history lies not. The world must become one promised land and all men priests of the Lord of Hosts; this is the final cause of the logic of history. Let those who are narrow-minded enough tie the world's destiny to the soil of a certain strip of country; we

> do not. We expect, and will see it come, the unification of the human family, the triumph of truth, and the domination of goodness.[18]

Wise believed that he was not alone in this ridicule, in this scornful repudiation. Morais was with him. It was not a question of reform *versus* orthodoxy, but of religion *versus* what seemed to him a ridiculous nationalism.[19] This did not keep him from expressing admiration for the Hebrew renaissance in Russia. Persecutions had served only:

> To intensify their pride of race, religion and history, instead of discouraging and humiliating them. These fellows seem to have backbone.[20]

He had begun to take notice of "Thomas Hirzl [sic!] with his novel scheme of the 'Jewish state'" in 1896, and remarked that Herzl was in London.[21] Several weeks later he published a lengthy account of Herzl's appearance before a meeting of the Maccabaeans, and of the reported objections of Lucien Wolf. This was done by Wise without adverse comment.[22] But later he contended that Herzl had met with no genuine degree of success in attempting to "play the part of the modern Messiah."[23]

We come now to the critical period insofar as Wise's views on Zionism are concerned, the time of the convoking and actual meeting of the First World Zionist Congress in Basel in the summer of 1897. We shall treat the stages of Wise's reactions to all this in some detail.

In the beginning the Zionist Congress did not seem to Wise cause for alarm:

> The announcement that Dr. Herzl had called a Zionist Congress to meet in Munich [it was later changed to Basel], August 25 to 27, need alarm no one. There is no reason to fear that mischief may be done to our fellow-believers, or their status as loyal citizens of their respective countries in any way affected. The men at the head of that pseudo-congress, except perhaps Max Nordau, are harmless zealots, most of them standing with one foot in the sixteenth century.[24]

He followed this shortly by reprinting an article culled from the *New York Independent*,[25] calling this proposal to establish a Jewish state "utterly impracticable and foolish."

Then came the meeting of the Central Conference of American Rabbis in Montreal. It was held from July 6 to July 10, 1897. In his presidential address Dr. Wise spoke as follows:

> I consider it my duty also, Reverend Colleagues, to call your attention to the political projects now engaging a considerable portion of our co-religionists in Europe and also in our country. . . . I refer, of course, to the so-called "Friends of Zion," *Chovaveh Zion*, who revive among certain classes of people the political, national sentiment of olden times, and turn the mission of Israel from the province of religion and humanity to the narrow political and national field, where Judaism loses its universal and sanctified ground and historical significance.

Wise went on to ascribe the rise of this movement to persecutions, which caused many to turn back to their national memories:

> At last politicians seized upon the situation, and one of them called Dr. Herzl, proposed to establish and constitute at once the Jewish State in Palestine, worked the scheme, and placed it so eloquently before the Jewish communities, that the utopian idea of a Jewish State took hold of many minds, and a congress of all "Friends of Zion" was convoked to the city of Munich, to meet there in August next. However, all this agitation on the other side of the ocean concerned us very little. We are perfectly satisfied with our political and social position. . . .

All this had been much discussed among Eastern Jews in the United States, and some delegates had been appointed to the Basel Congress. Some rabbis had been advocating:

> Those political schemes . . . and compromised in the eyes of the public the whole of American Judaism as the phantastic dupes of a thoughtless Utopia, which is to us a *fata morgana*, a momentary inebriation of morbid minds, and a prostitution of Israel's holy cause to a madman's dance of unsound politicians.
>
> The honor and position of the American Israel demand imperatively that this Conference, which does represent the sentiment of American Judaism, minus the idiosyncrasies of those late immigrants, do declare officially the American standpoint in this unpleasant episode of our history.[26]

A Committee on the President's Message was appointed, consisting of Max Landsberg, M. Mielziner, and M. Samfield. They brought in the following response to the president's suggestions:

> That we totally disapprove of any attempt for the establishment of a Jewish state. Such attempts show a misunderstanding of Israel's mission, which from the narrow political and national [in the original, "rational," by error] field, has

been expanded to the promotion among the whole human race of the broad and universalistic religion first proclaimed by the Jewish Prophets. Such attempts do not benefit, but infinitely harm our Jewish brethren, where they are still persecuted, by confirming the assertion of their enemies that the Jews are foreigners in the countries in which they are at home, and of which they are everywhere the most loyal and patriotic citizens. . . .[27]

Thereafter, Wise was convinced that Zionism was only a "bubble," which had already "burst and dissolved into nothingness." A clipping from the *Church Economist* predicted failure for the whole scheme, and the *New York Sun* called it "visionary."[28] Wise argued that Nordau would not long lend his name and prestige to this fatuous movement:

It is a temporary rush of the loyal blood to the head. He will in a year or two review this project with his wonted sarcasm and pessimism.[29]

Wise reminded his readers that Herzl had never been a religious Jew, and underlined the deep differences between orthodoxy and the new Zionism:

None can leap over two thousand years of history and commence anew, where all things were left then.[30]

In September, Wise published a long article in which again he predicted a speedy demise for Zionism, and also that Jews would pay little attention to it:

Go to the fantasts and the fanatics with your Basle-Herzl projects. We, dwelling in the heart of civilization, who have practical understanding, have no use for such hallucinations.[31]

An article of his on this timely topic was printed in *The New York Times*. Here he turned back to Jewish history—to assert that one could be a Jew in ancient times without being a resident of Judea, that long ago Jews had become good citizens of many lands:

If facts are eloquent witnesses and prove anything, they prove, in this case at least, that the Jews do not wish to and will not go back to Palestine; furthermore, that most of them, being citizens of this and other countries of advanced civilization approaching the ideals of Moses, want no Jewish state; would join none, if the establishment of such a State were possible. They will not separate themselves from the powerful organizations of the great nations of the world to set up a miniature

> statelet, a feeble dwarf of a government of their own in Palestine or in any other country.

The Basel Congress, he contended, was really Russian, with a few interlopers from Germany and Austria. All of them were impractical men:

> . . . Everything is possible in dreamland or in Utopia. That Congress in Basle was a novelty, a gathering of visionary and impractical dreamers who conceived and acted a romantic drama, and applauded it all by themselves.[32]

The full reports of the Congress began to arrive in America, and Wise wrote on the basis of this more complete record:

> . . . We know now why the secular press had but a few lines of report of the meeting. The reason was that it was absolutely of no importance. . . . The whole business was a farce, a crazy antic of irresponsible men. . . . We could laugh at the whole business, especially at the pitiable outcome of the much advertised meeting, did we not fear that the world at large would take it as indication of the existence of a desire for a separate national life among the entire body of Jews, a feeling which we know does not exist.[33]

The following week Wise continued. This installment was somewhat more moderate in tone and in content:

> We are not ready yet to render a verdict on the feasibility, practicability or desirability of this colonization project of the Zionists, although we are in full sympathy with them in seeking remedies for the impoverished, oppressed and downtrodden Jews of Russia, Roumania and other anti-Semitic countries, where the rights of man are denied or begrudged to the Jew. Anyhow we will try to do them justice.[34]

Wise was not always left unanswered. On October 28, 1897, he printed in the *Israelite* a letter from Bernard Felsenthal, rabbi in Chicago, claiming that he himself had always been a Zionist and that he was not alone. Felsenthal listed these men, who—he thought—were on his side—some of the names quite interesting and remarkable: Gustav Gottheil, Richard Gottheil, Pereira Mendes, Joseph Krauskopf, Charles Hoffman of Philadelphia, Harry Friedenwald of Baltimore, and Dr. Herz of Syracuse.[35]

The movement was certainly not confined to Europe, Western or Eastern. Societies sprang up in the communities of America. Upon this Wise commented:

> Most of them may be classed as socialists, idle dreamers, who fancy they have discovered a panacea for Jewish ills, as they have already done for the world at large. . . . At present they are harmless and will be as long as they confine themselves to talking and writing, but should they make any attempt to stimulate and assist emigration to Palestine with more than words, they will do infinite hurt, they will surely sacrifice the welfare, probably the lives, of those they send there.[36]

In the same spirit Wise wrote that it would be a "good riddance" if some of those who were talking would go to Palestine.[37] In the United States the movement—according to him—was the exclusive possession of Russian immigrants, "and will remain limited to that much wronged and much abused class of hapless people."[38]

The following year the second Zionist Congress took place. Of it Wise wrote:

> Two long cherished principles prevent us from taking any part in the Zionist movement as it presents itself now. The first is, we are American citizens, who will never violate our allegiance to our country and our attachment to its people. The second is, Judaism is to us a system of religion and ethics with a mission to mankind, entirely independent of nationality, politics, linguistical and ethnological, independent also of geographical location and social organization. . . . [39]

Again Wise came to the conviction that Zionism had died aborning:

> It may now be safely asserted that political "Zionism" has practically ceased to exist. . . . Quarreling among themselves, losing numbers, there is no hope for a *Judenstaat.* All that is left is the desire to help colonize Palestine, especially from Russia and Rumania. This kind of Zionism will recommend itself to every good man and all who can spare even a little should contribute to it. Should any measure of success attend the efforts of its adherents, good will after all have come out of Herzl's folly.[40]

But this more charitable and sympathetic judgment did not last long. Shortly thereafter Wise was placing on record that there had been a meeting in New York to select delegates to "another Zionistic convention at Basle," "to make us appear silly in the eyes of the world."[41] In advance of the Congress he wrote:

> The only class that will derive any advantage from the Congress will be the anti-Semites, whose strongest argument that Jews the world over are mere sojourners in countries, not a

> constituent part of their peoples, will receive unexpected support from the public acts and declarations of the Jews themselves.

To this he added the wry remark that we Jews have more than our share of fools.[42]

Once again he carried a long report of the second Congress. All the speeches—he wrote—were practically by Herzl and Nordau:

> . . . The Congress is most notable as a cry from the depths of the despair of a heart-broken people to whom the march of education and enlightenment has brought only a keener appreciation of the cruel wrongs that are being done them, without the least additional opportunities to lessen the resultant miseries.

Back of this "hopeless dream" is an appeal for justice.[43] At this Congress Nordau delivered a famous address on *Judennot* (Jewish need). But Wise did not share Nordau's pessimism, nor his sense of urgency in regard to Central Europe:

> We protest against the attempt to make us believe that we are outcasts and all our fellowmen are wicked devils, that we are expatriated and our neighbors are our despots, when in fact each of us lives in his own country and among his own people.[44]

He found it exceedingly difficult to understand how Gottheil and Stephen S. Wise could have sat silent during this tirade of Nordau's, without a word in defense of the position of Jews in America.[45] To this there was before long an answer by Gottheil, defending Nordau, and his own and Stephen S. Wise's conduct. *Contra* Isaac M. Wise, Gottheil asserted that the United States was not really free of the taint of anti-Semitism. Gottheil warned against insensate attacks on Zionism, which is "holy ground." Isaac M. Wise replied that Zionism is so far from sacred that it is a folly "on a par with the Sabbatai Zevi messiahship," that Gottheil was inflating into a mountain the molehill of prejudice at hotels:

> We have scant patience with any man who wants something better for Jews than the United States offers.[46]

At its meeting at Richmond, Va., the Union of American Hebrew Congregations had adopted also a strong resolution against "political Zionism" which asserted that no American Jew wanted to "go back."[47] Early in 1899 Wise published in the *Israelite* an article entitled "Concerning Ziomania," a word coined for the occasion:

> We consider the whole thing the wildest folly on the part of the rank and file and most of the leaders.[48]

With some sly satisfaction he remarked that no orthodox rabbis would go along with Zionism, and added a comment that he would not be opposed to colonization in Palestine, if the restrictions placed upon it by Turkey could be removed.[49]

Wise was very certain that anti-Semitism would not long be a serious menace to Jews. He was bold enough to predict that a relaxation of persecution in Russia would bring to a sudden end the whole wild dream of Zionism:

> The Czar of Russia could make a sudden end of the whole of Zionism by the revocation of all exceptional laws under which the Jews of that country suffer. One day after the emancipation of the Jews in Russia, Zionism would be dead. . . .[50]

In 1899 he penned some words on the Third Congress, chiefly to the effect that there were few non-Russians in attendance. He reported that the Congress had repeated its stand that "Jews are a nationality, and not a religious community," that it had denounced Reformers and rich men. The remainder will be found in "the Jargon papers," his flattering term for the Yiddish press.[51]

In contradiction to some of his earlier animadversions, he claimed that Zionism was practically pledged to the orthodox, and that—despite some declarations of the past—Zionism was not intended primarily to further colonization. He asserted that the spirit and content of the meeting had proved "the marked decadence of the cause," and that "from this meeting the future historian will date the beginning of the end."[52]

Many times Wise took the position that Zionism was the result solely of persecution, and that emancipation would demonstrate its folly.[53]

In his writing at this time there was the definite beginning of the charge that Zionism would cause an accusation of "dual loyalty" to be brought against Jews, especially in Western lands. Zionism was tending to make Jews aliens in the lands of their birth or adoption. Thus it would help anti-Semites.[54] Zionism was also—according to him—chiefly responsible for the restrictions Turkey had placed upon Jewish settlement in the Holy Land.[55]

Wise had written three fairly extensive and systematic articles setting forth his stand on Zionism. Two of these—before the Central Conference and in the *New York Times*—we have already treated. The third was in the *Hebrew Union College Journal* in December, 1899. We shall reproduce only the essential and significant sections:

> I understand under Zionism an extended *Bnai Brith* association for the benefit chiefly of Russian, Polish and Rumanian co-religionists or rather the large class of the poor among them. To contribute to this new *Bnai Brith* association and to cooperate with the body is an act of charity, like the dispensation of alms in any form.

But this the leaders of Zionism were making very difficult. The movement was "irreligious and anti-religious." It was unquestionably the result of anti-Semitism:

> Under the discussion of the parties, whether to direct the emigration to Palestine, or to Argentina, which was very lively in the newspapers, the question of nationality was evolved. It was dragged from the world's trouble into the troubled house of Israel, widening the breach in our own camp.
>
> And now, when the Jews of the West began to work and to speak the language of culture, and glorified Judaism, its history and literature before all the world, now came those Zionists to whip us again into the dark corner of isolation, Judaism and its grand literature with us and all our people behind us, wanting us to speak and to write Hebrew again, which nobody in all Christendom besides a few theologians and select students understand.
>
> . . . and now come these Zionists and proclaim us as members of a foreign nation, one that has not existed in fact nearly nineteen centuries, gives us all the lie, and brands us fossils and mummies, fit subjects for the museum.
>
> Still, as long as these gentlemen kept their business among themselves, the men in Israel could well afford to be charitable and let every man ride his hobby or his bicycle at his pleasure. But when four to five years ago Dr. Hertzl [sic!], Dr. Nordau and Co., came out with the grand scheme of establishing an independent Jewish State, called congresses in Basel, made a heathen noise the world over, added shame to blasphemy, folly to falsehood, the disgrace of a mountain travailing and bringing forth a mouse, and what a mouse! one that steals the honor and veracity and carries it into the fortresses of our antagonists —then Turkey spoke, and many of our best men and public bodies protested against the foolish project of fooling masses of Russian Jews and American newspaper writers, preachers, missionaries and anti-Semites.
>
> . . . they evidently—whatever other object they had in view—had this in view, to expose the Jewish communities as foolish and sentimental phantasts; and in this they succeeded well to a large extent. This chapter in the history of Zionism

> broke off the bridge between them and thinking Israelites. We can never identify ourselves with Zionism.[56]

One of Wise's habitual efforts during this time was to attempt to discredit Zionist leaders by hurling the spear of ridicule. Herzl, he wrote, was trying to be the Messiah. Except for Nordau most of the leaders were harmless zealots, with "one foot in the sixteenth century." He called them "harebrained," etc.[57] The local leaders in America were utterly insignificant men, idle dreamers, and—for the most part—"socialists."[58]

Many times Wise pointed out that Zionism was bitterly divided from within, in regard to orthodoxy, colonization, etc.[59] He claimed that the few leading Zionists in America were really in disagreement with Herzl's brand of Zionism.[60]

In a strange work—which we commented upon briefly in the Preface—the author (Dena Wilansky) gave these as the reasons for Wise's somewhat intemperate, if thoroughly sincere, attitude toward Zionism:

> Palestine as a Jewish state conflicted with his entire conception of the Mission of Israel: that we were to live among all nations until they had become monotheistic. He believed the Jewish commonwealth in Palestine to have been only a training-school for the development of the universalistic idea of the Fatherhood of God and the Brotherhood of man, and that, with the development of this idea, there was no further need for the national life of the Jews in Palestine.[61]

Given Wise's lifelong interpretation of Judaism and of the nature of the Jewish people, his intense distaste for Zionism and his fears concerning it were reasonable and cogent. At the outset of this work we assured the reader that we would not enter into a discussion of Wise's opinions, except in so far as we might aid in clarifying them, or occasionally in underlining some of their internal difficulties. We have striven to adhere to this policy, and we shall not transgress that practice now. It has been our effort to let him speak for himself, to listen to what he had to say in the crucial last years of the nineteenth century, when political Zionism was born. These were also the last few years of Isaac M. Wise's life.

He was unbending in his belief that Jews had long since ceased being a nation; that it was their destiny to missionarize for the belief in One God and in brotherhood and justice among men; that insistence upon this central task had become uniquely important in his own day, because the banner of "liberty, equality, and fraternity" had prepared the world for a swift and decisive *rapprochement* with Judaism credally and ethically.

There would be no point—and no fairness—in discussing here how little Wise's estimate of the reality and probable future of Zionism was borne out in the event, whether his judgment as to the effect of Zionism upon anti-Semitism or upon the status of Jews proved to be correct, or whether his prophecies regarding the early demise of the movement were prompted by clear vision or by an intense wish. All these opinions he shared with many others of that decade. We have set all this in its place, to relate his convictions concerning Zionism to his thought as a whole. Of this thought his immediate, consistent and strong antipathy was an integral and necessary part. It flowed from his universalism, his rationalism, his strong Americanism—as he interpreted these—his Jewish missionarism, and many other central themes of his lifelong credo concerning the tradition and destiny of Israel. This was an organic part of the whole man, as it was part of the "age" out of which he came, in which his mind was immersed and in which he lived and labored.

10

VI. The Time and Its Problems

A. THE MODERN AGE

In the first section of this book we devoted a chapter to the "spirit of the age," a phrase which Wise employed times without number and which was deeply meaningful for him as a central principle of his life and thought. He was a child of that unique period in the history of man which had witnessed the climactic growth of ideas and emotions long dormant: the natural rights of man, the inevitability of progress, the supreme role of reason, the irresistible march of liberty. Though at the time of his young manhood some of the first fine frenzy of the ideas disseminated by the French Encyclopedists, by the English libertarian philosophers, like John Locke, the theorists of the American Revolution, like Thomas Payne and especially Thomas Jefferson, had been dissipated and had made way for the imperialism of Napoleon, the restoration of the *ancien régime* in France, and the reactionary swing of Metternich and the Hohenzollerns: yet this philosophy and social program smouldered, expressed themselves in the writings of brave men, and moved myriads with unquenchable hope.

Wise was—as we have said—a child of that time, which had reached deeply into his mind and heart even through the feudal air of Bohemia. Though the latter decades of his life compelled him to take into account many discouraging events: pogroms, the Dreyfus trial, reactionary regimes, etc., he never lost his pristine faith, his conviction that his was a millennial time, that temporary setbacks could not long stay the triumph of freedom, of brotherhood, of democracy. No channel of his political or of his religious beliefs but ran with this ichor.

All through our account of his life this was evidenced in paragraph after paragraph, in one characteristic and optimistic utterance after another. To all this we shall now add a brief section, taken from some of his works, for the purpose of bringing together into one framework some of his own personal beliefs about the "modern age."

As a motto for the whole we might take one of his own "Aphorisms," written in 1873:

> Without reason, nature is no Cosmos; it is a Chaos.[1]

On December 22, 1852 Wise delivered a paper before the Hebrew Young Men's Literary Association of New York City, entitled "The End of Popes, Nobles and Kings, or the Progress of Civilization."[2] From this we shall insert here only those sentences which have a bearing upon his concept of the time. He began by asserting that as his own opponents:

> . . . are but the antagonists of rational progress, so my friends are but the champions of this principle.

The informing thesis of this essay was the story of the desperate struggle for liberty over the ages of the past:

> The nineteenth century offers to humanity the fruits of victory, the victory of civilization.

This victory had been won over the enemies of liberty, the first of whom were the Popes, who had lost "the power to govern the nations or to repress the march of liberty."[3] The second category of enemies were the petty tyrants, the self-styled nobility, who had so long held the people in servitude. These too the nineteenth century had "swept away . . . but one shower more and they have ceased to exist."[4] Thirdly there were the kings:

> . . . so the dominion of monarchs equally odious to human nature and opposed to liberty will also find its grave in the rushing waves of time.[5]

The peroration of the whole is a panegyric upon the American and French Revolutions, and of the new forces that have arisen to secure mankind forever from oppression:

> Philosophy first uttered the great motto: No *authority* and she routed the enemy; Religion came then and exclaimed: *No authority*, and also she was victorious; the Goddess of Political Liberty came last and exclaimed: *No authority*, and also she must be victorious; Science, Philosophy, Art and general education march on to the golden aim, on to victory, on to everlasting glory; her high standards wave, and they bear the inscription: Progress! No authority! literature! general education! Liberty! victory! and humanity![6]
>
> ". . . and when the nineteenth century will close, the enemies of liberty will be totally routed; thrones, and crowns and scepters will be dashed in pieces; and upon its ruins the banner of liberty will be unfurled; the nations will be free! and free men will reach out a brother's hand without distinction of religion, country, language, or colour; one mankind, one liberty; one fraternity, this is the triumph of civilization; and this triumph is on hand. . . ."

Even after he had been in America for some years, Wise had not lost the *raptus* of this early impassioned faith. Thus—under the title of "The Signs of the Time"—he wrote in the *Israelite* in 1860, certainly a year that might have given pause even to so stout a believer in the inevitability of progress:

> A mighty change has come over Europe since the French revolution celebrated its first triumph. Despots have become constitutional rulers, the nobility and clergy have lost most of their dominion and prerogatives, the peasants have been redeemed of their ignominious serfdom in almost all parts of Europe; mechanics, merchants, artists and scholars have occupied a proper sphere; public opinion and the press are the great lever in public movements; commerce and money are the *nervus rerum* of the governments and cosmopolitan ideas are operative everywhere, working out an entire revolution in public government. . . .
>
> Here in this blessed land the revolution, the forerunner of the French revolution, gave us everything we could ask for; it gave for the first time to the world unlimited liberty of conscience, the most precious boon a man can possess.[7]

And to this ecstatic summary he appended instances to show that the rights of Jews were gaining ground everywhere.

To this latter point he returned again and again. Among those who were being restored to their immemorial rights—as part of this final victory of freedom—were the Jews. This he emphasized in an article on "Modern Jews" in 1863:

> After the American revolution had proclaimed the equality of all men before the law, and France imitated it, to the terror of all the privileged classes of Europe (it is within the memory of many a man living still), the morning of the Hebrew people dawned, the primitive night of many centuries' duration gave way to a rising sun, which has not reached its meridian yet; for the rights of Hebrew citizens are still withheld by many a government . . . where the struggle between absolutism and constitutional government is not closed yet.[8]

On Passover, 1866, he spoke like a prophet who sees the "end of days" just over the horizon:

> The night is spent, the day breaks. Every year now witnesses the progress of a century; for most of the obstacles are removed, the ball, having rolled on so long and having met with so much resistance, has acquired a furious velocity. The time of redemption rapidly approaches. The day is nigh. Soon, very soon, all mankind will celebrate one Passover before the Lord.[9]

As the years passed, Wise noted the signs of that decline of the power of the papacy to which he had already adverted in his early address:

> Rome as a political power must fall.

It must give up its secular authority and devote itself to religion alone:

> Providence develops its wise design before our very eyes.[10]

In 1879 he wrote that the hopes of mankind were "being realized":

> The progress of liberty is the genuine Messiah.[11]

There is no reason for Jews longer to observe the Ninth of Ab as a day of mourning:

> The world rises from a long and bewildered delusion of mental and moral slavery to broad and clear daylight; we can mourn no longer.[12]

All lands will merge into a future world-republic. This the prophets had foreseen in ancient times, and this would come to pass in Wise's own day.[13]

Toward the end of his life his habitual optimism began to weaken, especially after the wave of Russian pogroms and the recrudescence of virulent anti-Semitism in Germany. Wise wrote sadly:

> . . . we poor optimists are sadly disappointed and made false prophets.[14]

Things were "going backward": wars, bad habits in clothes and food, the agitation for prohibition, the general indifference in regard to food forbidden in the Mosaic Law.

In the text of the biographical section of this work we noted some of Wise's reactions to the reports of the Dreyfus case. Rather amazingly he was not nearly as depressed or alarmed by it as was Theodor Herzl. It did not appear to Wise to prove that all his early libertarian ideas had been built on sand, but only that "royalty" and "Catholicism" were assaulting France.[15]

But in 1898 he wrote on the retrogression of mankind and the spread of materialism. Even his own strong faith in an era of progress and in the speedy triumph of Judaism was encountering obstacles and discouragements.[16] This was especially true in an article in which he wrote on "The Sunset of the Nineteenth Century." In this he recorded the fact that there had been much material prosperity and much progress, in the conquest of disease, in the physical conditions of the human race, in invention, etc. He believed that liberty had been born and would not die. Whether all this had made any fundamental improvement in "human nature" was still questionable. But he did believe that there had been decided progress in ethics:

> The climax of ethics is now in the love of liberty and equality among the governed and the sense of justice in the governing classes.

Even anti-Semites were appealing to justice. The sympathy with Dreyfus was a splendid sign. The end of the century, he contended, would find us "upon a height never reached before":

> The nations are approaching the ethical ideal; individuals only are immoral.[17]

Wise continued then with a description of progress in science and in the things of the intellect. But he could not help remarking upon the hypertrophy of the sentiment of nationalism:

> Another damper on our sympathies produced in this century is the narrow nationalistic theories, which slice the human family into numerous small bits, each prejudiced against all the others, and all of them in a state of hostility to each other.

In rationalism there had been genuine progress in breadth, if not in depth.[18] In the century the nations had lost much of their religion and the idealism that derived from it. There was too much wealth, too much of so-called science. But the reaction, Wise claimed, was beginning to set in. In some cases it had been dogmas that had been attacked rather than the essence of religion.[19] His last word was that there had nonetheless been genuine ethical progress:

> Reasoning on the subject as we do (that righteousness, as Judaism sees it, is central), and must do, we see in the sunset of the nineteenth century, a glorious triumph of religiousness, and a long step toward the fulfillment of the prophecies—"Back to Mosaism!"[20]

His strong initial messianism had suffered reverses. He had had to live through times when progress was neither clear nor sure, when—in fact—mankind seemed to be retrogressing. But he ended his life still informed by the faith that all these were only temporary defeats, perhaps only a symptom of the *chevlay hamoshiach* ["the travail of the Messiah"], and that the time could not be distant when all men would lift their eyes to the final dawning of the sun of liberty and brotherhood.

B. CIVIL RIGHTS

Many times Wise battled on behalf of the separation of Church and State, and for the civil rights of Jews, here and abroad. He had taken a lesson in his early years from Gabriel Riesser, and filled his articles—as he himself admitted—"with fire and brimstone" in defense of liberty and equality.[21] When the *Cincinnati Gazette* had called a Jewish merchant a "Shylock," Wise retorted with the epithet "scrofulous mongers," and continued:

> . . . we will . . . square accounts with the *Gazette*. We only wait for an opportune time to chastise again that priest-ridden, codfish aristocracy, designated the Cincinnati Gazette Co., who are British in politics, Henry VIII in religion, and Peter Amiens in fanaticism. Our time will come again to pay "eye for eye and tooth for tooth."[22]

Prejudice against Jews was, to him, religious in origin:

> . . . for every child was taught in school that the Jews crucified "our Lord," and every parson repeated it as often as possible.

To this he added the strong statement:

> The world has sinned more against the Jews than a hundred Christs could atone for on the cross.[23]

He had, however, little sympathy for Jews who tried to force their way into summer hotels, where they would gain the privilege of associating with "gamblers, hollow heads, the scum of society":

> It is not indispensible to show one's marriageable daughters at Saratoga. . . . Keep away from places where you are not wanted![24]

For Jewish rights Wise demanded full recognition. He filed protests all the way up to the President against Swiss discrimination in 1857. He was one of those who went to Lincoln in 1863 to ask for the repudiation of Grant's Order No. 11. He called on President Hayes in regard to the rights of American Jews in Russia:

> If we had any political influence, there would be no American minister at St. Petersburg and no Russian minister in Washington.[25]

He was especially determined and unremitting in his resistance to those who wanted to get Christianity into the Constitution, into Thanksgiving Proclamations, the Bible into the public schools, or to institute Christian national holidays. More than a few Jews were alarmed by Wise's boldness. But he was no respecter of persons, and not infrequently called even some Jewish higher-ups "imbeciles." He contended that his articles in the *Israelite* had lent courage to many a Jew who had been denying his own Jewishness, and that the same articles had put the Christian clergy on the defensive. His declared policy was to attack demagogs whenever they sought office:

> They must realize that the Jew can defend himself.[26]

He was not as patient as some of our contemporaries were, when this was, or is, called a "Christian nation." Thus he wrote in 1856:

> The Governor addresses himself to a Christian people, but he ought to know that the people of Ohio are neither Christian nor Jewish; they are a free and independent people.[27]

When attempts were made to amend the Constitution of the United States so that it would give recognition to Christianity, Wise fought them courageously and without apology. The cases were too numerous to describe, but it is obvious that from the time Wise came to Cincinnati in 1854 until his death in 1900 he was invariably vigilant, combating Blue Laws, Christian festivals in the schools and discrimination against Jewish chaplains during the Civil War. Here is a typical instance, on revising the Constitution of Ohio:

> Ohio will have a Constitutional Convention. Her constitution will be reshaped, to be the basis of legislation for the next twenty years. Look out in time. Plenty of obsolete and obnoxious clauses will turn up and *post festum* complaints come too late. It is necessary that some prominent Israelites be sent into that convention so that complaints be not necessary on our part. We call the attention of our friends to this point, especially of Cincinnati, Cleveland, Columbus, Dayton, etc. to be on the lookout on this subject.
>
> We want free schools and free colleges without any sort of religion in them. We want equal rights for all. We want State institutions purged of sectarianism. Wanting this, as we do, we must have our own men there to do it.[28]

In the campaign of 1876 Wise had urged the defeat of one Colonel Barnes, a Republican candidate in Hamilton County, who had supported a petition to Christianize the Ohio Constitution.[29]

In 1855 the Board of Education of Cincinnati adopted a resolution by which at the opening exercises of the schools a portion of the Bible was to be read. Upon this Wise published a long attack.[30] Some thirteen years later on November 1, 1869, the resolution was reversed by the Board. This initiated a fierce controversy. Certain citizens engaged counsel to seek to enjoin the Board of Education against excluding the Bible from the schools, claiming that the action of the Board had contravened public policy and morality. On this once again Wise took a decided stand in the *Israelite* of October 8, 1869.[31] In part Wise wrote:

> We are opposed to Bible reading in the schools. We want secular schools and nothing else. Nor has any state a shadow of right to support any other. As Jews we do not want any one to teach our young ones the religion of our fathers. We do it all ourselves. . . . The public schools are institutions for the education of free, intelligent, and enlightened citizens. That is all. To this end we need good secular schools and nothing else. The state has no religion. Having no religion, it cannot impose any religious instruction on the citizen, adult or child. The Bible is a book of religion—all admit this. By what right is it imposed on the public schools?[32]

The entire case came up before the Superior Court of Cincinnati, under Judges Hagans, Storer and Taft. The court granted the injunction against the Board of Education. Taft dissented. The Board carried the case to the Supreme Court of the State of Ohio, which reversed the judgment and confirmed the right of the Board of

Education to dispense with Bible-reading.[33] Wise's strong attitude and his many articles must have played a not inconsiderable part in this momentous process.

He was continually writing about the attempts in various places to denominate this a Christian country, or the American people a Christian people. Thus in 1860 he penned these words, directed to the Governor of Connecticut:

> We are not a *Christian people*, Sir, and the governor of a commonwealth ought to know the constitution of the United States and of his own state better than to call us anything except "We the people of the United States. . . ."[34]

At one time Wise wrote that American dedication to religious liberty was interestingly exemplified by the corner on which the Plum Street Temple stood—and stands—in Cincinnati. On the northwest corner stood—and stands—the City Hall; on the southwest corner the Catholic Cathedral; on the northwest corner then a new Unitarian Church; and on the remaining, southeast, corner, the temple of Bnai Yeshurun congregation.[35]

In the matter of Colonel Barnes, quoted above, Wise was violently taken to task by the *Toledo Blade*. Wise defended himself staunchly:

> It is a mistake to believe or to make others believe that the Christian sects can dominate over this country. . . . We stand or fall with the liberal phalanx of this country, come what may, because such is our conviction, and we have the moral courage to be there with our conviction. . . .[36]

In 1886 Archbishop Elder of the Catholic Church issued a pastoral letter, forbidding Catholics to be part of the choir at Jewish or Protestant services. Wise spoke on this the following Friday evening, utilizing as his text, Malachi (chapter 2, verse 10), "Have we not all one Father?" He defied the Archbishop to find any Biblical warrant for his action, to point out one line in the Jewish prayerbook to which a good Christian could not subscribe. No genuine sin was involved. It could become a sin only because the "infallible" Church declared it so: "To respect all religions must be catholicity."[37]

Late in his life, looking backward, Wise had the right to claim that he had never shirked his duty on the issue of civil and religious rights, whatever the cost:

> None can accuse us that we spared our arms or projectiles, our energy and capacity, when or whenever the enemy attacked

> the Jew or Judaism. We retaliated fiercely, stood like an iron wall around our camp, carried the war into Egypt, whenever Judaism was assailed, smote the Philistines hip and thigh, whenever the Jew was unjustly attacked.[38]

He must have attained a well-deserved reputation, for some years before—in March, 1873, to be exact—the *Catholic Guardian* had written of him:

> . . . one of the wildest vilifiers of our holy religion in America is a Jew—the Rabbi Wise of Cincinnati.[39]

This was and is one of the chief fronts of liberty, and Wise never shirked the issue, or took refuge from the particular by flight into generalities.

11

VII. *On Christianity*

A. ON CHRISTIANITY IN GENERAL

From the earliest period of his American career Isaac M. Wise gave evidence of a very great interest in the origin, history and character of Christianity, in its various epochs of relationship with Judaism, in the "agreements and disagreements" between the two, the person and meaning of the figure of Jesus, the place of Paul of Tarsus, the careers and messages of the Apostles, the evidence to be found in rabbinic Judaism in regard to these momentous times and problems, and other diverse aspects of the whole historic panorama. Quite early he appeared to comprehend that one of the organic changes in the position of Judaism that had been involved in the coming of the "modern age," in the enfranchisement of Jews, in the disappearance of the Ghetto, in the acquisition by Jews of modern culture and of their linking themselves with the political, economic and cultural destiny of Western mankind, must be a reconsideration of the position of Judaism toward Christianity. As long as there had been a deep gulf—of time as well as of faith—Jews could—for the most part—busy themselves with the absorbing concerns of their own life and tradition. But now things had to be clarified. The essential nature of the two had to be grasped and contrasted. And this had to be done, not by *a priori* generalizations as to the two systems of theology and ethics, but by a careful consideration of their origins, their respective histories, and their varying relationships along the course of the centuries. There were definite times when Wise labored hard to equip himself for much of this study. Certainly the exigencies of his life, his unbelievable multiplicity of tasks, made it out of the question for him to put all else aside, to become a master of the New Testament and of its literature and criticism, to go much beyond the training he had had in rabbinics in his student-days in Austria, to delve deeply into classical Greek and Latin sources. There is nothing amazing in the fact that he was not a great scholar, that he did not command the wide familiarity, the precise knowledge of comparative details, that would have enabled him to bring to bear upon his own ideas the critical apparatus, the delicate weighing of probabilities and interpretations, of the specialist. What is astonishing is that in the course of an exceedingly busy life he found time to write so much on all these aspects of Christianity and its relation to Judaism, that some of his work was genuinely pioneering, and that he came upon so many interesting—and sometimes novel—ideas.

To a certain extent he was forced in this direction by several causes. He found Jews in the United States fairly helpless when confronted with the rampant revivalists and missionaries of that stage of American culture. We have witnessed his method of meeting this menace, the courage and the directness he displayed in defense. But he knew that this was not enough, that it was upon too low a level, in the postures both of aggression and of repelling the attack. If Jews were to see themselves clearly, if he was to make progress toward his goal of enlightening them about their history, of arousing pride in their own Jewish heritage—not only as it was, but as it still is in our time—he would have to move to a broader and deeper level, to place Christianity and Judaism side by side, subject them to a careful scrutiny, make clear the deep, basic coincidences of doctrine and precept, but also their striking divergences. Psychologically—in reading this material—another impression is forced upon one. He himself found this fascinating! More and more he moved toward the feeling that, especially in Jesus, and in primitive Christianity, there was much that was Jewish, that was near in spirit and even in context to rabbinic Judaism, to the gentle Hillel and other envisoned seers of that time. He discovered for himself cross-references in the sayings of Jesus, facts that bore on the descriptions of the trial of Jesus in the Gospels, on the attitude of the New Testament toward the Pharisees, and upon many other things. All this, he felt, was not merely of value in itself, but ought to be of inestimable help in relation to the attitude of each toward the other, in mutual understanding, in shedding light upon one of the most confused and perplexing, as well as one of the most momentous, epochs in the history of man. Some of this derived from his informing optimism, his perennial belief that a universal religion was in the offing, that it was not beyond possibility that all men would slough off their peripheral beliefs and come together upon the great essentials of theology and ethics. Perhaps he himself would be able to contribute toward this, in bridging the gap, in casting across the ancient gulf a strand of brotherhood, which might be used to draw after it a rope and a foot-bridge!

There may be other ways in which to explain the remarkable number of works he found it possible to write in this field, most of which have sunk into complete oblivion, and are neither read nor even referred to any more. But, if so, they are not apparent. How shall we approach them? It is not possible to cover all Wise's writings about Jesus and Christianity in detail, or to indulge in any critical discussion of his ideas. All that we shall attempt to do is to set before the reader the substance of his ideas, select certain works and articles, which seem to us central for this purpose.

Let us begin with an enumeration of what Wise published, listed here not chronologically, but alphabetically:

"A Defense of Judaism *versus* Proselytizing Christianity," 1889 Cincinnati and Chicago, 129 pages.

"The Genealogy of Joseph, After Matthew," in the *Occident*, 1849-50, pages 375-6.

"Judaism and Christianity, Their Agreements and Disagreements," A Series of Friday evening lectures, at the Plum St. Temple, Cincinnati, Bloch and Co., 1883, 123 pages.

"Letters on Christianity," to the Rev. M. R. Miller, in the *Occident*, 1850-1, pages 232-7, 509-14, 594-9.

"The Martyrdom of Jesus of Nazareth," a historic-critical treatise of the last chapters of the Gospel. Cincinnati, Office of the *American Israelite*, 1874, 134 pages.

"The Origin of Christianity, and a Commentary to the Acts of the Apostles," Cincinnati, Bloch and Co., 1868, 135 pages.

"Paul and the Mystics," in the "Selected Writings of Isaac M. Wise," 1870, pages 352-75.

"Three Lectures on the Origins of Christianity," Cincinnati, Bloch and Co., 1873, 33 pages.

In addition to these major works there were a number of articles and lectures, published over the course of the years in the *American Israelite*. These we shall list, as we come to them, in due chronological order.

In a reminiscential series of articles toward the end of his life, Wise wrote that he had always treated Christianity "with respect," but that this had not kept him from meeting it "on philosophical grounds." He claimed also that, because of his tone and method, he had lost no friends. This had not, however, applied to his early brushes with missionaries, who had been abusing Judaism. With them he had decided to carry the battle into their own territory, but always in an "objective and factual" manner. He had early planned his series of works on Christianity, Jesus, and the relations of Christianity to Judaism. Part of his plan was the translation into English, and the publication in the *Israelite*, of the second part of the work of G. A. Wislicenus on the New Testament.

Before proceeding to a detailed consideration of some of his writings, we shall review a number of references to Christianity in the *Israelite*. These—again—we shall treat chronologically, without arranging them as to subject-matter.

In 1855 Wise took notice in the *Israelite* of the new dogma of the Immaculate Conception, adopted by Catholicism. He quoted some of the sentences from the proclamations on this subject by the church, and continued:

> Can any man read this without blushing? In the year 1855, A.D., when the nations boast of learning and enlightenment, the collective wisdom of Rome who best know the moral and mental condition of the civilized world, declare that any and every man not believing the immaculate conception of Miss Mary, the frivolous bride of Joseph of Nazareth, is a heretic; hence should be roasted alive, if Rome had the power to do so, and will at any rate go to hell after death. . . .[1]

In 1856 he published an article—obviously done with some care—on the "History of the Doctrine of the Trinity."[2]

In 1862, for some numbers of the ninth volume of the *Israelite*, he included a series—by himself—on "The Israelites' Arguments *versus* Christianity."[3] This was a forerunner of more extended works to come later.

In 1863—in the same source—he published an article entitled "The Sermon on the Mount and the Decalogue." In this he admitted the richness of sentiment of the "Sermon," "but we can not discover in it anything of importance to ethics."[4]

His essential optimism on the entire problem, to which we have referred above, was evidenced in a note in 1866; a paragraph in an editorial heralding the new year of the *Israelite:*

> We know the Christian sources, and, because we know them, we can not believe in them. We firmly believe that the day is not very distant when all Christians will understand the Christian story, as it originally was intended, as a legend, to convert the Heathens to the Monotheism and the ethics of Israel.

Certainly hopefulness could go no farther!

In the early months of 1867 he began the publication of "The Acts of the Apostles, Critically Reviewed," issued the following year under the title, "The Origin of Christianity, and a Commentary to the Acts of the Apostles," and listed in our bibliography above.[5]

He was not to be numbered among those rabbis who trembled before the Church, whether Protestant or Catholic. In the following year he printed some bold words as to the record of persecution of the Roman Church:

> Rome's political sins . . . in this century are grievous. They prove that, as a state, the Church has outlived her time, and would do no longer . . . We see the antagonism to all human interests, against which the world fights, cherished and eulogized in Rome, and held in readiness for the destruction of the world's civilization.[6]

He was not permitting a year to go by without some work in this field. In 1868 he announced the publication of "The Origin of Christianity," and wrote that in Bohemia—like all other rabbis—he had paid little attention to the New Testament. His experiences in Albany, his studies at the State Library, and his contacts with "men of other principles and other doctrines," had convinced him that he would have to acquire an acquaintance with Christian literature. He looked for a book of defense of Judaism and could discover none. He began—he wrote—with the orthodox Christian authors and continued with the liberals. Thereafter he turned to the New Testament itself, and—he claimed—devoted to it much close study, which he had been carrying forward since 1854. He asserted that he had established these points: that Jesus and his disciples were not fictions; that they were mentioned in the Talmud; that he had discovered the true identity of Paul of Tarsus; that the New Testament could not be understood fully without reference to rabbinic literature; that there were to be found in both the same kinds of miracles, also moral and theological speculation. He hoped that he had "fixed the Genesis of Christianity in history," and had contributed toward a "better understanding between Christianity and Judaism."[7]

In 1869 one comes upon this statement—which had probably been made frequently by others even then—that the Jews are the best Christians. Wise quoted at length from a lecture he had given on "The Religion of Jesus," on March 7, 1869, before the First Congregational Church of Cincinnati:

> I hope and pray that love and the law of love become the guiding star to all brother pilgrims upon the path of truth and virtue to eternal life and eternal happiness.[8]

It seemed to Wise, too, that the chief difference between the two faiths requiring elucidation was that of the doctrine of the Trinity. Thus, in commenting upon a sermon by Henry Ward Beecher on this doctrine, he wrote:

> It is the unfinished business of Christianity, which will turn up and annoy the house so long, until finally disposed of as a useless burden.

He continued with the statement that Beecher had put up a very poor argument in favor of the dogma, dwelling chiefly on the idea of the "Holy Ghost."[9]

In the same year during the summer Wise began a series of lectures under the title "Jesus Himself," an attempt to sift out all in the New Testament that seemed to him to have been written later, and to be untrue to classical Jewish tradition.[10]

Later we shall come to his argument that Paul was identical with Elisha ben Abuyah, known to Jewish tradition as *Acher* [the other one], who lived at the end of the first and the beginning of the second century. The rabbis came to hate Elisha, so that they could not bear to pronounce his real name, and most of his real life has disappeared from the sources. He was a scholar, a student of Greek, and perhaps an authority on matters of religious practice. There is some reference to his study of the works of the Sadducees. Like three other sages he was supposed to have "entered heaven," and to have seen things which ran counter to Jewish monotheism. He was also accused later of having lured pupils away from the study of the Torah, of having betrayed the Pharisees during the Hadrianic persecution, and of having become an apostate to Judaism. There was a tradition that Elisha had lost his belief in the reward of virtue. His desertion at so tragic a time made his name live in infamy in the rabbinic sources, and excited the great wrath of Akiba and others. He was the teacher of the famous Rabbi Meir, and perhaps was friendly with him even after his own supposed apostasy. There are also many legends that became associated with *Acher's* name and memory. Wise's belief that this was in reality Paul of Tarsus was repeated in the *Israelite* in the spring of 1870.[11]

Like a host of others Wise was disturbed and alarmed by the announcement by the Catholic Church of the dogma of papal "infallibility." He devoted some space to an attempt to expose the inconsistencies the doctrine involved, and the deep rift it would tend to create between Catholics and Protestants.[12]

Sometimes—he wrote—he was asked why he did not let Christianity alone, why he did not desist from his own attacks and from his constant treatment of it from his own—presumably Jewish—point of view. To this he replied that he would be quite willing to enter into an agreement: that, if Christians, especially Christian divines and scholars, would cease attacking Judaism, trying to convert Jews, he would stop talking about Christianity. Then, "we will make no use of our arms." But he closed with the Biblical words, "For Zion's sake I will not be silent" (Isaiah, chapter 62, verse 1).[13]

In "The Martyrdom of Jesus of Nazareth," a historic-critical treatise of the last chapters of the Gospel, published in 1874, Wise had written:

> The decline of the Church as a political power proves beyond doubt the decline of the Christian faith. The conflicts of Christianity and State all over the European continent, and the hostility between the intelligence and dogmatic Christianity (science and religion), demonstrate the death of Christology in the consciousness of modern culture. It is useless to shut our eyes to these facts. Like rabbinic Judaism, dogmatic Christianity was the product of ages without typography, telescopes, microscopes, telegraphs and the power of steam. These right arms of intelligence have fought the titanic battles, conquered and demolished the ancient castles, and remove now the debris, preparing the ground upon which there shall be reared the gorgeous temple of humanity, one universal republic, one universal religion of intelligence, and one great universal brotherhood. This is the new covenant, the gospel of humanity and reason.[14]

In an editorial paragraph in 1876 Wise asserted that simple facts teach that Christianity represents a retrogression in history. Prior to the American and French Revolutions:

> it was the fortress of absolutism, and now it is an echo of olden times, believed in by the illiterate masses, reshaped by reformers, and rejected by philosophers, philanthropists and patriots.[15]

On many occasions, in passing articles as well as in his published works, Wise was trying to define his attitude toward the gospels:

> When we say that the Gospels are legendary, we do not mean that they consist of allegories, fables, or any other form of pure fiction; we mean to say they were written to be used for public reading in the Christian churches of the second century, when the Emperor Hadrian had forbidden the use of the Jewish Scriptures for that purpose. Therefore, the Gospels were written in the homiletic style of the Jews, called *Derashah* [homiletical interpretation]; a story of incidents in the life or death of Jesus was so arranged or invented for the purpose, to fit a Bible verse according to the exegese of that time.[16]

To say the least, this is a novel theory of the origin of the gospels! Part of his idea also, the conclusion to which he came after some years, was that:

> The literature of the primitive Christians consisted of epistles and apocalypses only. The Gospels came after them.[17]

Though this is not far removed from some of the theories of modern scholars in regard to the books that circulated in the primitive Church, it is still much too precise and apodictic in its present form.

Naturally as part of his whole approach and purpose Wise devoted considerable attention to the anti-Pharisaic passages in the New Testament. These interested him, not only because of their obvious anti-Semitic bias, their consistent misrepresentation—so obvious to a Jew possessing even a smattering of knowledge—but also because they were part of the key to the actual age of the Gospels. In 1881 he began a series of articles on "A Review of the Anti-Pharisaic Speeches in the Gospels." These chapters—he said—had actually been written and published by him some twelve years earlier, but where we do not know.[18]

The following year Wise announced a series of lectures on "Judaism and Christianity, their Agreements and Disagreements." This was, of course, the basis of the book which he published the following year.[19]

Some years later he commented upon the many books on Christianity that were then appearing:

> . . . the whole trial, crucifixion, and resurrection stories in the Gospels are parts of a drama written in the second century, and there is very little if any history in it; hence the whole matter must be treated under the rules of dramatic canon. . . .[20]

On this entire topic his most careful treatment—especially by comparison with rabbinic sources about legal procedure—was in the book entitled *The Martyrdom of Jesus of Nazareth,* published fourteen years before this comment.

The same year he delivered an address, published the following year, on "A Defense of Judaism *versus* Proselytizing Christianity." In one of the sections of this he wrote on the docrine of salvation and damnation in Christianity:

> Rationalistic Judaism to this very day looks upon it as being the most narrow-minded dogma of all religious creeds known in history, and the source of unspeakable misery to millions besides the sufferers from the Crusades, Inquisition, and *autos-da-fé.*[21]

He went on with a treatment of the quotations of the New Testament from the Old, especially those from Isaiah, chapter 53, utilized as supposedly irrefutable evidence of Jesus as the Messiah and of the whole story of the Crucifixion. It was Wise's conviction that the evangelists took the story from Paul:

> There is nothing in the Torah, nothing in Isaiah, which could honestly be considered as support to justify the stories of the gospel upon which Christology is based.[22]

In the next article (No. XIII) he took up the supposed references to Christianity in the Psalms. He concluded by showing that the headings of the Psalms in Christian translation are "perversions":

> . . . all Christological quotations from them are utterly erroneous. There is no Christology in the Psalms.[23]

Only a week or two later he announced the appearance of the book which would contain these complete lectures and which would explain clearly why a Jew must refuse to embrace Christianity.[24]

A paragraph of more than passing interest, one that goes along with some of Wise's ideas to which we shall come later, was in the *Israelite* some years later:

> It would be interesting to ascertain whether Philo's *Logos* grew out of the Palestine *Metathron* [literally "sharer of the throne," an expression used especially in apocalyptic Jewish literature for the pre-existent Messiah], or *vice versa.* In time, it appears, both *Logos* and *Metathron* are of equal origin. It is sure that Paul's Son of God grew out of the Hebrews' *Metathron,* as they were almost synonymous and occupy the same offices in heaven, after both have lived on earth. It is also sure that the *Logos* of John

> the Evangelist grew out of Philo's *Logos* by personification of a metaphysical term. If the priority of either was established, it could be decided, who is the original biographer of Jesus, Paul with his Son of God, or John with his *Logos,* as now we have in Christendom two distinct Jesuses, one of Paul and another of John.[25]

This is interesting, and in our own time much light has been shed on the relation between Philo and the New Testament, as well as on Jewish antecedents of the whole concept of "intermediators" and "instruments."

On one matter Wise was quite unwavering. Anti-Semitism must be traced back to the fanaticism of the early Church:

> This is the cause of that raging vice, that epidemic pestilence called anti-Semitism. It is a new edition of the old original sin and universal depravity in Christendom.[26]

Even in his very last years Wise's interest in this whole field did not wane. In 1899 he was writing a series on "The Judaism of the Bible and the Christianity of the Church." In this he contended that the real difficulty was to be discovered not in the religion of Jesus, but in the dogmatic faith of Christianity. Against chronic Jewish optimism and meliorism Christianity sets a fundamental and pervasive pessimism.[27]

We close this section with three quotations, the precise origin of which we cannot find. In the first, Wise accused Christians of idolatry:

> Where in principle is the difference between those who knelt to a statue of Jupiter, or those who kneel before cross and crucifix? Where is the difference between those who worshiped Zoroaster's Ormuzd to protect them against Ahriman, and those who worship Jesus to protect them against Satan? The difference, it appears to us, is in words only.[28]

In the second, Wise referred to a theory which he developed at length in a book, called "The Origin of Christianity":

> The whole messianic plot originated in Alexandria by making allegories of Scriptural events and turning the political fabric of the ancient Hebrews into a mysterious scheme of salvation.[29]

He added that Judaism pictured man in the image of God, while Christianity had pictured God in the image of man.[30]

The third is a quotation from the work called "Paul and the Mystics" (1870):

> Paul conceived the idea of carrying into effect what all the prophets, and all the pious Israelites of all ages hoped and expected, the denationalization of the Hebrew ideal and its promulgation in the form of universal religion among the Gentiles, so that the whole human family might be united beneath the banner inscribed with the motto: "One God and one humanity." All Jews of all ages hoped and expected that the kingdom of heaven would encompass all nations and tongues; but Paul undertook to realize this hope; this is his title to greatness.[31]

For the remainder of this chapter we shall treat at greater length two works of Wise, one on "Judaism and Christianity, Their Agreements and Disagreements" (1883); and the second, his lectures on "The Origin of Christianity, and a Commentary to the Acts of the Apostles" (1868).

In both cases we shall not outline the books as a whole. This would lead us too far afield and would not be germane to the general purpose of this work and of this section of it, which is quite simply to set forth the gist of Wise's own thought. We shall, therefore, discuss or cite only those sections which add something to our knowledge of him.

We begin with the former of the two works, published in 1883.

In complete conformity with his lifelong approach Wise wrote that all through these lectures he would rest his case upon reason:

> Be not alarmed, if cherished beliefs examined under the light of free thought appear untenable, for there is no salvation in self-delusion, as there is none in the *Fata Morgana* for the traveler in the wilderness.[32]

There is no redemption save in truth. In the past Jews have not ventured to discuss the true relations of the two faiths, for they would have been done to death for attempting it. Many cruel historic instances exemplify this fact, and even among Jews there was not invariably free speech. The silence of Judaism was chronically misconstrued to mean that "Judaism had no apology for its doctrines, and no arguments against its opponents."[33] But now there is free thought in America; it is now possible boldly to enter into this discussion. It will prove to be a two-edged sword, cutting into both faiths.

The two great faiths agree on the following tenets: there is one God, who is to be worshiped:

> That much has been gained in the world's progress, that all civilized nations believe in the living God of Israel.[34]

This agreement is more apparent than real, for they differ in their definitions, Christianity adding to monotheism the doctrine of the trinity.

Both believe that the physical universe is God's creation, that spirit precedes matter, that God is immanent, that man's spirit comes from God, that the soul is immortal, and that there will be some kind of reward and punishment.

If Judaism and Christianity agree on so much, why do they disagree at all, and why does one persecute the other? Their disagreements have caused infinite misery, tears and bloodshed.

Wise continued with a section devoted to the Bible, the greatest of all books, by the consent of all nations and all faiths:

> Because one portion thereof is a direct revelation from on high, it is maintained, a momentary crevice in heaven's impenetrable dome, through which mortals beheld the glory of the Majesty on High; and another portion was written down by men, divinely inspired, for truth, righteousness, the salvation and happiness of man.[35]

The Bible is a broad and majestic river, other books are only small streams that bear no comparison. He continued with an attempt to explain his concept of revelation:

> Appealing to reason, there is no cause why the supernatural manifestations of inspiration, prophecy, and revelation should not be accepted as facts.[36]

But Judaism cannot agree to the claim of Christianity that all inspiration proceeds from the Holy Ghost. In Judaism inspiration is "natural and rational,"[37] limited to the inborn capacities of persons. Wise cited many Talmudic dicta to this effect. To Christians a prophet is a divinely commissioned man, who predicts the future, who works miracles. The Hebrew prophets wrought no miracles, and were not foretellers of the future.[38] In Judaism the prophet was a man and a patriot, a "man of God," a "sublime and patriotic statesman," a popular orator, a mouthpiece of truth and righteousness, who personified free press and free speech in Israel.[39] These men are the glory of the human family.[40] Great as they were, they were never regarded by Judaism as the "organ of revelation." There was only one:

> If the Sinaitic revelation is true, the whole must be true, and requires no other evidence.[41]

In this one revelation all the rest was contained: the laws of Moses, and the content of the prophetic message. Then Wise went on to a comparison of the Jewish and the Christian evidences of revelation, which in the latter case make it synonymous with authority. The miracles of the New Testament are not evidence. The Sinaitic revelation was in broad daylight, "with a force of internal evidence."[42] Either this is all invention, or all fact! The whole history of the Jewish people is "perhaps the most conclusive evidence. What right has any rational man to doubt it?" Upon this revelation both Christianity and Islam build. All three endorse the Sinaitic revelation. This is a great point of agreement.[43]

There is a half-digression about the laws of Moses, some of which are temporal and some eternal. Moses himself pointed out which laws were for the time and which were eternal and universal, not only for Jews, but for "all human beings who are of Israel in spirit and practice."[44]

The next section is a comparison of "Sinai and Calvary," from the ethical standpoint.[45] An ethical government was always the goal of the Hebrew state. Here Wise inserted a remark that all religions are beneficial to man, and that no sensible man will oppose religion in any form.[46] He conceded that Christianity is deeply related to Judaism. Jesus added nothing essential and abrogated nothing essential. His main object was the establishment of the Kingdom of Heaven, a Jewish goal. But Christianity has interpreted this as meaning a Kingdom not of this world, but in the next life. But this, Wise claimed, is clearly a misinterpretation. The Sermon on the Mount is fully parallel to Bible and Talmud in its ethical meliorism. Christian morals are Jewish.[47] In addition to the principles of Jewish ethics, however, Christianity took over some Roman elements, which tended to neutralize and sometimes to destroy the former. Christianity helped build up despotisms and sometimes indulged in the worship of many gods or of demi-gods. The Sabbath was abolished.[48] They have violated God's law against killing. Much misery and lawlessness resulted from the repudiation of the Sinaitic charter:

> All revolutions signify the rise of the human family toward the ethical standpoint of the Sinaic revelation. . . .[49] there is only one standard of ethics, and that is the Revelation on Mt. Sinai.

All ethics rests on the postulate of freedom. Man may obey or disobey. For the rabbis there was no Satan, only the "evil impulse" [*yetzer hora*]. Divine grace has meaning—but only for a man who helps himself. After the earliest days of primitive Christianity the faith adopted ethical doctrines, which infringed upon these basic principles, especially the doctrine of vicarious atonement, which reached its climax in the writing of Augustine; the doctrine of original sin, the possibility of redemption only through grace; predestination; eternal damnation, etc. Judaism affirms the freedom which Christianity denies. Upon the rejection of freedom no moral system can be built. Implicitly the modern civilized world accepts Jewish and not Christian doctrine in these respects. A criminal may not plead that Satan did it. The fundamental concepts of constitutional government are Jewish.[50]

Next Wise turned to the idea of Providence [with a digression on the untenability of atheism].[51] How reconcile the idea of Providence with that of the freedom of the will? Wise rested his case in reality only upon an outright assertion that there is no genuine conflict between God's omniscience and man's freedom,[52] but the case has not even the force of the discussion of this difficult theological and philosophical problem by Saadya, by Maimonides and others. He quoted Maimonides to the effect that we are at liberty to accept God's law or to rebel against it.

In men the deep instinct toward duty is the Holy Ghost or the *ruach hakodesh* ["the holy spirit"]. Man must conform to a standard of rectitude which ascends toward the height of holiness. He interrupts the argument to appeal to Christians not to believe that there is no corner in heaven for Jews, to see to it that intolerance stops at that threshold, not to make of God an arbitrary despot:

> If you do not do it for the sake of the Father, do it for the sake of the Son, that he appear not so much smaller than that rabbi who formulated the Jewish doctrine: "Pious Gentiles partake of the life and bliss eternal."[53]

At least let us live at peace with one another on earth.

All men have in them the inclination to do evil, and all sin to some extent. But God forgives sins, and no one else can. The Second Commandment implies that the good is imperishable, the evil only temporary.[54] Jews cannot believe in a devil or in hell, in fire or in brimstone. To invent this terrifying and terrible doctrine was a crime, perhaps to frighten people into the lap of the Church. The true means of atonement are repentance and reform, to repay evil with good.

The next section of the work is devoted to one of the beliefs which meant most to Wise, the belief in immortality, which he declared to be universal. He claimed that Moses accepted it; so did Josephus and the sects of his time, the Second Book of Maccabees, and various other biblical and post-biblical writings. But it is not wise to overemphasize the belief, for it would tend to make ethics self-centered, "otherworldly."[55] In the New Testament, Jesus cites a proof of immortality taken from the Torah (Matthew, chapter 22, verse 31).

Most of the doctrines reviewed are basic in both Judaism and Christianity, their disagreements are on subordinate points. Nothing could be more mistaken than to charge that Judaism is a "tribal religion":

> Confused and defective reasoners still fancy a Jewish nationality and government, the restoration of the throne of David under a Messiah king, of which there is no idea in the Sinaic revelation, or the laws of Moses. . . .[56]

Both Mohammedanism and Christianity err in confining salvation to "the faithful." It was only after the Council of Nice [sic] that the Church came to the full doctrine of the Trinity. The rabbis said that this was not as bad as paganism, and that beneath it lay agreements in principle.[57]

Wise returned then to the doctrines of heaven and hell, Satan, etc. In the Talmud too there are many passages which parallel Christian teaching about eschatology, the dualism of good and evil. But the rabbis came to reject all this. Our concepts of the future beyond the grave are all negative, all merely assertions that it is not this or that.[58] Reward and punishment are facts, but heaven and hell are fictions, and dangerous ones at that.

Wise returned also to the problem of salvation, whether by works or by grace. The means to salvation are to be sought within man, not without. There is no better summation of this in Judaism than Micah's famous definition of religion: "He hath told thee, O man, what is good, and what the Lord thy God requires of thee: only to do justice, to love mercy, and to walk humbly with thy God" (Micah, 6:8). The forms of religion are temporal, the spirit is eternal. Many superstitions arise as part of religion. Concrete forms tend to thrust out the spirit. It is not faith, but deeds, that are the prerequisite to salvation.[59]

Man's own conscience is the chief instrument of his moral growth, the struggle between opposites that is perpetually enacted within him. His ally is repentance, and the gift of grace. The real "hell-fire" is shame. But Judaism teaches the adequacy of repentance, which is accomplished not through sacrifice, but by the remaking of the heart. The idea of vicarious atonement crept into Christianity, when it was thought that the death of its Founder must have had a special purpose. This was superimposed upon the ethical doctrines of Judaism, and no basis for it can be found in the Bible:

> This makes of Christianity a tribal and sectional religion in conflict with man's reason.[60]

In the end this must go. Man will require no Messiah, no baptism, no circumcision, no mediator.[61]

Wise continued with a review of the Judaism of history:

> Permit me to remark here that the peculiar hypothesis of modern critics who set Moses after the Prophets is historically illegitimate and philosophically untenable; because there is no cause to assume that the writers of the sacred history did not know better than their critics of from two thousand to three thousand years later; no cause to assume that the authors of the holiest books of mankind were willful impostors; no cause to assume that the loftiest and purely spiritual aspect of any religion or code of laws preceded its concrete, practical and popular state.[62]

He traced the history of the Jews, through the Exile to the Talmudic period. He discussed then the errors of the Rabbis in believing that every law of Moses was intended to be eternally binding. The multiplication of laws distracted Jews from the essence of the religion. But this was gradually corrected.[63] Wise ended with some sentences devoted to the beginnings of enlightenment and Reform:

> American Judaism is, in forms and methods, far ahead of the Jewish congregations in any and every other country, Germany not excepted.[64]

But beneath all these changes and developments the original covenant lies unchanged and unchangeable.

Wise had not the right to speak for Christianity, but to him it seemed that originally Christians were a Jewish sect, and that they remained so for a long time. Paul came and altered the fundamentals, abrogated the political laws, so that he might propagate the new faith among the Gentiles. The Church, which followed later, dealt in doctrines, in dogmas, not in laws. It was dogmatic and speculative. Its heads were primarily theologians, rather than ethical leaders.[65] Of all this the mass understood nothing. The Canon Law was beneficent in repressing lawlessness. But the starting point of Christianity—in the ethics of Jesus—had been lost sight of. Speculation and the legislation of priests had replaced the Sinaitic revelation. Protestantism reformed the disciplines of the Church, but not its informing ideas. But the era of the Emancipation came upon all this with devastating impact:

> This is the last phase of the Christian Reformation, the next step leads into the Sinaic revelation and the covenant as the sole foundation of positive religion.[66]

It should not be necessary to pause here and to sum up. A rather discursive work! And one that was intended, while forthright and clear, to conciliate rather than to indulge in polemics. Its chief emphasis was on the common ground of Judaism and Christianity, and on the vision of their rapprochement. In general the argument rested upon Wise's theological position, to which we have devoted some space previously: that there is but one revelation, that at Sinai, and that all men must return to it in the end, Christians as well as Jews. The work is quite strong in its contrast between the Christian emphasis upon grace, salvation, vicarious atonement, damnation, etc., and upon Jewish insistence that the moral process is real and accomplishes itself within the human soul. This was unquestionably what Wise discerned as the chief point of departure in Christianity, more momentous than the doctrine of the Trinity, or the myths about Jesus that began to crystallize after his death. But the whole was informed with a friendly spirit, which must have made it possible even for orthodox Christians to read it without animus.

12

VII. On Christianity

(Concluded)

B. ON JESUS AND CHRISTIANITY

As we have remarked in the preceding chapter, Isaac M. Wise was greatly interested not only in the study of Christianity from his own point of view, but also in the figure of Jesus. Of this there is a great deal of evidence, only a small part of which it will be possible for us to adduce. We shall follow the same course as hitherto, review rapidly some passing references, records of addresses and articles in the *Israelite,* and then finally proceed to one or two longer works, selected from among the number Wise wrote in relation to Jesus.

In 1859 he announced in his journal the beginning of a series of articles on "The Resurrection and Ascension of Jesus, Critically Expounded."[1] These led to another series devoted to "The Birth of Jesus, Critically Expounded."[2] Nor did he stop with what he did in these early years. The same interest and the same effort accompanied him all along his career. In 1863 he began a series on "The Legal Trial of Jesus of Nazareth." These addresses were probably the basis of a book he published later in German, examining the details of the trial of Jesus, especially in the light of rabbinic sources.[3]

In these earlier years, at the back of much of Wise's treatment of Jesus, lay the conviction that Jesus was not a historical person, but that this figure and story had been the artifacts of a movement. Here is an instance of this:

> After Strauss, Renan, Wislecenus and others who have enlightened the world in regard to the New Testament, neither Mr. Ronge nor any other honest man will venture his honor on the proposition, that Jesus of Nazareth ever existed, or, if he had an actual existence, that this or that passage in the New Testament was actually spoken or written by Jesus; or that he had suffered or done anything told of him by his biographers.[4]

This was the stand taken later, and expounded in a considerable number of works, by William Benjamin Smith, Arthur Drews, and others. One would have thought that with this Wise would have abandoned the effort to distinguish between true and false, or to disentangle a "historical Jesus." But his opinion evolved as he proceeded, as we shall see.

Thus—fifteen years later—he was writing of Jesus in quite a different spirit:

> The grand dower of the Jewish civilization is hope; the dream of human perfection, the triumph of the Eternal Right. . . . Jesus was not thrust into Jewish history by some miraculous intervention; he was not an outside phenomenon, but a real child of his people. Its blood was in his veins, its hope, its vast desire. He did not oppose himself to the Jewish religion, but to the wealthy classes. He represented the common people. He was a patriot all over and that which had been gathered in the long history of his race—the splendid national dream—was the ideal of his life. He went forth as a Jewish man full of enthusiasm for his nation's glory, and realizing the grandeur of its ideas, its magnificent faith that could not be destroyed. He was a living flash of Judea's "mighty stream of tendency." That which he gave to the world bloomed from the very soil that he trod—the hills that he looked on and the flowers that he gathered in his infancy. It was that which he caught from his mother's eye and her voice as she told him of his ancestors and all that they had suffered. A thousand years poured into him these wondrous inspirations. The temple was his teacher and the altar and golden roof and the rolling incense; and from all these he caught the mighty hope that has ever haunted the weary and oppressed; that there is such a thing as eternal right; that thought became through the tragedy of his life the deathless inheritance of the world.[5]

The purport of this is not immediately clear. Especially in the beginning it sounds as though it were contending that Jesus was an ardent Jewish patriot, a nationalist of Judea. But this is not so. Its primary intent was to depict Jesus as caught up in the ethical vision of Jewish tradition, passionately and forever.

Later—under the title of "The Modernized Jesus"—Wise attempted an estimate of the greatness and the limitations of Jesus as a personality:

> Jesus was neither philosopher nor statesman, neither genius nor prominent talent, and in all excellencies of reason he stood far below other great men of history. Like all other sensitive characters of this kind, he was too gentle and mild to be firm, strong and decided, and too much engaged in opposition to the religious forms of his age and people to be considered profoundly religious. In our days any man so engaged would be called an infidel or heretic all over Christendom. He was decidedly too one-sided a man, too visionary, to have a just claim to intellectual greatness; always provided, however, there is anything in the Gospels on which we might rely in regard to the life of Jesus.[6]

Wise was attracted greatly by the messianic boldness of much of Jesus' preachment, its emphasis upon the Jewish vision of "the kingdom of heaven":

> If I add that this is the kingdom of heaven which Jesus of Nazareth preached, if I add that in the estimation of Jesus of Nazareth the Jews are the best Christians, you may not agree with me. If I should venture the assertion, of which, like the prophets of old, I am morally certain, that *this is the religion of coming generations* [in the following phrase the original has "its" not "my"], my boldness might shock you. . . .[7]

This rather startling passage is not as revolutionary as it reads at first glance. It intended to say—in our opinion—merely that the vision which Jesus took from the great literary prophets, especially from Isaiah, that the world moves toward an ethical goal, "the kingdom of heaven" on earth, was thoroughly Jewish and the veritable vision of the future.

Let us turn aside for a moment for a few of Wise's words on Paul of Tarsus. He too interested Wise greatly, since he too was a Jew, a "Pharisee of the Pharisees," and since, in Wise's view, he was the real founder of Christianity. This Wise expounded at length in his book, "Paul and the Mystics."

> Few and far apart are the brilliant stars on the horizon of history. Strike out a hundred names and their influence upon the fate of man, and you have no history. . . . He [Paul] conceived the idea of carrying into effect what all the prophets, all pious Israelites of all ages, hoped and expected, the denationalization of the Hebrew ideal and its promulgation in the form of universal religion among the Gentiles.[8]

This was what Wise himself had urged again and again. His only dispute with Paul was not as to the goal, but only as to the way, the concessions and compromises Paul made to attain it. Wise then went on to claim that the rabbis called Paul *Acher*, as we have noted above. At this point Wise introduced no material to substantiate this assertion, but simply contented himself with a number of Talmudic tales about *Acher*.[9] This was a terrible time, in which even great men took refuge from its ills in mysticism. This Paul too did: in his own doctrines of vicarious atonement, bodily resurrection, the abrogation of the Law, and the inauguration of a new covenant. Within ten years of labor and travel Paul laid the foundations of a complete new civilization. The veritable apostles of Jesus regarded him as an unscrupulous interloper, and were utterly unable and unwilling to go along with the revolutionary character of his proposals, e.g. especially the abrogation of the Mosaic Law. But to Paul laws were local, and the spirit free. Paul's concepts and plans were passionately bent upon the one end, to convert the Gentiles.[10] The Epistles were often polemics against Paul's colleagues in Jerusalem, with whom he severed connections. Wise claimed that Paul did not die in Rome:[11]

> . . . If the orthodox creed is Christian, then Jesus of Nazareth was a Jew. If the religion and the theocracy which Jesus preached are to become the universal religion, all dogmas must fall, and God alone will be all in all. . . . The patriotic and enthusiastic Jesus, and the brave, bold, wise Paul are grand types of humanity among those hundred that shine on the horizon of history, and illumine the records of the human family.[12]

Next we shall set before the reader a swift résumé of one of Wise's works, "Three Lectures on the Origins of Christianity."[13] Wise began with some introductory words about the study of religions and of the Talmud. He enumerated the various books of Talmudic literature, both in Babylon and in Jerusalem, a library of no less than one hundred volumes, which reveal a perfect picture of the age in which Christianity originated. He declared that he would also utilize Roman sources. Just as he had treated the Old Testament (presumably in his "History of the Israelitish Nation") on the ground of reason, "so I have considered the Gospels and the Talmud."

There followed a sketch of the life of Jesus, not the founder of Christianity, but a Pharisaic doctor and patriot. Wise asserted that there were many references to Jesus in the Talmud.[14] He described the program and the principles of the Pharisees, the Sadducees, and the Essenes. Jesus wished to be the savior of the nation.[15] He was proclaimed the Messiah, which at once threw him and his followers into conflict with Rome. This signified not merely a spiritual but a temporal ruler as well. The climax of Jesus' career, intended to lead swiftly to the achievement of his purpose, was his entry into Jerusalem. But this was far from having the effect hoped for, and actually sealed his doom. He was captured and crucified by the Romans, as thousands of others had been.

Wise considered the role of Judas Iscariot, but his summation was:

> So Jesus sacrificed himself to save his friends and his people from the calamity which was in store for them [All of this is treated more at length and more critically in "The Martyrdom of Jesus of Nazareth" and in a "History of the Hebrews' Second Commonwealth."][16]

Like most of the Biblical prophets Jesus was opposed to the Levitical laws and institutions. The Temple in Jerusalem cooperated with the Roman oppressors; it must be closed, and opened again only when a genuine theocracy would become possible. Then there would be no sacrificial system, but instead the coming of the Kingdom of Heaven, the dominion of God over the nation, leading to the most "exalted democracy." Jesus came not to abolish the Law—in the best Mosaic sense—but to fulfill it. He advised his followers to observe the Law. He himself kept the Sabbath.[17] He never entertained the notion of founding a new religion. He wanted a return to the innermost spirit of Judaism, each man to be his own priest, and God alone king. Jesus sided with the Pharisees in their ethical breadth and freedom. Like Hillel[18] he admonished the people to obey the decisions of the Sanhedrin, "the Pharisees who sit in the seat of Moses."

As to the doctrine of bodily resurrection, which was in dispute between the Sadducees and the Pharisees, Jesus sided with the latter and strove to prove the truth of the doctrine from Moses. Wise entered into a consideration of the difficult dictum, "Render unto

Caesar. . . . ," and explained it as resting upon "contempt of money and power."[19] Jesus was also at one with the Pharisees in their teaching of a special Providence.

But Jesus asked too much. The Jewish people, his people, could not lay down their arms. The likelihood, however, is that many Pharisees listened to him, for his teaching was thoroughly congenial to them. The later anti-Pharisaical fury of the New Testament was a product of the second century, when anti-Semitism was rampant in the early Church, and its leaders had no knowledge whatsoever of the real Pharisees.

It was not true that the Jews killed Jesus. The only genuine question is, why did the Christians later blame them? Wise regarded this development as having been due to the desire of the early Christians to curry favor with the Romans:

> Politics, ethics and religion being then an indivisible unit (and, in a true sense of the term, they always will be), he was a religious, moral and political character in one person.[20]
>
> . . . This much is sure: Jesus was an enthusiastic and thoroughly Jewish patriot, who fully understood the questions of his age and the problems of his people, and felt the invincible desire to solve them. Had he lived in Palestine at any other time, he would have lived long enough to stand now prominently among the sages of the Talmud, and undoubtedly would have gained a high reputation. But he was too young, when he lost his life. There was no originality in his words. His disciples estranged him to the Jew. His followers made of the cross the symbol of persecution. Therefore, the Jews did not think of reclaiming him, who was actually theirs—their blood and flesh, mind from their mind, and intellect from their intellect. He taught and practised their law, their morals, and their wisdom, and felt their woes and their afflictions. He longed to be their redeemer, and was crucified; he taught their doctrines, and was deified; he unfurled their banner, and became the great captain of a mighty host. His martyrdom became the cause of a new era in the world's history. . . .

The second "Lecture" dealt with the Apostles and the Essenes. The belief in miracles, so strong in the New Testament, was then very common, especially among the Essenes. Wise recapitulated what had been written of this remarkable group, by Philo, Josephus, and the Talmud: their contemplative life, their asceticism, etc. With them Jesus shared only opposition to Levitical laws [this is now an utterly untenable position, in the light of what has recently been revealed by the Dead Sea Scrolls].

As to the apostles after the crucifixion! At first they believed in the persistence of Jesus' ideas. Thus Peter said: "Jesus was put to death in the flesh, but quickened in the spirit." In the beginning they did not turn to the idea of the resurrection of the body.[21] Spinoza thought that then the disciples saw an apparition, and he was followed in this rationalization by Renan. The next step was the searching of Scriptures for prophecies. After the departure of Pilate conditions in Palestine were improved. The Sanhedrin was restored. The disciples came from Galilee to Jerusalem, and had adopted many of the customs of the Essenes (common property, baptism, no sacrifices, the table as an altar, frequent prayer, the reading and expounding of Scriptures). Not much attention was paid them. But they differed from the Essenes in that they—the disciples—did not work. They were poor, hence they were called "Ebionites" [from *Evyonim*, "the poor"]. They were called Nazarenes in rabbinic sources, and *Minim* [a much-debated word, meaning "heretics,"—literally "classes," or "kinds"]. It was Peter who built up the early church. The new impetus came from his doctrine of the "second coming," which Peter claimed Jesus had promised. Aside from their espousal of poverty, and their belief in the resurrection of Jesus, the Ebionites differed in no wise from other Jews. They were neither hated, nor persecuted, in any fashion.

But how were the disciples and the primitive church to live? Jews could not accept the doctrine of the crucified Rabbi or Messiah, nor the idea of the Second Coming. The early church found no credence in Jerusalem and met with success only among foreigners.[22] Therefore the Nazarenes left the city at the time of the beginning of its siege by Vespasian in the year 66, and declared themselves noncombatants. There were then some five hundred of them.

Wise contended that the apostles had no new ethical ideas, and soon were in trouble with the Roman authorities, as well as with the Jewish. They were frequently arrested and warned to give up faith-healing. But their cause was once pleaded by the great Jewish sage, Gamaliel. Stephen, "the first martyr," was—Wise wrote—not killed by Jews, but by Romans. The disciples began going on evangelical tours ["*evangel*" equals "good news."] They gained few converts. Up to the year 53 there was no congregation outside Jerusalem. Nor did this group think of going to the "Gentiles." It was Paul who first came to this plan after he had studied Greek with Gamaliel. The other apostles were narrowly circumscribed in their circle of ideas. They met with some successes in Galilee, including the conversion of Rabbi Eliezer ben Hyrcan.[23] But most important of all was the conversion of Paul—by his own words—in a blinding vision on the road to Damascus after the stoning of Stephen. Paul laid the foundations of an original gospel of his own. It was he who was the actual founder of Christianity.

The third lecture was on "Paul and the Mystics."[24] This we shall not summarize here.

In "The Martyrdom of Jesus of Nazareth" Wise's thesis was somewhat different, namely, that Jesus died, taking upon himself the charge of insurrection in order to save the apostles, for he had been proclaimed King, as the apostles had planned. Jesus gave himself up for the purpose of preventing a rebellion in Jerusalem, which was then ripe.[25]

This work, dedicated to Isaac Adolphe Crémieux, noble son of Israel in France, "the true philanthropist and apostle of justice, freedom, and equality," began with a declaration that Wise was not writing as a Jew:

> He [the author] wears no sectarian shackles, stands under no local bias, and obeys no mandate of any particular school. Whatever he says or has said on subjects contained in the New Testament, in order to be understood correctly, must be examined from the only standpoint of reason.[26]

Wise warned that his ideas would be original, and that his sole object was "truth."

> The author believes to have overcome the prejudices which education and association impose, and to have reached a purely objective standpoint with the ability of impersonal judgment.[27]

Wise then presented what he regarded as his own credentials for this study, the sources he had studied. The work was being written to combat fanaticism. The eucharist—he claimed—had been the cause of endless dissension and persecution. He would attempt to prove that Jesus had not instituted the Lord's Supper, or the sacraments derived from it.[28] Also the charge that Jews crucified Jesus would be disproved. Wise then entered into the usual contention that—according to Christianity—someone had to kill Jesus, if he were to fulfill his mission to save mankind by his own sacrifice. But this—he asserted—was an immoral doctrine. God would not have decreed such a cruel necessity. Hence the crucifixion had not been decreed by God. The doctrine of vicarious atonement was also immoral, a superstition. Schleiermacher had abandoned the belief in the divinity of Christ, the vicarious atonement, and upon these doctrines the whole of classical Christianity rested and rests.

None of the Gospels was written in the first century. The oldest is Mark, which is unitarian in doctrine, and contained no anti-Pharisaic speeches. Internal criteria seem to place it between the years 120 and 138. Mark was the headmaster of an academy in Alexandria. Wise contended that the chronological order of the Gospels was probably as follows: Mark, Matthew, Luke, John. Each one presented a contrasting set of doctrines. All these Wise would note, and would place in their setting of contemporary literary and rabbinic sources.[29]

At that time all priests—even the High Priest—were appointed by Pilate, the Roman Procurator. They enjoyed no esteem among the people. Patriots regarded them as hirelings. Here and there among them was a good man. Wise then went on to examine in detail the accounts of the trial of Jesus.[30] Matthew added elders to those who judged Jesus.

There were—Wise continued—two different traditions as to the conspiracy against Jesus: one in Mark, and the other in Matthew. In Jewish law there was a prohibition against executing a criminal on Friday. There was only one exception, which did not apply to the case of Jesus.[31] The whole narration at this point is illogical and impossible. First there was a resolve not to have the trial on a feast-day, and then nonetheless it was held. The priests dreaded the revenge of Pilate, because of the popular demonstrations for Jesus, and the effect it would have had on their own status, if they did not act. In the name of political necessity they went ahead.[32] Josephus wrote that there were two million pilgrims in Jerusalem for the Passover. All this went along with the Jewish tradition of redemption on *Pesach*, though the doctrine of the "sacrificial lamb"—in the sense of vicarious atonement—runs counter to all Jewish ethics. Wise cited a number of Jewish cases.[33] In Jewish law not the state, but the person, is the main object of care.

The date of the Last Supper is given differently in the Synoptics and in John. The accounts seem to demonstrate that neither Mark nor Matthew had ever seen a *Seder*. Here again Wise reiterated his claim that Jesus had decided to sacrifice himself to prevent the slaughter of the people the next day, and hence Jesus *asked* Judas to betray him.

The next section is an explanation of the institution of the eucharist, which rested—Wise wrote—on a tragic misunderstanding. This came from the mind of Paul, and was taken over by the later gospels. Jesus' motives in sacrificing himself were magnanimous; but the dogmas built upon it were "childish."[34]

Jesus wavered before the prospect of martyrdom (this is omitted by John). Next came the accounts of the capture of Jesus. Surely this could not have come from any men acquainted with Jewish institutions. Probably, as John wrote, Jesus was captured by Roman soldiers. Nor is Judas' kiss of betrayal in John. The accounts of the trial that followed abound with confusion as between Annas and Caiaphas. The whole trial, the maltreatment of Jesus in the house of the High Priest, etc., were contrary to Jewish law. This could not have been a trial before the Sanhedrin, and the place given is wrong. Nor is the time right. As has been said, it could not have taken place on a Sabbath or at the time of the Feast. The trial would have occupied a minimum of two days. Every step of the account is impossible. In the time stated the witnesses could not have been examined, according to careful Jewish practice. The laws against false witnesses were scrupulously enforced. It is evident in every line that Mark was quite ignorant of Jewish law and custom.[35] In Jewish law it was also out of the question for Jesus to have admitted his crime. Even if all the judges had condemned him, the verdict would have been invalid under the circumstances. The question revolved about what was blasphemy in Jewish law. Not one point on this actually agrees with Jewish law. It reads like an unskilled invention of the second century. Next Wise devoted himself to Luke's account of the trial.

The fact is that we have no genuine knowledge of the fate of Jesus, from the time of his capture to his appearance before Pilate. The representation of Pilate is utterly preposterous in the light of history. In the New Testament he is depicted not as the tyrant he actually was, but as a weak and half-merciful man. The washing of hands was only a Jewish, not a Roman, custom. One of the objects of the Gospels was to show how magnanimous a Roman could be, and how bloodthirsty the Jews were. The additions of Matthew and Luke to the account in Mark are plainly malicious. The words, "His blood be upon us" is an imitation of David's curse upon Joab. The Gospel according to John had at its disposal only vague and contradictory traditions.[36] John has the people saying that they will not judge. John knew that only Pilate had power over life and death. The even more detailed description in this source was intended to throw all blame on the Jews. But the conduct of Pilate throughout his career is contrary to the account of the New Testament, especially as that conduct is described in Josephus and in Philo. Any rational study will show either that Jesus was not scourged and crucified, or that the alleged friendship of Pilate was a lie.[37]

Wise turned next to the crucifixion. He reviewed the fact that there is much negative evidence (*e silentio*); that the Talmud was ignorant of the manner of Jesus' death; that the crucifixion was denied by a sect in the apostolic age. The cross itself was symbolic in pre-Christian times. The Church adopted this Roman symbol of victory over the state's enemies. The whole treatment of the successive gospels evidenced a growing intent to incriminate the Jews, laboring certainly under the impulse to exonerate the Romans. Mark Antony had crucified Antigonus, one of the scions of the Maccabees. This might possibly have been the true source of the crucifixion story. "Acts" says that Jesus was "hanged." Mark was trying to establish the authority of Paul and of "Christ crucified." Wise reviewed some of the reasons because of which the crucifixion was not believed among the earliest Christians.[38] There was no such place as Golgotha in Jerusalem, and the term itself demonstrated that Mark knew no Hebrew. The words ascribed to Jesus on the cross are contradictory, and are in imitation of the Old Testament. All Greek quotations are from the Septuagint. The Talmudic sources show that Jews knew nothing of the crucifixion story.[39] From its beginning to its end the whole narration is a Midrashic treatment to prove the fulfillment of Biblical verses, especially those of Zechariah, chapter 14, which are carried out in ridiculous detail. Also of the end of the 22nd Psalm, and of Isaiah, chapter 53! The pious thief is an invention of Luke. The crucifixion of thieves was much too severe a penalty. All this was manufactured for the purpose of fulfilling prophecies, and was necessary to prop up the Jesus story on the Bible.[40]

The whole has no genuine relation to Jews or to the time. It cannot be supported as historical fact. The probability is that Jesus was turned over by Pilate to Roman soldiers, was hanged, and perhaps exposed. He was a martyr, but not in the Christian sense. Jesus had been unable to carry out his plan, the restoration of the "kingdom of heaven" in Israel. For this failure he laid down his life heroically. Among his immediate disciples there was not the slightest idea of vicarious atonement. This dogma derived from Paul, who dealt with pagans, and who therefore invented a religion intelligible to them. Here follows a fine passage by Wise:

> One of the falsehoods to be erased from the memory of Christendom, for the sake of truth and humanity, is the horrid and shocking mad-dog cry—the Jews crucified Jesus. What hell could invent of fiendish torments and diabolic scorns was employed in Christendom, to make the Jew miserable with Christian love. Every fanatic, imbecile, or robber assumed the right

> to trample and spit upon the Jew. Every crazy priest had a doctrine on hand to justify those barbarous outrages as the special work of Providence. Every smooth-faced hypocrite or sorrowful bigot in our days had something harsh in his heart against the Jew who killed Christ; as though these few persons described in the New Testament had been the Hebrew people, or it was anybody's fault now that a man was killed eighteen centuries ago. So tenacious, however, and unreasoning is fanaticism, that it must be burnt out of the soul to be overcome. As long as that source of hatred exists in Christendom, Christianity is no religion; it is a misfortune for weeping humanity.[41]

All this was then changed by pagans converted to Christianity into a myth of resurrection and atonement. Jesus did not die for a unique and original truth, for there was none in the gospels.[42] If one approaches the gospels critically, they burst asunder. It is hard to believe any part of them. All true religious precepts are in the Old Testament:

> That is the point where modern critics arrived, therefore the gospels have become books for the museum and the archaeologist, for students of mythology and ancient literature.[43]

Wise then predicted the death of "Christology":

> These right arms of intelligence have fought the titanic battles, conquered and demolished the ancient castles, and remove now the debris, preparing the ground upon which there shall be reared the gorgeous temple of humanity, one universal republic, one universal religion of intelligence, and one great universal brotherhood. This is the new covenant, the gospel of humanity and reason.[44]

This was a frank and fearless book, with some interesting comments based on deep familiarity with rabbinic sources, which bore upon the account of the trial and execution of Jesus. The treatment is lacking only in a critical-historical sense in certain respects, and perhaps reads strangely in places, for here Wise utilized the very kind of critical method which he deplored in application to the Old Testament.

A study of chapters, published in the *Israelite*, under the title "Jesus Himself,"[45] was recently written by Dr. Samuel Sandmel.[46] These too were an attempt to sift "fact" from "fiction" in the New Testament. Most of their conclusions are identical with those we have already described. Wise believed that the gospels were originally in Aramaic, that they came from a common, original Aramaic source. Here too Wise asserted that Jesus was thoroughly Jewish, that he never himself claimed Davidic descent, and that his real office was as the "Son of Man," the title of a prophet after the Babylonian exile. Dr. Sandmel believes this writing to be without lasting scientific value, but evidencing a good deal of shrewdness:

> He had neither the training nor the discipline for exact and lasting scholarship.[47]

But his work had its own kind of importance, to recover the original Jesus, to peel off layer after layer of legend and theology. If an age-old division was ever to be healed, it had to come about by Jews grappling with the Christianity of Jesus. And this, on many occasions, Wise tried to do.

C. ON MISSIONARIES

For the last of our treatment of Wise's attitude toward Christianity we shall add some of his words about missionaries. For a complete review the reader should turn back to Wise's encounters with missionaries, especially in the early days of his ministry in Albany, and to some of the things he said and wrote of them and of their methods then.

As a motto for the whole, we might place these sentences:

> The Jews cannot be Christianized; this is beyond question. The spirit of the age goes against trinitarianism and favors Monotheism. Moses is ahead of the Pope.[48]

Early in his Cincinnati career he wrote in his usual strain about missionaries:

> Let them convert themselves. . . . John Randolph, when importuned by a lady for subscriptions, to defray the expenses of missionaries to Greece, pointed to the naked negroes at her threshold: "The Greeks are at your door, madam," he said. So say we, look to your own apostates, you Christian ministers. . . . as long as you are corrupted, and as long as you attempt to coerce the lunatic, the imbecile, and the infant, so long shall we consider your agents as speculators in easy positions of life, too lazy to work and——perhaps too honest to steal.[49]

In the same year he drew up a list of twelve charges against missionaries, which he challenged them to refute.[50]

In almost every issue of the *Israelite* in its earliest years he was taking up this topic. There was a long series, called "A Peep into the

Missionary Efforts." He asked them there to "cast the first stone on your neighbor" only when they themselves would be guiltless.[51] In a later installment of the same series—the last one in fact—he wrote:

> No objections will be raised on our part, but is it not supremely ridiculous for a church with such internal feuds, to attempt to convert the believers in One God, to their mongrelism?[52]

He was fully ready to meet them, if they were to come to Cincinnati and to set up shop there: "Let them come here and meet us face to face."[53]

Even a liberal like Henry Ward Beecher, Wise took to task for repeating thoughtlessly some of the words on the Pharisees which had their source in New Testament prejudice and New Testament distortion.[54]

The missionaries—Wise claimed—were trying to bring "religion" to a people who already possessed far more than they:

> Nobody, however, will deny that the doctrines of righteousness, as revealed in the Old Testament, are correct and sufficient. Therefore, we can not see what they want of us. . . . The fashion to hamper [probably an error for "hammer"] annually on the conversion of the Jews, an enterprise which hitherto has proved a failure, appears to us absurd and unbecoming men of sound judgment and honest intentions. Let good be well.[55]

Wise was confident in these years, as he had been in Albany, that his defense of Jews had put a stop to, or at least had greatly reduced, the insults flung by Christians at Jews in missionary sermons and in demagogic speeches. "Let the Jew alone, or speak of him with due respect and consideration."[56]

He himself was constantly receiving letters from Christians about Christianity. In general he replied in this spirit:

> Your religion is good enough for you, and worthless for us. 3000 to 4000 years of successive thoughts, by inheritance, to speak with Darwin, have changed our constitutions completely. We can not assimilate anything that sounds, looks or smells like polytheism, idolatry or heathenism in any shape or form; and Christianity has got too much of that element to be digestible. Let us alone, as we never interfere with you. Save paper, money and missionaries, and care for the poor, needy and suffering.[57]

Nor did he regard this only as an insult to the intelligence of Jews. It was also a menace to civil and religious liberty. Wherever the "dicta of reason" were "under the clouds of mania," there any clear concept of human rights was bound to suffer.[58]

Jews who succumb to these blandishments—and there are but a few who do—never acquire any real, new faith. All that happens is that they lose their "native ethics and its virtues." The Christian spends about twenty million dollars annually on this conversion mania: "It is all a ghastly farce, and should be ended."

One of Wise's brave works was entitled "A Defense of Judaism Against Proselytizing Christianity." Written against missionary chieftains, it was for the purpose of showing why "the Israelite can not embrace Christianity."

Judaism, now denationalized, is a universal religion. The truth which it propounds is ineluctable. It does not seek converts,[59] but believes that in the end of days the nations will convince and convert themselves. It does not behold a sinner in every human being. It does not believe in a hell for unbelievers. In the ancient world Judaism did make converts, but after that it was forbidden to do so on pain of death. Christianity and Islam converted by the sword, and then by the pyre. Most anti-Jewish prejudices derive from the "conversion mania of Christianity."[69] This had brought untold misery among men, and is "an erroneous, dangerous and unreasoning superstition." Wise's purpose in this book was not to retaliate in like spirit, but quite simply to defend. Silence might foster the belief that Jews have naught to say.[61]

Missions to Jews are a miserable failure. In his own thirty-four years in Cincinnati there was but one Jewish girl who became a Christian. But thirty-seven Christians have embraced Judaism, and that without solicitation. Unless trained from childhood to put reason aside, no one can credit Christian dogmas.[62] It is criminal to try to alienate men from their kindred. But this Christians have done without compunction, especially in such tragic and incredible cases as that of Edgar Mortara. Bribery and dissimulation play a large role. Anyone leaving Judaism is a "renegade, who perjures his ancestors and rebels against the will of God."

Next Wise tried to answer the question: why do Jews reject what three hundred million accept? The answer is that, if you are truly civilized, how is it possible for you to accept the dogmas of Christianity? Why not embrace Judaism? The world is full of "men and scholars who seem to be unable to see the moral heroism in the Jews' conscience, faithfulness and self-denial in this tragedy of fifteen centuries' duration."[63] Jews know that the story upon which Christianity rests is untrue. Christians accept the authority of the New Testament. Jews deny it. Which is more reliable, the testimony of a handful (the disciples), or of a whole people? Millions of Christians also have protested against the dogmas of the Church. There is a majestic difference between this and the revelation on Sinai. Where can one find evidence for the "immaculate conception," for temptation by Satan, for resurrection, etc.? Even in the apostolic age some sects denied all this.

The argument based on miracles, in the New Testament, is incredible, and many Christians also reject it. The Jew has always thought that miracles prove nothing. And such miracles! Mary conceiving by the Holy Ghost, etc.! The Talmud too was full of miracles;[64] why not believe these too? The only rational conclusion is that miracles prove nothing. Judaism maintains no doctrine merely because it is supported by a miracle. This was expounded in detail by Maimonides.[65] Sinai was not a miracle; it rested upon "the soundness, rationality, universality, and pure humanism of the doctrine promulgated there, and not vice versa."[66]

What has a Jew to gain by adopting Christianity? His own faith is solid and sure, and that of Christianity weak and flimsy. Christians sometimes claim that the doctrine of immortality was brought into the world by Jesus. But it is really innate in man, and goes back to prehistoric times among Hebrews.[67] Every nation had a concept of God and of immortality. It was not necessary to have an innocent man crucified to prove what Jews already believed.[68] And in later Christianity this led to the intolerant dogma that salvation is only through Christ.

Universal salvation will come without a Messiah. It is promised to all men. This was followed by a blow directed at Darwin:

> It took a Christian savant, one that grew up under the pessimistic and degrading estimate of human nature, to hit upon the idea of man's descent from a brute, in none else would the idea of manhood become so debased.[69]

The teaching that all men are sinners is iniquitous. A wise God must have created the means by which all men could attain the deepest purpose of their existence. What kind of God would condemn nine-tenths of the human race to damnation?

> Such a God is an idol of human fabrication. . . . There is no fact known in nature or history and no law in logic to prove such an anomaly in God's government.[70]

God seeks no human victims. Thus the Christian God is very different from the Jewish. Only God is the redeemer and savior. Christianity has:

> Nothing to offer to the Hebrew except a little worldly advantage in a society benighted with childish prejudices, steeped in myths and selfishness.[71]

Not Christian dogma but sound morality is needed to gain mundane happiness. But Christianity says that it is not of this world. The real basis of ethics is borrowed from Judaism:

> With Moses the revelations of Deity closed; so much and no more the human mind is enabled to know of the Supreme Being, that He is and what He is, that He rules and how He rules.[72] Nothing was, nothing could possibly be added thereto.

This Christians knew at the outset, but became arrogant, intolerant and haughty.[73] Mundane happiness depends not on Christology, but on intelligence, common sense, and morality:

> We find Judaism in every point far above Christology, and can not condescend to it.[74]

The world at large will never accept a religion so out of harmony with reason:

> If there is no salvation in truth, there is certainly none in fiction.[75]

The whole fabric of Christian faith is without any real foundation in the Old Testament. The final, impudent claim that Jews do not understand their own Scriptures,[76] that only Christians understand its prophecies, is boundlessly absurd, absurdity compounded with absurdity:

> How could the ex-heathens of foreign tongues have understood the Hebrew Bible better than the Hebrew in his own country up to four hundred A.C.?"

The little work then goes into an extended analysis of the Biblical passages in question: in Moses, in Isaiah, Jeremiah, Psalms, Zechariah, etc. Into this we shall not follow Wise. Christians—he concluded—have turned the Bible upside down:

> However, when the officious conversionist comes to us with his sanctimonious wisdom, and with all fair or ugly means seeks to impose on us his Christology, we must resent the indignity and tell him, as plain as language can convey it, that no intelligent and honest Hebrew would retrograde from rational Judaism to that negation of reason which is called Christology.[78]

This can never become the religion of mankind.

This work was written in 1879, and published just before Wise's sixtieth birthday.

These two chapters should have contained enough of Wise's words about Christianity, its relation to Judaism, the place of Jesus, and the attacks and errors of missionaries, to have given the reader a reasonably adequate idea of what Wise thought. It is astonishing that in the midst of so many preoccupations, duties and strivings, he should have been able to find time to delve into the problems of the origins of Christianity, its relationship with rabbinic sources, its own internal, critical difficulties. We have already indicated our opinion of the reasons and hopes that prompted Wise to do all this. At the very least, it should be clear that this was one of the deep and constant interests of his mature years, and that according to his wont he related it to his vision of interreligious understanding, his unswerving conviction that mankind was moving toward unity and brotherhood.

13

VIII. *On Wise Himself*

A. HIS BOOKS

This chapter will be for the purpose of adding a number of glimpses into Isaac M. Wise, his work, his life and personality, which could not be included in the foregoing chapters. The contents will have to do not so much with his thought as with himself.

In 1879 he began a series of addresses at the Plum St. Temple on "Great Minds." This was devoted primarily to the great creative spirits of Jewish history. Philo of Alexandria was the first of whom he spoke.[1] The next lecture was devoted to Josephus.[2]

In the following year he announced a course of lectures, to begin the following Friday night, on "The Future Man," to consider "Biblical and Jewish Aspects of Future Relations."[3]

In 1887 Wise wrote and delivered a series on Jewish Apologetics, concentrating on Judaism's rejoinders to atheism and agnosticism. It appears that he was urged to do this by some of his friends in the congregation, who believed that it was an imperative task.[4]

In 1888 he delivered a series—to which we have referred at length in the preceding chapter—on "A Defense of Judaism *versus* Proselytizing Christianity." Later this was published in book form.[5]

At various other times he delivered numbers of lectures on "Jesus, the Apostles and Paul," on "The Ethics of Judaism," and on "Israel, Its Place in History."

Wise's literary labors were no mere pastime to him. His books were an integral part of his purpose with regard to Judaism in America. They were "speculative, controversial, and historical."[6] Some were devoted to the controversy between religion and science that was raging in the early 70's. Into the midst of this Wise plunged. His chief work was "The Cosmic God," and to this he gave many months of thought and labor. His second major work was "The Origin of Christianity and a Commentary on the Acts of the Apostles," in 1868.[7] His other works on Christianity we have listed in Chapter Eleven. Details regarding them will be found in the Bibliography. Concerning the first of these, "The Origin of Christianity," Wise declared that he wrote it:

> . . . with the utmost regard for religion, and for the Bible, with due reverence for Christianity, the important factor in the history of civilization, and with a profound regard for the religious feelings of good men.[8]

Wise himself translated part of the work of Adolf Wislecenus "*Bibel fuer denkende Leser*" [The Bible for Thoughtful Readers].

In 1880 Wise returned to his first love, historical study. He published the second volume of the history he had written in Albany. This was entitled "The History of the Hebrews' Second Commonwealth."[9] Among other things it was intended as a text for students at the Hebrew Union College, and covered the period from Zerubbabel and the return from Babylon to the fall of Jerusalem in the year 70. The work is replete with judgments on the origin and composition of the later books of the Bible, the Apocrypha, and the New Testament. It treats at some length the Great Synod and the rise of Jewish Jurisprudence. Up to that time it was the first attempt to treat Jewish history as an organic whole.

In 1887 Wise completed the publication of a series of articles called "The Essence of Religion, The Elements of Theology of Judaism, the Torah of Moses." This was followed by an "Apologetics of Judaism, That God Is What He Is, the Theology of Moses, Revelation, Inspiration, Prophecy, etc." The purport of all these lectures was that Judaism is an elaboration of the revelation on Mt. Sinai. He concluded with several articles on "The Authenticity and Last Edition of the Pentateuch," which were later included in the "Pronaos." This latter work we have outlined in some detail, and we refer the reader back to those pages. The lectures on "The Essence of Judaism" were published in 1861 as a text for confirmands. In 1872 excerpts of this book were republished under the title, "Judaism, Its Doctrines and Duties." This was not, in fact, the first American

Jewish catechism. Samuel Hirsch had written and published one in 1856, *Systematischer Katechismus der Israelitischen Religion* (A Systematic Catechism of the Israelite Religion), translated into English later on. Samuel Adler had written *Leitfaden fuer den Israelitischen Religionsunterricht* (Aids for Religious Instruction in Israel), published in 1868. And Leeser had issued a translation of Johlson's *Lehren der Mosaischen Religion* (Doctrines of Mosaic Religion). For the most part these were from a partisan point of view. Wise departed from these precedents and avoided apologetics and polemics.[10]

In 1866 Wise prepared the second volume of *Minhag America* for the use of his own congregation. It was soon in use in a large part of the country. In 1868, at the request of his congregation, he prepared "Hymns, Psalms, and Prayers":

> as an expression of our religious feelings, hopes and wishes in the language most acceptable and in the form most agreeable to our age.[11]

In this latter task Wise had the cooperation of Minna Kleeberg, Maurice and Nathan Mayer, Isidor Kalisch, and Wolf Rothenstein.

Wise was constantly writing novels and romances. Though he was compelled to toss these off, so that they would make the deadline of the *Israelite*, or of the *Deborah*, he did not take lightly the task of composing them. In them he strove to transmit a knowledge of Jewish history, its pathos and grandeur. In 1854 he wrote "The Convert," and "The Jewish Heroine" (translated from the Spanish). In the following year he wrote "The Catastrophe of Eger." "The Shoemaker's Family," "Resignation and Fidelity, or Life and Romance." In 1866 he published "Romance, Philosophy and Cabalah, or The Conflagration at Frankfort o.t. M." In 1855 he had written also "The Last Struggle of the Nation," which was later translated into French by Rabbin Dreyfous of Mulhouse, and published as "*Le lieu d'Israël*"; also in 1958 "The Combat of the People, or Hillel and Herod." He found time to write a play, "The First of the Maccabees," which was later on done into Hebrew by Dr. Bliden and J. Epstein in Jerusalem in 1894.

In German, Wise wrote *Die Juden von Landshuth, Der Rothkopf oder des Schulmeisters Tochter* (The Redhead, or the Schoolmaster's Daughter), *Baruch und sein Ideal.* These appeared serially in the *Deborah.*

We cannot conclude this section without giving an example of Wise's style in at least one of these works. It was typical of him and of the period. We reproduce a single paragraph from "The Last Struggle of the Nation":[12]

> It was a dark night. Rain poured down from obscure clouds in rushing currents. A hurricane-like wind swept over the plain of Esdrael, and reverberated in awful melodies from Mount Carmel. An unbroken silence reigned supreme in the plain below, and on the vine-covered Carmel, where the autumn leaves whistled the awful accords with the rushing wind and the breaking and shoaming [one wonders whether this was taken from the German *Schaum*, for there is no such word in English, or at least none we can discover] waves of the sea at its foot. Men and beasts had sought shelter under the roofs, none would expose himself to weeping and mourning nature.

There are a few other novels which we have neglected, and which we include for the sake of completeness: *The Wizard of the Forest*,[13] *The Rabbi of Bacharach*, which he called *An Anti-Romantic Romance*,[14] a novel called *A Little Bohemian*,[15] a queer story on the first page of the *Israelite*—whether by Wise or by someone else is not clear—called *That Terrible Dentist*.[16]

Most of the novels are rather amazingly vivid and interesting. Especially in the early years the English bears testimony to the fact that Wise had still much to learn. Here for example is a sentence from "The Combat of the People":

> Tears flew rapidly from her eyes.

Altogether he wrote eleven novels in English, sixteen in German, and also hundreds of unsigned poems.[17]

B. HIS LABORS AND PERSONALITY

In a series, "The World of My Books," written in 1897, and which we have already utilized considerably above, Wise claimed that this "versatility" was forced upon him. He detested writing, he said. But he took pride in defending his own works. Each of his books appeared to meet with a "conspiracy of silence," but he was undeterred. He himself did not like long, scholarly books. And when he was faced with a really lengthy novel, he read the beginning, the middle and the end. Finally—he asserted—he adopted a "homeopathic method," a bit at a time, reading slowly when he was studying erudite, intricate works, pencil in hand, occasionally quarreling with the author, jotting down many marginal annotations.[18] He found this such a drudgery, that he had been tempted to take an oath "never to torture humanity with a book." He knew only too well that the Bible had been right, and that "of the making of books there is no end." (Ecclesiastes, 12:12). But his impulses were stronger than reason, to achieve something in the world, something not ephemeral but lasting![19]

From the very beginning a large part of his time was consumed in traveling. To leaf through the *Israelite* is to come across column upon column of "Correspondence" which Wise was sending back from this city or that city—always keenly observant, chatty, easy-going and simple. While his primary motive was to further his own causes, to organize congregations, to dedicate synagogues, to win the support of individuals and communities, he found time always to see and to write about the vivid American scene, to comment upon the vagaries and foibles of men, to write to his people about political events and about many, many other things. In 1856 he was upon a trip which began in Indianapolis and Terre Haute, and which proceeded thence to St. Louis.[20] We shall follow some of these junketings from year to year, but we shall reluctantly have to resist the temptation to reprint paragraphs from them.

A lithograph of Wise, by one J. Shore, had appeared in 1859. Of it he himself wrote in the *Israelite:*

> It is the exact likeness of a man who boasts upon warmer friends and opponents than any other Rabbi in this country. Being requested to give a motto to the picture we wrote, "Yet truth will triumph. . . ."[21]

In 1860 he traveled to Indianapolis again, Lafayette and Fort Wayne. He wrote much of Judaism as it was then in Chicago.[22]

A second installment of a trip he made in the summer of the same year is quite vivacious—up the Ohio Valley, then to Cleveland, Buffalo and Rochester.

> Rochester is the Cincinnati of this part of the country.

In Albany there flooded back upon him many bitter, but also many more pleasant, memories. In New York he conjectured that there were then 35,000 Jews and but fifteen congregations. In Philadelphia —to which he went next—he counted seven congregations. He spent some time with Szold in Oheb Shalom, Baltimore, and wrote of him:

> A kind and good man and an eloquent preacher.

This entire journey was capped with these words:

> We love those who think likewise, but we can not hate those who think other-wise; and, if our opponents are fierce, we are otherwise, all the time Wise![23]

Obviously on occasion he was not above a pun or two.

In 1863 he journeyed to Pittsburgh, Washington and Baltimore. He had been reading Renan's *Life of Jesus:*

> Renan stands not on the summit of modern criticism; he appears to be afraid of the radical cure.

Nonetheless Wise thought that Renan went beyond Colenso, Davidson, Newman, and the *Westminster Review.*[24]

On a trip which he made to New York in 1864 he was struck by the magnitude of the city—then with no less than 40,000 Jews and about thirty congregations. But he found it lagging behind the rest of the country in rabbis, and in Reform.[25]

Later that summer he wrote an article, entitled "Notes by the Wayside" on a trip to Philadelphia, during which he paid a visit to David Einhorn.[26]

During all these years, as we have remarked, Wise was editing his two papers, writing, and writing—articles, editorials, novels, poems, and letters. This must have been a constant and heavy burden. Here is a description he set down of some of it in 1866:

> An editor has to use pens, scissors, and brains. Correct bad proofs, and revise worse manuscripts. Write puffs for nauseous medicines which he never tasted. Attend theatres, concerts, balls, races, exhibitions. In all of which he is expected to be deeply interested. Give descriptions of murders, riots and marriages, review new books, and answer all questions proposed to him by correspondents. He is expected to use all the lotions sent to him, swallow all the cough-drops, candies and pills, to bear testimony to their value. To hear all the news, and comment upon it. To be ever ready to do anybody a service, who asks it, free of all charge. To drink with every agent, mountebank and sporting-man, who wants a word or two said in the paper. To call on all distinguished strangers, and to show them the lions. To read over a thousand exchanges, and not omit to notice every mammoth beet, and Brobdignag-cabbage—to announce the arrival and departure of all eminent citizens, write obituaries of all friends, and biographical sketches of all dignitaries, puff all the best hotels, and lie about the poor ones. Who would be an EDITOR?[27]

In 1867 he himself asked the question—why did he travel so much and dedicate so many synagogues? Not for money, for he got none! Not for fame! Never did he seek invitations! He claimed that it was because he was trying boldly to tell the truth, and because he had made Reform popular among the people. The people he found pious and conservative. They needed to be made to think. Thus far, thank God!, he had never met with an accident, nor been stopped by sickness.[28]

In 1877 he made one of his most ambitious journeys, which carried him all the way out to San Francisco. From the Pacific he wrote:

> I am sitting here high and dry, that is, I sit in the fifth story of the Palace Hotel, and all California is dry, because the latter rain has failed and crops are short. The decline in mining-stocks is worse to all commercial interests than all the other causes combined. The business-men here look displeased, some gloomy. It is a dull season. . . .[29]

There is a letter he wrote in 1886 to Max Heller, in which these words occur:

> You have no idea perhaps of the perfect indifference I feel towards everything said or written against me. . . .[30]

In 1887 he was on the road, to Philadelphia, Columbus, etc.[31]

Years later—in 1897—Wise wrote claiming that the *Israelite*—in the thirty-five years he had been publishing it—had been what Henry Ward Beecher called it: "This is the brain of our Jews." It had been the primary agent in the change in the Jewish community from 1854 to 1897.[32]

The first book written by two of his disciples about his life sums him up in these words:

> Reformer and builder, a man of action, and craving still all his life for the teacher's chair. He was an author of philosophic works and at the same time a fluent journalist, who flung out effective but fugitive words every week. He was modest in virtue, but also assertive in truth; a veritable giant, and still the meekest of men.[33]

Wise wrote everything in longhand. He had tried dictating to a stenographer, when this came into vogue. But he was never able to adjust to this technique. He could not learn, or would not learn, to use a typewriter. Thus he condemned himself to tremendous physical drudgery, which continued to the end.[34]

He was a severe and trenchant critic, but a generous opponent. He did not descend into vulgarities and rarely read the papers of his enemies. His motto for the *Deborah* was "*Vorwaerts, meine Seele*" [Forward, my Soul]. For it he wrote his more intimate articles and sometimes liked to call it his "waste-basket." The *Deborah* died with him.

He was accounted an excellent teacher, but had most likely acquired the art with more than a little difficulty. There is an interesting letter in the Archives of the Albany congregation, March 13, 1852,[35] in German, of which the following is a free translation:

> Owing to conditions, regarding which I shall give proper explanations, I am compelled to inform you that it will be impossible for me to continue both as a teacher and rabbi, and, if I give up teaching, my salary as a rabbi will not be sufficient for my living expenses.
>
> The principle cause for my resigning as teacher is the behavior of my pupils. To keep order I am obliged to arm myself with a cane and punish the unmanageable crowd. Such a state of affairs is most distressing to me, and by no means in harmony with my character and my sentiments. Because of the unbecoming conduct of some of the pupils, I frequently leave the schoolroom a sick man. Aside from this, it is impossible for a man who, during the week, wages battles with a crowd of ill-behaved children, to conduct three services on the Sabbath. . . .

But the resignation was withdrawn.

Wise worked hard for the B'nai Brith, and was often orator at various benevolent and fraternal organizations. He became a member of the German Pioneer Society of Cincinnati, and for many years spoke at its annual meeting, usually on Washington's Birthday.[36] He himself was temperate in his habits, but could discern no harm in moderate drinking. By nature and conviction he was opposed to all sumptuary legislation. He preached boldly against the temperance crusade. Thus he wrote an essay, which was read before "The Friends of Inquiry":

> Is it morally wrong to take a glass of beer, wine or champagne at dinner or at any other time? Or is it hypocrisy for hypocrisy's sake that persons using such beverages do it secretly as long as they can hide the fact? Let us first see what might be called morally wrong. . . .[37]

His sympathies did not lie strongly with organized charity. This was perhaps a symptom of his time. He liked to help individuals by himself. Stories of his gullibility abounded, of his blind faith in every poor man, every beggar. He asked no questions. If he were told that the mendicant was almost certainly an impostor, he would shrug his shoulders. There are many anecdotes concerning his kindness. He could not be kept in overcoats. No one ever left his door empty-handed. At his death a great sheaf of paper was found, worthless, money he had lent, notes he had endorsed, accounts he had guaranteed. One Friday evening word came that a large number of Russian Jewish immigrants was at the station in Cincinnati, and that no one was there to take care of them. He took his old-fashioned high hat, emptied his own pockets, and sent the hat through the Temple. With the money in it he hastened to the depot.

He was the leading rabbi of his day, but his maximum salary was $6000 a year. It never occurred to him to ask for an increase. In his seventy-second year he was counseled to make a will. "I have nothing to bequeath," he said, "the world will laugh at me, if I leave a will."[38]

It was reported that he had ended his *Reminiscences* with the year 1857, three years after his assumption of his post in Cincinnati, because he could not bear to put on record his quarrels and battles with his living opponents. He refused to believe evil of people who were close to him. Not rarely his confidence was misplaced and this invariably caused him distress. Wise was very friendly with two Catholic Archbishops, Purcell and Elder, and with the leading clergymen of the city. Between him and Thomas F. Vickers, a minister of the Unitarian Church and later rector of the University of Cincinnati, there was a long and intimate friendship.

Daily Wise drove from College Hill into the city, a distance of about nine miles. The picture of the old man, smoking a great cigar, behind the jogging horse, was a very familiar one in the city.[39] When he was seated and not reading, he had the habit of sliding his glasses to the top of his head, as many of the pictures of him show. Then often he would forget they were there.

Until the very end his eyes were undimmed. His face was illuminated with a genial smile. His figure was much stooped in later years, from bending over a desk, reading and writing. Usually he wore black, with a white shirt and a white neckcloth; a high hat in winter, a broadbrim straw hat in summer. He had a cane in his hand perpetually. Walking with someone, he would stop often to talk, to make a point, then, when he had concluded, start again. Where the College was—on Sixth Street between Center and Mound—he could be seen daily surrounded by students and professors, like Socrates with his disciples.[40] He liked to go to market and shop for his family. He was a man of much simplicity, of incredible energy, and of a staunch spirit!

C. HIS GENERAL INTERESTS

Only a few things need to be added to the many references in the text of the biographical section of our work in regard to Wise's preoccupation with Jewish and general affairs.

All through his life his interest reached out to Jews everywhere. He printed countless paragraphs or longer articles about Jews "in odd corners," Jews in North Africa, or living by the Dead Sea. Many numbers of the *Israelite* contained a section headed "Foreign Record," which culled items from all over the world. He was perpetually describing the situation of the Jews under the Czars, in the Crimea, in Rumania, or even in India and Cochin-China. Here—for example—is an account of a visit by the King of Portugal to the Jews of Amsterdam;[41] or another—under the heading "Political News"—about the status of the Jews of Austria, Prussia and Switzerland. On another page there is an account of the banishment of the Jews from Gutenberg.[42] The following year a series of articles appeared on the Jews in Arabia Felix, especially in Sanaa, the capital of Yemen.[43] He was one of the first to carry material on the Jews of Kai-Feng-Fu, the original and mysterious Jews of China.[44]

But Wise's interest was not exhausted by his curiosity about Jews in their "national" distribution. He followed the careers of individual Jews—especially of those who were leading exceptional lives and contributing in some unusual direction to human happiness. In 1863 he penned a long article about Jacques Offenbach, one full of meat.[45]

In the next and last chapter we shall come to some of his strange and far-flung interests. But these were not always fantastic. In 1867 he wrote an article "What is the Shape of the Earth?", chiefly taken from *Galignani's Messenger* of Paris. In this he indulged in a criticism of some of the findings of science, surely a foolhardy undertaking for a rabbi.[46]

We have already noted at some length his opinions on evolution. Here is a paragraph containing a very flippant reply to Darwin:

> In the large library burned in Alexandria, and all the libraries burned elsewhere, and in all existing now, there is or was not one book written by an animal, not even an anthropomorphous ape; and yet Mr. Darwin ascribed the same kind of intelligence to man and beast. The same kind of force must manifest itself in the same kind of phenomena.[47]

In 1888 he was fortunate enough to be able to print a series of articles on the Beni Israel of India, a fascinating group of Jews, written by one Hacem Samuel Kehimer, a member of that community.

Jewish and non-Jewish, religious or scientific, contemporary or from the past, Wise's interests ranged over and delighted in a host of things. Nothing could be more unmistakable than that he was a man of avid curiosity, of vivid imagination, and of wide-ranging sympathies. He felt himself to be a citizen of a multitudinous world, sharer with all men in a time of widening brotherhood and of exciting human discovery. He was like a source of light, stationary in space, but speeding its beams in concentric spheres toward all things!

14

IX. Curiosa

A MAN CANNOT ABRADE SO MANY THINGS WITHOUT THROWING OFF some curiously colored sparks. In this respect Wise was no exception. Sometimes his curiosity led him into exotic places and into fantastic opinions. These are all part of the man. To see him whole these must be set here as part of the account. We have, therefore, gathered together a number of paragraphs under the heading of "Curiosa," out-of-the-way opinions, quixotic expressions, manifestations of personal idiosyncrasies implied in what he wrote. These too will not be arranged in formal fashion, in topical array, like a lawyer's brief. We shall simply follow him from year to year through the *Israelite* and glean from its pages these sheaves with their mutational ears, permitting them to make whatever impression they may upon the reader. Obviously among Wise's editorial chores was that of filling up the nooks and crannies of his paper. The printer had to be served! The column must come out full and compact! He was forever looking about, forever gleaning. But the way in which he did it, and what he found, both reveal the texture of his mind.

Here—for instance—he was writing "On the Dullness of Great Men," on those who—despite their genius—were without sparkle and color. He cited the cases of Descartes, La Fontaine (a strange instance, indeed!), Buffon, Marmontel, and others, especially dwelling upon reports as to their conversational powers, or their lack of them![1]

Somewhere Wise had been reading of speakers before an Illinois debating society, and this led him into a paragraph on scolding wives, by what association of thought it is not easy to discover.[2]

In thinking about human and religious problems, occasionally an analogy, a metaphor, would come glinting. The "Ephemeron" fly—doubtless its metamorphosis from pupa and larva—induced in him thoughts of immortality.[3]

He was not unaware of the widening world of astronomy of that era, of the casting of the plummet of the mind outward into illimitable space. Thus he wrote of "The Universe" and of the wonder and awe a study of it engenders.[4]

Wise was no "schoolmarm." He liked women and probably found it interesting to observe them. Here we find him commenting on how a woman should grow old gracefully, though how a mere man can know of this remains a mystery. It seemed to him that this depended on character more than upon cosmetics.[5]

In the same year—and again giving evidence of his interest in astronomy and cosmogony in general—Wise wrote a long article on "The Nebular Hypothesis."[6]

From this it is a long leap to an article entitled "Who Were the Etruscans?", in reality a review of a book which he had just been reading.[7]

And—even more strangely as to sequence—shortly thereafter he was writing an editorial on prize-fighting in Britain:

> The bull fight of the Spaniards is virtue in comparison to the brutal practice of human bullies.[8]

As witness to the diversity of his interests, the next year he carried an article on "Egyptian Chronology," on the ways and means by which ancient Egypt kept account of time.[9]

One of the curiosities of the time, which must have had more than a passing vogue, was table-tilting. On this Wise wrote under the title "Table Moving among German Israelites," and a reprint appeared in the same issue on "How Women Become Insane."[10]

In a single issue we find an article on "Beauty a Duty," not only the physical symmetry of youth, but the spirit and loveliness of maturity and age; and almost side by side with it an article on "Pythagoras and Plato," which put forward the thesis—following the rabbis—that in their travels these two sages had come to an acquaintance with Jewish sources. And in the next number there was a poetic paragraph on "Evening Twilight."[11]

In the following year Wise was writing on the longevity of animals;[12] on "Saving for Old Age";[13] and two years later on "The Desert of Sahara";[14] and on "The Phenomena of Sunstroke."[15]

He had no use for Spiritualism and decried it as a superstition, leading to many absurdities. But in Austria a new form of it had made its appearance, which seemed to him "more spiritual":

> But now spiritualism appears to us the tool of living spirits.[16]

In the very same issue is a paragraph on meteoric rain, a special instance of which had occurred in Europe and had been observed by millions.[17]

Many people in that time entertained a quite fantastic interest in the pyramids, cherishing the myth that these structures concealed deep, mystical secrets. Of this Wise wrote under the title "The Great Pyramid and Egyptian Life 4000 Years Ago."[18] Surely, however, this was not as far afield as an editorial paragraph on playing billiards and cards.[19]

A story that used to be retailed in Cincinnati was recounted by Wise himself. He wrote that he had amused his fellow-travelers on a steamboat going upstream on the Mississippi. He had repeated long strings of numbers, first forward, and then backward, without an error. In point of fact, this was the usual practice of utilizing Hebrew letters both as sounds and as numbers.[20]

In 1874 there was an article on "Glaciers," which Wise wrote after "Principal Forbes."[21]

But it would be a mistake to think that the eccentricity of some of his writing was only on recondite or exotic subjects. Once in a while he could indite a paragraph on his own personal reactions to the ordinary events of a clergyman's life, which is exceedingly striking and amusing:

> . . . at weddings the minister should no longer be allowed to kiss the bride. We have united in wedlock about fifteen hundred couples and never kissed the bride, because we looked upon it as a damnable custom, a modern translation of the *jus primae noctae* [sic!] which disgraced Christendom in the Middle Ages. . . .[22]

In the same vein he asked that people should not give so many diamonds to brides, but rather put the money into a good savings bank, buy a house, or use it as part of a future dowry.[23]

Wise's estimate of Richard Wagner's music was hopelessly distorted by his hatred of him as an anti-Semite. He could not hear of Wagner's music without thinking that it must be as evil as the man. Thus he thought it worthwhile to comment on a production of *Tristan und Isolde:*

> Richard Wagner has made a fiasco in Berlin with his new opera, "Tristan und Isolde." The *National Zeitung* expresses its astonishment that the royal stage has been given up to the promulgation of such weak and immoral "stuff."[24]

Only a short time later he wrote more of Wagner:

> That Wagner is more of a humbug than a composer is now admitted in Germany . . . operas without melodies, made of spectacle scenes and noisy Janissary orchestras, do not suit the German taste.[25]

This latter was occasioned by a production of the "Ring."

Not infrequently Wise took a rap at the sale of patent medicines, though he carried advertisements of some of them in his paper. Thus in 1877 he noted that this evil had grown to alarming proportions in Germany and Austria.[26]

Like every rabbi he was called upon to speak at out-of-the-way events and occasions. Thus he delivered a lecture by invitation to the Cincinnati College of Medicine and Surgery on February 26, 1877, and its subject was "Medical Ethics."[27]

We have already quoted some of his advice to preachers, both in general and to some of his beloved pupils. But he did not always write of this with deadly seriousness. Here was a paragraph, headed "How a Bad Sermon is Made":

> Take a small quantity of ideas, which everybody knows, paste them on a Bible text, put in two or three funny anecdotes, pour on them three or four quarts of filtered words, stir well with the quill of a spread eagle, spice well with patriotism, liberty and great nation pepper, throw the whole liquid upon paper, dry it in the moonshine of sentimentalities, then cut it in slices of equal size, and you have a sermon which will hurt nobody.[28]

Wise was following the course of invention, the new things which Edison and others were devising for the nation and for the world:

> The electric candle, whose light they tell us will soon replace that of coal gas, seems, as yet, not to have been brought into a practical shape for private uses; the telephone will render communication for short distances more convenient; the phonograph has not yet risen above the rank of an ingenious toy.[29]

His interests were wide ranging and sometimes landed him in very curious places. Why he included them in the *Israelite*, and how they came to him is a mystery. Here—for example—is an article on "How to Preserve a Piano," which may have had something to do with his own musical interests, or which he may have thought of simply as a service to some of his readers.[30]

As he glanced over papers from various parts of the world, Wise would come upon odd items, and often he would tuck them into his columns. In 1881 he described a "machine that measures thought," invented by a Doctor Mosso of Turin, Italy, which the good doctor had named a "plethusmograph."[31]

Whether he went often to theater we do not know. But it seems probable that he did, for in the following year his editorial page contained a paragraph which objected with some energy to the great amount of shooting on the stage, "fancy shooting," as it was called. Wise asserted that this ought to be prohibited by law.[32]

He harped on Wagner's music quite often, whenever—in fact—it came to his notice. At a May Festival in Cincinnati Theodore Thomas had presented some of it. Once again Wise declared that:

> The Wagner music, it may be set down as a fact, will be defunct after this, at least in this Western country. Exit Wagner![33]

It must have been just about that time that kindergartens were invented. Wise did not approve of them. He thought it was not good to put too much strain on the minds of children when they were very young, because it would tend to stunt their physical development and tire them out.[34]

Another evidence of the wide gamut of his interests was in an article in 1897 on Jewish references to chess (perhaps especially in Abraham Ibn Ezra), chiefly in the Middle Ages, and also for women.[35]

Sometimes, however, his humor and his whimsicality played closer to home. Like almost every rabbi he was disturbed by the indifference of some of his flock, their apparent lethargy. Of this he wrote amusingly in 1893:

> We have quite a respectable number of lackadaisical members in the congregation; they look as pensive, tired, over-satiated, and dull as that old bachelor after a long debauch, although the Germans call it *Maechteldraetig*, which is of the feminine gender. It is not utter indifference, it is merely an affected pensiveness, a sort of mimical "I do not care, I know it all anyhow," "I have no special use for it." It is after all but skin deep. The slightest explosion of events or thoughts changes the physiognomy. A patent remedy, if but of momentary effect,

> applied by Rabbi Akia of old and many old teachers down to Rabbi Eleazar Flackels of Prague, is to tell them a conundrum, however quaint, simple, foolish or otherwise, then put some grains of spicy truth into the solution, a few drops of sarcasm would not hurt, and it will work like a charm in changing the lackadaisical to some kind of brilliancy. Preachers and other public speakers will find it very useful to have a dozen or two of such conundrums ready made on hand, to use one or two of them in proper time and place.[36]

Another comment by Wise on his own editorial tasks was in the following rules he thought useful for an editor:

> Mind your own business; think before you print; do not meddle in private affairs; do not write on things on which you are no authority; never quarrel for the sake of quarreling; never throw suspicion on the motives of the one you quarrel with. Here is the holy seven![37]

The very last of these curiosities, of these digressions of his interest and talent was appropriately enough again on Richard Wagner, whom in 1898 Wise accused of defaming Jewish composers [only too correctly!], also of stealing the march of *Die Meistersinger* from "The Prophet" by Giacomo Meyerbeer, a Jewish composer who had befriended Wagner and whom he berated. Wise claimed that the copy was quite inferior to the original.[38]

Thus ends this random list, which we have introduced merely for purposes of spice, to be added to the serious fare that has preceded it. These filled the interstices of his mind. They meant no more than this.

Appendices

Appendix One

BIBLIOGRAPHY

Much of this Bibliography is drawn, in content and form, from that on Isaac M. Wise, compiled by Adolph S. Oko, then Librarian of the Hebrew Union College, and published as part of the life of Isaac M. Wise by his grandson, Judge Max B. May. It is on pages 399 to 408. To it we have added much that has appeared later (the book was published in 1916), and correlative material in various related fields. In the foreword Oko noted that the Bibliography did not include any thorough references to the files of the *American Israelite*, the *Asmonean*, and the *Deborah*. It does not include Wise's speeches in the Proceedings of the Union of American Hebrew Congregations, and only about half of the contributions Wise made to the *Occident*.

We shall list not only the writings of Isaac M. Wise himself, but also those about him, those that refer in part or in passing to him; books that cover our introductory chapters on the background in Europe; and finally a long list of references, to various magazines in various languages, compiled by Gotthard Deutsch as part of his general Index on contemporary Jewish matters.

The Writings of Isaac M. Wise

(Compiled alphabetically, not chronologically)

American Judaism. Its record from New Year, 5646 A.M., to Dec. 1887 (in the *American Jews' Annual*, 1888), pp. 35-47.

American Judaism. A Record of American Judaism from the year 5645 A.M. (in the *American Jews' Annual*), Cincinnati, 1885.

Aphorisms on Ethics, 1891 (included in SWIW).

The Apologetics of Judaism, 1887 (included in SWIW).

Les Asmonéens, Drame en cinq actes, en prose, tiré du Roman, "The First of the Maccabees" by Isaac M. Wise, par M. le docteur Bliden; avec autorization de l'auteur. Traduction par I. Epstein. Printed in Jerusalem; École de filles de Saffed, 1893; 111 pages; 16°.

New Edition of the Babylonian Talmud, English translation. Original text, formulated and punctuated by Michael L. Rodkinson. Revised and corrected by the Rev. Dr. Isaac M. Wise, vol. 1-2—Tractate Sabbath, N. Y., New Amsterdam Book Co. (cop. 1896).

Chapter in Continuation of my "History of the Israelitish Nation." Chap. XIII (588-536 B.C.E.). In AMI, Cincinnati, 1855-56, vol. 2, pp. 225-26.

The Combat of the People; or Hillel and Herod. A historical romance of the time of Herod I. Cincinnati, Bloch and Co., 1859. 151 pages, 8°. Appeared originally in AMI.

The Cosmic God. A fundamental philosophy in popular lectures. Cincinnati, Office AMI and DEB, 1876. 181 pages, 1 portrait, 8°.

A Defense of Judaism *versus* Proselytizing Christianity, 1889, AMI, Cincinnati and Chicago. Preface, pp. 5-129, 8°.

The Divine Service for American Israelites for the Day of Atonement (appended: A selection of Psalms—in Hebrew), Cincinnati, Bloch and Co., 1866, 55 pages, 16°.

The Divine Service of American Israelites for the New Year, Cincinnati, Bloch and Co. (a copy of that of 1866), 212 pages, 16°. In Hebrew and English. Oko notes, "This and the next were from Part II of *Minhag America*, and were 'in use throughout the country until the appearance —in 1894—of the second volume of the *Union Prayerbook*.'" Referred to in SWIW, p. 98.

The Effects of Biblical Theology. A Sermon delivered at Charleston, S. C., In OCC, 1850-1, pp. 217-31.

The End of Popes, Nobles, and Kings, or The Progress of Civilization (a lecture), delivered before the Hebrew Young Men's Literary Association of the City of New York (Dec. 22, 1852), J. Muehlhaeuser, Printer, N. Y., 1852, 20 pages, 12°.

Erklaerung, Aufruf an die Rabbinern, Redactuere und Herausgeber juedischer Zeitschriften in Europa im Namen der Humanitaet und speciell im Namen eines betrogenen Weibes, Harriet Silbermann aus Chicago. Juedische Zeitschrift fuer Wissenschraft und Leben. Breslau, 1862, 8°. Jahrgang I, pp. 163-64.

An Essay on the Temperance Question. Cincinnati, 188-(?), 8 pages, 8°. Read before the Friends of Inquiry in Cincinnati.

The Essence of Judaism: for teachers and pupils, and for self-instruction. Cincinnati, Bloch and Co., 1861, 65 pages, 16°. Oko adds: "With the publication of this book the popularization of Biblical Judaism began." This comment is from a MSS note by the author on a fly-leaf of the HUC library copy.

The Essence of Judaism: for teachers and pupils, and for self-instruction. Second edition, Cincinnati, Bloch and Co., 1868, 80 pages, 16°.

The Ethics of Judaism (in "Judaism at the World's Parliament of Religions"), Cincinnati, 1894, pp. 99-106, 8°.

The First of the Maccabees. Cincinnati, Bloch and Co., 1860. 180 pages, 8°. The original was in AMI, and treats "of the period from the arousal of the Jewish people by the Asmonean and his sons to the rededication of the Temple at Jerusalem."

The First of the Maccabees. A historical novel. Cincinnati, Bloch Publishing and Printing Co., 180 pages, 8°. The same edition as the preceding, with a new cover.

The Fourth of July, Sermon. In the "American Jewish Pulpit," 1881, pp. 219-26.

Freedom, Justice, and Fidelity. A Passover Sermon (in CCAR "Sermons by American Rabbis"), Chicago, 1896, pp. 180-88.

Future Reward and Punishment. Also in OCC, 1849-50, pp. 86-89 (delivered originally at Congregation Shaar Hashamayim, New York).

Gebetbuch fuer den Offentlichen Gottesdienst, und die Privat-Andacht. Theil I. Geordnet and uebersetzt von der in der Cleveland Conferenz ernannten liturgischen Commission, den Rabbinern, Kalisch, Rothenheim, und Wise. Cincinnati, Bloch u. Co., 1857, iv, pp. 5-171, 16°.

Gebete der Israeliten in America (Verbessert von der Conferenz). Appended: Gebete zur oeffentlichen und haeuslichen Andacht. Sammlung von Gebete fuer alle Verhaeltnisse des Lebens, fuer Frauen und Maedchen. Cincinnati, Bloch and Co. (this is the copy of 1873), pp. 6-271, 16°. In Hebrew and German.

The Genealogy of Joseph, after Matthew. In OCC, 1849-50, pp. 375-76.

Genius in History and the History of Genius. A lecture delivered in St. Louis (to be found in CCAR, "Sermons by American Rabbis," Chicago, 1896, pp. 200-216).

Hebrew Monotheism: A Dedicatory Sermon, in the "American Jewish Pulpit," Cincinnati, 1881; pp. 199-208.

The History of the Hebrews' Second Commonwealth, with special reference to its literature, culture, and the origin of rabbinism and Christianity. Cincinnati, Bloch and Co., 1880, 386 pages, 8°.

History of the Israelitish Nation, from Abraham to the Present Time. Derived from original sources. Vol. I, Albany, J. Munsell, 1854, xxiv, 560 pages, 8°.

The History of the K.K.Bene Yeshurun of Cincinnati, Ohio, from the date of its organization. Published in commemoration of the 50th anniversary of its incorporation, by a committee of the board of trustees. Cincinnati, Feb. 28, 1892 (by Isaac M. Wise and Max B. May). Bloch Printing Co., 1892, 471 pages, 4 plates, 1 portrait, 8°.

Adolph Huebsche, Biographie (to be found in Huebsche, Adolph, A Memorial, New York, 1885) 8°, pp. i-xiii.

Hymns, Psalms, and Prayers, in English and German. By Isaac M. Wise and others. Cincinnati, Bloch and Co., published in 1868, 263 pages, 16°. A note in it: "With the present volume, the author concludes his labour for the *Minhag America*. . . . All original pieces in this volume written by others than the author are marked with their respective names. Pieces adapted from other collections are also properly noted. All other pieces are claimed by the author as his own productions."

Introduction (I, Reading of Scriptures. II, Expounding Scriptures. III, The *Maggid* and *Darshon*. IV, The Retrogression. V, The Sermon in America). In CCAR, "Sermons by American Rabbis," Chicago, 1896, pp. vii-xiv, 8°.

An Introduction to the Theology of Judaism. Delivered at the World's Congress of Religions (the publisher not given here), pp. 1-22.

Hymns and Prayers, in English and German. By Isaac M. Wise and others. Cincinnati and Chicago; Bloch Publishing and Printing Co., 1890, ix, pp. 10-263, 16°.

Slight typographical alterations from that previously noted (note by Oko).

Introduction to a Bibliography of the Jewish Periodical Press (in "Judaism at the World's Parliament of Religions," Cincinnati, 1894), pp. 402-409.

An Introduction to the Theology of Judaism, delivered at the World's Congress of Religions, published Cincinnati, 1894, 22 pages, 8°.

A Jewish State Impossible. An article in the New York Times on Zionism, September 8, 1897.

Judaism and Christianity, Their Agreements and Disagreements. A series of Friday evening lectures, delivered at the Plum St. Temple, Cincinnati, Bloch and Co., 1883, 123 pages, 8°.

Judaism: Its Doctrines and Duties. Cincinnati, Office of the AMI (the copy of 1872), 83 pages, 12°.

This is "The Essence of Judaism" (1861) rewritten "in the popular and catechetic form," to which is added "the main Scriptural passage to each paragraph."

The Law, *Hebrew Review,* Cincinnati, 1880. v. 1, pp. 12-31.

This (Oko) is a discussion of the essay, the argument of which was delivered orally by Wise at the Conference of the Rabbinical Literary Association, July 14, 1880, on pp. 74-79. Reprinted in SWIW, 1900, pp. 125-52.

A Lecture, delivered January 7, 1869, before the Theological and Religious Library Association of Cincinnati. Oko gives the title as "Our Country's Place in History" (*vide supra*), pp. 1-7.

Letters on Christianity, to the Rev. M. R. Miller, OCC, 1850-51, pp. 232-37, 309-14, and 594-99.

Letter to a Gentleman Who with his Family Wishes to Embrace Judaism, 1860 (source not given). In SWIW, pp. 400-06.

The Main Lesson of Israel's Sanctuary, A Sermon. In "The American Jewish Pulpit," 1861, Cincinnati, pp. 209-18.

The Light, A Sermon, delivered at the syngagogue, Shaar Hashamayim, in New York, March 3, 5609 (OCC, Phila., 1849-50, 8°, Vol. 7, pp. 12-25).

The Martyrdom of Jesus of Nazareth. A historic-critical treatise of the last chapters of the Gospel. Cincinnati, Office of the AMI (copy of 1874), 134 pages, 8°.

This is headed "Only truth in the name of Jehovah" (II Chron. Chap. 17, verse 15).

The Massorah and the Massoretic Text, *Hebrew Review,* Cincinnati, 1881-82. vol. 2, pp. 107-17. (Reads "To be continued," but no more appeared.)

Men More Instructive than Words. Sketch of a Chanuccah Sermon, in "The American Jewish Pulpit," Cincinnati, 1881, pp. 185-89.

The Messiah. Also in OCC, 1849-50, pp. 181-92, and 229-44 (delivered at Shaar Hashamayim, New York). Part I, The Mission of the People of Israel. A sermon, delivered at Albany, February 12, 5609. ". . . the intolerant and fanatical lectures of a minister of the Baptist Church in this city gave rise to this course of lectures. They were delivered before a numerous audience of Jews and Christians.").

Minhag America. The daily prayers for American Israelites, as revised in conference. Cincinnati, The Bloch Publishing and Printing Co., 1887 (a copy of that of 1872), 138 pages, 16°. The Hebrew differs from the previous edition only in slight typographical alterations.

Minhag America. The daily prayers, for American Israelites (a school edition) Cincinnati, The Bloch Publishing and Printing Co. (a copy of that of 1872), 138 pages, 16°, Hebrew only.

Minhag America, Cincinnati, The Bloch Publishing and Printing Co., 1889 (a copy of that of 1872), 3 p. 1. pp. 6-271. 16°. Hebrew and English edition, frequently reprinted.

Minhag America. The daily prayers for American Israelites, as revised in conference (Appended: Select prayers—in English—for various occasions in life). Cincinnati, Bloch and Co. (a copy of that of 1872) 3 p. 1. pp. 6-271. 16°. In Hebrew and English.

Minhag America. Daily prayers. Seventh revised stereotype edition. Cincinnati, Bloch and Co., 1870, 160 pages, 16°. This is in Hebrew only.

Minhag America. Gebetbuch fuer den oeffentlichen Gottesdienst und die Privat-Andacht. Zweite verbesserte Ausgabe. Cincinnati, Bloch and Co., 1864 (copied from 1861), 4 p., pp. 6-149, 16°. Hebrew and German side by side. The Hebrew text from the plates of the 1857 edition.

Minhag America. The daily prayer, part I. Revised and compiled by the committee of the Cleveland Conference. Translated by Isaac M. Wise, Cincinnati, Bloch and Co., 5617 (1857), iv, pp. 5-120, 16°.

Minhag America. A form of worship for American Israelites in Hebrew. Also issued together with the following English and German versions. Cincinnati, Bloch and Co., 1857, 144 pages, 16°.

Moreh Nebuchim. Liber ductor perplexorum. OCC, v.8 (1850-51), pp. 31-34. A description of the contents of Maimonides' work.

Moses, The Man and Statesman. A lecture. Cincinnati, Bloch and Co., 1883. 28 pages, 8°. Reprinted in SWIW, 1900, pp. 153-78.

The Origin of Christianity, and a Commentary to the Acts of the Apostles. Cincinnati, Bloch and Co., 1868, vii, pp. 10-535, 12°.

The Outlines of Judaism, an argument before the convention of the "Free Religious Association." Boston, Mass., 1869. In SWIW, pp. 212 ff.

Paul and the Mystics. 1870. In SWIW, pp. 352-75.

Presidential Addresses, delivered at the CCAR. YEARBOOKS, 1891-1899 (v. i., pp. 11-21; v. 2, pp. 6-11; v. 3, pp. 1-10; v. 4, pp. 24-29; pp. 67-76; v. 5, pp. 6-11; v. 6, pp. 11-19; v. 7, pp. vi-xiii; v. 8, pp. 8-16; v. 9, pp. 22-31).

Principles of Judaism, Nos. I-IV, OCC, 1850-51, pp. 492-96, and 541-44; v. 9 (1851-2), pp. 14-19, 187-95, and 298-305. These are in the form of letters to the editor.

Pronaos to Holy Writ, establishing, on documentary evidence, the authorship, date, form, and contents of each of its books and the authenticity of the Pentateuch. Cincinnati, R. Clarke and Co., 1891, 193 pages. 8°. Reviewed by Israel Abrahams in *The Jewish World,* London, 1914, May 6, pp. 24-25.

A Record of American Judaism for 5646 A.M. American Jews' Annual, Cincinnati, 1886, pp. 52-68, 8°.

Reformed Judaism, 1871. In SWIW, pp. 260-351.

Reminiscences. Translated from the German and edited with an introduction by David Philipson, Cincinnati, L. Wise and Co., 1901. 367 pages, 1 plate, 3 portraits, 8°.

Reminiscences (of Max Lilienthal). In The Hebrew Review, vol. 2, pp. 184-190, 8°. Published anonymously.

Rosh Hashanah, A Sermon, in The American Jewish Pulpit, Cincinnati, 1881, pp. 127-37, 8°.

Selected Writings. With a biography by the editors, David Philipson and Louis Grossmann. Published under the auspices of the Alumni Association of the HUC, Cincinnati, R. Clarke and Co., 1900. 419 pages, 8°.

A Sketch of Judaism in America, American Jews' Annual, Cincinnati, 1894, pp. 37-55, 8°.

The Sources of the Theology of Judaism, 1887. In SWIW, p. 197.

Three Lectures on the Origins of Christianity. Cincinnati, Bloch and Co., 1873, 33 pages, 8°. Lecture I, Jesus, the Pharisee; II, The Apostles and the Essenes; III, Paul and the Mystics (Lecture III reprinted in SWIW, 1900), pp. 352-75.

The Wandering Jew, A lecture, Cincinnati, 1877, 12 pages, 8°. Originally printed in AMI, Vol. 29, No. 15. Reprinted in SWIW, pp. 179-96. This treats of the part the Jew has played in the world's civilization.

The Word of God. A Sabbath *Nachamu* sermon, in "The American Jewish Pulpit," 1891, pp. 227-34.

The World of My Books, in DEB, Vol. XLII, beginning Sept. 17, 1896, No. 12; ending No. 38, March 18, 1897. Not completed. In German. Translated and separately published. An off-print in the "American Jewish Archives," June, 1954. Translated, with an Introduction and Explanatory Notes, by Albert H. Friedlander, Cincinnati.

Zionism. In the Hebrew Union College Journal, Cincinnati, 1899-1900, vol. 4, pp. 45-47, 8°.

Books About Isaac M. Wise

Biographical and Other Essays

The Americanization of Isaac Mayer Wise, by Jacob Rader Marcus. Privately printed, Cincinnati MCMXXXI (1931). Material drawn from memoirs and writings of Isaac M. Wise, from the *Asmonean* of March 17-24, 1854, where he writes of his life in Bohemia; from the *Reminiscences;* and from *The American Israelite*. Actually an Address on Founders' Day, at the Hebrew Union College, March 28, 1931.

The Attitude of Isaac M. Wise toward Zionism and Palestine. American Jewish Archives, Vol. III, No. 2, January 1951, pp. 3-21.

Isaac Mayer Wise, Pioneer of American Judaism by Jos. H. Gumbiner, Union of American Hebrew Congregations, 1959.

Isaac Mayer Wise, the Founder of American Judaism, A Biography, by Max B. May, A.M., Judge of the Court of Common Pleas, Hamilton County, Ohio; illustrated, G. P. Putnam's Sons, N. Y. and London. The Knickerbocker Press, 1916.

Isaac Mayer Wise's "Jesus Himself," by Samuel Sandmel, of the Faculty of the Hebrew Union College, Cincinnati, Ohio. Marcus Festschrift Volume.

Rabbi in America, the Story of Isaac M. Wise, by Israel Knox; Little, Brown, and Co., New York, 1957; 173 pages.

The Rabbi, the Man, and His Message, by Leo M. Franklin, 1938.

Sinai to Cincinnati, Lay Views on the Writings of Isaac M. Wise, etc., by Dena Wilansky, Renaissance Book Co., New York, 1937.

Collateral Books About Wise

American Jewry and the Civil War, by Bertram W. Korn, Jewish Publication Society of America, 1957, 331 pages.

As Yesterday When It Is Past, a History of the Isaac M. Wise Temple—K.K.B'nai Yeshurun—of Cincinnati, in Commemoration of the Centenary of its founding, by James G. Heller, Cincinnati, 1942, 250 pages.

Centenary Papers and Others, David Philipson, 1919.

Eventful Years and Experiences, Studies in 19th Century American Jewish History, by Bertram W. Korn, American Jewish Archives, Cincinnati, 1954, 249 pages.

History of Beth Emeth Congregation, of Albany, published in 1910.

The Jewish Encyclopedia, New York and London, Funk and Wagnalls Co., 1907.

Judaism at the World's Parliament of Religions, published by the Union of American Hebrew Congregations, Cincinnati, 1894.

The Reform Movement in Judaism, Second Edition, by David Philipson, Macmillan Company, New York, 1931 (originally published in 1907), 503 pages.

Universal Jewish Encyclopedia, edited by Isaac Landman, published in New York in 1943.

Yearbooks, the Central Conference of American Rabbis, from 1889 to 1900.

Books on European and American History in the 17th and 18th Centuries

The Cambridge Modern History, Planned by Lord Action, Vol. VI, the 18th Century, N. Y., Macmillan Co., Cambridge England, at the University Press, 1934, 887 pages. The first edition was published in 1904.

Grant Moves South, by Bruce Catton, Little, Brown and Co., 1960.

Man and the Western World, by John Geise, Hinds, Hayden and Eldredge, N. Y. and Phila., Revised to 1947, 1080 pages.

World History, by J. C. Revill, Longmans, Green and Co., London, etc., 1953, 760 pages.

The Age of the Democratic Revolution, A Political History of Europe and America, 1760-1800, by R. R. Palmer, Princeton Univ. Press, 1959.

Books About European Jews, also in Austria and Bohemia

Aus Zwei Jahrhunderten, von N.M. Gelber, Beitraege zur Neueren Geschichte der Juden. Published by R. Loewit, Wien und Leipzig, 1924, 265 pages.

History and Destiny of the Jews, by Jos. Kastein, translated from the German by Huntley Patterson, Viking Press, N.Y., 1934. 464 pages.

History of the Jews, by Heinrich Graetz, Phila., Jewish Publication Society of America, revised Edition, Vol. V., 766 pages.

A History of the Jewish People, by Margolis and Marx, Jewish Publication Society of America, Phila., 1927, 752 pages.

History of the Jews, by Solomon Grayzell, Phila., Jewish Publication Society of America, 1947, 835 pages.

Jahrbuch der Gesellschaft fuer Geschichte der Juden in der Czechoslovak Republik, 6th Annual Volume, Prague, 1934, Taussig and Taussig, Prague; Zur Geschichte der Juden in Boehmen in den letzten Jahren Josefs II und unter Leopold II. Von Regierung Rat Dr. Ludwig Singer.

Materialen zur Geschichte der Juden in Boehmen, von Dr. M. H. Friedlander, Bruenn, Verlag von Bernhard Epstein, 1888, 77 pages.

Appendix Two

BIBLIOGRAPHY

The Deutsch Index

During his lifetime the late Gotthard Deutsch, Professor of History at the Hebrew Union College, made a voluminous collection of index-cards, compiling historic data, references, etc. Part of it was devoted to facts and articles that had to do with the life and work of Isaac M. Wise. The collection is now in the American Jewish Archives at the Hebrew Union College in Cincinnati, Ohio. We list those that have to do with Wise, even though some of them refer to magazines and articles which have already been treated in the body of the foregoing text. We include Deutsch's comments, expanding abbreviations for the sake of clarity.

AMI Wise attacked by Emil G. Hirsch and his father, Samuel Hirsch, AMI, Dec. 3, 1880, p. 179.

AMI Wise on the subject of Divorce; Vol. 3, No. 13, pp. 96 ff.; pp. 120 ff.; also in No. 25, 1862, p. 91; No. 28, July 9, 1862, pp. 109 f.

AMI On the Ten Commandments as the basis of all laws, on the ground of Halevi's *Kuzari,* and Nachmanides' commentary to Canticles. Cf. also American Jewish Review Vol. 1, No. 18. Reference in AMI, Oct. 15, 1860, p. 124.

AMI Again on the Ten Commandments and the Law. AMI, July 29, 1881, p. 36.

AMI On the Ten Commandments and the Mosaic Law; an article strongly endorsing Wise's ideas, which appeared in the Hebrew Review. This also strongly condemns Kohler's point of view. AMI, March 11, 1861, p. 293.

AMI Defending Wise's theory of the Ten Commandments, refers to the Tosefta (Shabuot III, edition Zuckermandel, pp. 449-50, where an infidel is defined as one who does not keep the commandments, and only the last six commandments are quoted). AMI, May 13, 1881, p. 356.

AMI Wise reads a paper at the convention of the Rabbinical Literary Association in Milwaukee, July 13, 1880, claiming that the Ten Commandments are immutable. Also in AZJ for 1880, p. 521.

AMI Wise's mother, Regina, died in Peoria, Ill., June 11, 1880. AMI, June 18, 1880.

AMI Unsigned editorial, Oct. 10, 1879, p. 4: "The modern redeemer of the Jews was no particular man, the two revolutions, American and French . . . were the redeemers in the bloody garments prophesied by Isaiah (chap. 63).

AMI "Every word of the Bible is true, historically, ethically, metaphysically or poetically. The great art of expounding it correctly is to distinguish which is which." AMI, Dec. 12, 1879, p. 4.

AMI The story of the serpent in Genesis had for its object "to dethrone the brutal god" (the serpent god), as he [the author of Genesis] did in many other instances. AMI, Sept. 26, 1879, p. 4.

AMI "A Polish gentleman translated Shakespeare's *Romeo and Juliet* into Hebrew verse. What a waste of time!" AMI, Sept, 12, 1879, p. 6.

AMI "No Jewish congregation will succeed in establishing permanently a Sunday service." AMI, Aug. 3, 1879, p. 4.

AMI Opening address at the HUC, Sept. 1, 1879, "this shall be an orthodox Jewish academy . . . in which Jewish learning for its own sake shall be fostered . . . none of the heterodoxies of the Middle Ages . . . none of the ingenious hypotheses in mythology and philology . . . the Massoretic text of the Bible is the rock of foundation." AMI, Sept. 5, 1879, p. 4.

AMI An editorial, "Maimonides also calls Prophets and Hagiography *Divray kabalah* (the words of tradition), accepted, received traditional Scriptures in contradistinction to the Pentateuch." AMI, March 18, 1881, p. 300.

AMI Takes issue with Kaufmann Kohler, who in a paper published in the Hebrew Review, said that he follows German Protestant Theology about Higher Criticism. Wise says this would be enough to make him reject it. AMI, Feb. 4, 1881, p. 252.

AMI "Bible criticism is actually a shapeless conglomeration of hypotheses in which there is vastly more error . . . than truth, more philological quibbling and self-fabricated historical items than grains of fact." In an editorial, AMI, Jan. 9, 1880, p. 4.

AMI Wise condemns the practice of discriminating between German and Russian Jews, saying that this thing must be stopped. AMI, Feb. 26, 1881, p. 276.

AMI Refers to a letter in the Cincinnati Enquirer, of Jan. 2, 1878, by David Rosenberg (a converted Jewish missionary, probably), who advocated a Jewish state in Palestine, under American protection, and for the purpose of spreading Christianity among Jews. Wise writes that Jews do not wish to go to Palestine.

AMI An article, Sept. 8, 1876, which pleads for complete equality for women in the synagogue. There is a satirical reply by L.N. Dembitz, which alludes to Wise's marrying a woman to the brother of her deceased husband, without *Halitzah*. Dembitz inquires how a woman would feel, if she were called to the Torah to read Leviticus chap. 18. Dembitz also says that Wise asks for union, but causes disunion. Wise replies: "If any body of men would ever assume the function of governing my conscience or conviction, and bid me to say so and not otherwise, that body would have to count me out, for I give permission to no human being to silence my conviction or conscience. . . ." Wise then proceeds to justify his own practice: if a man is permitted to marry the sister of his lost wife, then why not vice versa? In Sept. 15, 1876.

AMI Wise on a report that Jews have bought Palestine. Editorial: "The American Jews are Americans, as the German Jews are Germans . . .

and will positively not go back to Palestine as long as there is a speck of civilization in their respective countries . . . all those rumors are falsehoods supported in England by the opponents of Disraeli and the supporters of Gladstone. AMI, Jan. 26, 1877, p. 7.

AMI Wise in criticism of S. Solis-Cohen: "we . . . think the habitable globe must be one holy law, every city a Jerusalem, every house a temple of the Most High, and every person an anointed priest. None of your racial narrowness for us . . . to lift the world above it, is the very object of the Jewish people." AMI, Nov. 1, 1878.

AMI Wise, "The Jew's nationality has been before this latter event [that is, the destruction of Jerusalem] independent of every soil; it has been and is now in his blood, in the purity of his race, in his belief, modes of thinking and feeling; it is all intellectual and moral without any reference to soil, climate, and outer circumstances." AMI, Jan. 24, 1879, p. 4.

AMI Wise discusses Laurence Oliphant's scheme for colonizing Palestine (Cf. the JE Vol. IX, p. 393), and says: "We want no Jewish princes, no Jewish country or government. The world is our country and justice our prince. We want freedom and equal rights for all with equal duties." AMI, June 26, 1880, p. 6.

AMI Wise announces that he has been elected rabbi of Anshe Chesed in New York with a salary of $8000, insurance of $15,000, and a guarantee of a pension of $15,000 in the event of his retirement. AMI, Aug. 15, 1873.

AMI Two orthodox congregations in Cincinnati, Shearith Israel and Ahabath Achim, pass resolutions, asking Anshe Chesed, New York, to release Wise, for he cannot be spared in Cincinnati, on account of the proposed theological College. AMI, Oct. 24, 1873, p. 7.

AMI Discusses Geiger's proposal (In *Juedische Zeitung* VIII, pp. 90-91), that civil divorce should be regarded as enough. I.M. Wise says: "We can not do it. . . . As long as marriage is connected with religious feeling, divorce can not be justly without it." AMI, Nov. 25, 1870, p. 8.

AMI Wise pleads for the retention of Hebrew in the services, and for educational purposes. AMI, Dec. 17, 1869, p. 8.

AMI Wise says that a rabbi cannot act contrary to the wishes of his congregation (?), AMI, July 15, 1870, p. 11.

AMI Wise pleads for establishment of a Jewish Publishing Society, April 9, 1869.

AMI He is married to Selma Bondi, April 24, 1876. In AMI, April 28, 1876.

AMI Wise opposes the continued use of German in America, not only because of the presence of anti-Semitism in Germany. "We for our part have always been opposed to perpetuating the German in the American synagogue, because we do not wish to be strangers at home." AMI, May 13, 1881, p. 256.

AMI "Maimonides calls the Prophets and Hagiographae *divray kabalah*, 'accepted,' 'received,' 'Traditional,' in contradistinction to the Pentateuch, which is 'Written Law,' 'Scripture.'" AMI, March 16, 1881, p. 300.

AMI Wise's rationalistic view on Jesus. June 24, 1881, p. 406.

AMI Kohler had introduced Sunday services, June 13, 1881, at Congregation Beth El, N.Y., probably to check the movement towards Ethical Culture. Wise condemns this move strongly. June 24, 1881, pp. 402 and 404.

AMI Some case where a meat-inspector had taken a bribe. Wise writes: "The . . . case convinces us again of the necessity of our *Shehitah* and *Bedika* laws. . . . The *Shohet* cannot be bribed so easily. Our laws need some improvement, but on the whole they are an excellent protection against numerous diseases. March 18, 1870, p. 9.

OCC A. Jacobson, probably of New York, charges Wise with duplicity. In New York, Wise has withheld his liberal views. But in Har Sinai in Baltimore, Wise blamed the people for eating *terefah,* and advocated placing fruits on the pulpit on *Sukkot,* instead of the traditional *Esrog.* Joseph Levy of Syracuse reports that Wise, in that city, boasted that his congregation let him off of services on week-days, because he would not lay *tefillin,* and that he said smoking a cigar did not violate the Sabbath. OCC, Vol. VIII, 1860, p. 140.

OCC An Article on Feb. 14, 1849, Wise wrote: "I am a Reformer . . . none can stop the stream of time, but I have always the *halacha* for my basis. . . . I have brought my people so far to observe the Sabbath." OCC, Vol. VI, pp. 616-17.

OCC Court verdict in Wise's favor, declaring that Spanier had had no right to interfere with Wise's duties. Spanier was fined $1000 and costs, on May 17, 1851. OCC, Vol. IX, 1851, pp. 166-67.

OCC "The learned stand at such an elevation above the people . . . that they can lead the congregations as they please. We have in our mind especially . . . Dr. Isaac M. Wise, who seems to have obtained almost unlimited control over entire districts and he would be irresistible, were it not that an antagonistic influence of a more radical kind yet, has been brought forward in the person of Dr. Einhorn." OCC, Vol. XXV, 1867, pp. 422-23.

SINAI Einhorn reviews the rationalistic interpretation of miracles in Wise's History. SINAI, Vol. I, pp. 8-9.

DEB Wise condemns the radical reformers, especially the abrogation of Hebrew, and of the reading of the Torah. DEB, 1872, also AMI, 1872, p. 132.

AZJ Wise attacked for his inconsistency by Ludwig Philippson, 1856, he did not deny the coming of the Messiah (p. 207).

OCC Leeser replies to the article in the ASM of April 25, 1854, by Wise. Leeser charges Wise with fondness for notoriety, and claims he has no right to call himself "Doctor." And, after Wise "edited a newspaper miscalled the Israelite," Leeser claims he had to correct Wise's English, and "Wise himself has not been able to cleanse himself from the charge of falsifying Scriptures." OCC, Vol. XII, pp. 148-53, 353-58.

OCC Leeser attacks Wise, "for rude, anonymous criticisms which appeared to the disgrace of the conductor in the Cincinnati paper." There is a good satirical poem in Hebrew, entitled *yehi or* ("Let there be light"). Again Leeser insinuates that Wise has no doctor's diploma. He says "Wise is all things to all men"; "the erratic conduct, erroneous published works and unwise declarations of the rabbi of the Cincinnati B'nai Jeshurun Congregation." This refers to Wise's attempt to form a *Beth Din* with Lilienthal and Rothenheim. OCC, Vol. XIII, pp. 164, 365, 403, 421, 426, and 459.

OCC Leeser's view that people who deny the authorities cannot expect religious sentiments in their flocks. He refers to Wise's attacks on certain ceremonies, like *tefillin, tsitsith, lulab,* and Wise's theology that the Ten Commandments are all of Judaism, though at the same time Wise considers them human (?). Leeser appeals that polemics be stopped, and each work for Judaism in his own way. OCC, Vol. XVII, p. 205.

OCC A Baltimore German paper contains an advertisement, giving notice that Congregation Oheb Shalom had introduced reforms in 1858, had adopted Minhag *RV'K* (in Hebrew) representing the initials of Rothenheim, Wise and Kalisch. OCC, Vol. XVI, p. 358.

AMI Wise proves from the parallelism of Isaiah chap. 32, vs. 9, and Genesis, Chap. 4, vs. 23, that Isaiah knew Genesis (this is about the Higher Criticism). AMI, 1881, Aug. 19, p. 60.

AMI Wise pleads for a Synod, at a rabbinical conference in Chicago, declaring that American Judaism then consisted of mere negations. Wise was violently abused by Samuel Hirsch. AMI, Aug. 19, 1881, p. 59.

OCC A Hebrew letter by Wise addressed to Illowy, dated the 6th of Adar (March 6), 1854. The Hebrew, Deutsch writes in the Index, is often quite faulty, and cites instances. OCC, Vol. XII, pp. 33-38.

OCC "The Effect of Biblical Theology," a sermon delivered by Wise at Charleston, S.C. OCC, Vol. VIII, pp. 217-31.

OCC "Future Reward and Punishment," in OCC, Vol. VII, pp. 86-89. . . . M. N. Noah . . . denies the existence of the devil, hell and brimstone, together with all popular absurdities of this kind. I have done the same in the OCC of the year 5608. OCC, Vol. VIII, p. 86.

ASM A letter from Wise on the organization of the ASM, Vol. I, No. 3, Nov. 9, 1849, signed Rabbi Wise, D.D.

AZJ A controversy with Jastrow. 1867, p. 842.

AZJ Reports that 2000 copies of Wise's History have been sold; 1854, pp. 161 and 260.

AZJ an enthusiastic description of Wise's activities in Cincinnati, by Dr. R . . . d (A. Rosenfeld), 1854, pp. 654 ff.

DER ISRAELIT Wise is attacked and it is charged that his daughter was converted to Christianity, and married a Christian. Only the second half is true. DER ISR. 1884, p. 781.

AMI An unsigned article, but obviously by Wise, reports that, when he came to the United States in 1846, there were 31 synagogues, having 3000 families, one Jewish paper, and no charitable institution. AMI, June 20, 1873, p. 4.

MENORAH An article by Kohler on "Dr. I.M. Wise and American Judaism." "Many of us who opposed and ridiculed Isaac M. Wise for his lack of learning, lack of principle, lack of system, shown in whatever he wrote and published, must give him credit. . . ." etc. MEN, Vol. 26, pp. 240-44 (1899)

MENORAH Article on Wise, interesting, written by one of his opponents M(oritz) E(llinger). Vol. 28, pp. 215-19(1899).

AHIASAF A Hebrew translation of Wise's "First of the Maccabees," appearing in Jerusalem, and made by Epstein. AHIASAF, 1895, No. 6, p. 424.

AZJ A letter by Leeser, describing Wise's plans for the Cleveland Conference, Vol. 20, 1856, p. 574.

AZJ Wise's prayer at the opening of the U.S. Congress, 1893, No. 7, appendix, p. 4.

AZJ "Isaac M. Wise und das Amerikanische Judenthum," by Prof. G. Deutsch. Wise's life, position, and accomplishments. AZJ, 1900, p. 184.

ARCHIVES ISRAELITES Wise speaks at memorial services for Lincoln, with a Catholic priest and a Protestant minister, 1865, p. 507.

ARCHIVES ISRAELITES Wise occupies the pulpit of Sheerith Israel of San Francisco, Calif., 1873, p. 701.

DER ISRAELITISCHE VOLKSLEHRER A controversy with David Einhorn, 1856, No. 10, p. 48.

DER ISRAELITISCHE VOLKSLEHRER Wise's plans for Reform, 1857, No. 55, p. 299.

DER ISRAELITISCHE VOLKSLEHRER Describes life in Cincinnati, 1858, No. 47, p. 255.

DIE GEGENWART Wise's plans for Confirmation, 1869, No. 15, p. 148.

DIE NEUZEIT Wise's achievements, 1882, No. 38, p. 321.

DIE NEUZEIT Wise's speech at a Methodist Congress, 1895, No. 28, p. 312.

DIE WELT An obituary, 1900, No. 15, p. 10.

HAKARMEL Wise's reforms in Cincinnati, 1863, p. 49.

HAMAGID A sermon by Wise on America, Vol, 2, 1858, p. 19.

HAMAGID Wise's reforms, Vol. 4, 1861, p. 196.

HAMAGID Wise writes on the problem of the *agunah*, Vol. 6, p. 103.

HAMAGID A decision on Jewish divorce, Vol. 6, 1863, p. 167.

HAMAGID Wise on the Board of Delegates, Vol. 6, 1863, p. 179.

HAMAGID With Lilienthal Wise confers with Lincoln on Grant's Order to expel Jews from the area, Vol. 7, p. 60.

HAMAGID Wise nominated to be State Senator, Vol. 7, p. 348.

HAMAGID Conversation at Steinway Hall about Jesus, Vol. 15, 1872, p. 116.

HAMAGID the founding of HUC, Vol. 16, p. 507-8.

HAMAGID Wise censured for his humanism and materialism, No. 27, p. 295.

HAMAGID Wise denies that one of his disciples had intended to become a *meshummed*. Vol. 29, p. 129.

HAMAGID Congratulates Wise on 55 years of being an American Reform rabbi, 1879, p. 211.

HAMAGID L'ISRAEL Sermon by Wise on Jewish-Christian relations, Vol. 1, No. 4, 1895, p. 39.

HAMAGID L'ISRAEL Wise's 75th birthday; an appreciation by the orthodox, Vol. 5, 1896, p. 149.

HAMAGID L'ISRAEL An article by Wise on the problems of Sabbath observance, Vol. 7, p. 45, 1898.

HAMELITZ His daughter marries a Gentile, 1884, p. 638.

HAMELITZ Wise speech on immigration (from HAZOFEH of Cincinnati), 1889, No. 234, pp. 3-4.

HAZEFIRAH On Wise, 1878, p. 53.

HAZEFIRAH Wise's reforms, and his salary (in a letter from New York), 1885, p. 1.

HAZEFIRAH Wise and Christians, 1889, p. 3.

HAZEFIRAH A Council for Russian Refugees, 1892, p. 84.

HAZEFIRAH Wise's article on the Decalogue refuted (by W. Shor writing from pp. 390 ff. Wise attacked for his jingoism by a New York correspondent, 1865, pp. 624 ff.)

Wise is charged with a desire to oust the German rabbis. Philippson adds that is not worthwhile to oppose him, 1868, pp. 1021 ff.

AZJ Wise is appointed a member of the *Beth Din* by Lilienthal. Wise's congregational work is praised by Lilienthal, who gives him credit for having made people close their stores on the Sabbath. To the *Beth Din* Wise submits a proposed *Minhag America.* AZJ, 1847, pp. 26, 145, and 364.

AMI A question from Victoria, Texas: ". . . we have no objection as to when and where good people meet to worship God and listen to divine instruction, but a Jew must not give his sanction to the Sunday Sabbath, which has no other historical ground than the alleged resurrection of Jesus." Dec. 1, 1871, p. 2.

OCC Wise's History, in Albany, 1854, is criticized by Leeser for its rationalist tendencies; by Abr. Rice, who calls Wise—in Hebrew—a "false prophet"; and by Illowy, who uses the same term, and who specifically condemns Wise's statements: that the man who fought with Jacob was a Bedawi; that the voice of God speaking to Abraham, when he was about to sacrifice Isaac, and later to Laban, was the voice of conscience; that the first-born in Egypt were killed by the Israelites; that the miracle of the Red Sea was due to Moses's knowledge of the tides; that the prophets were visionaries. Illowy adds that he knew Wise in former years as orthodox. OCC, Vol. XI, pp. 520-21 and 613-19.

AMI Wise objects to the Philadelphia Platform of 1869 as merely negative, declaring Jews not a nation, but without a positive statement. He is opposed to Einhorn's ritual, which makes *Tisha b'Ab* a holiday, "because we do not know the plans of Providence." April 22, 1870.

OCC Wise is called a thorough orthodox Talmudist, and himself protests against being classed with the German Reformers; he works successfully to have stores closed on the Sabbath. OCC, Vol. V, pp. 107-11, 119, 158-63, 260, and 415.

OCC Leeser springs to the defense of the Board of Delegates, which was attacked in the *Deborah* as being composed of insignificant persons, "If only little men we were, why did not the western sun come to shed its light on the benighted assembly which only wanted him to have one *man* among them?" OCC, Vol. XXIII, p. 236.

OCC A Sermon, "The Light," delivered by Wise in New York March 3, 1849, denounces Reform for abrogating the Sabbath and circumcision, to escape "the disgrace of exclusion" (page 15), and the "wild rage of Reform," the "Christianizing of the Jewish religion (ibid.), and those who exclaim 'Judaism is in a good enough position as it is,' while indifference increases, and who 'armed with their outward ceremonies, laugh to scorn the progress of time.'" Leeser takes strong exception to all this. OCC, Vol. VII, pp. 12-25.

OCC Wise signs a protest, with five other rabbis, against the Board of Delegates, which had appealed to Congress to alter the law that Jews might be appointed as chaplains. The protestants said that the Board of Delegates represented congregations which did not have any regularly ordained rabbis. Leeser replies: "Where did the one in Chicago (Felsenthal), or Dr. Wise in Cincinnati, ever obtain ordination?" OCC, Vol. XIX, p. 508.

OCC Wise writes articles on "The Principles of Judaism (Vol. IX, pp. 14-25, 187-99, and 298-305), chiefly critical of the doctrine of Resurrection. There are notes by Leeser, which call Wise an "able reasoner," and "consistent," but challenge the statement that Halevi and Abr. Ibn Ezra were excommunicated. 1896, p. 806.

HAZEFIRAH On the importance of the CCAR, 1898, p. 1342.

IL CORRIERE ISRAELITICO Wise's 45th anniversary in Cincinnati, 1899, p. 69.

IL VESSILIO ISRAELITICO Wise speaks on the beliefs of Judaism, 1875, p. 256.

IL VESSILIO ISRAELITICO An obituary, 1900, p. 150.

ISRAELITISCHE WOCHENSCHRIFT Wise's 25th anniversary as rabbi in Cincinnati. 1875, No. 24, p. 197.

ISRAELITISCHE WOCHENSCHRIFT Wise's theology, 1870, No. 31, p. 257.

ISRAELITISCHE WOCHENSCHRIFT Wise's controversy with Einhorn, 1871, No. 4, p. 30.

ISRAELITISCHE WOCHENSCHRIFT A criticism of Wise, 1871, No. 30, p. 236.

ISRAELITISCHE WOCHENSCHRIFT The differences between German and Polish Jews, 1870, No. 32, p. 267.

ISRAELITISCHE WOCHENSCHRIFT Wise on Marriage Laws, 1872, No. 35, p. 280.

ISRAELITISCHE WOCHENSCHRIFT Wise elected rabbi of Anshe Chesed, N.Y., 1873, No. 39, p. 317.

ISRAELITISCHE WOCHENSCHRIFT The founding of the HUC, 1875, No. 39, p. 321.

ISRAELITISCHE WOCHENSCHRIFT Wise's speech on the HUC, 1879, No. 66, p. 399.

ISRAELITISCHE WOCHENSCHRIFT Wise resents it that Jews are honoring Felix Mendelssohn, 1880, No. 1, p. 7.

ISRAELITISCHE WOCHENSCHRIFT A Review of the "History of Jews During the Second Temple," 1880, No. 24, p. 208.

ISRAELITISCHE WOCHENSCHRIFT A proposal by Wise of a Jewish jury, 1880, No. 45, p. 379.

ISRAELITISCHE WOCHENSCHRIFT A controversy with E.G. Hirsch, 1881, No. 9, p. 82.

ISRAELITISCHE WOCHENSCHRIFT Wise on the divisions of Scriptures, 1881, No. 11, p. 95.

ISRAELITISCHE WOCHENSCHRIFT Wise's attitude toward the proposed Synod, 1881, No. 15, p. 135.

JESCHURUN Wise's attitude toward Jewish divorce, 1862, No. 7, p. 352.

JESCHURUN Wise refutes an attack in JESCHURUN against a *trefe* meal at Confirmation, 1883, No. 40, p. 710.

MONATSCHRIFT FUER GESCHICHTE UND WISSENSCHAFT DES JUDENTHUMS A controversy with David Einhorn. 1856, pp. 14 f.

MONATSCHRIFT etc., Wise nominated to be Ohio State Senator, 1863, p. 476.

REVUE ISRAELITE On Wise, 1871, p. 506.

SYNODALBLATT A controversy with Lilienthal over the burial of the uncircumcised, 1871.

SYNODALBLATT On the marriage to the brother-in-law of a widow (*yebamah*), 1872, p. 243.

ZEITUNG DES JUDENTHUMS An appeal by Wise for religious schools; he is eager for a Union; as to relations between Jews and Christians; 1847, No. 51, p. 741.

Glossary

Hebrew, German, Latin, French, Spanish

A fortiori, a Latin logical term: if one thing is true, then another following it must be more obviously so.

Agunoth, Hebrew plural, from *Agunah;* literally "tied in" or "shut in", a deserted woman, who may not remarry, unless the death of her husband is certified by two witnesses.

Am Ha'aretz, Hebrew, originally merely "the people of the land"; by later usage an ignorant man.

Am Ha'aratzuth, Hebrew, nominal, abstract; the condition of being an *Am Ha'aretz*, or ignorance itself.

Amoraim, Hebrew, the generations of rabbis and scholars who compiled the Talmud.

Autos da fé, Spanish, literally "acts of faith", executions under the Inquisition, usually by burning at the stake.

Baba Metziah, Aramaic, a tractate of Mishna and Talmud on damages.

Bath Kol, Hebrew, literally "daughter of a Voice," a heavenly voice, indicating the will of God, often in rabbinic literature.

Beth Din, Hebrew, literally "house of justice," a court constituted in a Jewish community.

Beth Hachayyim, Hebrew, literally "house of life," a cemetery.

Beth Hamidrash, Hebrew, a Hebrew school.

B'nai Brith, Hebrew, literally "sons of the Covenant," a Jewish fraternal order, international in character.

Bochur, Hebrew, literally "a young man," customarily for a Jewish student.

B'rocho, Hebrew, a "blessing," not only in general, but the many specific blessings for specific occasions in traditional Judaism.

Cabbalah, or *Kabbalah*, Hebrew, literally "tradition," "that which has been received," actually in reference to mystical works in Jewish literature, the greatest of which was the *Zohar* (q.v.), of the 13th century.

Casus belli, Latin, a "cause for war."

Chamisha Asar B'Shvat, Hebrew, the 15th day of the month *Shvat*, in the Hebrew calendar, the New Year for trees, according to the school of Hillel.

Channucah, Hebrew, literally "dedication," the historic feast, eight days, in December, commemorating the victory of the Maccabees in the second century B.C.E., and the rededication of the temple in Jerusalem.

Cheder, Hebrew, a Hebrew primary school.

Chevlay Hamoshiach, Hebrew, literally "the pangs of the Messiah," a traditional teaching that the Messianic time will be preceded by tragedy and terror, like the travail of birth.

Chochmath Yavan, Hebrew, literally "the wisdom of Greece," used as a generic term for non-Jewish learning.

Chovave Zion, Hebrew, one of the early Zionist groups, the name meaning "Friends of Zion," or "Lovers of Zion."

Chovoth, in full, *Chovoth Hal'vavot,* Hebrew, "The Duties of the Heart," a beautiful work on ethics by Bachya ben Joseph ibn Pakudah, in 1040.

Chummesh, Hebrew, the "Five," the Five Books of Moses in Hebrew.

Conditio sine qua non, Latin, a condition that is indispensable.

Conseil d'État, French, State Council.

Dayyan, Hebrew, a judge.

De jure, Latin, "by law," usually in contrast to "*de facto,* in fact."

Dementia praecox, Latin, a mental abnormality afflicting chiefly adolescents.

Derashah, Hebrew, literally a "homiletical interpretation"; same root as *Midrash,* in contrast with a strictly legal, *Halachic* one.

Die Wissenschaft des Judenthums, German, literally "The Science of Judaism," a school of critical and evolutionary study of Jewish sources, in the 19th century.

Din, Hebrew, "judgment" or "decision," connoting the verdict of Jewish law on an action or an attitude.

Ding'-an-sich, German, a Kantian term, the "thing-in-itself," that is, matter as distinct from human perception.

Ebionites, or in Hebrew *Evyonim,* literally "the poor," a name for the early Christians, who were supposed to have espoused poverty.

Elohism and *Jahvism,* the theory that passages utilizing different Hebrew names for God, in the Torah, belong to sources different in authorship and time.

Engherzig, German, literally "narrow-hearted."

E silentio, Latin, "from silence," an argument drawn from the silence of a time or documents concerning a person or event.

Essenes, a semi-monastic Jewish group, described in Josephus, Philo, etc., who separated from the community and led a fairly ascetic life. Much new light on them in the Dead Sea Scrolls.

Ex officio, Latin, "by virtue of his office."

Ex parte, Latin, in the interest of one side only.

Galuth, Hebrew, equivalent to *Golus,* q.v.

Gemara, Hebrew, one of the Hebrew terms for the Talmud.

Golem, Hebrew, a mythical artifact, in the form of a man, which did the bidding of the *hohe Reb Loew* at the end of the 16th century in Prague.

Golus, Hebrew, "exile."

Goy, Hebrew, at first and literally "nation," later used for a non-Jew therefore "Gentile"; plural *Goyim.*

Haggadah, haggadic, Hebrew, those sections of rabbinic literature, not *Halacha,* dealing not with law but with tales, explanations, homilies, gnomic laws, legends, etc.

Haggadah, Hebrew, literally "narration, based on the injunction in Exodus, "And thou shalt tell thy son on that day. . . . ," the picturesque ritual devised by centuries for the evening of the Passover, the *Seder.*

Halachah, or *Halachic,* Hebrew, nominal and adjectival forms: that part of the rabbinic law which has to do with statute, with its legal authority and context.

Halitzah, Hebrew, a ceremony, based on biblical law, if a man refuse, under the *Yibum*, the Levirate marriage, to wed the childless widow of his brother, which provides that he must go through a public service of disapprobation or disgrace.

Hallel, Hebrew, literally "praise," a section of the prayer-book, consisting of Psalms 113-118 in praise of God, recited on the holidays.

Hameassef, a Hebrew periodical, meaning "The Gatherer," published 1784-1811.

Handelsschule, German, a Trade School.

Haskalah, Hebrew, "enlightenment," used for a modernist cultural movement in Eastern Europe.

Hatarat Haroah, Hebrew, literally chiefly "permission used to teach" among Ashkenazic Jews for the ordination of rabbis.

Hazan, plural *Hazanim*, Hebrew, "cantor," "cantors."

Hazir, Hebrew, "swine," "swine's flesh."

HIAS, "Hebrew Immigrant Aid Society."

Jahvism and *Elohism*, the theory that passages in the Torah utilizing different names for God belong to different sources in authorship and time.

Jus primae noctis, Latin, (in the text *noctae* by error for *noctis*), the "right of the first night," an alleged mediaeval practice, by which the overlord had the right to sleep the first night with the newly-wedded bride.

Kinnoth, Hebrew, literally "laments," recited in the synagogue on the 9th day of Ab, the anniversary of the destruction of Jerusalem.

K'lal and *P'rat*, two hermeneutic terms in rabbinic literature, the "general" and the "particular," a logical distinction.

Koferim b'ikor, Hebrew, "those who deny a central principle of belief"; in the Jewish sense, a heretic.

Kol Nidre, Hebrew, a strange and controversial prayer, at the beginning of the service for the evening of *Yom Kippur*, which asks absolution for all oaths that may be taken during the year.

Kosher, Hebrew, ritually fit according to the dietary laws; the abstract noun *Kashruth*, the state of being *Kosher*.

Kuzari, Hebrew, "About the *Khazars*," a philosophic work in defense and elucidation of Judaism, written in Arabic, about the beginning of the twelfth century, by the Spanish-Jewish poet and philosopher, Jehuda Halevi.

Lacunae, Latin, "holes," actually omissions.

Landsmannschaften, German, associations of Jews by the land of their derivation.

Machzor, Hebrew, part of the traditional Jewish liturgy, used for the holidays.

Massorah, Hebrew, the work of the generations of Jewish scholars, who devoted themselves to fixing the tradition of the text of the Bible.

Megillah, Hebrew, literally "scroll," used for any one of the five scrolls in the Bible (Job, the Song of Songs, Ruth, Lamentations, and Esther); but customarily in Jewish usage referring to the Book of Esther, read on Purim.

Melamed, Hebrew, a teacher.

Meshulochim, singular *Meshuloch*, Hebrew, literally "emissaries," Jews sent out by philanthropic or educational institutions to solicit financial aid.

Metathron, Greek taken into Hebrew, literally "one who shares the throne," much used in apocalyptic books and some rabbinic literature, for the idea of the pre-existent Messiah.

Mezuzah, Hebrew, a small metal box, affixed to the doorpost of a Jewish home, with special Hebrew sentences in it from the *Sh'ma*, and bearing one of the names of God, *Shaddai*, "the Almighty"; based on a literal observance of the section in "And thou shalt love the Lord thy God," which reads: "And thou shalt write them upon the doorposts of thy house."

Midrash Rabbah, Hebrew, the main compilation in rabbinic times of the homilies upon biblical texts, one of the chief sources of Jewis legends, ethics, etc.

Mikva, Hebrew, a ritual bath for women, provided for in orthodox practice.

Milath Gerim, Hebrew, the circumcision of proselytes, (literally "strangers").

Minhag, Hebrew, a custom among Jews, sometimes more tenacious than a law.

Minhag America, literally "the custom" or "usage" of America, a prayer-book, in Hebrew, German, and English, compiled by Isaac M. Wise, about 1855, with the aid of several others.

Minim, Hebrew, literally "classes," or "kinds"; but in rabbinic literature signifying "heretics," those who have departed from fundamental Judaism, or other sects "outside the Law."

Minyan, Hebrew, literally "number," used to indicate the count of ten men, needed for a traditional Jewish service, in most cases, a quorum.

Misheberach, Hebrew, literally "He who blessed," an opening word of prayer by the reader, for those called up to read a portion of the *Torah*.

Mishna, the codification of the rabbinic, or Oral law, finished by Jehuda Hanasi about 200 C.E.

Mishne Torah, Hebrew, Maimonides' great codification of the Talmudic law, about the middle of the 12th century.

Mitzvoth, Hebrew, literally "commandments," utilized in general for "duties," or even "privileges," and in the synagogue for the privilege of participating in the reading of the *Torah*.

Moreh Nevuchim, Hebrew, Maimonides' great philosophical work, *The Guide of the Perplexed*, written in Arabic, and published about 1160.

Morenu, Hebrew, "our teacher," a title for a rabbi.

Motzi, Hebrew, the prayer in Hebrew before partaking of a meal, before breaking bread.

Mutatis mutandis, Latin, "necessary changes having been made."

Nervus rerum, Latin, literally "the nerve of things," connoting the heart or essence of the matter.

Odium theologicum, Latin, controversy, or hatred, between theologians and/or scholars.

Parnass, Parnassim, Hebrew, probably originally from the Greek, which came eventually to mean the president of a Jewish congregation, but only in modern times.

Parnosoh, Hebrew, "sustenance," "support," "livelihood."

Pesach, Hebrew, the festival of the Passover, seven days in the Spring, commemorating the Exodus.

Peschitta, the oldest Syriac translation of the Bible (and also of the New Testament), made over the course of several centuries, probably begun in the first Christian century.

Pharisees, the rabbinical party in ancient Judea, believing in a democratization of the faith, in the Oral as well as in the Written Law, much persecuted under the later Hasmoneans and the Romans.

Piutim (or *Piyyutim*), Hebrew, liturgical hymns or poems, written mostly in the Talmudic era, and up to the 7th century (the word probably derived from the Greek for "poet"), found in the *Machzor*, the holiday prayer-book.

Post festum, Latin, after the event.

Pronaos, Greek, a preface or introduction.

Rabbinerversammlungen, German, rabbinic assemblies, of which there were four in central Europe, to which this term was in the main applied, in the middle of the 19th century.

Reshith Chochmah, Hebrew, "the beginning of wisdom," a popular ethical Cabbalistic work by Elijah de Vidas (16th century).

Rishus, Hebrew, literally "wickedness," but which came to mean "prejudice."

Rosh Ha-shono, the Jewish New Year, the first of the month Tishri, signalized by a solemn service and the blowing of the *Shofar*, or "ram's horn."

Ruach Hakodesh, Hebrew, "the Holy Spirit," the Spirit of God, a phrase used often in the Bible, and probably the basis of the Holy Ghost as a member of the Christian Trinity.

Sadduccees, probably deriving from "Zadok," as a priestly caste, the party of the priests and the wealthy, close to the Temple, opposed to the Pharisees, and having religious principles quite different from theirs.

Schlemiehl, (perhaps a Hebrew term from a name in the *Torah*), now signifying a feckless person; taken over into some modern European usage, as in Chamisso's *Peter Schlemiehl*.

Schutzjuden, German, literally "protected Jews," but actually a term that meant the legal helplessness of Jews.

Seder, Hebrew, literally "arrangement," the family meal on the eve of the first day of the Passover, with many picturesque prayers and ceremonies, commemorating the Exodus.

Sedrah, Hebrew, that part of the *Torah* assigned for reading on a particular Sabbath.

Seelenfeier, German, literally "a solemn ceremony of souls," standing for the *Yizkor*, the Memorial Service of *Yom Kippur*.

Sefer Hachayyim, Hebrew, a "Book of Life," here meaning a Memorial Volume.

Selichoth, Hebrew, penitential prayers, recited in the synagogue before *Rosh Ha-shono* and also between *Rosh Ha-shono* and *Yom Kippur*, at midnight, the oldest of the *Piutim* (q.v.).

Semicha, Hebrew, literally "laying on of hands," the ceremony of ordination.

Septuagint, the oldest Greek translation of the Bible, made in Egypt in the middle of the third century B.C.E.

Sequelae, Latin, consequences, necessary concomitants.

Shnoder, Hebrew, from a Hebrew prayer before the reading of the *Torah*, *Baruch sh'nodar*, "Blessed be he who vows," used for those who come up to read, and pledge a contribution to the synagogue.

Shabbos, Hebrew, the Jewish Sabbath.

Shabuoth, Hebrew, the Feast of Weeks, one of the three Jewish agricultural festivals; also of the giving of the Law on Mt. Sinai; used in Reform Judaism for Confirmation.

Shamash, Hebrew, the sexton of the synagogue.

Shechita, Hebrew, the ritual method of slaughtering, by Jewish traditional practice.

Sh'elah, Hebrew, a "question," usually part of the phrase *Sh'elot u-t'shuvot,* "Questions and Answers," a voluminous Jewish literature, by rabbis and scholars, in reply to legalistic, ritual, and many other questions directed to them through the ages, a most important source for Jewish life and thought.

Shidduch, Hebrew, a wedding, a match.

Sh'mona Esreh, the "eighteen benedictions" in Hebrew, a very important section of the *Siddur,* or Jewish traditional liturgy.

Shochet, Hebrew, a ritual butcher.

Sholom Aleichem, Hebrew, "peace be with you," the Hebrew greeting; also a song for Sabbath Eve.

Shulchan Aruch, Hebrew, literally "The Set Table," the authoritative codification of the Talmudic law, by Joseph Caro, approximately in 1565.

Sifre Torah, Hebrew, literally "The Books of the Law," or the scroll of the Law as used in the synagogue.

Simchath Torah, Hebrew, the "Joy of the Law," just after the end of the eight days of *Sukkoth,* the celebration at which the end and the beginning of the *Torah* are read; processions with the scrolls about the synagogue, etc.

Sukkoth, the "Feast of Booths," in the autumn, after *Yom Kippur,* the festival of the harvest, of dwelling in booths in the Wilderness period, a thanksgiving.

Esrogim, from *Esrog,* Hebrew, a citrus fruit, like an elongated lemon, (mentioned in the *Torah*), used as part of the celebration of *Sukkoth.*

Ta'anith, Hebrew, a tractate of the *Mishna* and of the Babylonian *Talmud,* on Fasts.

Taharoth, Hebrew, a tractate of the *Mishna* about cleanliness.

Tallis, Hebrew, the white and blue prayer-shawl with a knotted fringe, used by traditional Jews, and described and ordained in *Numbers,* etc.

Talmid, Hebrew, a pupil, one who learns.

Talmud Yelodim, Hebrew, literally "the instruction of children."

Tana'im, Hebrew, literally "teachers," those rabbinical authorities of the generation of the *Mishna.*

Tephillin, Hebrew, "phylacteries," wound about the arm, and placed on the forehead, in accordance with a literal interpretation of the prayer in the *Sh'ma,* "And thou shalt love the Lord thy God," etc., especially the sentence, "And thou shalt bind them for a sign upon thy hand, and they shall be as frontlets between thine eyes."

Torah, Hebrew, or sometimes as Wise spelled it *Thorah,* the Pentateuch, the Five Books of the Law, from Genesis through Deuteronomy.

Tovu vaBohu, Hebrew, in Genesis, chap. 1, vs. 2, "waste and empty," or chaos.

Trephah, Hebrew, the converse of *Kosher,* ritually unfit to eat, contrary to the dietary laws.

Tsitsis, Hebrew, the fringes at the corners of the *Arba Kanfot* (four corners) and of the *Tallis* (q.v.), in accordance with Numbers and Deuteronomy.

Targum, Hebrew, literally "translation," one of the Aramaic translations of the Bible.

Tisha b'Av, Hebrew, the ninth day of the month of Ab, usually in late summer, the day on which twice, once by Nebuchadnezzar, and once by Titus, the Temple on Zion was destroyed; and on which the book of Lamentations is chanted.

Tur, a codification of the Law by Jacob ben Asher (died in Spain about 1340), the main authority upon Talmud law until the appearance of the *Shulchan Aruch.*

Yeshiva, Hebrew, a Jewish institute of higher learning, devoted chiefly to the study of the Talmud.

Yesode Hatorah, a section of the Code of Maimonides (see *Mishne Torah,* sometimes called *Yad Hachazakah,* or *Yad,* "The hand," literally "the foundations of the Law.")

Yetzer hora, Hebrew, "the evil impulse," or "instinct." Judaism believed man had both, this and *Yetzer hatov,* the impulse to do good, but not that these represented a basic dualism, or the objective existence of evil or of a devil.

Yomim Noro'im, Hebrew, literally "the awesome days," the great holy days of the autumn in the Jewish calendar, specifically *Rosh Ha-shono* and *Yom Kippur.*

Zichron Ya'akov, Hebrew, one of the earliest of the agricultural settlements of Jews in Palestine, founded with the aid of Baron de Rothschild, the name meaning "The Memory of Jacob."

Zohar, Hebrew, the greatest work of Jewish mysticism, a commentary on the Pentateuch, ascribed to Rabbi Simeon ben Yochai, partly in Aramaic, and partly in Hebrew, which appeared first in Spain in the 13th century.

Notes

A PREFATORY CRITICAL NOTE

It did not seem wise to interrupt the narrative of Part Two of this book with technical and critical discussion, except in one or two places and more or less in passing. But it was made clear to the attentive reader, we believe, that most of the material in our early chapters was derived, ultimately, from Isaac M. Wise's own account of these years of his life in his *Reminiscences*, published originally in German in *Die Deborah*, and appearing with a fair degree of regularity from July 3, 1874 to August 11, 1875. Thus these articles describe events that took place either thirty or twenty years earlier, since they narrate the facts covered during the first eleven years of his life in the United States, from 1846 to 1857. At the latter year they cease, as we point out in the preceding text, because Wise did not wish to set down in this form his opinion of many events and persons that were still contemporary or alive.

Much of the material that precedes this, concerning his childhood and youth, also his ancestry, as reference to the notes will show, was taken from two sources: *Selected Writings*, published by David Philipson and Louis Grossmann in 1900, which begins with a biographical sketch; and *Isaac Mayer Wise, the Founder of American Judaism*, a Biography by Max B. May, his grandson, published in 1916. The *Reminiscences*, incidentally, were translated by David Philipson and published in 1901.

Several questions must be considered in this prefatory note. How reliable were Wise's own words? And to what extent can we rely upon accounts of his life by two of his disciples, and by his own grandson? Our own principle has been a simple one: in every case, where doubt as to the accuracy of his own memory was raised or where it seemed likely that his biographers had been swayed by their own predilections, we have instituted additional investigation to check up as far as it has proved possible.

Perhaps it will be useful to indicate some instances. Doubtless Wise himself was ultimately responsible for the description of his rabbinical and secular training in Bohemia, Austria, and Hungary, and also for the account of his ordination (which is to be found on pp. 14-34 of Part Two). None of our sources gives us the exact date of his ordination, but what we know of it is on p. 37 of the same part. Here he recorded that he had received *S'micha* at the hands of Rappaport, Samuel Freund, and Ephraim Loeb Teweles. This is chiefly in the early biographical sketch by Philipson and Grossmann. Some doubt has been cast on these facts. Some have asserted that Wise had no diploma of ordination, when he arrived in the United States in 1846. He was present at the third *Rabbinerversammlung* in Frankfort in 1845, and wrote concerning this. (This was in the *American Israelite* of Feb. 14, 1895, as part of a Series, "The Difficulty in Defining Judaism.") Some of the doubts as to Wise's truthfulness about his ordination spring from two references in writings by Leeser, one early in Wise's life in America, in which Leeser refers to him as a "school-master," and a second in a bitter polemical rejoinder by Leeser in the *Occident*, 1854, pp. 158-63. Here Leeser wrote that he would like to see "the diploma which constitutes Dr. Wise a doctor of divinity." Unless we mistake the meaning, Leeser did not here refer to Wise's ordination, but to Wise's possession of an academic degree of "divinity." But, at any rate, in the heat of controversy, and since Wise had not infrequently cast aspersions on Leeser's ability even to read "unpunctuated Hebrew," the statement was to be expected.

This is, as far as we know, in these words of Leeser, the only claim that can be found that Wise (as certainly did a number of others in pulpits in the United States then) had invented the fact of his ordination. But Wise's own account is circumstantial, names those who ordained him, and also his immediate recommendation by Rappaport to the pulpit in Radnitz. Concerning this last we have one small item of substantiation. This was in a letter from Isidor Lewi, a son of an old Albany friend, from Wise's earliest American days (described on p. 478 of Part Two). It is true that, as the text of the letter showed, Lewi's visit to Radnitz was forty-four years after Wise had fled from it. Some people met in Radnitz recalled that Wise had delivered his last sermon there on the last day of the Passover. That Wise could not take his certificate of ordination with him, considering the manner in which he, his wife and child had to leave Bohemia, even without a passport, is hardly to be wondered at. Regarding the matter as a whole, and Wise's almost life-long contact with such men as Dr. Stein in Germany, it is impossible to believe that Wise had manufactured the whole tale of his ordination by Rappaport, Freund, and Teweles, and that Leeser was correct in calling him a "school-master."

Similarly, and as a mere matter of accuracy, some doubt has been cast on Wise's account of the origin of his family name (p. 4 of Part Two taken from Max May's biography, p. 22). The objection has been made that the title, *Haham* (or *Chacham*) was used only among Sephardic Jews, and also in the case of the Turkish chief-rabbi, the

Haham-Bashi. My own grandfather, who was a layman, but a very learned one, who devoted almost all his time to study and neglected and lost his business in Prague, was, as my sure recollection tells me, known as *Haham.* In a letter in the *Israelite* a correspondent asserts that there were three titles used in connection with the Bohemian synagogue: *Morenu* (an ordained rabbi); *Haham* (an exceptionally learned layman); and *Haver* ("comrade," probably a simple member). My friend Dr. Solomon B. Freehof of Pittsburgh looked for *responsa* that might bear on this point. He cited the work of Edward Dukess. In *Iva l'Moshov* Dukess uses the title *Haham* for two rabbis; he entitled Rabbi Z'vi Ashkenazi as *Haham Z'vi,* and explains that Ashkenazi had distinguished himself in his earliest youth, in the city of Brod in Moravia, through his "unusual mental keenness [Freehof's words], . . . and that is why he was universally called *Haham.*" Dukess claimed that the rabbis in Bosnia were known as *Haham,* speaks of Isaac Bernays as "the *Haham* Bernays," and adds "and the reputation of his wisdom preceded him and he was called *Haham,* described by all as *Haham* Bernays." One might assume, adds Dr. Freehof, that the use of the term *Haham* was because there was a Portuguese congregation in Hamburg (where Bernays was rabbi), but this was not so, for the family was so called before they came to the city near the North Sea. Dr. Freehof's conclusion was "that *Haham* was a frequent title for rabbis among Sephardim, but was used in a non-technical sense occasionally among the Ashkenazim, especially in Bohemia and Moravia."

All this in letters to me personally from Dr. Freehof. In a further letter he added: "One thing seems certain to me: If Isaac M. Wise says definitely that his grandfather was called by the title *Haham,* and if, in addition, your father had such a memory, it is clear that the title must have been used at least in Bohemia." Dr. Freehof quotes Salo Baron in *The Jewish Community* (Vol. II, p. 62), who in turn quotes Rashi "as saying that the *Haham* mentioned in the Talmud means the one who is appointed over the city to answer ritualistic questions. So evidently for Rashi to call a rabbi *Haham* was not strange." Dr. Freehof conjectured that the title *Haham* was possibly used in some districts as *Haver* and *Morenu* were used in the later Middle Ages, as a title of dignity for a scholar who was not a professional or not officially the rabbi of the community. That their fellow-Jews wanted to bestow such a title was due to the specific fact in Jewish law that scholars who were not officially rabbis had certain special rights. They were freed from the necessity of paying communal taxes (see *Yore Deah,* 243:2, note of Isserles). Also, although not professionally rabbis, such scholars were often supported so that they could devote themselves to study (see Baron III, p. 126, note 27). (See also M. Frank, *Kehillat Ashkenaz,* Tel Aviv, 1938, p. 19, who says that many communities had unordained *Hahamim.*) "This must have been a local use, but there is no ground to deny it, since there was social and religious need for such a title." With this evidence, for much of which we are deeply grateful to Dr. Freehof (whose scholarly ability to find such references is remarkable), there is no good reason for casting doubt on Wise's contention that the name Wise, "Weise," was derived from the title of *Haham,* either conferred on his grandfather in Durmaul, or by which affectionately and in admiration he was known.

In the text, and in notes, we have already treated the doubt of Wise's recollection, written in Dr. Bertram Korn's book (*Eventful Years and Reminiscences,* The American Jewish Archives, Cincinnati, 1854). This is based on the fact that Wise erred in calling Judah P. Benjamin a Senator from Louisiana in 1850, when in fact Benjamin was not elected to the Senate until 1853, three years after this. We have treated this entire matter in an extended footnote, under chap. 13 of Part Two (note 15), to which the reader should refer. Most of the material in this section was extracted from Wise's *Reminiscences,* pp. 181 ff. Dr. Korn also casts doubt on Wise's assertion that Benjamin had some pride in his inherited religion. Into this we shall not go farther at this point, except to remark that these appear to us minor objections, and that the main fact of the "get-together" Wise had with Webster, Maury, and Benjamin was certainly correct, and not imagined or manufactured; and that there is no sufficient ground to doubt this main circumstance.

We come now to another moot point, one, at least, that was raised by one of those who read the manuscript of this book. In chap. 13 of Part Two (pp. 199-200) we reproduced material from the *Reminiscences,* pp. 217-19. This had to do with the proposal in the Legislature of New York that chaplains for both houses be selected, and with Wise's fight to secure for himself (and perhaps for Catholics too) fair play and equal rights, which the Protestant clergymen had striven to deny them. Wise also had the prayer he had delivered before the Senate reprinted in the *Asmonean* (Vol. 4, p. 12, July 9, 1851). There is extended reference to all this in Dr. Korn's *Eventful Years and Experiences* (The American Jewish Archives, Cincinnati, 1954), in which the claim is made that "no corroborating evidence for this 'battle of the clergy' has been preserved; the documents cannot be located, nor do the Albany newspapers mention the problem" (op. cit., p. 117). It is true, unfortunately, that there is no reference to the matter in the records of the Albany congregation (*Congregation Beth Emeth,* 1838-1938) which reprints a history written in 1910 by the Rev. Dr. Max Schlesinger and Hon. Simon W. Rosendale.

We have striven to the utmost to discover any contemporary evidence concerning this entire incident. But what we have found is meager indeed. This must not be taken to signify that Wise was entirely in the wrong. In fact, the material which we shall now adduce indicates, to our way of thinking, that he was correct about the whole tale, but that his memory betrayed him about dates, etc. Unfortunately a careful review of the records (*Journal*) of the Assembly and of the Senate of the State of New York for the years 1850, 1851, 1852, has not enabled us to find the resolution to which Wise referred. Nor do the Indexes list such a resolution. But the Minutes do give the names of the clergymen who opened the session with prayer (although in some cases it is noted that "no clergyman was present"). Let us examine these listings for a few moments. In the Senate in 1850, a long list of clergymen might here be adduced, obviously chosen—with some slight variations probably due to convenience or to their own personal preferences—in alphabetical order. Wise delivered a prayer before the Senate in April, 1850. In 1851, he was again among those who delivered invocations, in that year on January 24 and 26. And again in 1852 he gave a prayer before the Senate, three times, on January 12, 14, and 16.

The complete list is also given for the Assembly, but Wise's name does not occur in the year 1850, though the list of clergymen corresponds in the main with that giving prayers in that year before the Senate. In 1851 Wise delivered prayers before the Assembly on June 25 and 27; and in 1852 on January 13 and 15. From all this it is clear that the date he gives in his own *Reminiscences,* namely that a resolution was adopted by both houses on January 2, 1852, cannot be correct. This is also demonstrated by the prayer, which we have reproduced in the text (which was in ASM, No. 12, July 9, 1851). This prayer is probably one of those given by Wise before the Assembly, either on June 25 or 27, as noted in the preceding paragraph. This also indicates that his recollection concerning the resolution, and its date in 1852, cannot be correct. We went carefully over the daily press in Albany at this time (Wise contended that the events were covered in the *Albany Evening Atlas*), but were unable to find the paragraph or paragraphs to which he referred.

To what conclusion does all this lead? Quite simply to an error in dates, and to no more! From the records of the Senate and the Assembly of New York, it is clear that before April 1850 in the Senate, and June 1851 in the Assembly, no rabbi had been included among those clergymen opening the sessions with prayer, and that from those dates onward, while he remained in Albany, Wise *was* so included. It should be noted also that the clergyman, whose name Wise mentions in the *Reminiscences* (p. 218) as having "objected," was one of those whose names are recorded in both Senate and Assembly records as having opened sessions with prayer. The name of "Senator Thayer," who, according to Wise (p. 219) moved "that I be appointed chaplain of the Senate temporarily until the clergy should have obeyed the law," is not to be found among the list of Senators, in the *Journal,* of any of these years.

We believe that this whole story is an excellent illustration of the general principle we have been following. Wise was wrong about details, dates, etc., but almost certainly right about the story itself. This we believe the records of the Legislature, to which we have referred above, seem to indicate. There were no rabbis included in the beginning. He was the first, and he did begin just at this period. The prayer, to which we have referred, was reproduced in the *Asmonean* of 1851, so that we do not depend solely upon his recollections of twenty or thirty years later. We have been unable, in general, to discover any single incident, or claim, which would tend to cast doubt upon the veracity, or reliability, of his recollections in general, though—obviously and naturally—he was occasionally wrong about minor matters: dates, titles (as with "Senator" Benjamin), etc. It is important to note this, for there has been a tendency in some comments about Wise to adopt the attitude that he was not to be believed, that his own accounts of his life were constantly colored and warped.

There are doubtless other matters of historical accuracy, and of detail, that might have been here considered. In general, it is obvious that for many statements made by Wise, or doubtless largely reproduced from his own words or records by Philipson and Grossmann, or by Max B. May, one can find no corroborating evidence. It would be far better if such evidence could be found. Wherever it has been possible to reproduce it, as, e.g., in the case of his violent struggle with Spanier, in the records of the *Asmonean* and the *Occident* and of the Albany Journals, we have placed all of it, fully and frankly, before the reader. Though we have occasionally attempted to assess its validity, it ought to be possible for a critical reader to make up his own mind by careful perusal of the sources for himself. It is possible that, after the publication of this book, other doubts will be cast on various incidents or historical occurrences, herein described. The author will be very grateful for such criticism, where it does not derive from mere pettiness as to detail, or from general skepticism concerning Wise's veracity. Comments of this kind will be welcomed, and will be taken account of in any future editions, if future editions under the will of God there ever prove to be. Meanwhile, the notes that are hereinafter furnished afford every reader the opportunity of judging the source from which statements have been taken, and therefore the credence that may, or may not, be placed in them.

It must be reiterated, as was implied in the Preface of the whole work, that this was not intended as a "critical" biography of Wise, to assess his place in American Jewish history or even in Reform Judaism. Nor was it intended as an evaluation of the worth of his programs and ideas. What seemed to us to be needed was a complete account of his life, his work, and his thought. Beginning with this, critical studies of his concept of Reform, of the ultimate meaning of his creation of the three main institutional agencies he conceived, of his own part in the Pittsburgh Platform, and of the historical connotation and subsequent influence upon Reform and upon American Judaism of that Platform, of many of his own ideas here adduced, and of the way in which he fits into any concept of the place and meaning of Judaism in American life, may follow, to the extent that they have not already been made. It was not our purpose even to enter into a description or an evaluation of Reform, to the extent that Israel Knox did in his work, *Rabbi in America, the*

Story of Isaac M. Wise (Little, Brown and Co., 1957). But, since this is primarily in intent a work of sources and of material, it is especially important, as the writer would be the first to concede, that it should be as accurate as possible and that it should draw upon all that is or may be available. Criticism from this point of view will be very germane and acceptable.

Key to the Notes

To facilitate the use of the notes as references, and to save space, references are in the great majority of cases given in abbreviated form. Works utilized are indicated by combinations of capitalized letters. These will be readily found in the following list, which we place before the Notes in alphabetical order:

ADR, "The Age of the Democratic Revolution," by R. R. Palmar.
AIMW, "The Americanization of Isaac M. Wise."
AJ, "American Judaism," by Isaac M. Wise.
AJA, The American Jews' Annual.
AJCW, "American Jewry and the Civil War," by Bertram W. Korn.
AMI, The American Israelite, earlier The Israelite.
ARAJ, "A Record of American Judaism," by Isaac M. Wise.
ARCH, The American Jewish Archives, Cincinnati, Ohio.
ASM, "The Asmonean," a Periodical.
AWZ, "The Attitude of Isaac M. Wise Toward Zionism and Palestine," a pamphlet by M. Weinman.
AYWP, "As Yesterday When It is Past," by J. G. Heller.
AZJ, "Aus Zwei Jahrhunderten," von N. M. Gelber.
BPHB, "By Paths in Hebrew Bookland," by Isaac M. Wise.
CCAR, The Central Conference of American Rabbis.
CG, "The Cosmic God," by Isaac M. Wise.
CMH, The Cambridge Modern History.
DEB, "Die Deborah," a Periodical.
DI, Index, compiled by Gotthard Deutsch.
DJPC, "Defense of Judaism versus Proselytizing Christianity," by Isaac M. Wise.
EPNK, "The End of Popes, Nobles, and Kings," by Isaac M. Wise.
EYAE, "Eventful Years and Experiences," by Bertram W. Korn.
GHJ, "History of the Jews," by Heinrich Graetz.
GJB, Zur Geschichte der Juden in Boehmen, von Ludwig Singer.
HCJ, "Half a Century of Judaism," by Joseph Krauskopf.
HDJK, "History and Destiny of the Jews," by Jos. Kastein.
HIN, "The History of the Israelitish Nation," Vol. I, by Isaac M. Wise.
HJG, "History of the Jews," by Sol. Grayzell.
HPP, "Hymns, Psalms, and Prayers," by Isaac M. Wise.
HR, "The Hebrew Review," a Quarterly.

HUC, The Hebrew Union College.
HUCJ, "The Hebrew Union College Journal," a Periodical.
IBJP, "An Introduction to a Bibliography of the Jewish Periodical Press," by Isaac M. Wise.
ITJ, "An Introduction to the Theology of Judaism," by Isaac M. Wise.
IWJH, "Isaac M. Mayer's 'Jesus Himself,'" by Sam'l Sandmel.
IWMM, "Isaac Mayer Wise," by Max B. May.
IWRM, "Reminiscences," by Isaac M. Wise.
JAC, "Judaism and Christianity," by Isaac M. Wise.
JE, "The Jewish Encyclopedia."
LOC, "A Lecture on the Origin of Christianity," by Isaac M. Wise.
MGJ, "Materialen zur Geschichte der Juden in Boehmen," von Dr. H. H. Friedlander.
MJN, "The Martyrdom of Jesus of Nazareth," by Isaac M. Wise.
MMH, "History of the Jewish People," by Margolis and Marx.
MWW, "Man and the Western World," by John Geise.
OCC, "The Occident," a Periodical.
OCPH, "Our Country's Place in History," by Isaac M. Wise.
PAJHS, "Publications of the American Jewish Historical Society."
PHW, "Pronaos to Holy Writ," by Isaac M. Wise.
RMJ, "The Reform Movement in Judaism," by David Philipson.
SI, "Sinai," a Periodical.
STC, "Sinai to Cincinnati," by Dena Wilansky.
SUL, "Some Unpublished Letters of Ethical Importance," by David Philipson.
SWIW, "Selected Writings of Isaac M. Wise," by Philipson and Grossmann.
UAHC, The Union of American Hebrew Congregations.
UJE, The Universal Jewish Encyclopedia.
WHR, "'World History," by J. C. Revill.
WMB, "The World of My Books," by Isaac M. Wise.

Notes

Part One

CHAPTER ONE

1. CMH, Vol. VI, Preface, xii.
2. AMI, Vol. 31, Nov. 25 and Dec. 19, 1884, p. 1.
3. MWW, chap. 17, p. 748.
4. WHR, Section IX, "The Modern Age," beginning on p. 479.
5. MWW, chap. 17, p. 734.
6. CMH, Vol. VI, Preface, pp. v and vi.
7. CMH, Vol. VI, Preface, p. viii.
8. CMH, Vol. VI, Preface, pp. x-xi.
9. CMH, Vol. VI, Preface, p. xiii.
10. CMH, Vol. VI, chap. 18, pages 626-56.
11. ADR, pp. 4-5.
12. ADR, pp. 16-17.
13. ADR, p. 213.
14. ADR, p. 282.
15. WHR, Section IX, p. 499.
16. WHR, Section IX, pp. 501 f.
17. WHR, Section IX, p. 504.
18. WHR, Section IX, pp. 504-17.
19. CMH, Vol. VI, chap. 23, pp. 787-89.
20. CMH, Vol. VI, chap. 23, pp. 794-96.
21. CMH, Vol. VI, chap. 23, pp. 814-15.
22. CMH, Vol. 8, chap. 1, p. 2.
23. CMH, Vol. 8, chap. 1, pp. 2-3.
24. CMH, Vol. 8, pp. 5-7.
25. CMH, Vol. 8, chap. 25, pp. 773-76.
26. WHR, Section IX, p. 498.
27. CMH, Vol. 8, chap. 1, pp. 12-14.
28. MMW, chap. 17, p. 739; WHR, Section IX, p. 498; MWW, chap. 17, pp. 736-37.
29. CMH, Vol. 6, chap. 24, p. 824; MWW, chap. 17, p. 740.
30. MWW, chap. 17, page 740; CMH, Vol. 8, chap. 1, pages 29-32.
31. MWW, chap. 17, pp. 728 ff.

CHAPTER TWO

1. HDJK, pp. 365-66.
2. Cf. HDJK, pp. 377-78; GHJ, Vol. V, p. 337; HDJK, pp. 362-63.
3. GHJ, Vol V., p. 336.
4. For example, see the extended and laudatory treatment of Mendelssohn's life and work in Graetz, Vol. V.
5. Quoted in IMWW, pp. 1-3.
6. E.g., HDJK, pp. 369 ff. and HJG, pp. 543 ff.
7. GHJ, Vol. 5, p. 292.
8. *Ibid.*, p. 295.
9. *Ibid.*, pp. 296, 299, 302, 304, 307, 313, 325.
10. *Ibid.*, pp. 332, 364, 370. Also HJG, pp. 542-45; and HDJK, pp. 369-70.
11. HJG, p. 547.
12. HDJK, p. 371.
13. *Ibid.*, p. 380.
14. GHJ, Vol. V., pp. 361-62.
15. *Ibid.*, p. 416.
16. HDJK, p. 388.
17. MMH, p. 622; GHJ, Vol. V., p. 423.
18. GHJ, Vol. V., pp. 407 f.
19. *Ibid.*, p. 418.
20. *Ibid.*, p. 421.
21. HJG, pp. 572-73; MMH, p. 608.
22. MMH, p. 609.
23. GHJ, Vol. V., p. 439; HJG, p. 573.
24. HJG, p. 573.
25. HDJK, p. 389.
26. GHJ, Vol. V., p. 456; HJG, p. 573; HDJK, p. 390.
27. MMH, p. 611.
28. GHJ, pp. 501 f.; HJG, p. 579; MMH, p. 617; GHJ, Vol. V, pp. 501, 507, and 509; HDJK, p. 391; HJG, p. 579; Cf. also MMH, p. 620, and pp. 623-24.
29. HDJK, p. 390. Cf. Index for Wise's later action about Switzerland.
30. MMH, p. 620; HJG, p. 579; MMH, p. 627.
31. HJG, 575; GHJ, Vol.V., pp. 456 f.; MMH, p. 612.
32. HJG, p. 575.
33. GHJ, Vol. V., p. 477; HDJK, pp. 384-85.
34. HDJK, pp. 384-85; MMH, p. 612.
35. GHJ, Vol. V., p. 477.
36. *Ibid.*, pp. 581 f.; MMH, pp. 612-13.
37. GHJ, Vol. V., p. 482.
38. MMH, p. 613.
39. GHJ, Vol. V., pp. 482 f., 489; HDJK, p. 385; HJG, p. 576; MMH, p. 613; GHJ, p. 489.
40. HDJK, p. 385.
41. GHJ, Vol. V., p. 491.
42. HDJK, pp. 385-86.
43. GHJ, Vol. V., p. 489.
44. *Ibid.*, p. 493; HDJK, p. 388; HJG, p. 578; MMH, p. 513.
45. MMH, p. 614; GHJ, Vol. V., p. 495.
46. HDJK, p. 389; GHJ, Vol. V., pp. 497 f.; MMH, pp. 614-15.

47. HJG, pp. 576-78.
48. GHJ, Vol. V., p. 519; HJG, p. 581; MMH, p. 633; HDJK, p. 396.
49. GHJ, Vol. V., p. 519.
50. HJG, p. 581.
51. MMH, p. 633; HDJK, p. 396.
52. HJG, p. 582; GHJ, Vol. V., pp. 423-25, and 515; HDJK, p. 395; MMH, pp. 635-36.
53. HJG, p. 589.
54. HJG, p. 591.
55. HJG, p. 592, also Cf. Index concerning Gabriel Riesser.
56. HDJK, pp. 387-391.
57. *Ibid.*, p. 394.
58. *Ibid.*, pp. 397-98.
59. HJG, p. 587.
60. *Ibid.*, p. 588.
61. *Ibid.*, p. 596.
62. MMH, p. 636.
63. *Ibid.*,

CHAPTER THREE

1. HDJK, p. 364.
2. JE, under "Austria."
3. HDJK, p. 361.
4. JE, *loc. cit.*
5. GHJ, Vol. V., p. 253.
6. JE, *loc. cit.*; also GHJ, Vol. V., p. 252.
7. JE, *loc. cit.*
8. *Ibid.*
9. JE; GJB, p. 210; MGJ, pp. 75-76; HGJ, pp. 359-70; HDJK, pp. 381-82.
10. JE.
11. *Ibid.*
12. The figures given in various sources differ widely as to the number of Jews in Galicia, taken into Austria as part of the third partition of Poland. The lowest is that given here. The highest is 250,000.
13. JE.
14. *Ibid.*
15. HJG, p. 507 f., and p. 523.
16. GHJ, Vol. V., p. 523.
17. HJG, p. 579.
18. MMH, p. 624.
19. JE.
20. *Ibid.*
21. *Ibid.*
22. *Ibid.*
23. *Ibid.*
24. HJG, p. 593.
25. MMH, pp. 624-25, gives the permitted number in Bohemia as 14,000, and GJB gives it as 8600 families under the "Patent" of April 3, 1789. GJB, p. 207. The number in the text is taken from MGJ, p. 72.
26. MGJ, p. 72.
27. GHJ, p. 254; HDJK, p. 361.

28. MGJ, p. 73.
29. JE.
30. JE, under "Austria."
31. GJB, pp. 206-07.
32. JE, under "Bohemia"; MGJ, p. 75.
33. GJB, pp. 194 and 207.
34. *Ibid.*, p. 194.
35. *Ibid.*, pp. 198 and 210.
36. *Ibid.*, p. 212.
37. *Ibid.*, p. 212.
38. GJB, pp. 237-38.
39. *Ibid.*, p. 286.
40. *Ibid.*, pp. 289-90.
41. The first part from *Ein Aktenstueck zur Geschichte der boehmischen Juden in Vormaerz*, p. 122. AZJ. The latter part from AZJ, p. 124.
42. Cf. *The Jews of Austria,* by Wertheimer, Leipzig, 1842; also A. Stern, *Die Geschichte der Juden in Boehmen,* Bruenn, 1904.
43. AZJ, p. 123.
44. GJB, p. 285.
45. IWMM, p. 7.
46. "Recollections of Bohemia," in ASM, March 17 and 24, 1854, Vol. 9, Nos. 22 and 23, pp. 175 ff. Reprinted complete, for those who wish to see the original text in IWMM, pp. 7-21.

Part Two

CHAPTER ONE

1. IWMM, p. 7.
2. Part One, chap. Two.
3. IWMM, p. 7.
4. Cf. pages 125, 158, 195.
5. SWIW, p. 1.
6. Cf. JE, article.
7. STC, p. 16.
8. IWMM, p. 7; SWIW, p. 1.
9. SWIW, p. 1.
10. IWMM, pp. 22-23.
11. Cf. JE, article.
12. IWMM, p. 22.
13. SWIW, p. 1.
14. IWMM, p. 22.
15. HUCJ, March, 1899, Article by Max Heller, "Dr. Wise as a German."
16. IWMM, p. 22.
17. HUCJ, *loc. cit.*
18. SWIW, p. 2.
19. IWMM, pp. 22-23.
20. IWMM, p. 24; AMI, Vol. 29, No. 2.
21. IWMM, p. 23; SWIW, p. 2.
22. SWIW, p. 2; IWMM, p. 23.
23. SWIW, p. 2; IWMM, p. 23.

24. SWIW, p. 2; IWMM, pp. 24-5.
25. WMB, p. 29.

CHAPTER TWO

1. SWIW, p. 2.
2. SWIW, p. 2.
3. SWIW, p. 2; IWMM, p. 25.
4. SWIW, p. 2; IWMM, p. 25.
5. SWIW, p. 3; IWMM, p. 25.
6. SWIW, p. 3; IWMM, p. 25.
7. SWIW, p. 3; Cf. Philipson's "Old European Jewries," Philadelphia, 1894, p. 104.
8. SWIW, pp. 4-5.
9. SWIW, p. 5.
10. SWIW, *ibid.*
11. SWIW, *ibid.*
12. SWIW, p. 6.
13. SWIW, *ibid.* Samuel Freund.
14. SWIW, *ibid.*

CHAPTER THREE

1. SWIW, p. 7.
2. SWIW, *ibid.*
3. SWIW, *ibid.*
4. AMI, Vol. 35, April 25, 1889, p. 4.
5. JE, *ad loc.*
6. SWIW, p. 7.
7. SWIW, *ibid.*
8. SWIW, pp. 7-8.
9. SWIW, p. 8.
10. JE, *ad. loc.*
11. SWIW, pp. 8-9.
12. SWIW, p. 9.
13. SWIW, *ibid.*
14. JE, *ad. loc.*
15. SWIW, p. 9.
16. SWIW, *ibid.*
17. SWIW, *ibid.*
18. HUCJ, March, 1899.
19. SWIW, p. 9.
20. SWIW, *ibid.*
21. SWIW, *ibid.*

CHAPTER FOUR

1. SWIW, p. 10.
2. WMB, p. 6; SWIW, p. 10.
3. SWIW, p. 10.

4. WMB, p. 6; IWMM, p. 31; SWIW, p. 10.
5. IWMM, pp. 31-32, SWIW, p. 10.
6. IWMM, *ibid.*
7. IWMM, pp. 31-32; SWIW, pp. 10-11.
8. IWMM, pp. 31-32; SWIW, p. 11.
9. SWIW, p. 11.
10. IWMM, p. 37.
11. WMB, p. 7.
12. IWMM, pp. 31-32.
13. WMB, p. 7.
14. WMB, p. 6.
15. STC, quoted on p. 29, no source given.
16. IWMM, pp. 37-38.
17. Résumé of RMJ, pp. 162 ff.
18. IWMM, pp. 38-39.
19. IWMM, p. 39.
20. IWMM, p. 36.
21. IWMM, p. 36; SWIW, pp. 11-12.
22. SWIW, p. 12; IWMM, p. 36; SWIW, pp. 12-13.
23. IWMM, p. 37; SWIW, p. 13.

CHAPTER FIVE

1. WMB, p. 8; quoted from *Deborah,* Vol. 42, No. 14, October 1, 1786, p. 5.
2. IWMM, p. 41.
3. IWMM, p. 39; SWIW, p. 14.
4. AIMW, p. 7.
5. SWIW, p. 14.
6. AIMW, pp. 7-8.
7. IWMM, pp. 40-41.
8. SWIW, p. 14.
9. SWIW, pp. 14-15; IWMM, p. 41.
10. IWMM, p. 41.
11. SWIW, p. 15; AIMW, p. 8.
12. JE, *ad loc.*
13. JE, *ibid.*
14. JE, *ibid.*
15. SWIW, p. 15.
16. SWIW, *ibid.*; IWMM, p. 41.
17. JE, *ad loc.*
18. SWIW, p. 15; IWMM, p. 41.
19. JE, *ad loc.*
20. SWIW, p. 15; IWMM, p. 41.
21. JE, *ad loc.*
22. SWIW, p. 15; IWMM, p. 41.
23. JE, *ad loc.*
24. SWIW, p. 15.
25. IWMM, p. 42; from AMI, Vol. 29, N.S., No. 24.
26. IWRM (Cincinnati, 1901), p. 13.
27. SWIW, p. 15; IWMM, p. 42.

28. IWRM, pp. 14-16.
29. SWIW, p. 15; IWRM, p. 13.
30. IWMM, pp. 42 f.; AIMW, p. 8.
31. SWIW, p. 22; IWRM, pp. 16-17; IWMM, p. 43.
32. IWRM, p. 17.
33. IWRM, pp. 17-18.
34. JE, Vol. XII, article "United States," p. 370, "Statistics."
35. SWIW, p. 20.
36. IWMM, p. 47.
37. SWIW, p. 20.
38. SWIW, *ibid.*
39. AYWP, pp. 24-25.
40. RMJ, p. 469; AYWP, p. 21; IWRM, pp. 149 ff. and 155 ff.; SWIW, p. 21.
41. SWIW, p. 21.
42. SWIW, p. 22.
43. IWMM, p. 48.
44. AYWP, pp. 79-80.
45. IWMM, p. 47.
46. AIMW, p. 8.

CHAPTER SIX

1. IWRM, p. 25.
2. WMB, p. 8.
3. IWRM, p. 26.
4. IWRM, *ibid.*
5. IWRM, p. 28.
6. IWRM, pp. 25-26.
7. IWRM, p. 29.
8. IWRM, p. 19; IWMM, pp. 48-49; SWIW, p. 23.
9. IWRM, pp. 24-25; IWMM, pp. 50-51.
10. WMB, p. 8; IWMM, p. 51.
11. IWRM, pp. 20-25.
12. IWRM, p. 23.
13. IWRM, p. 24.
14. IWRM, p. 25.
15. JE, *loc. cit.*
16. IWRM, pp. 19-20.
17. SWIW, pp. 24-25.
18. IWRM, p. 27.
19. IWRM, pp. 27-28.
20. IWMM, p. 52.
21. IWMM, *ibid.*
22. IWMM, *ibid.*
23. IWRM, p. 28.
24. IWRM, *ibid.*
25. WMB, p. 8.
26. WMB, p. 9; IWRM, p. 30; IWMM, p. 52.
27. IWRM, pp. 29-30.
28. IWRM, p. 30.
29. IWRM, pp. 31-32.

30. IWRM, p. 32.
31. WMB, p. 9.
32. IWRM, pp. 32-3; WMB, p. 9; SWIW, p. 25.
33. IWMM, p. 53; WMB, p. 9; IWRM, p. 32.
34. IWMM, p. 53; IWRM, p. 32.
35. IWRM, p. 33, p. 38, p. 41; WMB, p. 9.
36. IWMM, p. 53; IWRM, p. 34.
37. WMB, p. 9.
38. IWRM, p. 36; WMB, p. 9; SWIW, p. 25.
39. IWRM, pp. 36-40.
40. IWRM, p. 40.
41. IWRM, *ibid.*
42. IWRM, p. 38; IWMM, p. 53; WMB, p. 9.
43. IWRM, p. 41.
44. IWRM, *ibid.*
45. IWRM, pp. 41-2.
46. IWRM, pp. 42-3.
47. IWRM, pp. 43-4; WMB, p. 10.
48. IWMM, p. 53; IWRM, p. 44; WMB, p. 10.
49. IWRM, pp. 44-6.
50. IWMM, p. 53; IWRM, p. 46; SWIW, p. 25.
51. WMB, p. 10; SWIW, p. 25; IWMM, p. 53; IWRM, pp. 46-47.
52. IWRM, p. 46.

CHAPTER SEVEN

1. OCC, Feb. 1, 1847.
2. AYWP, pp. 24-5.
3. AMI, Vol. 41, Feb. 14, 1895. Series, "The Difficulty in Defining Judaism."
4. *Ibid.*
5. IWRM, p. 46; IWMM, p. 57.
6. WMB, pp. 1-2.
7. OCC, Feb. 1, 1847. WMB, p. 11. SWIW, p. 29.
8. *Ibid.*
9. IWWM, p. 67. WMB, p. 11, from DEB, Vol. XLII, No. 15, Oct. 8, 1896, pp. 4-5.
10. WMB, p. 11.
11. WMB, p. 12.
12. AMI, March 7, 1895, Vol. 41, No. 7.
13. WMB, p. 13.
14. *Ibid.*
15. IWRM, p. 47. IWMM, p. 57.
16. IWRM, p. 47.
17. IWRM, p. 47.
18. *Ibid.*
19. AMI, Vol. 41, Feb. 14, 1895.
20. WMB, p. 11.
21. IWRM, p. 72. IWMM, p. 61.
22. IWMM, pp. 63 f.
23. IWMM, p. 58; IWRM, pp. 50-1.
24. IWRM, p. 51.

25. *Ibid.*
26. IWRM, p. 53.
27. Liturgical poems from the Middle Ages chiefly; Lamentations and Prayers for Pardon, in the days before the High Holy Days.
28. SWIW, p. 29. IWMM, pp. 63 f.
29. AMI, Vol. 41, Feb. 14, 1895.
30. *Ibid.*
31. IWMM, p. 61.
32. IWMM, p. 61; IWRM, p. 49; SWIW, pp. 29-30.

CHAPTER EIGHT

1. IWRM, p. 54.
2. IWRM, p. 55
3. IWRM, p. 57.
4. OCC, Vol. 5, p. 109 (quoted in IWMM, pp. 64-5).
5. The strange ceremony, when a man refuses, or is not permitted, to marry his brother's childless widow, a part of the legislation about the Levirate marriage.
6. Women whose husbands have disappeared, or died, but without witnesses. They may not, under Jewish law, remarry.
7. IWRM, pp. 55-6; IWMM, pp. 65-6.
8. OCC, Vol. 5, pp. 158 ff., 1847.
9. *Ibid.*
10. IWRM, pp. 55-6; IWMM, p. 65-6; SWIW, p. 31; AMI, Vol. 41, Feb. 14, 1895, p. 4.
11. SWIW, p. 32; cf. OCC, Vol. 5, p. 158; IWMM, p. 67.
12. An obvious error, since Jews first came to the American colonies in 1654.
13. IWRM, pp. 56-7.
14. *Ibid.*
15. AMI, Vol. 41, Feb. 14, 1895, p. 4.
16. IWRM, pp. 78-80; IWMM, pp. 69-70; IWRM, p. 81.
17. JE, *ad. loc.*
18. AMI, Vol. 41, Feb. 14, 1895, p. 4. For Cleveland Conference, see later under year 1855. Cf. also SWIW, pp. 30 f.
19. IWRM, p. 62.
20. AYWP, p. 12.
21. IWRM, p. 62.
22. IWMM, p. 67.
23. IWMM, p. 68.
24. SWIW, pp. 33 f.
25. IWRM, pp. 65-68.
26. IWRM, pp. 59-60.
27. IWRM, p. 62; IWMM, pp. 68-9; SWIW, pp. 32 f., also pp. 34-5.

CHAPTER NINE

1. IWRM, p. 84; IWMM, pp. 72 ff.
2. Encyc. Britt. *ad loc.*
3. IWRM, pp. 82-3.

4. Encyc. Britt. *ad loc.*
5. IWRM, p. 83.
6. IWRM, p. 105.
7. IWRM, pp. 108 f.
8. IWRM, p. 84.
9. *Ibid.*
10. IWRM, p. 86.
11. AMI, Vol. 41, Feb. 14, 1895, p. 4; OCC, 1848, pp. 431-35; IWMM, pp. 72 f.; IWRM, pp. 85-6; OCC, Vol. 6, p. 313, and p. 321, "Call" on pp. 431-35, December issue, 1848; IWMM, pp. 79-80, and 81.
12. OCC, Kislev 24, 5609.
13. OCC, Vol. 6, pp. 313 and 321.
14. AMI, Vol. 41, Feb. 14, 1895, p. 4.
15. AYWP, p. 68.
16. OCC, Vol. 7, No. 2, pp. 61-72, May, 1849 (quoted in EYAE, p. 37).
17. EYAE, pp. 38-9.
18. IWRM, p. 76, also p. 69.
19. *Ibid.*
20. IWRM, p. 73.
21. *Ibid.*
22. IWRM, p. 76.
23. IWRM, p. 97.
24. IWRM, pp. 97-100, also pp. 95-6, also p. 118.
25. SWIW, pp. 35-6, AMI, Vol. 38, No. 50, June 9, 1892, p. 4 has a note to the effect that Confirmation had been introduced in Germany twenty years before this time, which was forty years before this article was written. Wise claims that it was the idea of Leopold Stein in Burgkunstadt, Bavaria. Who was the first to have it in the United States is a question. Probably Merzbacher had had it a year earlier in New York than Wise did in Albany. Philipson in RMJ, ascribes it first to Joseph Abraham Friedlander, chief rabbi of the Duchy of Westphalia in 1833 (p. 36); later it had been introduced in Fuerth by Dr. Loewi (p. 77).
26. IWRM, pp. 97-100, also pp. 95-6, and pp. 119-20.
27. IWRM, pp. 112, 114.
28. IWRM, pp. 114-16.
29. IWRM, p. 116.
30. IWRM, p. 80.
31. IWRM, pp. 100-02.
32. IWRM, p. 87.
33. IWRM, pp. 87-8.

CHAPTER TEN

1. OCC, Vol. 6, p. 581, March, 1849.
2. IWMM, p. 82.
3. *Ibid.* Cf. OCC, *loc. cit.*
4. OCC, Adar, 5609—March, 1849.
5. *Ibid.*
6. OCC, Vol. 7, pp. 12-15.
7. OCC, Sivan, 5609, pp. 267-70, this is March, 1849.
8. ARCH, II, publication II, No. 1 (June, 1949), pp. 21-46.

9. AMI, Vol. 25, No. 5, Aug. 2, 1878, p. 4.
10. OCC, Kislev, 5610, December, 1849, Vol. 7, No. 9.
11. IWRM, p. 90, also pp. 82-3.
12. IWRM, p. 92. IWMM, p. 83.
13. IWRM, p. 88.
14. IWRM, pp. 125, 126.
15. IWRM, p. 94.
16. IWRM, pp. 94-5.
17. IWMM, pp. 89 f.
18. IWRM, pp. 124-25.
19. IWRM, p. 125; IWMM, pp. 88, 89.
20. OCC, Vol. 7, No. 4, July, 1849; second installment in No. 5, August, 1849.
21. IWRM, pp. 121-22.
22. *Ibid.*
23. EYAE, pp. 39-41.
24. JE, *ad loc.*
25. EYAE, pp. 39-41.
26. IWMM, p. 86.

CHAPTER ELEVEN

1. AMI, Vol. 41, Feb. 21, 1895, p. 4.
2. IWRM, p. 126; SWIW, p. 36; IWMM, p. 91; AIMW, p. 5.
3. IWRM, pp. 126-27.
4. IWMM, pp. 91 f.; IWRM, pp. 126 ff.
5. IWRM, pp. 130-31; IWMM, pp. 92 f.
6. IWMM, p. 93.
7. IWMM, pp. 93 f.; IWRM, pp. 132, 139-41. AMI, Vol. 41, Feb. 21, 1895.
8. IWMM, pp. 93 f.; also pp. 94 f.; IWRM, p. 136.
9. IWRM, pp. 132, 136.
10. AIMW, p. 5; IWRM, p. 136.
11. IWRM, p. 138.
12. *Ibid.* also p. 149; AIMW, p. 5.
13. IWMM, pp. 95-6; IWRM, p. 141.
14. IWRM, p. 141.
15. IWRM, p. 142; OCC, Vol. 7, p. 217, 1850; IWMM, p. 96; SWIW, p. 37.
16. IWRM, p. 143.
17. *Ibid.*, AMI, Vol. 41, Feb. 21, 1895, p. 4.
18. IWRM, pp. 143, 147.
19. IWRM, pp. 147-49; IWMM, pp. 96 f.; AMI, Feb. 21, 1895, Vol. 41, p. 4.
20. IWRM, p. 147; SWIW, pp. 37 f.; AMI, Vol. 41, Feb. 21, 1895, p. 4.
21. AMI, Vol. 41, Feb. 21, 1895.
22. *Ibid.*
23. IWRM, p. 147; SWIW, pp. 37 f.; IWMM, pp. 96 f.; IWRM, p. 145.
24. IWRM, p. 149; IWMM, p. 98; AMI, Vol. 41, Feb. 21, 1895. SWIW, p. 37.
25. AMI, Vol. 41, Feb. 21, 1895; SWIW, p. 37; IWRM, p. 151; IWMM, pp. 98 f.
26. IWRM, pp. 151-52; IWMM, pp. 98 f.; AMI, Vol. 41, Feb. 21, 1895.
27. OCC, Letter dated July 8, 1850.

CHAPTER TWELVE

1. AMI, Vol. 12, Jan. 26, 1866, p. 236.
2. AMI, Vol. 41, Feb. 21, 1895, p. 4.
3. SWIW, pp. 37 f.; IWRM, pp. 152-53.
4. IWRM, p. 155.
5. *Ibid.* p. 156.
6. IWMM, pp. 100-02; IWRM, p. 157.
7. IWRM, p. 157.
8. IWMM, pp. 100 f.
9. IWRM, p. 157.
10. IWRM, p. 157 f.; History of Beth Emeth Congregation, Albany (pub. 1910), pp. 46-7; IWMM, p. 102.
11. IWMM, pp. 102-03.
12. AYWP, pp. 71-2.
13. IWMM, p. 103.
14. *Ibid.*, p. 104.
15. IWRM, p. 158.
16. *Ibid.*, p. 159.
17. IWRM, p. 159.
18. IWRM, p. 161.
19. IWRM, pp. 161-62.
20. *Ibid.*
21. IWRM, p. 162.
22. IWRM, pp. 162-63
23. *Ibid.*
24. IWRM, pp. 164-65. IWMM, p. 104.
25. IWRM, p. 164.
26. IWRM, p. 165; SWIW, p. 38; also IWRM, p. 166.
27. *Albany Evening Atlas,* Sept. 7 and 9, 1850. Text in ARCH.
28. OCC, June, 1851, quoted in IWMM, p. 107, cf. also p. 105.
29. IWRM, pp. 166-67.
30. IWRM, p. 167.
31. *Ibid.*, also pp. 168-69.
32. IWRM, pp. 172-74.
33. OCC, 1850, pp. 255-57.
34. OCC, 1850, same issue.
35. OCC, 1850, pp. 306-12.
36. *Ibid.*
37. OCC, 1850, pp. 422-24.
38. AMI, Vol. 6, Nov. 11, 1859, p. 148.
39. RMJ, pp. 173-81.

CHAPTER THIRTEEN

1. WMB, p. 14. From DEB., Vol. 42, No. 17, Oct. 22, 1896; IWMM, p. 108.
2. IWMM, pp. 109-10; IWRM, p. 174.
3. AMI, Vol. 41, Feb. 21, 1895, p. 4.
4. IWRM, p. 176.

5. SWIW, p. 40; IWRM, p. 176.
6. IWRM, pp. 176-77.
7. IWRM, p. 178.
8. *Ibid.*
9. OCC, Vol. 8, p. 474 (quoted in IWMM, p. 111), October, 1850.
10. IWRM, p. 178.
11. *Ibid*
12. IWRM, p. 184.
13. Encyclop. Britt. *ad loc.*
14. *Ibid.*
15. IWRM, p. 185; IWMM, pp. 111 f.

Here it is necessary to take up in detail a very interesting and careful consideration of this account in Wise's *Reminiscences,* by Dr. Bertram W. Korn in his *Eventful Years and Experiences* (The American Jewish Archives, Cincinnati, 1954), in a chapter entitled "Judah P. Benjamin as a Jew," originally published in the Publications of the American Jewish Historical Society, No. XXXVIII, Pt. 3, March, 1949, pp. 153-71. Dr. Korn casts considerable doubt on the accuracy of Wise's memory in regard to this entire meeting with Webster, Maury, and Judah P. Benjamin. He is entirely correct in saying that Benjamin did not become Senator from Louisiana until 1853. Since Wise wrote his *Reminiscences* very much later, and did not publish them in *Die Deborah,* in German, until the issues beginning with July 3, 1875 and ending with August 11, 1875, it is evident that they represent his recollections of more than twenty years later. There are inaccuracies that creep into them in a number of places.

The question is whether these inaccuracies vitiate the value of the entire account. Webster *was* Secretary of State in the winter of 1850-51, when Wise was in Washington. Dr. Korn asserts that "so far as we know, Benjamin was nowhere near Washington during the time of Wise's visit." (p. 85, *op. cit.*). But this judgment is open to serious doubt. We do not possess an accurate enough account of Benjamin's days to state positively that Benjamin could not have been there. In 1848, Benjamin had been admitted to practice before the Supreme Court of the United States, and might well have been in Washington, either on legal business or upon a visit, at the time of which Wise writes. It is certainly not possible to assert definitely that Wise had imagined Benjamin's presence.

Nor is the date of Wise's visit to Washington as vague as Dr. Korn makes out. It is of course quite correct that Wise's chronology in the *Reminiscences* is quite unspecific at this point. He says merely that his new congregation was organized after *Rosh Ha-shono,* 1850, and that thereupon he left for New York, Baltimore, and Washington to lecture and to collect funds for it. But there are several checks which enable us to date it with considerable accuracy. We have quoted in the text an account from the *Occident* of his address at Rodef Shalom in Philadelphia; this was in the issue of October, 1850. This could not have got into print as quickly as this, had not Wise been in Philadelphia shortly before then. From this it seems clear that Wise must have left Albany almost immediately after the *Yomim Noro'im,* and must have been in Philadelphia at the end of September, and probably, almost certainly, in Washington early in October, 1850.

Finally, Dr. Korn has as his main point that, while Benjamin probably never denied his Jewishness, nor apostatized, neither is there any reliable indication, among the various tales and stories that have come out, that he was actively associated with a synagogue, and that he rose in defense of Jewish rights on the several occasions when he might have in the Senate or elsewhere.

Nor does it seem to me that Wise's account states or implies that Benjamin was an informed or an active Jew. Benjamin is reported simply to have differed with Wise, Maury, and Webster, claiming that Judaism and Unitarianism do not resemble one another, and a bit later on (p. 188) that he [Benjamin] "yet insisted that he had no coreligionists beside the Jews." Wise also says that it was painful to him to find that Benjamin compared very badly with Webster in Benjamin's ignorance of the Bible, and in his "confused notion of Orthodox Portuguese Judaism." He adds that Benjamin "rarely heard anything about it, and was never guided by it." The total picture given by Wise is, therefore, not as misleading, nor does it fail to correspond with what is known of Benjamin as a Jew nearly as greatly as one would be led to think by Dr. Korn's account.

The point is important only as an examination of the value of Wise's recollections as a whole. The conclusion to which one should probably come is that, while Wise was mistaken as to Benjamin's being a Senator at the time, the meeting with Webster, Benjamin, and Maury, most likely did take place, at the period and in the manner Wise recounts. The additional negative evidence, cited by Dr. Korn, that Wise failed to mention this meeting with Benjamin, in a bitter political statement about Benjamin in AMI, Vol. 7, No. 30, p. 238 (Jan. 25, 1861), or in his obituary sketch on Benjamin in AMI, Vol. 30, No. 46 (May 16, 1884), is interesting, but not decisive, for to neither case was the conversation in Washington germane.

Perhaps it is unnecessary to belabor the entire question, for it is not crucial in Wise's life. It is hard to believe, after an examination of all the evidence available, and of Wise's clear knowledge, for example about Maury—who was at the same two chats in Washington—that Wise was completely mistaken, that his memory was deceiving him, and that he knew nothing of Benjamin except by report.

16. IWRM, pp. 191-92.
17. *Ibid.*, p. 185.
18. *Ibid.*, pp. 186-87.
19. *Ibid.*, pp. 187-88.
20. *Ibid.*, pp. 191-92.
21. AMI, Vol. 41, Feb. 21, 1894, p. 4; IWMM, p. 112; IWRM, p. 192-93.
22. IWRM, pp. 192 f.
23. IWRM, p. 195.
24. *Ibid.*
25. IWRM, pp. 195-99.
26. IWRM, p. 199.
27. *Ibid.*, pp. 199-200.
28. ARCH.
29. IWRM, p. 213.
30. SWIW, p. 39; OCC, under "News Item," 1851, p. 477; IWMM, pp. 120 f.

31. RMJ, Note, p. 473: "The congregation *Anshe Emeth* of Albany, New York, under the leadership of Isaac M. Wise in 1851 (introduced first the "family-pew"); see *Reminiscences of Isaac M. Wise,* edited by the author, 212, Cincinnati, 1901."
32. IWRM, pp. 210-14; IWMM, pp. 121 f.
33. IWMM, pp. 123-44.
34. *Ibid.*, pp. 119-20.
35. IWRM, pp. 217-19; the prayer itself from ASM, Vol. 4, p. 12, July 9, 1851 (quoted in IWMM, pp. 120-21). The prayer itself was delivered in June. For the entire subject of priority in prayers before the Congress and State legislatures, cf. Korn, EYAE, "The First Jewish Prayer in Congress," pp. 98-124, originally in HUC College Annual, XXIII, part II (1951-52), pp. 95-125. References to Wise's prayer and its text, on pp. 116-18 of EYAE.
36. IWMM, pp. 113 f., also p. 119.
37. OCC, 1851, pp. 492-96. Wise's letter is dated Albany, Nov. 13, 5611 (1851).
38. IWMM, pp. 113-20 for entire series and controversy.
39. *Ibid.*
40. *Ibid.*
41. OCC, 1851, pp. 492-96. Letter dated Albany, Nov. 13.
42. OCC, Third Installment, 1851, pp. 14-19, Feb. 13, 5611 (1851).
43. OCC, Fourth Installment, 1851, pp. 187-95.
44. OCC, Fifth Installment, July 9, 1851, pp. 298-305.
45. *Ibid.*
46. OCC, July 9, 1851.

CHAPTER FOURTEEN

1. IWRM, pp. 208-09.
2. IWRM, p. 205.
3. WMB, p. 15; AMI, Vol. 41, Feb. 21, 1895.
4. IWRM, pp. 201 f.
5. Announcement and Lyon's note in ASM, Sept. 10, 1852 (quoted in IWMM, pp. 128 ff.), Vol. 6, No. 25; WMB, p. 15; IWRM, pp. 206-08.
6. IWMM, p. 131, on a seminary pp. 135-36; WMB, p. 16.
7. IWMM, pp. 127 f.
8. IWRM, p. 203 f.
9. ASM, April 12, 1854.
10. IWRM, pp. 207-08.
11. IWRM, pp. 212-13.
12. IWMM, pp. 126 f., quoting from ASM, Vol. 5, Dec. 18, 1851.
13. IWRM, footnote on p. 215.
14. IWRM, pp. 215-17.
15. AYWP, pp. 80-1.
16. IWRM, pp. 219-22.
17. IWMM, pp. 136 f.; citation from ASM, April 28, 1853.
18. WMB, p. 16.
19. *Ibid.*
20. Introduction to "History of the Israelitish Nation," Vol. I, pp. xv. to xvi., quoted in SWIW, pp. 42-3.
21. IWMM, pp. 124-25, also pp. 140-43; IWRM, pp. 230-31.

22. IWMM, pp. 142-43; IWRM, p. 225.
23. IWRM, pp. 227-28; at length in AMI, Vol. 41, March 7, 1895. also IWRM, pp. 230 f.; WMB, pp. 17 f.
24. IWRM, pp. 230 f. Also, AMI, March 7, 1895, Vol. 41.
25. IWRM, pp. 230 f.; OCC, 1854, pp. 33-8.
26. WMB, p. 17
27. ARCH, August 4, 1854, photostat of letter.
28. OCC, 1854, pp. 16-9.
29. OCC, Jan. 16, 1854.
30. OCC, 1854, pp. 148-53.
31. OCC, 1854, pp. 315-19.
32. OCC, 1854, pp. 398-401.
33. IWRM, pp. 232 f.
34. *Ibid.*

CHAPTER FIFTEEN

1. IWRM, p. 233.
2. IWMM, p. 143.
3. AMI, Vol. 41, March 7, 1895.
4. DEB, Vol. XLII, No. 18, Oct. 29, 1896, pp. 4-5.
5. IWRM, pp. 234-35; IWMM, pp. 143-44.
6. IWRM, pp. 233-34.
7. *Ibid.*
8. IWMM, pp. 144-45.
9. AMI, Vol. 41, March 7, 1895.
10. IWRM, pp. 235-36.
11. IWRM, p. 237; AYWP, p. 79.
12. IWMM, p. 145.
13. AYWP, p. 79.
14. AMI, Vol. 32, NS No. 18, May 2, 1879; IWMM, pp. 145-46.
15. IWMM, p. 146.
16. AYWP, p. 80, 81.
17. IWMM, p. 146; IWRM, p. 238.
18. IWRM, p. 238.
19. IWRM, p. 239.
20. IWRM, pp. 239-40.
21. AYWP, pp. 6-7 (cited from "The Civilization of the Old Northwest," by Beverly W. Bond, Jr., Macmillan, New York, 1914); and "The Cincinnati Miscellany," by Charles Cist; Caleb Clark, Cincinnati, 1845; "Cincinnati in 1841, Its Early Annals and Future Prospects," by Charles Cist, Cincinnati, 1841.
22. AYWP, p. 8; from "The Centennial History of Cincinnati and Representative Citizens," by Charles T. Greve, Vol. I, Chicago, 1904.
23. AYWP, pp. 10-12; from "The Domestic Manners of the Americans," by Mrs. Trollope; Whittaker, Treacher and Co., London, 1832.
24. AYWP, pp. 12-14; cf. "Cincinnati Sonst und Jetzt," by Armin Tenner, Mecklenberg and Rosenthal, Cincinnati, 1878.
25. AYWP, p. 14; from "In Early Cincinnati," by Henry A. and Mrs. Kate B. Ford, quoting Rev. J.S.. Buckingham.
26. AYWP, pp. 15-16.

27. AYWP, pp. 17-18.
28. AYWP, p. 18; from "The Cincinnati Miscellany," by Charles Cist, Caleb Clarke, Cincinnati, Vol. II, 1845.
29. AYWP, pp. 20-21.
30. AYWP, pp. 21-23, in part quoting AMI, June 18, 1858.
31. AYWP, pp. 24-31, quotation from p. 27.
32. AYWP, p. 29, 31.
33. AYWP, p. 32; Gutheim was for all the latter part of his life rabbi of Temple Sinai in New Orleans, with a brief, unsatisfactory interval at Temple Emanuel in New York. He died while serving the New Orleans congregation in 1886, and was succeeded by Rabbi Maximilian Heller in 1887.
34. AYWP, p. 35; from booklet in Hebrew Union College, published by the congregation and containing Gutheim's address.
35. AYWP, pp. 36-37.
36. AYWP, pp. 36-38, from the Anniversary Booklet, 1892.
37. AYWP, pp. 38-41; partly from *Occident,* November, 1848. AYWP, p. 68.
38. AYWP, pp. 68-72; also quoting *Occident,* November, 1852. Letter of Henry Mack on AYWP, p. 70, from *Occident,* July, 1852.
39. AYWP, pp. 72-76.
40. AYWP, p. 75, 76.
41. IWRM, pp. 240-50; IWMM, pp. 159-60; IWRM, p. 240 as to Woodruff House, etc.
42. IWRM, pp. 240-41.
43. IWRM, pp. 241-42.
44. *Ibid.*
45. IWRM, pp. 243-45.
46. IWRM, pp. 245-47.
47. IWRM, pp. 246-47.
48. IWRM, pp. 247-48.
49. IWRM, pp. 247-49.
50. IWRM, pp. 249-50.
51. IWRM, p. 250; AMI, Vol. 41, March 7, 1895.
52. AMI, Vol. 41, March 7, 1895. Salmon P. Chase, an American statesman and jurist, born in New Hampshire, Jan. 13, 1808, graduated from Dartmouth College, and removed to Cincinnati in 1830. He associated himself in 1836 with the anti-slavery movement, frequently serving as lawyer for fugitive slaves. Some of his appearances before the Supreme Court on key cases at this controversial time won him much attention. He left the Whig Party, joined the Liberty Party, but soon realized that a third party movement could not succeed. Later they combined with the Democrats, and Chase drafted the famous Free-Soil platform, in 1848, which nominated Van Buren. He was elected to the Senate in 1849. He classed himself with the Independent Democrats and spoke often and ably on anti-slavery. But gradually he became convinced of the futility of trying to influence the Democrats for a reasonable policy, and he was one of the first to envisage the creation of the Republican Party. He was first Republican Governor of Ohio from 1855-59. Second only to Seward, he was an outstanding Republican. He failed to get the nomination in 1860, despite his strong, unequivocal views on slavery, because his opinions on "protection" were not orthodox enough for the Party. He served as Secretary of the Treasury in

Lincoln's Cabinet from 1861-64, and rendered service of inestimable value. He was chiefly responsible for two major changes: the establishment of a national banking system, and the issue of a legal tender paper currency. He was exceedingly ambitious, had some temperamental differences with Lincoln, and retired at last from the Cabinet. A few months later he was appointed a member of the Supreme Court to succeed Taney, and held this position until his death in 1873. In his later years he drifted back toward the Democratic Party, and tried unsuccessfully to get the nomination in 1872. He was one of the ablest leaders during the crucial period of the Civil War, and deserves high rank among American statesmen. (from the Encyc. Brit. *ad loc.*)

53. WMB, p. 18.
54. IWMM, p. 148.
55. IWMM, pp. 148-49, from ASM, Vol. 9, No. 23.
56. IWMM, pp. 147-48.
57. IWMM, p. 147.
58. IWRM, p. 251.
59. IWRM, p. 251-52; IWMM, p. 150, quoting from ASM, April 28, 1854.
60. IWRM, p. 252.
61. *Ibid.*
62. IWRM, p. 253.
63. IWRM, pp. 253-54; AYWP, pp. 88-9.
64. IWRM, p. 254.
65. AMI, Vol. 41, 1895.
66. AMI, Vol. 41, March 7, 1895.

CHAPTER SIXTEEN

1. WMB, p. 19; SWIW, pp. 101-02, IWMM, p. 160.
2. SWIW, pp. 101-02.
3. IWRM, p. 257.
4. IWRM, pp. 257-58., IWMM, p. 159.
5. AMI, Vol. 25, No. 42, April 25, 1879.
6. IWRM, pp. 260-61.
7. SWIW, p. 55.
8. IWRM, pp. 261-63.
9. IWMM, pp. 159-61.
10. IWMM, pp. 161-63; IWRM, pp. 276-79.
11. IWRM, pp. 277-78.
12. IWMM, p. 161-63; IWRM, pp. 278-79.
13. IWMM, p. 163; IWRM, p. 279.
14. IWRM, pp. 263-64.
15. IWRM, pp. 264-65.
16. IWRM, p. 265.
17. ARCH.
18. AMI, Vol. 1, No. 19, p. 150, Nov. 17, 1854.
19. AMI, Vol. 1, No. 19, p. 148, Nov. 17, 1854.
20. AYWP, p. 23.
21. IWRM, pp. 279-81.
22. IWRM, p. 281.

23. IWRM, p. 283-91. Cf. also Jacob R. Marcus.
24. IWRM, pp. 304-05.

CHAPTER SEVENTEEN

1. SWIW, pp. 55-56; WMB, pp. 19-20; IWRM, pp. 265-70.
2. WMB, pp. 19-20.
3. WMB, p. 20.
4. WMB, pp. 20-22, from DEB, Vol. 42, No. 19, pp. 4-5, Nov. 5, 1896.
5. WMB, p. 21.
6. WMB, p. 22.
7. AMI, Vol. 1, No. 9, Sept. 8, 1854.
8. AMI, Vol. 25, No. 1, p. 4, July 5, 1878.
9. *Ibid.*
10. IWMM, pp. 195-205, from IWRM pp. 265-72.
11. AMI, Vol. 1, No. 23; IWMM, pp. 205-07 (AMI of Dec. 15, 1854).
12. IWRM, pp. 272-74
13. IWRM, p. 271.
14. IWRM, pp. 272-73. Eisenmenger was an anti-Jewish fanatic, born in Mannheim in 1654, and died in Heidelberg in 1704. He devoted himself to Jewish studies for the sole purpose of finding things with which to damn and slander Jews. His main work, *Entdecktes Judenthum*, has been the chief arsenal for slanders on the Talmud down to our own time. It appeared in Frankfort in 1700. At one time Eisenmenger negotiated for blackmail to suppress the work. It is a distortion throughout, resting upon mistranslations, perversion by taking passages out of context, etc. Unfortunately it has been periodically republished in new editions.
15. AMI, Vol. 39, No. 1, July 7, 1892.
16. IWRM, pp. 292-93.
17. IWRM, pp. 346-47.
18. AMI, Vol. 1, No. 34, p. 271, March 2, 1855.
19. AMI, Vol. 40, No. 47, May 24, 1894; IWRM, p. 293.
20. IWRM, pp. 326-27.
21. *Ibid.*
22. IWRM, pp. 285-86; SWIW, p. 57; AMI, Vol. 1, No. 12, p. 101, Oct. 6, 1854.
23. AMI, Vol. 1, No. 13, p. 101, Oct. 6, 1854.
24. IWRM, pp. 285-86.
25. IWRM, pp. 289-90.
26. IWRM, pp. 290-91.
27. IWRM, pp. 305-06.
28. IWRM, pp. 325-26.
29. IWRM, p. 325.
30. IWMM, p. 207.
31. AMI, Vol. 3, No. 19, Nov. 14, 1856; cited in IWMM, pp. 207-08.
32. AMI, Vol. 1, No. 2, July 21, 1854; cited in IWMM, p. 259.
33. AMI, Vol. 1, No. 3, July 28, 1854; cited in IWMM pp. 259-60.
34. ASM, spring of 1855; cited in IWMM, p. 260.
35. AMI, Vol. 1, No. 37, March 23, 1855; cited in IWMM, pp. 260-61.
36. AMI, Vol. 1, No. 14, p. 110, Oct. 13, 1854.
37. AMI, Vol. 1, No. 15, p. 114, Oct. 20, 1854.
38. AMI Vol. 1, No. 21, p. 164, Dec. 1, 1854.

39. AMI, Vol. 1, No. 21, p. 175, Dec. 1, 1854.
40. AMI, Vol. 1, No. 27, p. 212, Jan. 12, 1855.
41. In the dictionary "pomology" the "science and practice of fruit-raising."
42. AMI, Vol. 1, No. 38, p. 300, March 30, 1855.
43. AMI, Vol. 1, No. 39, p. 398, April 6, 1855.
44. AMI, Vol. 2, No. 5, pp. 37-8, Aug. 10, 1855.
45. AMI, Vol. 2, No. 9, p. 70, Sept. 7, 1855; also No. 10, p. 77, Sept. 14, 1855.
46. AMI, Vol. 2, No. 14, p. 108, Oct. 12, 1855.
47. AMI, Vol. 2, No. 18, p. 149, Nov. 9, 1855.
48. AMI, Vol. 2, No. 19, p. 156, Nov. 16, 1855.
49. AMI, Vol. 2, No. 27, p. 220, Jan. 11, 1856.
50. AMI, Vol. 2, No. 52, p. 420, July 4, 1856.
51. AMI, Vol. 3, No. 7, p. 30, Aug. 25, 1856.
52. AMI, Vol. 5, No. 21, Nov. 26, 1858.

CHAPTER EIGHTEEN

1. IWRM p. 307.
2. AMI, Vol. 1, No. 29, p. 229, Jan. 26, 1855.
3. AMI, Vol. 1, No. 31, p. 244, Feb. 9, 1855.
4. AMI, Vol. 1, No. 34, p. 268, March 2, 1855.
5. *Ibid.*
6. AMI, Vol. 1, No. 35, p. 276, March 9, 1855.
7. "The fifteenth day of the month of Sh'vat," the New Year for trees.
8. AMI, Vol. 1, No. 40, p. 317, April 13, 1855.
9. AMI, Vol. 1, No. 41, p. 325, April 20, 1855.
10. AMI, Vol. 2, No. 4, p. 29, Aug. 3, 1855.
11. AMI, Vol. 2, No. 6, p. 44, Aug. 17, 1855; IWRM, pp. 307-08; IWMM, pp. 323-24.
12. AMI, Vol. 2, No. 8, Aug. 31, 1855.
13. IWMM, p. 164.
14. AMI, Vol. 2, No. 11, p. 81, Sept. 21, 1855.
15. AMI, Vol. 2, No. 12, p. 92, Sept. 28, 1855.
16. AMI, Vol. 2, No. 15, p. 115, Oct. 12, 1855.
17. AMI, Vol. 2, No. 17, p. 132, Oct. 26, 1855; IWRM, cf. complete from pp. 312-23.
18. AMI, Vol. 2, No. 17, p. 132, Oct. 26, 1855.
19. *Ibid.*
20. AMI, Vol. 2, No. 18, p. 148, Nov. 9, 1855; IWRM, pp. 313-14.
21. AMI, Vol. 2, No. 17, p. 132, Oct. 26, 1855.
22. *Ibid.*
23. AMI, Vol. 2, No. 18, p. 148, Nov. 9, 1855.
24. IWRM, p. 316.
25. IWRM, p. 315.
26. IWRM, p. 315.
27. IWRM, pp. 316-20.
28. From "Some Unpublished Letters," etc., ARCH. David Einhorn, one of the leaders of the Reform movement in the United States, was born in Bavaria in 1809. He was thus almost ten years older than Wise. He was made *Morenu* in 1826 and pursued philosophical studies in Würzburg and Munich. In 1838 he became rabbi of a congregation in Wellhausen, but

had difficulties with the government. He held several other pulpits, participated in the Frankfort conference of 1845, at which Wise was present, and argued against Frankel. He attended also the Breslau Conference in 1846. Delitsch later charged him with heresy, but he defended himself successfully. His position became more and more perilous, because of the reactionary government, and he determined to migrate to America. This he did in this very year, 1855, and became rabbi of Har Sinai congregation in Baltimore. Very soon he started a monthly in German, to favor "radical reform," called *Sinai.* In 1858, he issued a prayer book, called *Olat Tamid,* which was widely used. Before and during the Civil War he denounced slavery unsparingly. He was threatened for this, and had to flee in 1861. He went to Philadelphia, where he became rabbi of Congregation Keneseth Israel. In August, 1866, he removed to New York, to the pulpit of Adath Yeshurun. His co-workers were Samuel Adler and Samuel Hirsch. He retired near his seventieth year. Two of his daughters were married to Kaufmann Kohler and to Emil G. Hirsch. He was the author of two books, and of many controversial articles. He was also supposed to have been a magnificent preacher.

Samuel Adler was also a German rabbi, born in the same year as Einhorn. He was graduated from the Frankfort Gymnasium, and studied at the Universities of Bonn and Giessen. His first pulpit was in the city of Worms, later in Alzey. He was called to Temple Emanu-El in New York in 1857, to succeed Merzbacher. He was the leader of the congregation until 1874, and was succeeded by G. Gottheil. He was a thorough Talmudist, and an excellent Jewish scholar in general. He too attended the rabbinical conferences in Germany, three of them in fact: at Brunswick, Frankfort, and Breslau. He was a devoted advocate of Reform, and wrote some excellent articles. He was the father of Felix Adler, the founder of the Ethical Culture Society. He passed away in 1891.

29. "Some Letters of Ethical Importance," ARCH
30. *Ibid.*
31. IWRM, pp. 317-18.
32. IWRM, pp. 318-19.
33. IWRM, pp. 319-20.
34. IWRM, pp. 320-21.
35. AMI, Vol. 2, No. 19, p. 157, Nov. 16, 1855.
36. AMI, Vol. 2, No. 20, p. 164, Nov. 23, 1855.
37. AMI, Vol. 2, No. 21, p. 172, Nov. 30, 1855.
38. AMI, Vol. 2, No. 24, p. 196, Dec. 21, 1855.
39. AMI, Vol. 2, No. 26, p. 212, Jan. 4, 1856.
40. AMI, Vol. 2, No. 30, p. 244, Feb. 1, 1856.
41. AMI, Vol. 2, No. 32, p. 266, Feb. 15, 1856.
42. IWRM, pp. 321-22.
43. AMI, Vol. 2, No. 34, p. 275, March 1, 1856.
44. AMI, Vol. 2, No. 40, April 12, 1856.
45. AMI, Vol. 2, No. 45, p. 356, May 9, 1856.
46. AMI, Vol. 3, No. 11, p. 84, Sept. 19, 1856.
47. *Ibid.*
48. AMI, Vol. 3, No. 33, p. 260, Feb. 20, 1857.
49. AMI, Vol. 4, No. 9, p. 69, Sept. 4, 1857.

50. Cf. UJE *ad loc.*
51. IWMM, p. 325; AMI, Vol. 5, Dec. 31, 1858.
52. IWRM, pp. 343-44; IWMM, pages 331-35.
53. WMB, p. 23.
54. AMI, Vol. 4, No. 10, p. 76, Sept. 11, 1857.
55. IWMM, p. 164; AMI, Vol. 4, No. 13, p. 102, Oct. 2, 1857; IWRM, pp. 345-346; AMI, Vol. 5, No. 7, p. 54, Aug. 20, 1858.
56. IWRM, pp. 347-48; IWMM, pp. 163-64.
57. AMI, Vol. 5, No. 26, Dec. 31, 1858; IWMM, pp. 333-35.

CHAPTER NINETEEN

1. EYAE, pp. 58-78.
2. IWRM, pp. 310-11.
3. IWRM, p. 311.
4. ASM, Vol. 12, No. 2, p. 12, April 27, 1855, cited in EYAE, p. 69.
5. AMI, Vol. 2, No. 13, p. 102, Oct. 5, 1855; cited in EYAE, p. 69.
6. AMI, Vol. 2, No. 2, p. 12, July 20, 1855; cited in EYAE, p. 69.
7. AMI, Vol. 2, No. 10, Sept. 14, 1855, p. 76.
8. SWIW, p. 55.
9. IWRM, pp. 275-76.
10. IWRM, pp. 283-84.
11. ARCH.
12. IWMM, p. 160.
13. IWMM, pp. 160-61.
14. IWRM, pp. 258-59.
15. IWRM, pp. 259-60.
16. IWRM, pp. 281-83.
17. No. 560 of the *Orach Chayyim.*
18. AMI, Vol. 1, No. 45, p. 356, May 18, 1855.
19. IWRM, p. 285.
20. IWRM, p. 309.
21. IWRM, p. 310.
22. IWRM, pp. 322-23.
23. AMI, Vol. 3, No. 1, p. 4, July 11, 1856.
24. AMI, Vol. 3, No. 18, Nov. 7, 1856; cited in IWMM, pp. 265-66.
25. IWRM, pp. 328-29.
26. IWRM, p. 331.
27. IWRM, pp. 332-34.
28. IWRM, pp. 337-39.
29. IWRM, pp. 340-43.
30. AMI, Vol. 3, No. 34, p. 268, Feb. 27, 1857.
31. AYWP, pp. 50-1.
32. AMI, Vol. 5, No. 11, p. 86, Sept. 17, 1858.
33. AMI, Vol. 2, No. 28, p. 227, Jan. 18, 1856.
34. EYAE, p. 90.
35. AMI, Vol. 2, No. 28, p. 227, Jan. 18, 1856.
36. AMI, Vol. 4, No. 5, p. 33, Aug. 7, 1857.
37. AMI, Vol. 4, No. 7, p. 58, August 21, 1857.
38. AMI, Vol. 4, No. 14, p. 108, Oct. 9, 1857; also same volume, No. 18, p. 142, Nov. 6, 1857.

39. AMI, Vol. 4, No. 18, p. 142, Nov. 6, 1857.
40. AMI, Vol. 4, No. 19, Nov. 13, 1857.
41. AMI, Vol. 5, No. 8, p. 62, Aug. 27, 1958.
42. With permission of the University of Chicago, from ARCH.

CHAPTER TWENTY

1. Dedicated September 22, 1848. AYWK, p. 32.
2. IWMM, pp. 166-67.
3. AMI, Vol. 7, No. 13, p. 102, Sept. 28, 1860.
4. IWMM, pp. 167-68.
5. AMI, Vol. 6, p. 236, January 27, 1860.
6. AMI, Vol. 6, p. 4, July 8, 1859.
7. AMI, Vol. 5, No. 21, April 29, 1859; Vol. 5, No. 43, March 9, 1860; Vol. 6, p. 284.
8. IWMM, pp. 267-68.
9. AMI, Vol. 7, p. 140, Nov. 2, 1860. Cited in IWMM, p. 268.
10. AMI, Vol. 5, No. 43, April 20, 1859. IWMM, p. 262.
11. AMI, Vol. 5, p. 388, June 10, 1859.
12. AMI, Vol. 5, p. 348, May 6, 1859.
13. DEB, Vol. 42, No. 28, p. 5, Jan. 7, 1897; quoted in WMB, p. 27.
14. AMI, Vol. 6, p. 276, March 2, 1860.
15. AMI, Vol. 6, p. 236, Jan. 27, 1860.
16. AMI, Vol. 5, p. 364, May 30, 1859.
17. AJCW, p. 10.
18. AMI, Vol. 5, No. 26, p. 204, Dec. 31, 1858.
19. AMI, Vol. 5, No. 24, p. 188, Dec. 17, 1858.
20. AMI, Vol. 5, No. 27, p. 213, Jan. 7, 1859.
21. AMI, Vol. 5, No. 27, p. 212, Jan. 7, 1859.
22. AMI, Vol. 5, p. 308, April 1, 1859.
23. AMI, Vol. 5, No. 49, p. 389, June 10, 1859; also AJCW, p. 10.
24. AMI, Vol. 2, No. 19.
25. AMI, Vol. 2, No. 25, Dec. 28, 1855.
26. IWMM, p. 226.
27. AMI, Vol. 6, No. 44, May 4, 1859; and IWMM, p. 224.

CHAPTER TWENTY-ONE

1. "America as a Civilization," by Max Lerner, Simon and Schuster, N.Y., 1957, p. 7.
2. IWMM, p. 243.
3. EYAE, pp. 130-31.
4. AMI, Vol. 7, No. 28, p. 221, Jan. 11, 1861.
5. *Ibid.*
6. EYAE, pp. 126-27.
7. AMI, Dec. 14, 1860, Vol. 7, No. 24.
8. AMI, Vol. 7, No. 26, p. 205, Dec. 28, 1860.
9. AMI, Vol. 7, No. 27, Jan. 4, 1861; and issues to No. 32, Feb. 8, 1861; in AJCW, p. 40.
10. AMI, Vol. 7, No. 26, p. 205, Dec. 28, 1860. EYAE, pp. 125-26.

11. AMI, Vol. 7, No. 27, Jan. 4, 1861.
12. AMI, Vol. 7, No. 42, April 19, 1861; IWMM, pp. 245 f.; AJCW, p. 40.
13. EYAE, p. 125.
14. AYWP, p. 97.
15. AYWP, p. 98.
16. EYAE, p. 139.
17. Entire chapter in EYAE, "Isaac Mayer Wise on the Civil War," pp. 125-50; Above passage quoted on pp. 138-39. Based on following references from AMI: Vol. 7, No. 37, p. 292, March 15, 1861; No. 45, p. 356, May 10; Vol. 8, No. 1, p. 4, July 5, 1861; No. 3, p. 20, July 19, 1861; Cf. also Vol. 8, No. 30, p. 236, Jan. 24, 1862; Vol. 10, No. 2, p. 12, July 10, 1863; Vol. 11, No. 8, p. 60, Aug. 19, 1864.
18. AMI, Vol. 9, p. 52, Aug. 15, 1862.
19. AMI, Vol. 9, No. 19, p. 147, Nov. 14, 1862; AJCW, p. 40.
20. AMI, Vol. 9, p. 268, Feb. 27, 1863.
21. AMI, Vol. 10, p. 84, Sept. 11, 1863.
22. AMI, Vol. 11, No. 8, p. 60, Aug. 19, 1864; in AJCW, p. 43.
23. AMI, Vol. 10, No. 16, p. 122, Oct. 16, 1863; Vol. 11, No. 11, p. 124, Oct. 14, 1864; in AJCW, p. 112.

CHAPTER TWENTY-TWO

1. EYAE, pp. 127-28.
2. Passim, AMI, Vol. 7, No. 22, p. 173, Nov. 30, 1860; No. 24, p. 188, Dec. 14; No. 26, p. 205, Dec. 28; No. 31, p. 244, Feb. 1, 1861; No. 37, p. 292, March 15; No. 48, p. 381, May 31; Vol. 8, No. 16, p. 124, Oct. 18, No. 30, p. 236, Jan. 24, 1862; quoted in AJCW, pp. 24-5.
3. AMI, Vol. 9, No. 2, p. 14, July 11, 1862; in AJCW, p. 61.
4. AJCW, p. 61, and note on p. 259, No. 21.
5. AJCW, Chap. IV, pp. 56-97.
6. EYAE, p. 134.
7. EYAE, *Ibid.*
8. EYAE, p. 131.
9. Cf. also Louis Ruhames, "The Abolitionists and the Jews," in PAJHS, Vol. 42, 1952, No. 2, pp. 131-55.
10. Cf. Lincoln's letter to Canisius, May 17, 1859, the Chicago Historical Society; in EYAE, note to p. 148, and p. 132.
11. AMI, Vol. 7, No. 30, p. 238, Jan. 25, 1861; in EYAE pp. 132-33; also AMI, Vol. 7, No. 38, p. 301, March 22, 1861; Vol. 8, No. 35, p. 278, Feb. 28, 1862; in AJCW, pp. 26-7.
12. AMI, Vol. 7, No. 22, p. 173, No. 30, 1860; in AJCW, p. 25; cf. also No. 24, p. 188, Dec. 14; No. 26, p. 205, Dec. 28; No. 31, p. 244, Feb. 1, 1861; No. 37, p. 292, March 15; No. 48, p. 381, May 31; Vol. 8, No. 16, p. 124, Oct. 18; No. 30, p. 236, Jan. 24, 1862.
13. AMI, Vol. 7, No. 29, p. 229, Jan. 18, 1861; in EYAE, pp. 133-34.
14. AMI, Vol. 9, No. 4, p. 46, July 25, 1862; in AJCW, p. 40.
15. In D. Barbee, "President Lincoln and Dr. Hurley," p. 11; quoted in AJCW, p. 25.
16. AMI, Vol. 9, No. 34, p. 268, Feb. 27, 1863; from EYAE, p. 133.
17. AJCW, p. 26.
18. AMI, Vol. 7, No. 6, p. 205, Dec. 28, 1860; in AJCW, p. 25.

19. AMI, Vol. 7, No. 29, p. 230, Jan. 18, 1861; in EYAE, p. 128.
20. AMI, Vol. 8, No. 25, p. 196, Dec. 20, 1861, Cf. also AMI, Vol. 9, No. 34, p. 268, Feb. 27, 1863; in EYAE, pp. 128-29.
21. AMI, Vol. 11, p. 60, Aug. 19, 1864.
22. AMI, Vol. 9, No. 20, p. 156, Nov. 11, 1864; also No. 26, p. 204, Dec.23. In EYAE, p. 130.
23. AMI, Vol. 11, No. 19, pp. 48-9, Nov. 4, 1864; in AJCW, Note 29, on p. 252.
24. EYAE, pp. 129-30.
25. AMI, Vol. 11, No. 26, p. 204, Dec. 23, 1864; in AJCW, p. 25.
26. AMI, Vol. 11, p. 204, No. 26, Dec. 23, 1864.
27. Max J. Kohler, "The Jews and the Anti-Slavery Movement," American Jewish Historical Society, Vols. v-vi, p. 150.
28. IWMM, pp. 244-45.
29. Philip S. Foner, "The Jews in American History, 1854-1865," New York, 1945, p. 60.
30. EYAE, note on p. 147.
31. AJCW, p. 17.
32. AJCW, p. 17; M.J. Raphall, "The Bible View of Slavery," reprinted in E.M.F. Mielziner's, "Moses Mielziner," 1823-1903, pp. 212-24.
33. EYAE, p. 127-28.
34. AMI, Vol. 43, No. 52, p. 4, June 24, 1897.
35. AMI, Vol. 14, No. 52, p. 4, July 3, 1868; in EYAE, p. 128.

Since this chapter was written, a new book has appeared, entitled *Grant Moves South,* by Bruce Catton (Little, Brown and Co., 1960). In Chapter Seventeen, especially on pp. 352 ff., Catton treats the entire matter of Grant's Order No. 11. He adduces some very interesting new material, which, as far as I know, is to be found nowhere else, and which may certainly have something to do with Wise's later somewhat modified attitude toward Grant.

This chapter asserts that Grant's trouble began with his own father, Jesse, who was "making book with the very traders who were Grant's worst trial—coming in, sly and insinuating, to help the men whose patriotism, as Grant believed, was to be measured by dollars and cents." According to the account that follows (pp. 352-53), the elder Grant had formed a partnership with three Cincinnati brothers, Henry, Harmon, and Simon Mack, who traded as Mack and Brothers. Jesse and the Macks were to go South to buy cotton, in the area where Ulysses S. was, and then split the profits they made. (The source for this is a lawsuit instituted by Jesse Grant against the Mack brothers in 1863, non-suited and described in the New York Tribune, Sept. 19, 1872. There are some other sources given in a note on p. 525.)

It took Grant a while to see what these men, with his father, were after, Catton goes on to write. They were, as a matter of fact, putting up for sale Grant's "own authority." A Chicago newspaperman, Sylvanus Cadwallader, wrote that Grant was "bitter, indignant, and mortified." Catton continues by saying that Grant "put his fury into an order, which would leave a queer enduring stain on his own name." Then follows the text of Order No. 11, as we have given it in our own pages, in chapter 23 of

Part Two. Catton contends that the Jewish character of this order was due to the Mack brothers being Jewish, though the truth was that the word "Jew" was being used by some army officers in much the same fashion that "superheated Southerners at the same time were using the word 'Yankee'—as a catch-all epithet which epitomized everything that was mean, grasping, and without conscience." Another passage from a letter of Grant's, written to the Assistant Secretary of War, is here produced, quite anti-Jewish in tone (taken from O.R.—probably "Official Records"—cf. Note 10, p. 525). This, writes Catton, uses the word "Jews" and "cotton traders" interchangeably. Speaking with "a rabbi" after the war, Grant tried to explain what he had done:

> You know, during war times these nice distinctions were disregarded. We had no time to handle things with kid gloves. But it was no ill-feeling or a want of good-feeling towards the Jews. If such complaints would have been lodged against a dozen men each of whom wore a white cravat, a black broadcloth suit, beaver, or gold spectacles, I should probably have issued a similar order against men so dressed. (From an interview with "Rabbi Browne" in the *Chicago Tribune*, Dec. 18, 1862. For other sources, cf. Note 13 Catton, p. 525.)

Catton then concludes with a few additional comments, but claims that at the time this Order did not make nearly the stir that it did in "later years." We set all this in a Note, for it casts a very interesting additional light on the entire affair.

CHAPTER TWENTY-THREE

1. AJCW, chiefly chapter 6, pp. 121-55, *et seq.*
2. AJCW, pp. 122-23.
3. AMI, Vol. 10, No. 24, p. 188, Dec. 11, 1863; in EYAE, p. 144.
4. AMI, Vol. 9, No. 25, Dec. 26, 1862; IWMM, pp. 228-29.
5. AMI, Vol. 9, No. 26, Jan. 2, 1863.
6. IWMM, pp. 230-31.
7. IWMM, p. 232.
8. AJCW, p. 123.
9. AMI, Vol. 9, p. 212, Jan. 9, 1863.
10. His old friend, Salmon P. Chase.
11. AMI, Vol. 9, p. 226, Jan. 30, 1863.
12. AMI, Vol. 9, p. 228, Jan. 23, 1863.
13. AJCW, p. 126.
14. AMI, Feb. 28, 1868.
15. AMI, Dec. 4, 1868.
16. AMI, Dec. 4, 1868.
17. EYAE.
18. Cf. AJCW, pp. 166-73.
19. EYAE, p. 142.
20. AMI, Vol. 10, No. 24, p. 188, Dec. 11, 1863.
21. EYAE, p. 143.
23. AJCW, p. 61.

22. AMI, Vol. 8, No. 17, p. 132, Oct. 25, 1861; in EYAE, pp. 144-45.
24. AMI, Vol. 8, No. 20, p. 157, Nov. 15, 1861, and *passim;* AJCW, p. 65.
25. AMI, Vol. 27, Nos. 16 and 17, Oct. 20 and 27, 1875; IWMM, pp. 211-13.
26. AMI, Vol. 8, No. 3, p. 23, July 19, 1861; AJCW, p. 57.
27. AMI, Vol. 8, No. 20, p. 157, Nov. 15, 1861; No. 23, p. 177, Dec. 6, 1861; No. 25, p. 196, Dec. 20, 1861; No. 44, p. 348, May 2, 1862; in AJCW, p. 61.
28. AMI, Vol. 8, No. 36, pp. 283, 285, March 7, 1862; EYAE, p. 140.
29. EYAE, pp. 154-55.
30. AMI, Vol. 9, No. 4, p. 46, July 25, 1862; in AJCW, p. 40.
31. AMI, Vol. 10, No. 37, pp. 292-93, March 11, 1864.

CHAPTER TWENTY-FOUR

1. AMI, Vol. 7, p. 172, Nov. 30, 1860.
2. AMI, Vol. 7, No. 33, p. 262, Feb. 15, 1861; in AJCW, p. 41; also AYWP, p. 97.
3. AMI, Vol. 7, No. 37, p. 294, March 15, 1861; AJCW, p. 41; AYWP, p. 97.
4. EYAE, pp. 136-37.
5. AMI, Vol. 7, p. 244, Feb. 1, 1861.
6. IWRM, p. 327.
7. AMI, Vol. 7, No. 49, p. 386, July 7, 1861.
8. "The Americanization of Isaac M. Wise," by Jacob Rader Marcus, pp. 8-10; cf. also AJCW, p. 41.
9. *Cincinnati Enquirer,* Sept. 6, 1863; in AKCW, pp. 41-42.
10. AMI, Vol. 10, p. 92, Sept. 19, 1863.
11. AMI, Vol. 10, No. 12, pp. 92-93, Sept. 18, 1863. Reprinted in the *Jewish Record,* No. 3 of Vol. 3, Sept. 25; and also in the *New York Times;* cf. AJCW, p. 42.
12. AJCW, p. 42. Cf. the *Cincinnati Daily Gazette*, Sept. 11, 1863.
13. AJCW, p. 42; cf. *Cincinnati Daily Gazette*, Sept. 11, 1863.
14. *The Jewish Record,* Vol. 3, No. 3, p. 2, Oct., 9, 1863; AJCW, p. 43.
15. *Cincinnati Enquirer*, Sept. 11, 1863; in AJCW, p. 43.
16. *Cincinnati Daily Gazette*, Sept. 7, 1863; AJCW, p. 42.
17. AMI, Vol. 9, p. 94, Sept. 19, 1862.
18. EYAE, p. 125.
19. AMI, Vol. 7, p. 334, April 19, 1861.
20. AMI, Vol. 7, No. 48, p. 381, May 31, 1861; Vol. 13, No. 1, p. 5, July 6, 1866; in AJCW, p. 41.
21. The Board of Delegates became part of the Union of American Hebrew Congregations in 1878.
22. AJCW, pp. 72-74.
23. AMI, Vol. 9, p. 156, Nov. 21, 1862.
24. AMI, Vol. 12, p. 276, 1866.
25. AMI, Vol. 10, No. 7, Aug. 14, 1863; in IWMM, pp. 269-71.
26. AYWP, p. 97.
27. AMI, Vol. 9, p. 308, April 3, 1863.
28. AMI, Vol. 7, p. 252, Feb. 8, 1861.
29. From an article by Isaac M. Wise Jr., on the College Hill Farm, written in 1883; in ARCH.

CHAPTER TWENTY-FIVE

1. Quoted in Hertz, "The Tribute of the Synagogue to Abraham Lincoln," N.Y., 1927, pp. 161-62; AJCW, p. 212.
2. AMI, Vol. 9, No. 43, April 21, 1865; in IWMM, p. 245.
3. AMI, Vol. 11, No. 43, p. 348, April 28, 1865.
4. AJCW, p. 189.
5. AMI, Vol. 11, No. 43, p. 339, April 21, 1865.
6. AJCW, pp. 210-11; quoted in Hertz, op. cit., pp. 96-97.
7. AMI, Vol. 11, No. 43, p. 340, April 21, 1865.
8. AMI, April 21, 1865.
9. AMI, Vol. 14, No. 3, p. 4, July 19, 1867; No. 12, p. 4, Sept. 20; in EYAE, p. 141.
10. AMI, Vol. 14, p. 4, Sept. 20, 1867.
11. AMI, Vol. 14, No. 31, p. 4, Feb. 7, 1868; Vol. 38, No. 23, p. 4, Dec. 3, 1891.
12. OCC, Vol. 24, No. 5, p. 239, August, 1866.
13. EYAE, p. 141.
14. AMI, Vol. 14, No. 35, p. 4, March 6, 1868; EYAE, p. 142.
15. AMI, Vol. 13, p. 4, Dec. 28, 1866.
16. AMI, Vol. 14, No. 50, p. 4, June 19, 1868.
17. AYWP, p. 101.
18. AYWP, pp. 101-02; IWMM, p. 168.
19. AYWP, p. 102; IWMM, p. 168.
20. AMI, May 19, 1865; AYWP, p. 102-04.
21. AYWP, *ibid.*
22. AMI, Vol. 11, p. 373, May 19, 1865.
23. AMI, Vol. 13, p. 5, July 20, 1866.
24. AYWP, p. 105.
25. SWIW, p. 104.
26. AYWP, pp. 105-10; based on AMI, Vol. 13, p. 5, Aug. 31, 1866; and on the Fiftieth Anniversary Booklet.
27. AMI, *Ibid.*
28. AYWP, pp. 133-34.
29. AMI, Vol. 46, No. 20, Nov. 16, 1899; IWMM, p. 171.
30. IWMM, p. 168.
31. *New York Times,* Vol. 55, No. 45, 1870.
32. IWMM, p. 169.
33. AMI, Vol. 11, p. 420, June 30, 1865.
34. AMI, Vol. 12, p. 117, Oct. 3, 1865.
35. AMI, Vol. 12, p. 324, April 13, 1866.
36. AYWP, p. 54.
37. AMI, Vol. 12, p. 412, June 29, 1866.
38. AMI, Vol. 14, p. 4, July 19, 1867.
39. AMI, Vol. 14, p. 4, August 2 and 9, 1867.
40. SWIW, p. 102.
41. AMI, Vol. 13, p. 5, Oct. 5, 1866.

CHAPTER TWENTY-SIX

1. AMI, Vol. 15, p. 4, April 9, 1869.
2. IWMM, pp. 272-75; also p. 335.
3. SWIW, p. 73.
4. Cf. *Protokolle der Rabbiner Conferenz, abgehalten zu Philadelphia, vom* 3 *bis zum* 6 November, 1869; N. Y., 1870, pp. 39-41.
5. At the Brunswick Conference, *vide* RMJ, p. 154; at the Frankfort Conference, *vide* RMJ, pp. 275 f; etc.
6. SWIW, p. 73.
7. AMI, Vol. 16, p. 8, Nov. 12, 1869.
8. RMJ, pages 354-55; AMI, Vol. 16, p. 8, Nov. 12, 1869.
9. AMI, Vol. 16, p. 8, Nov. 12, 1869.
10. AMI, Vol. 16, p. 8, Nov. 19, 1869.
11. AMI, Vol. 16, p. 8, April 29, 1870.
12. AMI, Vol. 16, p. 8, May 6, 1870.
13. AMI, Vol. 16, p. 8, May 13, 1870.
14. AMI, Vol. 16, p. 8, June 17, 1870.
15. AMI, Vol, 17, p. 8, Nov. 4, 1870.
16. AMI, Vol. 17, p. 8, Nov. 4, 1870.
17. AMI, Vol. 17, p. 8, Nov. 11, 1870.
18. AMI, Vol. 17, p. 8, Nov. 18, 1870.
19. SWIW, p. 74.
20. AMI, Vol. 17, p. 8, June 9, 1871.
21. AMI, Vol. 17, p. 8, June 16, 1871.
22. AMI, Vol. 17, p. 8, June 23, 1871.
23. AMI, Vol. 18, No. 1, p. 8, July 7, 1871.
24. AMI, Vol. 18, No. 6, p. 8, Aug. 11, 1871.
25. AMI, Vol. 16, No. 34, Feb. 1870; IWMM, p. 275.
26. AMI, Vol. 16, p. 10, July 30, 1869.
27. AMI, Vol. 16, p. 5, Aug. 6, 1869.
28. AMI, Vol. 16, p. 8, Dec. 17, 1869.
29. AMI, Vol. 16, p. 8, March 4, 1870.
30. AMI, Vol. 16, p. 8, April 1, 1870.
31. AMI, Vol. 17, p. 8, July 15, 1870.
32. AMI, Vol. 17, p. 8, July 29, 1870.
33. AMI, Vol. 17, p. 8, Aug. 12, 1870.
34. AMI, Vol. 17, p. 8, Sept. 9, 1870.
35. AMI, Vol. 18, No. 4, p. 8, July 28, 1871.
36. AMI, Vol. 18, No. 14, Oct. 6, 1871.
37. AMI, Vol. 19, No. 16, Oct. 18, 1872.
38. IWMM, p. 278.
39. *New York Jewish Times,* June 30, 1871, Vol. 2, No. 18.
40. IWMM, p. 278.
41. AMI, Vol. 15, June 11, 1869, p. 4.
42. AMI, Vol. 15, p. 4, June 11, 1869.
43. AMI, Vol. 16, p. 8, Dec. 24, 1869.
44. AMI, Vol. 16, p. 89, Dec. 31, 1869.
45. AMI, Vol. 16, p. 10, May 27, 1870; STC, p. 14.
46. EYAE, pp. 98-124.

47. STC, p. 45.
48. AMI, Vol. 16, p. 8, June 10, 1870.
49. AMI, Vol. 17, p. 8, Dec. 23, 1870.
50. RMJ, p. 433.
51. AMI, Vol. 18, No. 19, p. 8, Nov. 10, 1871.
52. AMI, Vol. 18, No. 31, p. 8, Feb. 2, 1872.
53. AMI, Vol. 18, No. 33, p. 8, Feb. 16, 1872.
54. AMI, Vol. 19, No. 9, p. 8, Aug. 30, 1872.
55. AMI, Vol. 19, No. 13, p. 8, Sept. 27, 1872.
56. AMI, Vol. 19, No. 17, p. 8, Oct. 25, 1872.

CHAPTER TWENTY-SEVEN

1. *New York Jewish Times,* Vol. 5, No. 22, July 25, 1873; IWMM, pp. 285-86.
2. UJE, Vol. 10, p. 530.
3. SWIW, p. 81; on Oct. 10, 1872.
4. AMI, Vol. 20, No. 6, p. 4, Feb. 7, 1873.
5. IWMM, p. 171.
6. AMI, Vol. 20, No. 14, April 4, 1873; IWMM, pp. 279-80; SWIW, p. 81.
7. AMI, Vol. 20, No. 14, April 14, 1873.
8. AMI, May 18, 1873; IWMM, pp. 279 f.
9. AMI, Vol. 20, No. 22, May 30, 1873.
10. AMI, Vol. 20, No. 23, June 6, 1873.
11. AMI, Vol. 20, No. 24, June 13, 1873.
12. AMI, Vol. 20, No. 25, June 20, 1873; IWMM, pp. 281-84.
13. AMI, Vol. 20, No. 26, June 27, 1873.
14. IWMM, p. 291; RMJ, p. 510.
15. SWIW, pp. 81 f.
16. AMI, Vol. 21, No. 2, July 18, 1873.
17. IWMM, p. 292.
18. AMI, Vol. 25, No. 9, Sept. 3, 1873; IWMM, pp. 295-97.
19. SWIW, pp. 82 f.
20. *Ibid.*
21. Proceedings, Cincinnati Convention, UAHC, Vol. 1, 1873-79, p. 14; SWIW, pp. 82-4.
22. AMI, Vol. 21, No. 20, May 15, 1874, p. 1; Vol. 21, No. 2, p. 4, July 3, 1874.
23. IWMM, pp. 287 ff.
24. AMI, Vol. 21, No. 4, pp. 5-6, July 17, 1874.
25. AMI, Vol. 21, No. 4, p. 4, July 31, 1874.
26. AMI, Vol. 22, April 23, 1875.
27. AMI, Vol. 22, No. 44, p. 4, May 19, 1875.
28. AMI, Vol. 23, No. 4, p. 4, July 30, 1875.
29. AMI, Vol. 23, No. 8, p. 5, Aug. 27, 1875.
30. AMI, Vol. 23, No. 13, p. 4, Oct. 1, 1875.
31. AMI, Vol. 23, No. 3, July 21, 1876.
32. SWIW, p. 82; IWMM, p. 277.
33. AMI, Vol. 20, No. 18, May 2, 1873.
34. AMI, Vol. 21, No. 5, p. 4, Aug. 7, 1874.
35. AMI, Vol. 21, No. 51, p. 252, 1874; SWIW, p. 84.
36. AMI, Vol. 21, No. 5, p. 4, Aug. 7, 1874.
37. AMI, Vol. 22, No. 5, p. 4, Aug. 6, 1875.

38. AMI, Vol. 22, No. 9, Sept. 3, 1875.
39. AMI, Vol. 25, No. 9, Sept. 3, 1875; IWMM, pp. 295-96.
40. AMI, Vol. 22, No. 9, p. 4, Sept. 3, 1875.
41. IWMM, p. 294.
42. AMI, Vol. 23, No. 14, Oct. 8, 1875; IWMM, pp. 298-99.
43. WMB, p. 35.
44. President's Report, HUC, Sept. 10, 1876, p. 319; also Annual Report, July 1877, p. 377.
45. IWMM, p. 298.
46. IWMM, pp. 296-98.
47. IWMM, p. 299.
48. AMI, Vol. 22, No. 16, p. 4, Oct. 22, 1875.
49. AYWP, p. 56.
50. *Ibid.*
51. AMI, Vol. 22, No. 47, p. 4, June 9, 1876.
52. IWMM, p. 316.
53. SWIW, pp. 391-96; IWMM, pp. 316-17.
54. IWMM, p. 314.
55. UAHC Proceedings, pp. 4163-64, in IWMM, pp. 314-15.
56. IWMM, pp. 299 f.
57. IWMM, p. 310.
58. IWMM, *Ibid.*
59. *Ibid.*
60. IWMM, p. 312.
61. *Ibid.*
62. UAHC Report, p. 546.
63. AYWP, p. 115.
64. AYWP, p. 116.
65. *Ibid.*
66. AMI, Aug. 18, 1873; IWMM, pp. 174-75.
67. AYWP, pp. 116-17.
68. AMI, Vol. 21, No. 14, Oct. 3, 1873; IWMM, pp. 175-77.
69. AYWP, p. 118.
70. AMI, Vol. 21, No. 13, p. 4, Dec. 11, 1874.
71. STC, p. 287.
72. In ARCH.
73. AMI, Vol. 22, No. 42, p. 4, April 28, 1876.
74. AMI, Vol. 23, No. 15, p. 6, Oct. 13, 1876.
75. AMI, Vol. 22, June 25, 1875.
76. AMI, Vol. 20, No. 8, p. 4, Feb. 21, 1873; EYAE, p. 141.
77. AJCW, p. 159.
78. AMI, Vol. 23, No. 18, Nov. 3, 1876.
79. AYWP, p. 134; IWMM, p. 178.
80. AMI, Vol. 20, No. 1, Jan. 3, 1873.
81. AMI, Vol. 21, No. 1, July 4, 1873.
82. AMI, Vol. 21, No. 26, Dec. 26, 1873.
83. AMI, Vol. 21, No. 12, p. 4, Dec. 4, 1874.
84. AMI, Vol. 22, p. 4, June 4, 1875.
85. AMI, Vol. 22, No. 1, p. 4, July 2, 1875.

CHAPTER TWENTY-EIGHT

1. AMI, Vol. 25, No. 43, p. 4, May 2, 1879.
2. AMI, Vol. 23, No. 17, April 25, 1879; IWMM, pp. 178-185.
3. AMI, Vol. 26, p. 4, Aug. 15, 1879.
4. AMI, Vol. 25, No. 23, Dec. 6, 1878.
5. AMI, Vol. 26, p. 4, June 18, 1880.
6. AMI, Vol. 27, p. 44, Aug. 5, 1880.
7. WMB, p. 36.
8. WMB, p. 36.
9. WMB, pp. 36-37.
10. DEB, Vol. 42, No. 34, pp. 4-5, Feb. 18, 1897.
11. AMI, Vol. 23, No. 34, p. 4, Feb. 23, 1877.
12. AMI, Vol. 23, No. 50, p. 4, June 22, 1877.
13. AMI, Vol. 24, No. 3, p. 4, July 20, 1877.
14. AMI, Vol. 24, p. 4, May 10, 1878.
15. IWMM, p. 304.
16. AMI, Vol. 25, No. 3, p. 4, July 19, 1878.
17. AMI, Vol. 25, No. 6, p. 4, Aug. 9, 1878.
18. AMI, Vol. 27, p. 36, July 30, 1880.
19. ARCH.
20. IWMM, p. 301.
21. *Cleveland Jewish Review and Observer*, Nov. 26, 1915; IWMM, pp. 301-2.
22. IWMM, pp. 303-04.
23. ARCH.
24. IWMM, pp. 300-01.
25. IWMM, p. 301.
26. AMI, Vol, 26, p. 4, Sept. 5, 1879.
27. AMI, Vol. 26, p. 4, Oct. 31, 1879.
28. AMI, Vol. 26, p. 4, Jan. 23, 1880.
29. IWMM, p. 300.
30. AMI, Vol. 26, p. 4, Aug. 1, 1879.
31. AMI, Vol. 24, p. 4, May 31, 1878.
32. AMI, Vol. 27, p. 28, July 23, 1880.
33. AMI, Vol. 27, p. 108, Oct. 1, 1880.

CHAPTER TWENTY-NINE

1. ARCH.
2. AMI, Vol. 28, p. 100, Sept. 23, 1881.
3. AMI, Vol. 28, No. 42, pp. 331-32, April 14, 1882.
4. AMI, Vol. 30, No. 15, p. 4, Oct. 12, 1883.
5. AMI, Vol. 30, No. 28, p. 4, Jan. 11, 1884.
6. AMI, Vol. 30, No. 50, p. 4, June 27, 1884.
7. AMI, Vol. 31, No. 16, p. 4, Oct. 17, 1884.
8. AMI, Vol. 28, p. 180, Dec. 2, 1881.
9. AMI, Vol. 28, p. 252, Feb. 3, 1882.
10. AMI, Vol. 28, p. 388, June 2, 1882.
11. AMI, Vol. 29, p. 78, Sept. 22, 1882.

12. AMI, Vol. 30, No. 18, p. 4, Nov. 2, 1883.
13. AMI, Vol. 30, No. 20, p. 4, Nov. 16, 1883.
14. AMI, Vol. 31, No. 23, p. 4, Dec. 5, 1884.
15. AMI, Vol. 27, p. 232, April 22, 1881.
16. AMI, Vol. 29, No. 38, p. 324, March 30, 1883.
17. AMI, Vol. 29, No. 43, p. 404, June 8, 1883.
18. IWMM, p. 304.
19. AMI, Vol. 29, No. 45, p. 5, June 22, 1883.
20. AMI, Vol. 31, No. 1, p. 4, July 4, 1884.
21. AMI, Vol. 31, No. 7, p. 4, Aug. 15, 1884.
22. AMI, Vol. 22, p. 21, July 15, 1881.
23. Cf. *Hebrew Review*, pp. 12-32 and also 25-152; SWIW, p. 75.
24. RMJ, p. 459.
25. AMI, Vol. 28, p. 20, July 15, 1882.
26. AMI, Vol. 31, No. 2, p. 4, July 11, 1884.
27. AMI, Vol. 30, No. 4, p. 4, July 27, 1883.
28. AMI, Vol. 30, No. 5, p. 4, Aug. 3, 1883.
29. AMI, Vol. 30, p. 4, May 9, 1884.
30. History of Cong. Rodeph Shalom, pp. 95-6.
31. From the ARCH of the Hebrew Union College.

CHAPTER THIRTY

1. IWMM, p. 309.
2. AMI, Vol. 31, No. 38, p. 4, March 20, 1885.
3. AMI, Vol. 32, Nos. 4 and 5, p. 4, July 21 and 28, 1885.
4. AMI, Vol. 34, p. 4, Aug. 5, 1887.
5. AMI, Vol. 34, p. 4, Aug. 12, 1887.
6. AMI, Vol. 34, p. 4, Aug. 26, 1887.
7. AMI, Vol. 34, p. 4, July 22, 1887.
8. AMI, Vol. 33, No. 45, p. 4, May 6, 1887.
9. AMI, Vol. 34, p. 8, July 22, 1887.
10. AMI, Vol, 35, p. 8, July 20, 1888.
11. *American Hebrew,* Vol. 26, No. 3. Feb. 25, 1886.
12. IWMM, p. 309.
13. AMI, Vol. 32, No. 46, p. 4, May 14, 1886.
14. AMI, Vol. 34, p. 4, March 30, 1888.
15. AMI, Vol. 21, No. 2; IWMM, p. 337.
16. AMI, Vol. 36, No. 39.
17. AMI, Vol. 31, No. 44, May 1, 1885.
18. Italics Wise's.
19. AMI, Vol. 32, No. 19, p. 4, Nov. 6, 1885.
20. The foregoing sections all from an article, "A Record of American Judaism for A.M. 5646" (1886-87), by Wise.
21. RMJ, p. 355.
22. RMJ, p. 371.
23. RMJ, pp. 374-75.
24. August 13, 1896.
25. SWIW, pp. 75-6.
26. AMI, Vol. 32, No. 22, p. 4, Nov. 27, 1885.
27. AMI, Vol. 32, No. 23, p. 4, Dec. 4, 1885.

28. AMI, Vol. 32, No. 28, p. 4, Jan. 8, 1886.
29. AMI, Vol. 32, No. 32, p. 4, Feb. 5, 1886.
30. AMI, Vol. 32, No. 37, p. 4, March 12, 1886.
31. AMI, Vol. 32, No. 39, p. 4, March 26, 1886.
32. AMI, Vol. 32, No. 43, p. 4, April 23, 1886.
33. AMI, Vol. 32, No. 48, p. 4, May 28, 1886.
34. AMI, Vol. 32, No. 48, p. 4, May 28, 1886.
35. *Juedische Zeitschrift*, Vol. 8.
36. AMI, Vol. 32, No. 49, p. 4, June 4, 1886.
37. AMI, Vol. 33, No. 2, p. 4, July 9, 1886.
38. AMI, Vol. 33, No. 12, p. 4. Sept. 17, 1886.
39. AMI, Vol. 31, No. 32, p. 4, Feb. 6, 1885.
40. AMI, Vol. 32, No. 3, p. 4, July 17, 1885.
41. AMI, Vol. 31, No. 35, p. 4, Feb. 27, 1885.
42. AMI, Vol. 32, No. 11, p. 4, Sept. 11, 1885.
43. AMI, Vol. 32, No. 5, p. 5, July 31, 1885.
44. AMI, Vol. 32, No. 18, p. 4, Oct. 30, 1885.
45. AMI, Vol. 34, p. 4, Dec. 9, 1887.

CHAPTER THIRTY-ONE

1. AMI, Vol. 25, No. 46, May 16, 1889; IWMM, p. 338.
2. YEARBOOK, CCAR, No. 4, Atlantic City, July 11, 1894.
3. AMI, Vol. 36, No. 2, p. 4, July 11, 1889.
4. AMI, Vol. 36, No. 3, p. 4, July 18, 1889.
5. YEARBOOK, CCAR, July 9-10, Detroit, 1889; RMJ, p. 493; AMI, Vol. 36, No. 3, page 4, July 18, 1889.
6. YEARBOOK, CCAR, 1898-99, p. 10; SWIW, p. 78.
7. IWMM, p. 337.
8. WMB, p. 38.
9. SWIW, p. 78.
10. YEARBOOK, CCAR, Cleveland, 1890; IWMM, p. 339; AMI, Vol. 36, No. 35, p. 4, Feb. 27, 1890.
11. AMI, Vol. 36, No. 38, p. 4, March 20, 1890.
12. AMI, Vol. 36, No. 42, p. 4, April 17, 1890.
13. YEARBOOK, CCAR, 1899, p. 28; RMJ, p. 493.
14. SWIW, p. 77.
15. AMI, Vol. 38, No. 31, p. 4, Jan. 28, 1892.
16. AMI, Vol. 39, No. 18, Nov. 3, 1892.
17. IWMM, p. 339.
18. AMI, Vol. 37, No. 44, p. 4, May 7, 1891.
19. AMI, Vol. 39, No. 22, Dec. 1, 1892.
20. AMI, Vol. 37, No. 36, p. 4, March 12, 1891.
21. AMI, Vol. 39, No. 9, Sept. 1, 1892.
22. IWMM, pp. 185-86. From the *Commercial-Gazette*, Cincinnati.
23. AMI, Vol. 35, p. 4, April 11, 1889.
24. AMI, Vol. 35, p. 6, April 18, 1889.
25. AYWP, vii.
26. AMI, Vol. 38, No. 2, p. 4, Jan. 7, 1892.
27. AMI, Vol. 38, No. 36, March 3, 1892.

28. AMI, Vol. 36, No. 40, p. 4, April 3, 1890.
29. AMI, Vol. 37, No. 29, p. 4, Jan. 22, 1891.
30. AMI, Vol. 39, No. 12, Sept. 22, 1892.
31. AMI, Vol. 35, p. 4, Jan. 10, 1889.
32. AMI, Vol. 36, No. 9, p. 4, Aug. 29, 1889.
33. AMI, Vol. 37, No. 9, p. 4, Aug. 28, 1890.
34. AMI, Vol. 37, No. 7, p. 4, Aug. 14, 1890.
35. AMI, Vol. 35, p. 4, March 14, 1889.
36. AMI, Vol. 35, p. 4, May 30, 1889.
37. AMI, Vol. 38, No. 22, p. 4, Nov. 26, 1891.
38. AMI, Vol. 39, No. 17, Oct. 27, 1892.
39. AMI, Vol. 39, No. 23, Dec. 8, 1892.
40. Deuteronomy, 34: 7.

CHAPTER THIRTY-TWO

1. AMI, Vol. 45, p. 4, Sept. 8, 1898, and Dec. 30, 1897.
2. AMI, Vol. 40, No. 28, Jan. 11, 1894.
3. AMI, Vol. 39, No. 30, Jan. 26, 1893.
4. AMI, Vol. 39, No. 36, March 9, 1893.
5. AMI, Vol. 39, No. 38, March 23, 1893.
6. AMI, Vol. 44, p. 4, April 21, 1898.
7. AMI, Vol. 44, p. 4, April 28, 1898.
8. AMI, Vol. 44, p. 4, May 12, 1898.
9. AMI, Vol. 44, p. 4, May 26, 1898.
10. AMI, Vol. 44, p. 4, Jan. 29, 1898.
11. AMI, Vol. 46, p. 4, July 20, 1899.
12. AMI, Vol. 41, No. 4, July 26, 1894.
13. IWMM, p. 340.
14. AMI, Vol. 41, p. 4, May 16, 1895.
15. IWMM, pp. 340 f.
16. AYWP, p. 61; IWMM, p. 187.
17. AMI, Vol. 27, No. 19, Nov. 10, 1876; IWMM, pp. 190-92.
18. AMI, Vol. 46, No. 12, Sept. 21, 1899; IWMM, p. 190.
19. SWIW, p. 87.
20. AMI, Vol. 40, No. 51, June 21, 1894.
21. IWMM, p. 340.
22. AMI, Vol. 41, Aug. 23, 1894.
23. AMI, Vol. 41, p. 4, Dec. 20, 1894.
24. AMI, Vol. 41, p. 4, Jan. 10, 1895.
25. Original letter in ARCH.
26. Original letter in ARCH.
27. AMI, Vol. 39, No. 40, April 6, 1893.
28. DEB, Vol. 42, No. 38, pp. 4-5, March 19, 1897; WMB, p. 38; AMI, Vol. 39, No. 48, June 1, 1893.
29. AMI, Vol. 40, No. 4, July 27, 1893.
30. AMI, Vol. 40, No. 7, Aug. 17, 1893.
31. Formerly of Cincinnati.
32. Original letter in ARCH.
33. AMI, Vol. 39, No. 33, Feb. 16, 1893.
34. AMI, Vol. 40, Nos. 17 and 18, Oct. 26, and Nov. 2, 1893.

35. AMI, Vol. 44, p. 8, March 31, 1898.
36. YEARBOOK, CCAR, Vol. 9, March 13-18, 1899.
37. AYWP, p. 60.
38. AMI, Vol. 45, No. 37, p. 2, March 16, 1899.
39. AMI, Vol. 45, p. 1, No. 37, March 16, 1899.
40. IWMM, pp. 186-87.

CHAPTER THIRTY-THREE

1. Translated from the German by B. Bettmann.
2. IWRM, pp. 351-54.
3. *Ibid.*
4. IWMM, pp. 392-93.
5. IWRM, pp. 351-54.
6. IWMM, pp. 392-93.
7. AMI, Vol. 46, p. 4, March 29, 1900.
8. IWRM, pp. 351-54.
9. AMI, *loc. cit.*
10. IWMM, pp. 389-92.
11. IWRM, pp. 351-54.
12. AMI, *loc. cit.*
13. AMI, Vol. 46, p. 4, March 29, 1900; also p. 6, April 5, 1900.
14. AMI, Vol. 46, p. 6, April 5, 1900.
15. IWMM, pp. 392-93.
16. AMI, Vol. 46, p. 6, April 5, 1900.
17. IWMM, pp. 392-93.
18. AMI, Vol. 46, p. 6, April 5, 1900.
19. AMI, Vol. 46, No. 45, p. 1, May 30, 1900.
20. Talmud, Berachot, p. 28.
21. SWIW, pp. 113-20.
22. AMI, Vol. 46, p. 4, April 5, 1900.
23. YEARBOOK, CCAR, Vol. 10, Buffalo, July 5, 1900.
24. *Ibid.*

Part Three

CHAPTER ONE

1. Page 426.
2. His own translation.
3. CG. p. 6.
4. *Ibid.*, pp. 10-11.
5. *Ibid.*, p. 12.
6. *Ibid.*, p. 13.
7. *Ibid.*, p. 15.
8. *Ibid.*, p. 17.
9. *Ibid.*, p. 20.
10. *Ibid.*, p. 22.
11. *Ibid.*, p. 28.

12. *Ibid.*, p. 29.
13. *Ibid.*, p. 33.
14. *Ibid.*, p. 38.
15. *Ibid.*, p. 41.
16. *Ibid.*, p. 42.
17. *Ibid.*, p. 43.
18. *Ibid.*, p. 43.
19. *Ibid.*, p. 46.
20. *Ibid.*, p. 48.
21. *Ibid.*, p. 51.
22. *Ibid.*, p. 52.
23. *Ibid.*, p. 52.
24. *Ibid.*, p. 68.
25. *Ibid.*, p. 71.
26. *Ibid.*, p. 73.
27. *Ibid.*, p. 81.
28. *Ibid.* pp. 83-4.
29. *Ibid.*, p. 88.
30. *Ibid.*, p. 91.
31. *Ibid.*, p. 93.
32. *Ibid.*, pp. 103-04.
33. *Ibid.*, p. 115.
34. *Ibid.*, p. 125.
35. *Ibid.*, p. 132.
36. *Ibid.*, p. 135.
37. *Ibid.*, p. 137.
38. *Ibid.*, p. 146.
39. *Ibid.*, p. 152.
40. *Ibid.*, p. 155.
41. *Ibid.*, p. 161.
42. *Ibid.*, p. 162.
43. *Ibid.*, pp. 164-65.
44. *Ibid.*, p. 166.
45. *Ibid.*, p. 177.
46. *Ibid.*, p. 170.
47. *Ibid.*, p. 180.
48. AMI, Vol. 14, p. 4, Jan. 24, 1868.
49. AMI, Vol. 43, p. 4, Aug. 13, 1896.
50. AMI, Vol. 28, p. 348, April 28, 1882.
51. AMI, Vol. 10, p. 133, Oct. 10, 1863.
52. AMI, Vol. 14, p. 4, May 8, 1868.
53. AMI, Vol. 27, p. 20, July 16, 1880.
54. AMI, Vol. 34, p. 4, Oct. 7, 1887.
55. AMI, Vol. 34, p. 4, Oct. 14, 1887.
56. STC, p. 20.
57. *Ibid.*

CHAPTER TWO

1. AMI, June 22, 1899; STC, p. 30.
2. AMI, April 30, 1896.
3. AMI, Vol. 29, No. 45, p. 420, June 22, 1883.

4. AMI, Vol. 13, p. 4, July 13, 1866.
5. AMI, Vol. 31, No. 18, p. 4, Oct. 31, 1884.
6. SWIW, p. 400.
7. AMI, Vol. 27, p. 188, Dec. 10, 1880.
8. AMI, Vol. 6, p. 364, May 18, 1860; Vol. 33, No. 13, p. 4, Sept. 24, 1886.
9. AMI, Vol. 30, No. 12, p. 4, Sept. 21, 1883.
10. AMI, Vol. 38, No. 17, p. 4, Oct. 22, 1891.
11. AMI, Vol. 45, p. 4, Sept. 8, 1898; Cf. also Vol. 43, p. 4, Aug. 6, 1886.
12. AMI, Vol. 6, No. 18, p. 140, Nov. 4, 1859.
13. AMI, Vol. 34, p. 4, Aug. 19, 1887.
14. AMI, Vol. 37, No. 5, p. 4, July 31, 1890.
15. AMI, Vol. 40, No. 22, Nov. 30, 1893.
16. AMI, Vol. 23, No. 8, Aug. 25, 1876.
17. AMI, Vol. 1, p. 196, Dec. 29, 1854.
18. AMI, Vol. 24, No. 13, p. 5, Oct. 12, 1877.
19. AMI, Nov. 30, 1883; STC, p. 30.
20. AMI, Vol. 36, No. 36, p. 4, March 6, 1890.
21. AMI, Vol. 7, p. 116, Oct. 12, 1860.
22. AMI, Vol. 34, p. 4, Nov. 18, 1887; p. 4, Nov. 25, 1887.
23. AMI, March 28, 1895, p. 4.
24. "An Introduction to the Theology of Judaism," pp. 1-2.
25. SWIW, pp. 197 ff.
26. SWIW, p. 199.
27. SWIW, p. 205.
28. SWIW, p. 213.
29. SWIW, p. 213.
30. PHW, p. 12.
31. PHW, p. 27.
32. PHW, pp. 153 f.
33. PHW, p. 170.
34. PHW, p. 181.
35. PHW, p. 183.
36. PHW, pp. 183-84.
37. PHW, pp. 188 f.
38. AMI, Vol. 11, p. 164, Nov. 18, 1854; Vol. 12, p. 140, Nov. 3, 1865.
39. AMI, Vol. 12, p. 404, June 2, 1866.
40. AMI, Vol. 13, p. 4, March 22, 1867.
41. AMI, Vol. 13, p. 4, March 29, 1867.
42. AMI, Vol. 13, p. 4, April 15, 1867; Vol. 26, p. 4, Dec. 12, 1879.
43. AMI, June 13, 1862; STC, pp. 29-30.
44. AMI, p. 4, May 9, 1895.
45. AMI, Vol. 15, p. 4, May 21, 1869.
46. AMI, p. 4, Oct. 3, 1895.
47. STC, pp. 83-84; SWIW, p. 174; AMI, Vol. 44, p. 4, Feb. 17, 1898; Vol. 37, No. 9, p. 4, Aug. 28, 1890.
48. STC, pp. 84-85.
49. AMI, Vol. 33, No. 32, p. 4, Feb. 4, 1887.
50. AMI, Vol. 38, No. 34, p. 4, Feb. 18, 1892.
51. AMI, Vol. 30, No. 17, p. 4, Oct. 26, 1883.
52. AMI, p. 4, May 30, 1895.
53. Letter in ARCH; Cf. also AMI, Vol. 15, p. 4, Jan. 1, 1869.

CHAPTER THREE

1. PHW, pp. 3-4.
2. AMI, Vol. 26, No. 16, p. 4, Oct. 17, 1879.
3. AMI, Vol. 27, p. 140, Oct. 29, 1880.
4. AMI, Vol. 27, p. 300, March 18, 1881; Vol. 34, p. 4, Oct. 28, 1887
5. AMI, Vol. 28, p. 317, March 31, 1882; Vol. 31, No. 19, p. 4, Nov. 7, 1884.
6. AMI, Vol. 31, No. 37, p. 4, March 13, 1885; Vol. 34, p. 4, Oct. 21, 1887; Vol. 34, p. 4, Jan. 27, 1888; Vol. 36, No. 34, p. 4, Feb. 20, 1890; Vol. 29, No. 41, p. 388, May 25, 1883.
7. AMI, Vol. 34, p. 4, Dec. 16, 1887.
8. AMI, p. 4, May 23, 1895.
9. AMI, Vol. 43, p. 4, Aug. 13, 1896.
10. AMI, Vol. 46, p. 4, Oct. 26, 1899.
11. AMI, Vol. 46, p. 4, Dec. 28, 1899.
12. AMI, Vol. 26, p. 4, Jan. 9, 1880.
13. AMI, Vol. 13, p. 4, Nov. 23, 1866.
14. HIN, Volume I, Introduction, pp. xv–xvi.
15. Genesis Rabba, 5:4; and Exodus Rabba, 21:6.
16. AMI, Vol. 27, p. 356, May 13, 1881.
17. AMI, Vol. 34, p. 4, Dec. 23, 1887.
18. AMI, Vol. 34, p. 4, Dec. 30, 1887.
19. AMI, Vol. 35, p. 4, Nov. 30, 1888.
20. AMI, Vol. 34, p. 4, Sept. 2, 1887.
21. Given in YEARBOOK, CCAR, pp. 117 ff.
22. CCAR, p. 118.
23. STC, p. 34; AMI, May 14, 1875.
24. Beginning AMI, Vol. 28, p. 204, Dec. 16, 1881.
25. AMI, Vol. 28, Jan. 13 and 20, 1882.
26. AMI, Vol. 28, p. 244, Jan. 27, 1882.
27. AMI, Vol. 28, p. 268, Feb. 17, 1882.
28. STC, p. 29.
29. STC, p. 29.
30. STC, pp. 32-33.
31. STC, *Ibid.*
32. Issue of May 5, 1854.
33. RMJ, p. 336.
34. AMI, Vol. 12, p. 180, Dec. 8, 1865.
35. From "The Wandering Jew," 1877; In SWIW, p. 196.
36. For date of publication, etc., Cf. the Bibliography.
37. SWIW, p. 231; "Aphorisms" written in 1891.
38. SWIW, p. 241.
39. SWIW, pp. 125 *et. seq.*
40. SWIW, p. 134.
41. SWIW, pp. 137-38.
42. SWIW, pp. 151-52.
43. AMI, Vol. 7, p. 90, Sept. 14, 1860.
44. AMI, Vol. 10, No. 16, pp. 124-25, Oct. 16, 1863.
45. AMI, Vol. 23, No. 32, p. 4, Feb. 16, 1877; Vol. 27, p. 220, Jan. 7, 1881; Vol. 29, No. 33, p. 284, Feb. 23, 1883.

46. AMI, Vol. 34, p. 4, Dec. 9, 1887.
47. AMI, Vol. 34, p. 4, Jan. 20, 1888; Vol. 34, p. 4, Jan. 27, 1888.
48. AMI, Vol. 34, p. 4, Feb. 10, 1888; also p. 4, Feb. 17, 1888.
49. AMI, Vol. 41, p. 4, Nov. 8, 1894.
50. AMI, Vol. 45, p. 4, Sept. 1, 1898.

CHAPTER FOUR

1. RMJ, p. 353.
2. ASM, Feb. 24, 1854.
3. AMI, Vol. 2, No. 19, p. 164, Nov. 23, 1855.
4. AMI, Vol. 2, No. 21, p. 180, Dec. 7, 1855.
5. AMI, Vol. 2, No. 23, p. 188, Dec. 14, 1855.
6. SINAI, Vol. 1, No. 1; SWIW, p. 66.
7. AMI, Vol. 2, Feb. 15, 1856.
8. AMI, Vol. 2, March 7, 1856.
9. AMI, Vol. 2, No. 36, p. 292, March 14, 1856.
10. AMI, Vol. 2, p. 348, May 3, 1856.
11. AMI, Vol. 5, p. 348, May 6, 1859.
12. AMI, Vol. 30, No. 33, p. 4, Feb. 22, 1884.
13. YEARBOOK, CCAR, Vol. 5, p. 11.
14. RMJ, p. 389.
15. YEARBOOK, CCAR, Vol. 5, p. 52.
16. *Ibid.*, p. 61; RMJ, p. 360.
17. YEARBOOK, CCAR, Vol. 6, pp. 16-17.
18. *Ibid.*, p. 61; RMJ, p. 360.
19. YEARBOOK, CCAR, Vol. 5, p. 61.
20. STC, p. 64-65.
21. AMI, Vol. 1, No. 30, p. 236, Feb. 2, 1855.
22. AMI, Vol. 1, No. 31, p. 244, Feb. 9, 1855.
23. AMI, Vol. 11, No. 11, p. 84, Sept. 9, 1864.
24. AMI, Vol. 22, No. 2, p. 4, July 9, 1875.
25. AMI, Vol. 34, p. 4, April 27, 1888.
26. AMI, Vol. 36, No. 17, p. 4, Oct. 21, 1889.
27. AMI, Vol. 37, No. 32, p. 4, Feb. 12, 1891.
28. *Op. cit.*
29. AMI, Vol. 45, p. 4, June 1, 1899; Vol. 37, No. 33, Feb. 12, 1891.
30. AWZ, p. 7; AMI, Vol. 40, No. 19, Nov. 9, 1893; Vol. 36, No. 17, Oct. 24, 1889.
31. SWIW, p. 387.
32. AMI, Vol. 3, No. 17, p. 132, Oct. 31, 1856.
33. AMI, Vol. 32, No. 14, p. 4, Oct. 2, 1885.
34. ARCH, Holograph letter to Max Heller, Sept. 5, 1886.
35. ARCH, Holograph letter to Rev. J. L. Mayerberg, May 23, 1888.
36. ARCH, Holograph letter to Edw. N. Calisch, Jan. 21, 1889.
37. ARCH, Holograph letter to Edw. N. Calisch, April 2, 1891.

CHAPTER FIVE

1. AMI, Vol. 33, No. 19, p. 4, Nov. 5, 1886.
2. AMI, Vol. 17, p. 9, June 2, 1871.
3. AMI, Vol. 18, No. 20, pp. 8-9, Nov. 17, 1871.

4. AMI, Vol. 31, No. 2, p. 4, July 11, 1884.
5. AYWP, p. 3.
6. AMI, Vol. 42, p. 4, Feb. 13, 1896.
7. AMI, Vol. 16, Feb. 11, 1870.
8. AMI, Vol. 30, No. 42, p. 4, April 25, 1884.
9. AMI, Vol. 32, No. 40, p. 4, April 2, 1886.
10. *American Jews' Annual*, 1888.
11. AMI, Vol. 43, No. 1, July 2, 1896.
12. YEARBOOK, CCAR, Vol. 6, p. 12, Milwaukee, 1896.
13. AMI, Vol. 18, Nos. 22-31, from Dec. 1, 1871 to Feb. 2, 1872.
14. SWIW, pp. 295-339.
15. Cf. also SWIW, pp. 260-90.
16. AMI, Vol. 12, p. 364, May 18, 1866.
17. AMI, Vol. 14, p. 4, Jan. 3, 1868.
18. AMI, Vol. 15, p. 4, April 30, 1869.
19. AMI, Vol. 34, p. 4, July 29, 1887.
20. *Ibid.*
21. SWIW, p. 65.
22. SWIW, *Ibid.*
23. SWIW, p. 67.
24. AMI, Vol. 2, March 7, 1856.
25. ASM, March 3, 1854.
26. AMI, Vol. 1, July 28, 1854.
27. AMI, Vol. 2, p. 44, Aug. 17, 1855.
28. AMI, Vol. 6, p. 20, July 22, 1859; Vol. 11, p. 20, July 15, 1864.
29. AMI, Vol. 10, p. 164, Nov. 20, 1863.
30. AMI, Vol. 13, p. 4, Jan. 11, 1867; Vol. 13, p. 4, March 1, 1867; Vol. 15, p. 4, Dec. 4, 1868.
31. AMI, Vol. 26, p. 4, March 19, 1880.
32. AMI, Vol. 34, p. 4, July 1, 1887.
33. YEARBOOK, CCAR, pp. 17 f., July 13, 1880.
34. AMI, Vol. 41, p. 4, Jan. 4, 1895.
35. AMI, Vol. 44, p. 4, Oct. 28, 1897.
36. AMI, Vol. 45, p. 4, April 20, 1899; Cf. also Vol. 5, No. 15, p. 124, Oct. 28, 1858.

CHAPTER SIX

1. OCC, Vol. 23, p. 145.
2. AMI, Vol. 12, No. 4, p. 29, July 28, 1865.
3. AMI, Vol. 23, No. 9, p. 4, Sept. 1, 1876; Vol. 17, p. 8, Jan. 13, 1871.
4. AMI, Vol. 30, No. 19, p. 4, Nov. 9, 1883.
5. AMI, Vol. 37, No. 31, p. 4, Feb. 5, 1891.
6. RMJ, p. 503.
7. RMJ, p. 15.
8. AMI, Vol. 5, No. 49, p. 389, June 10, 1859; Cf. also AYWP, pp. 92-93, as to the introduction of the organ in Cincinnati.
9. AYWP, p. 91.
10. AMI, Vol. 4, No. 4, p. 28, July 31, 1857.
11. AYWP, p. 94.
12. AMI, Vol. 4, No. 3, p. 20, July 24, 1857.
13. AMI, Vol. 5, No. 26, p. 205, Dec. 31, 1858.

14. AMI, Vol. 13, p. 4, July 20, 1866.
15. AMI, Vol. 27, p. 364, May 20, 1881.
16. AMI, Vol. 29, No. 45, p. 420, June 22, 1883.
17. ARCH, Holograph letter to Max Heller, Nov. 30, 1896; the paper was read at Montreal, and appears in YEARBOOK, CCAR, No. 8, p. 60.
18. YEARBOOK, CCAR, Montreal, Vol. 8, pp. 91-92 and 66-128.
19. RMJ, p. 502, with the necessary references.
20. ARCH, Holograph letter to Rev. Julius Mayerberg, Feb. 20, 1891.
21. AMI, Vol. 32, No. 25, p. 4, Dec. 18, 1885.
22. AMI, Vol. 32, No. 52, p. 4, June 28, 1886.
23. AYWP, p. 83.
24. AMI, Vol. 43, p. 4, Feb. 4, 1897.
25. AMI, Vol. 23, No. 13, pp. 4-5, 1876.
26. AMI, Vol. 38, No. 20, p. 4, Nov. 12, 1891.
27. AMI, Vol. 2, No. 5, p. 36, Aug. 10, 1855.
28. STC, p. 70; AMI, Jan. 8, 1858.
29. AMI, Vol. 16, p. 8, May 6, 1870.
30. AMI, Vol. 17, p. 8, Nov. 25, 1870.
31. AMI, Vol. 23, No. 10, p. 4, Sept. 8, 1876.
32. SWIW, pp. 397-99.
33. SWIW, p. 399.
34. AMI, Vol. 25, No. 37, p. 4, March 14, 1879.
35. AMI, Vol. 30, No. 25, p. 4, Dec. 14, 1883.
36. E.g. AMI, Vol. 36, No. 19, p. 4, Nov. 7, 1889.
37. AMI, Vol. 37, No. 21, p. 4, Nov. 27, 1890.
38. AMI, Vol. 39, No. 21, Nov. 24, 1892.
39. AMI, Vol. 44, p. 4, March 10, 1898.
40. AMI, Vol. 2, p. 372, May 23, 1856.
41. AMI, Vol. 2, p. 380, May 23, 1856.
42. AMI, Vol. 3, No. 1, p. 4, July 11, 1856.
43. AMI, Vol. 3, No. 38, p. 300, March 27, 1857.
44. ARCH, Holograph letter to Adler, Dec. 1, 1857, in German.
45. AMI, Vol. 24, p. 4, May 10, 1878.
46. AMI, Vol. 27, p. 220, Jan. 7, 1881.
47. AMI, Vol. 27, p. 236, Jan. 21, 1881.
48. AMI, Vol. 27, p. 244, Jan. 28, 1881.
49. AMI, Vol. 28, p. 132, Oct. 21, 1881.
50. AMI, Vol. 29, No. 36, p. 308, March 16, 1883.
51. AMI, Vol. 32, No. 4, p. 4, July 21, 1885.
52. AMI, Vol. 32, No. 6, p. 4, Aug. 7, 1885.
53. AMI, Vol. 35, No. 18, p. 4, Nov. 2, 1888.
54. AMI, Vol. 41, p. 4, March 14, 1895.
55. AMI, Vol. 41, p. 4, March 21, 1895.
56. AMI, Vol. 43, p. 4, Dec. 17, 1896.
57. AMI, Vol. 45, p. 4, March 2, 1899.
58. Cf. YEARBOOKS, CCAR, Vols. XIII to XVI, p. 172.

CHAPTER SEVEN

1. STC, p. 62.
2. STC, pp. 61-62.
3. AMI, Vol. 1, No. 42, p. 332, April 27, 1855.

4. AMI, Vol. 3, No. 32, p. 253, Feb. 13, 1857.
5. AMI, Vol. 3, No. 49, p. 388, June 12, 1857.
6. AMI, Vol. 5, No. 28, p. 220, Jan. 14, 1859.
7. AMI, Vol. 12, p. 180, Dec. 8, 1865.
8. AMI, Vol. 12, p. 204, Dec. 29, 1865.
9. AMI, Vol. 15, p. 4, Aug. 28, 1868.
10. AMI, Vol. 24, No. 16, p. 4, Nov. 2, 1877.
11. STC, p. 49; from AMI, 1878.
12. AMI, Vol. 26, p. 4, June 18, 1880.
13. AWZ, p. 9; AMI, Vol. 41, No. 44, May 2, 1885; Vol. 44, No. 5, July 29, 1897; No. 21, Nov. 21, 1897; No. 37, March 10, 1898; Vol. 45, No. 4, July 7, 1898; No. 18, Nov. 3, 1898; No. 30, Jan. 26, 1899.
14. STC, pp. 77-78.
15. STC, p. 78; in AMI, 1894.
16. STC, p. 88.
17. AMI, Vol. 27, p. 292, March 11, 1881.
18. AMI, Vol. 28, p. 260, Feb. 10, 1882.
19. AMI, Vol. 28, p. 301, March 17, 1882.
20. AMI, Vol. 28, p. 372, May 19, 1882.
21. AMI, Vol. 28, p. 380, May 26, 1882.
22. AMI, Vol. 29, p. 138, Oct. 20, 1882.
23. AMI, Vol. 33, No. 31, p. 4, Jan. 28, 1887.
24. AMI, Vol. 41, p. 4, Oct. 11, 1894.
25. AMI, Vol. 43, p. 4, June 10, 1897.

CHAPTER EIGHT

1. AMI, Vol. 44, No. 36, March 3, 1898; AWZ, p. 15.
2. AWZ, p. 17; AMI, Vol. 31, No. 34, Feb. 20, 1885; No. 25, Dec. 19, 1884; Vol. 31, No. 42, April 17, 1885; Vol. 33, No. 13, Sept. 23, 1887.
3. AWZ, pp. 17-18; AMI, Vol. 36, No. 43, April 24, 1890.
4. AWZ, p. 18; AMI, Vol. 37, No. 37, March 12, 1891; Vol. 38, No. 11, Sept. 10, 1891; Vol. 38, No. 38, March 17, 1892; Vol. 30, No. 43, April 27, 1893.
5. AWZ, p. 18; AMI, Vol. 40, No. 5, Aug. 3, 1893.
6. AMI, Vol. 43, No. 32, Feb. 4, 1897; No. 39, March 25, 1897.
7. AWZ, p. 18.
8. AMI, Vol. 26, p. 4, Nov. 14, 1879.
9. AMI, Vol. 29, p. 36, Aug. 4, 1882.
10. AMI, Vol. 29, p. 78, Sept. 22, 1882.
11. AMI, Vol. 29, p. 211, Dec. 22, 1882.
12. AMI, Vol. 29, No. 31, p. 268, Feb. 9, 1883.
13. AMI, Vol. 29, No. 33, p. 284, Feb. 23, 1883.
14. AMI, Vol. 29, No. 41, p. 388, May 25, 1883.
15. AMI, Vol. 34, p. 4, Nov. 25, 1887; Cf. also Vol. 38, No. 15, p. 4, Oct. 8, 1891.
16. SWIW, p. 189.
17. AMI, Vol. 29, No. 2, July 14, 1882; Vol. 33, No. 13, Sept. 23, 1887.
18. AMI, Vol. 39, No. 43, April 27, 1893; Vol. 42, No. 35, Feb. 27, 1896; Vol. 33, No. 13, Sept. 23, 1887.
19. AMI, Vol. 38, No. 11, Sept. 20, 1891; Vol. 31, No. 42, April 17, 1885; Vol. 46, No. 7, Sept. 17, 1899; Vol. 32, New Series No. 10, No. 4, Jan. 24, 1879; Vol. 26, No. 26, June 25, 1880; Vol. 28, No. 27, May 19, 1882.
20. AMI, Vol. 34, No. 21, Nov. 18, 1887.

21. AMI, Vol. 17, No. 32, Feb. 3, 1871; Vol. 32, No. 51, June 18, 1886.
22. AMI, Vol. 15, No. 18, Nov. 6, 1868; Vol. 16, No. 38, March 25, 1870; Vol. 33, No. 19, Nov. 5, 1885.
23. AMI, Vol. 37, No. 51, June 18, 1891.
24. AMI, Vol. 6, No. 29, Jan. 20, 1860.
25. AMI, Vol. 9, No. 41, April 17, 1863.
26. AMI, Vol. 14, No. 9, Aug. 30, 1867; Vol. 16, No. 38, March 25, 1870.
27. AMI, Vol. 39, No. 15, Oct. 13, 1892.
28. AMI, Vol. 38, No. 38, March 17, 1892; Vol. 37, No. 51, June 18, 1891.
29. AMI, Vol. 6, Jan. 20, 1860; June 18, 1891; March 17, 1892.
30. AMI, Vol. 30, No. 11, Sept. 14, 1883.
31. AMI, Vol. 41, No. 39, March 25, 1894.
32. AMI, Vol. 45, No. 29, Jan. 19, 1899; Vol. 45, No. 32, Feb. 9, 1899.
33. AMI, Vol. 30, No. 20, Nov. 16, 1883; Vol. 33, No. 25, Dec. 17, 1886; Vol. 34, No. 9, Aug. 26, 1887; Vol. 45, No. 48, June 1, 1899; Vol. 36, No. 50, June 12, 1890; Vol. 43, No. 6, Aug. 6, 1896.
34. AMI, Vol. 34, No. 15, Oct. 7, 1887; Vol. 35, No. 36, March 7, 1889; Vol. 35, No. 37, March 14, 1889; Vol. 39, No. 26, Dec. 29, 1892.
35. AWZ, pp. 19-20; AMI, Vol. 35, No. 5, Aug. 3, 1888; Vol. 35, No. 47, May 23, 1889; Vol. 36, No. 46, May 15, 1890; Vol. 37, No. 22, Nov. 27, 1890; Vol. 37, No. 44, April 30, 1891; Vol. 39, No. 15, Oct. 13, 1892; also AWZ, p. 20; AMI, Vol. 36, No. 43, April 24, 1890; Vol. 35, No. 22, Nov. 30, 1888; Vol. 41, No. 8, Aug. 23, 1894; Vol. 43, No. 48, May 27, 1897.
36. AWZ, p. 20; AMI, Vol. 35, No. 21, Nov. 23, 1888; Vol. 36, No. 50, June 13, 1890; Vol. 37, No. 49, June 4, 1891; Vol. 40, No. 40, April 5, 1894.
37. AWZ, p. 20 AMI, Vol. 29, No. 20, Nov. 16, 1877; Vol. 30, No. 7, Aug. 17, 1883; Vol. 45, No. 16, Oct. 20, 1898.
38. AMI, Vol. 6, No. 30, p. 228, Jan. 20, 1860.
39. AMI, Vol. 9, p. 324, April 17, 1863.
40. AMI, Vol. 14, p. 4, Aug. 30, 1867.
41. AMI, Vol. 26, p. 4, Feb. 13, 1880.
42. AMI, Vol. 28, p. 180, Dec. 2, 1881.
43. AMI, Vol. 29, p. 12, July 14, 1882.
44. AMI, Vol. 29, No. 35, p. 300, March 9, 1883.
45. AMI, Vol. 31, No. 34, p. 4, Feb. 20, 1885; Cf. also Vol. 33, No. 7, p. 4, Aug. 13, 1886; No. 42, p. 4, April 15, 1887.
46. AMI, Vol. 34, p. 4, July 15, 1887.
47. AMI, Vol. 38, No. 4, p. 4, July 23, 1891.
48. AMI, Vol. 38, No. 8, p. 4, Aug. 20, 1891.
49. AMI, Vol. 38, No. 11, p. 4, Sept. 10, 1891.
50. AMI, Vol. 40, No. 5, Aug. 3, 1893.
51. AMI, Vol. 40, No. 34, Feb. 22, 1894.
52. AMI, Vol. 42, p. 4, Dec. 19, 1895.
53. AMI, Vol. 44, p. 4, Nov. 4, 1897.

CHAPTER NINE

1. SWIW, p. 176.
2. SWIW, p. 384.
3. ASM, Vol. 6, No. 27, Oct. 22, 1852; IWMM, p. 343.
4. AMI, Vol. 15, No. 1, July 10, 1869; IWMM, p. 343.

5. AMI, Vol. 17, No. 38, March 17, 1871; IWMM, p. 344.
6. AMI, Vol. 32, No. 24, Jan. 1879; IWMM, pp. 344-47.
7. AMI, Feb. 13, 1880; July 14, 1882; AWZ, p. 5.
8. E.g. Jan. 24, 1879; AWZ, p. 5.
9. AMI, Vol. 3, No. 35, March 6, 1857; Vol. 18, No. 24, Dec. 15, 1871; Vol. 44, No. 41, April 7, 1898; AWZ, p. 7.
10. AMI, Vol. 14, No. 43, May 1, 1868; Vol. 44, No. 19, Nov. 4, 1897; AWZ, p. 14.
11. AMI, Vol. 42, No. 25, Dec. 19, 1895; Vol. 42, No. 30, Jan. 25, 1896; AWZ, p. 15.
12. OCC, "The Principles of Juadism," second installment, pp. 541-44.
13. AMI, Vol. 15, p. 4, Dec. 25, 1868.
14. AMI, Vol. 27, No. 23, p. 180, Dec. 3, 1880.
15. AMI, Vol. 44, p. 4, Dec. 23, 1897.
16. AMI, Vol. 45, p. 4, Feb. 16, 1899.
17. YEARBOOK, CCAR, Vol. 1, pp. 25-26.
18. AMI, Vol. 23, No. 11, p. 5, Sept. 15, 1876.
19. AMI, Vol. 23, No. 31, p. 6, Feb. 9, 1877.
20. AMI, Vol. 33, No. 34, p. 4, Feb. 18, 1887.
21. AMI, Vol. 43, No. 1, p. 4, July 2, 1896.
22. AMI, Vol. 43, p. 5, July 30, 1896.
23. AMI, Vol. 43, p. 4, Aug. 20, 1896.
24. AMI, Vol. 43, p. 4, May 6, 1897.
25. *New York Independent*, issue of May 20, 1897.
26. YEARBOOK, CCAR, Vol. 7, pp. x-xii.
27. *Ibid.*, pp. xli f., July 8, 1897; also RMJ, pp. 496-97.
28. AMI, Vol. 44, p. 4, Aug. 5, 1897.
29. AMI, Vol. 44, p. 4, Aug. 26, 1897.
30. AMI, Vol. 44, p. 4, Sept. 2, 1897.
31. AMI, Vol. 44, p. 4, Sept. 9, 1897.
32. AMI, Vol. 44, p. 4, Sept. 16, 1897.
33. AMI, Vol. 44, p. 4, Sept. 23, 1897.
34. AMI, Vol. 44, p. 4, Sept. 30, 1897.
35. AMI, Vol. 44, p. 4, Oct. 28, 1897.
36. AMI, Vol. 44, p. 4, Nov. 4, 1897.
37. AMI, Vol. 44, p. 4, Nov. 18, 1897.
38. AMI, Vol. 44, p. 4, Feb. 17, 1898.
39. AMI, Vol. 44, p. 4, March 17, 1898.
40. AMI, Vol. 44, p. 4, June 23, 1898.
41. AMI, Vol. 45, p. 4, July 7, 1898.
42. AMI, Vol. 45, p. 4, Aug. 25, 1898.
43. AMI, Vol. 45, p. 4, Sept. 8, 1898.
44. AMI, Vol. 45, p. 4, Sept. 29, 1898.
45. AMI, Vol. 45, p. 4, Oct. 6, 1898.
46. AMI, Vol. 45, p. 4, Oct. 13, 1898.
47. AMI, Vol. 45, p. 4, Dec. 22, 1898.
48. AMI, Vol. 45, p. 4, Jan. 19, 1899.
49. AMI, Vol. 45, p. 4, Feb. 9, 1899.
50. AMI, Vol. 46, p. 4, Aug. 10, 1899.
51. AMI, Vol. 46, p. 4, Aug. 24, 1899.
52. AMI, Vol. 46, p. 5, Dec. 7, 1899.

53. AWZ, p. 6; AMI, Vol. 42, No. 35, Feb. 27, 1896; Vol. 43, No. 52, June 24, 1897; Vol. 44, No. 15, Oct. 7, 1897; No. 19, Nov. 4, 1897; Vol. 46, No. 6, Aug. 10, 1899.
54. AWZ, p. 8; AMI, Vol. 43, No. 49, June 3, 1897; Vol. 44, No. 13, Sept. 23, 1897; No. 41, April 7, 1898; Vol. 46, No. 16, Oct. 19, 1899; Vol. 45, No. 29, Jan. 19, 1899; Vol. 46, No. 15, Oct. 12, 1899.
55. AWZ, p. 9; AMI, Vol. 45, No. 27, Jan. 5, 1899; Vol. 46, No. 16, Oct. 19, 1899; No. 36, March 8, 1900.
56. HUC Journal, Dec., 1899; Vol. IV, pp. 45-47.
57. AWZ, p. 12; AMI, Vol. 43, No. 8, Aug. 20, 1896; No. 45, May 6, 1897; No. 46, May 13, 1897; No. 52, June 24, 1897.
58. AMI, Vol. 44, No. 19, Nov. 4, 1897; AWZ, p. 13.
59. AWZ, p. 14; AMI, Vol. 44, No. 10, Sept. 2, 1897.
60. AWZ, p. 14; AMI, Vol. 44, No. 21, Nov. 18, 1897; Cf. *also* No. 41, April 7, 1898; Vol. 44, No. 49, June 2, 1898; Vol. 45, No. 4, July 7, 1898.
61. STC, p. 107.

CHAPTER TEN

1. STC, p. 20; AMI, Feb. 21, 1873
2. EPNK, Published by J. Muhlhaeuser, 195 Division St., N.Y.
3. EPNK, p. 11.
4. EPNK, p. 16.
5. EPNK, p. 17.
6. EPNK, p. 20.
7. AMI, Vol. 6, p. 260, Feb. 17, 1860.
8. AMI, Vol. 10, p. 196, Dec. 18, 1863.
9. AMI, Vol. 12, p. 308, March 30, 1866.
10. AMI, Vol. 15, p. 4, Oct. 23, 1868.
11. STC, p. 104.
12. AMI, Vol. 27, p. 28, 1880.
13. AMI, Vol. 27, No. 22, p. 173, Nov. 26, 1880.
14. STC, pp. 100-01; AMI, May, 1881.
15. STC, p. 104.
16. AMI, Vol. 44, p. 4, Jan. 29, 1898.
17. AMI, Vol. 46, p. 4, Jan. 4, 1900.
18. AMI, Vol. 46, p. 4, Jan. 11, 1900.
19. AMI, Vol. 46, p. 4, Jan. 18, 1900.
20. AMI, Vol. 46, p. 4, Jan. 25, 1900.
21. AIMW, p. 19.
22. AIMW, p. 19.
23. AIMW, pp. 19-20.
24. AIMW, p. 20.
25. AIMW, p. 20.
26. AIMW, p. 21.
27. IWMM, p. 208; from AMI, Vol. 3, No. 19, Nov. 14, 1856.
28. IWMM, pp. 210-11; AMI, Vol. 20, No. 31, Jan. 24, 1873.
29. IWMM, p. 211.
30. AMI, Vol. 17, No. 14, Sept. 28, 1855; IWMM, pp. 246-47.
31. AMI, Vol. 17, No. 14.
32. IWMM, pp. 247-48.

33. *Board of Education* vs. *Minor*, 23, Ohio State Reports, 211; IWMM, pp. 248 f.
34. AMI, Vol. 7, No. 18, p. 146, Nov. 2, 1860.
35. AMI, Vol. 16, p. 8, Oct. 15, 1869.
36. AMI, Vol. 23, No. 16, p. 4, Oct. 20, 1876.
37. AMI, Vol. 33, No. 25, p. 4, Dec. 17, 1886.
38. STC, pp. 38-39; AMI, July, 1899.
39. STC, pp. 38-39.

CHAPTER ELEVEN

1. AMI, Vol. 1, No. 36, p. 284, March 16, 1855.
2. AMI, Vol. 1, No. 30, p. 237, Feb. 2, 1856.
3. AMI, Vol. 9, *passim,* July 11, 1862.
4. AMI, Vol. 10, p. 148, Nov. 13, 1863. Probably reprinted from the AZDJ.
5. AMI, Vol. 13, Jan. 4, 1867 *et seq.*
6. AMI, Vol. 14, p. 4, Nov. 8, 1867.
7. AMI, Vol. 14, p. 4, May 8, 1868.
8. AMI, Vol. 15, p. 4, March 12, 1869.
9. AMI, Vol. 15, April 23, 1869.
10. AMI, Vol. 16, p. 8, July 9, 1869.
11. AMI, Vol. 16, p. 8, April 15, 1870.
12. AMI, Vol. 17, p. 9, Aug. 19, 1870.
13. AMI, Vol. 17, p. 8, Sept. 2, 1870.
14. STC, p. 100.
15. AMI, Vol. 23, No. 1, July 7, 1876.
16. AMI, Vol. 27, p. 44, Aug. 6, 1880.
17. AMI, Vol. 27, p. 60, Aug. 20, 1880.
18. AMI, Vol. 28, p. 140, Oct. 28, 1881.
19. AMI, Vol. 29, p. 146, Oct. 27, 1882.
20. AMI, Vol. 34, p. 5, June 8, 1888.
21. AMI, Vol. 35, p. 4, Dec. 7, 1889, fifth installment.
22. AMI, Vol. 36, p. 4, Jan. 24, 1889.
23. AMI, Vol. 36, p. 9, Feb. 7, 1889.
24. AMI, Vol. 35, p. 4, Feb. 14, 1889.
25. AMI, Vol. 42, p. 4, Oct. 10, 1895. Italics throughout this paragraph not Wise's, but mine.
26. AMI, Vol. 45, p. 4, June 29, 1899.
27. AMI, Vol. 46, p. 4, Dec. 7, 1899.
28. Quoted in STC, p. 38.
29. *Ibid.*, pp. 47-48.
30. *Ibid.*, p. 50.
31. *Ibid.*, p. 63.
32. JAC, p. 5.
33. *Ibid.*
34. JAC, p. 7.
35. JAC, p. 10.
36. JAC, p. 12.
37. JAC, p. 13.
38. JAC, p. 14.
39. JAC, p. 17.

40. JAC, p. 19.
41. JAC, p. 20.
42. JAC, p. 26.
43. JAC, p. 27.
44. JAC, p. 31.
45. JAC, beginning p. 40.
46. JAC, p. 43.
47. JAC, pp. 45-46.
48. JAC, p. 48.
49. *Ibid.*
50. JAC, p. 53.
51. JAC, p. 57.
52. JAC, p. 61.
53. JAC, p. 66.
54. JAC, p. 67.
55. JAC, p. 73.
56. JAC, p. 80.
57. JAC, pp. 81-82.
58. JAC, p. 88.
59. JAC, p. 96.
60. JAC, p. 102.
61. JAC, p. 103.
62. JAC, p. 106.
63. JAC, p. 112.
64. JAC, p. 115.
65. JAC, p. 119.
66 JAC, p. 122.

CHAPTER TWELVE

1. AMI, Vol. 5, No. 35, p. 260, Feb. 18, 1859.
2. AMI, Vol. 5, p. 372, May 27, 1859.
3. AMI, Vol. 10, p. 52, Aug. 14, 1863.
4. AMI, Vol. 12, p. 164, Nov. 24, 1865.
5. AMI, Vol. 25, p. 4, Jan. 23, 1880.
6. AMI, Vol. 26, p. 4, March 26, 1880.
7. SWIW, p. 220.
8. SWIW, p. 352.
9. SWIW, p. 354.
10. SWIW, p. 367.
11. SWIW, p. 372.
12. SWIW, p. 368.
13. Here referred to as LOC; Cf. Bibliography.
14. LOC, p. 8; Cf. note by Silverman.
15. LOC, p. 12.
16. LOC, p. 15.
17. LOC, p. 19.
18. LOC, p. 20.
19. LOC, p. 22.
20. LOC, p. 27.
21. LOC, p. 33.

22. Cf. Acts; LOC, p. 43.
23. LOC, p. 51.
24. Which is in SWIW, pp. 352-75.
25. STC, p. 45.
26. MJN, Pref. ii.
27. MJN, Introduction, p. 10.
28. MJN, p. 11.
29. MJN, p. 14.
30. MJN, p. 16.
31. MJN, p. 19.
32. MJN, p. 23.
33. MJN, pp. 26-27.
34. MJN, p. 52.
35. MJN, p. 73.
36. MJN, p. 92.
37. MJN, p. 99.
38. MJN, pp. 108-09.
39. MJN, p. 113.
40. MJN, p. 123.
41. MJN, p. 129.
42. MJN, p. 132.
43. MJN, p. 133.
44. MJN, p. 134.
45. Begun AMI, July 9, 1869, ending April 1, 1870—to be continued, but never was.
46. In AMI.
47. IWJH, p. 8.
48. STC, p. 44.
49. AMI, Vol. 1, No. 8, p. 61, Sept. 1, 1854.
50. AMI, Vol. 1, No. 13, Oct. 6, 1854.
51. AMI, Vol. 1, No. 26, p. 204, Jan. 5, 1855.
52. AMI, Vol. 1, No. 30, p. 237, Feb. 2, 1856.
53. AMI, Vol. 3, No. 19, p. 147, Nov. 14, 1856.
54. AMI, Vol. 12, p. 340, April 27, 1866.
55. AMI, Vol. 12, p. 396, June 15, 1866.
56. AMI, Vol. 19, No. 11, p. 8, Sept. 13, 1872.
57. AMI, Vol. 23, No. 48, p. 4, June 8, 1877.
58. AMI, Vol. 35, p. 4, Oct. 5, 1888.
59. DJPC, p. 6.
60. DJPC, p. 8.
61. DJPC, p. 9.
62. DJPC, p. 11.
63. DJPC, p. 18.
64. DJPC, p. 27.
65. DJPC, p. 29.
66. DJPC, p. 30.
67. DJPC, pp. 32 ff. for proofs.
68. DJPC, p. 35.
69. DJPC, p. 40.
70. DJPC, p. 43.
71. DJPC, p. 45.

72. DJPC, p. 49.
73. DJPC, p. 50.
74. DJPC, p. 59.
75. DJPC, p. 60.
76. DJPC, p. 65.
77. DJPC, p. 66; "A.C." doubtless "After Christianity."
78. DJPC, p. 127.

CHAPTER THIRTEEN

1. AMI, Vol. 26, p. 4, Oct. 31, 1879.
2. AMI, Vol. 26, p. 6, Nov. 7, 1879.
3. AMI, Vol. 27, p. 148, Nov. 5, 1880.
4. AMI, Vol. 34, p. 4, Nov. 11, 1887.
5. AMI, Vol. 35, p. 4, Nov. 9, 1888.
6. SWIW, p. 89.
7. SWIW, p. 90.
8. SWIW, p. 91.
9. SWIW, p. 94.
10. SWIW, p. 97.
11. HPP, p. 5.
12. AMI, Vol. 3, No. 7, p. 49, Aug. 22, 1856.
13. Beginning AMI, Vol. 7, No. 36, p. 281, March 8, 1861.
14. Beginning AMI, Vol. 11, No. 10, p. 73, Sept. 2, 1864.
15. Part II, in AMI, Vol. 27, No. 22, p. 171, Nov. 26, 1880.
16. AMI, Vol. 27, No. 26, p. 203, Dec. 24, 1880.
17. STC, p. 14.
18. WMB, p. 4.
19. Up to here in DEB, Vol. 42, No. 12, Sept. 17, 1896, pp. 5-6.
20. AMI, Vol. 3, No. 1, p. 14, July 11, 1856.
21. AMI, Vol. 5, p. 374, May 27, 1859.
22. AMI, Vol. 6, p. 214, Jan. 6, 1860.
23. AMI, Vol. 7, p. 68, Aug. 31, 1860.
24. AMI, Vol. 10, No. 29, 1863.
25. AMI, Vol. 10, p. 412, June 24, 1864.
26. AMI, Vol. 11, p. 44, Aug. 5, 1864.
27. AMI, Vol. 12, No. 43, p. 341, April 27, 1866.
28. AMI, Vol. 13, p. 4, June 14, 1867.
29. AMI, Vol. 24, No. 6, p. 4, Aug. 10, 1877.
30. ARCH, Letter of June 7, 1886.
31. AMI, Vol. 34, Sept. 23, 1887.
32. AMI, Vol. 44, p. 4, July 1, 1897.
33. SWIW, p. 111.
34. IWMM, pp. 251 f.
35. Cited in IWMM, p. 356.
36. IWMM, p. 358.
37. IWMM, p. 362.
38. IWMM, p. 358.
39. IWMM, p. 381.
40. IWMM, p. 384.
41. Vol. 1, *passim.*

42. AMI, Vol. 3, p. 52, Aug. 23, 1856.
43. AMI, Vol. 4, No. 15, Oct. 16, 1857.
44. AMI, Vol. 4, No. 37, p. 293, March 10, 1858.
45. AMI, Vol. 10, p. 116, Oct. 9, 1863.
46. AMI, Vol. 12, No. 43, p. 341, April 27, 1867.
47. AMI, Vol. 21, No. 3, p. 4, July 17, 1874.

CHAPTER FOURTEEN

1. AMI, Vol. 2, No. 42, p. 339, 1856.
2. AMI, Vol. 4, No. 16, p. 122, Oct. 23, 1857.
3. AMI, Vol. 5, No. 5, p. 37, Aug. 6, 1858.
4. AMI, Vol. 5, No. 9, p. 69, Sept. 3, 1858.
5. AMI, Vol. 5, No. 8, p. 70, Sept. 3, 1859.
6. AMI, Vol. 5, p. 348, May 6, 1859.
7. AMI, Vol. 6, No. 36, March 9, 1860.
8. AMI, Vol. 6, p. 348, May 7, 1860.
9. AMI, Vol. 7, p. 132, Oct. 26, 1860.
10. AMI, Vol. 7, No. 40, p. 317, April 5, 1861.
11. AMI, Vol. 7, Nos. 47 and 48, p. 370, May 24, and May 31, 1861.
12. AMI, Vol. 9, No. 12, p. 93, Sept. 26, 1862.
13. AMI, Vol. 9, No. 12, Oct. 3, 1862.
14. AMI, Vol. 10, No. 36, p. 285, March 4, 1864.
15. AMI, Vol. 10, p. 404, June 17, 1864.
16. AMI, Vol. 13, p. 4, Dec. 21, 1866.
17. AMI, Vol. 13, p. 5, Dec. 21, 1866.
18. AMI, Vol. 14, No. 44, May 8, 1868.
19. AMI, Vol. 14, p. 4, Jan. 10, 1868.
20. AMI, Vol. 19, No. 20, p. 8, Nov. 22, 1872.
21. AMI, Vol. 21, No. 3, p. 5, July 10, 1874.
22. AMI, Vol. 21, No. 6, p. 4, Aug. 14, 1874.
23. AMI, Vol. 22, No. 6, p. 5, Aug. 13, 1875.
24. AMI, Vol. 23, No. 4, July 28, 1876.
25. AMI, Vol. 23, No. 13, Sept. 29, 1876.
26. AMI, Vol. 23, No. 31, Feb. 9, 1877.
27. AMI, Vol. 23, No. 35, p. 4, March 2, 1877.
28. AMI, Vol. 24, May 3, 1878.
29. AMI, Vol. 25, No. 27, Jan. 3, 1879.
30. AMI, Vol. 26, p. 1, Jan. 23, 1880.
31. AMI, Vol. 27, No. 43, p. 331, April 22, 1881.
32. AMI, Vol. 29, p. 194, Dec. 8, 1882.
33. AMI, Vol. 30, No. 47, p. 4, June 6, 1884.
34. AMI, Vol. 30, No. 49, p. 4, June 20, 1884.
35. AMI, Vol. 44, p. 4, Nov. 18, 1897.
36. AMI, Vol. 39, No. 32, Feb. 9, 1893.
37. AMI, Vol. 39, No. 36, March 9, 1893.
38. AMI, Vol. 44, p. 4, Feb. 17, 1898.

Index

INDEX